Microsoft®

PROGRAMMING MICROSOFT® SQL SERVER 2000 WITH MICROSOFT VISUAL BASIC® .NET

Microsoft® .net

Rick Dobson

PUBLISHED BY
Microsoft Press
A Division of Microsoft Corporation
One Microsoft Way
Redmond, Washington 98052-6399

Library of Congress Cataloging-in-Publication Data
Dobson, Rick, 1944-

Programming Microsoft SQL Server 2000 with Microsoft Visual Basic .NET / Rick Dobson.

p. cm.

Includes index.

ISBN 0-7356-1535-7

1. Microsoft Visual BASIC. 2. Microsoft.net framework. 3. SQL server. 4. Client/server computing. I. Title.

QA76.73.B3 D63 2002
005.75'85--dc21 2002025450

Printed and bound in the United States of America.

1 2 3 4 5 6 7 8 9 QWE 7 6 5 4 3 2

Distributed in Canada by H.B. Fenn and Company, Ltd.

A CIP catalogue record for this book is available from the British Library.

Microsoft Press books are available through booksellers and distributors worldwide. For further information about international editions, contact your local Microsoft Corporation office or contact Microsoft Press International directly at fax (425) 936-7329. Visit our Web site at www.microsoft.com/mspress. Send comments to *mspinput@microsoft.com*.

Acquisitions Editor: Anne Hamilton
Project Editor: Dick Brown
Technical Editors: Dick Brown and Jean Ross

Body Part No. X08-68738

Table of Contents

Part II SQL Server 2000 Data Access, Data Manipulation, and Data Definition

Foreword

During my five years at Microsoft, I've been helping developers understand technologies such as Microsoft Visual Studio, Microsoft SQL Server, and Microsoft Office Developer. During the past two years, I have worked on the Microsoft Office XP *Visual Basic Language Reference*, and now, the MSDN Office Developer Center. In the monthly column on MSDN, *Office Talk*, I have written articles to help Office developers understand the .NET platform and how it affects their current and future development efforts.

As I write this foreword to Rick Dobson's book on programming Microsoft SQL Server solutions with Microsoft Visual Basic .NET, I think back to my own experiences developing software applications with Visual Basic. My first experience with Visual Basic was learning the language using version 3.0. I remember picking up my first Visual Basic beginner's book and being excited as I developed my first few "Hello, World" applications. I couldn't believe how quick and easy it was to develop software applications that operated similarly to other popular shareware programs of that time.

However, during that time I also discovered some of the shortcomings of Visual Basic as an enterprise-level development language. It was then that I turned my attention to C++. I remember being very frustrated at trying to learn the language, trying to understand concepts such as pointers, memory allocation, and true object-oriented programming. I took classes on C++ at the local university, but I got even more frustrated having to wait months until I was taught how to create the simplest Microsoft Windows form, something I did in just a couple of minutes using Visual Basic. In my frustration, I gave up trying to learn C++ and have been using Visual Basic to develop software applications ever since.

As each new version of Visual Basic was released, I readied myself to learn new software development technologies. First it was ActiveX control development. Then it was calling the Windows API. Next it was DHTML Applications. Then it was database development using Microsoft SQL Server. It always seemed as though I had to learn a new language and a new development paradigm for every new technology that came along. I kept thinking that there had to be an easier and more unified approach.

Well, now we've reached the advent of the Microsoft .NET platform, and with it, a revolution in the Visual Basic language, Microsoft Visual Basic .NET. I believe that Visual Basic .NET will provide software developers with new opportunities for quickly and easily designing integrated software applications that connect businesses and individuals anytime, anywhere, and on virtually any software device. With advances in the Visual Basic .NET language, Visual Basic .NET developers will finally be on a par with their C++ and C# counterparts, participating in many high-end development projects. With Visual Studio .NET features such as cross-language debugging, along with Visual Basic .NET conformance to the common type system and the common language runtime, organizations can drive down their development costs by tapping into the wide range of skills that Visual Basic .NET developers now possess.

True object-oriented programming is now available in Visual Basic .NET, including features such as inheritance and method overloading. It's now simpler to call the Windows API by using the .NET Framework Class Libraries. Web application development is now as easy as developing Windows forms–based applications. Database application development is made easier by uniting disparate data object libraries such as DAO, RDO, OLE DB, and ADO under ADO.NET, utilizing the power of XML to consume and transmit relational data over computer networks. And a new technology, XML Web services, allows Visual Basic .NET developers to host their software applications' logic over the Web. Additionally, a big issue for software developers today is that of software application deployment and versioning. If you don't agree, just ask any software developer about "DLL hell," and you're bound to get an earful. For many .NET applications, the .NET platform features "copy and paste" or XCOPY deployment. (Users simply copy your application files from the source media to any single directory and run the application.) And because .NET no longer relies on the registry, virtually all DLL compatibility issues go away.

With this book, Rick aims to give you the skills you need to program SQL Server solutions with Visual Basic .NET. I know you will find Rick's book helpful. Rick brings his experience to bear from three previous books: *Programming Microsoft Access Version 2002* (Microsoft Press, 2001), *Programming Microsoft Access 2000* (Microsoft Press, 1999), and *Professional SQL Server Development with Access 2000* (Wrox Press Inc., 2000). Rick also brings his experience of leading a successful nationwide seminar tour. More important, I know you will enjoy Rick's book because of his deep interest in Visual Basic .NET and SQL Server, and in helping you, the professional developer, understand and apply these technologies in your daily software application development projects.

Paul Cornell
MSDN Office Developer Center
http://msdn.microsoft.com/office
Microsoft Corporation
February 2002

Acknowledgments

This section offers me a chance to say thank you to all who helped make this book possible. I wish to offer special recognition to five support resources.

First, the folks at Microsoft Press have been fantastic. Dave Clark, an acquisitions editor, selected me to write the book just months after I completed another book for Microsoft Press. Dick Brown, my project editor, staunchly stood up for his perception of how to make the book's organization and content clear to you without being petty or boring to me. Dick also lightened my load substantially by showing a real knack for editing my text without distorting the original intent. When Dick was especially busy, he handed off some of his load to Jean Ross, who also did an admirable job. Others at Microsoft Press who contributed to my well-being in one way or another include Aaron Lavin and Anne Hamilton.

Second, I had excellent working relations with several professionals within Microsoft. Paul Cornell, a widely known technical editor at Microsoft, was kind enough to share his insights on how to present .NET concepts compellingly. I want to thank Paul especially for writing the Foreword to this book. Karthik Ravindran served as the MSXML Beta Product Lead Engineer at Microsoft Product Support Services during the time that I wrote this book. He provided valuable technical content about the SQL Server 2000 Web releases. Other Microsoft representatives providing moral and technical support for this book include Richard Waymire and Jan Shanahan.

Third, I want to express my appreciation to the many readers, seminar attendees, and site visitors who took the time to tell me what I did right or wrong for them, and also to those who shared their technical support questions with me. It is through this kind of feedback that I am able to know what's important to practicing developers. I encourage you to visit my main Web site (*http://www.programmingmsaccess.com*) and sign the guest book. The entry form includes space for you to leave your evaluation of this book or your question about a topic covered in the book. I promise to do my best to reply personally. In any event, I definitely read all messages and use them so that I can serve you better with future editions of this, and other, books.

Fourth, I want to tell the world how grateful I am to my wife, Virginia. Without Virginia's warm support, love, and care, this book would be less professional. She relieves me of nearly every responsibility around the house when I undertake a book project. In addition, she offers strategic advice on the issues to address and their style of coverage. When I run out of time, she even pitches in with the proofreading.

Fifth, it is important for me to give praise and glory to my Lord and Savior, Jesus Christ, who I believe gave me the strength and wisdom to write this book. In addition, He gave me health during the long gestation period that resulted in the birth of this book. It is my prayer that the book prove to be a blessing to you.

Introduction

Anyone who buys a book—or considers buying it—wants to know who the book is for, what sets it apart from others like it, and how the book is organized. This introduction covers those three questions, and it also discusses system requirements, sample files, and support.

- **First, who is the book for?** There are at least two answers to this question. One answer is that the book targets *professional developers* (and others aspiring to be professional developers). The second group the book addresses is *those who want to build full-featured, secure SQL Server solutions with Visual Basic .NET.*
- **Second, what's special about the book?** I hope you come to believe that the most important answer to this question is that the book considered *quality and depth of coverage more important than rushing to market.* The book will arrive on bookshelves more than three months after the official release of the .NET Framework. It is my wish that you derive value from the extra time taken to develop the many code samples and the in-depth discussions of advanced topics, such as class inheritance, ASP.NET, and XML Web services.
- **Third, how is the book organized?** The short answer is that there are two main sections. One section introduces SQL Server concepts as it demonstrates *T-SQL (Transact SQL) programming* techniques. After conveying SQL Server basic building blocks in the first part, the second part reveals how to put those parts together with *Visual Basic .NET and related technologies* into SQL Server solutions for handling common database chores.

The three support items include a brief description of the book's companion CD and how to use it, Microsoft Press Support Information for this book, and a summary of system and software requirements for the sample code presented in the book.

Who's the Book For?

This book targets professional Visual Basic and Visual Basic for Applications developers. From my seminar tours and Web sites (*http://www.programmingmsaccess.com* and *http://www.cabinc.net*), I know that these professionals are driven by a passion to deliver solutions to their clients through applying the most innovative technologies their clients will accept. In-house developers are the go-to persons for getting results fast—particularly for custom in-house systems and databases. Independent developers specialize in serving niche situations that can include under-served business needs and work overflows. In both cases, these professionals need training materials that address practical business requirements while showcasing innovative technologies without wasting their time. This book strives to serve this broad need in two specific areas.

This book is for developers looking for code samples and step-by-step instructions for building SQL Server 2000 solutions with Visual Basic .NET. The book focuses on the integration of SQL Server 2000 with .NET technologies tapped via Visual Basic .NET. It is my firm belief that you cannot create great SQL Server solutions in any programming language without knowing SQL Server. Therefore, this book goes beyond traditional coverage of SQL Server for Visual Basic developers. You'll learn T-SQL programming techniques for data access, data manipulation, and data definition. A whole chapter equips you to secure your SQL Server solutions. In addition, there's plenty of content in this book on Visual Basic .NET and related technologies, such as ADO.NET, ASP.NET, XML (Extensible Markup Language), and XML Web services. The presentation of these technologies demonstrates coding techniques and explores concepts that equip you to build better solutions with SQL Server 2000 databases. In addition, the book highlights innovations introduced through the Web releases for SQL Server 2000 that integrate SQL Server 2000 tightly with Visual Basic .NET.

This isn't a book about XML, but three of the book's 13 chapters focus in whole or in part on XML. Therefore, those seeking practical demonstrations of how to use XML with SQL Server and Visual Basic .NET will derive value from this book. If you have looked at any of the computer magazines over the past couple of years, you know that XML is coming to a solution near you. However, the rapid pace of XML innovation may have dissuaded some from jumping on the bandwagon while they wait to see what's going to last and what's just a fad. In the book's three chapters on XML technology, you'll learn about XML documents, fragments, and formatting as well as related technologies, such as XPath (XML Path Language) queries, XSLT (Extensible Stylesheet Language Transformation), and WSDL (Web Services Description Language).

What's Special About This Book?

There are several features that make this book stand apart from the flood of books on .NET. One of the most important of these is that this book didn't rush to market but rather shipped months after the release of the .NET Framework. This allowed me enough time to filter, examine, and uncover what were the most useful and innovative features for Visual Basic .NET developers building SQL Server solutions. For example, the book includes a whole chapter on creating solutions with XML Web services. That chapter includes two major sections on the SQL Server 2000 Web Services Toolkit, which didn't ship until the day of the .NET Framework release.

The .NET Framework content is at a professional level, but it isn't just for techies. This book doesn't assume any prior knowledge of the .NET Framework. It *does* assume that you get paid for building solutions programmatically and that at least some of those solutions are for SQL Server databases. Therefore, the book explains basic .NET concepts and demonstrates how to achieve practical results with those concepts through a huge collection of .NET code samples.

This book is about building solutions for SQL Server 2000. I include coverage of the many special features that tie Visual Basic .NET and SQL Server 2000 closely to one another. Although there is coverage of general .NET database techniques, this book dives deeply into T-SQL programming techniques so that you can create your own custom database objects, such as tables, stored procedures, views, triggers, and user-defined functions. In addition, there is separate coverage of the XML features released with SQL Server 2000 as well as separate coverage of the XML features in the first three Web releases that shipped for SQL Server 2000. There are numerous code samples throughout the book. These will equip you to build solutions with Visual Basic .NET, T-SQL, and combinations of the two.

Finally, this book is special because of the unique experiences of its author, Rick Dobson. I have trained professional developers in Australia, England, Canada, and throughout the United States. This is my fourth book in four years, and you can find my articles in popular publications and Web sites, such as *SQL Server Magazine* and *MSDN Online*. As a Webmaster, my main site (*http://www.programmingmsaccess.com*) serves hundreds of thousands of sessions to developers each year. I constantly examine their viewing habits at the site to determine what interests them. In addition, my site features scores of answers to technical support questions submitted by professional developers. My goal in offering answers to these questions is to stay in touch with practicing developers worldwide so that my new books address the needs of practicing, professional developers.

How's the Book Organized?

There are two main parts to this book tied together by an introductory part. Part II, the first main part, dwells on SQL Server techniques. Part III builds on the SQL Server background as it lays a firm foundation in .NET techniques for Visual Basic .NET developers. Part I, the introductory part, demonstrates ways to use SQL Server and Visual Basic .NET together.

Part I, Introduction

Part I, which includes only Chapter 1, has three main goals. First, it acquaints you with the basics of Visual Basic .NET within Visual Studio .NET. You can think of Visual Basic .NET as a major upgrade to the Visual Basic 5 or 6 that you are probably using currently. This first section introduces some concepts that you will find useful as you initially learn the landscape of Visual Basic .NET. The second goal of Chapter 1 is to introduce ADO.NET. If you think of Visual Basic .NET as a major upgrade to Visual Basic 6, ADO.NET is more like a major overhaul of ADO. In two sections, you get an introduction to ADO.NET classes—particularly as they relate to SQL Server—and you get a chance to see a couple of beginner samples of how to create SQL Server solutions with Visual Basic .NET and ADO.NET. The third goal of the introductory part is to expose you to Query Analyzer. This is a SQL Server client tool that ships with all commercial editions of SQL Server 2000. You can think of it as an IDE for T-SQL code. Most of the book's first part relies heavily on T-SQL, and therefore having a convenient environment for debugging and running T-SQL code is helpful. The final section of Chapter 1 addresses this goal.

Part II, SQL Server

Part II consists of six relatively short chapters that focus substantially on programming SQL Server 2000 with T-SQL. Chapter 2 and Chapter 3 introduce T-SQL and SQL Server data types. If you are going to program SQL Server and create efficient, fast solutions, you must learn SQL Server data types, which is one of the main points conveyed by Chapter 2. Many readers will gravitate to Chapter 3 because it introduces core T-SQL programming techniques for data access. You'll apply the techniques covered in this chapter often as you select subsets of rows and columns in data sources, group and aggregate rows from a table, process dates, and join data from two or more tables. Chapter 3 also considers special data access topics, such as outer joins, self joins and subqueries.

The next pair of chapters in Part II, Chapter 4 and Chapter 5, take a look at programming database objects that you will use for data access and data manipulation, such as views, stored procedures, user-defined functions, and triggers. These database objects are important for many reasons, but one of the most important is that they bundle T-SQL statements for their easy reuse. It is widely known that the best code is the code that you don't have to write. However, if you do have to write code, you should definitely write it just onc, and then reuse it whenever you need its functionality. Stored procedures are particularly desirable database objects because they save compiled T-SQL statements that can deliver significant speed advantages over resubmitting the same T-SQL statement for compilation each time you want to perform a data access or data manipulation task. Chapter 4 and Chapter 5 are also important because they convey T-SQL syntax for using parameters and conditional logic that support dynamic run-time behavior and user interactivity.

One of the most important features of SQL Server 2000 is its XML functionality. Because XML as a topic is changing so rapidly, Microsoft adopted a strategy of upgrading the SQL Server 2000 XML functionality through Web releases. Although those with SQL Server 2000 can download the Web releases without charge from the Microsoft Web site, the Web releases are fully supported. Chapter 6 introduces core XML functionality introduced with SQL Server 2000 as well as functionality from the first two Web releases. In particular, you can learn in this chapter about IIS virtual directories as well as formats for XML documents and schemas. You also learn about templates in virtual directories that facilitate data access and data manipulation tasks over the Web.

Chapter 7 closes out the SQL Server part of the book with an in-depth look at programming SQL Server security. In these times, security has grown into a monumental topic, and this chapter can keep you out of trouble by blocking hackers from getting into or corrupting your database. You learn such topics as how to create and manage different types of login and user accounts and how to control the permissions available to individual accounts as well as groups of accounts. By learning how to script accounts and permissions with T-SQL, you simplify revising and updating security as conditions change (for example, when users leave the company or when new, sensitive data gets added to a table).

Part III, .NET

Chapter 8 starts the .NET part of the book with a review of selected .NET topics that are covered in the initial look Chapter 1 offered at the .NET Framework. This chapter provides an overview of the architecture for .NET solutions, and it drills down on two topics: ASP.NET and XML Web services. The general purpose of this chapter is the same as Chapter 1, which is to introduce concepts. The emphasis in Chapter 8 isn't how you do something, but rather what are the major technologies enabling you to do something. Chapter 1 and Chapter 8 are both relatively short chapters, but you may find them invaluable if you are the kind of person who benefits from high-level overviews of a collection of topics.

Chapter 9 starts with a close examination of how to use Windows Forms with Visual Basic .NET. It then shifts its focus to a review of traditional class processing concepts via Visual Basic .NET as an introduction to class inheritance, a new object-oriented feature that makes its first appearance in Visual Basic with Visual Basic .NET. Next the treatment of classes progresses to the handling of built-in events as well as the raising of custom events. Finally the chapter closes with an examination of the new exception handling techniques for processing run-time errors.

Chapter 10 is a how-to guide for solutions to typical problems with ADO.NET. Before launching into its progression of samples showing how to perform all kinds of tasks, the chapter starts with an overview of the ADO.NET object model that covers the main objects along with selected properties and methods for each object. The how-to guide focuses on data access tasks, such as selecting rows and columns from SQL Server database objects, as well as data manipulation tasks, such as inserting, updating, and deleting rows in a table. Working through the samples in the how-to guide offers a hands-on feel for using the *System.Data.SqlClient* namespace elements to perform typical tasks.

Chapter 11 switches the focus to the Web by addressing the creation and use of ASP.NET solutions. This chapter starts by introducing basic elements that you need to know in order to use ASP.NET to create great Web solutions with Visual Basic .NET. These include learning what happens as a page does a round-trip from a browser to a Web server and back to the browser—particularly for data associated with the page. Other preliminary topics that equip you for building professional Web solutions include running the same page in multiple browser types and sniffing the browser for cases in which you want to send a page optimized for a specific kind of browser type. Management of session state is a major topic in the chapter, and you learn how to use enhancements to Session variables for Web farms as well as the new view state variables, a non-server-based technique for managing state in ASP.NET solutions. The last two sections in the chapter deal with ADO.NET topics in ASP.NET solutions and the new automatic data validation features built right into ASP.NET.

The last two chapters in the book explore how XML interplays with Visual Studio .NET and SQL Server 2000. For example, Chapter 12 examines special tools in Visual Studio .NET to facilitate the design and editing of XML documents and schemas. In addition, you learn how to designate XPath queries that accept run-time input for returning SQL Server result sets inside Visual Basic .NET programs. The chapter demonstrates techniques for processing the XML document associated with all ADO.NET data set objects. In the chapter's last section, I present a couple of code samples that illustrate how to program static HTML pages based on XML documents with XSLT.

Chapter 13 drills down on XML Web services by demonstrating several different approaches for creating Web services as well as consuming XML output from Web services. Web services behave somewhat like COM objects in that you can set up server applications for client applications. The server applications expose methods to which the client applications can pass parameters. XML comes into play with Web services in a couple of areas. First, Web services represent their inputs and outputs via WSDL, an XML-based language that formally describes an XML Web service. Second, Web services return data to their clients as XML documents or document fragments.

System Requirements

The requirements for this book vary by chapter. I developed and tested all samples throughout this book on a computer equipped with Windows 2000 Server, SQL Server Enterprise Edition, and the Enterprise Developer Edition of Visual Studio .NET, which includes Visual Basic .NET. To use this book, you'll need to have Visual Basic .NET or Visual Studio .NET installed on your computer. (See Chapter 1 for more information on versions of Visual Basic .NET and Visual Studio .NET.) In addition, you'll need SQL Server 2000, and for some of the chapters, you'll need SQL Server 2000 updated with Web releases 1, 2, and 3. Chapter 6 gives the URLs for downloading Web releases 1 and 2. Chapter 12 gives two different URLs for downloading Web Release 3—one with the SQL Server 2000 Web Services Toolkit and the other without it.

For selected chapters, you can run the samples with less software or different operating systems than the one that I used. For example, chapters 2 through 5 will run on any operating system that supports a commercial version of SQL Server 2000, such as Windows 98 or a more recent Windows operating system. Chapter 7 requires an operating system that supports Windows NT security, such as Windows 2000 or Windows XP Professional. Chapter 6, Chapter 11, and Chapter 13 require Microsoft Internet Information Services (IIS). In addition, Chapter 6 requires the installation of Web releases 1 and 2. For Chapter 11, your system needs to meet the minimum requirements for ASP.NET. (See a note in the "How Does ASP.NET Relate to ASP?" section of Chapter 8.) Several of the samples in Chapter 13 require Web Release 3 and its associated SQL Server 2000 Web Services Toolkit.

Sample Files

Sample files for this book can be found at the Microsoft Press Web site, at *http://www.microsoft.com/mspress/books/5792.asp*. Clicking the Companion Content link takes you to a page from which you can download the samples.

Supplemental content files for this book can also be found on the book's companion CD. To access those files, insert the companion CD into your computer's CD-ROM drive and make a selection from the menu that appears. If the AutoRun feature isn't enabled on your system (if a menu doesn't appear when you insert the disc in your computer's CD-ROM drive), run StartCD.exe in the root folder of the companion CD. Installing the sample files on your hard disk requires approximately 15.3 MB of disk space. If you have trouble running any of these files, refer to the text in the book that describes these programs.

Aside from the sample files that this book discusses, the book's supplemental content includes a stand-alone eBook installation that will allow you to access an electronic version of the print book directly from your desktop.

Support

Every effort has been made to ensure the accuracy of this book and the contents of the companion CD. Microsoft Press provides corrections for books through the World Wide Web at the following address:

http://www.microsoft.com/mspress/support

To connect directly to the Microsoft Press Knowledge Base and enter a query regarding a question or an issue that you may have, go to:

http://www.microsoft.com/mspress/support/search.asp

If you have comments, questions, or ideas regarding this book or the companion content, or questions that are not answered by querying the Knowledge Base, please send them to Microsoft Press via e-mail to:

mspinput@microsoft.com

Or via postal mail to:

Microsoft Press
Attn: *Programming Microsoft SQL Server 2000 with Microsoft Visual Basic .NET* Editor
One Microsoft Way
Redmond, WA 98052-6399

Please note that product support is not offered through the above mail address. For product support information, please visit the Microsoft Support Web site at:

http://support.microsoft.com

Part I

Visual Basic .NET and SQL Server 2000 Fundamentals

1

Getting Started with Visual Basic .NET for SQL Server 2000

This book aims to give professional developers the background that they need to program SQL Server applications with Microsoft Visual Basic .NET. This overall goal implies three guidelines:

- First, the book targets practicing developers. In my experience, these are busy professionals who need the details fast. These individuals already know how to build applications. They buy a book to learn how to build those applications with a specific set of tools.
- Second, the book is about building applications for SQL Server 2000. This focus justifies in-depth coverage of SQL Server programming topics—in particular, T-SQL, Microsoft's extension of the Structured Query Language (SQL).
- Third, the book illustrates how to program in Visual Basic .NET, but with particular emphasis on database issues for SQL Server 2000. Special attention goes to related .NET technologies, such as the .NET Framework, ADO.NET, ASP.NET, and XML Web services.

My goal in this chapter is to equip you conceptually for the rest of the book. Therefore, this chapter includes material that acquaints you with application development techniques and topics for SQL Server 2000 and Visual Basic .NET. The discussion of the samples in this chapter generally aims to convey broad approaches instead of how to run the sample. All the remaining chapters except for Chapter 8, another conceptual chapter, have samples with instructions aimed at professional developers.

I believe that the overwhelming majority of professional Visual Basic developers have no hands-on familiarity with Visual Basic .NET and its related technologies. If you already knew Visual Basic .NET, it wouldn't make any sense to buy a book describing how to use it. This chapter therefore focuses on how to get started with Visual Basic .NET and one of its core related technologies for those building SQL Server applications—ADO.NET. I also believe that most Visual Basic developers don't have an intimate knowledge of SQL Server—especially for creating user-defined objects, such as tables, views, and stored procedures. This capability can empower you to build more powerful and more secure applications. As you learn about database objects and how to create them in Chapter 2 through Chapter 7, reflect back on the Visual Basic .NET coverage in this chapter and how to marry database creation techniques and Visual Basic .NET development techniques. One of the best tools to build database objects is SQL Server 2000 Query Analyzer. This chapter's closing section conveys the basics of Query Analyzer that you need to follow the samples in Chapter 2 through Chapter 7.

Visual Studio .NET, the Visual Basic .NET IDE

Visual Studio .NET is the new multilanguage integrated development environment (IDE) for Visual Basic, C#, C++, and JScript developers. If you are developing solutions for Visual Basic .NET, I definitely recommend that you use Visual Studio .NET as your development environment. This section demonstrates how to get started using Visual Studio .NET for developing solutions with Visual Basic .NET.

Visual Basic .NET is available as part of Visual Studio .NET in four editions:

- Professional
- Enterprise Developer
- Enterprise Architect
- Academic

All four editions of Visual Studio .NET include Visual Basic .NET, Microsoft Visual C# .NET, Microsoft Visual C++ .NET, and support for other languages. In addition, Microsoft offers Visual Basic .NET Standard, which doesn't include Visual C# .NET or Visual C++ .NET.

Because this book targets professional Visual Basic developers creating SQL Server applications, it uses the Enterprise Developer Edition of Visual Studio .NET. You may notice some differences if you're using another edition.

Visual Studio .NET can be installed on computers running one of five operating systems: Windows 2000, Windows NT, Windows XP, Windows ME, and Windows 98. Not all the .NET Framework features are available for each operating system. For example, Windows 98, Windows Me, and Windows NT don't support developing ASP.NET Web applications or XML Web services applications. The samples for this book are tested on a computer running Windows 2000 Server, which does support all .NET Framework features.

Starting Visual Studio .NET

To open Visual Studio .NET, click the Start button on the Windows taskbar, choose Programs, and then choose Microsoft Visual Studio .NET. Visual Studio displays its integrated development environment, including the Start Page (unless you previously configured Visual Studio to open differently). From the Start Page, you can configure Visual Studio to work according to your development preferences, and you can start new solutions as well as open existing projects.

Configuring Visual Studio .NET for Visual Basic .NET

Use the links on the left side of the Start Page to begin configuring Visual Studio .NET for developing solutions in Visual Basic .NET. Click the My Profile link to open a pane in which you can specify an overall profile as well as individually indicate your preferences for Keyboard Scheme, Window Layout, and Help Filter. You also can designate the initial page that Visual Basic .NET displays. When you are beginning, it may be particularly convenient to choose Show Start Page. As a Visual Basic developer who has worked with Visual Basic 6, you might feel most familiar with a layout that reflects your prior development environment. Figure 1-1 shows these My Profile selections.

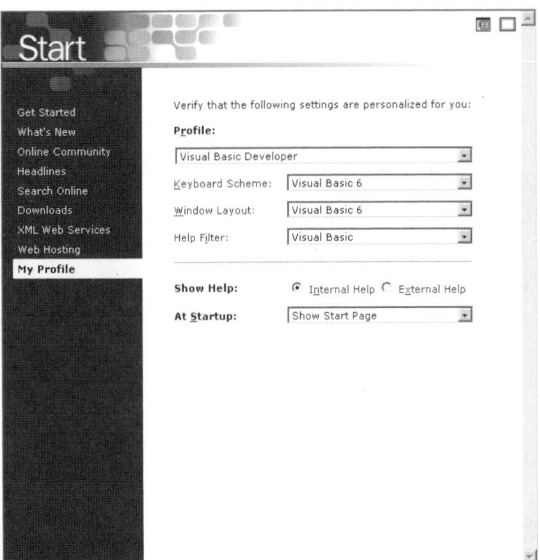

Figure 1-1. My Profile selections for starting Visual Studio .NET for a Visual Basic developer.

Using the Start Page

After setting your profile, you can return to the initial Start Page pane by choosing the Get Started link from the menu on the left border. If you had created previous solutions, the last four modified projects would appear on the Projects tab of the Start Page. The tab shows project names along with date last modified. If a project you want to view doesn't appear on the list, you can click the Open Project link to display the Open Project dialog box and then navigate to a directory containing the previously created solution. Select the project's folder that you want to open in the IDE, and double-click the solution file (.sln) for the project. The next section illustrates this process in the context of a sample project.

To create a new solution, click the New Project link to open the New Project dialog box. If you saved preferences such as those shown in Figure 1-1, the dialog will automatically select Visual Basic Projects in the Project Types pane of the New Project dialog box. On the right, you can select a template for launching a project. Table 1-1 shows the project template names along with a brief description available from the Enterprise Developer Edition of Visual Studio .NET. Choosing a template (by clicking OK after selecting a template) opens a project ready for creating the type of solution that you want to develop. When Visual Studio .NET saves the template to start a new project, it specifies either a file folder or a Web site for the template's files; you can override the default names for the file folder and Web site.

> **Note** Not all the project template types in Table 1-1 are available with the non-Enterprise (or Standard) editions of Visual Studio .NET. In addition to the empty projects, the Standard editions make available the Windows Application, ASP.NET Web Application, ASP.NET Web Service, and Console Application templates.

Table 1-1 Visual Basic .NET Project Template Types

Template Name	Creates A
Windows Application	Windows application with a form
Class Library	Windows application suitable for a library of classes without a form
Windows Control Library	Project for developing custom reusable form controls for Windows applications
ASP.NET Web Application	Web application on a Web server
ASP.NET Web Service	XML Web service on a Web server
Web Control Library	Project for developing custom reusable controls for Web applications
Console Application	Command line application that operates in an MS-DOS–style window (the Console)
Windows Service	Windows service, formerly NT service, application that runs in the background without its own custom user interface
Empty Project	Local project with no custom style
Empty Web Project	Web project with no custom style
New Project In Existing Folder	Blank project in an existing folder

There are two main categories of templates: Web projects and local projects. Web projects permit a browser to serve as the client for a project. Web projects are optimized for form processing on the Web server. Local projects offer custom form user interfaces with the capability of processing on a local workstation. Local projects can provide richer environments more conducive to client-side programming, but local projects don't offer the wide accessibility of solutions running from a Web server.

Creating and Running a Console Application

When you select a Console Application template and click OK to launch a new project, Visual Studio .NET responds by opening a project with a blank module. In addition to the Module window, Visual Studio displays Solution Explorer and the Properties window. You can enter code directly into the Module window, which appears as a tab that you can select alternately with the Start Page. Figure 1-2 shows a code sample in the Main subroutine that prompts for a first and second name before combining them and displaying them in the Console (the computer's monitor). The code is also available as MyNameIsFromConsole in the Chapter 1 folder on the companion CD for this book. Although Visual Basic developers didn't previously have Console applications routinely available, this sample should be very easy to follow. The final two lines present an instruction and cause the window to remain open until the user responds to the instruction. This allows the user to view the full name in the Console window.

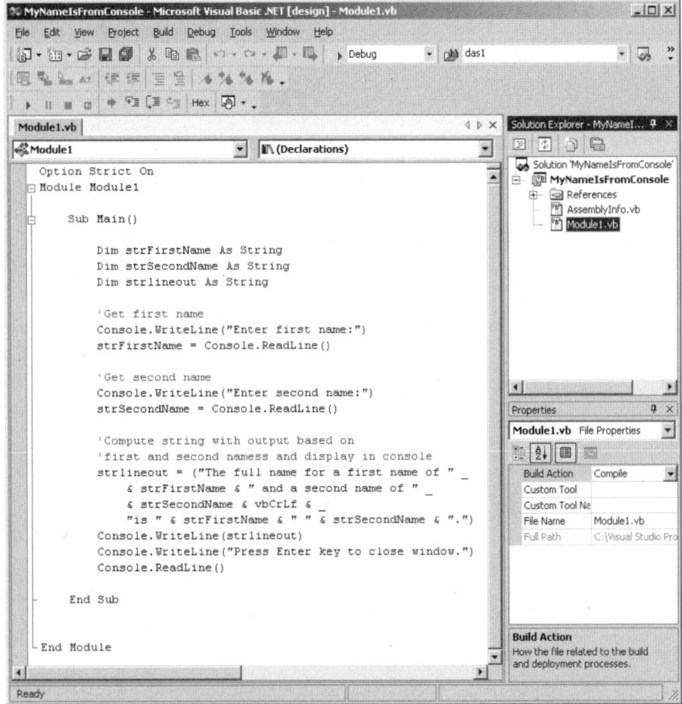

Figure 1-2. A Console application for displaying a full name based on user input for first and second names.

To the right of the Module window are two other windows. The top one of these is Solution Explorer. It shows the file structure for the solution. Solution

Explorer indicates in its first line that the solution consists of just one project. Below that line appears the name of the project, MyNameIsFromConsole. Within the project are three entries: one each for the References, AssemblyInfo.vb, and Module1.vb elements within the solution's project. By default, the Properties window is below Solution Explorer. In the Full Path property text box is an excerpt showing the path to Module1.vb on my computer. When you click the project name in Solution Explorer, the Project Folder text box in the Properties window displays the path of the directory holding the solution's files. It is this directory that you copy to deploy your solution on another computer with the .NET Framework installed. The solution won't run without the common language runtime on the computer to which you copy the directory containing the .NET Framework solution. See Chapter 8 for more detailed coverage of the .NET Framework, including the runtime and distributing .NET Framework solutions as assemblies of files in folders.

You can test run the application by choosing Start from the Debug menu, or by pressing F5. This opens the Console window with a prompt to enter a first name. After you close your application and save any changes to it, your solution appears on the Start Page for recent solutions. If you start Visual Studio .NET and the solution you want to open doesn't appear on the Projects tab of the Start Page, you can also open the solution by clicking Open Project. In the Open Project dialog box, choose the file with the .sln extension and the solution's name (MyNameIsFromConsole). A solution can contain just one .sln file, but it can contain multiple projects.

You also can run the solution and open the Console window directly from Windows Explorer without using Visual Studio .NET. Open the bin subdirectory within the directory containing the assembly folder for the solution. Then double-click the MyNameIsFromConsole.exe file. This opens the Console window with the prompt for a first name.

An Overview of ADO.NET Capabilities

ADO.NET encapsulates the data access and data manipulation for the .NET Framework. This section gives you an overview of the topic that equips you for a starter sample in the next section. Microsoft chose the name ADO.NET for the .NET Framework data access component to indicate its association with the earlier ADO technology for data access. While there are some similarities in syntax between ADO.NET and ADO (particularly for connection strings), many will find the differences are more obvious than the similarities. These differences substantially upgrade ADO.NET over ADO in two key areas—scalability and XML (Extensible Markup Language) interoperability. As a result, you will be able to create database applications with ADO.NET that serve more users and share more data than you did with ADO. See Chapter 10 for a more intensive examination of ADO.NET. Chapter 12 explicitly explores interoperability between ADO.NET and XML.

.NET Data Provider Types

Your .NET Framework solutions require .NET *data providers* to connect to data sources. These providers are different from those used with ADO, but there are distinct similarities in some of the ways you use them. With .NET data providers, your solutions can connect, read, and execute commands against data sources. The .NET providers also offer selected other functions, such as the management of input and output parameters, security, transactions, and database server errors.

Visual Studio .NET ships with two .NET data providers—the SQL Server .NET data provider and the OLE DB .NET data provider. In addition, you can download an ODBC .NET data provider from the Microsoft MSDN download site (*http://msdn.microsoft.com/downloads/default.asp*).

> **Note** As I write this chapter, the ODBC .NET data provider just became available with the rollout of the shipping version of Visual Studio .NET. You can download it from *http://msdn.microsoft.com/downloads/default.asp?url=/downloads/sample.asp?url=/msdn-files/027/001/668/msdncompositedoc.xml*. The URLs for resources sometimes change. You can always search for the ODBC .NET data provider at the MSDN download site to obtain its current download location.

The three providers taken together offer fast, highly focused access to selected data sources as well as general access to a wide range of possible data sources. The SQL Server .NET data provider is optimized for SQL Server 7.0 and SQL Server 2000. This data provider connects directly to a SQL Server instance.

The OLE DB .NET data provider connects to OLE DB data sources through two intermediate layers—the OLE DB Service Component and the classic OLE DB provider introduced along with ADO. The OLE DB Service Component manages connection pooling and transaction services. The classic OLE DB provider, in turn, directly connects to a database server. Microsoft explicitly tested the OLE DB .NET data provider with SQL Server, Oracle, and Jet 4.0 databases. Use the OLE DB .NET data provider to connect to the SQL Server 6.5 version and earlier ones. This provider is also good for connecting to your Microsoft Access solutions based on the Jet 4.0 engine.

The OLE DB .NET data provider definitely doesn't work with the OLE DB provider for ODBC data sources (MSDASQL). Because the .NET OLE DB data provider doesn't connect to ODBC data sources, you require the ODBC .NET data provider for connecting to ODBC data sources from your .NET Framework solutions.

There are four main .NET data provider classes for interacting with a remote data source. The names of these classes change slightly for each type of provider, but each .NET data provider has the same four kinds of classes. The names for the SQL Server .NET data provider classes for interacting with SQL Server instances are *SqlConnection*, *SqlCommand*, *SqlDataReader*, and *SqlDataAdapter*. You can use the *SqlDataReader* class for read-only applications from a SQL Server data source. Two especially convenient ways to display results with a *SqlDataReader* class are in a message box or the Visual Studio .NET Output window. The *SqlDataAdapter* class acts as a bridge between a remote SQL Server data source and a *DataSet* class instance inside a Visual Basic .NET solution.

A data set in a Visual Studio solution is a fifth type of ADO.NET class. A data set can contain multiple tables. A sixth ADO.NET class is the *DataView* class, which acts like a view based on a table within a *DataSet* object. Windows Forms in Visual Basic .NET applications can bind only to tables within a *DataSet* object and *DataView* objects. I examine the *DataSet* object later in this section. Chapter 10 includes a systematic summary of all six ADO.NET classes that reviews selected properties and methods of each class. The overview of ADO.NET classes in Chapter 10 is supported by numerous code samples that illustrate how to manipulate instances of the classes programmatically.

> **Note** In order to use abbreviated names, such as those listed in this section for the SQL Server .NET data provider class instances, your application needs a reference to the *SqlClient* namespace. You can create such a reference with an *Imports System.Data.SqlClient* statement just before a Module declaration.

SqlConnection Class

An instance of the *SqlConnection* class can interface directly with a SQL Server data source. Use a constructor statement to instantiate a *SqlConnection* object from the *SqlConnection* class. The *constructor statement* is a new type of syntax for .NET Framework solutions. This type of statement permits you to declare, instantiate, and pass startup parameters to an object based on a class. With the *SqlConnection* constructor statement, you can specify a connection string as an argument for the constructor statement. Alternatively, you can assign the connection string to the *SqlConnection* object after its instantiation with a property assignment statement for the *ConnectionString* property. The following line shows the syntax to instantiate a new *SqlConnection* object, *MySQLCnn1*, with a connection string designating integrated security to the mydb database on the myserver instance of SQL Server. You don't have to explicitly indicate a provider because the constructor statement reveals the type of provider through its reference to the *SqlConnection* class.

```
Dim MySQLCnn1 As New _
SqlConnection("Integrated Security=SSPI;" & _
"Data Source=myserver;Initial Catalog=mydb")
```

After instantiating a *SqlConnection* object, you need to invoke its *Open* method before the object can link another object based on one of the other SQL Server .NET data provider classes, such as *SqlCommand*, *SqlDataAdapter*, or *SqlDataReader*, to a SQL Server instance. Invoke the *Close* method to recover the resources for a *SqlConnection* object when your solution no longer needs it. The *Close* method rolls back any pending transactions and releases the connection to the connection pool. The *Dispose* method is also available for removing connections, but it invokes the *Close* method and performs other .NET administrative functions. Microsoft recommends the *Close* method for removing a connection. Unclosed connections aren't returned to the connection pool.

SqlCommand and *SqlDataReader* Classes

One way to put a connection to use is to employ it along with the *SqlCommand* and *SqlDataReader* objects. A *SqlDataReader* object can maintain an open forward-only, read-only connection with a SQL Server database. While the *SqlDataReader* using a *SqlConnection* object is open, you cannot use the *SqlConnection* object for any other purpose except to close the connection. Closing a *SqlDataReader* object releases its associated *SqlConnection* object for other uses. The *SqlDataReader* class doesn't have a constructor statement. You declare the *SqlDataReader* object with a *Dim* statement and assign a result set from a *SqlCommand* object to a *SqlDataReader* with the *ExecuteReader* method of the *SqlCommand* object. Finally, invoke the *SqlDataReader* object *Read* method to open a row from the result set in the *SqlDataReader*.

The *SqlCommand* object can serve multiple functions, including processing a T-SQL statement against a connection. When used in this fashion, the *SqlCommand* can take two arguments. The first can be a T-SQL data access statement, such as `SELECT * FROM MyTable`. The second *SqlCommand* argument designates the source connection for the T-SQL statement. For example, you can use the name of a *SqlConnection* object, such as *MySQLCnn1*.

Figure 1-3 shows the route from a SQL Server data source to a *SqlDataReader* object. Although the *SqlConnection* and *SqlCommand* objects support two-way interaction with a data source, the *SqlDataReader* object allows read-only access to the result set from the T-SQL statement serving as an argument for a *SqlCommand* constructor. Because a *SqlDataReader* object cannot specify its own data source, a *SqlDataReader* object must link to a *SqlConnection* object through an intermediate *SqlCommand* object.

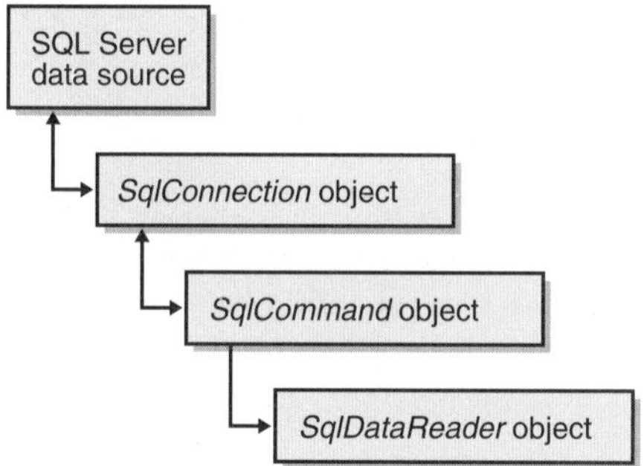

Figure 1-3. A schematic illustrating the route by which a *SqlDataReader* object returns values to an application.

The *SqlCommand* object can do more than provide a result set to the *SqlDataReader* object. The discussion of the *SqlDataReader* object described the use of the *SqlCommand* object *ExecuteReader* method. Three related methods highlight some contrasting *SqlCommand* object functionality.

- Invoke the *ExecuteNonQuery* method to perform two types of actions. First, use this method to perform data definition tasks, such as creating stored procedures and views. Second, the *ExecuteNonQuery* method can enable data manipulation tasks, such as inserts, updates, and deletes.

- Next, you can apply the *ExecuteScalar* method to a *SqlCommand* object when you want to return a single value from a *SELECT* statement. The method returns the first column from the first row of a result set. If you program this cell to be an aggregate value such as a *count* or *sum*, you can readily extract that single value with the *ExecuteScalar* method.

- Finally, the *ExecuteXMLReader* method opens a T-SQL source statement with a *FOR XML* clause into an *XMLReader* object. Chapter 6 contains extensive coverage of the *FOR XML* clause. Objects for dealing with XML will be covered in Chapter 12.

The *SqlDataAdapter* Class and the *DataSet* Class

You use objects based on the *SqlDataAdapter* class in combination with objects based on the *DataSet* class. A *DataSet* object, which is an instance of the *DataSet* class, represents an in-memory cache of data retrieved from a database. The *DataSet* object offers a disconnected data source as opposed to the always-connected data source for *SqlDataReader* objects. As a consequence, using the *SqlDataAdapter* and *DataSet* objects instead of a *SqlDataReader* object improves application scalability. This scalability improvement results because the *DataSet* doesn't persist a connection to its underlying data source over the whole of its lifetime as does the *SqlDataReader* object. While the *SqlDataReader* isn't as scalable as the *SqlDataAdapter*/*DataSet* combination, the *SqlDataReader* can provide faster performance from a remote data source because it delivers data in the style of a forward-only, read-only cursor—the classic firehose delivery model.

> **Note** The term *firehose* refers to the fact that data gushes out of a forward-only, read-only cursor.

The *SqlDataAdapter* and *DataSet* objects combine to enable both data access and data manipulation capabilities. This is important because *SqlDataReader* objects provide strictly data access capabilities (that is, you cannot perform update, insert, or delete tasks with a *SqlDataReader* object). Use the *SqlDataAdapter Fill* method to populate a *DataSet* object with values from a SQL Server data source. Because a single *DataSet* object can work with multiple *SqlDataAdapter* and OLE DB *DataAdapter* objects, you can populate a single *DataSet* object with heterogeneous data sources from multiple database servers. For example, you can populate a single data set with tables, views, or stored procedures from two different SQL Server instances or from Access and Oracle data sources in addition to a SQL Server data source. Furthermore, you can join all the data sources within a *DataSet* object on fields with common data types.

Use the *SqlDataAdapter Update* method to transfer changes from a *DataSet* object to its underlying data sources. When users perform insert, update, and delete operations against the contents of a *DataSet* object, those modifications don't transfer to the data sources for the *DataSet* object until your application invokes the *Update* method for a *SqlDataAdapter* object underlying the data source. Despite its name, the *Update* method can process all three types of data manipulation operations. However, you need a custom *SqlCommand* object to accommodate each type of data manipulation task. Therefore, a *SqlDataAdapter* can relate to a remote data source through more than a single *SqlCommand* object. Between the time you populate the *DataSet* object and the time your application invokes the *SqlDataAdapter Update* method, it's possible for the underlying data source on a SQL Server instance to change. Any changes can cause exceptions because the original values in a data set can be different from the current values in the SQL Server data source. The *SqlDataAdapter* has events and properties to help manage exceptions that can occur during an update process. Figure 1-4 presents a schematic diagram summarizing how *SqlDataAdapter* and *DataSet* objects exchange data with an underlying data source. By contrasting this diagram with the one in Figure 1-3, you can easily spot an important difference between the *SqlDataReader* and a *DataSet* object supplied by a *SqlDataAdapter* object. The capability of performing data manipulation with the *DataSet* object is a critical feature that means many applications will rely on a *DataSet* object instead of a *SqlDataReader* object.

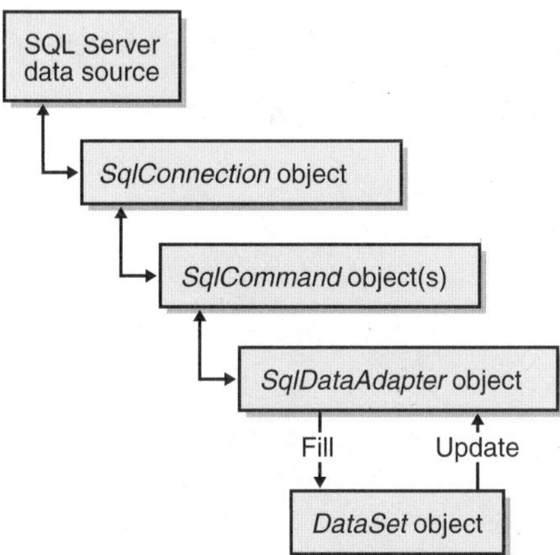

Figure 1-4. A schematic illustrating the route by which *SqlDataAdapter* and *DataSet* objects exchange values with a SQL Server data source.

The *DataSet* object offers an object model for managing the individual elements within it. The *DataSet* object consists of a *DataTable* collection (along with other elements). This collection can contain one or more tables. You can create these tables with the *SqlDataAdapter Fill* method when you initially populate a *DataSet* object from a SQL Server data source. The *SelectCommand* property, which is a T-SQL statement or a stored procedure, for a *SqlDataAdapter* object can serve as the basis of a table in the *DataTable* collection for a *DataSet* object. You can use multiple *SqlDataAdapter* objects to add more than one table to a *DataSet* object. Each table has a rich object model that permits the designation of primary keys and foreign keys as well as constraints to manage data integrity within a table. One very practical use for the *DataTable* collection and the object model for individual tables is that you will use it to navigate among the values within a *DataSet* object.

> **Note** In addition to referencing the column values of rows within an individual *DataTable* in a *DataSet* object, you can reference the schema of *DataTable* objects within a *DataSet* object. This is particularly convenient when you want to create a table that you want to populate with data from an XML document.

The *DataSet* object supports four key methods for exchanging its data with XML documents. Two of the methods are used for writing XML documents based on a *DataSet* object, and two are for reading XML documents into a *DataSet* object. Within each pair, one method focuses just on transferring schema information and the other focuses on transferring data as well as schema information.

A Starter ADO.NET Sample

This section presents a starter sample to illustrate some of the concepts described in the preceding section. Don't worry about following the details of the example. Instead, pay attention to how easy it is to get started with ADO.NET. This section reinforces the presentation of basic ADO.NET concepts described in the preceding section with simple drag-and-drop techniques and a little code included to tie objects together or enable selected functionality. See Chapter 10 for a collection of code samples that illustrate how to program ADO.NET objects when you require customized solutions not readily available from the graphical development environment. Most professional developers get called on to do the hard work that goes beyond dragging and dropping objects. After all, if it were easy, they wouldn't need you. However, it is nice to start out by seeing how easy it is to create a simple solution mostly by dragging and dropping.

> **Note** For those who want the sample from this section as a point of departure, it is available on the book's CD as the GraphicalDataBind solution.

Adding a *SqlDataAdapter*, *SqlConnection*, and *DataSet*

You can drag a *SqlDataAdapter* object to a form just like a text box or a combo box in Visual Basic 6. There is even a wizard to help you configure the *SqlDataAdapter* object. Figure 1-5 shows the opening screen immediately after dragging a *SqlDataAdapter* object to the startup blank form, *Form1*, for a Windows application. You can use this wizard to specify two ADO.NET objects.

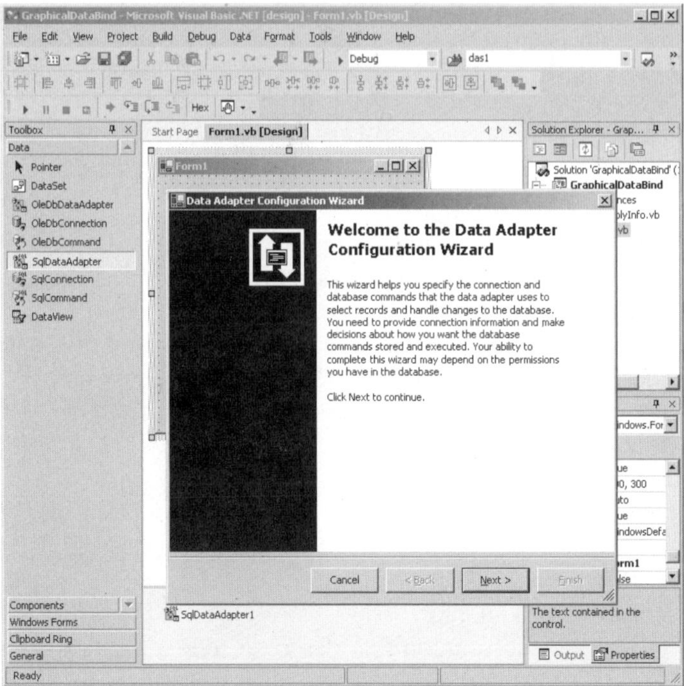

Figure 1-5. The Data Adapter Configuration Wizard enables you to graphically configure a *SqlDataAdapter* object and its related *SqlConnection* object for use with a Windows form.

First, you can designate a SQL Server database to which to connect; this creates a *SqlConnection* object. This wizard offers several routes for specifying a database connection. For example, you can pick a previously created connection, or you can create a new collection from the Data Link Properties dialog box. This dialog box lets you specify the common connection string arguments, such as a database server, a type of authentication, and a database name. In this starter sample, I used the default connection to the Northwind database.

Second, you can specify a data source within a database connection using a SQL string or a stored procedure. For this starter application, I used `SELECT CategoryID, CategoryName FROM Categories` as the SQL string source for the *SqlDataAdapter* object. Although a graphical designer is available for building query statements, you will be severely hampered as a SQL Server developer if you don't learn T-SQL, the dialect of SQL that SQL Server supports. In addition, you will find a grasp of T-SQL important for crafting the statements for the *SqlCommand* objects that enable you to build solutions that update a SQL Server data source from a Windows application.

After you finish configuring the Data Adapter Configuration Wizard, the component tray will open below your blank form. The tray will hold the two objects that the wizard created—a *SqlDataAdapter* object and a *SqlConnection* object. Because a *SqlDataAdapter* object is merely a bridge between a remote data source and a data set in a Windows application, you will need to create a data set. Then your *SqlDataAdapter* object can fill the data set with data from the remote data source specified by your replies to the Data Adapter Configuration Wizard.

Immediately after a *SqlDataAdapter* object is created, three links are displayed near the bottom of the Properties window for the object. One of these links reads Generate Dataset. Clicking the link opens the Generate Dataset dialog box, in which you designate an existing data set or specify the name for a new one. Figure 1-6 shows the specification of a new data set named *DsCategories* for the *SqlDataAdapter* created with the Data Adapter Configuration Wizard. When you click OK within the Generate Dataset dialog box portrayed in Figure 1-6, Visual Basic .NET adds a new object named *DsCategories1* to the tray below the form. In addition, Visual Basic .NET adds an XML schema named DsCategories.xsd to the solution that describes the data set. You can view the schema for the data set graphically or as XML code by double-clicking the file's name in Solution Explorer. The schema's graphical view is interactive so that you can change the data type specification for columns and make other design changes to the *Categories* table. The Properties window for the *DsCategories.xsd* shows the name of the table specification as *Categories*. At this point, you have completed the creation of the *DsCategories* data set, which contains a *DataTable* named *Categories*.

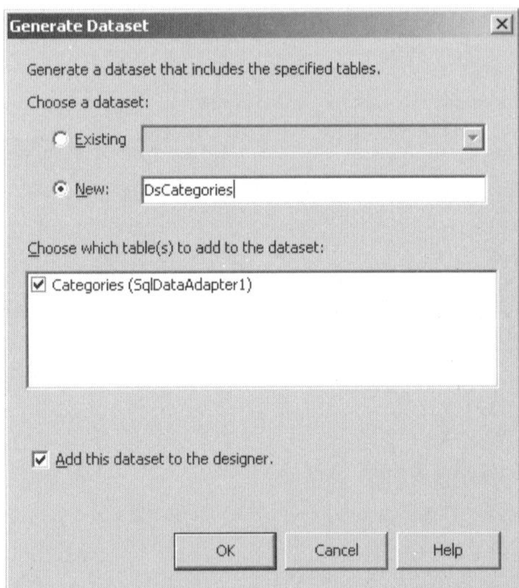

Figure 1-6. You need to add a data set before you can use a *SqlDataAdapter*. You can add the data set as simply as giving it a name in the Generate Dataset dialog box.

> **Note** Although the Generate Dataset dialog box shows the data set name as *DsCategories*, Visual Basic .NET assigns *DsCategories1* as the data set name in the tray below *Form1*.

After adding a *SqlDataAdapter* object and a *DataSet* object to an application, you can preview the data that the *SqlDataAdapter* will bring to the application. Clicking the Preview Data link in the Properties window for a *SqlDataAdapter* object opens the Data Adapter Preview dialog box. Click the Fill DataSet button to display the data in the dialog box. Because of the SQL statement used when configuring our *SqlDataAdapter* object, the button populates the form with a table that shows the *CategoryID* and *CategoryName* column values from the Northwind database. Don't confuse clicking the button on the form with populating the data set for use with a Windows form. Filling the *Categories* data table in the *DsCategories* data set with data values from a SQL Server instance and displaying the values on a Windows form requires two more steps. First you need to invoke the *Fill* method for the *SqlDataAdapter* object. Second you need to bind form controls, such as text boxes, to columns in the local *Categories* data table.

Filling a Data Set and Binding Controls to It

A logical place to fill a data set for use with a form is the form *Load* event procedure. A single line of code in the template will fill the data set. Run the line of code from the form *Load* event to make the contents for the data set available as soon as the form opens. The following code segment illustrates the syntax for invoking the *SqlDataAdapter Fill* method to populate a data set. The event procedure is for *Form1*, which is the default startup object for a Windows application. The *Fill* method takes two arguments in this situation. First you specify the data set name. Second you designate the *DataTable* name within the data set. You must name a *DataTable* object because one data set can hold multiple *DataTable* objects. Leaving out the *DataTable* name will cause an error.

```
Private Sub Form1_Load(ByVal sender As System.Object, _

    ByVal e As System.EventArgs) Handles MyBase.Load

    SqlDataAdapter1.Fill(DsCategories1, "Categories")

End Sub
```

After you fill the data set, you can bind it to controls on a form. For example, I added two text boxes to Form1 for the starter ADO.NET application. You can do this with the Toolbox just as in prior Visual Basic versions. What's new is that there is now a *DataBindings* property. You can graphically bind the *Text* property for a text box control to a column in the *Categories* data table. Figure 1-7 shows how to bind the *Text* property for *TextBox1* to the *CategoryID* column in the *Categories* data table. The Form1.vb Design tab shows *TextBox1* selected on *Form1*. The Properties window reveals the assignment of the *CategoryID* column to *TextBox1*. Selecting a column from the *Categories* data table completes the task. I followed the same process for *TextBox2*, but I selected *CategoryName* instead.

If you run *Form1* by pressing the F5 key, you see the form with two text boxes showing the *CategoryID* and *CategoryName* column values for the first row from the *Categories* data table. While it is nice to see data in the text boxes, applications typically seek to allow users to at least browse through data. To enable browsing, you need controls that let a user navigate through the rows of the *Categories* data table.

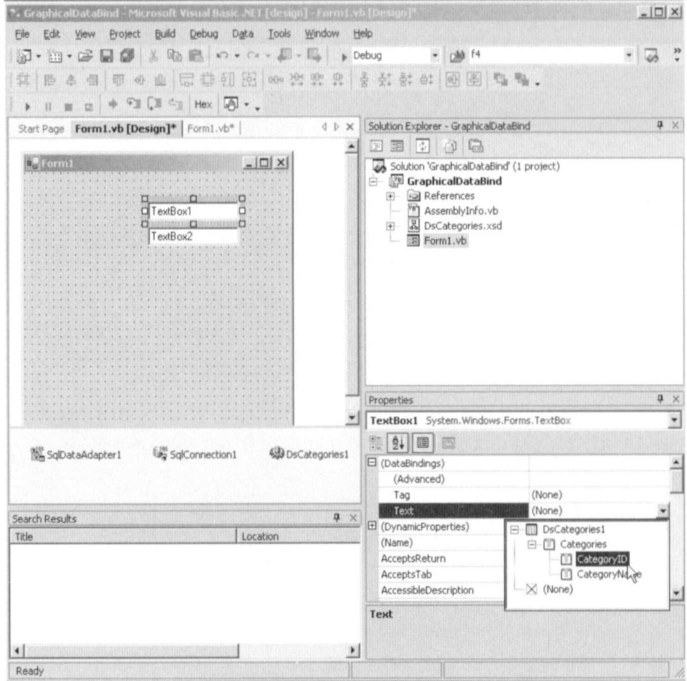

Figure 1-7. Use the *DataBindings* property to bind the *Text* property of a text box control to a column in a *DataTable* object.

Navigating Through Rows

A row of button controls can provide the basis for a navigation bar. All we need are *Text* property settings indicating the navigation each button provides and event procedures for the *Click* event of each button that navigates through the rows in the *Categories* data table. I added four button controls to *Form1* with event procedures to control navigation in response to click events. For example, Figure 1-8 shows the text boxes after the button control on the far right has been clicked. Notice that the last row (for *CategoryID* 8 in the *Categories* data table) shows in the top text box.

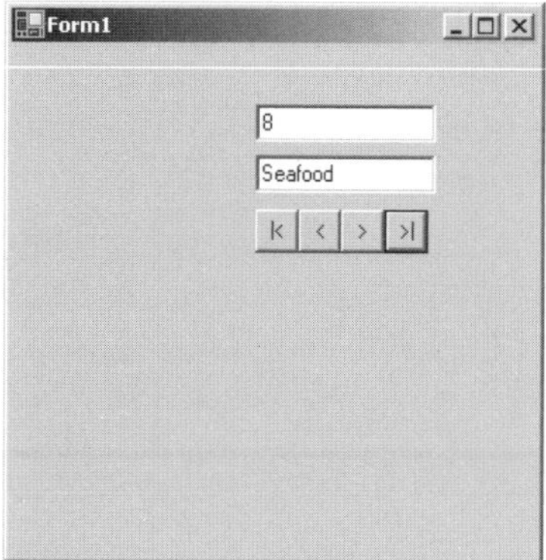

Figure 1-8. *Form1* in the starter ADO.NET sample after the last-row button (>I) has been clicked displays column values from the corresponding row in its text box controls.

The following set of *Click* event procedures for *Button1* through *Button4* shows how easy it is to control navigation. The buttons from left to right navigate to the first row, the previous row, the next row, and the last row. The procedures update the *Position* property of the *BindingContext* property on the form for the *Categories DataTable* in the *DsCategories1* data set. This manipulation, in turn, affects all text box controls bound to the *Categories* data table. Chapter 10 drills down more deeply into the object model supporting these manipulations. The important point to notice here is that the code doesn't have to handle moving past the beginning or ending row because ADO.NET is smart about recognizing either end of a rowset, such as the *Categories* data table.

```
Private Sub Button1_Click(ByVal sender As System.Object, _
   ByVal e As System.EventArgs) Handles Button1.Click


    'Move to the first row.
    Me.BindingContext(DsCategories1, "Categories").Position _
        = Me.BindingContext(DsCategories1, "Categories"). _
            Position.MinValue

End Sub

Private Sub Button2_Click(ByVal sender As System.Object, _
    ByVal e As System.EventArgs) Handles Button2.Click

    'Move to the previous row.
    Me.BindingContext(DsCategories1, "Categories").Position _
        -= 1

End Sub
```

```
Private Sub Button3_Click(ByVal sender As System.Object, _
    ByVal e As System.EventArgs) Handles Button3.Click

    'Move to the next row.
    Me.BindingContext(DsCategories1, "Categories").Position _
            += 1

End Sub

Private Sub Button4_Click(ByVal sender As System.Object, _
    ByVal e As System.EventArgs) Handles Button4.Click

    'Move to the last row.
    Me.BindingContext(DsCategories1, "Categories").Position _
        = Me.BindingContext(DsCategories1, "Categories"). _
        Position.MaxValue

End Sub
```

Using Query Analyzer

Query Analyzer is your friend for debugging T-SQL statements. Because T-SQL is so important to SQL Server development, mastering this tool can be part of what makes you into a great SQL Server developer.

What's Query Analyzer For?

Query Analyzer is one of the client tools that ships with SQL Server 2000. This is another way of saying that Query Analyzer isn't part of the database server. You are authorized to use Query Analyzer, and the other client tools, by the allocation of a Client Access License to your workstation. Although the client tools don't ship with MSDE 2000 (Microsoft SQL Server 2000 Desktop Engine), they are available with any regular version of SQL Server 2000, such as the Enterprise, Standard, Developer, and Personal editions.

I think of Query Analyzer as sort of an IDE for running T-SQL statements. This client tool is a real help for anyone programming solutions for SQL Server. Query Analyzer will help you to easily and quickly debug your T-SQL code. Although you can program and debug T-SQL directly with Visual Basic .NET and ADO.NET, Query Analyzer provides a much richer environment that makes your T-SQL coding go much faster. Even if an application calls for running T-SQL inside of a Visual Basic .NET application, I often find it convenient to debug the statement in Query Analyzer before inserting the T-SQL code into my Visual Basic .NET application.

There are at least five reasons to become comfortable with T-SQL, and using Query Analyzer may be one of the best ways to do that.

- You can build richer query statements that return precisely the data you want without having to resort to a graphical query builder. Indeed, some query operations, such as those performed by the *UNION* function, cannot be represented by graphical query designers.
- You can create data manipulation statements for updating, inserting, and deleting rows. Graphical query builders aren't always effective at creating these statements.
- You can program security topics, such as creating SQL Server logins and controlling access to database objects and server administration functions.
- You can program the creation of databases and the objects within them, such as tables, stored procedures, and user-defined functions. Several chapters within this book include scripts to create databases and populate those databases with objects automatically.
- You can take advantage of programming features, such as *IF...ELSE* statements, local variables, parameters, and return values to build flexibility and user interactivity into your applications.

Many T-SQL samples are especially designed for use with Query Analyzer. For example, these samples set the database context for T-SQL code with a *USE* statement. This statement explicitly targets Query Analyzer and doesn't run from most other SQL Server clients, such as Visual Basic .NET. Books Online, the SQL Server Help system, follows this convention with its samples. Therefore, a basic familiarity with Query Analyzer will help you to take advantage of the rich collection of samples in Books Online. In addition, the T-SQL samples in this book follow the same convention. Therefore, this section gives you a brief introduction to Query Analyzer. You will have ample opportunity to reinforce and extend the understanding this section conveys with the T-SQL samples throughout the balance of this book. In fact, the commentary for these samples sometimes describes how to run code in Query Analyzer.

Making a Connection with Query Analyzer

To start Query Analyzer, click the Start button on the Windows taskbar; choose Programs, then Microsoft SQL Server, and then Query Analyzer. When you start Query Analyzer this way, you will be greeted with the Connect To SQL Server dialog box. Recall that Query Analyzer is a client tool. Therefore, you can use it with any SQL Server instance that you can connect to and for which you have access permission. If you are connecting to the local instance of SQL Server on your computer for which you are the administrator, you can designate the SQL Server as "(local)" and choose Windows Authentication. (See Figure 1-9.) The settings in Figure 1-9 are suitable for connecting to SQL Server with any Windows login. Click OK to complete the connection to the server.

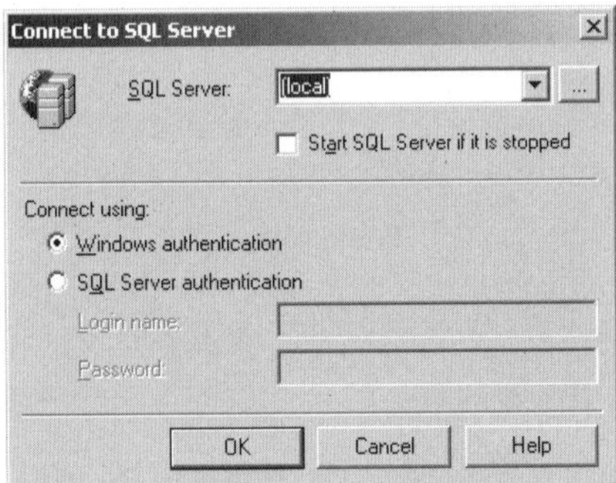

Figure 1-9. The connection settings for logging in to the local instance of SQL Server with Windows authentication.

Query Analyzer offers the normal flexibility in how you connect to a SQL Server instance. As I already noted, you can connect with any Windows login that a SQL Server instance recognizes. In addition, you can use SQL Server authentication. If you select SQL Server Authentication rather than Windows Authentication in the Connect To SQL Server dialog box, Query Analyzer enables the Login Name and Password text boxes so that you can specify a SQL Server login and password. In addition, you can connect to any other SQL Server instance besides the local default one. If you know the name of the instance to which you want to connect, type the name in the SQL Server combo box in the Connect To SQL Server dialog box. Otherwise, click the browse button (...) next to the combo box. This opens a dialog box that lists SQL Server instances currently active on the network to which your workstation connects. Select an instance name to specify a connection to that server.

See Chapter 7 for more about SQL Server security and logging in to SQL Server instances with different types of logins. Until Chapter 7, one safe approach to running the samples is to connect as a member of the sysadmin server role, such as the SQL Server administrator. Members of the sysadmin server role have unrestricted permission on a SQL Server instance. Chapter 7 gives guidelines and procedures for restricting the permissions for an application's users.

Running, Saving, and Opening T-SQL Scripts

When Query Analyzer opens as described in the preceding section, it will connect a user to the default database for the login that the user specified in the Connect To SQL Server dialog box. The default is the master database unless a database administrator changed the standard default database specification when adding a new login.

Because most user-defined queries don't interrogate the master database, which is a system database, you will usually want to change the database context before writing any SQL query statements. You can employ the *USE* statement for this. Just follow *USE* with the name of the database for which you want to write a query. The following statement directs Query Analyzer to run query statements against the pubs database (until another *USE* statement or some other specific instruction to use another database). The pubs database is one of the sample databases that is installed automatically with SQL Server 2000.

```
USE pubs
```

Figure 1-10 shows this simple *SELECT* statement for the *authors* table in the pubs database:

```
SELECT au_fname, au_lname, state
FROM authors
WHERE contract = 1
```

The *SELECT* statement appears after the *USE* statement in the Editor pane, which is where you type T-SQL statements in Query Analyzer. The statement selects three column values from the *authors* table if a row has a *contract* column value equal to 1. You can see the result set from the query statement in the Results pane that appears below the Editor pane, as shown in Figure 1-10. Query Analyzer automatically displays the Results pane when you run a query, but you can also show and hide it by pressing Ctrl+R.

By default, Query Analyzer displays the result set in the Results pane within a spreadsheetlike grid. At the bottom of the Results pane are a Grids tab and a Messages tab. You can click the Messages tab to see general feedback from SQL Server about how a query statement operated. For example, the Messages tab for the query in Figure 1-10 says, "(19 row(s) affected)", which corresponds to the number of rows the query statement returns. Warnings and error feedback from a SQL Server instance appear in the Messages pane.

You also can choose to display the result set in the Results pane as text in columns. In that case, there is only a Results tab at the bottom of the Results pane, and both the result set and messages are displayed in the pane. To specify whether you want to set the result set in a grid or in text, choose Options from the Tools menu, then choose the Results tab, and then use the combo box at the right of the Options dialog box to specify Results To Text, Results To Grids, or Results To File.

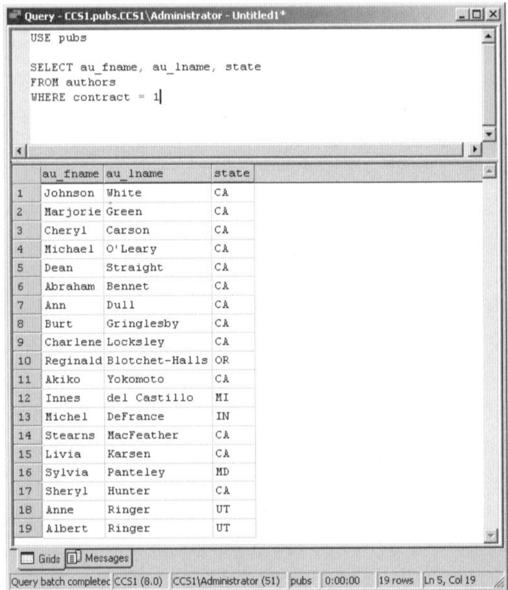

Figure 1-10. A query statement for the pubs database and its result set run from Query Analyzer.

After creating a T-SQL script, you can save it so that you or others can reopen it and use it again later. Most of the sample files for Chapter 2 through Chapter 7 are saved scripts with the .sql extension. To save a script file for the first time or resave an existing script file with a new name, choose Save As from the File menu, navigate to a desired folder with the Save Query dialog box, enter a filename, and click Save. These steps will save the current script in the designated folder with the filename that you specify with the .sql extension. For example, I followed these steps to save the script shown in Figure 1-10 to my computer. I saved the file as AuthorsQuery.sql in the Chapter01 folder of the SQL Server Development With VBDotNet directory on my C drive.

There are several ways to open a script file. For example, immediately after connecting to a SQL Server instance for a new Query Analyzer session, you can choose Open from the File menu, navigate in the Open Query File dialog box to the folder with the script file (.sql), highlight the filename, and click Open. These steps open an Editor pane in Query Analyzer with the saved script file. Figure 1-11 shows the opened script file saved in the preceding paragraph in an Editor pane. Notice that the title bar for the pane includes the path along with the filename and extension.

The Object Browser will also script objects for you. To automatically create a script for an object, right-click an object such as the *Categories* table, and choose Script Object To New Window As and then the Create command. This feature allows you to see the T-SQL script behind your favorite objects to learn how to make more objects like them or to help you change their design to meet expanded objectives.

As you build up your collection of databases and the objects within them, you might start to find special value in the Object Search component within Query Analyzer. You can open the Object Search dialog box by pressing the F4 key or by choosing Object Search from the Tools menu and then Open. You can open multiple Object Search dialog boxes at the same time. The dialog box lets you search for any object or subset of objects, such as views or stored procedures, by name or even a part of a name. Figure 1-13 shows an excerpt from the results in a search for any type of database object that begins with Categ in any database on the currently connected SQL Server instance. As you can see, objects beginning with Categ for their name are very popular in the Northwind database. (Other databases outside the excerpt shown also have objects beginning with Categ.)

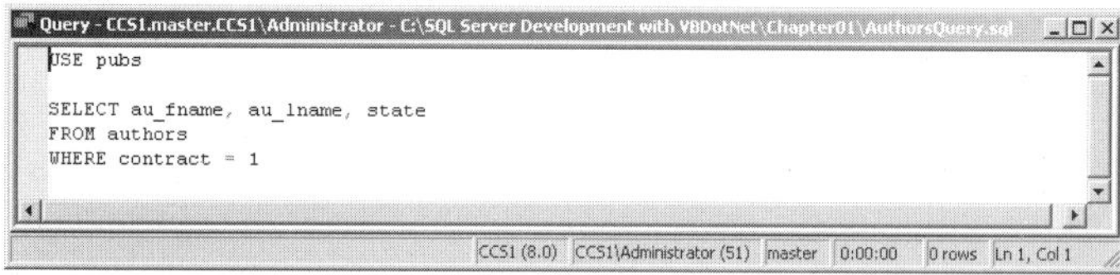

Figure 1-11. An opened T-SQL script from a saved .sql file. The path and filename in the title bar indicate the source of a .sql file.

Selected Other Topics

There's lots more to Query Analyzer, but the preceding introduction equips you for the ways in which this book exploits the tool. In this section, I briefly highlight a couple of my favorite other uses for Query Analyzer.

The Object Browser is a convenient tool for exploring the databases and the objects within them on a connected SQL Server instance with a tree-type interface. You can use this Query Analyzer component to examine the database objects within a database. You can show or hide the Object Browser by pressing the F8 key or by choosing Object Browser from the Tools menu and then the Show/Hide command. Figure 1-12 shows the Object Browser window expanded to display the column names and data type specifications for the *Categories* table (dbo.Categories) in the Northwind database. I often find it convenient to drill down into a database design and check the spelling of column names. Being able to quickly look up the data type for a column in a table is particularly convenient when you are declaring a search parameter for a column in a table; use the wrong data type, and you may not get a match, even with the right value.

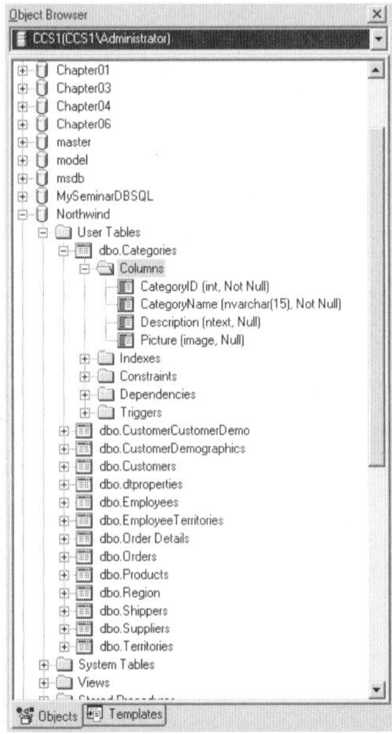

Figure 1-12. The Object Browser opened to show the names and data types for the columns in the Northwind database.

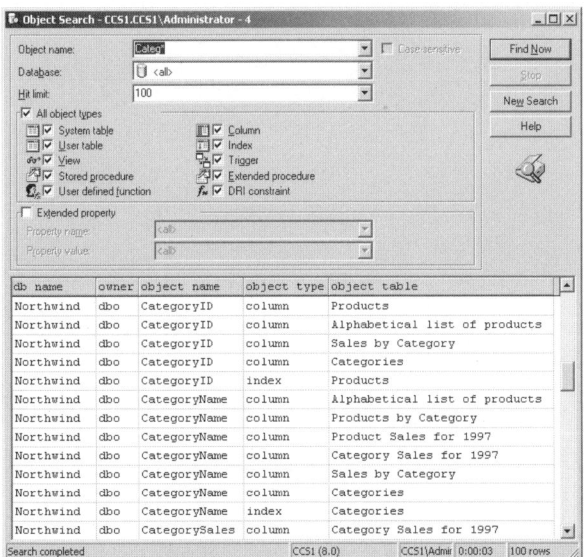

Figure 1-13. You can use the Object Search dialog in Query Analyzer to search for objects by name (or even part of a name).

Part II

SQL Server 2000 Data Access, Data Manipulation, and Data Definition

2

Tables and Data Types

This chapter targets the design and programming of SQL Server tables with T-SQL (Transact Structured Query Language). SQL Server database administrators and developers use T-SQL for programming database administration and data access. By data access, I mean selecting records from a database. T-SQL is generally compatible with the SQL-92 standard endorsed by ANSI (American National Standards Institute) and ISO (International Standards Organization). However, Microsoft optimized and streamlined T-SQL for use with SQL Server.

Any developer who wants to use Visual Basic .NET to build custom SQL Server solutions will be severely handicapped without a good grasp of SQL Server data types and tables, as well as T-SQL. Several subsequent chapters in this part of the book will explore selected other database objects, such as views, stored procedures, and user-defined functions, from design and implementation perspectives with T-SQL. The next part of the book builds on this foundation as it demonstrates how to create custom SQL Server solutions with Visual Basic .NET.

This chapter begins with an exploration of SQL Server data types. Next it provides an overview of different types of tables. A series of T-SQL samples illustrates core table design issues and solutions. These samples introduce you to programming techniques for SQL Server tables. By understanding how to script database objects, such as tables, you can readily duplicate those database objects across multiple servers. For example, a Visual Basic developer can build a solution on one server and then readily transport the objects for use on another server—just by running the scripts for the objects. You can also adapt the script from one object as a starting point for other, similar, objects. A clear understanding of table scripting techniques will help you to automate table design. This frees resources for focusing on the needs of clients for your databases.

Chapter Resources

There are two key resources for this chapter. First, a SQL Server database named Chapter 02 illustrates many of the design concepts used throughout this chapter. Second, a collection of T-SQL sample scripts illustrates coding techniques for creating tables and working with the resources within a table.

The Chapter's T-SQL Sample Scripts

The T-SQL sample collection for this chapter illustrates key design and implementation issues for scripting SQL Server database objects. All the sample scripts that you see in this chapter are available on the book's companion CD. The samples are all saved with the .sql extension, so you can open and run each of them from Query Analyzer. As you learned in Chapter 1, Query Analyzer is a graphical tool that ships with Microsoft SQL Server 2000. As you read and run the sample scripts, you might find it helpful to learn more about the structure of the Chapter02 database by browsing it with SQL Server Enterprise Manager, which also was discussed in Chapter 1.

The Chapter's Sample Database

The script in this section creates a new version of the Chapter02 database. Subsequent T-SQL code samples will create additional tables in the database and demonstrate techniques for working with tables.

Prepare to create the Chapter02 database by starting Query Analyzer and connecting to the SQL Server instance you are using. Log in as **sa** or with a user ID that belongs to the sysadmin fixed server role. This book drills down on security explicitly in Chapter 7, where you will learn how to fine-tune database and user security settings. When users connect to a SQL Server database through your Visual Basic .NET applications, they must identify themselves through the security accounts discussed in Chapter 7. Until that chapter, using a login that belongs to sysadmin will work for all samples.

Copy or type the following T-SQL script into the Editor pane in Query Analyzer, and press F5 to run the script to create the database. Alternatively, you can open the script directly from Query Analyzer: choose Open from the File menu, and then navigate to the location of the script. Notice that the first comment in the sample is "CreateSampleDB"—the name of the sample file. I use this convention for all the samples in the book to make it easier for you to locate and open them from Query Analyzer.

Attaching a Database to a New SQL Server Instance

I regularly read on the SQL Server newsgroups of folks asking how to attach a database to a server. These developers want to take a database and its objects developed on one server and run them on another server. Their need can be as simple as copying a database application they are developing on their desktop to their laptop so they can work on it while away from the office. Alternatively, they may want to copy a database from headquarters or one branch office to one or more other branch offices.

Although there are wizards for this kind of thing, it is nice to know how to program the administration of this kind of task for your own custom solutions. This capability liberates you from the canned wizard solution and gives you more flexibility in how you work with SQL Server. At its most elementary level, this can be as simple as attaching a pair of database files to a new server instance. In the context of this chapter, a completed version of the Chapter02 database is on the book's CD. Therefore, you might care to copy a version to another instance of SQL Server besides the one you use to test the samples for this chapter. The instance can be on another computer or the same computer.

Start to migrate the Chapter02 database by copying the Chapter02_dat.mdf and Chapter02_log.ldf files from the CD to the Data folder for the SQL Server instance to which you want to attach the completed database. After clearing the read-only attribute settings for the files, you can run the following script from Query Analyzer. The script attaches the chapter's two database files to the default instance of the SQL Server to which Query Analyzer connects. By changing *MSSQL* to *MSSQL$MYOTHERINSTANCE*, you can attach the database files to a SQL Server instance named *MYOTHERINSTANCE*. You must copy your database files to the Data path for the SQL Server instance in the *sp_attach_db* statement before running the script.

```
--AttachSampleDB
--Run the script from the master database.
USE master

--Update the paths for the data and log files so they
--are appropriate for your computer.
EXEC sp_attach_db @dbname = N'Chapter02',
   @filename1 =
    N'c:\Program Files\Microsoft SQL Server\MSSQL\Data\Chapter02_dat.mdf',
   @filename2 =
    N'c:\Program Files\Microsoft SQL Server\MSSQL\Data\Chapter02_log.ldf'
```

The initial *USE* statement in the script specifies the source database so that the sample runs from the SQL Server master database. Next the script removes any prior version of the Chapter02 database on the server. This ensures that you can always create a new copy of the database. After removing any prior version, the code invokes the *CREATE DATABASE* statement. This statement assigns the logical filenames Chapter02_dat and Chapter02_log to the data and log files for the database. Although your SQL Server databases can have more files, these two are necessary for populating a database and performing backup operations. Update the operating system file paths so that they are appropriate for your computing setup.

```
--CreateSampleDB
--Execute statements from the master database.
USE master
GO

--Drop any prior version of Chapter02 database.
IF EXISTS (SELECT *
    FROM   INFORMATION_SCHEMA.SCHEMATA
    WHERE  CATALOG_NAME = N'Chapter02')
DROP DATABASE Chapter02
GO

--Create new version of Chapter02 database.
CREATE DATABASE Chapter02
ON
(NAME = Chapter02_dat,
    FILENAME =
    'c:\program files\microsoft sql server\mssql\data\Chapter02_dat.mdf',
    SIZE = 1)
LOG ON
(NAME = Chapter02_log,
    FILENAME =
    'c:\program files\microsoft sql server\mssql\data\Chapter02_log.ldf',
    SIZE = 1,
    MAXSIZE = 5)
GO
```

Data Types for Tables

Tables are the building blocks for SQL Server applications because they store the data for the entities that an application models. Likewise, columns are the building blocks of tables because tables store their data as column values. SQL

Server applications can often have tables with numerous rows, so it is important to specify the data type for columns to ensure that they use the minimum amount of storage. When you specify the data type, you are indicating the kind of data that the column is going to contain. Making these assignments correctly speeds the performance of your SQL Server applications while also conserving storage space. In addition, the validity of your database model for a real-world system can depend on the use of proper data types.

In many circumstances, your applications can denote data with one of the data types built into SQL Server—the system data types. When your application needs more definition than these system data types allow natively, you can create user-defined data types that refine the system data types. However, your ability to fashion valuable user-defined data types depends on your grasp of the system data types.

If you are familiar with data types, you may want to skip this section and refer to it as needed. But if you are new to SQL Server programming or need a refresher on data types, read on.

System Data Types

It is useful to think about the system data types in six groups. In addition to the six homogeneous categories, there is a collection of special, or miscellaneous, system data types. The six homogeneous groups of data types pertain to:

- Character data
- Unicode data
- Numeric data
- Monetary data
- Date and Time data
- Binary data

Character Data

Character data consists of alphanumeric character sequences. Therefore, you can represent any combination of numbers and words with character data, such as "123 Mulberry Lane", "$1,000,000", "Your name goes here:" or "Rick Dobson". SQL Server has three character data types: *char*, *varchar*, and *text*. The following table briefly summarizes them.

Data Type Name	Data Type Description
char	For fixed-length character data up to 8000 characters. Use *char(n)* to specify, with *n* as the number of characters. The storage size is *n* bytes. Appropriate when all the column values are the same length (or when this is very nearly true).
varchar	For variable-length character data up to 8000 characters. Use *varchar(n)* to specify, with *n* as the maximum number of characters. The storage size for any *varchar* column value is the actual size, where 1 byte equals 1 character. Appropriate when there is substantial variability in length between column values.
text	For variable-length character data that can grow to 2^{31}-1 (2,147,483,647) characters in the SQL Server instance's code page format. Although some of these code pages permit double-byte format for representing characters, the length of a *text* data type column value is still the number of characters, where 1 character equals 1 byte.

SQL Server supports implicit and explicit conversion between data types. SQL Server handles implicit conversions automatically; you use the *CAST* and *CONVERT* functions to convert between types explicitly. The *CONVERT* function is a proprietary extension of the *CAST* function that offers extra conversion capability not available from *CAST*, which is SQL-92 compliant. See the "CAST and CONVERT" topic in SQL Server Books Online for more detail on conversion between SQL Server data types.

Implicit conversions don't depend on the transformation of a value by the *CONVERT* or *CAST* function. Implicit conversion also applies to the conversion of a result from combining or comparing two or more values with different data types. A variety of Books Online topics clarify implicit conversion, including the "CAST and CONVERT" topic. For example, see the "Data Type Conversion," "Data Types and Table Structures," and "Data Type Precedence" Books Online topics. You can use the Search tab in Books Online to search for these topics. The Books Online search engine will often return multiple topics for any search string, even when you specify a precise search topic title. Scan the list of titles returned by the search engine for the exact one you seek.

Unicode Data

Unicode is a 16-bit character encoding standard. SQL Server data types for Unicode correspond to SQL character data types—*nchar*, *nvarchar*, and *ntext* for fixed-length, variable-length, and very long Unicode data. One key distinction is that the Unicode format for translating bits to characters relies on a single standard translation table that uses 2 bytes per character. The character data formats use a collection of different code pages most of which assign 1 byte per character. This distinction gives Unicode format the capacity to represent more than 65,000 characters, while non-Unicode character data typically represents only 256 characters at a time (or per code page). The Unicode codes that have been assigned represent characters in most of the written languages of the world.

Character data uses system-level tables called code pages to determine how to translate bits to characters. Different countries can rely on different code pages to represent their character set. For applications that run in many different countries, it can be challenging to find a single code page with valid and consistent bit-to-character translations for all languages. Using Unicode data resolves this problem because its code page accommodates 2^{16} characters. The price for this easier cross-country applicability is that each character has a size of 2 bytes instead of the 1 byte per character. As a result, the maximum number of characters for Unicode data types is half that of corresponding character data types.

The following table summarizes the three Unicode data types. These data types align with the character data types, but they have different length and applicability.

Data Type Name	Data Type Description
nchar	For fixed-length character data up to 4000 characters in length with a Unicode data format. Use *nchar(n)* to specify, with *n* as the number of characters. The storage size in bytes equals twice the number of characters. Corresponds to the *char* data type in terms of applicability except for its broader usefulness for representing characters from multiple languages.
nvarchar	For variable-length character data up to 4000 characters in length. Use *nvarchar(n)* to specify, with *n* as the maximum number of characters. The storage size for any nvarchar column value is the actual size, where 2 bytes equal 1 character. Corresponds to the *varchar* data type in terms of applicability except for its broader usefulness for representing characters from multiple languages.
ntext	For variable-length character data that can grow to 2^{30}-1 (1,073,741,823) characters in the Unicode code page format. Corresponds to the *text* data type in terms of applicability except for its broader usefulness for representing characters from multiple languages.

> **Note** In the case of column data type specifications, precede the character data type name with an *n* to denote the matching Unicode data type name. Represent character constants in SQL Server with single-quotation mark delimiters. Use a leading *N* to represent a Unicode constant. For example, a character constant appears as `'my character constant'`. However, the matching Unicode equivalent appears as `N'my Unicode constant'`.

Numeric Data

Numeric data consists of numbers only. You can perform arithmetic operations on numeric data, and you can compare numeric values along a numeric scale, which can differ from comparisons based on collations for character data and Unicode data. SQL Server has three general categories for numeric data: integer data, decimal data, and approximate data. Within each of these categories, there are one or more specific data types. Beyond that, the numeric data categories denote different classes of numbers or ways of representing numbers.

Integer Data Integer data types denote values that SQL Server represents exclusively as whole numbers. The integer data types include *tinyint*, *smallint*, *int*, and *bigint*. The data types differ primarily in the magnitude of the number that they can represent, but the *tinyint* data type differs in that it cannot represent negative values as can the others. Integer data types, particularly *int*, are commonly used along with the *IDENTITY* property to specify automatically incrementing column values that serve as the primary key for a table.

The next table lists the integer data types along with brief summaries of their capabilities. Your applications should generally use the smallest data type possible. However, use a data type with sufficient range for your needs because SQL Server rejects column values outside the limits for a data type. Calculations, such as aggregations in views, work differently for *tinyint* and *smallint* values. In these cases, SQL Server automatically promotes the return value to the *int* value range. Therefore, the sum of a set of *tinyint* column values can exceed 255, but no individual *tinyint* column value can exceed 255.

The *tinyint/smallint* promotion policy doesn't apply to calculations based on *int* column values; SQL Server doesn't automatically promote a return value outside the *int* limits—even if the result is within the *bigint* limits. Instead, SQL Server returns an error. In addition, the *bigint* data type doesn't work with all functions that the other integer data types can use, and there are special functions for selected tasks, such as counting instances and returning rows affected by queries, in which the quantities exceed the *int* range to fall in the bigint range. See the "Using *bigint* Data" topic in Books Online for more detail on the special restrictions that apply to the *bigint* data type.

Data Type Name	Data Type Description
tinyint	For values in the range 0 through 255. Each *tinyint* column value is 1 byte long.
smallint	For values from -2^{15} (-32,768) through $2^{15}-1$ (32,767). Each *smallint* column value consumes 2 bytes of storage.
int	For values from -2^{31} (-2,147,483,648) through $2^{31}-1$ (2,147,483,647). Each *int* column value requires 4 bytes of storage.
bigint	For values from -2^{63} (-9,223,372,036,854,775,808) through $2^{63}-1$ (9,223,372,036,854,775,807). Each *bigint* column value requires 8 bytes of storage.

Decimal Data The decimal data category is a single numeric category with two equivalent SQL Server data types: *numeric* and *decimal*. You can use them interchangeably, but *decimal* is probably the more common data type name. Like the integer data types, the decimal data types precisely represent values. However, decimal data types differ from integer data types in three ways. First, decimal data type values allow for places after the decimal. (Recall that integer data types restrict you to whole numbers.) Second, decimal data type specifications permit a variable precision (or total number of digits). The total number of digits, which can range from 1 through 38, includes digits to the right and left of the decimal point. Third, you can designate a decimal data type for a column with variable scale (or digits to the right of the decimal point).

> **Note** The *decimal* data type in SQL Server 2000 and the *Decimal* data type in Visual Basic .NET aren't the same. The *Decimal* data type in Visual Basic can represent numbers with values from 1 through 28 digits to the right and left of the decimal point. This distinction (1 through 28 vs. 1 through 38) is important. Unless proper precautions are taken, you can encounter overflow errors as you extract column values with a *decimal* data type from a SQL Server table into your Visual Basic .NET application. If you know the numbers in the SQL Server table exceed the values that Visual Basic .NET can represent with its *Decimal* data type, consider representing the SQL Server *decimal* data type values with another data type in Visual Basic .NET, such as *Double*, which has a range from -1.79E + 308 through 1.79E + 308.

Designate a decimal category value with *decimal(p,s)* or *numeric(p,s)*. The *p* value represents the precision; the *s* value denotes the scale. The precision must be less than or equal to 38 but greater than or equal to the scale. The scale must be less than or equal to the precision, but the scale has to be greater than or equal to 0. The maximum data range for *decimal* type values is from $-10^{38} + 1$ through $10^{38} - 1$. This range substantially exceeds the limits of any integer data type. The same holds true for the two monetary data types that SQL Server offers. (We'll review these shortly.)

> **Note** Columns with the *decimal* data type specification can also serve as an auto-incrementing primary key when you assign an *IDENTITY* property to the column. Set the scale to 0 for this application of the data type.

The length in bytes for the *decimal* data type specification depends on the precision. The following table summarizes the relationship between storage requirements and precision for decimal data types.

Precision	Storage Bytes
1–9	5
10–19	9
20–28	13
29–38	17

Approximate Data All the prior numeric data types precisely represented data values. This avoids rounding error. The two approximate data types allow you to represent data values without perfect precision (but extremely close to the exact value). In exchange for reduced precision requirement, the approximate data types offer a much wider range than the previous data types. When you need to represent numbers beyond the range of the preceding numeric category data types, the approximate data types offer a viable alternative (for example, in engineering applications working with very large or small values). Approximate data types also enable your applications to use less storage space when reduced precision is acceptable for your needs.

The two SQL Server approximate data types are *real* and *float*. The *real* data type offers the smaller range and precision, but it requires just 4 bytes per data value. Its range extends from -3.40E + 38 through 3.40E + 38. The *float* data type extends from -1.79E + 308 through 1.79E + 308, but each *float* data type value requires 8 bytes of storage. Therefore, the *float* data type offers increased range and precision relative to the *real* data type, but *float* data type values consume 4 more bytes per column value. Both data types follow the IEEE (Institute of Electrical and Electronic Engineers) 754 specification for approximate data types. SQL Server uses the round up mode, which is one of four rounding modes in the 754 specification.

Monetary Data

SQL Server has two data types for representing monetary data. Both are accurate to the nearest ten-thousandth of a monetary unit. The *smallmoney* data type has a range from -214,748.3648 through 214,748.3647. SQL Server requires 4 bytes of storage for each value with this data type. The *money* data type has a range that starts at -922,337,203,685,477.5808 and runs through 922,337,203,685,477.5807. This data type consumes 8 bytes of storage for each column value. With either data type, you can use a currency symbol, such as $, and a decimal point when inputting values, but you shouldn't input values with commas. In other words, use $1234.5678 instead of $1,234.5678.

As you can see, the two monetary data types are two possible variations of the decimal data type in terms of its precision and range. For example, you can represent *smallmoney* data types with *decimal*(10,4). The money data type has *decimal*(19,4). When you need to represent monetary data with other formats, use alternative decimal specifications, such as *decimal*(19,2) or *decimal*(38,2).

Date and Time Data

SQL Server has two data types for internally representing date and time values. These data types differ in precision as well as range. Before diving into the details of each data type, note that SQL Server data types for date and time values always contain both a date and a time value. In addition, while SQL Server uses one of two internal formats for storing date and time values, it displays date and time values as strings. In addition, you will frequently input a new date or time column value as a string. When designating a date or a time value with a string, you can designate just the date, just the time, or both the date and the time.

The *smalldatetime* data type has the shorter range of the two data types for dates and times. This data type includes dates from January 1, 1900, through June 6, 2079. Within any given day, *smalldatetime* data type values represent time from 12:00 A.M. (midnight) through 11:59 P.M., to the nearest minute. The *smalldatetime* data type rounds down to the nearest minute for all values of 29.998 seconds or less. Conversely, it rounds up to the nearest minute for all values of 29.999 seconds or more. You can designate a *datetime* value with a character string to the nearest one-thousandth of a second, such as 'January 1, 1900 12:00:29.998', for implicit conversion as input to columns with a *smalldatetime* data type specification. Each *smalldatetime* column value requires 4 bytes of storage—two for the date and two for the time.

The other data type for date and time values is *datetime*. Values in *datetime* format can range from January 1, 1753, through December 31, 9999. As with the *smalldatetime* data type, the *datetime* data represents time from midnight. However, the precision is to the nearest 3.33 milliseconds. Therefore, you can represent the first time value after midnight as '00:00:00:003'. SQL Server rounds *datetime* values internally to the nearest millisecond within its precision. For example, time values to the nearest millisecond progress from '00:00:00:000' to '00:00:00:003' to '00:00:00:007'. The *datetime* data type specification consumes 8 bytes of storage—4 bytes for the date and 4 bytes for the time.

Binary Data

Binary data represents data in its native binary format. For example, a GUID, or globally unique identifier, appears as a 16-byte binary data stream. SQL Server represents each byte with two hexadecimal numbers. The decimal number 17, for example, appears as 11 in hexadecimal format, which corresponds to 00010001 as a byte. Hexadecimal formatting uses the letters A through F to denote the decimal values 10 through 15. Therefore, the hexadecimal number 9F translates to 159 in decimal format, or 10011111 as the bits for a byte. SQL Server frequently denotes hexadecimal values for input and display with a leading 0x; that is, a zero followed by a lowercase x. Of course, the internal representation contains just the binary representation for data.

There are three data types for binary data in SQL Server. When you are working with data strings of 8 KB or less, use either *binary* or *varbinary*. For longer binary data streams, such as Word documents or Excel worksheets in Office 97 or Office 2000, use the *image* data type. The following table summarizes the three binary data types.

Data Type Name	Data Type Description
binary	For fixed-length binary data up to 8000 bytes in length. Use *binary(n)* to specify, with *n* as the number of bytes. The storage size is *n* bytes. Appropriate when all the column values are the same length.
varbinary	For variable-length binary data up to 8000 bytes in length. Use *varbinary(n)* to specify, with *n* as the maximum number of bytes. The storage size for any *varbinary* column value is the actual size of a bit stream in bytes. Appropriate when not all column values are the same length.
image	For variable-length character data that can grow to 2^{31}-1 (2,147,483,647) bytes. Use this data type when your binary data exceeds 8 KB for any column values. Although the data type's name is *image*, it accommodates any binary data, including bitmap or GIF image files as well as Word .doc files.

Special System Data Types

Four remaining system data types complete the set available for specifying columns in a table: *timestamp*, *bit*, *uniqueidentifier*, and *sql_variant*. These data types don't fit into any one category. This section addresses each of the data types individually.

The *timestamp* data type is a binary variable that tracks the latest addition or revision of a row throughout a database. It is a sequential number—somewhat like an *autonumber* in Access or an integer with an *IDENTITY* property setting in SQL Server. However, it pertains to an entire database instead of a single table within a database. Whenever a user adds a new row or revises a value in a row of a table with a *timestamp* column, the *timestamp* column value increases by 1. SQL Server represents this *timestamp* value as an 8-byte binary value. If the largest *timestamp* value throughout any row in any table of a database is 0x13579BDF, the next *timestamp* value will be 0x13579BE0.

Note Columns declared with a *timestamp* data type don't contain *datetime* or *smalldatetime* values. Microsoft announced its intention to reference the *timestamp* data type as the *rowversion* data type in future SQL Server versions.

The *bit* data type is for representing True/False or Yes/No data. In SQL Server, a *bit* data type with the value 1 is equivalent to True or Yes. The *bit* value 0 corresponds to False or No. You can, optionally, make a *bit* data type nullable so that it can have the value 0, 1, or NULL. Values in *bit* format consume 1 bit, and SQL Server packs *bit* data values 8 bits to the byte to conserve space. Therefore, 1 through 8 *bit* data type columns in a row require 1 byte of storage. The ninth through the sixteenth *bit* data type columns add a second byte of storage for each row.

The *uniqueidentifier* data type specifies a 16-byte GUID. Since a GUID is unique in space and time, the *uniqueidentifier* is a candidate for identifying rows across multiple installations of SQL Server, such as by state in the United States or by country. However, because of its size, using a *uniqueidentifier* can slow an application and consume storage disproportionately. The severity of this *uniqueidentifier* weakness escalates with the number of rows in a table. Consider using an *int* (or even a *bigint*) column with an *IDENTITY* property along with a second column to denote place. This alternative approach to uniquely identifying records at multiple locations can make an application run faster and consume less storage. Also, the *uniqueidentifier* doesn't work well for the full range of SQL Server functions; see the "*uniqueidentifier*" and "Using *uniqueidentifier* Data" topics in Books Online for more detail.

A *sql_variant* data type specification enables a column in a table to accept a mixed collection of data values based on any other system data type except *text*, *ntext*, *timestamp*, *image*, and *sql_variant*. All other system data types require the values in a column to be of one data type. You can't enter character data into a column with an *int* data type. With a *sql_variant* data type specification, a single column can contain *char*, *int*, and *datetime* data values all in a single column. The *sql_variant* data type name derives its name because of its similarity to the Visual Basic *Variant* data type.

The mixed data type values in a *sql_variant* column can cause its values to behave differently when you're comparing *sql_variant* values with values of another data type or when you're sorting a table by the values in a *sql_variant* column. See the "Using sql_variant Data" topic in Books Online for more details on this topic.

Data Type Name	Data Type Description
timestamp	The *timestamp* data type has a *binary*(8) data format unless you make it nullable. A nullable *timestamp* data type has a *varbinary*(8) data format. SQL Server automatically generates *timestamp* values; your application or your users have no need to populate a *timestamp* column.
bit	Primarily for modeling attributes that can have one of two states. However, the data type also does permit NULL values. SQL Server optimizes storage of *bit* data type values so that the first 8 take up to 1 byte, the next 8 a second byte, and so on.
uniqueidentifier	A 16-byte binary number that represents its value as 32 hexadecimal characters. The format for displaying the hexadecimal characters is xxxxxxxx-xxxx-xxxx-xxxx-xxxxxxxxxxxx. Use the *NewID* function to generate a new *uniqueidentifier*. You can specify a *uniqueidentifier* value either with a character string representing the 32 hexadecimal characters or with a binary number. However, always use the *NewID* function when you must ensure the uniqueness of the *uniqueidentifier* value.
sql_variant	For storing multiple other kinds of data type values in a single column. This SQL Server data type bears a resemblance to the Visual Basic *Variant* data type.

> **Note** Two additional SQL Server types do not represent individual numbers or string values. These are the *table* and *cursor* types. The *table* type can represent a whole result set of values, such as a table returned by a user-defined function. Chapter 5 demonstrates the use of this SQL Server type. The SQL Server *cursor* type refers to server-side cursors. Many developers prefer to avoid this type because it can degrade database performance.

User-Defined Data Types

User-defined data types enable you to define custom data types based on system data type and nullability. You and your developer team can then apply these user-defined data types in multiple tables throughout a database. The scope of a user-defined data type is the current database, but you can copy the script defining a user-defined database to other databases.

Use the *sp_addtype* and *sp_droptype* system stored procedures to add and drop user-defined data types to and from a database. When you add a user-defined data type with *sp_addtype*, specify its name, base data type, and nullability by position or with parameter name assignments. After creating a user-defined data type, you can assign it to table columns throughout a database. If you add a user-defined data type to the model database, every new user-defined database will have the user-defined data type. This is because SQL Server uses the model database as a starting point for all user-defined databases. The *sp_droptype* system stored procedure can generally remove a user-defined data type from a database, but this system stored procedure won't succeed if any tables exist with columns defined by the user-defined data type.

> **Note** System stored procedures, such as *sp_addtype* and *sp_droptype*, gain focus as a general topic in Chapter 4.

The *sp_addtype* system stored procedure allows you to specify a user-defined data type in terms of its base data type. For example, you can designate a postal code data type with a char(5) or a char(9) base data type. However, users can still enter values other than numbers in the postal code character fields. To specify constraints that apply to user-defined data types, designate a SQL Server Rule object and bind the rule to the user-defined data type; use the *sp_bindrule* system stored procedure to bind a rule. Then developers can specify new tables with columns specified by user-defined data types that convey the rule. This approach for applying rules bound to user-defined data types works for the creation of new tables but not for the modification of existing columns in existing tables. For implementation details of user-defined data types, see the Books Online topics for *sp_addtype*, *sp_droptype*, and *sp_bindrule*.

> **Note** Examine the pubs sample database in Enterprise Manager for several examples of how to apply user-defined data types in a database.

Scripting Tables

The "Data Types for Tables" section earlier in this chapter described the most fundamental elements of a table. However, it didn't demonstrate how to apply those elements to the construction of a table. This section introduces T-SQL statements and syntax rules for creating tables. The section also examines issues relating to the processing of selected data types and the modifying of a table's design.

Creating a Table

You use the *CREATE TABLE* statement to create a new table. Before invoking the statement, you must designate a database to hold your new table. Specify this database with the *USE* statement. The following sample script assigns its new table, *EmailContacts*, to the Chapter02 database; recall that the "Chapter Resources" section includes a script for creating a fresh copy of this database. Within the *CREATE TABLE* statement, you can specify column names for the table along with data types and other settings for each column. The script creates a table named *EmailContacts* with four columns named *ContactID*, *FirstName*, *LastName*, and *Email1*. The *ContactID* column serves as a primary key. The column's specification includes a name (*ContactID*), a data type (*int*), and a specification for its nullability (*NOT NULL*); and the last keyword designates the column as a primary key. Because the table includes additional columns, the column declaration ends with a comma.

The remaining three declarations within the *CREATE TABLE* statement specify columns for holding contact data. Each of these declarations begins with a column name followed by a data type and a nullability assignment. A comma separates the declaration for each column. In contrast with the column serving as the primary key for the table, the three columns for storing contact data can be null. This allows a user to create a row for a contact at one time and then populate the row at a later time. SQL Server has a default setting for the nullability of columns that you can configure. The default configuration is for ANSI compatibility, which allows nulls for new columns. Nevertheless, it is good practice to designate the nullability of columns explicitly.

```
--CreateEmailContactsTable_01
--Execute statements after USE from Chapter02 database
USE Chapter02
--Create EmailContacts with three columns.
CREATE TABLE EmailContacts
(
ContactID int Not Null PRIMARY KEY,
FirstName nvarchar(20) NULL,
LastName nvarchar(35) NULL,
Email1 nvarchar (255) NULL
)
GO
```

The script will work the first time you run it. However, if you try to run the script a second time, it will fail with a message reminding you that the *EmailContacts* table is already in the database. In order to rerun the *CREATE TABLE* statement successfully, you can conditionally drop the *EmailContacts* table. You need to drop the table conditionally because the *DROP TABLE* statement will fail if the table isn't already in the database. While you're editing the preceding script, it might be nice to add some data and then run a simple *SELECT* query to see how to insert and retrieve data from the table. The next script demonstrates techniques for achieving these results.

This next script illustrates broad design issues for running T-SQL scripts in Query Analyzer. For example, the *USE* statement designates a source database to use for running the statement. *USE* isn't a T-SQL statement; rather, it is a keyword for Query Analyzer that instructs it to connect to a database on the server for the current Query Analyzer session. If the database doesn't exist on the connection, Query Analyzer returns an error message. Notice also that batches of T-SQL statements are delimited by the *GO* keyword. This is a keyword for Query Analyzer as well. The *GO* keyword instructs Query Analyzer to interpret and run the preceding T-SQL statements. Position the *GO* keyword in scripts to ensure that a set of statements will run before you start another set of statements. This keyword is convenient for isolating errors.

After the *USE* statement, the script tests for the prior existence of the *EmailContacts* table. If it does exist in the current database, the script invokes a *DROP TABLE* statement to remove the prior version of the table. An *IF EXISTS* statement based on an *INFORMATION_SCHEMA* view is a common means of testing for the existence of a database object. *INFORMATION_SCHEMA* views return metadata about many classes of SQL Server database objects besides tables. A subsequent section dwells on this topic more specifically.

The *CREATE TABLE* statement is identical to the preceding T-SQL listing. However, in the context of this sample, you can rerun the script repeatedly without encountering an error message about the object already existing. After creating the table, the following listing populates the table with two rows. It uses the *INSERT INTO* statement to add rows. Because these statements designate column values for all the table's columns in the order in which they appear in the table, the statements can simply reference the *VALUES* keyword followed by the column values for a row.

```
--CreateEmailContactsTable_02
--Execute statements after USE from Chapter02 database.
USE Chapter02
GO

--Remove prior version of EmailContacts if it exists.
IF EXISTS
```

```
    (
    SELECT *
    FROM INFORMATION_SCHEMA.TABLES
    WHERE TABLE_NAME = 'EmailContacts'
    )
DROP TABLE EmailContacts

--Create EmailContacts with three columns.
CREATE TABLE EmailContacts
(
ContactID int Not Null PRIMARY KEY,
FirstName nvarchar(20) NULL,
LastName nvarchar(35) NULL,
Email1 nvarchar (255) NULL
)
GO

--Populate EmailContacts and run a SELECT query.
INSERT INTO EmailContacts
    VALUES(1,'Rick', 'Dobson', 'rickd@cabinc.net')
INSERT INTO EmailContacts
    VALUES(2,'Virginia', 'Dobson', 'virginia@cabinc.net')
SELECT * FROM EmailContacts
GO
```

A *SELECT* statement closes the script. When the *SELECT* statement runs, Query Analyzer displays the result set in the Results pane, as shown in Figure 2-1.

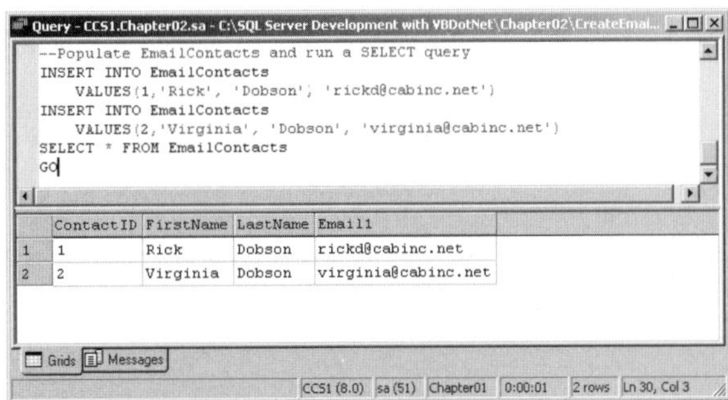

Figure 2-1. The result set from the script to create, populate, and list values for the *EmailContacts* table.

Viewing Metadata

Metadata is the information about data, such as a database server and its objects, including databases, tables, and keys. So far, this chapter has reviewed two main T-SQL samples. One of these created a database—Chapter02. The other created a table—*EmailContacts*—within the database. In turn, the table has several columns, and one of those columns is defined as a primary key. It is often useful to be able to generate reports that contain information about the contents of a database server and its objects. For example, the previous sample showed that determining whether a table already existed in a database would allow your application to avoid an error—trying to create a new table with the same name as an existing one. SQL Server *INFORMATION_SCHEMA* views can derive this kind of information for your applications. This section examines this capability by demonstrating it.

The following T-SQL script includes four batches of statements—each terminated by the *GO* keyword—that illustrate different uses and formats for deriving metadata with *INFORMATION_SCHEMA* views. The initial batch demonstrates the syntax for reporting the databases within a connection. In this case, the connection is the one based on your login to Query Analyzer and the master database for the SQL Server instance. The master database is one of the system databases that SQL Server creates when you install it. This database is vital to the proper operation of a SQL Server instance. One function of this database is to track information about all the databases on a SQL Server instance. The *SCHEMATA* view of the *INFORMATION_SCHEMA* returns a high-level summary of that information.

The next batch of T-SQL statements begins by changing the context for the statements from the master database to the Chapter02 database. This batch returns all the columns from the *TABLES* view of the *INFORMATION_SCHEMA* for which the table's name doesn't begin with either *sys* or *dtp*. While users can create tables with names that begin with either of these character strings, SQL Server uses tables beginning with these characters to manage a database. Therefore, excluding tables that begin with those characters can return information about user-defined tables. Of course, if your application creates any tables beginning with these prefixes, they won't appear in the result set for the *TABLES* view.

> **Note** The *TABLES* view for *INFORMATION_SCHEMA* returns information about views as well as tables. Specify a *TABLE_TYPE* column value of *VIEW* in the *WHERE* clause for a *SELECT* statement to return only views.

With the *COLUMNS* view of the *INFORMATION_SCHEMA*, you can return information about columns in a database. The third batch illustrates this application. It also reveals a new syntax for specifying the database serving as the source for the view. Notice that the specification of the view name has three parts. The first of these is the database name—Chapter02. Designating a database name as the first part removes the need to designate a database context with a *USE* statement. This is because no matter what database context the statement executes, it always extracts information from the database—that is, the first part of the *INFORMATION_SCHEMA* view name. The second and third parts follow the convention for the preceding batches except for the name of the specific *INFORMATION_SCHEMA* view (*COLUMNS*). The sample also includes a *WHERE* clause to reference a particular table—in particular, *EmailContacts*. Without the *WHERE* clause, the T-SQL statement in the batch will return information for all the columns within the Chapter02 database, including those from system and user-defined tables.

The final batch shows the *INFORMATION_SCHEMA* syntax for reporting about the keys in a database. These include the primary keys, foreign keys, and unique keys. The information is really about the columns on which an application defines its keys. As with the preceding batch, this sample restricts the result only to keys for the *EmailContacts* table.

```
--INFORMATION_SCHEMA_Samples
--List databases on current server.
USE master
SELECT * FROM INFORMATION_SCHEMA.SCHEMATA
GO

--List user-defined tables in Chapter02 database.
USE Chapter02
SELECT * FROM INFORMATION_SCHEMA.TABLES
WHERE NOT(SUBSTRING(TABLE_NAME,1,3) = 'sys'
    OR SUBSTRING(TABLE_NAME,1,3) = 'dtp')
GO

--List all columns in EmailContacts table.
SELECT * FROM Chapter02.INFORMATION_SCHEMA.COLUMNS
WHERE TABLE_NAME = 'EmailContacts'
GO

--List data on columns constrained as keys in
--the EmailContacts table.
SELECT * FROM Chapter02.INFORMATION_SCHEMA.KEY_COLUMN_USAGE
WHERE TABLE_NAME = 'EmailContacts'
GO
```

Figure 2-2 displays an excerpt from the result set for the preceding script. The return for each batch begins with a new set of column headers. The list of databases includes our user-defined database, Chapter02, along with the two SQL Server sample databases, pubs and Northwind, as well as the four system databases. The second header shows just one row for the lone table in Chapter02. The third header rows reveal the names of the four columns within the *EmailContacts* table. This view provides much additional information about each column, such as its nullability, data type, and related settings, including its precision and scale if appropriate. The row for the last set of column headers provides information about the lone key for the *EmailContacts* table. This is the table's primary key. Each key has a name, which appears in the *CONSTRAINT_NAME* column. Because our syntax for the creation of the table didn't specify a name for the primary key, the last row of output in Figure 2-2 shows the system-generated name for the table's primary key in the *CONSTRAINT_NAME* column. A subsequent sample in the "Scripting Keys and Indexes" section illustrates the syntax for assigning a specific name to a primary key.

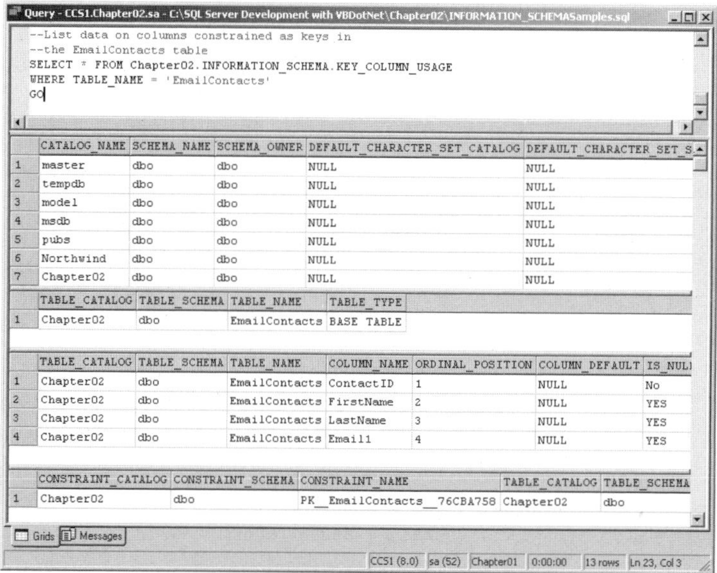

Figure 2-2. Sample output from a set of four T-SQL batches illustrating the behavior of *INFORMATION_SCHEMA* views.

INFORMATION_SCHEMA offers many more views besides those illustrated in the preceding four batches. For example, you can gather information about check constraints for column values, table constraints, stored procedures, and user-defined functions. Refer to the "Information Schema View" topic in Books Online for an overview of the *INFORMATION_SCHEMA* views along with links defining the result set for each type of view available.

Working with Column Data Types

The "Creating a Table" section introduced the *CREATE TABLE* statement syntax and demonstrated how to declare typical system data types such as *int* and *nvarchar*. Applying this framework will enable you to assign the other data types to columns as well. In spite of the simplicity of the overall approach, there are special issues for some data types, and one data type hasn't been covered yet. This section reviews these issues.

Comparing *timestamp* and *datetime* Data Types

Those who are migrating to SQL Server may be confused at first by the *timestamp* data type and whether it has anything to do with *datetime* data (it doesn't). The *rowversion* alias for *timestamp* actually summarizes the purpose of the *timestamp* data type more precisely. This may be one reason why Microsoft plans to use the *rowversion* name more prominently in the future.

The following script contrasts the *timestamp* and *datetime* data types. The contrast relies on two tables, *t1* and *t2*, each with three columns, *col1*, *col2*, and *col3*. The *col1* column has an *int* data type and offers a value for programmatically populating rows in each table. The *col2* and *col3* columns populate automatically. The data type for *col2* is *datetime*, but it has a *DEFAULT* constraint that assigns the current time automatically. Users and your application's code can override this default value. The *timestamp* data type also automatically populates *col3* in both tables. However, for this data type, only SQL Server updates the value. This occurs with the insertion of a new row or the revision of any value in an existing row.

After creating the *t1* and *t2* tables, the script does a couple of operations to contrast *timestamp* and *datetime* data types. The script inserts a record into each table with a delay of 1 second between each insertion. The *WAITFOR DELAY* statement actually suspends the operation of SQL Server for the duration of its argument. Therefore, the insertion for table *t2* can occur more than 1 second after the insertion for table *t1* because SQL Server requires time to perform the operation. After running a *SELECT* query to show the column values in tables *t1* and *t2*, the script next updates the value of *col1* in table *t2*. Then it reruns the SELECT query to demonstrate the impact of the operation on the column values in the sample. At the sample's conclusion, the script removes the *t1* and *t2* tables from the Chapter02 database.

```
--CompareTimestampToDatetime
--Execute statements after USE from Chapter02 database.
USE Chapter02

--Create two tables named t1 and t2.
CREATE TABLE t1
(
```

(continued)

```
col1 int,
col2 datetime DEFAULT GETDATE(),
col3 timestamp
)
CREATE TABLE t2
(
col1 int,
col2 datetime DEFAULT GETDATE(),
col3 timestamp
)
GO

--Insert a row in tables t1 and t2 with
--a one-second delay between tables.
INSERT INTO t1 (col1) VALUES (1)
WAITFOR DELAY '00:00:01'
INSERT INTO t2 (col1) VALUES (1)
GO

--Run queries on tables t1 and t2.
SELECT 't1' AS 'Table Name', * FROM t1
SELECT 't2' AS 'Table Name', * FROM t2
GO

--Update column col1 in table t2.
UPDATE t2 SET col1 = col1 + 2
GO

--Re-run queries on tables t1 and t2.
SELECT 't1' AS 'Table Name', * FROM t1
SELECT 't2' AS 'Table Name', * FROM t2
GO

--Drop tables t1 and t2.
DROP TABLE t1
DROP TABLE t2
GO
```

Figure 2-3 shows the Results pane from Query Analyzer for the preceding script. The *col2* value for the second row is 1 second plus a SQL Server clock tick (3 milliseconds) behind the *col2* value for the first row. This clock tick is the time that it takes to complete the row insertion for table *t2*. The *col3* values for the first and second rows are displaced by 1. Because the insertion for table *t2* occurred immediately after the one for table *t1*, this is appropriate. If other insertions took place between the initial insertion for table *t1* and table *t2*, the difference in the binary value for *col3* would be greater. The update of *col1* for table *t2* demonstrates this point.

The second pair of rows in Figure 2-3 also displays the column values for tables *t1* and *t2* after an update to *col1* in table *t2*. In the case of table *t1*, the *col3* value remains unaltered. However, the *col3* value for table *t2* grows by 1 from its initial value after the insertion. This increased value reflects the impact of the update to *col1* in table *t2*. While the second pair of rows varies from the first pair for *col3* in Figure 2-3, the *col2* values are identical between the first and second pair of rows. This is because updating values of other columns has no impact on the *datetime* values in *col2*, but updating any value in a row does impact the value of the *timestamp* column value in the row.

> **Note** You can have just one column per table with a *timestamp* data type.

	Table Name	col1	col2	col3
1	t1	1	2001-08-18 01:48:56.450	0x000000000000009F

	Table Name	col1	col2	col3
1	t2	1	2001-08-18 01:48:57.453	0x00000000000000A0

	Table Name	col1	col2	col3
1	t1	1	2001-08-18 01:48:56.450	0x000000000000009F

	Table Name	col1	col2	col3
1	t2	3	2001-08-18 01:48:57.453	0x00000000000000A1

Figure 2-3. Sample output contrasting the behavior of *datetime* and *timestamp* data types.

Using *sql_variant* Data Type Values

The *sql_variant* data type is the only data type that lets you store different data types in the same column. This capability is useful for storing a collection of values in a column in which you don't know in advance what types of values you'll have. This can arise in a situation in which you let a user define values on an ad hoc basis.

Consider a table that stores miscellaneous information about contacts. Sometime your application may need to store a money data type, another time a user may want to specify a date, and in yet other cases, your application may need to designate a variable-length character value. This kind of scenario is typical of situations in which your application needs to characterize elements but the complete set of elements and their attributes isn't known at the time that you develop the application.

The following script assigns a set of extended properties to a table of contacts identified by a *ContactID* column. Notice that the *CREATE TABLE* statement uses three columns to characterize the contacts. The most important column is *PropValue*, which has a *sql_variant* data type. This column stores the actual value that characterizes a contact. In some cases, the contact characteristic is a monetary value, in other cases it is a date, and in still other cases it is a string value, such as the name of a favorite sport or store. *PropID* and *PropName* describe the characteristic for the contact. *PropName* makes it easy to follow what the *PropValue* column values describe without requiring another table to decode the *PropID* column values. A subsequent sample will return to the *ContactExtProps* table and link it to other tables containing contact and property names. In addition, that sample will add a primary key to the table. These refinements aren't necessary to demonstrate the behavior of *sql_variant* data types.

The *INSERT INTO* statements that add values to the *PropValue* column use *CAST* functions to establish sub data types within the *sql_variant* column. This isn't strictly necessary, but the *CAST* function confirms the ability of the *sql_variant* data type to accept multiple other data types.

```
--SQL_variantSample
--Execute statements after USE from Chapter02 database.
USE Chapter02
GO

--Remove prior version of ContactExtProps if it exists.
IF EXISTS
    (
    SELECT *
    FROM INFORMATION_SCHEMA.TABLES
    WHERE TABLE_NAME = 'ContactExtProps'
    )
DROP TABLE ContactExtProps
GO

--Create ContactExtProps with four columns.
CREATE TABLE ContactExtProps
(
ContactID int NOT NULL,
PropID int NOT NULL,
PropName nvarchar(20),
PropValue sql_variant
)
GO

--Populate ContactExtProps with values.
INSERT INTO ContactExtProps
    VALUES(1, 1,'Birthday', CAST('9/9/1944' AS datetime))
```

```
INSERT INTO ContactExtProps
    VALUES(1, 2, 'Salary', CAST(50000 AS money))
INSERT INTO ContactExtProps
    VALUES(1, 3, 'Bonus', CAST(30000 AS money))
INSERT INTO ContactExtProps
    VALUES(1, 4, 'Favorite Sport', 'Boxing')
INSERT INTO ContactExtProps
    VALUES(2, 1, 'Birthday', CAST('1/1/1950' AS datetime))
INSERT INTO ContactExtProps
    VALUES(2, 2, 'Salary', CAST(60000 AS money))
INSERT INTO ContactExtProps
    VALUES(2, 3, 'Bonus', CAST(40000 AS money))
INSERT INTO ContactExtProps
    VALUES(2, 5, 'Favorite Store', CAST('Tailspin Toys' AS nvarchar(20)))
GO

--Select all records with a Favorite Store property.
SELECT ContactID, PropName, PropValue
FROM ContactExtProps
WHERE PropName = 'Favorite Store'
GO

--Select Salary and Bonus properties and add one to
--money data type for Salary and Bonus properties.
SELECT ContactID, PropName, Cast(PropValue AS money)+1, PropValue
FROM ContactExtProps
WHERE PropID >=2 and PropID <=3
GO

--This SELECT fails because sql_variant doesn't implicitly
--convert to other data types (for example, money)
SELECT ContactID, PropName, Cast(PropValue AS money), PropValue+1
FROM ContactExtProps
WHERE PropID >=2 and PropID <=3
GO
```

Three *SELECT* queries at the end of the preceding script illustrate some of your options for extracting data from columns declared with a *sql_variant* data type. The first *SELECT* query includes *PropValue*, the *sql_variant* data type, in the *SELECT* list for a query, but it uses a column defined with the *nvarchar* data type in a *WHERE* clause. This *SELECT* query succeeds and returns the name of the favorite store for any record that has the *PropName* value 'Favorite Store'.

The second *SELECT* query uses *PropID*, a column with an *int* data type, in the *WHERE* clause to extract records with information about salary and bonus for contacts in the *PropValue* column. This sample transforms the sql_variant data type for *PropValue* to a money data type in the *SELECT* list. Then it adds 1 to the transformed value. This addition operation succeeds because it works with the explicitly converted *sql_variant* data type.

The last *SELECT* query tries the same addition task as the second *SELECT* query, but its *SELECT* list relies on an implicit transformation of the *sql_variant* data type to a data type that supports addition. Because SQL Server doesn't support this transformation for a *sql_variant* source data type, the last *SELECT* query fails. Figure 2-4 displays the output from the first two successful query statements.

	ContactID	PropName	PropValue
1	2	Favorite Store	Tailspin Toys

	ContactID	PropName	(No column name)	PropValue
1	1	Salary	50001.0000	50000.0000
2	1	Bonus	30001.0000	30000.0000
3	2	Salary	60001.0000	60000.0000
4	2	Bonus	40001.0000	40000.0000

Figure 2-4. Notice that the *PropValue* column, which has *a sql_variant* data type, returns values with different data type formats, such as variable-length character strings and money.

Using Computed Columns in Tables

A computed column adds a virtual column to a table based on an expression that draws on one or more other columns within the table. You can specify a computed column with a *CREATE TABLE* (or an *ALTER TABLE*) statement. You can use a computed column in a *SELECT* list, a *WHERE* clause, or an *ORDER BY* clause. In addition, computed columns can participate in the definition of an index or primary key. You can also use a computed column in the definition of a *UNIQUE* constraint. When you're using a computed column to help define a primary key or an index, the expression must be deterministic. In other words, the expression must generate the same result all the time based on the same input. An expression based on *GETDATE* isn't appropriate for a computed column that will serve as a column for an index. This is because the result will change each time you open the table.

Despite the wide range of uses for computed columns, there are several circumstances in which you cannot use them. For example, you cannot specify nullability for computed columns. This is because SQL Server automatically determines whether a computed column is null based on its input and the expression for combining the computed columns in question. Even non-nullable inputs can generate null results if an expression generates an underflow or overflow. In addition, you cannot specify inputs or modify the contents of columns with *INSERT INTO* or *UPDATE* statements. Yet another application that doesn't permit the use of computed columns is that which defines *FOREIGN KEY* and *DEFAULT* constraints.

The following script sample illustrates the syntax for specifying a computed column and shows an example of how to use it. The *CREATE TABLE* statement designates three columns for the *ProjectedDeliveryDates* table. The first column is autoincrementing, with default settings for the *IDENTITY* column property. The second column has a *datetime* data type for accepting order dates. The third column is a computed column. The expression for the column uses the *DateAdd* function to compute a projected delivery date based on the table's *OrderDate* column.

> **Note** The *IDENTITY* property permits you to set the seed value and the step value for an autoincrementing series. Its default seed and step values are both 1. You can specify alternate seed and step values by adding parentheses after the keyword. For example, use *IDENTITY*(100, 10) to specify a series that starts at 100 and progresses in steps of 10.

```
--ComputedColumnSample
--Execute statements after USE from Chapter02 database.
USE Chapter02
GO

--Remove prior version of ProjectedDeliveryDates if it exists.
IF EXISTS
    (
    SELECT *
    FROM INFORMATION_SCHEMA.TABLES
    WHERE TABLE_NAME = 'ProjectedDeliveryDates'
    )
DROP TABLE ProjectedDeliveryDates

--Create ProjectedDeliveryDates with three columns.
CREATE TABLE ProjectedDeliveryDates
(
OrderID int IDENTITY Not Null PRIMARY KEY,
OrderDate datetime Not Null,
ProjectedDeliveryDate AS DateAdd(day, 10, OrderDate)
)
GO
```

(continued)

```
--Populate ProjectedDeliveryDates.
INSERT INTO ProjectedDeliveryDates
Values(GetDate())
INSERT INTO ProjectedDeliveryDates
Values('9/1/01')

--Display date and time for projected delivery.
SELECT OrderID, OrderDate, ProjectedDeliveryDate
FROM ProjectedDeliveryDates

--Display just date for projected delivery.
SELECT OrderID, OrderDate,
    LEFT(ProjectedDeliveryDate,12)
    AS 'ProjectedDeliveryDate'
FROM ProjectedDeliveryDates
GO
```

After inserting order dates based on either the *GETDATE* function or a string representing a date, the script queries the *ProjectedDeliveryDates* table with two separate *SELECT* queries. The first *SELECT* query statement demonstrates the computed column as part of the list for the statement. For this statement, the *ProjectedDeliveryDate* column displays both the date and the time. However, your application may require just the date. The second query statement shows how to crop the time value out of the display. Figure 2-5 presents the output from both *SELECT* statements.

	OrderID	OrderDate	ProjectedDeliveryDate
1	1	2001-08-18 11:59:35.797	2001-08-28 11:59:35.797
2	2	2001-09-01 00:00:00.000	2001-09-11 00:00:00.000

	OrderID	OrderDate	ProjectedDeliveryDate
1	1	2001-08-18 11:59:35.797	Aug 28 2001
2	2	2001-09-01 00:00:00.000	Sep 11 2001

Figure 2-5. This example shows the use of a computed column to display a projected date for the delivery of an order in either of two representations—one that includes a time and another that shows only a date.

Adding Check Constraints

Check constraints are among the most simple of the constraint types available to database developers and administrators. Basically, a check constraint allows you to restrict the values entering a column—somewhat in the way that data type specifications do. (Users cannot enter a character string into a column with an int data type.) However, check constraints base their restriction on a Boolean expression that evaluates to *True* or *False*. The constraint expression can draw on one or more column values from the table to which it applies. A column constraint applies to an individual column, and a table constraint references two or more columns. The value *False* for the expression violates the constraint. SQL Server rejects the insertion of a record with a value that violates a constraint. You can use this behavior to maintain the integrity of the column values in the tables of your database applications.

The following script has three batches of statements. First the script adds a column check constraint to the *EmailContacts* table initially generated in the "Creating a Table" section. The first batch also tests the constraint by attempting to insert a row with a column value that violates the constraint. In the second batch, the script shows how to disable a constraint. This batch attempts to insert the same record that failed in the first batch, but this time the insertion succeeds. The third batch drops the constraint from the *EmailContacts* table and deletes the record added in the second batch.

You can use the *ALTER TABLE* statement to add a column check constraint to a table, such as *EmailContacts*. The *ALTER TABLE* statement permits the modification of a table after its creation. Besides adding check constraints, you can add other constraints, such as primary or foreign keys, and new columns. To add a constraint, use the *ADD* keyword followed by *CONSTRAINT*. You can optionally assign a constraint name. Specifying a constraint name is particularly convenient if your application has a need to disable or remove a constraint. If you don't explicitly name your constraints, SQL Server automatically assigns a name. The *CHECK* keyword specifies the type of constraint. Finally, the expression trailing the *CHECK* keyword represents the condition for which the check constraint tests. In the sample script, the constraint evaluates the *Email1* value to ensure that it contains the @ symbol. E-mail addresses that don't include this symbol are invalid.

```
--ColumnCheckConstraintSample
USE Chapter02

--Add CHECK constraint to require at
--least one @ in Email1.
ALTER TABLE EmailContacts
ADD CONSTRAINT ch_EmailContacts_Email1_for@
CHECK (CHARINDEX('@',Email1)<>0)

--Test constraint with an Email1 value
--that contains no @; the INSERT statement fails.
INSERT INTO EmailContacts
    VALUES (3,'Karl', 'Doel', 'Doel.hlcofvirginia.com')
GO
```

(continued)

```
--Disable the constraint.
ALTER TABLE EmailContacts
NOCHECK CONSTRAINT ch_EmailContacts_Email1_for@

--Test the disabled constraint with an Email1 value
--that contains no @; the INSERT statement succeeds.
INSERT INTO EmailContacts
    VALUES (3,'Karl', 'Doe1', 'Doe1.hlcofvirginia.com')
GO

--Drop the constraint and delete bad Email1 row.
ALTER TABLE EmailContacts
DROP CONSTRAINT ch_EmailContacts_Email1_for@
DELETE FROM EmailContacts
WHERE LastName = 'Doe1'
GO
```

Scripting Keys and Indexes

This section drills down on techniques for scripting primary keys, foreign keys, and indexes in your tables. Each topic begins with a brief description of background issues before the discussion of a sample or two that illustrate typical uses for the topic.

Primary Keys

Primary keys have two especially distinctive features. First, each row must have a unique primary key value. Second, no primary key value can be null—even if it is the only null record in a table. It is common, but not mandatory, to base primary keys on a single column with an *IDENTITY* property setting. A primary key can span multiple columns.

Each primary key creates an *index*. An index is a database object that supports fast access to the rows within a table or view. Any one SQL Server table can have up to 250 indexes, but only one of these can be clustered. A clustered index physically orders the records for a table in storage according to the index values. Because a clustered index can speed performance so much, you should reserve the clustered index so that it serves your application's most heavily used lookup requirement. You can make either the index for the primary key or another index the clustered index for a table. With a standard SQL Server installation, a primary key declaration makes the primary key clustered by default. However, you can explicitly declare a primary key as nonclustered.

As mentioned previously, the primary key can have its name assigned either by the system or by a user. The following script sample re-creates the *EmailContacts* table. If you check the sample in that section, you will observe that the primary key declaration doesn't include a name for the primary key.

The following script re-creates the generation of the *EmailContacts* table, but this sample does explicitly name the primary key. The sample also demonstrates the use of the *sp_pkeys* system stored procedure—once before dropping the first version of the *EmailContacts* table and a second time after creating a new version of the table with a user-defined name for the primary key. The *sp_pkeys* system stored procedure has a result set with a separate row for each column in the primary key. The columns of the result set report such items as the database name, the table name, and the primary key name.

The primary key declaration in this section performs identically to the one in the "Creating a Table" section except for the assignment of a name to the primary key. In this instance, the sample uses the *CONSTRAINT* keyword. This is optional for a primary key, but its use can remind you that the primary key is a member of the family of constraints, including check constraints and foreign key constraints. The name for the primary key appears immediately after the *CONSTRAINT* keyword. The following script also explicitly declares the primary key as clustered. You can replace the keyword *CLUSTERED* with *NONCLUSTERED* to avoid physically ordering the records in the table according to *ContactID* values.

```
--CreateEmailContactsTableWithPKName
--Execute statements after USE from Chapter02 database.
USE Chapter02
GO

--Print primary key columns and remove prior version
--of EmailContacts, if the table exists.
IF EXISTS
    (
    SELECT *
    FROM INFORMATION_SCHEMA.TABLES
    WHERE TABLE_NAME = 'EmailContacts'
    )
    BEGIN
        EXEC sp_pkeys 'EmailContacts'
        DROP TABLE EmailContacts
    END

--Create EmailContacts with three columns while
--explicitly assigning a name to the primary key.
CREATE TABLE EmailContacts
(
ContactID int Not Null
    CONSTRAINT pk_EmailContacts_ContactID PRIMARY KEY CLUSTERED,
FirstName nvarchar(20),
LastName nvarchar(35),
Email1 nvarchar (255)
)
```

(continued)

```
GO

--Populate EmailContacts and run a SELECT query
INSERT INTO EmailContacts
    VALUES(1,'Rick', 'Dobson', 'rickd@cabinc.net')
INSERT INTO EmailContacts
    VALUES(2,'Virginia', 'Dobson', 'virginia@cabinc.net')
SELECT * FROM EmailContacts
GO

--List primary key columns in EmailContacts.
EXEC sp_pkeys 'EmailContacts'
```

Figure 2-6 shows the output from the preceding script. The results below the first and third column headers reveal the output from the *sp_pkeys* system stored procedure before and after the naming of the primary key. The first set of column headers shows the system defined name for the primary key. The third set of column headers shows the output from the *sp_keys* stored procedure after the assignment of a name to the primary key. Notice how the *PK_NAME* column value in the last row of Figure 2-6 matches the name assigned to the primary key in the preceding script.

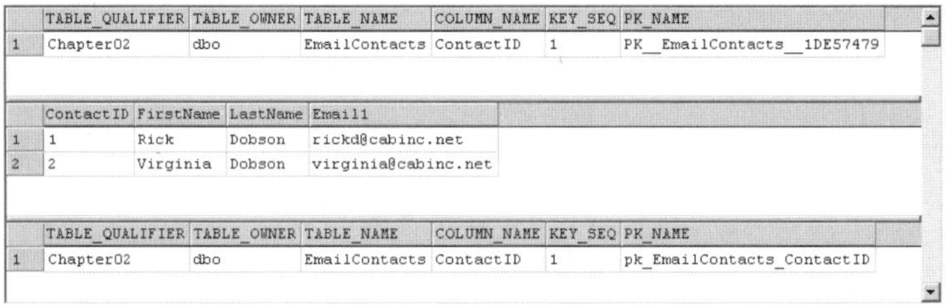

	TABLE_QUALIFIER	TABLE_OWNER	TABLE_NAME	COLUMN_NAME	KEY_SEQ	PK_NAME
1	Chapter02	dbo	EmailContacts	ContactID	1	PK__EmailContacts__1DE57479

	ContactID	FirstName	LastName	Email1
1	1	Rick	Dobson	rickd@cabinc.net
2	2	Virginia	Dobson	virginia@cabinc.net

	TABLE_QUALIFIER	TABLE_OWNER	TABLE_NAME	COLUMN_NAME	KEY_SEQ	PK_NAME
1	Chapter02	dbo	EmailContacts	ContactID	1	pk_EmailContacts_ContactID

Figure 2-6. Sample output demonstrating primary key names assigned by the system (top row) and by the preceding script (bottom row).

Recall that the "Using *sql_variant* Data Type Values" section initially created the *ContactExtProps* table. When it was created in that section, the script didn't create a primary key for it. In addition, the *ContactExtProps* table includes a column, *PropID*, designed to link to another table that defines names to match the *PropID* values. The next script creates a table, *ExtProps*, that matches the *PropID* int values with names in a column of variable-length character strings. The script then proceeds to use the *sp_pkeys* system stored procedure to determine whether a primary key column is already in the *ContactExtProps* table. A value of 0 for *@@ROWCOUNT* specifies no primary key. If the value is greater than 0, the procedure drops the existing primary key. Next the procedure uses an *ALTER TABLE* statement to create a new primary key based on two columns—*ContactID* and *PropID*. This primary key designation permits each contact to have multiple properties but no more than one setting for any one property. The foreign key sample in the next section will demonstrate how to link the *ContactExtProps* table to the *EmailContacts* and *ExtProps* tables.

```
--CreateExtProps
--Execute statements after USE from Chapter02 database.
USE Chapter02
GO

--Remove prior version of ExtProps, if it exists.
IF EXISTS
    (
    SELECT *
    FROM INFORMATION_SCHEMA.TABLES
    WHERE TABLE_NAME = 'ExtProps'
    )
DROP TABLE ExtProps
GO

--Create ExtProps.
CREATE TABLE ExtProps
(
PropID int,
PropName nvarchar(20),
)

--Populate ExtProps with values.
INSERT INTO ExtProps
    VALUES(1, 'Birthday')
INSERT INTO ExtProps
    VALUES(2, 'Salary')
INSERT INTO ExtProps
    VALUES(3, 'Bonus')
INSERT INTO ExtProps
    VALUES(4, 'Favorite Sport')
INSERT INTO ExtProps
    VALUES(5, 'Favorite Store')
GO

--Drop primary key for ContactExtProps.
EXEC sp_pkeys ContactExtProps, dbo, Chapter02
IF @@ROWCOUNT > 0
ALTER TABLE ContactExtProps
DROP CONSTRAINT pk_ContactExtProps_ContactID_PropID
GO

--Add Primary Key based on ContactID and PropID.
ALTER TABLE ContactExtProps
```

(continued)

```
ADD CONSTRAINT pk_ContactExtProps_ContactID_PropID
    PRIMARY KEY NONCLUSTERED
    (
    ContactID,
    PropID
    )

--List primary key columns in ContactExtProps.
EXEC sp_pkeys 'ContactExtProps'
```

The preceding script closes by invoking the *sp_pkeys* system stored procedure. The output from the procedure appears in Figure 2-7. Notice that it contains two rows—one for each column that contributes to the primary key for the *ContactExtProps* table.

	TABLE_QUALIFIER	TABLE_OWNER	TABLE_NAME	COLUMN_NAME	KEY_SEQ	PK_NAME
1	Chapter02	dbo	ContactExtProps	ContactID	1	pk_ContactExtProps_Contac..
2	Chapter02	dbo	ContactExtProps	PropID	2	pk_ContactExtProps_Contac..

Figure 2-7. Output from the *sp_pkeys* system stored procedure that shows a primary key defined on two columns.

Foreign Keys

Foreign keys are column values in one table that point to the primary key or unique key in another table. Specifying a foreign key enforces referential integrity between the two tables. Referential integrity requires all new records added to the table with the foreign key to match either a primary or a unique key value in the other table if it isn't null. You can optionally specify actions to occur when you update or remove a primary or unique key in the table on the other end of the foreign key relationship. Specifically, you can cascade the change from the table with the primary or unique key to the one with the foreign key. Alternatively, you can choose no action to occur in the table with the foreign key as a consequence of updates to the table with the primary or unique key.

The following script adds a couple of foreign keys to the *ContactExtProps* table. The first foreign key uses the *ContactID* in the *ContactExtProps* table to refer to the primary key for the *EmailContacts* table. The second foreign key uses the *ContactExtProps* table via its *PropID* column values to refer to the *ExtProps* table. Because the *ExtProps* table doesn't initially have a primary or a unique key, the table cannot participate in a foreign key relationship. Therefore, the script first adds constraints to the *PropID* column in *ExtProps* so that it serves as the table's primary key. Then it declares the foreign key relationship between the *ContactExtProps* table and the *ExtProps* table. Although the first foreign key doesn't declare any cascading action, the declaration for the second foreign key specifies cascading updates. The script sample illustrates the syntax for designating cascading updates in its declaration. After the second foreign key declaration, the script tests the cascading update behavior by making a change to a *PropID* value in the *ExtProps* table and then verifying that the update cascades to the corresponding *PropID* value in the *ContactExtProps* table. The script sample concludes by restoring the values and the database design to their former state before the addition of either foreign key. This makes it possible to rerun the script without any manual setup activity between runs.

You add a foreign key to a table as a constraint. The syntax for performing this task has at least three steps, and it can have more if you specify a cascading action. Begin the foreign key declaration inside an *ALTER TABLE* statement. After you open the *ALTER TABLE* statement, the first step is to indicate that you want to add a constraint with the *ADD* and *CONSTRAINT* keywords. You can, optionally, assign a name to the foreign key constraint. Next add the *FOREIGN KEY* keyword and follow it with parentheses containing the names of the columns from the current table participating in the relationship. Third add *REFERENCES* as a keyword. Follow this keyword with the name of the table to which the relationship refers. Then, in parentheses after the table name, add the column names from that table that participate in the relationship. By default, update and delete actions don't cascade from the table with the unique key or primary key to the table with the foreign key. However, you can optionally add an *ON UPDATE* or *ON DELETE* clause to the foreign key declaration. Include in either clause *CASCADE* to transfer the action from the table with the primary or unique key to the one with the foreign key.

```
--ForeignKeysSamples
--Beginning of first FOREIGN KEY sample.
USE Chapter02

--Remove FOREIGN KEY constraint if it exists already.
EXEC sp_fkeys @fktable_name = N'ContactExtProps'
IF @@ROWCOUNT > 0
BEGIN
    ALTER TABLE ContactExtProps
    DROP CONSTRAINT ContactExtProps_fkey_ContactID
END

--Then, add a new FOREIGN KEY constraint.
ALTER TABLE ContactExtProps
ADD CONSTRAINT ContactExtProps_fkey_ContactID
FOREIGN KEY (ContactID)
REFERENCES EmailContacts(ContactID)

--Verify addition of new constraint.
EXEC sp_fkeys @fktable_name = N'ContactExtProps'
--End of first FOREIGN KEY sample
```

(continued)

```
--Beginning of second FOREIGN KEY sample.
--Convert PropID in ExtProps to NOT NULL.
ALTER TABLE ExtProps
ALTER COLUMN PropID int NOT NULL
GO

--Then, define a primary key on PropID.
ALTER TABLE ExtProps
ADD CONSTRAINT pk_PropID PRIMARY KEY CLUSTERED (PropID)
GO

ALTER TABLE ContactExtProps
ADD CONSTRAINT ContactExtProps_fkey_PropID
FOREIGN KEY (PropID)
REFERENCES ExtProps(PropID)
ON UPDATE CASCADE

--Verify addition of new constraint.
EXEC sp_fkeys @fktable_name = N'ContactExtProps'
GO

--List ExtProps and ContactExtProps rows before
--update to ExtProps.
SELECT * FROM ExtProps
SELECT * FROM ContactExtProps

--Then, make a change in ExtProps that
--cascades to ContactExtProps.
UPDATE ExtProps
SET PropID = 50 WHERE PropID = 5

--List ExtProps and ContactExtProps rows after
--update to ExtProps.
SELECT * FROM ExtProps
SELECT * FROM ContactExtProps
GO
--End of second FOREIGN KEY sample.

--Do cleanup chores.
--Start to restore by resetting PropID values.
UPDATE ExtProps
SET PropID = 5 WHERE PropID = 50

--Next, drop FOREIGN KEY constraints.
ALTER TABLE ContactExtProps
DROP CONSTRAINT ContactExtProps_fkey_ContactID

ALTER TABLE ContactExtProps
DROP CONSTRAINT ContactExtProps_fkey_PropID
```

```
--Then, drop PRIMARY KEY constraint first .
ALTER TABLE ExtProps
DROP CONSTRAINT pk_PropID

--Finally, restore NULL setting for column.
ALTER TABLE ExtProps
ALTER COLUMN PropID int NULL
GO
--End of restore from second FOREIGN KEY sample.
```

Figure 2-8 shows two excerpts from the preceding script's output. The top panel shows the *ExtProps* table rows over the *ContactExtProps* table rows. This is before an update of the *PropID* value 5 to a new value of 50 in the *ExtProps* table. The bottom panel shows the same two tables after the update of the value in the *ExtProps* table. Notice that the change to the *ExtProps* table cascades to the *ContactExtProps* table.

	PropID	PropName
1	1	Birthday
2	2	Salary
3	3	Bonus
4	4	Favorite Sport
5	5	Favorite Store

	ContactID	PropID	PropName	PropValue
1	1	1	Birthday	1944-09-09 00:00:00.000
2	1	2	Salary	50000.0000
3	1	3	Bonus	30000.0000
4	1	4	Favorite Sport	Boxing
5	2	1	Birthday	1950-01-01 00:00:00.000
6	2	2	Salary	60000.0000
7	2	3	Bonus	40000.0000
8	2	5	Favorite Store	Tailspin Toys

	PropID	PropName
1	1	Birthday
2	2	Salary
3	3	Bonus
4	4	Favorite Sport
5	50	Favorite Store

	ContactID	PropID	PropName	PropValue
1	1	1	Birthday	1944-09-09 00:00:00.000
2	1	2	Salary	50000.0000
3	1	3	Bonus	30000.0000
4	1	4	Favorite Sport	Boxing
5	2	1	Birthday	1950-01-01 00:00:00.000
6	2	2	Salary	60000.0000
7	2	3	Bonus	40000.0000
8	2	50	Favorite Store	Tailspin Toys

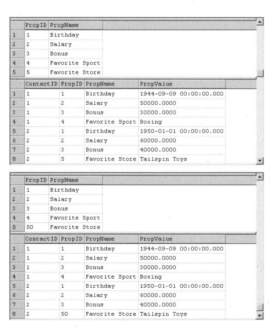

Figure 2-8. The top and bottom panels show the *ExtProps* table over the *ContactExtProps* table before and after a change to the *ExtProps* table.

Indexes

Many databases can achieve performance gains through the addition of an index. Indexes are great at speeding lookups and sorts. On the other hand, there are times when the overhead associated with maintaining an index can slow an application. This is particularly true when one or more indexes overlap with a clustered primary key. Often developers and administrators have to resort to timing runs for typical tasks to determine the best configuration of indexes for a database application. With this in mind, the value of being able to add and drop indexes programmatically is considerable as you perform your timing runs to discern the optimal index configuration.

The last script in this chapter illustrates several techniques for working with indexes that you are likely to find useful. The script begins by creating a user-defined stored procedure, *ListUserDefinedIndexes*, that lists the indexes for user-defined tables in a database. (You'll read much more about stored procedures in Chapter 4.) See Figure 2-9 for sample output. This procedure draws on both the *sysobjects* and *sysindexes* tables—two system catalog tables. While you should generally avoid manipulating system tables, some advanced developers find it useful to do so. The *Name* column from the *sysobjects* table (*sysobjects.name*) returns the table for an index, and the *Name* column from the *sysindexes* table (*sysindexes.name*) is the name for a specific index in a table (if there is one). The *indid* column presents the index identifier column values. An *indid* value of 1 indicates a clustered index, such as one created with the *CREATE INDEX* statement or one associated with a primary key. Values of *indid* between 2 and 250 are for nonclustered indexes. An *indid* value of 0 indicates there is no clustered index for a table. The *indid* column value also conveys information about tables containing large data types, such as *text*, *ntext*, and *image*. See the "Table and Index Architecture" topic in Books Online for additional detail.

> **Note** Instead of using the *ListUserDefinedIndexes* stored procedure in the script below, you can use the system stored procedure *sp_helpindex* to collect information about indexes. This system stored procedure works similarly to *sp_pkeys* and *sp_fkeys*, but it provides information for indexes. However, *ListUserDefinedIndexes* gives you exposure to techniques for working with system catalog tables, which are a rich source of content about a database's design.

You can add an index to a table with the *CREATE INDEX* statement. The listing below initially demonstrates the syntax for creating an index based on one column. Follow *CREATE INDEX* with the name of your index. Then follow the index name with an ON clause. In the *ON* clause, include the table name with the column or columns for the index. Place the column name in parentheses after the table's name.

The sample illustrates the application of the *CREATE INDEX* syntax twice. The first use of the statement is for adding an index based on the *LastName* column in the *EmailContacts* table. This example demonstrates how to use the *CREATE INDEX* statement as described in the preceding paragraph. A second application of the statement shows how to create a unique index based on two columns from the *ContactExtProps* table—namely, *ContactID* and *PropID*. The syntax for this example uses the *UNIQUE* keyword. This keyword is appropriate for a table with a candidate key because it specifies a second index that is unique for each record besides the primary key. In other words, the column(s) contributing to a unique index are candidates for the primary key. By default, the *CREATE INDEX* statement generates nonclustered indexes. However, you can insert *CLUSTERED* after either *CREATE* or *UNIQUE* (if it is present) to make a clustered index.

Use the *DROP INDEX* statement to remove a user-defined index (for example, one you create with the *CREATE INDEX* statement). The syntax for the *DROP INDEX* statement uses a two-part name to designate the index to drop. The first part is the table name, and the second part is the index name. A period delimits the two parts. Our stored procedure lists the indexes for primary keys and system-defined indexes. You can delete the index for a primary key by dropping the key. If the SQL Server settings for a server permit it, you can remove the index for a foreign key directly from the *sysindexes* table. See the "How to set the allow updates option (Enterprise Manager)" and "Error 259" topics in Books Online for more detail on directly manipulating system catalog tables, such as *sysindexes*.

```
--IndexSamples
USE Chapter02
--Create a stored procedure to list for user-defined
--tables object name from sysobjects, and name and
--indid from sysindexes.
IF EXISTS(SELECT * FROM INFORMATION_SCHEMA.ROUTINES
    WHERE ROUTINE_NAME = 'ListUserDefinedIndexes')
DROP PROCEDURE ListUserDefinedIndexes
GO
CREATE PROCEDURE ListUserDefinedIndexes
AS
SELECT sysobjects.id AS [sysobjects.id],
    sysindexes.id AS [sysindexes.id],
    sysobjects.name AS [sysobjects.name],
    sysindexes.name AS [sysindexes.name], sysindexes.indid
FROM sysobjects INNER JOIN sysindexes
ON sysobjects.id = dbo.sysindexes.id
```

(continued)

```
WHERE (LEFT(sysobjects.name, 3) <> 'sys')
    AND (sysobjects.name <> N'dtproperties')
GO

--List indexes data.
EXEC ListUserDefinedIndexes

--Create an Index for LastName in EmailContacts.
CREATE INDEX ind_EmailContacts_LastName
ON EmailContacts(LastName)

--List indexes data.
EXEC ListUserDefinedIndexes

--Remove previously created index.
DROP INDEX EmailContacts.ind_EmailContacts_LastName

--Remove primary key for ContactExtProps based
--on ContactID and PropID.
EXEC sp_pkeys ContactExtProps, dbo, Chapter02
IF @@ROWCOUNT > 0
ALTER TABLE ContactExtProps
DROP CONSTRAINT pk_ContactExtProps_ContactID_PropID
GO

--List indexes data.
EXEC ListUserDefinedIndexes
GO

--Create an Index for LastName in EmailContacts.
CREATE UNIQUE INDEX ind_ContactExtProps_ContactID_PropID
ON ContactExtProps(ContactID, PropID)

--List indexes data.
EXEC ListUserDefinedIndexes
GO

--Attempt to enter a record with duplicate key values for
--ContactID and PropID.
INSERT INTO ContactExtProps Values (1, 1, 'Birthday', '9/9/1964')
GO

--Remove previously created index.
DROP INDEX ContactExtProps.ind_ContactExtProps_ContactID_PropID

--List indexes data.
EXEC ListUserDefinedIndexes
GO
```

```
--Insert and then delete record with duplicate values for
--ContactID and PropID columns.
INSERT INTO ContactExtProps Values (1, 1, 'Birthday', '9/9/1964')
DELETE FROM ContactExtProps WHERE PropValue = '9/9/1964'
GO
```

Besides syntax issues, the preceding sample script illustrates design issues for working with indexes, such as testing the behavior of a unique index. To isolate the effect of the index, the script drops a primary key that requires uniqueness on the same two columns as the *ind_ContactExtProps_ContactID_PropID* index. The test for the validity of this unique index is an attempt to enter a record with a duplicate key value. After failing, the script drops the unique index and confirms that you can add the record if the unique index isn't present; the script closes by removing the test record.

Figure 2-9 shows an excerpt from the beginning of the script with the output from the first two uses of the *ListUserDefinedIndexes* stored procedure. The main point to take away from the output is that the first listing of indexes doesn't include a reference to *ind_EmailContacts_LastName*, but the second one does. In between the two runs of the *ListUserDefinedIndexes* stored procedure, the script invokes the *CREATE INDEX* statement to generate the index. The two result sets also show the indexes for clustered and nonclustered primary keys. For example, *pk_EmailContacts_ContactID* is a clustered primary key; notice that its *indid* value is 1. The index for the nonclustered primary key, *pk_ContactExtProps_ContactID_PropID*, has an *indid* value of 2. Finally, the *_WA_Sys_PropID_77BFCB91* index is for a foreign key from a preceding sample. SQL Server didn't remove the index when the script dropped the key.

	sysobjects.id	sysindexes.id	sysobjects.name	sysindexes.name	indid
1	2009058193	2009058193	ContactExtProps	ContactExtProps	0
2	2009058193	2009058193	ContactExtProps	pk_ContactExtProps_ContactID_PropID	2
3	2009058193	2009058193	ContactExtProps	_WA_Sys_PropID_77BFCB91	3
4	517576882	517576882	EmailContacts	pk_EmailContacts_ContactID	1
5	1074102867	1074102867	ExtProps	ExtProps	0
6	2089058478	2089058478	ProjectedDeliveryDates	PK__ProjectedDeliver__7D78A4E7	1

	sysobjects.id	sysindexes.id	sysobjects.name	sysindexes.name	indid
1	2009058193	2009058193	ContactExtProps	ContactExtProps	0
2	2009058193	2009058193	ContactExtProps	pk_ContactExtProps_ContactID_PropID	2
3	2009058193	2009058193	ContactExtProps	_WA_Sys_PropID_77BFCB91	3
4	517576882	517576882	EmailContacts	pk_EmailContacts_ContactID	1
5	517576882	517576882	EmailContacts	ind_EmailContacts_LastName	2
6	1074102867	1074102867	ExtProps	ExtProps	0
7	2089058478	2089058478	ProjectedDeliveryDates	PK__ProjectedDeliver__7D78A4E7	1

Figure 2-9. These two result sets identify the addition of an index, *ind_EmailContacts_LastName*, to the *EmailContacts* table. By contrasting the first with the second listing, you can see the effect of the *CREATE INDEX* statement for *ind_EmailContacts_LastName*.

3

Programming Data Access with T-SQL

This chapter presents T-SQL programming techniques for data access. You can use these techniques in many environments—in Query Analyzer, encapsulated within views, in stored procedures and user-defined functions—and in Visual Basic .NET. When you finish working through this chapter, you should possess a foundation for extracting precisely the data you need from a SQL Server database for any application.

The objective of this chapter is to demystify T-SQL data access techniques so that you can create T-SQL *SELECT* statements as easily as you used to write DAO and ADO data access code. Although the chapter assumes you're working in Query Analyzer, the techniques you learn will apply equally when you use T-SQL statements in Visual Basic .NET.

The chapter begins by introducing the *SELECT* statement and describing how to filter columns and rows from a row source, such as a table. Next the chapter focuses on techniques for aggregating data across a whole row source as well as specific groups within the row source. The chapter explores particular techniques for *money* and *datetime* variables, and the *datetime* topic gains a section of its own. The concluding section examines ways of combining row sources with joins and subqueries. If you have had difficulty understanding joins before, spend some time with the script samples in the chapter and the accompanying commentary to build your grasp of this important capability.

> **Note** By the term *row source*, I refer to a collection of rows from a database. Although this can be a table, it can also be a view based on one or more tables. In addition, a row source can be the result set generated by a stored procedure or a table-valued user-defined function.

The T-SQL samples for this chapter are available in an .sql file on the companion disk. You can use the scripts as starting points for your own custom extrapolations of the techniques. You can run all the samples from Query Analyzer if you have the Northwind and pubs databases installed on a SQL Server instance to which you can connect.

Introduction to Data Access with T-SQL

Creating efficient, speedy, and flexible data access solutions for SQL Server data will inevitably involve programming T-SQL. In particular, you will require a firm foundation in the design of *SELECT* statements. This section introduces the *SELECT* statement by reviewing its architecture. You'll find code samples designed to illustrate the basic operation of the statement's main elements, including the *SELECT* list as well as the *FROM* and *WHERE* clauses, and you'll be introduced to the topic of calculated columns.

Overview of the *SELECT* Statement

Learning the syntax and clauses for the *SELECT* statement is the surest way to guarantee your productivity with SQL Server. As mentioned in the introduction to this chapter, you can use the *SELECT* statement in SQL batches for Query Analyzer, views, stored procedures, and user-defined functions. It is common to use the *SELECT* statement for data access with SQL Server.

A *SELECT* statement can generate a set of values. SQL Server literature calls the values returned by a *SELECT* statement its *result set*. A typical *SELECT* statement can return a scalar value, a single column of values, or a two-dimensional array of values. In normal data access scenarios, the two-dimensional array of values will be the most common design for a result set.

At a minimum, a *SELECT* statement includes a *SELECT* list and a *FROM* clause. The list designates the columns that populate a result set. You can use the entries in the *SELECT* list to filter columns and calculate new columns based on the row source for the *SELECT* statement. The *FROM* clause designates the row source for a *SELECT* statement. The row source for a typical *SELECT* statement can be a table, a view, a user-defined function, or even a subquery. This subquery is simply another *SELECT* statement. At a minimum, a *SELECT* statement used for data access must include a list and a *FROM* clause argument. The *FROM* clause must appear after the *SELECT* list. As with other *SELECT* clauses, you separate the *FROM* clause from the *SELECT* list by a space or a carriage return.

You won't always want to see all the data from the source specified in the *FROM* clause. The *SELECT* list enables you to specify a subset of the row source's columns that should be included in the result set. Similarly, the *WHERE* clause enables you to designate a subset of the rows. The *WHERE* clause supplies the criteria used to filter rows in the argument for a *FROM* clause. The *WHERE* clause is optional. If you don't use a *WHERE* clause, the *SELECT* statement includes all the rows designated by the *FROM* clause in its result set. When you do use a *WHERE* clause, be sure to reference columns in the *FROM* clause argument. A general way of denoting the syntax for a basic *SELECT* statement is:

```
SELECT select_list
FROM row_source
WHERE criteria_expressions
```

Ordering Data in the Result Set

The rows in a relational data source don't have any special order. However, you'll often want the result set from a *SELECT* statement to be arranged a certain way—for example, in alphabetical or numeric order based on one or more columns. You can achieve this with the *ORDER BY* clause. The columns you designate to use for the ordering can originate with the row source in the *FROM* clause, or they can be calculated columns. You can designate ascending (*ASC*) or descending (*DESC*) sort orders for any column in an *ORDER BY* clause. Ascending order is the default. That means you have to specify an order only when you require a descending order. The *ORDER BY* clause should always come after all other *SELECT* statement clauses except for the *COMPUTE* and *COMPUTE BY* clauses (which I'll describe shortly).

Grouping Data in the Result Set

Just as you'll probably want to arrange data in a result set in a certain way, you'll often want to group data to make it more useful. With the *GROUP BY* clause, you can group sets of rows in a result set. This clause is especially useful when you want to apply an aggregate function to one or more columns in a row source. Aggregate functions are useful for developing summary statistics, such as the count, sum, or average of column values by group. The result sets generated with the *GROUP BY* clause support business decision making. For example, you can use the clause to develop total sales by region of the country or by product category.

The *GROUP BY* clause works hand-in-hand with the *HAVING* clause. The *HAVING* clause enables you to filter groups in the same way that the *WHERE* clause permits you to filter rows. The *GROUP BY* and *HAVING* clauses belong after the *FROM* and *WHERE* clauses in a *SELECT* statement. Just as with the *WHERE* clause, the *HAVING* clause is optional. If you do include it, position it after the *GROUP BY* clause. (Later in the chapter, I provide a sample script that uses *HAVING*.)

Generating Summary Values with *COMPUTE* and *COMPUTE BY*

In addition to making a result set more useful by ordering and grouping, you'll sometimes find that a summary of the data is just as important as the data itself. That's when you might decide to use the *COMPUTE* and *COMPUTE BY* clauses to generate not only detail (the rows in the result set) but also summary values (aggregate totals and subtotals).

You'll recall that the *GROUP BY* clause returns a single result set. In contrast, *COMPUTE* and *COMPUTE BY* generate multiple result sets. With the *COMPUTE BY* clause, a *SELECT* statement prepares a separate result set for the rows in each group and another collection of result sets with the summary statistics for each group. The *COMPUTE BY* clause designates aggregate functions, columns for their application, and grouping columns all in one clause.

The *COMPUTE* clause can generate two result sets—one containing all the rows in the row source for a *SELECT* statement and a second result set with summary statistics for the full set of rows. The *COMPUTE* clause creates grand total statistics, but the *COMPUTE BY* clause creates subtotal statistics for each group.

> **Note** The *COMPUTE BY* and *COMPUTE* clauses contrast with other techniques for preparing totals and subtotals, such as the *ROLLUP* and CUBE operators. For more detail on these operators, see the Books Online topics "Summarizing Data Using ROLLUP" and "Summarizing Data Using CUBE."

You can use the *GROUP BY* and *COMPUTE BY* clauses in the same *SELECT* statement. When you use the two clauses together, the *COMPUTE BY* summary statistics apply to the groups of rows specified in the *GROUP BY* clause. Applying the *COMPUTE BY* clause without the *GROUP BY* clause permits the *COMPUTE BY* clause to generate results for individual rows designated by the *FROM* clause.

Whenever you designate either the *COMPUTE BY* or *COMPUTE* clause, it should always appear as the last clause in the *SELECT* statement. When you use both, the *COMPUTE* clause belongs after the *COMPUTE BY* clause.

I provide more detail on ordering, grouping, and aggregating result sets later in this chapter.

Specifying Columns and Rows

You use the *SELECT* statement to return a result set or sets from a row source. However, you won't always want to return all columns and rows in the row source. *SELECT* offers you various ways of filtering out what you don't want.

Returning All Columns

The most elementary *SELECT* statement is that which designates the return of all columns from each row within a row source. There are two different ways to do this. The most familiar uses an asterisk (*) to denote all the columns in a row source. For example, if you wanted to create a result set with all the column values for each row in the *Customers* table, you could use the following code:

```
--SelectAllColumns
--Select all columns from all rows.
USE Northwind
SELECT *
FROM Customers
```

Notice that the USE keyword specifies the Northwind database as the database context for the statement. Unless you explicitly designate otherwise, your *SELECT* statement will apply to the current database. Subsequent samples will illustrate how to override this default selection.

> **Note** The *USE* keyword is an instruction to Query Analyzer. This keyword is not a part of T-SQL. You set the database context differently for other SQL Server clients.

There is another, less common, approach to returning all columns that achieves the same result as using an asterisk: you can separately denote each column name in the *Customers* table. The following code shows the first couple of column names, an ellipsis, and the last name from the *Customers* table in the Northwind database. (Note that SQL Server syntax doesn't allow an ellipsis; it's used here with a few column names to represent the full list of *Customers* columns.)

```
USE Northwind
SELECT CustomerID, CompanyName, ..., Fax
FROM Customers
```

The two different approaches will generate equivalent results for the standard *Customers* table in the Northwind sample database. However, in some circumstances they can return divergent result sets. If you add a new column to the *Customers* table, the initial sample will return the new column along with the old. On the other hand, the second sample that lists the individual columns will omit the new column because its name isn't in the *SELECT* list. So which approach is best? The answer depends on your needs. In general, evaluate very carefully whether you need all the columns from a row source. You can speed an application's performance by choosing just the columns that an application truly requires.

Returning a Subset of Columns

You can filter out unwanted columns in many different ways. The following sample returns values for all rows in the *Customers* table, but only from the *Country*, *City*, and *CompanyName* columns. Because there are 91 customers in the Northwind database, this result set has three columns and 91 rows—one for each row in the table.

```
--SelectSomeColumns
--Select some columns from all rows.
SELECT Country, City, CompanyName
FROM Customers
```

You may have noticed that unlike the previous code sample, this one doesn't include a specific reference to the Northwind database. That's because Query Analyzer will continue to use Northwind until you specify a different database with a new *USE* statement. All the remaining samples in this chapter assume that the database is Northwind.

> **Note** The elements in a *SELECT* list and the argument in a *FROM* clause are examples of identifiers for database objects. SQL Server has precise rules for naming objects and using object names as well as a rich collection of Books Online topics for describing them. For example, see the topic "Using Identifiers" for a delineation of the four rules for regular identifiers. When dealing with objects that contain identifiers with embedded spaces, such as the *Order Details* table, you can often appropriately refer to them by enclosing their identifiers in brackets or single quotation marks—for example, `FROM [Order Details]`.

Returning a Subset of Rows

Just as you can limit which columns are returned, you also can limit which rows are in the result set. The following script returns *Country*, *City*, and *CompanyName* column values for a subset of the rows in the *Customers* table. The expression in the *WHERE* clause denotes the precise subset—namely, those customers from a country beginning with either the letter B or C. That filtering is done by using the *SUBSTRING* function to examine just the first character in each *Country* column value. I will show you a simpler way to express this in a subsequent sample, but you'll likely find this exposure to the *SUBSTRING* function useful.

Any legitimate expression works in a *WHERE* clause. Your expression can apply to the values for any column designated by the row source in the *FROM* clause.

The code also demonstrates the use of the *ORDER BY* clause. Because of the two arguments in the clause, the result set appears in alphabetical order by country. Within each country, the cities are, in turn, sorted in alphabetical order.

```
--SomeColumnsFromSomeRows
--Select some columns from some rows.
SELECT Country, City, CompanyName
FROM Customers
WHERE SUBSTRING(Country,1,1)<='C' and LEFT(Country,1)>'A'
ORDER BY Country, City
```

The result set from the *SELECT* statement contains 14 rows, instead of the 91 rows in the preceding sample. This difference isn't significant for a single user. However, if many users repeatedly run a query that returns less than one-sixth as many rows, your overall network performance will improve.

The following sample repeats the code from the previous one but also prints the number of rows returned, using a custom format. By default, SQL Server will report the number of rows affected, which is the number of rows in a result set for a *SELECT* statement. The sample turns off the default message with the *SET NOCOUNT ON* statement. Then it declares a local string variable—*@strRows*—for its custom report about the number of rows returned. The *@@ROWCOUNT* global variable returns the number of records affected by the last T-SQL statement. Because this function returns an integer, a *CAST* function is used to convert the numeric value returned by *@@ROWCOUNT* to character data. The character data is then concatenated with a string that informs the user how many rows are in the result set, which the *PRINT* statement sends to the Messages Pane in Query Analyzer.

```
--CustomCount
--Select some columns from some rows
--with custom count of rows affected.
```

```
SET NOCOUNT ON
Declare @strRows nvarchar(50)
SELECT Country, City, CompanyName
FROM Customers
WHERE SUBSTRING(Country,1,1)<='C' and SUBSTRING(Country,1,1)>'A'
ORDER BY Country, City
SET @strRows = 'Rows returned = ' + Cast(@@ROWCOUNT AS nvarchar)
PRINT @strRows
SET NOCOUNT OFF
```

Using the *LIKE* Operator with Wildcards

Many developers and end users creating T-SQL statements for data access will use the *LIKE* operator to specify a pattern match. This operator appears in *SELECT* statements within the *WHERE* clause.

The *LIKE* operator typically works with one of three wildcard parameters—%, _, and ^. The % parameter represents any set of 0 or more characters. You can use it at the beginning or end of a search string. The _ parameter designates a single character in a search string. You can position the _ parameter at the beginning or end of a search string or within a search string. The ^ parameter specifies that return values *not* match a pattern. This parameter always appears in a search string within square brackets. You can apply it to an individual character or a range of characters. Square brackets can denote a pattern range with or without the ^ parameter.

The following code demonstrates the use of the % parameter to return all rows in the *Customers* table of the Northwind database with U as the first letter of their *Country* column value. The return set includes rows with the *Country* column values USA and UK.

```
--Return rows with Country values beginning with U.
SELECT CompanyName, Country
FROM Customers
WHERE Country LIKE 'U%'
```

By applying the _ parameter in the argument for a *LIKE* operator, a *SELECT* statement can return just rows that contain USA instead of UK. The *'U_A'* argument fails to match rows with the *Country* column value UK.

```
--Return rows with Country values beginning with U followed
--by any character, the letter A and any other characters.
SELECT CompanyName, Country
FROM Customers
WHERE Country LIKE 'U_A'
```

Using the *LIKE* Operator with Wildcards *(continued)*

With the ^ operator in square brackets, we can return all rows from the *Customers* table except those that start their *Country* column value with U.

```
--Return rows with Country values that don't begin with U.
SELECT CompanyName, Country
FROM Customers
WHERE Country LIKE '[^U]%'
```

Using the square brackets to denote a range can simplify some expressions. For example, you can return rows from the *Customers* table that have *Country* column values beginning with either B or C with the square brackets and the *LIKE* operator. The following *SELECT* statement shows the syntax.

```
--Return rows with Country values beginning with B or C.
SELECT CompanyName, Country
FROM Customers
WHERE Country LIKE '[B-C]%'
```

Calculated Columns

A calculated column is one that doesn't appear within the row source for a *SELECT* statement. Instead, you specify the calculated column with an expression inside the *SELECT* statement. Because normalized tables aren't supposed to contain columns that depend on other columns in the same table, you will often need to develop calculated columns when working with properly designed databases. For example, you can compute extended price in terms of quantity, price, and discount for the line items in a table of order details. In addition, you can compute how late a shipment or a payment is by computing the difference between dates.

The following sample illustrates how to specify a calculated column as well as how to use the *CAST* function to transform the data type for a calculated result. The script lists four regular columns from the *Order Details* table in the Northwind database and also a couple of calculated columns that compute extended price. The calculated columns each multiply one regular column value by another to compute extended price, but they differ in formatting. Although *Quantity* is a *smallint* data type and *UnitPrice* is a *money* data type, `Quantity*UnitPrice` returns a result with a *money* data type. However, multiplying by `(1-Discount)` converts the data type for the expression to a *real* data type. Without any conversion, the extended price will appear in scientific notation (with an E in the result). The sample shows how to convert the result to either a *money* data type or a *decimal* data type with two places after the decimal point. Both of these conversions preserve the extended price result as a numeric value.

> **Note** See the "Data Type Precedence" topic in Books Online for an introduction to how SQL Server returns results when there is a calculation between column values with different data types.

```
--AddCalculatedColumn
--Add a calculated column to the result set formatted
--to two different numeric formats.
SELECT OrderID, Quantity, UnitPrice, Discount,
    CAST(Quantity*UnitPrice*(1-Discount) AS money) AS 'Price as money',
    CAST(Quantity*UnitPrice*(1-Discount) AS dec(9,2)) AS 'Price as dec(9,2)'
FROM [Order Details]
```

Figure 3-1 displays an excerpt from the result set for the preceding script. The two columns on the right show the outcome from the two *CAST* functions. The label to the right of each *CAST* function appears as the column heading in the result set excerpt. The *CAST* function that converts extended price to *money* shows four places to the right of the decimal point. This is the scale for the *money* data type. The *CAST* function that transforms the extended price into a *decimal* data type shows just two places after the decimal point. This is consistent with the dec(9,2) data type specified in the *CAST* function.

	OrderID	Quantity	UnitPrice	Discount	Price as money	Price as dec(9,2)
1	10248	12	14.0000	0.0	168.0000	168.00
2	10248	10	9.8000	0.0	98.0000	98.00
3	10248	5	34.8000	0.0	174.0000	174.00
4	10249	9	18.6000	0.0	167.4000	167.40
5	10249	40	42.4000	0.0	1696.0000	1696.00
6	10250	10	7.7000	0.0	77.0000	77.00
7	10250	35	42.4000	0.15000001	1261.4000	1261.40

Figure 3-1. An excerpt showing the result of two different *CAST* functions for a *real* data type.

The next sample illustrates how to compute and report the difference between two *datetime* values. The T-SQL batch uses the *DATEDIFF* function to compute the difference between two local variables. While this sample isn't explicitly for column values, the same techniques apply to calculated column values. (See the "Performing Date Arithmetic" section for details that specifically pertain to column values.) The *GETDATE* function returns a current date and time. The batch deposits the current date and time into two different local variables—*@dtStart* at the top of the batch and *@dtEnd* in the next-to-last statement. The *DATEDIFF* function computes the difference between these two local variables. The *DATEDIFF* function enables you to extract the difference between *datetime* values in any of several units. Using ms as the first argument extracts the difference in milliseconds. You can use a procedure like this one for a quick snapshot of the time it takes to run some T-SQL statements. Other, more comprehensive, performance measures are available from SQL Server; see, for example, "Query Window Statistics Pane" in Books Online for more detail.

> **Note** A local variable in T-SQL operates like a memory variable in Visual Basic. Chapter 3 provides explicit coverage of T-SQL local variables.

```
--ComputeWithDatediff
--Demonstrates use of DATEDIFF function to compute
--a difference in milliseconds.
DECLARE @dtStart datetime
DECLARE @dtEnd datetime
DECLARE @intOrderID int
SET @intOrderID = 10700
SET @dtStart = GETDATE()
SELECT OrderID, Quantity, UnitPrice, Discount,
    CAST(Quantity*UnitPrice*(1-Discount) AS money) AS 'Price as money',
    CAST(Quantity*UnitPrice*(1-Discount) AS dec(9,2))'Price as dec(9,2)'
FROM [Order Details]
WHERE OrderID < @intOrderID
SET @dtEnd = GETDATE()
SELECT DATEDIFF(ms, @dtStart, @dtEnd) 'Time to run (ms)'
```

Aggregating and Grouping Rows

T-SQL aggregate functions can apply to all the rows in a result set or just subsets of them, such as those identified with a *GROUP BY* clause. For example, you can count the number of overall rows in a row source, or you can count the rows by country (or by any other value on which you group rows). You can choose to return aggregate values and the rows they summarize, or just the aggregate values.

Summary of Aggregate Functions

Table 3-1 itemizes the aggregate functions by listing their names with a short description. The purpose of many of these functions is implied by their name. For further details about functionality and syntax, search Books Online for a topic with the function name.

Table 3-1 Summary of T-SQL Aggregate Functions

Name	Description
AVG	Returns an average
BINARY CHECKSUM	Can return the binary check sum for a row
CHECKSUM	Computes a checksum for use in constructing hash indexes
CHECKSUM AGG	Performs a checksum computation for a group
COUNT	Counts the items in a group or overall row source; returns an *int* value
COUNT BIG	Like Count function but returns a *bigint* value
GROUPING	For use with *CUBE* and *ROLLUP* operators
MAX	Returns maximum value in a column
MIN	Returns minimum value in a column
SUM	Returns sum of values in a column
STDEV	Computes standard deviation for the sample of values in a column
STDEVP	Computes standard deviation for the population of values from which a column samples
VAR	Computes variance for the sample of values in a column
VARP	Computes variance for the population of values from which a column samples

Aggregating Without Grouping

Like some of the other aggregate functions, the *COUNT* function has multiple forms. For example, `COUNT(*)` returns the number of values in a row source, including null and duplicate values. The *WHERE* clause can constrain the range of rows over which `COUNT(*)` computes a result. In the next sample, the row source includes all customers from a country starting with the letter B or C. Because the *Customers* table in the Northwind database has a primary key, the rows are all unique. This *SELECT* statement returns a scalar value of 14, which is the number of rows in the *Customers* table meeting the criterion expression in the *WHERE* clause. Notice that like an earlier sample in this chapter, this code limits countries to those starting with the letter B or C but does so using *LEFT* and *IN* rather than *SUBSTRING*. You can use either method, but this one requires a little less typing.

```
--CountRows
--Count all rows meeting a criterion.
SELECT Count(*)
FROM Customers
WHERE LEFT(Country,1) IN ('B','C')
```

You can use the *COUNT* function to return just the number of non-null values within a column by replacing the asterisk with the name of a specific column. Any rows with null values for a specific column in the row source for the query won't be tallied as part of the return value for the *COUNT* function. Changing the asterisk to a specific column name—*Country*—won't change the result in the previous sample because there aren't any null values in the *Country* column. But you can change the result by using the *DISTINCT* keyword as a predicate to the specific column. Position the keyword inside the parentheses trailing the function. The following script illustrates this syntax. The query statement returns the value 3 because there are only three distinct countries in the *Customers* table starting with the letter B or C—Belgium, Brazil, and Canada.

```
--CountIncidences
--Count distinct incidences.
SELECT Count(DISTINCT Country)
FROM Customers
WHERE LEFT(Country,1) IN ('B','C')
```

Aggregating with Grouping

It is common to use aggregate functions when grouping on one or more columns. For instance, instead of just computing the total count of customers, you can derive more detailed information by computing the count of customers by city and country. One approach to performing this type of calculation uses a *GROUP BY* clause in a *SELECT* statement. When you add a *GROUP BY* clause, this, in turn, places restrictions on the entries in a *SELECT* list. It is typical to have just two types of entries in the list—aggregate functions, such as *COUNT* and *SUM*, for specific columns; and columns that appear in the *GROUP BY* clause.

The columns in the *GROUP BY* clause determine the span over which an aggregate function computes. By adding *Country* to the *GROUP BY* clause and including *Country* and *COUNT(CustomerID)* in the list for a *SELECT* statement, you can compute the count of customers by country. The *GROUP BY* clause can take multiple columns as arguments. Therefore, adding *City* to both the *GROUP BY* clause and the *SELECT* list tells the *COUNT* function to count the customers by cities within country. The following script illustrates this approach for customers who come from countries beginning with the letter B or C.

```
--CountCustomers
--Count column value instances meeting a criterion
--that is grouped and ordered by two columns.
SELECT Country, City, Count(CustomerID) '# of Customers'
FROM Customers
WHERE LEFT(Country,1) IN ('B','C')
GROUP BY Country, City
ORDER BY Country, City
```

The result set from the preceding script (see Figure 3-2) shows how the 14 customers from countries beginning with B or C are distributed by country and city. It shows customers in nine cities within three countries. The most customers in any city are in São Paulo, Brazil. The closing *ORDER BY* clause arranges the rows in the result set alphabetically by city within country.

	Country	City	# of Customers
1	Belgium	Bruxelles	1
2	Belgium	Charleroi	1
3	Brazil	Campinas	1
4	Brazil	Resende	1
5	Brazil	Rio de Janeiro	3
6	Brazil	Sao Paulo	4
7	Canada	Montréal	1
8	Canada	Tsawassen	1
9	Canada	Vancouver	1

Figure 3-2. A result set showing grouping by city within country for a count of customers.

The result set for the preceding script counts the customers by city, but it doesn't break out results separately by group or provide any subtotals for the number of cities within each country. You can use the *COMPUTE BY* and *COMPUTE* clauses of a *SELECT* statement to generate results like these. The following script shows how to use the *COMPUTE BY* clause to split the results by country and add a count of the number of cities within each country. A *COMPUTE BY* clause requires a matching *ORDER BY* clause; both clauses must specify the same column name as an argument. In this sample, notice that *Country* appears in the *COMPUTE BY* and *ORDER BY* clauses. The final *COMPUTE* clause adds a count of the total number of cities across all countries in the collection of result sets for the *SELECT* statement.

```
--CountCustomersInSpecifiedCountries
--Count column value instances meeting a criterion that is
--grouped and ordered by two columns and subtotaled by
--one column.
SELECT Country, City, Count(CustomerID) AS '# of Customers'
FROM Customers
WHERE LEFT(Country,1) IN ('B','C')
```

```
GROUP BY Country, City
ORDER BY Country
COMPUTE Count(City) BY Country
COMPUTE Count(City)
```

The script generates seven result sets that appear in a single Results Pane within Query Analyzer, as shown in Figure 3-3. A separate column header denotes the beginning of each result set. The top result set shows the count of customers by city within Belgium. The second result set displays a count of the number of cities in Belgium. The next two pairs of result sets provide comparable information for customers from Brazil and Canada. The final result set shows the total count of cities across the preceding result sets for each country.

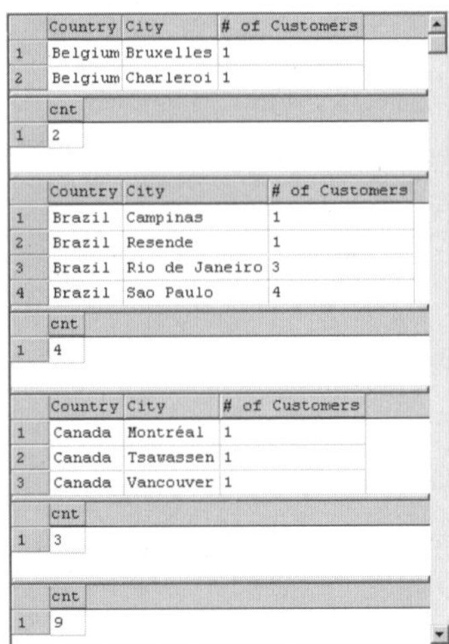

	Country	City	# of Customers
1	Belgium	Bruxelles	1
2	Belgium	Charleroi	1

	cnt
1	2

	Country	City	# of Customers
1	Brazil	Campinas	1
2	Brazil	Resende	1
3	Brazil	Rio de Janeiro	3
4	Brazil	Sao Paulo	4

	cnt
1	4

	Country	City	# of Customers
1	Canada	Montréal	1
2	Canada	Tsawassen	1
3	Canada	Vancouver	1

	cnt
1	3

	cnt
1	9

Figure 3-3. A collection of result sets demonstrating the operation of the *COMPUTE BY* and *COMPUTE* clauses.

The next example returns to a more basic application of the *GROUP BY* clause, but this script demonstrates the aggregation of a calculated column—namely, extended price based on the *Quantity*, *UnitPrice*, and *Discount* columns in the *Order Details* table. Because the script groups by *OrderID* column values, the result set displays the total extended price for all the items within each order. This script groups by *OrderID*, and it also aggregates by *OrderID*. The count of a single *OrderID* column value within an order returns the number of line items for an order. The sum of the expression for extended price provides the total extended price for an order. This is the first sample script in this book that illustrates the syntax for the *HAVING* clause. In this instance, the clause restricts the entries in the result set to orders with a total extended price of more than $11,000. The final *ORDER BY* clause in the script is necessary to arrange the rows in descending order based on total extended price.

```
--CountAndSum
--Count one real column (OrderID) and SUM one calculated column
--to get total Extended Price for each order.
--Format money data type as characters for display.
SELECT OrderID, COUNT(OrderID) 'Line items',
    '$' +
    CONVERT(varchar,CAST(SUM(Quantity*UnitPrice*(1-Discount)) AS money),1)
    AS 'Extended Price'
FROM [Order Details]
GROUP BY OrderID
HAVING SUM(Quantity*UnitPrice*(1-Discount)) > 11000
ORDER BY SUM(Quantity*UnitPrice*(1-Discount)) DESC
```

Notice the use of a *CAST* function nested within a CONVERT function. The *CAST* function transforms the *real* total extended price for an order into a *money* value. The *CONVERT* function represents the *money* value as a character string formatted for currency with comma delimiters between every three digits to the left of the decimal point and just two digits to the right of the decimal point. A string expression adds a leading currency sign. The *CONVERT* function offers three different styles for rendering currency as a character value. The third argument for the *CONVERT* function designates the style. The following table summarizes the effect of each possible value for the third argument. The default value is 0.

CONVERT Style Argument Values for Rendering Money	Style Argument Format Effects
0	No commas, but just two digits to the right of the decimal point
1	Commas separating every three digits to the left of the decimal point and just two digits to the right of the decimal point
2	No commas, and four digits to the right of the decimal point

Processing Dates

Dates are different from other data types, and processing them can be tricky. For one thing, SQL Server typically saves date values in a numeric format with either a *datetime* or a *smalldatetime* data type. For another, dates represent a calendar in which the total days per month aren't consistent from one month to the next. Also, you can group dates by day, week, month, quarter, and year. Fortunately, SQL Server offers some highly useful functions to simplify the use of dates that don't apply to other data types. This section explores some of these functions and other techniques that can help you process dates with SQL Server.

Counting by Year and Month

It is common to need to aggregate data by year and month. This section provides four code samples that demonstrate how to do it. In particular, the script tackles the problem of counting the orders per period of time, such as by year or by month within a year.

Counting by Year

The first sample generates a result set that accumulates the number of orders by year. It takes just three lines to do this. The first is a *SELECT* statement with a list that includes two entries. The first entry is the *DATEPART* function for the *OrderDate* from the *Orders* table. The *DATEPART* function returns an integer that reflects a part of a *datetime* value, such as the month number for a date. The function takes two arguments. The first argument denotes the date part to extract. The sample uses yyyy to extract the year as a four-digit number. The second argument is the actual *datetime* value. This can be an expression or a column value. The sample references the *OrderDate* column value from the *Orders* table. In order to accumulate a quantity by year, the T-SQL sample includes the same *DATEPART* function as the argument for a *GROUP BY* clause. The second list entry is a *COUNT* function. The function uses *OrderID* as its argument to count the number of orders within a year.

```
--CountOrdersByYear
--Count one column by year date part.
SELECT DATEPART(yyyy, OrderDate), COUNT(OrderID)
FROM Orders
GROUP BY DATEPART(yyyy, OrderDate)
```

The *DATEPART* function is extremely flexible. It can extract any of 11 different date parts from a *datetime* value. You can also use the *DATEPART* function with *smalldatetime* values, but the function cannot extract milliseconds for *smalldatetime* values because the data type doesn't support this level of precision. The function offers multiple arguments for specifying which date parts to extract. At a minimum, you can designate date parts by their name or their abbreviation. Many date parts give you the choice of two abbreviations for referencing them. You can use the *DATEPART* function with one of its parts to replace the *Year*, *Month*, and *Day* functions. Table 3-2 shows the possible date part arguments available for the *DATEPART* function.

Table 3-2. Arguments for the *DATEPART* Function

Date Part Name	Date Part Abbreviation
year	*yy, yyyy*
quarter	*qq, q*
month	*mm, m*
dayofyear	*dy, y*
day	*dd, d*
week	*wk, ww*
weekday	*dw*
hour	*hh*
minute	*mi, n*
second	*ss, s*
millisecond	*ms*

Counting by Month

Developing a result set that returns the number of orders by month within year builds on the techniques that you learned previously. It is just a matter of putting the elements together correctly. You include three items in the list for the *SELECT* statement to return the year, month, and count of orders in a time period. Specify the *Orders* table as the argument for the *FROM* clause. In the *GROUP BY* clause, use a *DATEPART* function statement to return the year followed by a comma and a *DATEPART* function to return the month, like this:

```
GROUP BY DATEPART(yyyy, OrderDate), DATEPART(mm,OrderDate)
```

Because we want the result rows ordered by month within year, the *SELECT* statement requires an *ORDER BY* clause with the same arguments as the *GROUP BY* clause.

The following script shows the *SELECT* list items. The first two items in the list match the arguments for the *GROUP BY* clause. The last *SELECT* list argument is the aggregate function, *COUNT*, that counts the number of orders per date unit. This sample design is very general. You can use any other aggregate function or more aggregate functions than those in the sample. For example, you can add a *DATEPART* function to count orders by week within year instead of or in addition to month within year.

```
--CountOrdersByYearAndMonth
--Count one column by year and month date parts of another.
SELECT DATEPART(yyyy, OrderDate) AS 'Year',
    DATEPART(mm,OrderDate) AS 'Month',
    COUNT(OrderID) AS 'Orders'
FROM Orders
```

```
GROUP BY DATEPART(yyyy, OrderDate), DATEPART(mm,OrderDate)
ORDER BY DATEPART(yyyy, OrderDate), DATEPART(mm,OrderDate)
```

Figure 3-4 shows an excerpt of the results from the script. Notice that months are represented by their number. They are sorted within year, which also happens to be a number. At least some of your clients are bound to request the replacement of the month numbers with names.

	Year	Month	Orders
1	1996	7	22
2	1996	8	25
3	1996	9	23
4	1996	10	26
5	1996	11	25
6	1996	12	31
7	1997	1	33
8	1997	2	29
9	1997	3	30
10	1997	4	31
11	1997	5	32
12	1997	6	30

Figure 3-4. An excerpt from a result set that displays the number of orders by month within year.

The next script illustrates an approach to generating the report in Figure 3-4, but with names instead of numbers to designate months. You can use the *DATENAME* function to extract a month name as a character string from a date. The *DATENAME* function takes two arguments—just like the *DATEPART* function. Both functions use the same codes to represent date parts, and the two also use a *datetime* value as the second argument. (You can use a *small-datetime* value as well.) In the case of a month date part, the *DATENAME* function provides the month's full name, such as January or February, instead of a number, such as 1 or 2.

```
--ShowMonthNames
--Count one column by year and month date parts of another
--column while showing month names instead of month numbers.
SELECT DATEPART(yyyy, OrderDate) AS Year,
    DATENAME(mm, OrderDate) AS Month,
    COUNT(OrderID) AS Orders
FROM Orders
GROUP BY DATEPART(yyyy, OrderDate),
    DATENAME(mm, OrderDate)
ORDER BY DATEPART(yyyy, OrderDate)
```

However, there's a problem. The script sorts the result set by month name, but the alphabetical order of the months doesn't correspond to their temporal order. That's why the months in the result set are arranged alphabetically within each year rather than chronologically. One solution to this problem is to set up a one-to-one correspondence between the month names returned by the *DATENAME* function and the month numbers returned by the *DATEPART* function.

The following script shows an approach to mapping month names to month numbers that relies on only the *SELECT* list items along with the *GROUP BY* and *ORDER BY* clauses. The *SELECT* list contains three terms: the year returned by the *DATEPART* function, the month name returned by the *DATENAME* function, and the *COUNT* function to compute the number of orders by year and month. (Any other aggregate function would work as well.) Because the *DATENAME* function appears in the *SELECT* list, it must also be an argument for the *GROUP BY* clause. The trick is to place the *DATENAME* function in the *GROUP BY* clause in between the first *DATEPART* function for year and a second *DATEPART* function for month. Because month names map perfectly to month numbers, the two *GROUP BY* arguments after the *DATEPART* for year group the rows in an identical way. The *DATENAME* argument for month has to appear in the *GROUP BY* clause because you need it in the *SELECT* list. In addition, the *DATEPART* function that returns a month's number in the *GROUP BY* clause is also necessary because the *ORDER BY* clause requires it as its second argument. The output from the following script matches the output in Figure 3-4 except that the second column shows month names instead of month numbers.

```
--ShowMonthNamesChronologically
--Count one column by year and month date parts of another
--column while showing month names instead of month numbers.
--Order months by names chronologically, not numerically.
SELECT DATEPART(yyyy, OrderDate) AS Year,
    DATENAME(mm, OrderDate) AS Month,
    COUNT(OrderID) AS Orders
FROM Orders
GROUP BY DATEPART(yyyy, OrderDate),
    DATENAME(mm, OrderDate),
    DATEPART(mm, OrderDate)
ORDER BY DATEPART(yyyy, OrderDate), DATEPART(mm, OrderDate)
```

Performing Date Arithmetic

The "Calculated Columns" section demonstrated how to take advantage of SQL *datetime* local variables to compute the difference between two *datetime* values. That illustrates date arithmetic. This section drills down more deeply into the topic.

Let's start out with a sample that screens orders to find those with an estimated arrival date that is later than the required date for the order. These are late orders because they arrive at the customer after the required date. The

SELECT list for the sample includes *OrderID* and three *datetime* columns: *OrderDate*, *RequiredDate*, and *ShippedDate*. Because the time of day that an order ships is immaterial, the three *datetime* columns are in *LEFT* functions that strip off just the first 11 characters for display. This permits the display of the dates in three parts: a three-character part for the month, up to two digits for the display of the day number in the month, and a four-digit field for the year. A single blank character delimits the first part from the second part and the second part from the third part.

The *WHERE* clause for the following *SELECT* statement performs the date arithmetic. The expression for the clause returns all rows from the *Orders* tables whose *RequiredDate* is less than *ShippedDate* plus 3. Values in *datetime* format represent one day with an integer value of 1. By adding 3 to the *ShippedDate* column value, the *WHERE* clause expression computes a projected arrival date that is three days after the order ships. If the projected arrival date is greater than the *RequiredDate* column value, the order is late. The *SELECT* statement includes only late orders in its result set.

```
--ListLateOrders
--List just date portion of datetime column values
--with a criterion based on day offset between two columns.
SELECT OrderID, Left(OrderDate,11) 'OrderDate',
    Left(RequiredDate,11) 'RequiredDate',
    Left(ShippedDate,11) 'ShippedDate'
FROM Orders
WHERE RequiredDate < ShippedDate + 3
```

The result set from the preceding script is useful for getting a basic grasp of late orders, but all it does is list the orders. The viewer of the result set is responsible for computing the number of days that an order is late as well as finding those orders that missed the required date by a wide margin. The following script remedies both of these weaknesses. The remedy fashions a solution based on date arithmetic.

The sample's arithmetic with *datetime* values relies on the *DATEADD* and *DATEDIFF* functions. It uses these two system functions to compute the number of days that an order is late. With the *DATEADD* function, the following script adds 3 days to *ShippedDate* to compute a projected arrival date. The script computes the number of days an order is late by depending on two expressions. First the *WHERE* clause expression filters for just those rows in which the projected arrival date value is greater than the *RequiredDate* column value. The orders on these rows from the *Orders* table are late. Second the script computes the number of days that an order is late. The expression for computing this nests the expression for the projected arrival date value inside a *DATEDIFF* function with the *RequiredDate* column value. *DATEDIFF* explicitly references days as the metric for computing the difference between the two values. This

DATEDIFF function appears in the *SELECT* list and in the *ORDER BY* clause. The *SELECT* list for this *DATEDIFF* function includes in the result set the number of days that an order is late; the name of this calculated column is *Days Late*. The *ORDER BY* clause includes the *DESC* keyword so that SQL Server will sort the result set with the latest orders listed first.

```
--CalculateDaysLate
--Demonstrates uses of DATEDIFF for Days Late calculation
--and DATEADD for day offset in criterion expression.
SELECT OrderID, Left(OrderDate,11) 'OrderDate',
    Left(RequiredDate,11) 'RequiredDate',
    Left(ShippedDate,11) 'ShippedDate',
    DATEDIFF(day,RequiredDate,DATEADD(day, 3, ShippedDate)) 'Days Late'
FROM Orders
WHERE RequiredDate < DATEADD(day, 3, ShippedDate)
ORDER BY DATEDIFF(day,RequiredDate,DATEADD(day, 3, ShippedDate)) DESC
```

The last sample script in this section illustrates how to aggregate a calculated value and then group it by quarter within year. The sample also shows the syntax for filtering groups defined by a *GROUP BY* clause with a *HAVING* clause.

The script does its aggregating with a *SUM* function defined on the *DATEDIFF* expression for computing the number of days an order is late. This *SUM* function requires a *GROUP BY* clause. The one in the sample specifies an order's year and quarter as grouping column values. Two separate *DATEPART* functions derive the year and quarter for an *OrderDate*. The *SELECT* list contains three items—the two *DATEPART* functions for the year and quarter and the *SUM* function for the number of days late. A *HAVING* clause includes two separate expressions to filter groups in the result set. First, only groups with a year value greater than 1996 can belong to the result set. Second, the *HAVING* clause excludes the group corresponding to the second quarter of 1998. The *SELECT* statement's final line is an *ORDER BY* clause that ensures rows appear in order by quarter within year.

```
--DaysLatePerQuarter
--Demo Sum aggregate function of DATEDIFF with GROUP BY and HAVING clauses.
SELECT DATEPART(yyyy, OrderDate) AS 'Year',
    DATEPART(q, OrderDate) AS 'Quarter',
    SUM(DATEDIFF(d, RequiredDate, DATEADD(day, 3, ShippedDate))) AS 'Days Late'
FROM Orders
WHERE (DATEDIFF(d, RequiredDate, DATEADD(day, 3, ShippedDate)) > 0)
GROUP BY DATEPART(yyyy, OrderDate), DATEPART(q, OrderDate)
HAVING DATEPART(yyyy, OrderDate) > 1996 AND
    NOT(DATEPART(yyyy, OrderDate) = 1998 AND DATEPART(q, OrderDate) = 2)
ORDER BY DATEPART(yyyy, OrderDate), DATEPART(q, OrderDate)
```

Joins and Subqueries

Joins are a powerful technique for combining two or more row sources in a single *SELECT* statement. This section introduces joins with a review of T-SQL techniques for creating inner joins between two tables. Then it goes on to explore other formulations for inner joins and other kinds of joins. The section closes with a couple of samples demonstrating ways of formulating *SELECT* statements with subqueries. This approach is a way of making *SELECT* statements dynamic because the subquery can return the most current value to the *SELECT* statement referencing it.

An Inner Join Between Two Tables

By using an inner join, your database solutions can refer simultaneously to the content from two different row sources. So far, the samples in this chapter have focused on just one table. For example, some samples used the *Order Details* table to develop an expression for extended price. Other samples worked with the days that an order was late. These samples used the *Orders* table. No sample processed content from both the *Orders* and *Order Details* tables in a single solution. Inner joins enable this type of functionality. An inner join most typically merges two tables when their values match on a common field, such as a primary key from one table and its matching foreign key in another table.

The first join sample lists two columns from two different tables—the *Orders* and *Order Details* tables. The *SELECT* statement returns the *OrderID* column from the *Orders* table and the ProductID column from the *Order Details* table. The *OrderID* column appears in both tables. Therefore, the *SELECT* statement must use a table qualifier to indicate from which table to extract the *OrderID* column values. The *JOIN* keyword in the *FROM* clause designates the two tables contributing column values to the result set from the *SELECT* statement. The *ON* keyword points to the columns within each table on which to join the tables.

```
--JoinColumns
--Join columns from two tables.
SELECT Orders.OrderID, ProductID
FROM Orders JOIN [Order Details]
ON (Orders.OrderID = [Order Details].OrderID)
```

The next sample uses the *OrderID* column values from the *Orders* table to merge its content with matching records based on *OrderID* in the *Order Details* table. An inner join implements the merge. As a result of the merge, a single *SELECT* statement can access content from both tables. The result set for the

SELECT statement returns both the *Days Late* calculated column from the *Orders* table and the *Ext. Price* calculated column from the *Order Details* table.

You can specify an inner join with either the *FROM* clause or the *WHERE* clause of a *SELECT* statement. The following sample demonstrates the syntax for the *FROM* clause. Within the *FROM* clause, position the *JOIN* keyword between the two row sources participating in the inner join. It is immaterial which table is on the left and right sides of the *JOIN* keyword. You can optionally replace *JOIN* with *INNER JOIN*. Your *FROM* clause also requires an *ON* keyword. The argument for the *ON* keyword expresses how to merge the rows from the two sources for the join. The *ON* argument expression will often denote an equivalence between two column names, one from each of the row sources participating in the join. The *ON* keyword expression dictates which columns to compare and how to compare them between the two row sources. Notice that the expression includes a table name qualifier for the column name. This is one way to distinguish the source for a column. It is vitally important throughout a *SELECT* statement with a join to indicate the source for a column when the column has the same name for the row source on either side of the *JOIN* keyword. If the column doesn't have the same name in both row sources, the designation of a table name qualifier is optional.

The sample script instructs SQL Server to match *OrderID* column values from the *Orders* table with *OrderID* column values from the *Order Details* table. The result set contains just those rows from the *Order Details* table with matching *OrderID* values from the *Orders* table. Because a single order can spread across multiple rows in the *Order Details* table, column values from the *Orders* table repeat for each of the multiple rows within an order.

As with any *SELECT* statement, the *SELECT* list specifies the column names for the result set. The sample includes a mix of real and calculated columns. *OrderID* from the *Orders* table is a real column. All the other columns are calculated. The columns with the names *OrderDate*, *RequiredDate*, and *ShippedDate* merely apply a *LEFT* function to extract the date portion of a *datetime* value. The columns with the names *Days Late* and *Ext. Price* invoke more sophisticated expressions to calculate their column values. The last column, *Ext. Price*, references the *Order Details* table. The *WHERE* clause filters for orders projected to arrive after the *RequiredDate* value. The *ORDER BY* clause keeps the line item rows for an order together. Because the *OrderID* column is in both row sources for the join, it is necessary to use a table name qualifier for the column name.

```
--DaysLateUsingJoin
--List results from two tables based on day offset criterion.
SELECT Orders.OrderID, LEFT(Orders.OrderDate,11) AS 'OrderDate',
    LEFT(Orders.RequiredDate,11) AS 'RequiredDate',
    LEFT(Orders.ShippedDate,11) AS 'ShippedDate',
```

```
    DATEDIFF(day,RequiredDate,DATEADD(day, 3, ShippedDate)) 'Days Late',
    CAST([Order Details].Quantity*[Order Details].UnitPrice*
    (1-[Order Details].Discount) AS dec(9,2)) AS 'Ext. Price'
FROM Orders JOIN [Order Details]
ON (Orders.OrderID = [Order Details].OrderID)
WHERE RequiredDate < DATEADD(day, 3, ShippedDate)
ORDER BY [Order Details].OrderID
```

Figure 3-5 displays an excerpt from the result set for the preceding script. The *OrderID* column is from both row sources. The *OrderID* column value repeats for each line item within an order. The *OrderDate*, *RequiredDate*, *ShippedDate*, and *Days Late* columns are from the *Orders* table. The values in these columns repeat across the multiple rows within an order. Within the excerpt, the *Ext. Price* column values are unique for each row in the result set. The script calculates these column values based on three columns in the *Order Details* table.

	OrderID	OrderDate	RequiredDate	ShippedDate	Days Late	Ext. Price
1	10264	Jul 24 1996	Aug 21 1996	Aug 23 1996	5	532.00
2	10264	Jul 24 1996	Aug 21 1996	Aug 23 1996	5	163.63
3	10271	Aug 1 1996	Aug 29 1996	Aug 30 1996	4	48.00
4	10280	Aug 14 1996	Sep 11 1996	Sep 12 1996	4	43.20
5	10280	Aug 14 1996	Sep 11 1996	Sep 12 1996	4	384.00
6	10280	Aug 14 1996	Sep 11 1996	Sep 12 1996	4	186.00
7	10302	Sep 10 1996	Oct 8 1996	Oct 9 1996	4	1248.00
8	10302	Sep 10 1996	Oct 8 1996	Oct 9 1996	4	1019.20
9	10302	Sep 10 1996	Oct 8 1996	Oct 9 1996	4	441.60
10	10305	Sep 13 1996	Oct 11 1996	Oct 9 1996	1	1125.00
11	10305	Sep 13 1996	Oct 11 1996	Oct 9 1996	1	2227.50
12	10305	Sep 13 1996	Oct 11 1996	Oct 9 1996	1	388.80

Figure 3-5. An excerpt from a result set that displays content from two row sources.

Using Aliases Within an Inner Join

Because *SELECT* statements can get long and difficult to read with table name qualifiers, it is common to use aliases. An alias is an alternative name for a table that you specify within your *SELECT* statement. Use the alias as a short nickname for the original table name. You can specify your alias within the *FROM* clause immediately after specifying a table by its name. However, you can use an alias anywhere throughout a *SELECT* statement, such as in the *SELECT* list or the *ORDER BY* clause.

The following sample illustrates a join for the *titles* and *titleauthor* tables from the pubs database. The *FROM* clause designates the alias *t* for the *titles* table and *ta* for the *titleauthor* table. You can also see the use of these aliases in the *SELECT* list and *ORDER BY* clauses in this excerpt from the script on the following page.

```
SELECT ta.au_id, t.title, t.ytd_sales, t.price
FROM pubs..titles t JOIN pubs..titleauthor ta
ON (t.title_id = ta.title_id)
ORDER BY ta.au_id
```

The sample also illustrates the syntax for referring to a row source outside the current database context. Recall that all the samples throughout this chapter use the Northwind database, and they rely on an a *USE* statement from the second sample to specify the database connection for the sample. The following sample has the same database context, but it uses three-part names to reference a row source in another database—the pubs database. The first part is the database name, and the second part is the row source owner's name. When the owner's name is dbo (as in the current instance), you can leave the second part null (which means you end up with two consecutive periods). The third part is the row source name. In this sample, that is either *titles* or *titleauthor*.

There is one other special feature about the sample. It includes T-SQL code to print to the Messages Pane the number of rows in the result set. An earlier sample in the "Specifying Columns and Rows" section describes the approach applied in the sample below. The reason for explicitly counting the rows is to compare the number of rows in this result set, 25, with a subsequent sample that uses a different kind of join.

```
--InnerJoinWithAliases
--Inner join between authors titles and titleauthor.
--Returns 25 matching rows from both tables.
SET NOCOUNT ON
Declare @strRows nvarchar(50)
SELECT ta.au_id, t.title, t.ytd_sales, t.price
FROM pubs..titles t JOIN pubs..titleauthor ta
ON (t.title_id = ta.title_id)
ORDER BY ta.au_id
SET @strRows = 'Rows returned = ' + Cast(@@ROWCOUNT AS nvarchar)
PRINT @strRows
SET NOCOUNT OFF
```

An Inner Join Between Three Tables

It is often necessary to merge the results of more than two row sources in a single *SELECT* statement. However, you can join only two row sources at a time. The workaround to this predicament is to use a joined row source as one of the row sources for a new join. This section demonstrates how to implement this logic for the joining of three tables from the pubs database. This kind of join is particularly appropriate for modeling a pair of tables in a many-to-many relationship with a junction table between them. The general approach to developing joins in this section is applicable for more than three row sources. See the T-SQL script for the Invoices view in the Northwind database for a sample script that joins six tables.

> **Note** You can use Enterprise Manager to view the script for a database object. For more information on Enterprise Manager and other SQL Server 2000 tools, see Books Online.

The special syntax for a three-table join is in the *FROM* clause of your *SELECT* statement. Add tables to the *FROM* clause in the order that you want them to join—starting from the extreme left table. Join this table to one of your remaining two tables. Use the syntax previously presented for joining two tables. After the argument for the *ON* keyword, add a second instance of the *JOIN* keyword followed by the name of the third table. Next add a second instance of the *ON* keyword that specifies how to join the third table with the joined first and second tables. After specifying the *FROM* clause as described, you are free to refer to columns from any of the three tables. You can even create calculated columns that draw on columns from two or three tables.

The *FROM* clause in the following script demonstrates how straightforward it is to join three tables. This sample script joins the *titles* table with the *titleauthor* table. Then the script merges the joined *titles* and *titleauthor* tables with the authors table. The script illustrates the syntax for joining the three tables as well as the use of columns from all three tables in the *SELECT* list.

```
--InnerJoinWithThreeTables
--List results from three tables.
SELECT aut.au_fname, aut.au_lname, t.title, t.ytd_sales,
    t.royalty, ta.royaltyper
FROM pubs..titles t JOIN pubs..titleauthor ta
ON (t.title_id = ta.title_id) JOIN pubs..authors aut
ON (ta.au_id = aut.au_id)
```

In addition to listing columns from all three tables, you can use the join to compute calculated columns with inputs from two or more tables. The following script illustrates this design feature with a calculated column for royalty paid to an author for a title. The calculated column draws on ytd_sales and royalty from the *titles* table and royaltyper from the *titleauthor* table. Both royalty and royaltyper represent percentages as integers. Therefore, the calculated field divides the product for all three columns by 10,000.

```
--JoinWithCalculatedColumn
--List results from three tables, including a calculated column
--based on two tables.
SELECT aut.au_fname, aut.au_lname, t.title,
    CAST(t.ytd_sales * t.royalty * ta.royaltyper AS money)/10000,
    t.advance
FROM pubs..titles t JOIN pubs..titleauthor ta
ON (t.title_id = ta.title_id) JOIN pubs..authors aut
ON (ta.au_id = aut.au_id)
ORDER BY t.title, aut.au_lname, aut.au_fname
```

Outer Joins

An outer join contrasts with an inner join by adding in all the rows from a row source whether or not the row satisfies an expression for the *ON* keyword. There are three types of outer joins: a left outer join, a right outer join, and a full outer join. When performing one of these outer joins, replace *JOIN* or *INNER JOIN* with an appropriate alternative term, such as *LEFT OUTER JOIN*, *RIGHT OUTER JOIN*, or *FULL OUTER JOIN*. With a left outer join, all the rows from the row source on the left side of the *LEFT OUTER JOIN* keyword phrase appear in the result set whether or not they satisfy the expression in the argument for the *ON* keyword. A right outer join works similarly to a left outer join, but it adds in all the rows from the row source on the right of *RIGHT OUTER JOIN*. A full outer join adds in all the rows from row sources on both sides of *FULL OUTER JOIN*. Aside from the keyword phrase name, the syntax for the three types of outer joins is the same as for an inner join.

The following sample demonstrates the syntax for a left outer join between the *titles* table and the *titleauthor* table in the pubs database. Notice that the syntax exactly follows the preceding inner join sample between these tables except for the replacement of the *JOIN* keyword by the *LEFT OUTER JOIN* keyword phrase. In addition, the result set for this *SELECT* statement includes 26 rows instead of the 25 rows in the preceding sample. The extra row is from a book title that doesn't have an author designated for it. The preceding *SELECT* statement screened out this extra row because the *titles* table *title_id* column value had no match in the *titleauthor* table. However, because the *titles* table is on the left side of the *LEFT OUTER JOIN*, the join forces in the row from the *titles* table, although it has no corresponding *title_id* column value in the *titleauthor* table.

```
--LeftOuterJoin
--Left outer join between authors titles and titleauthor.
--Returns 26 rows (25 matching rows + 1 non-matching row
--from the titles table).
SET NOCOUNT ON
```

```
Declare @strRows nvarchar(50)
SELECT ta.au_id, t.title, t.ytd_sales, t.price
FROM pubs..titles t LEFT OUTER JOIN pubs..titleauthor ta
ON (t.title_id = ta.title_id)
ORDER BY ta.au_id
SET @strRows = 'Rows returned = ' + Cast(@@ROWCOUNT AS nvarchar)
PRINT @strRows
SET NOCOUNT OFF
```

One practical use for left and right outer joins is that of listing rows on one side of a join without a matching row on the other side. For example, we can use an adaptation of the preceding sample to list the specific row in the *titles* table that has no matching *title_id* column value in the *titleauthor* table. The following script demonstrates the syntax for the solution. Notice that the basis for the solution is a *WHERE* clause that screens for a null value from the table without the matching row.

```
--RowsWithNoMatch
--Find rows in the left table without a match in the right table.
SELECT ta.au_id, t.title, t.ytd_sales, t.price
FROM pubs..titles t LEFT OUTER JOIN pubs..titleauthor ta
ON (t.title_id = ta.title_id)
WHERE ta.au_id IS NULL
```

Self Joins and Cross Joins

Two special kinds of joins, which serve contrasting purposes, are self joins and cross joins. A self join merges a table with itself. Use a self join when you need to relate the values in one column to the values in another column of the same table. A cross join creates a result set that combines column values from all the rows in one row source with column values from all the rows in a second row source. This is different from an outer join because a cross join doesn't create any null values in its result set. You will typically use this kind of join when at least one of your row sources is very small, such as a scalar value or a row source with just a couple of rows.

Within the context of the Northwind database, the classic situation calling for the application of a self join is the task of returning the names of the managers from the Employees table. This table contains a separate row for each employee, with two sets of columns that contribute to the task. The first set includes the *EmployeeID*, *FirstName*, and *LastName* columns. The second set includes a single column, *ReportsTo*. The *ReportsTo* column contains the *EmployeeID* value for the manager to whom an employee reports. You can find the manager names by merging the *ReportsTo* column values in the second set with the *EmployeeID* values in the first set. The *FirstName* and *LastName* column values for the matching records are the manager names. Manager names will repeat for as many direct reports as they have. Therefore, adding a *DISTINCT* predicate to the *SELECT* statement removes the duplicates.

The syntax for a self join is the same as for an inner join. However, the same row source appears on both sides of the *JOIN* keyword. With a self join, the use of aliases is mandatory. It is through the aliases that you designate the left and right row sources. The following sample shows the T-SQL for finding the managers from the Employees table. Notice that the expression for the *ON* keyword matches the *ReportsTo* column values to the *EmployeeID* column values. The *DISTINCT* predicate after *SELECT* removes the multiple instances of manager names from the result set.

```
--SelfJoin
--Self join to find managers in Employees table.
SELECT DISTINCT em.ReportsTo, e.FirstName, e.LastName
FROM Employees em JOIN Employees e
ON (em.ReportsTo = e.EmployeeID)
```

The cross join does have its own keyword phrase to denote its join type. (Not surprisingly, the keyword phrase is *CROSS JOIN*.) The syntax is distinctive as well. This is because the *FROM* clause doesn't need the *ON* keyword to specify columns for comparing between the two row sources. A cross join automatically merges all the rows from one source with each row from the other source; in other words, it generates one row for each possible pairing of rows from the two sources. That means it's important that at least one of the row sources have just one row or very few rows. A cross join of two tables with just 10,000 rows each generates a result set with 100,000,000 rows! You can limit the size of the result set through *WHERE* clause arguments that restrict the rows participating in the cross join from either the left or the right row source.

The following sample shows a simple cross join that merges *CompanyName* column values from each row in the *Shippers* table with *OrderID* column values from the *Orders* table that are less than or equal to 10,249. Only two *OrderID* values match this condition, and there are just three rows in the *Shippers* table, so the result set for the cross join contains only six rows. The syntax for the cross join appears below, and Figure 3-6 shows the result set.

```
--CrossJoin
--Cross join selected rows from one table with all
--selected rows from a second table based on a
--WHERE clause.
SELECT OrderID, CompanyName
FROM Orders CROSS JOIN Shippers
WHERE OrderID <= 10249
```

	OrderID	CompanyName
1	10248	Speedy Express
2	10249	Speedy Express
3	10248	United Package
4	10249	United Package
5	10248	Federal Shipping
6	10249	Federal Shipping

Figure 3-6. The result set from a cross join of *CompanyName* from the *Shippers* table with two *OrderID* values from the *Orders* table.

Subqueries

A subquery is merely a *SELECT* statement nested in another *SELECT* statement. Sometimes the SQL literature calls the nested *SELECT* statement the inner query and the container for the nested *SELECT* query the outer query. You can nest queries at more than two levels, but there are memory and complexity limits for parsing statements that you might incur before reaching the specified limit of 32 levels of nesting. You can use many of the standard *SELECT* statement features in a subquery, but there are some restrictions; see "Subquery Fundamentals" and "Subquery Rules" in Books Online for the details. This section will illustrate a couple of approaches that do work.

Before diving into the specifics of the syntax, it is important to understand a couple of points about subqueries. First, for most *SELECT* statements that use a subquery, there's almost always an alternative that doesn't require a subquery. Frequently a join will provide the same functionality. In any event, SQL Server searches for the fastest way to execute the query no matter how you state the query. Second there are two basic kinds of subqueries. The first of these is a stand-alone *SELECT* statement that executes once inside another query. The second subquery type is a *SELECT* statement that SQL Server must execute once for each row in the outer query. This type of inner query is known as a correlated subquery. A correlated subquery can degrade performance if SQL Server cannot find an alternative to computing two *SELECT* statements for each row in the row source for the outer query.

The following script illustrates a subquery formulation for finding the names of the managers in the Northwind database. The inner query finds the *EmployeeID* for the two managers—but it doesn't return their names. The outer query returns the *FirstName* and *LastName* column values for the *EmployeeID* values returned by the inner query.

```
--SubqueryForManagers
--Subquery to find managers in Employees table.
SELECT FirstName, LastName
FROM Employees
WHERE EmployeeID IN
    (SELECT DISTINCT ReportsTo FROM Employees)
```

The self join sample in the preceding section illustrates an alternative formulation for returning the names of company managers. Because the inner query executes just once in the formulation in this section, there is no particular disadvantage to the subquery formulation. Also, there is no performance penalty with either option. Look at both designs, and consider which one makes the most sense to you.

The next sample demonstrates the application of a correlated subquery. The outer *SELECT* statement returns the *OrderID* column value as well as the number of line items and the total extended price for all orders with more than four line items. This outer query computes the extended price for each line and groups the line items for each order. The inner query computes the number of line items in the current order for the outer query, and the outer query takes this result and compares it with 4 to determine whether it should include or exclude the order. As you can see, the outer query must recompute the inner query for each row in its result set.

```
--CorrelatedSubquery
--Correlated subquery to filter on an aggregated column value.
SELECT OrderID, COUNT(OrderID) 'Line items',
    '$' +
    CONVERT(varchar,CAST(SUM(Quantity*UnitPrice*(1-Discount)) AS money),1)
FROM [Order Details] odout
WHERE (SELECT COUNT(OrderID) FROM [Order Details] odin
    WHERE odin.OrderID = odout.OrderID) > 4
GROUP BY OrderID
ORDER BY COUNT(OrderID)
```

Alternatively, we could replace the inner query with a *HAVING* clause, as shown in the following script. Correlated subqueries usually carry a performance penalty, so you have to evaluate carefully whether any benefit derived from the correlated subquery is worth the penalty. When you are formulating ad hoc queries for use a limited number of times, correlated queries may make sense if the subquery formulation is easier for you to state than other, more efficient, approaches.

```
--CorrelatedSubqueryWithHaving
--HAVING clause alternative to the preceding
--correlated subquery sample.
SELECT OrderID, COUNT(OrderID) 'Line items',
    '$' +
    CONVERT(varchar,CAST(SUM(Quantity*UnitPrice*(1-Discount)) AS money),1)
FROM [Order Details]
GROUP BY OrderID
HAVING COUNT(OrderID) > 4
ORDER BY COUNT(OrderID)
```

4

Programming Views and Stored Procedures

The preceding chapter introduced you to programming data access with T-SQL. This chapter builds on and goes beyond the introduction in two explicit ways: First it introduces views by describing their uses with various types of row sources. Second it introduces you to stored procedures by reviewing their uses and the statements for creating and altering them, and by focusing on the use of parameters and local variables that are often found in stored procedures.

A view is a container for a single *SELECT* statement. Your SQL Server applications can refer to the view name as a shortcut to the *SELECT* statement within the view. In this chapter, you will learn the syntax for creating and using views. Special attention goes to creating views for data on remote servers and for data in other database formats, such as Access and any ODBC data source.

Stored procedures are compiled sets of T-SQL statements. After introducing the syntax for creating stored procedures, the chapter drills down on the syntax for manipulating parameters and return status values, programming the insertion and deletion of rows as well as the updating of column values in row sources, and the return of conditional result sets from a stored procedure.

The resources for this chapter include a database, Chapter04, with completed versions of the sample views and stored procedures discussed as well as T-SQL scripts for creating the views and stored procedures from scratch. Unless explicitly stated, all scripts should be run from the Chapter04 database. See the "Chapter Resources" section in Chapter 2 for more detail on attaching database files to a server and creating a new blank database from which you can invoke the scripts. The chapter also references other commonly available databases, including the SQL Server Northwind database, the pubs database, and the Access Northwind database. The first two databases are installed with SQL

Server; the third database is installed with Access. For the references to remote servers, you will need an instance of SQL Server running on two different computers or two instances of SQL Server running on the same computer.

Introduction to Views

A SQL Server view is a virtual table. As with a table, you can use a view in many ways, but unlike a table, a view doesn't actually store rows of data. Instead, what it stores is a *SELECT* statement, such as one of those covered in Chapter 2. The result set of the *SELECT* statement constitutes the data available through a view. The *FROM* clause of the view's *SELECT* statement can reference other views as well as base tables.

Uses for Views

You can use views as a way of insulating users from the database design in the schema of a custom application. This benefit makes your applications more robust in the face of ongoing requirements to update schema designs. The *INFORMATION_SCHEMA* views discussed in several sections throughout Chapter 2 illustrate this use for views. This approach to exposing data permits your custom solutions to change an application's schema but still provide the same information to the end users of an application. All you need is to update the view so that it selects the same data as before the schema change.

You also can use views to *secure* either the rows or the columns from a base table. With the *SELECT* list and the *WHERE* clause for a view's *SELECT* statement, you can filter data from a base table. In other words, a view permits you to expose a subset of a row source. For example, you could base a Visual Basic .Net application on a view instead of a table if you wanted to restrict the access of the application users to just rows that match the criteria in the *WHERE* clause. This approach "secures" the rows filtered out of the view. Instead of filtering rows with a *WHERE* clause, you can exclude selected columns with sensitive data from a *SELECT* list, such as columns for salary and bonus. Again, by excluding data, you "secure" the data from those without authority to view it.

A view is particularly valuable for combining the data for two or more base tables into a single row source. The various join clauses enable this capability very flexibly. You can also use a *UNION* operator to combine the data from two or more tables. A *UNION* operator contrasts with join clauses by concatenating one row source after another. Join clauses stitch row sources together side by side.

> **Note** See "Combining Results with UNION" in Books Online as a starting point for more coverage of *UNION* queries.

Using the *OPENROWSET* function allows access to remote, heterogeneous data sources through a view. This function permits you to access non-SQL Server data from SQL Server views. In addition, you can return data and even join data from other computers. The *OPENROWSET* function depends on an OLE DB provider for connecting to a data source; the provider determines the type of functionality available from the source. This function is particularly appropriate for ad hoc queries. The *OPENROWSET* function works with whatever username and password your application supplies it.

Alternatives to the *OPENROWSET* function include the *OPENDATASOURCE* function and linked servers. Books Online recommends linked servers for frequently used connections to data sources outside the scope of the active SQL Server instance. (See the "Remarks" section of the "OPENDATASOURCE" topic.) Administering a linked server requires a login that belongs to the sysadmin or setupadmin fixed server role.

Another purpose for a view is the representation of aggregations from a base table. A view can count or sum column values in a base table overall or by groups. This capability of presenting data summaries confirms a view as a decision-support tool. Because views encapsulate *SELECT* statements for reuse, you can add new views to a database based on T-SQL queries developed by, or in coordination with, the end users of an application. This feature makes views desirable for extending the functionality of applications in ways that you know have user appeal.

It is important that you grasp the notion of a view as a virtual table because this conveys some powerful clues about the needs they can fulfill in a custom solution. Your applications can insert, update, and delete data through a view. These capabilities depend on the characteristics of the view. For example, you can perform insert/update/delete functions for views of a single base table but not for views that expose aggregates of a base table. The "Remarks" section of the "CREATE VIEW" topic in Books Online details rules for the modification of the row source behind a view.

You can index views to speed their performance—just as you can with tables. Indexed views deliver benefits when you're working with very large tables. See the "Creating an Indexed View" topic in Books Online for a starting point for learning more about indexed views.

Partitioned views represent a means of segmenting a table over multiple computers each running SQL Server; you aggregate the partitions of a view with *UNION* operators. Through partitioned views, a view on each server with a segment can browse, add, update, and delete rows in the whole table (across all servers). Partitioned views are a robust way of working with very large databases. See the "Creating a Partitioned View" topic in Books Online for help with preparing partitioned views.

Statements for Creating and Altering Views

You can generate and modify views with the T-SQL *CREATE VIEW* and *ALTER VIEW* statements. In its most basic form, a *CREATE VIEW* statement specifies a name for the view and a *SELECT* statement to designate its result set. Position the view's name after a space delimiter following the *CREATE VIEW* keyword phrase. Then use the *AS* keyword to separate the view's name from its *SELECT* statement. For example, you can create a new view with this syntax:

```
CREATE VIEW view_name
AS
SELECT list_of_columns
FROM base_table_name
```

View names are standard SQL Server identifiers. Therefore, they must follow the rules for all object identifiers. Refer to the "Using Identifiers" topic in Books Online for a summary of the rules for specifying identifiers. In addition, user-defined views are objects like other system and user-defined SQL Server objects. Because SQL Server objects share a common namespace, you may care to use prefixes to reflect the type of object and avoid name conflicts. For example, this chapter uses the vew prefix for all user-defined views.

Just as with tables and other database objects, you cannot create a new view with the same name as an existing view. You must remove the prior version of the view before creating a new view with the same name as an existing one in a database. The *DROP VIEW* statement supports the removal of an existing view. A couple of *INFORMATION_SCHEMA* views return the names of the views in a database. This chapter demonstrates the use of these views.

You can invoke the *ALTER VIEW* statement to change an existing view without deleting it totally. The *ALTER VIEW* statement preserves permissions set on a view and doesn't alter the dependency of an *INSTEAD OF* trigger or a stored procedure on a view.

Restrictions on *SELECT* Statements for Views

While you do have access to most of the *SELECT* statement functionality, there are some design limitations as well as some differences in behavior for *SELECT* statements in views. For example, a *SELECT* statement in a view cannot contain a *COMPUTE* or *COMPUTE BY* clause because either clause can return multiple result sets. Views must always return a single result set. In this way, a view emulates a table. The single result set from a view can serve as a table in many other T-SQL statements.

You cannot use an *ORDER BY* clause by itself in the *SELECT* statement for a view. The Books Online documentation at several points makes this assertion without bothering to note an important case that permits the use of an *ORDER BY* clause inside the *SELECT* statement for a view. In this special case, you use the *TOP* predicate inside the *SELECT* statement. Subsequent samples will demonstrate the syntax for this.

The *WITH CHECK OPTION* clause is a special clause that applies to *SELECT* statements inside views. This clause can restrict a user's ability to insert new records through a view or modify the values in the result set that a view exposes. The *WITH CHECK OPTION* clause requires that all modifications to the row source for a view comply with criteria statements in the *SELECT* statement for a view.

View Attributes

Three view attributes help to refine the functionality that a view provides. A view's attribute specification can appear following its name in a *CREATE VIEW* or *ALTER VIEW* statement. Use *WITH* as a keyword before the attribute name.

Using the *ENCRYPTION* attribute encrypts the *SELECT* statement for the view. Users get the same result set for an encrypted or unencrypted view, but the encrypted view protects the T-SQL statement for the view. If you need to modify a view in the future, save outside the database an unencrypted version of the view's *CREATE VIEW* statement. You can do this with Query Analyzer by saving the unencrypted T-SQL statement that was used for creating the encrypted view.

The *SCHEMABINDING* view attribute integrates a view with its row sources so that you cannot remove or change a row source for a view in a way that will modify the result set. To specify the *SCHEMABINDING* attribute for a view, you must designate all underlying row sources for the view with a two-part naming convention that designates the owner name and the name for the row source. If you create indexes for a view, you must also designate the *SCHEMABINDING* attribute for the view.

> **Note** The *SELECT* statement for a view with *SCHEMABINDING* cannot include a *SELECT* list with * in it if it is an indexed view.

The *VIEW_METADATA* attribute is the third attribute for a view. Specify this attribute for views that are intended for use with SQL Server 2000 Meta Data Services. You can invoke these services from either Enterprise Manager or a special stand-alone Microsoft Management Console snap-in. Meta Data Services is a specialized topic outside the scope of this book. See the "Meta Data Services Overview" topic in Books Online for an introduction to the uses for Meta Data Services.

Creating and Using Views

As explained earlier, creating a view permits you to expose a subset of a row source through the view. The *SELECT* statement for a view determines the subset that a view returns. Nesting a *SELECT* statement in a *CREATE VIEW* statement generates a new view with a result set determined by the *SELECT* statement. This section illustrates typical syntax conventions for the *CREATE VIEW* statement. It also presents some special requirements for *SELECT* statements nested in *CREATE VIEW* statements.

Creating and Selecting from a View

To create a view, you must have an initial row source. This row source can reside in the current database or in another database to which your view can connect. The most straightforward solution is to use a row source in the current database.

The following script creates a row source as a table named *EmailContacts* in the database for this chapter and then populates the table with a couple of rows. Next, after dropping the view if it already exists, the script creates a view based on the table. Finally, a *SELECT* statement provides a result set based on the view.

The portion of the script creating and populating the table is excerpted from Chapter 2 with a minor adaptation for its use in the database for this chapter. After the *INSERT INTO* statements, the script displays new code specific to views. Before invoking the *CREATE VIEW* statement, the script uses the *INFORMATION_SCHEMA.VIEWS* view to verify whether a view already exists with the name for the new view. If the view does exist, the script drops the prior version. You can also use the *INFORMATION_SCHEMA.TABLES* view for the same purpose.

After ensuring that the name for the new view won't conflict with an existing one, the script invokes the *CREATE VIEW* statement. This statement demonstrates the syntax for naming a view. Notice the vew prefix. While this prefix isn't strictly necessary, recall that names for views and tables occupy the same namespace. Therefore, you must specify a view's name distinctly from a table serving as the view's row source. Because the *EmailContacts* table resides in the same database as the view and its owner is the dbo user, you can use a one-part name that simply references the table's name in the *FROM* clause of the view's *SELECT* statement. After the creation of the view, the script invokes a new *SELECT* statement to return the view's result set. Notice that the *FROM* clause in the concluding *SELECT* statement refers to the view's name, *vewEmailContacts*.

```
--CreatevewEmailContacts
USE Chapter04
GO

--Remove prior version of EmailContacts if it exists.
IF EXISTS
    (
    SELECT *
    FROM INFORMATION_SCHEMA.TABLES
    WHERE TABLE_NAME = 'EmailContacts'
    )
DROP TABLE EmailContacts

--Create EmailContacts with three columns.
CREATE TABLE EmailContacts
(
ContactID int Not Null PRIMARY KEY,
FirstName nvarchar(20) NULL,
LastName nvarchar(35) NULL,
Email1 nvarchar (255) NULL
)
GO

--Populate EmailContacts.
INSERT INTO EmailContacts
    VALUES(1,'Rick', 'Dobson', 'rickd@cabinc.net')
INSERT INTO EmailContacts
    VALUES(2,'Virginia', 'Dobson', 'virginia@cabinc.net')
GO
```

(continued)

```
--Drop prior version of view if it exists.
IF EXISTS (SELECT TABLE_NAME FROM INFORMATION_SCHEMA.VIEWS
        WHERE TABLE_NAME = 'vewEmailContacts')
    DROP VIEW vewEmailContacts
GO

--Create view to select all columns for
--all rows from the EmailContacts table.
CREATE VIEW vewEmailContacts
AS
SELECT *
FROM EmailContacts
GO

--Select all columns for all rows from
--the vewEmailContacts view.
SELECT *
FROM vewEmailContacts
```

Contrasting Unencrypted and Encrypted Views

With minor extensions, the preceding sample can serve as a template for the creation of any view. The following script illustrates one of these extensions. It creates a view in the Chapter04 database that has the *Shippers* table in the Northwind database as its base table. While the row source for a view can reside in another database, the *CREATE VIEW* statement can create a view only in the current database. Similarly, the *DROP VIEW* statement can remove a view only from the current database.

An easy way to reference a row source from another SQL Server database is to use a three-part name. The first part refers to the alternate database name, Northwind in this case. The second part designates the owner of the object providing the row source. When the row source owner is the default dbo user, you can omit its explicit designation (as in the following script). The third name part denotes the name of the database object providing the row source for a view. Figure 4-1 shows the result set from the *SELECT* statement based on the *vewShippers* view. Notice that it matches the values in the *Northwind..Shippers* table, which is the source for the *vewShippers* view.

Notice that unlike the first code sample, this one doesn't include a specific reference to the Chapter04 database. That's because Query Analyzer will continue to use Chapter04 until you specify a different database with a new *USE* statement.

```
--CreatevewShippers
--Search for, and remove if found, the
--vewShippers view in the Chapter04 database.
```

```
IF EXISTS (SELECT TABLE_NAME FROM INFORMATION_SCHEMA.VIEWS
    WHERE TABLE_NAME = 'vewShippers')
    DROP VIEW vewShippers
GO

--Create a new version of the vewShippers
--view in the Chapter04 database from the
--Shippers table in the Northwind database.
CREATE VIEW vewShippers
AS
SELECT *
FROM Northwind..Shippers
GO

--Select all rows and columns from the
--vewShippers view in Chapter04.
SELECT * FROM vewShippers
```

	ShipperID	CompanyName	Phone
1	1	Speedy Express	(503) 555-9831
2	2	United Package	(503) 555-3199
3	3	Federal Shipping	(503) 555-9931

Figure 4-1. The result set from a view based on the *Shippers* table in the Northwind database.

The *ENCRYPTION* attribute isn't set by default. Setting encryption doesn't change the result set from a *SELECT* statement. Instead, it encodes the T-SQL for a view's definition. You can verify this by trying to display the script for a view. The *VIEW_DEFINITION* column for the *INFORMATION_SCHEMA.VIEWS* view returns the script for a view on each of its rows.

The following script demonstrates the syntax for invoking the *ENCRYPTION* attribute. The script also demonstrates the syntax for returning the script that defines a view. This script includes all comments as well as the operational T-SQL statements for creating the view; these statements include the *CREATE VIEW* statement for generating a new view and the *SELECT* statement for defining a view's result set. In this case, the *SELECT* statement is identical to the one in the preceding view. However, the *CREATE VIEW* statement includes the *WITH ENCRYPTION* clause that encodes the T-SQL for the view. After creating the view, the script performs a simple *SELECT* query to verify the contents of the view's result set. The final portion of the script creates another result set with the definition for each user-defined view in the current database, which is Chapter04 in the sample. Omitting all rows beginning with "sys" for their *TABLE_NAME* column value in the *INFORMATION_SCHEMA.VIEWS* view excludes all system views from the final result set.

```
--CreatevewShippersEncrypted
--Search for, and remove if found, the
--vewShippersEncrypted view in the Chapter04 database.
IF EXISTS (SELECT TABLE_NAME FROM INFORMATION_SCHEMA.VIEWS
       WHERE TABLE_NAME = 'vewShippersEncrypted')
    DROP VIEW vewShippersEncrypted
GO

--Create a new version of the vewShippersEncrypted
--view in the Chapter04 database from the
--Shippers table in the Northwind database.
CREATE VIEW vewShippersEncrypted
WITH ENCRYPTION
AS
SELECT *
FROM Northwind..Shippers
GO

--Select all rows and columns from the
--vewShippersEncrypted view in Chapter04.
SELECT * FROM vewShippersEncrypted

--List user-defined view names in Chapter04 database
--along with their scripts.
SELECT TABLE_NAME, VIEW_DEFINITION
FROM INFORMATION_SCHEMA.VIEWS
WHERE LEFT(TABLE_NAME,3) <> 'sys'
```

Figure 4-2 shows an excerpt from the result sets for the preceding scripts. This excerpt is from the Results pane of Query Analyzer with a Results To Grids setting. The top result set shows the same three rows as in Figure 4-1. This confirms that encrypting a view doesn't alter the result from its *SELECT* statement. The second result set in Figure 4-2 displays the names of the three views created to this point in the chapter. Next to each view name is the beginning of the script for the view. Because the scripts start with comments, the *VIEW_DEFINITION* column values start with these comments. With a Results To Text setting for the Results pane, you can examine the whole script for each view except *vewShippersEncrypted*. The *WITH ENCRYPTION* clause in the *CREATE VIEW* statement for this view secures its script so that the *VIEW_DEFINITION* column of the *INFORMATION_SCHEMA.VIEWS* view cannot expose the T-SQL that generates the view.

	ShipperID	CompanyName	Phone
1	1	Speedy Express	(503) 555-9831
2	2	United Package	(503) 555-3199
3	3	Federal Shipping	(503) 555-9931

	TABLE_NAME	VIEW_DEFINITION
1	vewEmailContacts	--Create view to select all columns for --all rows from the EmailContacts
2	vewShippers	--Create a new version of the vewShippers --view in the Chapter03 databas
3	vewShippersEncrypted	[illegible]

Figure 4-2. An excerpt showing the result set from an encrypted view as well as the *VIEW_DEFINITION* column values from the *INFORMATION_SCHEMA.VIEWS* view for three views in a database.

Sorting and Grouping Within a View

The *SELECT* statement that defines a view has generally the same syntax as that within a stand-alone script. For example, grouping rows to aggregate a column value works the same in both stand-alone scripts and those inside views. Similarly, the *IN* keyword in a *WHERE* clause works the same as well.

In contrast, the *ORDER BY* clause in a *SELECT* statement requires slightly different syntax inside a view than it does outside a view. In particular, *ORDER BY* inside a view requires the *TOP* predicate after the *SELECT* keyword. The *TOP* predicate, in turn, requires an argument to designate how many records to return. If you want all the rows from a source, follow *TOP* with *100 PERCENT*. You can designate any other percentage as well as a number for any number of rows. Trailing *TOP* with the number 10 without the *PERCENT* keyword returns the first 10 rows in the result set. When you use an *ORDER BY* clause, those rows will be the highest or lowest column values on a sort dimension depending on the sort order. The syntax for designating a sort order in an *ORDER BY* clause is the same in a *SELECT* statement in or out of a view.

The following script shows the creation and return of values from a view that groups and sorts column values. The *SELECT* statement for the view also includes a criterion that filters exclusively for countries beginning with the letter *B* or *C*. Chapter 3 included a similar stand-alone script for counting the number of customers by city within country. The *SELECT* statement in the following script is distinct because of its use of the *TOP* predicate. While the *TOP* predicate will work in a stand-alone script, it isn't necessary.

```
--CreatevewCustomersInCountryCity
--Search for, and remove if found, the
--vewCustomersInCountryCity view in the Chapter04 database.
IF EXISTS (SELECT TABLE_NAME FROM INFORMATION_SCHEMA.VIEWS
       WHERE TABLE_NAME = 'vewCustomersInCountryCity')
    DROP VIEW vewCustomersInCountryCity
GO
```

(continued)

```
--Create a new version of the vewCustomersInCountryCity
--view in the Chapter04 database.
--To use ORDER BY clause in view you need TOP predicate
--with modifier of 100 PERCENT.
CREATE VIEW vewCustomersInCountryCity
AS
SELECT TOP 100 PERCENT Country, City,
    Count(CustomerID) '# of Customers'
FROM Northwind..Customers
WHERE LEFT(Country,1) IN ('B','C')
GROUP BY Country, City
ORDER BY Country, City
GO

--Select all rows and columns from the
--vewCustomersInCountryCity view in Chapter04.
SELECT * FROM vewCustomersInCountryCity
```

Views for Remote and Heterogeneous Sources

It is often necessary to view data residing on another SQL Server instance or even in another type of database format. T-SQL provides several approaches to satisfying these kinds of requirements. The *OPENROWSET* function is a flexible approach because it can accommodate ad hoc queries as well as those performed on a regular basis. As mentioned previously, Books Online recommends that you use linked servers when it is necessary to query a remote or heterogeneous source on a regular basis. However, you can invoke the *OPENROWSET* function for a userid that doesn't have membership in the sysadmin or setupadmin fixed server roles. The *OPENROWSET* function depends only on the permissions for the userid passed to the other data source. This section presents a series of *OPENROWSET* samples designed to help you understand remote data access.

Creating a View for Another SQL Server Instance

One typical requirement is to view a SQL Server row source, such as a table, on another server. You can use the *OPENROWSET* function to perform this task, with arguments that specify a provider, other elements of a connection string, and a *SELECT* statement. The *OPENROWSET* function can serve as an argument for the *FROM* clause of a *SELECT* statement. This outer *SELECT* statement, in turn, must reside in a *CREATE VIEW* statement when your goal is to create a view in the current database that exposes a row source in another database.

When the inner *SELECT* statement—the one in the call to the *OPENROWSET* function—points at another SQL Server instance, the provider for the function should be SQLOLEDB. Next you can denote the remaining elements of the connection string for the other server in the following order: the server instance name, a SQL Server login for the server, and a password for the login. Follow the provider name by a comma, but use a semicolon for a delimiter after the server name and login name. A comma separates the password from the *SELECT* statement.

The following script creates a view on one SQL Server running SQL Server 2000 that points at a table on the cabxli server running the MSDE version compatible with SQL Server 7. You need two instances of SQL Server to evaluate this script, but you can name the instances anything you want. Just change the references to cabxli to the name of a SQL Server instance to which you can connect. By the way, the table is the *authors* table in the pubs database; MSDE doesn't routinely install with the pubs database. Because cabxli is an internal test server running Windows 98, the server is available with sa and an empty password. Production servers should *always* have a password for the sa login if you aren't forcing Windows authentication. The *SELECT* statement references the *authors* table in the pubs database on the cabxli server. The *ORDER BY* clause along with the *TOP* predicate sorts the result set by author first name within author last name.

The outer *SELECT* statement takes the *OPENROWSET* function as the argument for its *FROM* clause. The *SELECT* list for the outer *SELECT* statement lists the authors by first name, last name, and phone number, in that order.

```
--CreatevewAuthorsSortedOnCabxli
--Search for, and remove if found, the
--vewAuthorsSortedOnCabxli view in the Chapter04 database.
IF EXISTS (SELECT TABLE_NAME FROM INFORMATION_SCHEMA.VIEWS
        WHERE TABLE_NAME = 'vewAuthorsSortedOnCabxli')
    DROP VIEW vewAuthorsSortedOnCabxli
GO

--Create a new version of the vewAuthorsSortedOnCabxli
--view in the Chapter04 database from the
--Shippers table in the Northwind database.
CREATE VIEW vewAuthorsSortedOnCabxli
AS
SELECT au_fname, au_lname, phone
FROM OPENROWSET('SQLOLEDB','cabxli';'sa';'',
    'SELECT TOP 100 PERCENT * FROM pubs..authors ORDER BY au_lname, au_fname')
GO

--Select all rows and columns from the
--vewAuthorsSortedOnCabxli view in Chapter04.
SELECT * FROM vewAuthorsSortedOnCabxli
GO
```

Creating a View for an Access Database

It isn't uncommon to need to upgrade Access applications for the use of an Access database via a SQL Server solution. While you can perform a full-scale upsizing, it is possible that the *OPENROWSET* function can dramatically reduce the effort of working with Access data from SQL Server. That's because the function permits a SQL Server solution to view Access data without the need of transporting the data from Access to SQL Server. Therefore, you save the conversion effort. In addition, your clients avoid the disruption that could arise if their familiar Access solution were unavailable because you replaced it with a SQL Server application. At the same time, new applications can expose data from the Access database. So long as you don't expect to experience bottlenecks related to the capacity of the Access database, this approach bears consideration. In any event, the approach supports the easy availability of Access data from SQL Server views.

You can use an *OPENROWSET* function to connect with an Access database much like you use the function to connect with a SQL Server database on another SQL Server instance. The *OPENROWSET* function is the argument for the *FROM* clause of a *SELECT* statement. When connecting to an Access database, you must specify the Jet data provider followed by the path to the Access database file, a login name, and a password. The *OPENROWSET* function also has its own *SELECT* statement that specifies the row source in the Access database as well as any special settings, such as a *WHERE* clause.

The following script demonstrates a connection to an Access database file on the current computer. The path points to the default installation of the Northwind sample database for Access 2002. The connection string specifies a login by the admin user with an empty password. This is normal for an unsecured Access database file, such as the Access Northwind sample. The *SELECT* statement inside the *OPENROWSET* function call designates the return of all rows with a *Country* column value of USA. When designating a string in this instance, the normal syntax is to enclose the string argument, *USA,* with a pair of single quotation marks. However, within the *OPENROWSET* function, single quotation marks are already used around the *SELECT* statement, so it's necessary to use two single quotation marks on each side of *USA*. In the following script, the outer *SELECT* statement displays all the columns from the inner *SELECT* statement.

```
--CreatevewUSACustomersFromAccess
--Search for, and remove if found, the
--vewUSACustomersFromAccess view in the Chapter04 database.
IF EXISTS (SELECT TABLE_NAME FROM INFORMATION_SCHEMA.VIEWS
        WHERE TABLE_NAME = 'vewUSACustomersFromAccess')
    DROP VIEW vewUSACustomersFromAccess
GO
```

```
--Create a new version of the vewUSACustomersFromAccess
--view in the Chapter04 database from the Customers table
--in the Access Northwind database. (You should install the
--Northwind sample if it isn't already installed. Also, you
--may need to change the path to Northwind.)
CREATE VIEW vewUSACustomersFromAccess
AS
SELECT *
FROM OPENROWSET(
    'Microsoft.Jet.OLEDB.4.0',
    'c:\Program Files\Microsoft Office\Office10\Samples\Northwind.mdb';
    'admin';'',
    'SELECT * FROM Customers WHERE Country=''USA''')
GO

--Select all rows and columns from the
--vewUSACustomersFromAccess view in Chapter04.
SELECT * FROM vewUSACustomersFromAccess
GO
```

Creating a View for an ODBC Row Source

Viewing an ODBC data source may be the ultimate in flexibility because ODBC drivers are available for so many different types of databases. In addition, the MSDASQL provider, which is installed with Microsoft Data Access Components, offers a standard interface to ODBC data sources. The *OPENROWSET* function through its *SELECT* statement lets your applications choose a specific row source within a data source or even filter a row source to derive a new custom source for an application.

Using the *OPENROWSET* function to connect with a row source in an ODBC data source bears a strong resemblance to using the function to connect with SQL Server and Jet row sources. The main differences are in the connection string specifications. First you must designate the MSDASQL provider instead of the SQLOLEDB or Jet provider. Second you specify connection string elements that are appropriate for the data source to which you want to connect.

The following script shows the syntax for an application of the *OPEN-ROWSET* function with the MSDASQL provider for an ODBC data source. In fact, the sample connects to a SQL Server data source with the ODBC driver, but the general syntax issues are the same as for any data source. This sample requires two instances of SQL Server. For example, the connection string elements point to the cab2000 server running a SQL Server database. You can replace the reference to cab2000 with the name of any other instance of SQL Server on your network. The userid and password are, respectively, sa and password. The inner *SELECT* statement for the *OPENROWSET* function chooses all the rows from the *Orders* table in the Northwind database whose *OrderDate* is in 1998. A *WHERE* clause and a *DATEPART* function participate in the designation of an appropriate criterion for the *SELECT* statement. The outer *SELECT* statement returns all columns from the *Orders* table.

```
--Createvew1998OrdersOnCab2000
--Search for, and remove if found, the
--vew1998OrdersOnCab2000 view in the Chapter04 database.
IF EXISTS (SELECT TABLE_NAME FROM INFORMATION_SCHEMA.VIEWS
        WHERE TABLE_NAME = 'vew1998OrdersOnCab2000')
    DROP VIEW vew1998OrdersOnCab2000
GO

--Create a new version of the vew1998OrdersOnCab2000
--view in the Chapter04 database from the Orders table
--in the Northwind database on the Cab2000 server.
CREATE VIEW vew1998OrdersOnCab2000
AS
SELECT *
FROM OPENROWSET('MSDASQL',
    'DRIVER={SQL Server};SERVER=cab2000;UID=sa;PWD=password',
    'SELECT *
    FROM Northwind..Orders
    WHERE DATEPART(yyyy, OrderDate) = 1998')
GO

--Select all rows and columns from the
--vew1998OrdersOnCab2000 view in Chapter04.
SELECT * FROM vew1998OrdersOnCab2000
```

Joining Row Sources for a View

The value of being able to process remote and heterogeneous data sources multiplies when you can join two row sources from different servers or different databases. There are at least two approaches to this task. The first one is to create a *SELECT* statement that contains a *JOIN* operator. In this approach, each side of the join has its own explicit *OPENROWSET* function. The other approach is to create two new views, each based on its own *OPENROWSET* function. Then you can create a new, third, view that joins the two views. Either approach empowers an application to process concurrently row sources from different database servers in different database formats!

The following script shows the syntax for the first approach. Like several of the previous *OPENROWSET* function samples, this one requires two instances of SQL Server. The script joins rows from the *Orders* table in a SQL Server database with rows from the *Customers* table in an Access database file. The *OPENROWSET* function declarations follow the syntax of previous samples that used the functions separately as the source for a view. This script sample joins the *Customers* rows with the *Orders* rows based on their *CustomerID* column values. An advantage of nesting the two *OPENROWSET* functions as the argument for the *FROM* clause of the outer *SELECT* statement is that your application doesn't require separate views for each row source object that gets joined. This saves your application from opening the views.

```
--CreatevewAccessCustomersCab2000Orders
--Search for, and remove if found, the
--vewAccessCustomersCab2000Orders view in the Chapter04 database.
IF EXISTS (SELECT TABLE_NAME FROM INFORMATION_SCHEMA.VIEWS
        WHERE TABLE_NAME = 'vewAccessCustomersCab2000Orders')
    DROP VIEW vewAccessCustomersCab2000Orders
GO

--Create the vewAccessCustomersCab2000Orders view
--in the Chapter04 database from the
--OPENROWSET of CustomersFromAccess and
--OPENROWSET of 1998OrdersOnCab2000.
CREATE VIEW vewAccessCustomersCab2000Orders
AS
SELECT TOP 100 PERCENT c.CompanyName, c.ContactName, c.Phone,
    o.OrderID, LEFT(o.OrderDate, 11) 'Order Date'
FROM OPENROWSET('Microsoft.Jet.OLEDB.4.0',
    'C:\Program Files\Microsoft Office\Office10\Samples\Northwind.mdb';
    'admin';'',
    'SELECT *
    FROM Customers
    WHERE Country=''USA''') AS c JOIN
    OPENROWSET('MSDASQL',
        'DRIVER={SQL Server};SERVER=cab2000;UID=sa;PWD=password',
    'SELECT *
    FROM Northwind.dbo.Orders
    WHERE DATEPART(yyyy, OrderDate) = 1998')
    AS o
    ON c.CustomerID = o.CustomerID
ORDER BY c.CompanyName, o.OrderID
GO

--Select all rows and columns from the
--vewAccessCustomersCab2000Orders view in Chapter04.
SELECT * FROM vewAccessCustomersCab2000Orders
```

The next script shows the syntax for the alternative approach to joining two heterogeneous data sources. Again, you need two SQL Server instances to run the sample. This alternative joins two previously created views. In this instance, each view is from a prior sample in this chapter. In addition, the two views correspond to the *SELECT* statements for each of the nested *OPEN-*

ROWSET functions in the prior sample. Therefore, the result is identical for the next script and the prior script. However, the code for the next script is dramatically simpler. By segmenting the two *OPENROWSET* functions into separate views, the second approach makes it easier to debug the syntax. On the other hand, with this approach your application requires the additional overhead of managing two separate views. This includes creating, maintaining, and opening the views.

```
--Createvew2JoinedViews
--Search for, and remove if found, the
--vew2JoinedViews view in the Chapter04 database.
IF EXISTS (SELECT TABLE_NAME FROM INFORMATION_SCHEMA.VIEWS
        WHERE TABLE_NAME = 'vew2JoinedViews')
    DROP VIEW vew2JoinedViews
GO

--Create a new version of the vew2JoinedViews
--view in the Chapter04 database from
--two other previously existing views.
CREATE VIEW vew2JoinedViews
AS
Select TOP 100 PERCENT c.CompanyName, c.ContactName, c.Phone,
    o.OrderID, LEFT(o.OrderDate, 11) 'Order Date'
FROM vewUSACustomersFromAccess c JOIN vew1998OrdersOnCab2000 o
    ON (c.CustomerID = o.CustomerID)
ORDER BY c.CompanyName, o.OrderID
GO

--Select all rows and columns from the
--vew2JoinedViews view in Chapter04.
SELECT *
FROM vew2JoinedViews
GO
```

Introduction to Stored Procedures

Stored procedures are compiled batches of T-SQL statements. The batch of statements can contain nearly all the T-SQL statement types. While a stored procedure can return a result set the same way a view does, stored procedures are more powerful in several respects. A view is a virtual table; a stored procedure is more like a procedure in Visual Basic. You can pass it parameters, and it can return values through its result set, output parameters, and return status values. In fact, stored procedures can return multiple result sets, while views are limited to a single result similar to a table.

Uses for Stored Procedures

Stored procedures have four main uses. First, they can return one or more result sets. You can program a stored procedure to return multiple result sets as easily as including multiple *SELECT* statements within a single stored procedure. Another way stored procedures can return result sets is via output parameters. An output parameter is a scalar value. A scalar value is a single value, such as a string or an integer, that isn't a part of a rowset. While a result set can contain a scalar value, result sets normally contain sets of values. Output parameters provide an efficient means for stored procedures to return scalar values. Stored procedures can also return integer values that indicate how a stored procedure terminates. SQL Server documentation refers to these return values as return status values. When a stored procedure can follow any of several internal processing paths, return status values can indicate to a calling routine which path a stored procedure pursued.

A second major use of stored procedures is the processing of input parameters. These parameters enable your applications to control dynamically the things that a stored procedure returns. Not all T-SQL statements take parameters. In these circumstances, you can combine the use of parameters with control-of-flow statements, such as *IF...ELSE* statements, to determine what a stored procedure returns. One common use for parameters is in the *WHERE* clause of *SELECT* statements. By using input parameter values as criterion values for *WHERE* clause expressions, your applications can dynamically control a stored procedure's result set. When users set the parameter values, you enable users to control an application dynamically at run time.

A third major use for stored procedures is the management of insert/update/delete operations for row sources. In this context, a stored procedure provides value to an application without returning a result set, a parameter value, or a return status value. The procedure simply modifies a row source. Because stored procedures can set parameters based on user input and the procedures can use parameters for insert/update/delete operations, users can control the modifications to a row source at run time.

Fourth, you will learn how to use stored procedures as programs implemented with a batch of T-SQL statements. This fourth use underlies and extends the other three uses for stored procedures. These statements can include *SELECT* statements, other statements for insert/update/delete operations, and control-of-flow statements, such as *IF...ELSE* statements. In addition, you can specify any of four types of values—local variables, global variables, parameters, and return status values—to control the dynamic behavior of a stored procedure and how it communicates with its calling procedure.

> **Note** See the "Control-of-Flow" topic in Books Online for a good starting point that helps you to learn about traditional programming techniques for stored procedures. Another especially useful Books Online topic for learning about stored procedure programming is "Programming Stored Procedures."

Reusing T-SQL Statements with Stored Procedures

One of the major advantages of stored procedures is that they can package T-SQL statements for reuse. Four T-SQL statements help you manage these blocks of code. Two statements, *CREATE PROCEDURE* and *ALTER PROCEDURE*, enable the definition and refinement of the code within a stored procedure. With the *DROP PROCEDURE* statement, you can remove a stored procedure from a database. The *EXECUTE* statement permits you to run a stored procedure.

The *CREATE PROCEDURE* statement lets you create a stored procedure. You can abbreviate this statement as *CREATE PROC*. Follow the statement name with the name for your stored procedure. SQL Server has a rich collection of system stored procedures, which typically start with sp_. Chapter 2 includes examples of how to use system stored procedures with tables. System stored procedures are available for managing every aspect of SQL Server performance and administration. To avoid conflicts with system stored procedures, avoid starting your own user-defined stored procedures with the sp_ prefix. This chapter uses udp as a prefix for user-defined stored procedures. Like view names, stored procedures should follow the standard rules for SQL Server identifiers.

The *CREATE PROC* statements typically have three or four main elements. First, *CREATE PROC* declares the stored procedure and assigns a name to it. Second, you can specify one or more parameters for the procedure. The parameter declarations are optional. Third, the *AS* keyword serves as a transitional word between the declaration elements and the T-SQL code (the fourth element) that enables a stored procedure to perform a task. The following template illustrates how to arrange these stored procedure elements.

```
CREATE PROC procedurename
Parameter specifications
AS
T-SQL code
```

After you create a stored procedure, you can change its code in at least two different ways. First, you can invoke the *DROP PROCEDURE* (or *DROP PROC*) statement to remove the prior version and then invoke a new *CREATE*

PROC statement with the same name as the removed procedure. To delete an existing stored procedure with the *DROP PROC* statement, simply follow the keyword phrase with the name of the stored procedure that you want to remove. With this approach, you wipe out any permissions assigned to users for the dropped stored procedure. Alternatively, you can invoke the *ALTER PROCEDURE* (or *ALTER PROC*) statement. This allows you to respecify the parameters and the code within a stored procedure while it maintains any permission settings for the stored procedure that you modify. Except for the keyword declaring it, the *ALTER PROC* statement has the same format as the *CREATE PROC* statement.

Your applications can use the *EXECUTE* (or *EXEC*) statement to invoke a stored procedure initially created with a *CREATE PROC* statement. In its most basic representation, follow the *EXEC* keyword with the name of the stored procedure that you want to run. The syntax for the *EXEC* statement permits you to assign values for input parameters as well as accept output parameter and return status values. In addition, the *EXEC* statement can also return one or more result sets—depending on the T-SQL code that populates the stored procedure. This chapter includes numerous samples that illustrate the syntax for invoking stored procedures with the *EXEC* statement.

Using Parameters, Local Variables, and Global Variables

Although parameters, local variables, and global variables can, of course, be used elsewhere, using them with stored procedures especially enhances the value of the procedures in an application. There are two basic kinds of parameters—input parameters and output parameters. Parameter names must begin with the @ symbol. The remainder of a parameter's name must follow the standard SQL Server identifier conventions. Parameters have data types that correspond to those for table column values. (See Chapter 3.)

Input parameters permit you to customize the operation of a stored procedure at run time. For example, you can use input parameters to specify the column values for a stored procedure that adds a new row to a row source. The *CREATE PROC* and *ALTER PROC* statements permit you to assign default values for input parameters. These default values allow a stored procedure to use a parameter without testing for a null value even if the user omits the specification of a parameter when invoking the stored procedure.

Output parameters represent values developed from within a stored procedure. These can be values computed by the procedure or SQL Server. A stored procedure can pass back as an output parameter the *IDENTITY* value for a new row in a table so that another stored procedure can use the output parameter as a foreign key value for a new row in a related table. In this scenario, the output parameter value from one stored procedure serves as the input parameter value for a second one.

A local variable is a memory variable that you assign for use inside a stored procedure. Use the *DECLARE* keyword for designating local variables and the *SET* keyword for assigning values to a local variable. You can also assign a value to a local variable with a *SELECT* statement that returns a scalar value, such as the count of the number of rows in a table. The scope of a local variable is the stored procedure that declares the variable.

Like parameters, local variable identifiers must begin with the @ symbol. The remainder of the local variable name must follow standard SQL Server identifier conventions. The *DECLARE* statement for a local variable must include a data type for the variable. You can use any data type except for *text*, *ntext*, and *image*. A local variable's data type specification determines the type of content that the variable can hold. Local variables can be used in expressions and as arguments for control-of-flow statements to control the operation of a stored procedure. Local variables can work in coordination with parameters by accepting values from parameters and passing values to them.

Developers familiar with SQL Server versions prior to 7.0 may be familiar with the term *global variables*. SQL Server 2000 refers to these global variables as functions. A global variable function name starts with @@. These global variable functions return values to stored procedures that contain system information. You can display the full list of 33 @@ variable functions from the Index tab in Books Online by entering **@@** as the keyword. This chapter illustrates the use of the *@@ROWCOUNT* function, which returns the number of rows affected by the last T-SQL statement. Other @@ functions that I regularly find particularly convenient include *@@IDENTITY*, *@@ERROR*, and *@@DBTS*. These three functions return the last *IDENTITY* value inserted, the error number associated with the last T-SQL statement, and the current timestamp value within a database.

Creating and Using Stored Procedures

The purpose of this section is to introduce you to syntax for creating and using stored procedures. This section shows you typical ways of applying the *CREATE PROC* statement. In addition, you learn common ways of specifying the *EXEC* statement to run a stored procedure. The section illustrates techniques for designating input parameters when you create a stored procedure as well as ways of specifying input parameter values when you run a stored procedure.

Dynamically Selecting from a Row Source

One of the main advantages of stored procedures compared with views is that stored procedures permit the use of parameters. Both views and stored procedures can invoke *SELECT* statements. However, stored procedures let you assign values to parameters in *WHERE* clause expressions at run time. This capability means your applications can take input from users to designate which rows a stored procedure returns in its result set. With views, you would have to preprogram a different view for each set of rows you wanted.

The following script has three batches of T-SQL code. The first batch removes any prior version of the *udpListShippersRow* in the current database. The first batch uses the *INFORMATION_SCHEMA.ROUTINES* view to search for an existing stored procedure with the name *udpListShippersRow*. If one already exists with that name, the batch invokes the *DROP PROCEDURE* statement to remove it.

The second batch invokes the *CREATE PROC* statement to create a new stored procedure named *udpListShippersRow*. This procedure takes a single parameter named *@RowID* with an *int* data type. The procedure uses the parameter to specify the *ShipperID* column value for the row it returns; see the *WHERE* clause for the syntax of how to do this. The basic *SELECT* statement returns all the columns from the *Shippers* table in the Northwind database. You can tell from the syntax that this is the SQL Server version of the database. (Notice the *FROM* clause argument.) All the remaining stored procedure samples use just SQL Server databases.

The final batch consists of a single *EXEC* statement. The statement runs the stored procedure created in the previous batch and designates a value for the *RowID* parameter. Failing to specify a *RowID* parameter value causes the procedure to fail with an error message. Designating a nonexistent *ShipperID* column value with *RowID* produces an empty result set. On the other hand, specifying any of the existing *ShipperID* column values causes the procedure to generate a result set with all the columns for that row in the *Shippers* table.

```
--CreateudpListShippersRow
--Delete previous version of udpListShippersRow
--stored procedure if it exists.
IF EXISTS (SELECT ROUTINE_NAME
        FROM INFORMATION_SCHEMA.ROUTINES
        WHERE ROUTINE_TYPE = 'PROCEDURE' AND
        ROUTINE_NAME = 'udpListShippersRow')
    DROP PROCEDURE udpListShippersRow
GO

--Create udpListShippersRow with an
```

(continued)

```
--input parameter to specify a row.
CREATE PROC udpListShippersRow
@RowID int
AS
SELECT *
FROM Northwind..Shippers
WHERE ShipperID = @RowID
GO

--Run udpListShippersRow with an
--input parameter of 2.
EXEC udpListShippersRow 2
```

Returning a Sorted Result Set

Even a basic *SELECT* statement can yield benefits when it is made available from a stored procedure. For example, the use of the *ORDER BY* clause in a view requires the concurrent use of the *TOP* predicate. While this is certainly not complicated, it is just one more thing you have to remember to get right. The syntax for using the *ORDER BY* clause in a stored procedure is just like that in a stand-alone T-SQL script. In other words, you don't need a *TOP* predicate for your *SELECT* statement.

The following script shows the *ORDER BY* clause within a *SELECT* statement that determines the result set from a stored procedure. The *SELECT* statement generates a result set based on the *Shippers* table, with the rows sorted by *CompanyName* column values. This returns the rows in a different order than the default one based on the *ShipperID* column values. The script again relies on a three-part strategy. The first part removes an old version of the *udpShippersSortedByCompanyName* stored procedure. The second part invokes the *CREATE PROC* statement to add the new stored procedure. The third part runs the newly created stored procedure with the *EXEC* statement. Because this stored procedure doesn't take any parameters, you can just follow the *EXEC* keyword with the name of the stored procedure. There is no need for anything else after the *EXEC* keyword.

```
--CreateudpShippersSortedByCompanyName
--Delete previous version of udpShippersSortedByCompanyName
--stored procedure if it exists.
IF EXISTS (SELECT ROUTINE_NAME
        FROM INFORMATION_SCHEMA.ROUTINES
        WHERE ROUTINE_TYPE = 'PROCEDURE' AND
        ROUTINE_NAME = 'udpShippersSortedByCompanyName')
    DROP PROCEDURE udpShippersSortedByCompanyName
GO

--Create udpShippersSortedByCompanyName with an
--input parameter to specify a row.
CREATE PROC udpShippersSortedByCompanyName
```

```
AS
SELECT *
FROM Northwind..Shippers
ORDER BY CompanyName
GO

--Run udpShippersSortedByCompanyName.
EXEC udpShippersSortedByCompanyName
GO
```

Returning the Script for a View

Stored procedures are an extremely flexible tool. You can use *SELECT* statements in the full range of cases that use views and stand-alone T-SQL statements. For example, you can query *INFORMATION_SCHEMA* views to uncover information about the objects in a database. An advantage of a stored procedure is that the T-SQL it contains is compiled. A stand-alone T-SQL statement must be compiled before SQL Server can use it. Therefore, the stored procedure can run the same T-SQL code faster.

> **Note** The *sp_executesql* system stored procedure offers some of the benefits of stored procedures for stand-alone T-SQL *SELECT* statements.

The following script demonstrates the use of a stored procedure to query the *INFORMATION_SCHEMA.VIEWS* view. The result set for this view contains a row for each view in the current database. The view's *VIEW_DEFINITION* column returns the T-SQL script defining a view. The *TABLE_NAME* column returns the name for a view.

The stored procedure accepts a parameter that designates a view's name. The stored procedure's *SELECT* statement passes the T-SQL script for a view to a local variable, *@strDefinition*. The local variable accepts the value in the *VIEW_DEFINITION* column value for the row with a *TABLE_NAME* column value equal to the parameter passed to the stored procedure. Then a *PRINT* statement displays the contents of the local variable in the Messages pane.

The stored procedure's approach works for views with up to 8000 characters from the default code page for the computer on which you developed the stored procedure. This is because the *varchar* data type for the *@strDefinition* local variable has a maximum length of 8000 characters in the default code page for a computer. If you expect your view scripts to have more characters or your application runs on computers using multiple code pages, you need another approach for storing the view's T-SQL script. For example, you can use an output parameter instead of a local variable. Assign a *text* or an *ntext* data type to the parameter. When using the output parameter approach, you can print the script in the calling routine for the stored procedure. Recall that a *text* data type can hold up to 2^{31}-1 characters, and a data type value can hold up to 2^{30}-1 characters.

Users can alter the return value that appears in the Messages pane by changing the name of the view passed to the stored procedure. The *EXEC* statement to invoke the stored procedure encloses the parameter in single quotation marks. This is because the stored procedure assigns a *varchar* data type to the parameter storing a view's name.

```
--CreateudpScriptForView
--Remove prior version of stored procedure.
IF EXISTS (SELECT ROUTINE_NAME
        FROM INFORMATION_SCHEMA.ROUTINES
        WHERE ROUTINE_TYPE = 'PROCEDURE' AND
        ROUTINE_NAME = 'udpScriptForView')
    DROP PROCEDURE udpScriptForView
GO

--Create stored procedure to print definition
--for a view in the current database.
CREATE PROC udpScriptForView
@vewName varchar(128)
AS
DECLARE @strDefinition varchar(8000)
SET @strDefinition = (SELECT VIEW_DEFINITION
FROM INFORMATION_SCHEMA.VIEWS
WHERE TABLE_NAME = @vewName)
PRINT @strDefinition
GO

--Run stored procedure and pass view name.
EXEC udpScriptForView 'vewShippers'
GO
```

Processing Stored Procedure Outputs

One of the tasks that stored procedures serve especially well is getting data back to a calling procedure. Stored procedures can achieve this goal in several ways. First, they permit the transfer of data back to the calling procedure in the form of result sets. You can return multiple result sets from a single stored procedure. Second, a stored procedure can return scalar values via output parameters. Third, code calling a stored procedure can process return status values. In any one application, you can concurrently use any combination of these three processes for returning values. This section elaborates on them and demonstrates the syntax for implementing each.

Returning Two Result Sets from a Stored Procedure

It's simple to return multiple result sets from a single stored procedure: just include a separate *SELECT* statement for each result set that you want a stored procedure to return. In contrast, views can have only a single *SELECT* statement. Once you start using multiple *SELECT* statements in a stored procedure, you'll find that it has considerably more flexibility than returning rows from a table or view.

The following script creates a stored procedure with two result sets. The first result set contains a row with the name and creation date for each user-defined stored procedure in a database. Recall that the database context for these samples is Chapter04. (You can set the context with a *USE* statement.) To return just the user-defined stored procedures from the *INFORMATION_SCHEMA.ROUTINES* view, you need two criteria expressions. One expression selects just rows with a *ROUTINE_TYPE* column value of *PROCEDURE*. This expression filters out any user-defined functions. The second expression removes any rows with a *ROUTINE_NAME* column value that begins with dt_. Because SQL Server uses dt_ as a prefix for the stored procedures that it creates in a database, this expression leaves only user-defined stored procedures.

The second *SELECT* statement returns the value of the *@@ROWCOUNT* function. This function is always the value of records affected by the last T-SQL statement. In this case, the last one returns the names and creation dates of the user-defined stored procedures in a database, so the second *SELECT* statement returns the number of user-defined stored procedures in the current database context.

```
--CreateudpReturn2ResultSets
--Remove prior version of stored procedure.
IF EXISTS (SELECT ROUTINE_NAME
        FROM INFORMATION_SCHEMA.ROUTINES
        WHERE ROUTINE_TYPE = 'PROCEDURE' AND
        ROUTINE_NAME = 'udpReturn2ResultSets')
    DROP PROCEDURE udpReturn2ResultSets
GO

--Create stored procedure to return one result
--set for listing stored procedure names and dates
--and another with the count of the stored procedures.
```

(continued)

```
CREATE PROC udpReturn2ResultSets
AS
SELECT ROUTINE_NAME, CREATED
FROM INFORMATION_SCHEMA.ROUTINES
WHERE ROUTINE_TYPE = 'PROCEDURE' AND
    LEFT(ROUTINE_NAME,3) <> 'dt_'
ORDER BY CREATED DESC
SELECT @@ROWCOUNT 'Number of stored procedures'
GO

--Run stored procedure that returns two result sets.
EXEC udpReturn2ResultSets
GO
```

Figure 4-3 shows the output from running the *udpReturn2ResultSets* stored procedure. (This is the output from the preceding script.) Notice that the top result set contains *ROUTINE_NAME* and *CREATED* column values. This result has a row for each user-defined stored procedure. The last row includes the name and creation date for the eleventh stored procedure. The second result set contains a number that is the count of the number of user-defined stored procedures—11.

	ROUTINE_NAME	CREATED
1	udpReturn2ResultSets	2001-09-06 20:08:58.487
2	udpReturnStatusValue	2001-09-06 19:35:12.863
3	udpReturn1StringParameter	2001-09-06 19:31:56.193
4	udpReturn1ResultSet1Parameter	2001-09-06 19:29:33.827
5	udpScriptForView	2001-09-06 18:11:17.553
6	udpShippersSortedByCompanyName	2001-09-06 15:44:08.590
7	udpListShippersRow	2001-09-06 14:18:59.623
8	udpLongestLateOrdersWithTop	2001-09-05 19:46:10.023
9	udpLongestLateOrders	2001-09-05 19:28:52.420
10	udpParamsForInsertUpdateDelete	2001-09-05 12:31:52.680
11	udpInsertUpdateDeleteSamples	2001-09-05 12:03:07.550

	Number of stored procedures
1	11

Figure 4-3. The return from a user-defined stored procedure that specifies two result sets.

Returning One Result Set and One Parameter Value

The preceding sample uses a *SELECT* statement to return a scalar value, namely the current value for *@@ROWCOUNT*. By entering the *@@ROWCOUNT* global variable function in a *SELECT* statement, the sample returns the current value of *@@ROWCOUNT* in a result set. The next sample illustrates how to return the *@@ROWCOUNT* value as an output parameter from a stored procedure. This involves a special declaration for the parameter inside the stored procedure as well as an assignment expression in the *EXEC* statement to retrieve the value for the output parameter. In the T-SQL code that calls the stored procedure, you need to transfer the output parameter to a local variable for use locally. In addition, the *EXEC* statement must explicitly designate the output parameter.

The following code shows the exact syntax for returning *@@ROWCOUNT* as an output parameter. First notice the line immediately after the *CREATE PROC* statement:

```
@NumberOfRows int OUTPUT
```

This line declares the parameter. Notice that it ends with the keyword *OUTPUT*. This keyword designates the *@NumberOfRows* parameter as an output parameter. Later in the stored procedure, a *SET* statement assigns the current value of *@@ROWCOUNT* to the *@NumberOfRows* parameter, like this:

```
SET @NumberOfRows = (SELECT @@ROWCOUNT)
```

This stored procedure diverges from the preceding one by explicitly invoking the *SET NOCOUNT* statement with the value *ON*. This statement suppresses the automatic SQL Server message about the number of rows affected, which happens to be the value of *@@ROWCOUNT*. At the conclusion of the stored procedure, the sample invokes the *SET NOCOUNT* statement a second time with the setting *OFF*. This second invocation of the *SET NOCOUNT* statement restores the default behavior of printing the rows affected by a T-SQL statement.

Using a parameter returned by a stored procedure also requires special syntax. First you need a local variable to accept the output parameter value. This is because you cannot work directly with the output parameter in the code that calls the stored procedure. The sample code declares a local variable named *@ReturnedParamValue* to store the output parameter value locally. Second you need an assignment statement. This statement must end with the *OUTPUT* keyword. In addition, the local variable must be on the right side of the equal sign, and the output parameter should appear on the left side. Third the output parameter returns an *int* data type value. However, the *Print* statement that reports the number of stored procedures requires a character data type, namely *varchar*. Therefore, the code applies the *CAST* function to the local variable storing the output parameter value; the function represents the integer value as a string. The expression for *@strForPrinter* combines a string constant with the *CAST* function value. The *PRINT* statement takes *@strForPrinter* as its argument to print the number of stored procedures with a brief descriptive label.

```
--CreateudpReturn1ResultSet1Parameter
--Remove prior version of stored procedure.
IF EXISTS (SELECT ROUTINE_NAME
        FROM INFORMATION_SCHEMA.ROUTINES
        WHERE ROUTINE_TYPE = 'PROCEDURE' AND
```

(continued)

```
        ROUTINE_NAME = 'udpReturn1ResultSet1Parameter')
    DROP PROCEDURE udpReturn1ResultSet1Parameter
GO

--Create stored procedure to return one result
--set for listing stored procedure names and dates along
--with another containing the count of the stored procedures.
CREATE PROC udpReturn1ResultSet1Parameter
@NumberOfRows int OUTPUT
AS
SET NOCOUNT ON
SELECT ROUTINE_NAME, CREATED
FROM INFORMATION_SCHEMA.ROUTINES
WHERE ROUTINE_TYPE = 'PROCEDURE' AND
    LEFT(ROUTINE_NAME,3) <> 'dt_'
ORDER BY CREATED DESC
SET @NumberOfRows = (SELECT @@ROWCOUNT)
SET NOCOUNT OFF
GO

--Run stored procedure that returns two result sets.
DECLARE @ReturnedParamValue int
DECLARE @strForPrinter varchar(100)
EXEC udpReturn1ResultSet1Parameter
    @NumberOfRows = @ReturnedParamValue OUTPUT
SET @strForPrinter = 'Number of stored procs: ' +
    Cast(@ReturnedParamValue AS varchar(3))
PRINT @strForPrinter
GO
```

Returning One String Parameter

The code you use to return a string value as an output parameter is essentially the same code you use to return a number value. The main distinction is the declaration of the data type for the parameter.

The following script returns the name of the oldest user-defined stored procedure in a database. It passes back the name of the stored procedure via an output parameter named *@strNameOfOldestSProc*. Notice that the output parameter declaration uses a *varchar* data type that is consistent with the maximum length of a SQL Server identifier. If your application runs in multiple locations that use different code pages, you may want to use an *nvarchar* rather than a *varchar* data type specification for the parameter.

In this case, the technique for finding the stored procedure is as interesting as the technique for declaring the output parameter. The *SET ROWCOUNT* statement tells SQL Server to stop processing a statement after the designated number of records. The *ORDER BY* clause in the *SELECT* statement sorts the stored procedures so that the name of the oldest stored procedure appears first. Therefore, stopping after processing the first row returns the oldest stored procedure.

The technique for processing an output parameter in the calling routine is about the same whether the output parameter has an *int* or a *varchar* data type. This particular sample appears slightly simpler than the preceding one mostly because it doesn't label the return value that is printed in the Messages pane. Because the local variable for holding the output parameter is already a string, there is no need to convert it so that it can be used as an argument for the *PRINT* statement.

```
--CreateudpReturn1StringParameter
--Remove prior version of stored procedure.
IF EXISTS (SELECT ROUTINE_NAME
        FROM INFORMATION_SCHEMA.ROUTINES
        WHERE ROUTINE_TYPE = 'PROCEDURE' AND
        ROUTINE_NAME = 'udpReturn1StringParameter')
    DROP PROCEDURE udpReturn1StringParameter
GO

--Create stored procedure to return one
--parameter with a string value.
CREATE PROC udpReturn1StringParameter
@strNameOfOldestSProc varchar(128) OUTPUT
AS
SET ROWCOUNT 1
SET @strNameOfOldestSProc = (SELECT TOP 1 ROUTINE_NAME
FROM INFORMATION_SCHEMA.ROUTINES
WHERE LEFT(ROUTINE_NAME,3) <> 'dt_'
    AND ROUTINE_TYPE = 'PROCEDURE'
ORDER BY CREATED)
GO

--Run stored procedure that returns one string parameter.
DECLARE @ReturnedParamValue varchar(128)
EXEC udpReturn1StringParameter
    @strNameOfOldestSProc = @ReturnedParamValue OUTPUT
PRINT @ReturnedParamValue
GO
```

Working with Return Status Values

Stored procedures considered to this point in the chapter proceed in a straight line from the first to the last statement in the procedure. However, this isn't a requirement. Control-of-flow statements, such as the *IF...ELSE* statement, make it possible for a stored procedure to execute conditionally. You can end the processing within a stored procedure with one or more *RETURN* statements at the end of each of several paths through the code. Each *RETURN* statement can pass back an *int* data type value to the calling procedure as it closes the stored procedure. Although you can have multiple *RETURN* statements with different return status values, any one invocation of a stored procedure can return just one return status value. This makes it possible for code invoking a stored procedure to know precisely at which line the stored procedure closed.

The following code sample creates a stored procedure that searches for a stored procedure by a name in a database. If the search finds a stored procedure with the target name, the return status value is 1. Otherwise, the return status value is 0. It is common to set return status values with a *RETURN* statement inside an *IF...ELSE* statement (although this sample's design is extraordinarily simple).

The calling T-SQL code for the stored procedure in the following sample causes the procedure to search for either of two names: *udpListShippersRow* or *SP1*. Make sure your database has a stored procedure named *udpListShippersRow* and that your database doesn't have a stored procedure named *SP1*. If you have been doing the samples in the order that they appear in this chapter, your Chapter04 database will have a stored procedure named *udpListShippersRow*. This lets you use the sample T-SQL code that calls the stored procedure to verify that the return status values reflect the presence or absence of a stored procedure. The calling T-SQL code for the stored procedure displays the return status value in a result set that contains either 0 or 1. These values match each of the return status values set in the stored procedure.

The syntax for capturing a return status value in a calling procedure deviates slightly from that for an output parameter. In both cases, you need a local variable to represent the value returned from the stored procedure. However, to capture the return status value, you use an assignment expression that sets the stored procedure equal to the local variable for the return status value. This assignment expression is actually integrated into the call of the stored procedure as an argument for an *EXEC* statement.

In the sample, a local variable specifies the value for the procedure to pass to the stored procedure. As the code appears, the calling code passes the name *udpListShippersRow*. However, you can comment out (with two leading hyphens) the assignment statement for the *@strProcName* local variable and remove the hyphens from the assignment statement that sets the local variable to SP1. This transition will cause the return status value to switch from 1 to 0.

```
--CreateudpReturnStatusValue
--Remove prior version of stored procedure.
IF EXISTS (SELECT ROUTINE_NAME
        FROM INFORMATION_SCHEMA.ROUTINES
        WHERE ROUTINE_TYPE = 'PROCEDURE' AND
        ROUTINE_NAME = 'udpReturnStatusValue')
    DROP PROCEDURE udpReturnStatusValue
```

```
GO

--Create stored procedure to pass back
--a return status value of 0 or 1.
CREATE PROC udpReturnStatusValue
@strName varchar(123)
AS
SELECT ROUTINE_NAME
FROM INFORMATION_SCHEMA.ROUTINES
WHERE ROUTINE_NAME = @strName AND ROUTINE_TYPE = 'PROCEDURE'
IF @@ROWCOUNT = 0
    RETURN 0
ELSE
    RETURN 1
GO

--Pass a procedure name to udpReturnStatusValue.
DECLARE @strProcName varchar(128)
DECLARE @return_status int

--Use the following SET statement for a 1.
SET @strProcName = 'udpListShippersRow'

--Use the following SET statement for a 0.
--SET @strProcName = 'SP1'

EXEC @return_status = udpReturnStatusValue @strProcName
SELECT @return_status AS 'Return Status'
```

Inserting, Updating, and Deleting Rows

Data manipulation is another area in which stored procedures shine—unlike views, which cannot execute the *INSERT INTO*, *UPDATE*, or *DELETE* statement. The capability of taking parameters as arguments with these statements permits a single stored procedure to modify a database in different ways at run time based on user input. This section has two main goals. First it introduces the syntax for the SQL Server data manipulation statements within a stored procedure. Second it illustrates how to perform data manipulation with parameter values for stored procedures.

Altering a Stored Procedure for Data Manipulation

The syntax for inserting, updating, and deleting rows from a row source is straightforward. The sample for this section separately illustrates how to perform each task for a table in the local database. In order to keep the sample easy to understand, the insert/update/delete code uses constants to work with specific values for a specific row.

In addition to clarifying the syntax for performing the task, the sample demonstrates how to alter an existing stored procedure to perform a different function. Recall that altering a stored procedure with the *ALTER PROC* statement allows you to preserve the permissions assigned for the stored procedure. If you drop and re-create a stored procedure, any user permissions for the old version of the stored procedure are lost unless you reassign them to the new version of the stored procedure. I don't necessarily recommend you alter a single stored procedure that you modify for each of three different functions in production systems. The sample design has the tutorial value of reinforcing your understanding of the technique for altering a stored procedure.

The sample reuses the same stored procedure for three tasks successively. First the script starts to create a new copy of the *udpInsertUpdateDeleteSamples* stored procedure by removing any existing version of the object from the database. Then the script invokes the *CREATE PROC* statement to make a fresh version of the stored procedure with the code to add a record to the *EmailContacts* table. (See the "Creating and Selecting from a View" section earlier in this chapter for the sample code to create and initially populate this table.) The stored procedure adds a new record to the table for Tony Hill.

The stored procedure demonstrates the use of the *INSERT INTO* statement for adding a new row to the *EmailContacts* table, like this:

```
CREATE PROC udpInsertUpdateDeleteSamples
AS
INSERT INTO vewEmailContacts
(ContactID, FirstName, LastName, Email1)
VALUES (3, 'Tony', 'Hill', 'tony@cabinc.net')
GO
```

The statement can work directly with tables, but the sample illustrates its capability of working with a view—namely, *vewEmailContacts*. An earlier sample in this chapter created this view. The *INTO* keyword is optional. In other words, you can specify *INSERT* with or without *INTO*. Notice the list of column names in parentheses following the *INTO* keyword and the view name. The syntax rules for the statement require this list when you are inserting values for some but not all columns or you are inserting column values in a different order than the one in which they appear in the row source. Because the sample assigns a value to each column in the order that the columns appear in the table, the list isn't mandatory. However, including the list is a good practice because it makes it clear which values the statement assigns to individual columns. The *VALUES* keyword is mandatory. This keyword marks the start of the values for the new row. Include the values that you want to add within parentheses.

> **Note** There are several interesting adaptations of the *INSERT INTO* or *INSERT* statement. For example, you shouldn't specify column values for columns with an *IDENTITY* property or computed columns because SQL Server automatically determines the values for these columns. In addition, you can transfer data from one table to another by using a *SELECT* clause within an *INSERT INTO* statement. See the "INSERT" topic in Books Online for the precise syntax to implement this. When you combine this feature with the *OPENROWSET* function or another means of selecting rows from a heterogeneous or remote data source, the *INSERT INTO* statement provides a conduit for transferring data between databases.

The initial version of the *EmailContacts* table has just two rows, for Rick Dobson and Virginia Dobson. Invoking the stored procedure with an *EXEC* statement adds a third row. The sample script runs the *EXEC* statement for the stored procedure and then performs a *SELECT* statement that returns all rows from the *EmailContacts* table. The result set from the *SELECT* statement confirms the addition of the new row to the table.

After inserting a new row, the sample script progresses by invoking the *ALTER PROC* statement:

```
ALTER PROC udpInsertUpdateDeleteSamples
AS
UPDATE vewEmailContacts
SET FirstName = 'Anthony', Email1 = 'anthony@cabinc.net'
WHERE ContactID = 3
GO
```

This statement modifies the syntax for the *udpInsertUpdateDeleteSamples* stored procedures from an insert procedure to an update procedure. The new version of the stored procedure changes the *FirstName* and *Email1* column values for the row added with the *INSERT INTO* demonstration.

The syntax for the *UPDATE* statement reveals how to change two column values within a single *UPDATE* statement. Start by following the *UPDATE* keyword with the name of a table or view that points at a table with column values you want to update. To use a view in this way (as the sample does), the view must permit updating of its underlying column values. After the *UPDATE* keyword and its target row source, you can start a new line with the *SET* keyword. Each update for a column value requires an assignment statement with the new value for the column. Delimit successive assignment statements with commas.

The *WHERE* clause is particularly critical with *UPDATE* and *DELETE* statements because it specifies to which row(s) to apply the statement. In the script below, using the *WHERE* clause expression `ContactID = 3` indicates that the *UPDATE* statement applies to just the row for Tony Hill, who has a *ContactID* column value of 3.

After altering the stored procedure, you must run it for the change to have an effect. The *EXEC* statement achieves this. A *SELECT* statement confirms that the update occurred. The row for Tony Hill includes new values for its *FirstName* and *Email1* columns.

The last part of the sample script shows how to alter a stored procedure for the addition of a *DELETE* statement. This statement doesn't require a list, as is common with the *SELECT* statement. That's because the *DELETE* statement removes one or more rows at a time; the statement doesn't operate on individual columns within a row. The *FROM* clause in the sample denotes the row source from which to remove rows. The *WHERE* clause is critical. Use your *WHERE* clause expression to designate which rows to remove from the row source. Without a *WHERE* clause, the *DELETE* statement removes all rows from its row source.

> **Note** If you do want to remove all rows, you can specify the statement as `DELETE` *rowsourcename*, such as `DELETE pubs..authors` to remove all the rows from the *authors* table in the pubs database. However, when you want to remove all the rows from a table with many rows, two other techniques will do the job faster. Invoke the *TRUNCATE TABLE* statement to remove all the rows from a table without logging the deletions to the log file while preserving the table's design. Alternatively, you can invoke the *DROP TABLE* statement to remove concurrently the contents and the design for a table.

The last part of the following script creates a stored procedure that removes the row with a *ContactID* column value of 3 by applying the *DELETE* statement. Then the script executes the stored procedure to remove the row with a *ContactID* value of 3. Finally the script concludes by invoking a *SELECT* statement that displays the remaining rows in the *EmailContacts* table. Figure 4-4, after the script, shows the three result sets it produces.

```
--CreateudpInsertUpdateDeleteSamples
--Remove prior version of stored procedure.
IF EXISTS (SELECT ROUTINE_NAME
        FROM INFORMATION_SCHEMA.ROUTINES
        WHERE ROUTINE_TYPE = 'PROCEDURE' AND
        ROUTINE_NAME = 'udpInsertUpdateDeleteSamples')
    DROP PROCEDURE udpInsertUpdateDeleteSamples
GO

--Insert into a table via a view.
CREATE PROC udpInsertUpdateDeleteSamples
AS
INSERT INTO vewEmailContacts
(ContactID, FirstName, LastName, Email1)
VALUES (3, 'Tony', 'Hill', 'tony@cabinc.net')
GO

--Confirm new result set.
EXEC udpInsertUpdateDeleteSamples
SELECT * FROM EmailContacts
GO

--Modify table column values via a view.
ALTER PROC udpInsertUpdateDeleteSamples
AS
UPDATE vewEmailContacts
SET FirstName = 'Anthony', Email1 = 'anthony@cabinc.net'
WHERE ContactID = 3
GO

--Confirm new result set.
EXEC udpInsertUpdateDeleteSamples
SELECT *
FROM vewEmailContacts
GO

--Delete newly added row directly from table.
ALTER PROC udpInsertUpdateDeleteSamples
AS
DELETE
FROM EmailContacts
WHERE ContactID = 3
GO

--Confirm new result set.
EXEC udpInsertUpdateDeleteSamples
SELECT * FROM EmailContacts
GO
```

	ContactID	FirstName	LastName	Email1
1	1	Rick	Dobson	rickd@cabinc.net
2	2	Virginia	Dobson	virginia@cabinc.net
3	3	Tony	Hill	tony@cabinc.net

	ContactID	FirstName	LastName	Email1
1	1	Rick	Dobson	rickd@cabinc.net
2	2	Virginia	Dobson	virginia@cabinc.net
3	3	Anthony	Hill	anthony@cabinc.net

	ContactID	FirstName	LastName	Email1
1	1	Rick	Dobson	rickd@cabinc.net
2	2	Virginia	Dobson	virginia@cabinc.net

Figure 4-4. The return from views that successively insert, update, and delete rows from a row source.

Performing Database Maintenance with Parameters

Typically, you won't run data manipulation statements, such as *INSERT INTO*, *UPDATE*, and *DELETE*, with constants as in the preceding sample. The purpose for the preceding script was to provide a basis for describing the syntax for including data manipulation statements in stored procedures. The real power of stored procedures with these statements is that you can pass parameters to the procedures to specify the rows that the statements insert, update, or delete from a row source.

The sample script in this section builds on the prior one by demonstrating the syntax for using parameters with data manipulation statements. Again, the emphasis is on clarity, so the script accomplishes the same kind of tasks as the preceding one. A significant change, however, is that the target row source is from another database on the same server—the Northwind SQL Server database. The script in this section follows the model of the previous one by altering one stored procedure instead of creating three separate stored procedures—one for inserting, another for updating, and a third for deleting. Because of the similarity of this script's design to the preceding one, I will explain just the first part of the script for inserting a new record. Like the preceding sample, this one switches back and forth between using a table and a view as a row source for the data manipulation statements. This is to reinforce your understanding that you can perform database maintenance chores with either type of object serving as a row source.

After removing any prior version of the *udpParamsForInsertUpdateDelete* stored procedure, the script creates a new version that includes an *INSERT INTO* statement. The *CREATE PROC* statement for creating the stored procedure has two input parameters—one for the *CompanyName* column value and another for the *Phone* column value. A comma delimits the two parameter declarations.

The data type settings follow those for the columns in the Northwind *Shippers* table. The parameter names appear again in parentheses after the *VALUES* keyword. These parameters replace the string constants used in the preceding script sample. The code illustrating the syntax for the *UPDATE* and *DELETE* statements follows the same pattern. First it declares the parameter. Second it uses the parameters as variables in database maintenance statements.

The *EXEC* statement for the stored procedure specifies values for passing to the stored procedure. This is one way your Visual Basic .NET applications can use values entered by users as part of data manipulation statements. Chapter 10 illustrates how to use Visual Basic .Net for this kind of task. The user input sets the parameter values in the code that calls the stored procedure. After adding the new record to the *Shippers* table in the Northwind database by calling the stored procedure, the script invokes a *SELECT* statement to display all the rows in the *Shippers* table.

```
--CreateudpParamsForInsertUpdateDelete
--Remove prior version of stored procedure.
IF EXISTS (SELECT ROUTINE_NAME
        FROM INFORMATION_SCHEMA.ROUTINES
        WHERE ROUTINE_TYPE = 'PROCEDURE' AND
        ROUTINE_NAME = 'udpParamsForInsertUpdateDelete')
    DROP PROCEDURE udpParamsForInsertUpdateDelete
GO

--Insert values into a table in another database.
CREATE PROC udpParamsForInsertUpdateDelete
@newCompanyName nvarchar(40),
@newPhone nvarchar (24)
AS
INSERT INTO Northwind..Shippers
(CompanyName, Phone)
VALUES (@newCompanyName, @newPhone)
GO

--Confirm new result set.
EXEC udpParamsForInsertUpdateDelete
    'CAB Delivers', '(123) 456-7890'
SELECT *
FROM Northwind..Shippers
GO

--Modify table column values in another database
--via a view pointing at the table in this database.
ALTER PROC udpParamsForInsertUpdateDelete
@newPhone nvarchar(24),
@newCompanyName nvarchar(40)
AS
```

(continued)

```
UPDATE vewShippers
SET Phone = @newPhone
WHERE CompanyName = @newCompanyName
GO

--Confirm new result set.
EXEC udpParamsForInsertUpdateDelete
    '(234) 567-8901', 'CAB Delivers'
SELECT *
FROM vewShippers
GO

--Delete newly added row in other database
--from view pointing at row in this database.
ALTER PROC udpParamsForInsertUpdateDelete
@newCompanyName nvarchar(40)
AS
DELETE
FROM vewShippers
WHERE CompanyName = @newCompanyName
GO

--Delete newly added row directly from table.
EXEC udpParamsForInsertUpdateDelete 'CAB Delivers'
SELECT * FROM Northwind..Shippers
GO
```

Programming Conditional Result Sets

Even though a stored procedure is compiled, it can still execute in different ways at run time, depending on the values of parameters. The preceding section showed how to accomplish this for insert/update/delete operations. This section shows how you can modify the output from a procedure at run time in a more advanced way than setting values for *WHERE* clause expressions. This section starts with a sample that lists the views in a database. If there are no views in the database, it doesn't display the column headers for itemizing views. The second and third samples show how to return the top *x* rows with a *SELECT* statement. Users can vary the number of rows returned.

Conditionally Listing Objects

A *SELECT* statement displays the column headers for a result set even if the result set is empty. If you happen to be returning multiple result sets from a stored procedure, the writing of headers for empty result sets can clutter the

Results pane and distract attention from populated result sets. In any event, you may prefer to avoid printing the column headers for an empty result set—after all, there's nothing to itemize below the headers.

The sample for this section tests whether the result set for a *SELECT* statement has any rows before sending its output to the Results pane. The logic is to perform an aggregate query that tests for the existence of items satisfying a *WHERE* clause criterion. If the count of returned rows is greater than 0, the procedure executes a *SELECT* statement that returns the individual items. Otherwise, the stored procedure just writes a statement to the Messages pane saying there are no items in the result set.

This sample enumerates the views in a database connection. A *USE* statement at the top of the script specifies the target database. This book has two custom databases so far. The database for this chapter, Chapter04, has nine views. Chapter01, the database for this book's first chapter, has zero views. Therefore, by changing the *USE* statement to point at one or the other database, the sample script can demonstrate conditional outputs from the sample stored project.

The stored procedure uses a local variable, *@intViews*, to store the result from a *SELECT* statement with a *COUNT* function. The function aggregates the number of virtual tables (or views) in a database. The *INFORMATION_SCHEMA.TABLES* view is the row source for the *SELECT* statement. An *IF...ELSE* statement branches to the *IF* block or the *ELSE* statement depending on the value of *@intViews*. If the local variable is greater than 0, the procedure executes the *BEGIN...END* block in the *IF* clause of the *IF...ELSE* statement. Whenever you need to conditionally execute more than one statement in either clause of an *IF...ELSE* statement, you must group the statements between *BEGIN* and *END* keywords as the sample demonstrates.

The two statements in the *BEGIN...END* block print the number of views in the database connection to the Messages pane and show the result set for a *SELECT* statement listing the individual view names in the Results pane. If *@intViews* is 0, the procedure merely prints a sentence to the Messages pane saying there are no views. Because this requires just one statement, the *ELSE* clause doesn't require a *BEGIN...END* block. To unclutter the Messages pane, the procedure invokes the *SET NOCOUNT ON* statement at its start and restores the default setting (*SET NOCOUNT OFF*) at its close.

Because the stored procedure for this sample is meant for a one-time execution, the script drops the stored procedure at its conclusion. Therefore, the stored procedure isn't strictly necessary for this sample. Feel free to modify the sample to remove the creation of the stored procedure. In any event, learn the *IF...ELSE* design guidelines presented in the sample.

```
--CreateudpCountAndListViews
--Designate database context.
USE Chapter04
GO

--Remove prior version of stored procedure.
IF EXISTS (SELECT ROUTINE_NAME
        FROM INFORMATION_SCHEMA.ROUTINES
        WHERE ROUTINE_TYPE = 'PROCEDURE' AND
        ROUTINE_NAME = 'udpCountAndListViews')
    DROP PROCEDURE udpCountAndListViews
GO

--Create procedure to count and list views in the
--current database connection.
CREATE PROC udpCountAndListViews
AS
SET NOCOUNT ON
DECLARE @intViews int
SET @intViews = (SELECT COUNT(TABLE_NAME)
    FROM INFORMATION_SCHEMA.TABLES
    WHERE TABLE_TYPE = 'VIEW' AND
        LEFT(TABLE_NAME,3) <> 'sys')
IF (@intViews) > 0
BEGIN
    PRINT 'There were ' +
        CAST(@intViews AS varchar(3)) + ' views in the connection.'
    SELECT TABLE_NAME
    FROM INFORMATION_SCHEMA.TABLES
    WHERE TABLE_TYPE = 'VIEW' AND
        LEFT(TABLE_NAME,3) <> 'sys'
END
ELSE
    PRINT 'There are no views in the connection.'
SET NOCOUNT OFF
GO

--Run the procedure to report on the views in
--the current database connection.
EXEC udpCountAndListViews
GO

--Drop the procedure from the current database connection.
DROP PROCEDURE udpCountAndListViews
GO
```

Returning *X* Items with the *TOP* Predicate

A typical request on SQL Server newsgroups is, "How do I return just the top *x* items, where I can vary the value of *x*?" The question is sometimes phrased as, "How do I use the *TOP* predicate to return a variable number of items from a row source?" The *TOP* predicate alone can't solve this problem because it can accept only a constant as the number of items to return.

One way to use a *TOP* predicate to return more than a single number of items from a row source is to nest *SELECT* statements with *TOP* predicates within the clauses of an *IF...ELSE* statement. Because you can nest *IF...ELSE* statements within one another indefinitely, this approach permits you to fine-tune the level of precision on how many rows to return if you are willing to nest enough *IF...ELSE* statements within one another.

The next sample returns either the top 5 or 10 orders with the longest delay in shipping after the required date for an order. An input parameter value controls which of these two result sets the stored procedure returns. If the input parameter, *@NumberOfOrders*, is less than or equal to 5, the stored procedure returns the 5 orders with the longest delays in shipping. If the value of *@NumberOfOrders* is 6 or greater, the procedure returns the 10 orders with the longest delays in shipping. This is the first sample in the chapter to assign a default value to a parameter. The equal sign in the parameter declaration shows the syntax for assigning a default value of 5. Because of this default value, the procedure returns the 5 records with the longest delays if the *EXEC* statement that invokes the *udpLongestLateOrdersWithTop* stored procedure fails to designate a parameter value.

A single *IF...ELSE* statement passes control to one of the two *SELECT* statements in its clauses based on the *@NumberOfOrders* parameter value. The *SELECT* statement in the *IF* clause uses a *TOP* predicate with an argument of *5*. On the other hand, the *SELECT* statement in the *ELSE* clause has exactly the same syntax except that its *TOP* predicate has an argument of *10*.

The *EXEC* statement for invoking the stored procedure passes the parameter value *7*. Because this is greater than 5, the procedure returns the 10 orders with the longest shipping delays after the required date. The parameter value *100*, *1,000*, or *10,000* will still return just 10 rows in the result set. This is because the stored procedure supports just two different *TOP* predicate argument values. You can alter the procedure by adding nested *IF...ELSE* statements to accommodate more *TOP* predicate argument values.

```
--CreateudpLongestLateOrdersWithTop
--Remove prior version of stored procedure.
IF EXISTS (SELECT ROUTINE_NAME
        FROM INFORMATION_SCHEMA.ROUTINES
```

(continued)

```
        WHERE ROUTINE_TYPE = 'PROCEDURE' AND
        ROUTINE_NAME = 'udpLongestLateOrdersWithTop')
    DROP PROCEDURE udpLongestLateOrdersWithTop
GO

--Create proc for itemizing late orders
--with one of two TOP predicates.
CREATE PROC udpLongestLateOrdersWithTop
@NumberOfOrders int = 5
AS
IF @NumberOfOrders <= 5
SELECT TOP 5 OrderID,
    CAST((RequiredDate - ShippedDate) AS int)
        'Days shipped after required',
    CustomerID
FROM Northwind..Orders
WHERE (RequiredDate - ShippedDate) IS NOT NULL
ORDER BY (RequiredDate - ShippedDate)
ELSE
SELECT TOP 10 OrderID,
    CAST((RequiredDate - ShippedDate) AS int)
        'Days shipped after required',
    CustomerID
FROM Northwind..Orders
WHERE (RequiredDate - ShippedDate) IS NOT NULL
ORDER BY (RequiredDate - ShippedDate)
GO

--Run proc to list orders with the shipped
--date farthest behind the required date with
--one of two TOP predicates.
EXEC udpLongestLateOrdersWithTop 7
GO
```

Returning *X* Items with *SET ROWCOUNT*

The *SET ROWCOUNT* statement provides a more flexible technique for returning a variable number of records from some *SELECT* statements. The *SET ROWCOUNT* statement can stop a T-SQL statement after a fixed number of rows. Furthermore, the argument for the *SET ROWCOUNT* statement can be a parameter. This permits your application to set the number of rows to return at run time.

The following script demonstrates the syntax for returning a variable number of rows shipped after their required date. Because this script uses the *SET ROWCOUNT* statement, it can return a variable number of rows with just a single *SELECT* statement. Before the *SELECT* statement, the stored procedure assigns the *@NumberOfOrders* parameter as the argument for the *SET ROWCOUNT* statement. The declaration for the *@NumberOfOrders* parameter again assigns the default value 5 to the parameter. Therefore, the procedure will return five rows even if a user fails to set a parameter when invoking the stored procedure.

> **Note** The *SET ROWCOUNT* statement will override a *TOP* predicate argument if the *SET ROWCOUNT* argument is the smaller of the two.

The *EXEC* statement for the stored procedure designates the parameter value 7—just like the preceding sample script. However, in this instance, the stored procedure returns precisely 7 rows instead 10 rows. Furthermore, the *SELECT* statement will always return the precise number of rows designated by the parameter value up to the maximum number of rows available from the *SELECT* statement without a *SET ROWCOUNT* statement.

```
--CreateudpLongestLateOrdersWithoutTop
--Remove prior version of stored procedure.
IF EXISTS (SELECT ROUTINE_NAME
        FROM INFORMATION_SCHEMA.ROUTINES
        WHERE ROUTINE_TYPE = 'PROCEDURE' AND
        ROUTINE_NAME = 'udpLongestLateOrdersWithoutTop')
    DROP PROCEDURE udpLongestLateOrdersWithoutTop
GO

--Create proc for itemizing late orders.
CREATE PROC udpLongestLateOrdersWithoutTop
@NumberOfOrders int = 5
AS
SET ROWCOUNT @NumberOfOrders
SELECT OrderID,
    CAST((RequiredDate - ShippedDate) AS int)
        'Days shipped after required date',
    CustomerID
FROM Northwind..Orders
WHERE (RequiredDate - ShippedDate) IS NOT NULL
ORDER BY (RequiredDate - ShippedDate)
GO

--Run proc to list seven orders with the shipped
--date farthest behind the required date.
EXEC udpLongestLateOrdersWithoutTop 7
GO
```

5

Programming User-Defined Functions and Triggers

This chapter completes the book's review of database objects that facilitate the reuse of T-SQL code. The beginning of the chapter introduces user-defined functions (UDFs). Your applications can apply UDFs as if they were built-in functions. The chapter explores the different kinds of UDFs that you can create and illustrates scenarios for developing and applying them. The last part of the chapter deals with triggers. Visual Basic developers are likely to find it useful to think of triggers as event procedures for tables and views. This chapter's coverage of triggers starts with an overview of the key concepts for designing and applying triggers and concludes with a series of four samples that demonstrate the kinds of uses to which you can put triggers. The main purpose of the samples is to highlight syntax conventions for different types of triggers and illustrate broad design issues. The T-SQL inside a trigger can reference other database objects. For example, the last trigger sample references a UDF defined earlier in the chapter.

The resources for this chapter include the Chapter05 database, with completed versions of the sample UDFs discussed as well as T-SQL scripts for creating the UDFs and triggers from scratch. Unless explicitly stated, all scripts are to be run from the Chapter05 database. If you run the scripts from another database context, such as the master database, you can generate errors unrelated to the sample logic and syntax. See the "Chapter Resources" section in Chapter 2 for more detail on attaching database files to a server and creating a new blank database from which you can invoke the scripts. This chapter also references the SQL Server Northwind database. This database is installed with SQL Server 2000.

Introduction to User-Defined Functions

A *user-defined function* permits a developer to save a body of T-SQL code and then reuse it. UDFs can return both scalar values and tables. In fact, SQL Server 2000 introduces a new data type, *table*, for representing the return of a table from a UDF. Visual Basic developers will feel comfortable with UDFs because in many ways they perform like function procedures in Visual Basic. You can pass UDF values through parameters, and they return a value—namely, a scalar value or a table.

> **Note** The *table* data type wasn't discussed in the review of data types in Chapter 2 because that chapter focuses on the creation of permanent tables that are part of a database. You can refer to a permanent table directly. Permanent tables cannot include columns with a *table* data type. A table returned by a UDF isn't permanent. The returned table is available only through the UDF that returns it. Many uses for temporary tables can be served by tables returned from UDFs. You can also use the *table* data type in stored procedures and T-SQL batches. Search for "table data type" from the Index tab of Books Online for more details on this data type.

Overview of UDF Types

SQL Server 2000 offers three types of UDFs:

- You can write a *scalar function* to return a scalar value, such as a conversion routine for representing the value of British pounds in U.S. dollars or Fahrenheit degrees in Centigrade degrees.
- A UDF can return a table based on a single *SELECT* statement. SQL Server calls this an *inline table-valued function.*
- With a *multistatement table-valued function*, you can declare the columns and compose a UDF return based on multiple statements. For example, you can insert result sets from two or more *SELECT* statements in the table returned by a UDF. In addition, multistatement table-valued functions don't restrict you to *SELECT* statements for populating the returned table.

Scalar UDFs

A scalar UDF returns a single value. The computations inside a UDF cannot affect any entity outside the UDF. SQL Server documentation refers to this property as UDFs having no side effects. The number of input parameters for a UDF can range from 0 through 1024. Just as with input parameters for stored procedures, you can assign default values for UDF input parameters. UDF parameters don't support user-defined or *timestamp* data types. In addition, UDF parameters cannot be nonscalar, such as a table-valued UDF. The return from a UDF can have any column data type except *text*, *ntext*, *image*, and *timestamp*. UDFs don't support output parameters. A UDF's return value is its sole form of output.

You can use a scalar UDF anywhere in a UDF that you can use a scalar value, such as the list for a *SELECT* statement. Other uses for scalar UDFs include arguments in *WHERE*, *HAVING*, *ORDER BY*, and *GROUP BY* clause expressions. Your code can also put scalar UDFs to use in *SET* statements for local variables in stored procedures and T-SQL batch scripts within Query Analyzer. In addition, UDFs are useful within data manipulation statements for adding new values and updating existing ones. Yet another UDF application is inside table declarations for check constraints and computed values. When using UDFs for computed columns with indexes, the UDF must be deterministic—that is, it must always return the same value given the same input.

> **Note** *Determinism* is a relatively new concept for functions, views, and stored procedures. See the "Deterministic and Nondeterministic Functions" topic in Books Online for an introduction to this topic for SQL Server 2000.

Inline Table-Valued UDFs

An inline table-valued UDF performs similarly to a view. It differs from a scalar UDF in that the inline UDF returns a table instead of a scalar value. Both types of UDF can accept input parameters. Because a view and an inline UDF depend on a single *SELECT* statement—but the UDF accepts a parameter—the inline UDF offers the functionality of a parameterized view. In addition, a view can serve as the source for an inline UDF. If your view involves a complex *JOIN* statement with indexes and therefore schema binding, the inline UDF can deliver the power of the view with a much simpler syntax than the T-SQL statement underlying the view, and it offers the advantages of selections based on parameters. You can invoke *INSERT*, *UPDATE*, and *DELETE* statements with inline table-valued UDFs serving as a source in the *FROM* clause provided the inline table-valued UDF draws on a *SELECT* statement or a view that permits data manipulation.

> **Note** See a discussion of issues that enable updatable views in the "Remarks" section of the Books Online "CREATE VIEW" topic. See also the "Rules for Updating Results" topic in Books Online for guidance on *SELECT* statements that generate updatable result sets.

Multistatement Table-Valued UDFs

Multistatement table-valued UDFs and inline table-valued UDFs both return tables, but there are two important differences. First, as the name implies, you can use multiple statements to define the result set from a multistatement table-valued UDF. In addition to multiple *SELECT* statements, you can draw on other T-SQL statements, such as *DECLARE* and assignment statements; *IF...ELSE* statements; and *INSERT*, *UPDATE*, and *DELETE* statements for table variables local to the function. Second, multistatement table-valued UDFs return read-only tables. Recall that inline table-valued UDFs permit updating their base tables through the UDF.

Statements for Creating and Managing UDFs

You can create and manipulate UDFs with statements performing familiar functions for other SQL Server database objects. These statements are *CREATE FUNCTION*, *ALTER FUNCTION*, and *DROP FUNCTION*. Because of the divergence in types of UDFs, the syntax for the *CREATE FUNCTION* and *ALTER FUNCTION* statements differs as well; there are three variations of each of these two statements to match the corresponding UDF types. In contrast, a single *DROP FUNCTION* syntax suffices for all three UDF types. Trail the keyword phrase with the name of the function that you want removed from a database. You can use the *INFORMATION_SCHEMA.ROUTINES* view to detect the existence of a previously existing version of a UDF.

The *CREATE FUNCTION* statement for a scalar UDF has several important arguments with a variety of variations beyond those depicted in the following template. The *function_name* argument is a standard SQL Server identifier. However, as with other objects, you may care to use a prefix to make it easy to identify UDF objects vs. other types of objects. This chapter uses *udf* as the first three characters of all UDF names.

The input parameters for a UDF reside within parentheses following the function name. Start each parameter name with the @ sign, and then make the rest of the parameter name characters follow SQL Server identifier rules. Designate a data type for each parameter with a space delimiter after the parameter name. Delimit multiple parameter declarations with commas. You can optionally designate a default value for parameters with an equal sign (=) followed by a value after the data type specification for any parameter with a default value.

Designate a data type for the scalar UDF with the *RETURNS* keyword. The *RETURNS* keyword and its trailing data type specification make up the *RETURNS* clause within the *CREATE FUNCTION* statement. Use the *AS* keyword to mark the transition from function declarations to T-SQL code for the function.

The T-SQL code for a scalar UDF must appear between *BEGIN* and *END* keywords. The *RETURN* keyword within the *BEGIN...END* block marks the expression that specifies the return value from the scalar UDF. The *RETURN* keyword and its expression argument are another critical clause within the *CREATE FUNCTION* statement, as shown in this code template:

```
CREATE FUNCTION function_name (parameter_names and data types)
RETURNS data type for return value
AS
BEGIN
    T-SQL statements for UDF
    RETURN (expression for scalar return value)
END
```

The following *CREATE FUNCTION* statement template illustrates the syntax for creating an inline table-valued UDF. The function name and parameter declarations follow the same conventions as for the *CREATE FUNCTION* statement for a scalar UDF. The *RETURNS* and *TABLE* keywords together make up the *RETURNS* clause for an inline UDF. This clause designates a table as the return data type from the UDF. The template follows the return data type specification with the *AS* keyword that marks the transition between the declarations and the T-SQL code for the function. When you're generating an inline table-valued UDF, the only T-SQL code is a single *SELECT* statement that serves as the argument for the *RETURN* keyword. The *SELECT* statement is the equivalent of the expression for the scalar return value in the preceding template.

```
CREATE FUNCTION function_name (parameter_names and data types)
RETURNS TABLE
AS
RETURN (SELECT statement)
```

The *CREATE FUNCTION* template for a multistatement table-valued UDF that appears next has a different design from that of either of the two preceding templates. In fact, the template borrows elements from each of the preceding templates and adds its own unique element. The function name and parameter declarations are the same as in the preceding two templates. The *RETURNS* keyword denotes a *table* data type (with the *TABLE* keyword) as the return data type for the function. The syntax of a *CREATE FUNCTION* statement for a multistatement table-valued UDF requires a table name between the *RETURNS* keyword and the *TABLE* keyword. The table name follows the same conventions as parameters and local variables. (Don't forget the leading @ sign.) Another unique element of the *CREATE FUNCTION* template for a multistatement table-valued UDF is the column declarations area that appears after the *TABLE* keyword specifying the return data type and the *AS* keyword. Column declarations include column names, data type specifications, and optional column specifications for the primary key, a unique index, or a check constraint. The *RETURNS* clause for a multistatement table-valued UDF starts with the *RETURNS* keyword and runs through the column specifications. The T-SQL statements in the *BEGIN...END* block must include one or more *INSERT* statements that refer back to the table name in the *RETURNS* clause. These *INSERT* statements populate the table returned by the UDF. The T-SQL code in your *BEGIN...END* block can optionally include *UPDATE* and *DELETE* statements that assist in refining the result set returned by the UDF. The *RETURN* keyword within the *BEGIN...END* block signals the end of processing in the UDF.

```
CREATE FUNCTION function_name (parameter_names and data types)
RETURNS table_name TABLE
(column declarations)
AS
BEGIN
T-SQL statements for UDF
RETURN
END
```

CREATE FUNCTION statements support the assignment of two optional function specifications, using the keywords *ENCRYPTION* and *SCHEMABINDING*. Designate either of these specifications following a *WITH* keyword. Place the designation just before the *AS* keyword. If you invoke the *ENCRYPTION* option, remember to preserve an unencrypted version of your function for future editing. After invoking the *SCHEMABINDING* option for a UDF, any tables or views on which the function relies cannot change until you either drop the UDF or modify the UDF with the *ALTER FUNCTION* statement. Several special rules apply when you apply the *SCHEMABINDING* option to a function. See the "Arguments" section of the "CREATE FUNCTION" topic in Books Online for the rules.

Comparing UDFs with Views and Stored Procedures

UDFs share elements in common with both views and stored procedures. On the other hand, UDFs also differ from views and stored procedures in some important ways. Understanding these similarities and differences will help you decide when to choose each kind of object for a database chore and whether it is appropriate to reformulate an object in one format to another format.

Views and table-valued UDFs both have result sets. In addition, the inline table-valued UDF even relies on a single *SELECT* statement just like a view. The similarities between inline table-valued UDFs and views means that you can use either for viewing and updating data. An important distinction is that the inline table-valued UDF permits input parameters in its *SELECT* statement. Therefore, an inline table-valued function delivers the features of a view with the added flexibility afforded by parameters. The multistatement table-valued function has its own column declarations, and it can contain multiple *SELECT* statements as well as other kinds of T-SQL statements that modify the values returned by the function. These extra statements provide added flexibility for the creation of the result set from a multistatement table-valued UDF relative to either an inline table-valued UDF or a view. On the other hand, your applications can never modify the base tables for a multistatement table-valued UDF through the UDF.

Stored procedures can return scalar values and result sets just as UDFs can. In addition, both stored procedures and UDFs accept parameters that the objects can use to help compute outputs. Stored procedures can return one or more result sets, but table-valued UDFs always return a single result set. The result sets from a stored procedure are available for viewing in Query Analyzer when you run a stored procedure, and you can pass the result sets to temporary tables for additional programmatic manipulation. The result set from table-valued UDFs is available for use directly in the *FROM* clause of *SELECT* statements. Additionally, you must pass scalar returns from stored procedures to local variables before you can programmatically manipulate them outside the stored procedure. On the other hand, you can use a scalar UDF just like a scalar value in a T-SQL script. Stored procedures do counter these UDF advantages by offering a richer array of output types. In addition to offering multiple result sets, a stored procedure can concurrently return a result set, multiple output parameters, and a return status value. UDFs don't offer this richness of output types.

Creating and Invoking Scalar UDFs

Scalar UDFs are a flexible development tool. This is for two primary reasons. First, they make it easy to encapsulate T-SQL statements for reuse. Second, it is simple to reference scalar UDFs in T-SQL scripts and other SQL Server objects. Three scalar function samples in this section confirm how easy it is to encapsulate T-SQL expressions in UDF functions. The section also highlights ways of referencing scalar UDFs in different T-SQL contexts.

Creating a Scalar UDF Without Parameters

Scalar functions can compute all kinds of results. It is common in database applications to need the next higher number in a series, such as when one or more rows in a child table need a foreign key value matching the identity column value for the row most recently inserted into a parent table. The *@@IDENTITY* function can supply this value automatically when you are inserting new rows into a table. However, there are times when the return value from the *@@IDENTITY* function isn't desirable because your application needs to add refinements to the basic behavior. Even outside the autoincrementing context, an application can readily require the next higher value in a series. The sample in this section shows how to satisfy this requirement with a scalar UDF.

The following script creates a table with a single column, *col1*, and then populates the column with five row values: 1, 5, 9, 4, 12. *INSERT INTO* statements add the values to the table. Because the row values are primary key values, any *SELECT* statement without an *ORDER BY* clause for the table arranges the rows in ascending order from 1 through 12.

After creating and populating the table, the script adds a new scalar UDF to the Chapter05 database. The *USE* statement at the top of the script sets the database context for this sample. All the other samples in this chapter are for the same database context, although subsequent samples don't explicitly include the *USE* statement for the Chapter05 database. By checking the *INFORMATION_SCHEMA.ROUTINES* views, the script can detect whether a prior version of the *udfOneHigherThanMax* UDF exists in the Chapter05 database. If one already exists, the script removes it with the *DROP FUNCTION* statement.

Next the *CREATE FUNCTION* statement demonstrates the application of basic UDF specifications. Before dwelling on the statement's format, notice the *GO* keyword immediately preceding it. A *CREATE FUNCTION* statement must start its own T-SQL batch. Notice also that parentheses follow the function name. Parentheses are necessary whether or not your UDF has parameters. The *RETURNS* statement declares the scalar return value from the function as an *int* data type. This is consistent with the data type for the *col1* column in the *MyTable* table created and populated earlier in the sample. The scalar UDF has just a single operational statement that selects the maximum value from the *col1* column in the *MyTable* table and then adds 1 to it. However, the syntax rules for all scalar UDFs require the standard *AS* keyword and a *BEGIN...END* block. The *SELECT* statement for computing the integer 1 higher than the maximum in *col1* appears within parentheses in the *RETURN* clause for the *CREATE FUNCTION* statement. The expression within the clause computes the value that the scalar UDF returns.

After the *CREATE FUNCTION* statement, a T-SQL script invokes the scalar UDF inside a *SELECT* statement. This returns the value 13 in a result set with one row and one column. Notice the owner specification for the UDF—namely, dbo. Recall that dbo designates any member of the sysadmin fixed server role who creates an object. Function names must be unique for a database by the function's owner.

> **Note** By default, permission to create a UDF is available to members of the sysadmin fixed server role as well as the db_owner and db_ddladmin fixed database roles. Members of the sysadmin and db_owner roles can grant permission to create UDFs to other logins. See the "Permissions" section in the "CREATE FUNCTION" Books Online topic for more detail about permissions to create and administer UDFs. The Books Online topics for all data definition language (DDL) T-SQL statements have a "Permissions" section. Chapter 7 drills down on SQL Server security.

```
--udfHigherThanMax
--Specify database context.
USE Chapter05

--Remove prior version of table MyTable.
IF EXISTS(SELECT * FROM INFORMATION_SCHEMA.TABLES
WHERE table_name = 'MyTable')
DROP TABLE MyTable

--Create table MyTable.
CREATE TABLE MyTable
(
col1 int PRIMARY KEY
)
GO

--Populate MyTable with either 4 or 5 rows.
--Comment out last INSERT INTO statement for 4 rows.
INSERT INTO MyTable VALUES(1)
INSERT INTO MyTable VALUES(5)
INSERT INTO MyTable VALUES(9)
INSERT INTO MyTable VALUES(4)
INSERT INTO MyTable VALUES(12)
GO
```

(continued)

```
--Drop old version of user-defined function if it exists.
IF EXISTS(SELECT * FROM INFORMATION_SCHEMA.ROUTINES
    WHERE ROUTINE_NAME = 'udfOneHigherThanMax')
    DROP FUNCTION udfOneHigherThanMax
GO

--Create function to find value 1 greater than maximum.
CREATE FUNCTION udfOneHigherThanMax()
RETURNS int
AS
BEGIN
    RETURN(SELECT MAX(col1)+1 FROM MyTable)
END
GO

--Must reference function owner's name (dbo) for syntax to work.
SELECT dbo.udfOneHigherThanMax()
GO
```

Creating a Scalar UDF with a Parameter

Redesigning the *udfOneHigherThanMax* UDF with an input parameter can achieve two benefits. First, the redesign demonstrates the detailed syntax for passing parameters to functions. Second, the redesign offers the opportunity to create a new scalar UDF that returns a value that is *x* units higher than the current maximum *col1* column value.

The following script illustrates how to achieve both of these benefits. The script starts by dropping any prior versions of the *udfXHigherThanMax* UDF if it exists. Next the *CREATE FUNCTION* starts the design of a new scalar UDF. The parentheses after the function name include a parameter declaration. Recall that the initial sample included the parentheses, but they didn't enclose anything. The name of the parameter for this UDF is *@x*, and its data type is *int*, which matches the data type of the values in *col1*. The matching data type specification for the column values and the parameter eliminates the need for a conversion when the function adds *@x* to the maximum value in the *col1* column.

With the *udfXHigherThanMax* UDF, users can specify the return of a value *@x* units higher than the maximum value in *col1*. The *SELECT* statement after the *CREATE FUNCTION* statement illustrates the syntax for passing a parameter to a function. Simply enclose the value in parentheses after the function name. The sample denotes a parameter value of 2, but any parameter value that yields a legitimate *int* value for the UDF is acceptable. All parts of the function call are mandatory. First you must specify a function owner; the sample designates the dbo user. Second, after the function name, you must include parentheses. When there is a parameter (as in this instance), you must specify a parameter value unless the parameter has a default value in its declaration.

```
--udfXHigherThanMax
--Drop old version of user-defined function if it exists.
IF EXISTS(SELECT * FROM INFORMATION_SCHEMA.ROUTINES
    WHERE ROUTINE_NAME = 'udfXHigherThanMax')
    DROP FUNCTION udfXHigherThanMax
GO

--Create function to compute x units higher than maximum.
--Demonstrates use of parameters.
CREATE FUNCTION udfXHigherThanMax(@x AS int)
RETURNS int
AS
BEGIN
    Return(SELECT MAX(col1) + @x FROM MyTable)
END
GO

--Must reference function owner's name (dbo) for syntax to work.
SELECT dbo.udfXHigherThanMax(2)
GO
```

Using Scalar UDFs in T-SQL Scripts

The first two samples highlighted the syntax for creating scalar UDFs. However, they merely echoed the return value from the UDF. One significant reason for using UDFs is their ability to be used directly in T-SQL statements. This section creates a new UDF and illustrates the syntax for referencing the UDF at several locations within a *SELECT* statement as well as in a T-SQL script with an *IF…ELSE* statement and in string expressions for local variables.

The *udfDaysShippedLate* scalar UDF returns the numbers of days that an order shipped before or after its required date. After removing any prior version of the scalar UDF, the procedure invokes the *CREATE FUNCTION* statement to start the creation of the new version of the *udfDaysShippedLate* UDF. This UDF requires three items to compute its return value: the order ID, the required date, and the shipped date for the order. The UDF accepts the order ID as a parameter named *@TargetID*. Two *SELECT* statements return the required and shipped dates from the *Orders* table in the Northwind database. Although the database context for the function is the Chapter05 database, the UDF can refer to the Northwind database using the standard three-part naming convention. The built-in *DATEDIFF* function computes the difference in days between the required and shipped dates so that orders shipping after the required date have a positive value. The script uses the return from the built-in function with its arguments as the expression for the *RETURN* clause. This clause passes back a value from the scalar UDF.

```
--udfDaysShippedLate_a
--Drop old version of user-defined function if it exists.
IF EXISTS(SELECT * FROM INFORMATION_SCHEMA.ROUTINES
        WHERE ROUTINE_NAME = 'udfDaysShippedLate')
    DROP FUNCTION udfDaysShippedLate
GO

--Create function to compute difference in days between
--required date and shipped date for an order.
CREATE FUNCTION udfDaysShippedLate(@TargetID AS int)
RETURNS int
AS
BEGIN
DECLARE @TargetShippedDate datetime
DECLARE @TargetRequiredDate datetime

SET @TargetShippedDate = (SELECT ShippedDate
    FROM Northwind..Orders
    WHERE OrderID = @TargetID)
SET @TargetRequiredDate = (SELECT RequiredDate
    FROM Northwind..Orders
    WHERE OrderID = @TargetID)
RETURN (DATEDIFF(d, @TargetRequiredDate, @TargetShippedDate))
END
GO
```

The next script is a *SELECT* statement that demonstrates the syntax for referencing a scalar UDF in the list for the statement and in the *WHERE* and *ORDER BY* clauses of the statement. The list for the statement includes four columns for each order: *OrderID*, the *udfDaysShippedLate* value, the shipped date, and the required date. The input parameter specified for the scalar UDF is *OrderID*. This causes the UDF to return the difference between the required and shipped dates for the order on each row of the *SELECT* statement's result set. The *FROM* clause designates the *Orders* table in the Northwind database.

Without any additional clauses, the list and the *FROM* clause for the *SELECT* statement would return a row for each row in the *Orders* table with rows arranged by *OrderID* value, the primary key for the *Orders* table. However, the two additional clauses change this. First, the *WHERE* clause causes the statement to return rows just for those orders that shipped one or more days after the required date. The *udfDaysShippedLate* UDF helps to specify the expression for the clause. The UDF's representation is the same as in the *SELECT* statement's list. Second, the *ORDER BY* clause specifies that the rows in the result set be sorted from the order that shipped the latest to the order that shipped the least late.

```
--udfDaysShippedLate_b
--Syntax for user-defined function in list, WHERE, and
--ORDER BY clauses of SELECT statement to return
--orders shipped after required date.
SELECT OrderID, dbo.udfDaysShippedLate(OrderID) 'Days Shipped Late',
    LEFT(ShippedDate, 11) 'Shipped Date',
    LEFT(RequiredDate, 11) 'Required Date'
FROM Northwind..Orders
WHERE dbo.udfDaysShippedLate(OrderID) > 0
ORDER BY dbo.udfDaysShippedLate(OrderID) DESC
```

Figure 5-1 shows an excerpt from the result set for the preceding *SELECT* statement. The second column shows the return values from the UDF. You can confirm its calculation with the help of the last two columns. Notice also that rows appear in order based on the value in the second column, which displays the UDF values for each row. Figure 5-1 shows the Results pane. However, the Messages pane contains the number of rows affected, or returned, by the *SELECT* statement. It is only 37, which is substantially less than the full number of 830 rows in the original *Orders* table.

	OrderID	Days Shipped Late	Shipped Date	Required Date
1	10777	23	Jan 21 1998	Dec 29 1997
2	10726	18	Dec 5 1997	Nov 17 1997
3	10423	18	Feb 24 1997	Feb 6 1997
4	10970	17	Apr 24 1998	Apr 7 1998
5	10515	16	May 23 1997	May 7 1997
6	10827	11	Feb 6 1998	Jan 26 1998
7	10660	9	Oct 15 1997	Oct 6 1997
8	10663	9	Oct 3 1997	Sep 24 1997

Figure 5-1. An excerpt from a result set based on a *SELECT* statement that uses a scalar UDF in its list as well as its *WHERE* and *ORDER BY* clauses.

The next script shows another type of application for the *udfDaysShippedLate* UDF. This script uses the UDF in an expression that serves as the condition for an *IF...ELSE* statement. Because the value for the UDF appears elsewhere in the script besides the condition for the *IF...ELSE* statement, the script saves the UDF's value in a local variable, *@DaysBeforeAfter*. This assignment saves having to recompute the function each time the script needs the UDF's value.

The script computes and displays one of two possible messages based on the *udfDaysShippedLate* UDF value. If the scalar UDF value is negative, the order shipped before the required date. Otherwise, the order shipped on or after the required date. The expression for the *IF...ELSE* statement captures whether the order shipped before or after the required date. The *IF* clause of the statement computes a statement saying how many days before the required date an order shipped. This can be any value from 1 day through the maximum number of days in the *Orders* table that an order shipped before its required date. The *ELSE* clause computes a statement detailing how many days after the required date an order shipped. The string expressions in the *IF* and *ELSE* clauses both reference the *@DaysBeforeAfter* local variable, which the script uses to store the return value from the *udfDaysShippedLate* UDF.

To see the script in operation, you need to run it with *OrderID* values for orders shipping before and after their required dates. The sample script includes two such *OrderID* values. As the script appears below, it computes a message for *OrderID* 10777, which shipped 23 days after its required date. You can comment out the *SET* statement assigning 10777 to the *@TargetID* local variable and remove the comment markers for the *SET* statement assigning 10248 to the local variable. This action permits you to run the script in a mode that computes a message for the number of days that an order shipped before its required date. In this instance, the order shipped 16 days before its required date.

```
--udfDaysShippedLate_c
--Invoke a user-defined function to compute a conditional message
--for the number of days that an order ships before or after its
--required date.
DECLARE @TargetID int
DECLARE @DaysBeforeAfter int
DECLARE @ShipMessage varchar (1000)

--Order 10248 shipped 16 days before its required date.
--Order 10777 shipped 23 days after its required date.
--SET @TargetID = 10248
SET @TargetID = 10777

--Save user-defined function value for reuse in script.
SET @DaysBeforeAfter = dbo.udfDaysShippedLate(@TargetID)

--Branch to compute one of two message formats based on the
--user-defined function value.
IF @DaysBeforeAfter < 0
    BEGIN
        SET  @ShipMessage = 'Order ' + CAST(@TargetID AS varchar) +
            ' shipped ' + CAST(-1 * @DaysBeforeAfter AS varchar) +
            ' days before the required date.'
        Print @ShipMessage
    END
ELSE
    BEGIN
        SET  @ShipMessage = 'Order ' + CAST(@TargetID AS varchar) +
```

```
                ' shipped ' + CAST(@DaysBeforeAfter AS varchar) +
                ' days after the required date.'
            Print @ShipMessage
        END
    GO
```

Creating and Invoking Table-Valued UDFs

Both inline UDFs and multistatement UDFs can return tables instead of scalar values. The inline UDF has the advantage of an exceedingly simple syntax. In addition, it supports parameters so that users can control its result set at run time. Multistatement UDFs are substantially more flexible than inline UDFs. The extra flexibility comes at the expense of more sophisticated T-SQL logic. SQL Server gives you a choice. You can incorporate the table-valued UDF that best fits your needs. The samples in this section will help you see some of the capabilities of both approaches so that you can make an informed choice.

Providing Parametric Views

Inline table-valued UDFs are always based on a single *SELECT* statement—just like a view. However, the inline table-valued UDF offers one significant advantage over a view. You can pass parameters to the *SELECT* statement for an inline table-valued UDF, but the syntax for the *CREATE VIEW* statement offers no opportunities for specifying parameters. Inline UDFs heighten the power of their advantage by offering it with an exceedingly simple syntax. Recall that all you have to do when creating an inline UDF is declare the return data type as *table* in the *RETURNS* clause and then specify a *SELECT* statement as the argument for the *RETURN* clause. You can reference an inline UDF in T-SQL statements just as you would a view except that you can pass the inline UDF parameter values.

The following script illustrates the syntax for saving a *SELECT* statement in a UDF. The *SELECT* statement provides a result set with a row for each order by a customer. The syntax for the statement joins the *Customers* and *Orders* tables in the Northwind database. Notice that the *SELECT* statement specifies the input parameter *@CustID* in its *WHERE* clause. The *SELECT* statement is the argument for the *RETURN* clause in a *CREATE FUNCTION* statement. The parentheses after the function name trailing the *CREATE FUNCTION* keyword phrase are where the UDF declares the *@CustID* parameter value.

The *SELECT* statement that concludes the following script illustrates the syntax for invoking an inline UDF. The sample specifies the return of all the columns from the source with the * character. You can designate individual columns in the list. The *FROM* clause designates the inline UDF as the source for the result set from the *SELECT* statement. In this application, it isn't essential that you specify the owner for the UDF. The function's name is sufficient for designating an inline UDF owned by the dbo user. The specification of the *@CustID* parameter in the parentheses after the UDF's name is critical because the function expects a parameter value and has no default value. This parameter allows the function to return the orders for a particular customer.

```
--udfOrdersForCustomerID
--Drop old version of user-defined function if it exists.
IF EXISTS(SELECT * FROM INFORMATION_SCHEMA.ROUTINES
        WHERE ROUTINE_NAME = 'udfOrdersForCustomerID')
    DROP FUNCTION udfOrdersForCustomerID
GO

--Create Inline table-valued function with a parameter.
CREATE FUNCTION udfOrdersForCustomerID(@CustID varchar(5))
RETURNS TABLE
AS
RETURN(
SELECT c.CompanyName, c.ContactName, c.Phone,
        o.OrderID, o.OrderDate
    FROM Northwind..Customers c JOIN Northwind..Orders o
    ON (c.CustomerID = o.CustomerID)
    WHERE c.CustomerID = @CustID
    )
GO

--Specify a parameter for table returned from function.
SELECT *
    FROM udfOrdersForCustomerID('BERGS')
GO
```

Using a Scalar UDF in the List for an Inline UDF

By combining different types of functions, you can add considerable flexibility to your applications. A scalar UDF returns a single value, but the single value can change depending on input parameter values. An inline UDF returns a result set that can contain multiple rows. By conditioning a scalar UDF on column values from the result set of an inline UDF, you can create new values that combine or extend the values in the source for the inline UDF.

The script sample in this section illustrates how to use a scalar UDF to define a column for the result set from an inline UDF. The script also shows how to use the column defined by the scalar UDF in the *WHERE* clause for *SELECT* statements invoking the inline UDF.

The script defines two UDFs. The first, *udfManagerName*, is a scalar UDF. This function returns the first and last name for an employee from the *Employees* table in the Northwind database. An expression in the list for the *SELECT* statement combines the *FirstName* and *LastName* fields into a single scalar value with a space delimiter between them. The *WHERE* clause for the *SELECT* statement includes a parameter for designating the *EmployeeID* column value. The return value from the scalar UDF is the name of the employee with an *EmployeeID* column value matching the input parameter.

The second UDF in the following script is an inline UDF, named *udfEmployeeExtensionManager*. The *SELECT* statement for the inline UDF specifies the *Employees* table in the Northwind database as its row source. The list for the *SELECT* statement designates four columns. Three come directly from the row source; these are an employee's first name, last name, and extension. The fourth column is the return value from the *udfManagerName* UDF. The parameter value passed to the scalar UDF is the *ReportsTo* column value from the *Employees* table. This column value is the *EmployeeID* for the manager to which an employee reports. The *SELECT* statement specifies an alias, Manager's Name, for the *udfManagerName* UDF return value. Notice that you can represent a single apostrophe within a string constant with two single apostrophes.

```
--udfEmployeeExtensionManager
--Drop old version of user-defined function if it exists.
IF EXISTS(SELECT * FROM INFORMATION_SCHEMA.ROUTINES
            WHERE ROUTINE_NAME = 'udfManagerName')
    DROP FUNCTION udfManagerName
GO

--Function to return the manager's name matching a ReportsTo column value.
CREATE FUNCTION udfManagerName (@reportsto int)
RETURNS varchar(40)
AS
BEGIN
    RETURN(SELECT DISTINCT FirstName + ' ' + LastName
            FROM Northwind..Employees WHERE
            EmployeeID = @reportsto)
END
GO

--Drop old version of user-defined function if it exists.
IF EXISTS(SELECT * FROM INFORMATION_SCHEMA.ROUTINES
            WHERE ROUTINE_NAME = 'udfEmployeeExtensionManager')
    DROP FUNCTION udfEmployeeExtensionManager
GO

--Inline table-valued function to return employee first name, last name,
--extension, and manager's name.
CREATE FUNCTION udfEmployeeExtensionManager()
RETURNS TABLE
```

(continued)

```
AS
RETURN(SELECT FirstName, LastName, Extension,
        dbo.udfManagerName(ReportsTo) 'Manager''s Name'
        FROM Northwind..Employees)
GO

--SELECT statement with inline table-valued function in its FROM clause.
PRINT 'Report for Full udfEmployeeExtensionManager Function'
SELECT *
FROM udfEmployeeExtensionManager()

--Print direct reports to Andrew Fuller.
PRINT 'Report for Andrew Fuller Direct Reports'
SELECT FirstName, LastName, Extension
FROM udfEmployeeExtensionManager()
WHERE [Manager's Name] = 'Andrew Fuller'

--Print direct reports to Steven Buchanan.
PRINT 'Report for Steven Buchanan Direct Reports'
SELECT FirstName, LastName, Extension
FROM udfEmployeeExtensionManager()
WHERE [Manager's Name] = 'Steven Buchanan'

--Print direct and indirect reports to Andrew Fuller.
PRINT 'Report for Andrew Fuller Direct and Indirect Reports'
SELECT FirstName, LastName, Extension
FROM udfEmployeeExtensionManager()
WHERE [Manager's Name] = 'Andrew Fuller'
UNION
SELECT FirstName, LastName, Extension
FROM udfEmployeeExtensionManager()
WHERE [Manager's Name] = 'Steven Buchanan'
```

After creating the two UDFs, the script illustrates with four different batches how to invoke the inline UDF containing a scalar UDF in its *SELECT* list. The first batch returns all the columns for all the rows in the result set from the inline UDF. This result set has four columns and nine rows: one column for each item in the list for the *SELECT* statement of the inline UDF and one row for each row in the *Employees* table—the base table for the *SELECT* statement. The following listing shows the result sets for each of the four samples.

The second and third batches show how to reference in the *WHERE* clause the column returned by the scalar UDF inside the inline UDF. The syntax for this reference uses the alias name for the function, Manager's Name, in the *SELECT* list from the inline UDF. The second sample returns all the direct reports to Andrew Fuller. The third sample returns the direct reports to Steven Buchanan. Because Steven Buchanan reports directly to Andrew Fuller, the direct reports to Steven report indirectly to Andrew Fuller.

The fourth batch constructs a *UNION* query statement that returns all the employees reporting directly or indirectly to Andrew Fuller. The *UNION* operator combines into one result set the results from the *SELECT* statements in the second and third samples. This final result differs from the one for the first sample in a couple of ways. First, it contains just three columns. There is no need for a column with the manager's name because all employees report directly or indirectly to Andrew Fuller. Second, this final result set contains just 8 rows as opposed to the 9 rows in the result set for the first sample. This is because Andrew Fuller doesn't appear in the list of employees reporting to him.

The following listing presents all the result sets returned to the Messages pane when you run the preceding sample from Query Analyzer with a Results In Text setting.

```
Report for Full udfEmployeeExtensionManager Function
FirstName  LastName             Extension Manager's Name
---------- -------------------- --------- ---------------------------------
Nancy      Davolio              5467      Andrew Fuller
Andrew     Fuller               3457      NULL
Janet      Leverling            3355      Andrew Fuller
Margaret   Peacock              5176      Andrew Fuller
Steven     Buchanan             3453      Andrew Fuller
Michael    Suyama               428       Steven Buchanan
Robert     King                 465       Steven Buchanan
Laura      Callahan             2344      Andrew Fuller
Anne       Dodsworth            452       Steven Buchanan

(9 row(s) affected)

Report for Andrew Fuller Direct Reports
FirstName  LastName             Extension
---------- -------------------- ---------
Nancy      Davolio              5467
Janet      Leverling            3355
Margaret   Peacock              5176
Steven     Buchanan             3453
Laura      Callahan             2344

(5 row(s) affected)

Report for Steven Buchanan Direct Reports
FirstName  LastName             Extension
---------- -------------------- ---------
Michael    Suyama               428
Robert     King                 465
Anne       Dodsworth            452

(3 row(s) affected)
```

(continued)

```
Report for Andrew Fuller Direct and Indirect Reports
FirstName  LastName             Extension
---------- -------------------- ---------
Anne       Dodsworth            452
Janet      Leverling            3355
Laura      Callahan             2344
Margaret   Peacock              5176
Michael    Suyama               428
Nancy      Davolio              5467
Robert     King                 465
Steven     Buchanan             3453

(8 row(s) affected)
```

Encapsulating More Logic with Multistatement UDFs

A multistatement table-valued UDF provides substantially more flexibility than is available from an inline UDF. While an inline UDF restricts you to a single *SELECT* statement, a multistatement UDF can contain multiple *SELECT* statements along with other kinds of T-SQL statements. The wide range of statements that you can place inside a multistatement UDF allows you to create more flexible functions that can simplify the logic of T-SQL statements that reference them or even recover from invalid input.

The following script contains a multistatement UDF that can return three different types of result sets. The UDF accomplishes this feat with the aid of a couple of input parameters and nested *IF...ELSE* statements that test the input parameter values. The *@ReportsTo* parameter designates the manager for whom to return a result set. The parameter has an *int* data type, and it denotes a manager's employee ID. The *@Indirect* parameter has a *bit* data type. The value 0 is for direct reports, and the value 1 is for the return of direct and indirect reports. The logic inside the *CREATE FUNCTION* statement accommodates one invalid pair of input parameters to demonstrate what you can accomplish with a multistatement UDF. This logic traps for a request of indirect reports for the manager whose *EmployeeID* value is 5. This request is invalid for the *Employees* table in the Northwind database because this manager has only direct reports. The function recovers from the request by supplying only direct reports to the manager.

After creating the multistatement UDF with a *CREATE FUNCTION* statement, the script launches four *SELECT* statements that reference the UDF. The parameters for the *SELECT* statements allow you to confirm the flexibility of the UDF. The first *SELECT* statement returns the direct reports to Andrew Fuller, whose *EmployeeID* is 2. The second *SELECT* statement returns the direct reports to Steven Buchanan, whose *EmployeeID* is 5. The third *SELECT* statement includes the *EmployeeID* value for Andrew Fuller again, but it sets *@Indirect* to

1. This permits the UDF to return the result for a union query instead of a simple parameter query (as in the first two *SELECT* statements). The fourth *SELECT* statement requests the direct and indirect reports for the manager whose *EmployeeID* is 5, namely Steven Buchanan. This requests passes control to the last *IF* clause in the UDF and returns just the direct reports for Steven Buchanan. The UDF could have printed a custom message with the *RAISERROR* statement.

```
--udfReportsTable
--Drop old version of user-defined function if it exists.
IF EXISTS(SELECT * FROM INFORMATION_SCHEMA.ROUTINES
            WHERE ROUTINE_NAME = 'udfReportsTable')
    DROP FUNCTION udfReportsTable
GO

--Create multistatement table-valued function.
CREATE FUNCTION udfReportsTable(@ReportsTo int, @Indirect bit)
RETURNS @TableOut TABLE(
FirstName varchar(10) NOT NULL,
LastName varchar(20) NOT NULL,
Extension varchar(4) NULL
)
AS
BEGIN
IF @Indirect = 0
    INSERT @TableOut
    SELECT FirstName, LastName, Extension
    FROM Northwind..Employees
    WHERE ReportsTo = @ReportsTo
ELSE
    IF @ReportsTo = 2
        INSERT @TableOut
        SELECT FirstName, LastName, Extension
        FROM Northwind..Employees
        WHERE ReportsTo = @ReportsTo
        UNION
        SELECT FirstName, LastName, Extension
        FROM Northwind..Employees
        WHERE ReportsTo <> @ReportsTo AND
            ReportsTo IS NOT NULL
    ELSE
        IF @ReportsTo = 5
            INSERT @TableOut
            SELECT FirstName, LastName, Extension
            FROM Northwind..Employees
            WHERE ReportsTo = @ReportsTo
RETURN
END
GO
```

(continued)

```
--Print direct reports to Andrew Fuller.
SELECT *
FROM udfReportsTable(2,0)

--Print direct reports to Steven Buchanan.
SELECT *
FROM udfReportsTable(5,0)

--Print direct and indirect reports to Andrew Fuller.
SELECT *
FROM udfReportsTable(2,1)

--Demo recovery from Indirect Reports request for Steven Buchanan.
SELECT *
FROM udfReportsTable(5,1)
```

Introduction to Triggers

Triggers enable developers to create stored procedures that fire automatically when an application makes changes to tables or views to which the triggers belong. This section introduces core concepts about what a trigger is, the different types of triggers available to developers, and statements for managing triggers in your applications.

Triggers Are like Event Procedures

Visual Basic developers may find it convenient to think of triggers as event procedures. Triggers encapsulate T-SQL code much like stored procedures except that triggers fire automatically when events happen for an object to which the trigger belongs. It is good practice to back up your trigger code independently of the objects to which they belong—especially as you are initially defining the objects for a project. This is because dropping an object removes any triggers associated with the object. There is no warning message about the existence of trigger code that you might want to save before removing an object.

The events that fire a trigger are inserts, updates, and deletes. With classic triggers, the events are for tables. These triggers actually fire after the initiation of a change event but before the commitment of a change to a database table. Within the code for a classic trigger, you can perform many different kinds of actions, such as rolling back the change to the table, performing data integrity checks, and archiving original and changed data. Before the introduction of declarative referential integrity and cascading updates and deletes, it was common to program this kind of behavior with triggers. Even now, if an application requires referential integrity between two tables in different databases, you must program it manually. Triggers represent a natural place to locate the code for programming referential integrity across two tables in different databases.

It is good practice to keep your trigger code short and uncomplicated. This is because a trigger fires whenever its event occurs. Therefore, an update trigger fires whenever a user tries to update a value in a table. The update doesn't commit until SQL Server completes the execution of the code in the trigger. If the code presents a message to the user, you especially want to keep the code brief so that the message returns to the user swiftly.

A trigger does have a decided advantage over an event procedure that you can assign to a form in Visual Basic. This is because the trigger always fires no matter how a user opens the object with the trigger. With an event procedure for a form that uses a SQL Server table for its row source, database users can bypass any logic in the event procedure by opening the table directly or opening the table with another form or user interface that doesn't have the event procedure. When you code your change directly against the database object with a trigger, the code fires no matter how users open the row source.

Types of Triggers

SQL Server offers two basic types of triggers. Within each type, you can have three event types that fire triggers: inserts, updates, and deletes. You can create a trigger for any combination of these three events.

The preceding section briefly described classic triggers. This is the first type of trigger. SQL Server documentation refers to this kind of trigger as an *AFTER* trigger. You can create an *AFTER* trigger only for a table. The name for the type of trigger indicates when the trigger fires—namely, after the start of a change to a table. You can have multiple *AFTER* triggers for the same change event. With the help of two system stored procedures, you can designate the first and last trigger to fire for a change event to an object. By designating a first and last trigger to fire, you can precisely control the order in which up to three triggers fire. However, remember that all the triggers eventually fire for a change event to an object. Therefore, the more triggers you have, the longer it takes for SQL Server to commit the insert, update, or delete action. In addition, multiple triggers can delay custom messages sent back to users.

> **Note** Invoke the *sp_settriggerorder* system stored procedure to control the order of execution for triggers. The procedure takes three arguments: one for the trigger name, another for the order of firing, and the third for the type of event.

The second type of trigger is an *INSTEAD OF* trigger. You can create *INSTEAD OF* triggers for both tables and views. This type of trigger fires before the change event for the object. Therefore, you cannot roll back a change to a table or view from an *INSTEAD OF* trigger because the event didn't occur yet. However, you can complete the action, or an alternative one, from within the trigger code. Unlike *AFTER* triggers, only one *INSTEAD OF* trigger can exist for each type of change event. If you apply a change event to a view and permit direct access to any base tables for the view, users can bypass the trigger for the view by opening the base tables.

inserted and *deleted* Tables

The *inserted* and *deleted* tables are two logical tables available within a trigger. The tables have the same structure as the table or view to which a trigger belongs. Each of the three change events impacts the contents of the *inserted* and *deleted* tables differently. These tables are convenient for archiving changes to a table. You can select which columns you archive and add any data that your requirements dictate, such as user identification, date, and time.

An *INSERT* statement populates the *inserted* table. *INSERT* statements don't populate the *deleted* table. The new column values for the inserted row are in the *inserted* table.

A *DELETE* statement populates the *deleted* table, but the statement leaves the *inserted* table empty. The *deleted* table will have as many rows as the *DELETE* statement removes from the table. The *TRUNCATE TABLE* statement doesn't log changes to the *deleted* table or fire triggers. In addition, the *DROP TABLE* statement doesn't fire a trigger. Instead, the statement removes the trigger along with the table.

An *UPDATE* statement populates both the *inserted* and *deleted* tables. The rows with the new values are in the *inserted* table. The rows with the old values are in the *deleted* table. As with the *DELETE* statement, the *inserted* and *deleted* tables can contain multiple rows for a single *UPDATE* statement.

Statements for Creating and Dropping Triggers

An array of T-SQL statements exist for creating and managing triggers. Many of these statements parallel those for other database objects, but some are special for triggers. (For example, you already read about the *sp_settriggerorder* system stored procedure.) You can make new triggers with the *CREATE TRIGGER* statement. This single T-SQL statement facilitates the creation of *AFTER* and *INSTEAD OF* triggers by the inclusion of a keyword phrase specifying the trigger type. The *DROP TRIGGER* statement works for either type of trigger, but there is no *INFORMATION_SCHEMA* view that displays the triggers in a database. The following samples demonstrate an approach to checking for the existence of a trigger based on the *sysobjects* table in a database. It is sometimes convenient to disable a trigger (for example, to enter new rows into a table that conflict with the logic in the trigger). Use the *ALTER TABLE* statement with the *DISABLE* keyword followed by the trigger name to disable an existing trigger. To restore the trigger, specify the *ENABLE* keyword followed by the trigger's name within an *ALTER TABLE* statement.

The *CREATE TRIGGER* statement is flexible because a single template accommodates both *AFTER* and *INSTEAD OF* triggers. In addition, you can specify either trigger type for any combination of the three possible events that can fire it. The trigger name following the *CREATE TRIGGER* keyword phrase is a normal SQL Server identifier. To make trigger names identify their object type, this chapter begins trigger names with the *trg* prefix. Designate the object to which a trigger belongs in the *ON* clause. Specify the object by following the *ON* keyword with the name of a table or view.

The next line is where the *CREATE TRIGGER* statement offers much of its flexibility. You can start the line with either the *AFTER* keyword or the *INSTEAD OF* keyword phrase to declare the trigger type. Because *AFTER* is the default trigger type, you don't need to specify the *AFTER* keyword to create an *AFTER* trigger. The *FOR* clause specifies the type of events that will fire an *AFTER* trigger. The syntax for the *INSTEAD OF* keyword doesn't require the *FOR* keyword (as is the case for *AFTER* triggers). The following code template shows all three events. However, you can designate any two or just one event. The event names in the *FOR* clause determine what actions fire a trigger. The *AS* keyword marks the transition from the trigger declarations to the T-SQL code that a trigger executes when it fires.

```
CREATE TRIGGER trigger_name
ON tablename or viewname
AFTER OR INSTEAD OF OR FOR INSERT, UPDATE, DELETE
AS
T-SQL statements for trigger
```

CREATE TRIGGER will fail if you try to create a new trigger with a name for a previously existing trigger. There are a couple of workarounds to this problem. First, you can modify the design of the old trigger with the *ALTER TRIGGER* statement. Second, you can conditionally drop the old version of a trigger. The syntax for checking on the existence of a previously existing trigger is different from that for tables, views, stored procedures, and UDFs. This is because there is no *INFORMATION_SCHEMA* view for listing triggers. However, you can use the *name* and *type* columns of the *sysobjects* table to verify the existence of a previously existing version of a trigger in a database. The *sysobjects* table is a table maintained by SQL Server that keeps track of the objects in a database. In the following template, control passes to the *DROP TRIGGER* statement only if the *sysobjects* table contains a row with a name column value equal to *triggername* and a type value equal to *TR*.

```
IF EXISTS (SELECT name FROM sysobjects
        WHERE name = 'triggername' AND type = 'TR')
    DROP TRIGGER triggername
```

You can use the same syntax for verifying the existence of many other database objects. Change *type* to *V* for views and *P* for stored procedures. Use *FN*, *IF*, and *TF* for scalar, inline, and multistatement UDFs, respectively.

Creating and Managing Triggers

Triggers are a valuable tool for managing your databases. The "Introduction to Triggers" section reviewed the basic concepts for using triggers, some potential applications, and basic syntax issues. This section provides four samples that illustrate the syntax for using triggers in database applications. The samples aren't as important themselves as the issues that they frame, such as how to use the *inserted* and *deleted* tables and how to enforce business rules. Review the samples to rapidly ramp up to speed on core trigger design and application issues. Then adapt and extend the samples for your own application development needs.

Protecting and Unprotecting a Table from Changes

Because triggers can fire whenever there is an attempt to change a table, it is possible to write a trigger that guards the contents of a table. For example, you can block all attempts to modify the contents of a table. You can selectively restrict the ability to delete rows, change column values in rows, or insert new rows into a table with *AFTER* triggers. You can protect a table's contents unconditionally, or you can condition the protection on a user's membership in security roles, the time of day, day of the week, or whatever. If you elect to block modifications with a trigger to a table unconditionally, you will probably encounter a need to disable the trigger occasionally. Disabling a trigger allows you to reinvoke it easily without having to re-create or modify it in any way. To reinvoke a disabled trigger, all you have to do is enable it. Recall that you can disable and enable a trigger with an *ALTER TABLE* statement for the table with the trigger that you want to disable temporarily.

The following script demonstrates the syntax for creating a trigger for the *MyTable* table created earlier in this chapter. (See the "Creating a Scalar UDF Without Parameters" section.) The trigger protects the table from inserts, updates, and deletes by rolling back the transaction associated with the trigger.

The script starts by removing any previous version of the *trgKeepMyTableUntouched* trigger and then begins a *CREATE TRIGGER* statement. Like most other *CREATE* statements, the *CREATE TRIGGER* statement must occur at the top of a batch. Therefore, the code to drop the old version ends with the *GO* keyword. The *ON* clause of the *CREATE TRIGGER* statement designates the *MyTable* table as the one to which the trigger will belong. The *FOR* clause indicates that the trigger will fire for insert, update, and delete events.

The first statement after the *AS* keyword is a *RAISERROR* statement that sends a custom message back to the Messages pane of Query Analyzer. An informational message issued from a trigger is useful for letting a user know that a trigger fired. The *RAISERROR* statement can serve other functions as well, but it is a robust alternative to the *PRINT* statement for sending messages to the Messages pane. The string for a custom message can be up to 400 characters. The trailing values 16 and 1 indicate the severity and state for the error. For simple informational messages, you can consistently apply these values. The second T-SQL statement in the script rolls back the transaction to modify the table. The *ROLLBACK TRAN* statement is an abbreviated version of the *ROLLBACK TRANSACTION* statement. In either form, this statement removes any inserted rows, restores any column values to their nonupdated state, and adds back any deleted rows. You will generally want to use the *ROLLBACK TRAN* statement as the last statement in a trigger because any statements after *ROLLBACK TRAN* can modify the table for a trigger.

```
--trgKeepMyTableUntouched
--Drop prior version of trigger.
IF EXISTS (SELECT name FROM sysobjects
        WHERE name = 'trgKeepMyTableUntouched' AND type = 'TR')
    DROP TRIGGER trgKeepMyTableUntouched
GO

--Create new trigger to keep MyTable table untouched.
CREATE TRIGGER trgKeepMyTableUntouched
ON MyTable
FOR INSERT, UPDATE, DELETE
AS
RAISERROR('Message from trgKeepMyTableUntouched.',16,1)
ROLLBACK TRAN
GO
```

The following script is a collection of T-SQL statements that demonstrates the behavior of the trigger as well as how to disable and restore the trigger. The first couple of batches in the script attempt to delete all rows from the *MyTable* table and modify a column value in the table. Neither batch succeeds because the *trgKeepMyTableUntouched* trigger protects the *MyTable* table from delete and update events (as well as insert events).

If it becomes essential to modify a table with a trigger that blocks changes, you can temporarily disable the trigger. The script demonstrates the syntax for the *trgKeepMyTableUntouched* trigger. You have to modify the *MyTable* table with the *ALTER TABLE* statement to disable its trigger. After disabling the trigger, the script changes the maximum value in the *col1* column. Then, in another batch, the script restores the initial maximum value. The scripts use a scalar UDF developed earlier in this chapter to accomplish these tasks. After successfully modifying the table with the trigger disabled, the script enables the trigger again for the *MyTable* table with the *ALTER TABLE* statement. Just to confirm the trigger's operation, the script again attempts to delete all rows from the table. The trigger fires and prints its informational message and rolls back the transaction to remove the rows from the table.

```
--Demo_trgKeepMyTableUntouched
--An attempt to delete all records fails with
--trigger error message.
DELETE
FROM MyTable
GO

--An attempt to update the maximum value in
--col1 in the MyTable table fails also.
UPDATE MyTable
SET col1 = dbo.udfOneHigherThanMax()
WHERE col1 = (SELECT MAX(col1) FROM MyTable)
GO

--Disable the trigger for MyTable without dropping it.
ALTER TABLE MyTable
Disable TRIGGER trgKeepMyTableUntouched
GO

--Update attempt for MyTable succeeds.
UPDATE MyTable
SET col1 = dbo.udfOneHigherThanMax()
WHERE col1 = (SELECT MAX(col1) FROM MyTable)

SELECT * FROM MyTable
GO

--Restoring update event also succeeds.
UPDATE MyTable
SET col1 = dbo.udfOneHigherThanMax() - 2
WHERE col1 = (SELECT MAX(col1) FROM MyTable)

SELECT * FROM MyTable
GO
```

```
--Re-enable trigger.
ALTER TABLE MyTable
Enable TRIGGER trgKeepMyTableUntouched
GO

--An attempt to delete all records fails again
--with trigger error message.
DELETE
FROM MyTable
GO
```

Archiving Changes to a Table

The logical tables *inserted* and *deleted* contain the changes that users make to a table. Unfortunately, the *inserted* and *deleted* tables are available only for the time that a trigger has control of an application. When the trigger closes, SQL Server in effect clears the tables. If you want to persist some subset of the changes to a table for permanent ready access, you can use triggers to save the contents of the logical *inserted* and *deleted* tables to a table in a SQL Server database. Because changes (inserts, updates, and deletes) affect the *inserted* and *deleted* tables differently, one approach is to create a separate trigger for each type of change. This simplifies the trigger logic, and it makes each type of change run faster than having one trigger that deciphers the type of change and then archives the *inserted* and *deleted* tables properly.

The following script creates three triggers to log inserts, updates, and deletes to the *MyTable* table in the *ChangeLogForMyTable* table. The script starts by removing the *trgKeepMyTableUntouched* trigger created in the previous sample. Recall that the previous trigger blocks all changes to the *MyTable* table. Next this procedure creates a fresh blank version of the *ChangeLog-ForMyTable* table. The table has four columns—one for the *col1* values from the *inserted* or *deleted* table, a second for the type of change, a third for the date and time of the change, and a fourth column for the login of the user making the change.

After creating a table to archive changes, the script creates a fresh copy of the *trgInsertToChangeLog* trigger. This trigger copies the *col1* value from the *inserted* table to a local variable. Then it uses the local variable in the *VALUES* clause of an *INSERT INTO* statement to persist the new value to the *ChangeLog-ForMyTable* table. The script uses a string constant—*INSERT*—to designate the type of change. The *CURRENT_TIMESTAMP* and *SYSTEM_USER* keywords denote built-in functions that return the current date and time as well as the login for the current user (the one who makes the change).

The *CREATE TRIGGER* statements for the *trgDeleteToChangeLog* and *trgUpdateToChangeLog* triggers persist the delete and update *col1* values to the

ChangeLogForMyTable table. When logging deletes, you use the *deleted* table instead of the *inserted* table. In the case of updates, you log the contents of the *deleted* and *inserted* tables to the *ChangeLogForMyTable* table. However, the basic design of delete and update triggers corresponds to the *trgInsert-ToChangeLog* trigger.

```
--trgInsertUpdateDeleteToChangeLog
--Drop prior version of trgKeepMyTableUntouched trigger.
IF EXISTS (SELECT name FROM sysobjects
        WHERE name = 'trgKeepMyTableUntouched' AND type = 'TR')
    DROP TRIGGER trgKeepMyTableUntouched
GO

--Remove prior version of ChangeLogForMyTable table.
IF EXISTS(SELECT TABLE_NAME = 'ChangeLogForMyTable'
            FROM INFORMATION_SCHEMA.TABLES)
    DROP TABLE ChangeLogForMyTable

--Create ChangeLogForMyTable table.
CREATE TABLE ChangeLogForMyTable
(
col1 int,
type varchar (10),
changedatetime datetime,
changeuser varchar(128)
)
GO

--Drop prior version of trgInsertToChangeLog trigger.
IF EXISTS (SELECT name FROM sysobjects
        WHERE name = 'trgInsertToChangeLog' AND type = 'TR')
    DROP TRIGGER trgInsertToChangeLog
GO

--Create trigger to monitor inserts.
CREATE TRIGGER trgInsertToChangeLog
ON MyTable
FOR INSERT
AS
DECLARE @col1value int
SET @col1value = (SELECT col1 FROM inserted)
INSERT INTO ChangeLogForMyTable VALUES(@col1value, 'INSERT',
CURRENT_TIMESTAMP, SYSTEM_USER)
GO

--Drop prior version of trgDeleteToChangeLog trigger.
IF EXISTS (SELECT name FROM sysobjects
        WHERE name = 'trgDeleteToChangeLog' AND type = 'TR')
```

```
    DROP TRIGGER trgDeleteToChangeLog
GO

--Create trigger to monitor deletes.
CREATE TRIGGER trgDeleteToChangeLog
ON MyTable
FOR DELETE
AS
DECLARE @col1value int
SET @col1value = (SELECT col1 FROM deleted)
INSERT INTO ChangeLogForMyTable VALUES(@col1value, 'DELETE',
CURRENT_TIMESTAMP, SYSTEM_USER)
GO

--Drop prior version of trgUpdateToChangeLog trigger.
IF EXISTS (SELECT name FROM sysobjects
        WHERE name = 'trgUpdateToChangeLog' AND type = 'TR')
    DROP TRIGGER trgUpdateToChangeLog
GO

CREATE TRIGGER trgUpdateToChangeLog
ON MyTable
FOR UPDATE
AS
DECLARE @col1value int
SET @col1value = (SELECT col1 FROM deleted)
INSERT INTO ChangeLogForMyTable VALUES(@col1value, 'UPDATE',
CURRENT_TIMESTAMP, SYSTEM_USER)
SET @col1value = (SELECT col1 FROM inserted)
INSERT INTO ChangeLogForMyTable VALUES(@col1value, 'UPDATE',
CURRENT_TIMESTAMP, SYSTEM_USER)
GO
```

The following script should be run immediately after you create the triggers with the preceding script. It also benefits from a fresh copy of the *MyTable* table, such as the one generated by the *udfHigherThanMax* script in the "Creating a Scalar UDF Without Parameters" section. The script makes a series of changes to the *MyTable* table. After each change, it uses *SELECT* statements to return the *MyTable* table and the *ChangeLogForMyTable* table. The first change is to add a new row with the value 25 for *col1*. Next it updates the value 25 to 26. Finally it deletes the row in the *MyTable* table with a *col1* value of 26.

```
--Demo_trgInsertUpdateDeleteToChangeLog
--Insert a new row into MyTable and display
--MyTable and ChangeLogForMyTable tables
INSERT INTO MyTable (col1)
VALUES (25)
```

(continued)

```
SELECT *
FROM MyTable
SELECT *
FROM ChangeLogForMyTable
GO

--Update inserted row value and display
--MyTable and ChangeLogForMyTable tables.
UPDATE MyTable
SET col1 = 26
WHERE col1 = 25

SELECT *
FROM MyTable
SELECT *
FROM ChangeLogForMyTable
GO

--Delete updated row and display
--MyTable and ChangeLogForMyTable tables.
DELETE
FROM MyTable
WHERE col1 = 26

SELECT *
FROM MyTable
SELECT *
FROM ChangeLogForMyTable
GO
```

Examining the Results pane contents will allow you to follow the changes to the *MyTable* table as well as the *ChangeLogForMyTable* table. The first display of the *ChangeLogForMyTable* table shows a table with just one row and a *col1* value of 25. In the next display of the table, you can see three rows. This is because an update adds two rows to the table. In its final appearance in the results pane, the *ChangeLogForMyTable* table contains four rows.

Enforcing a Business Rule on a Table

One of the classic uses for triggers is the enforcement of business rules. After all, the trigger always fires before a change event. The T-SQL in the trigger can assess the change to make sure it conforms to business rules before committing the change to a table. If a change value doesn't satisfy a business rule, the trigger can take an appropriate remedy, such as rejecting the change or revising the change and informing the user of any remedial action.

The next sample enforces a simple business rule. The rule is that users can insert only even numbers into *col1* of the *MyTable* table. Your normal business rules can be substantially more sophisticated than this sample, but the triggers to enforce those rules can still use the same logic. First you test the change value to make sure it adheres to the rule. Second, if the change value doesn't conform to the business rule, your trigger can perform an appropriate remedial action for the invalid change value. Third, if the change value satisfies the business rule, you insert it into the table.

> **Note** Before running the sample script in this section, make sure you drop all other triggers for the *MyTable* table that can conflict with the sample below. The sample script on the book's companion CD removes all prior triggers created for the *MyTable* table in this chapter. For brevity, the listing here doesn't show the code for dropping all these triggers.

The sample uses an *INSTEAD OF* trigger. Because this type of trigger fires before the change event, there is no need to roll back a transaction for an invalid action. The sample uses the modulo operator (%) to check whether a number divides evenly by 2. A remainder of 1 indicates an odd number. This outcome calls for a remedial action. The action in this instance is to add 1 to the input value from the *inserted* table, construct a message indicating the alternative action taken, and finally insert the new even number into the table. A remainder of 0 indicates an even number. Because even numbers satisfy the business rule, the trigger can just insert the value from the *inserted* table into *col1* of the *MyTable* table.

After the creation of the trigger, the script includes data manipulation and *SELECT* statements to test the trigger's logic. You can run the sample script and see the trigger automatically add 1 when the script attempts to input an odd number (25) into *col1* in the *MyTable* table. On the other hand, the trigger merely accepts the insert of an even number (24) into *col1* in the *MyTable* table.

```
--trgInsteadOfInsert
--Drop prior version of trgInsteadOfInsert trigger.
IF EXISTS (SELECT name FROM sysobjects
        WHERE name = 'trgInsteadOfInsert' AND type = 'TR')
    DROP TRIGGER trgInsteadOfInsert
GO

--Create an INSTEAD OF trigger.
CREATE TRIGGER trgInsteadOfInsert
ON MyTable
INSTEAD OF INSERT
```

(continued)

```
AS
DECLARE @col1value int
DECLARE @newcol1value int
DECLARE @strMsg varchar(400)

SET @col1value = (SELECT col1 FROM inserted)

--If inserted value is odd, make it even
--before inserting it.
IF @col1value%2 = 1
    BEGIN
        SET @newcol1value = @col1value + 1
        SET @strMsg = 'The value you want to insert is: '
            + CAST(@col1value AS varchar(3))
            + ', but it violates a business rule.' + CHAR(10) +
            '  Therefore, I insert '
            + CAST(@newcol1value AS varchar(3)) + '.'
        RAISERROR (@strMsg,16,1)
        INSERT INTO MyTable (col1) VALUES(@newcol1value)
    END
ELSE
    INSERT INTO MyTable (col1) VALUES(@col1value)
GO

--Try to insert an odd value into col1 in MyTable.
INSERT INTO MyTable (col1) VALUES(25)

--Display the col1 values in MyTable.
SELECT *
FROM MyTable

--Delete the next even value after the odd value.
DELETE
FROM MyTable
WHERE col1 = 26

--Display the col1 values in MyTable.
SELECT *
FROM MyTable

--Insert an even value into col1 in MyTable.
INSERT INTO MyTable (col1) VALUES(24)

--Display the col1 values in MyTable.
SELECT *
FROM MyTable

--Delete the new even col1 value in MyTable.
DELETE
```

```
FROM MyTable
WHERE col1 = 24

--Display the col1 values in MyTable.
SELECT *
FROM MyTable
```

Enforcing a Business Rule on a View

Two of the advantages of views are that they permit you to insulate your database schema from the user interface for an application and that you can selectively expose subsets from a table without exposing all the data in a base table. These features permit you to secure the base table or tables for a view from all or most users while you grant these same users access to a subset of the data from the base table or tables through a view. Unfortunately, *AFTER* triggers never applied to views, so previously you couldn't enforce business rules with triggers for views. SQL Server 2000 introduced *INSTEAD OF* triggers, which apply to views. Therefore, you can gain the benefits of exposing data through views and still be able to enforce business rules via triggers.

The sample in this section demonstrates the syntax for applying a business rule for inserts into a view. The view is *vewMyTable*. This view returns all the rows for the column in the *MyTable* table. The business rule is that the inserted *col1* value can be only 1 greater than the current maximum in *col1* of the *MyTable* table.

> **Note** As with the sample script from the preceding section, you should remove all triggers that can conflict with the new trigger. The version of the following sample on the book's companion CD removes all prior triggers created for the *MyTable* table in this chapter. For brevity, the listing here doesn't show the code for dropping all these triggers.

The script below starts with the creation of the *vewMyTable* view. Then the script moves on to create a fresh version of *trgInsteadOfInsertForvewMyTable*. No special action is necessary for creating a trigger for a view. In the *ON* clause for the *CREATE TRIGGER* statement, just name the view—*vewMyTable*, in this case. The trigger's logic uses the *udfOneHigherThanMax* UDF created earlier in this chapter. You should run the code to create this UDF if it isn't available. The logic for enforcing the business rule is the same as for the previous trigger, although the actual business rule is different. An *IF...ELSE* statement tests for the validity of the new value relative to the business rule. If the new value fails the test, the trigger performs a remedial action. This action prints a message letting the user know the new value is invalid. Because the trigger is an *INSTEAD OF* trigger, there is no need to roll back the insert. If the new value is valid, the trigger inserts the new value into *vewMyTable*.

After the script creates the trigger, the script goes on to test the trigger by trying to insert two new values. The first value violates the business rule, and the trigger rejects it. The second value satisfies the business rule, and the trigger inserts the new value into *col1* of the *MyTable* table. The final data manipulation statement in the script removes the value newly inserted into the *vewMyTable* view to restore the base table to its initial state.

```
--trgInsteadOfInsertForvewMyTable
--Drop prior version of vewMyTable view.
IF EXISTS(SELECT TABLE_NAME
            FROM INFORMATION_SCHEMA.VIEWS
            WHERE TABLE_NAME = 'vewMyTable')
    DROP VIEW vewMyTable
GO

--Create vewMyTable view.
CREATE VIEW vewMyTable
AS
SELECT *
FROM MyTable
GO

--Drop prior version of trgInsteadOfInsertForvewMyTable trigger.
IF EXISTS (SELECT name FROM sysobjects
        WHERE name = 'trgInsteadOfInsertForvewMyTable' AND type = 'TR')
    DROP TRIGGER trgInsteadOfInsertForvewMyTable
GO

--Create an INSTEAD OF trigger for a view.
CREATE TRIGGER trgInsteadOfInsertForvewMyTable
ON vewMyTable
INSTEAD OF INSERT
AS
DECLARE @col1value int
SET @col1value = (SELECT col1 FROM inserted)
IF @col1value > dbo.udfOneHigherThanMax()
    RAISERROR('Value too high.',17,1)
ELSE
    INSERT INTO vewMyTable (col1) VALUES(@col1value)
GO
```

```
--Attempting to insert a value of 100 fails
--through vewMyTable.
INSERT INTO vewMyTable (col1) VALUES(100)

SELECT * FROM vewMyTable
GO

--Attempting to insert a value one higher
--than the maximum value succeeds.
INSERT INTO vewMyTable (col1) VALUES(dbo.udfOneHigherThanMax())

SELECT * FROM vewMyTable
GO

--Remove inserted value.
DELETE
FROM vewMyTable
WHERE col1 = dbo.udfOneHigherThanMax()-1
GO
```

6

SQL Server 2000 XML Functionality

When Microsoft SQL Server 2000 was launched, Microsoft committed itself to providing the best Extensible Markup Language (XML) functionality possible. XML is important because it promises to revolutionize the way database and Web developers implement data access and data manipulation capabilities in their solutions. Microsoft said it would revise the initial release with timely updates that included new functionality reflecting the rapidly evolving XML standards and related development issues.

As this chapter was being prepared, Microsoft delivered on its commitment with the release of its latest update—the Microsoft SQL Server 2000 Web Services Toolkit. The toolkit follows two earlier releases: XML for SQL Server 2000 Web Release 1 and XML for SQL Server 2000 Web Release 2.

The Web Services Toolkit is based on SQLXML 3.0 and includes the SQLXML 3.0 installation package. Microsoft says that the features introduced in SQLXML 1.0 and SQLXML 2.0 are included in the SQLXML 3.0 package. See Chapter 12 for coverage of the compatibility of the toolkit with the two prior Web releases. In addition, see Chapter 13 for commentary and samples using the Web Services Toolkit.

You will gain from this chapter an overall understanding of XML functionality in SQL Server with an emphasis on access to that functionality via T-SQL, XML schemas and templates, and hypertext transport protocol (HTTP). Chapter 12 will refocus on XML so that you can build on the understanding presented here while you learn how to tap the XML capabilities in SQL Server with Visual Basic .NET and related technologies, such as ADO.NET. With XML, developers can build incredibly powerful solutions for retrieving and maintaining data over

Web connections. As the word gets out about how easy it is to create these solutions, you will become an evangelist for using XML with SQL Server.

This chapter relies on the Northwind sample database. The chapter samples add a couple of new views and user-defined functions to the database for use with XML files. T-SQL scripts for creating these objects are included with the sample files for this chapter. The main resource for the chapter is a collection of nearly 20 XML files along with an assortment of URLs. Some of the URLs demonstrate direct access to a SQL Server database, while other URLs invoke an XML file and access a SQL Server database indirectly through the XML file.

Overview of XML Support

In learning about XML functionality, it is important to recall that Microsoft introduced XML processing power to SQL Server 2000 in multiple waves. This means that selected XML features available from the initial version of SQL Server 2000 have been obsoleted, or at least deprecated, by subsequently introduced XML techniques. This is because Web Release 1 and Web Release 2—and now the Web Services Toolkit—added new XML functionality not available in the initial release.

The overview of XML capabilities in this section has two parts. First it briefly summarizes important XML features for the initial release of SQL Server 2000 and each of the first two Web releases. Second it provides helpful information for installing the Web releases. See Chapter 12 and Chapter 13 for more information about the latest Web release, the Microsoft SQL Server 2000 Web Services Toolkit.

Summary of XML Features by SQL Server Release

The initial release of SQL Server 2000 offered XML functionality in four main areas.

- The ability to access SQL Server via HTTP. This form of access relies on the creation of a Microsoft Internet Information Services (IIS) virtual directory for each database for which you provide access via HTTP.
- Support for XDR (XML-Data Reduced) schemas. You can use these schemas to create XML-based views of SQL Server row sources, and you can use a subset of the XML Path (XPath) query language to query these views. The full XPath specification is a World Wide Web Consortium (W3C) standard (as outlined at *http://www.w3.org/TR/xpath*).

- Retrieving and writing XML data. With the *FOR XML* clause for the T-SQL *SELECT* statement, SQL Server provides a route for reading its data sources and returning result sets in XML format. *OPENXML* is a new function that can return a rowset based on an XML document. Because T-SQL enables the use of the *OPENXML* function in a manner similar to that of the *OPENROWSET* function, you can use *INSERT* statements to populate data sources based on XML document contents.
- Enhancements for XML to Microsoft SQL Server 2000 OLE DB provider (SQLOLEDB). These XML improvements come along with version 2.6 of Microsoft Data Access Components. Using the new capabilities permits you to pass XML-formatted data to a *Command* object and return XML-formatted data from a *Command* object. In either case, the data passes as a *Stream* object.

Web Release 1 was last updated on February 15, 2001. This release adds selected new XML capabilities to the XML features introduced when SQL Server 2000 initially shipped in the fourth quarter of 2000. As you can see, Microsoft wasted no time enhancing the initial capabilities. Web Release 1 creates two major improvements along with a collection of minor ones.

- *Updategrams* enable transaction-based data manipulation using XML. Updategrams offer an XML-based syntax for inserting, updating, and deleting records in a SQL Server row source. You can specify transactions for sets of operations within Updategrams so that all the data manipulation tasks within a transaction occur or none occur. By using Updategrams instead of the *OPENXML* function, developers can improve the performance of their inserts, updates, and deletes while simplifying the coding.
- *XML Bulk Load* targets moving massive amounts of XML-based data into SQL Server. This feature addresses the needs of database administrators and others who regularly use either the *BULK INSERT* statement or the bcp utility. In a non-transaction-based mode, you can insert XML-formatted data faster than with Updategrams or the *OPENXML* function.
- Selected other Web Release 1 enhancements. New syntax offers you the ability to specify with a parameter the return of binary data from a SQL Server data source. Virtual directory management tools expand to offer more precise control over how users can access a database via a virtual directory. Syntax enhancements improve your ability to map XML schemas to SQL Server data sources and generally manage XML templates.

Web Release 2 continued the pattern of intermediate releases that enhance the XML functionality of SQL Server 2000. The last update for Web Release 2 was October 15, 2001, eight months after Web Release 1. In Internet time, this gap is long enough for a major upgrade—and Microsoft took advantage of the interval to offer significant new functionality. Web Release 2 is especially appropriate for those planning to develop solutions with a .NET language, such as Visual Basic .NET. I highlight four major areas of XML functionality and operation associated with Web Release 2:

- Compliance with the W3C schema specification known as XML Schema Definition (XSD). While this release doesn't drop support for the proprietary XDR schema specification, Microsoft adds new functionality that is compliant only with the industry-standard XSD. Adopting XSD schemas in your own work will ensure the interoperability of your applications with those of others who subscribe to the XSD specification.
- Client-side formatting permits the XML formatting of SQL Server rowsets on the IIS server rather than the database server. This offers potential scalability advantages because multiple virtual directories from different IIS servers can point to the same database on a database server. In addition, client-side formatting removes processing from a database server that might have other processing requirements besides those for one or more IIS servers.
- Two new data access components enhance XML processing capabilities. First, the SQLXMLOLEDB provider facilitates multiple objectives, including client-side formatting and ActiveX Data Objects (ADO) access to Web Release 2 functionality. SQLXMLOLEDB isn't a data provider; you use it in combination with SQLOLEDB, the SQL Server ADO data provider. Second, SQLXML Managed Classes explicitly expose the Web Release 2 object model, SQLXML 2.0, to the .NET Framework. By using these managed classes, Visual Basic .NET developers can apply DiffGrams as an alternative to Updategrams for data manipulation tasks.
- Side-by-side installation allows Web Release 2 to run on the same machine with Web Release 1. When using Web Release 2 in this fashion, developers need to explicitly reference the version they need for their applications. For example, client-side processing is exclusively available from virtual directories compliant with Web Release 2. Similarly, the XML Bulk Loading capability is dependent on Web release. Each Web release has its own distinct DLL for implementing the XML Bulk Loading feature. You must register the one that your application requires.

Web Release Installation

Both Web Release 1 and Web Release 2 are fully supported releases for SQL Server 2000. These releases shouldn't be confused with service packs that fix problems. While a Web release can remedy a problem, its main goal is to add new functionality not present in an earlier release. In order to install Web Release 1 or 2, your computer must have installed SQL Server 2000 RTM (Version 8.00.194).

You can obtain the Web releases from *http://www.microsoft.com/sql/downloads/*. Click the link labeled XML For SQL Server Web Release 1 (WR1) for Web Release 1. Click the link labeled XML For SQL Server Web Release 2 (SQLXML 2.0) for Web Release 2. You will typically be downloading the releases to a computer equipped with an IIS server. Therefore, you should take the normal precautions to guard against acquiring a virus during your Internet connection time.

After you complete installing a Web release, your Programs menu is updated with an item for the release. Web Release 1 adds a new menu item labeled Microsoft SQL Server XML Tools, which includes a single item—XML For SQL Documentation. This item opens the Software Development Kit (SDK) for the package, which includes documentation on the features of the release.

Web Release 2 adds SQLXML 2.0 to the Programs menu. The SQLXML 2.0 menu contains three items: Configure IIS, SQL 2.0 Documentation, and SQLXML 2.0 Readme. Configure IIS offers a new wizard for configuring a virtual directory to interact with SQL Server (updated from the wizard in the initial release). The installation of Web Release 2 also offers a new SQLISAPI filter and SQLXML DLL files for the middle tier that replace the versions shipping with the initial release of SQL Server 2000. Creating a virtual directory with the Configure IIS menu item permits your applications to take advantage of the new features enabled by these components. You can also use the new wizard to upgrade virtual directories to take advantage of features introduced with Web Release 2. Installing the files for Web Release 2 doesn't cause the removal or overwriting of the files for Web Release 1. It is this feature that permits you to tap the features of either release side by side on the same computer.

XML Formats and Schemas

XML is a rich and deep technology that promises to advance computing in the first decade of the twenty-first century as much as or more than Visual Basic did in the last decade of the twentieth century. This section delivers an introduction to XML-formatted data that particularly targets current and potential applications of XML with SQL Server. Subsequent sections will highlight how to use

XML with SQL Server 2000; this section focuses on three XML topics that will equip you to understand the material in those later sections. First I start by describing the overall syntax for XML documents. Second I present the basics of XML schemas as a device for validating XML documents. Third I review XML annotated schemas as a means of creating a view for a SQL Server data source.

XML Documents

XML is especially well suited for representing structured documents, such as invoices and row sources in a database. There is an immense body of literature about XML. Aside from this section, one place to start familiarizing yourself with XML conventions for representing data is the World Wide Web Consortium (W3C) site at *http://www.w3c.org/XML*. This site contains links to many valuable XML resources, such as the W3C Recommendation for XML 1.0. In addition, there are many XML-based technologies, such as XML Schema, XPath, XSL, and XSLT. Links at the W3C main Web site can serve as a starting point for learning about these related technologies.

A typical XML document can represent data with a collection of tags and a starting declaration. These tags are similar in some ways to HTML tags, but they differ in important ways. XML tags denote data elements instead of how to format data. HTML assigns a precise meaning to tags. For example, the *<p>* tag means start a new paragraph. XML, on the other hand, doesn't assign a predetermined meaning to a tag. Indeed, the same tag can have a different meaning in different XML documents, and it is even possible for one tag to have different meanings in the same XML document. By using namespaces, developers can resolve potential conflicts when the same tag has two or more different meanings in the same document.

XML literature typically refers to the tags in a document as *elements*. An element can contain other elements, a data value, or both other elements and a data value. Elements can have parent, child, and sibling relationships with one another. When an element contains another one, the container element is the parent element and the contained element is the child element. For example, *<ShipperID>*, *<CompanyName>*, and *<Phone>* tags can be child tags of a parent tag *<Shippers>* in an XML document with data for the *Shippers* table. The tags between a particular instance of *<Shippers>* and *</Shippers>* can denote a row in the *Shippers* table. XML documents that contain multiple occurrences of at least one tag, such as *<Shippers>*, must have one tag set that contains all other tags, such as *<root>* and *</root>*. This outermost tag set can occur just once within an XML document.

An XML tag (or element) can have one or more attributes. The use of attributes is optional. Attributes appear within the tag for an element, such as *<Shippers>*. You designate attributes with name-value pairs. The name denotes the attribute's name, and the value depicts its data value. Data values can appear in either single or double quotation marks following an equal sign behind the attribute name. You can represent the data for a table with element values, attribute values, or both.

The following document depicts the *Shippers* table data from the Northwind database represented with elements and no attributes. Notice that the first set of angle brackets (<>) declares the document as an XML document in version 1 format. The utf-8 designation for encoding denotes a convention for converting characters to bit sequences inside a computer. Because the *<Shippers>* tag is repeated three times in the document, a parent tag set that appears just once is necessary; the *<root>* and *</root>* tags meet this requirement. The name *root* has no special meaning; any other legitimate name for a tag, such as ShippersRoot, can replace *root*. The *<Shippers>* tag is the parent of the *<ShipperID>*, *<CompanyName>*, and *<Phone>* tags. These latter three tags are siblings of one another.

```
<?xml version="1.0" encoding="utf-8"?>
<!--Available in Chapter 06 code samples as shippers_elements.xml-->
<root>
    <Shippers>
        <ShipperID>1</ShipperID>
        <CompanyName>Speedy Express</CompanyName>
        <Phone>(503) 555-9831</Phone>
    </Shippers>
    <Shippers>
        <ShipperID>2</ShipperID>
        <CompanyName>United Package</CompanyName>
        <Phone>(503) 555-3199</Phone>
    </Shippers>
    <Shippers>
        <ShipperID>3</ShipperID>
        <CompanyName>Federal Shipping</CompanyName>
        <Phone>(503) 555-9931</Phone>
    </Shippers>
</root>
```

The next XML document shows the same data from the *Shippers* table as the preceding one. In this instance, the document's formatting represents data values with attributes instead of elements or tags. The declaration for this XML document instance is the same as in the preceding sample. Attributes appear in a paired arrangement—first the attribute name followed by an equal sign, and second the attribute value in double quotation marks. The column values for each row in the *Shippers* table appear within a separate *<Shippers>* tag in the document. The trailing / character within each *<Shippers>* tag is an alternative to designating *</Shippers>* to close the *<Shippers>* tag.

```
<?xml version="1.0" encoding="utf-8" ?>
<!--shippers_attributes.xml-->
<root>
    <Shippers ShipperID="1" CompanyName="Speedy Express"
    Phone="(503) 555-9831" />
    <Shippers ShipperID="2" CompanyName="United Package"
    Phone="(503) 555-3199" />
    <Shippers ShipperID="3" CompanyName="Federal Shipping"
    Phone="(503) 555-9931" />
</root>
```

Figure 6-1 shows the *Shippers* table in the XML format for each of the preceding XML document files. The figure reveals how the XML appears within a browser. Notice that you can read the data! Many other data formats don't appear so readable in a browser. XML's character-based format for representing data is one of the advantages of XML over other formats for representing data. In the browser view of shippers_elements.xml, you can collapse the data for any individual row in the *Shippers* table by clicking the minus sign (–) next to the opening *<Shippers>* tag for a row. You can collapse the data for all three rows by clicking the minus sign next to the opening *<root>* tag for either document.

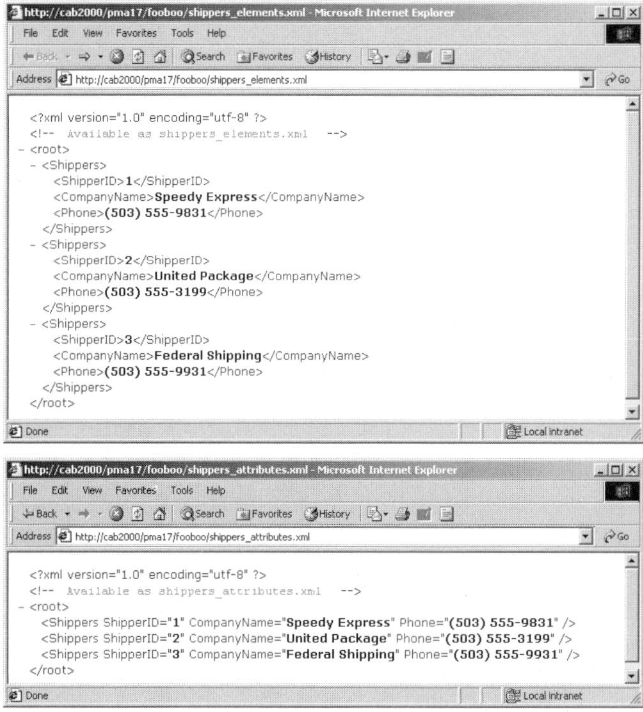

Figure 6-1. A pair of screen shots illustrating that users can readily examine the contents of an XML document in a browser.

XML Schemas

An XML schema provides a framework for describing the structure and validating the contents of an XML document. With an XML schema, you can know what values are legitimate for any tag or attribute instance. You can also use schemas to place constraints on the range of acceptable values for a data element. By specifying cardinality for elements with the *minOccurs* and *maxOccurs* element attributes, you can specify how many element instances are legitimate in an XML document. You can additionally designate whether an element has any attributes, and the relationships among elements.

The W3C approved on May 2, 2001, a recommendation (*http://www.w3.org/2001/XMLSchema*) that serves as the industry standard for expressing XML schemas. Developers refer to the W3C schema standard as an XSD schema. Starting with Web Release 2, SQL Server adopted this standard. Before Web Release 2, SQL Server worked with XDR schemas—a precursor of the XSD schema. This chapter uses exclusively XSD schemas.

The following script represents the shell for a schema. Notice that an XSD schema is an XML document because it starts with an XML declaration. This means that you can describe an XSD schema with the same syntax that you use for any XML document. In addition, notice the reference to the namespace at *http://www.w3.org/XMLSchema*. This namespace defines a set of tags and attributes for defining schemas as XML documents. The xsd designation for the namespace is arbitrary. (For example, you can use xs instead.) An XSD schema can have more than one namespace reference. Each namespace can reference a different set of tags and attributes. By using a distinct namespace designator for each namespace, you can resolve conflicts for identically named tags and attributes between two different namespaces. The shell refers to the tags and attributes with the xsd namespace designation. The schema tag or element, which marks the beginning and end of a schema, is from the namespace designated by xsd.

```
<?xml version="1.0" encoding="UTF-8"?>
<xsd:schema xmlns:xsd="http://www.w3.org/2001/XMLSchema">
...
</xsd:schema>
```

A basic understanding of several formatting conventions can help you get started writing your own schema (or at least equip you to read those written by others). Element declarations can be for a simple or a complex type. A complex type element has at least one child element or one attribute. You can explicitly define a child element within a parent element or refer to a child element defined elsewhere within a schema. A simple type element has neither a child element nor an attribute. In addition, the declaration for a simple type element classifies the data type for the element according to one of the built-in XSD data types. The XSD data types generally correspond to SQL Server data types. See the "Data Type Coercions and the sql:datatype Annotation" topic in the online documentation for Web Release 2 for a detailed discussion of the similarities and differences between SQL Server and XSD data types. In addition to elements, a schema can also specify attributes. According to the W3C convention, the attributes for a complex type element are designated following the specifications for or references to any child elements.

The following XML document is the XSD schema for the shippers_elements.xml document file presented in the preceding section. Following the schema tag with the namespace declaration, the schema declares a complex element type for the root tag. The root element is complex because it has child elements, namely, one or more *Shippers* elements. The exact upper limit for the number of *Shippers* elements within the root element is unbounded. (See the assignment for *maxOccurs*.) The *minOccurs* attribute for the choice specification doesn't appear in the schema, but its default value is 1. Therefore, to allow an XML document with no *Shippers* elements, designate the value 0 for *minOccurs*. Notice that the *Shippers* element doesn't appear nested within the root element declaration. Instead, the root element declaration uses the ref attribute to refer to the *Shippers* element.

The *Shippers* element declaration follows the root element declaration. The *Shippers* element has three child elements—*ShipperID*, *CompanyName*, and *Phone*. In the following schema, the declarations for the child elements appear nested within the *Shippers* element. Each child element has a data type derived from an XSD built-in data type, such as the *integer* or *string* data type. The *restriction* element in the child declarations denotes the data type for the child elements from the built-in data type. In the case of the *ShipperID* element, the declaration limits the element's values to integers. In the case of the *CompanyName* and *Phone* elements, the declarations limit the element values to strings. In addition, the maximum length is 40 and 24 for the *CompanyName* and *Phone* elements, respectively. By assigning *minOccurs* to 0, the schema permits the *Phone* element to be optional for each *Shippers* element. The *ShipperID* and *CompanyName* elements are required child elements for each *Shippers* element.

```
<?xml version="1.0" encoding="UTF-8"?>
<!--shippers_elements.xsd-->
<xsd:schema xmlns:xsd="http://www.w3.org/2001/XMLSchema">
    <xsd:element name="root">
        <xsd:complexType>
            <xsd:choice maxOccurs="unbounded">
                <xsd:element ref="Shippers"/>
            </xsd:choice>
```

```
        </xsd:complexType>
    </xsd:element>
    <xsd:element name="Shippers">
    <xsd:complexType>
    <xsd:sequence>
        <xsd:element name="ShipperID">
            <xsd:simpleType>
                <xsd:restriction base="xsd:integer"/>
            </xsd:simpleType>
        </xsd:element>
        <xsd:element name="CompanyName">
            <xsd:simpleType>
                <xsd:restriction base="xsd:string">
                    <xsd:maxLength value="40"/>
                </xsd:restriction>
            </xsd:simpleType>
        </xsd:element>
        <xsd:element name="Phone" minOccurs="0">
            <xsd:simpleType>
                <xsd:restriction base="xsd:string">
                    <xsd:maxLength value="24"/>
                </xsd:restriction>
            </xsd:simpleType>
        </xsd:element>
    </xsd:sequence>
    </xsd:complexType>
    </xsd:element>
</xsd:schema>
```

The schema for the shippers_attributes.xml document file appears next. The *Shippers* element in this schema has no child elements because of the layout of the shippers_attributes.xml document. Nevertheless, the *Shippers* element still requires a complex type element declaration because the *Shippers* element has three attributes. Notice that you can use the same *simpleType* elements for declaring attributes that you use for declaring elements in an XML document. In spite of using the same *simpleType* elements as the preceding schema, this schema differs from the preceding one by declaring *ShipperID*, *CompanyName*, and *Phone* as attributes instead of elements.

```
<?xml version="1.0" encoding="UTF-8"?>
<!--shippers_attributes.xsd-->
<xsd:schema xmlns:xsd="http://www.w3.org/2001/XMLSchema">
    <xsd:element name="root">
        <xsd:complexType>
            <xsd:choice maxOccurs="unbounded">
                <xsd:element ref="Shippers"/>
            </xsd:choice>
        </xsd:complexType>
```

(continued)

```
    </xsd:element>
    <xsd:element name="Shippers">
    <xsd:complexType>
        <xsd:attribute name="ShipperID">
            <xsd:simpleType>
                <xsd:restriction base="xsd:integer"/>
            </xsd:simpleType>
        </xsd:attribute>
        <xsd:attribute name="CompanyName">
            <xsd:simpleType>
                <xsd:restriction base="xsd:string">
                    <xsd:maxLength value="40"/>
                </xsd:restriction>
            </xsd:simpleType>
        </xsd:attribute>
        <xsd:attribute name="Phone" type="string">
            <xsd:simpleType>
                <xsd:restriction base="xsd:string">
                    <xsd:maxLength value="24"/>
                </xsd:restriction>
            </xsd:simpleType>
        </xsd:attribute>
    </xsd:complexType>
    </xsd:element>
</xsd:schema>
```

Annotated Schemas

Up until this point, I used schemas to specify the contents of XML documents. However, most of you reading this book probably care more about the data in your SQL Server database than in an XML document. XML documents are a convenient way of showing and sharing data over the Web. Instead of schemas merely defining XML documents, you would probably prefer that XML documents point to SQL Server databases and expose database contents. This role allows schemas to provide Web-based views for SQL Server database contents.

Annotated schemas when used with a virtual directory on an IIS server allow you to derive a view of the data in a SQL Server database. An annotated schema contains special elements and attributes that specify how to link it to a SQL Server database. The XML document that exposes the view can appear in a Web browser. The contents of the XML document will conform to the schema design and any parameters passed directly from the browser (or an intermediate XML document). A browser can both initiate the request for the XML view and display the view as an XML document. In addition, a browser can launch the process by pointing to an XML document in a virtual directory on an IIS server that invokes a schema linking to a row source. SQL Server has a special tool for creating virtual directories on IIS servers that point to specific SQL Server databases. These virtual directories permit annotated schemas to connect to a SQL Server database and derive a rowset.

> **Note** One of the innovations of Web Release 2 is that the formatting of the returned rowset can take place on the IIS server instead of SQL Server. By transferring the formatting of the returned rowset from the database server to the IIS server, Microsoft can eventually provide views based on annotated schemas for other than SQL Server databases.

This section introduces the basics of annotated schema design and use. A later section, "Virtual Directory Management," drills down on virtual directories. An annotated schema is an XML document just like a normal XSD schema. However, you normally write it without the XML version declaration. In addition, you must add a new namespace reference (*schemas-microsoft-com:mapping-schema*) to the schema shell to accommodate special annotation elements and attributes. This Microsoft mapping namespace supports the special features that permit annotation of XSD schema so they link to one or more row sources in a SQL Server database. The sql designator for the namespace is arbitrary; you can use any other legitimate XML name.

```
<xsd:schema xmlns:xsd="http://www.w3.org/2001/XMLSchema"
            xmlns:sql="urn:schemas-microsoft-com:mapping-schema">
...
</xsd:schema>
```

Two attributes for linking a schema to a row source in a database include the *relation* attribute and the *field* attribute. Precede these attribute names and any other that you use for annotating your schema with the designator for the Microsoft mapping namespace. The *relation* attribute creates a link between a complex element and a SQL Server row source. Using the *relation* attribute lets you create an alias in your annotated schema for the row source name in a SQL Server database. The schema will attempt to match the child elements and attributes for the complex element to the columns from the row source. If the attributes and child elements have names that match column names in the row source, you don't need to specify a *field* attribute for the attribute or element. If the attribute or child element name doesn't match the name for a column in the row source, you can specify the *field* attribute. With the *field* attribute, you can explicitly link an element or attribute to a column in the row source specified by a *relation* attribute.

> **Note** If a complex element name in a schema matches a row source name in a database, you don't need to designate the correspondence between the two with the *relation* attribute.

The following annotated schema demonstrates the use of the *relation* and *field* attributes. The schema formats an XML document with a complex element type named *xmlShippers* that has two child elements, *xmlCompanyName* and *xmlPhone*, and an attribute, *ShipperID*. Notice that the *relation* and *field* attributes appear with a sql prefix to specify the namespace for defining the attributes. The *sql:relation* attribute points the *xmlShippers* element to the *Shippers* row source. The *sql:field* attributes for the *xmlCompanyName* and *xmlPhone* elements link these elements to the *CompanyName* and *Phone* columns in the *Shippers* row source. Because the *ShipperID* attribute name matches a column in the *Shippers* row source, it doesn't require a *sql:field* attribute setting to link it to a column within the row source.

```
<xsd:schema xmlns:xsd="http://www.w3.org/2001/XMLSchema"
            xmlns:sql="urn:schemas-microsoft-com:mapping-schema">
<!--xmlShippersSchema.xml-->
  <xsd:element name="xmlShippers" sql:relation="Shippers" >
   <xsd:complexType>
     <xsd:sequence>
        <xsd:element name="xmlCompanyName"
                     sql:field="CompanyName"
                     type="xsd:string" />
        <xsd:element name="xmlPhone"
                     sql:field="Phone"
                     type="xsd:string" />
     </xsd:sequence>
     <xsd:attribute name="ShipperID" type="xsd:integer" />
    </xsd:complexType>
  </xsd:element>
</xsd:schema>
```

With three more steps, you can return an XML document based on the *Shippers* row source.

1. Save the annotated schema in a virtual directory configured to connect to the Northwind database. Because the Northwind table contains a table named *Shippers*, this defines the row source in the annotated schema.
2. Create a new XML document, called a template, that invokes the annotated schema. By invoking the query with XPath syntax, the template file can cause the annotated schema to return a view of the *Shippers* table as an XML document.
3. Navigate to the template from a browser to return the view specified by the template to the browser's document window.

The following XML document illustrates the syntax for referring to the preceding annotated schema in xmlShippersSchema.xml. The specification requires the schema to reside in a special template folder within the virtual directory, but you can explicitly designate another source for the annotated schema file. The actual query syntax simply references the element with the *sql:relation* attribute setting, namely xmlShippers. This form of an XPath query requests the return of all the rows from the *Shippers* table. The XPath query is equivalent to `SELECT * FROM Shippers` in T-SQL.

```
<ROOT xmlns:sql="urn:schemas-microsoft-com:xml-sql">
<!--xmlShippersSchemaT.xml-->
  <sql:xpath-query mapping-schema="xmlShippersSchema.xml">
    /xmlShippers
  </sql:xpath-query>
</ROOT>
```

The top screen shot in Figure 6-2 shows the *Shippers* table in XML format based on the annotated schema in xmlShippersSchema.xml and the template file (xmlShippersSchemaT.xml) that queries the schema. The browser's Address box shows the path to the template file that contains the XPath query. The template resides on an IIS server named ccs1. The template is in the template folder of the MyNwind virtual directory. The use of the name *template* for the template folder is arbitrary. Any other name will serve equally well. The XML document in the browser window follows the format of the annotated schema. Notice that *ShipperID* appears as an attribute, but *xmlCompanyName* and *xmlPhone* appear as elements. Whereas the data values are from the *Shippers* table in the Northwind database, the element and attribute names are from the annotated schema.

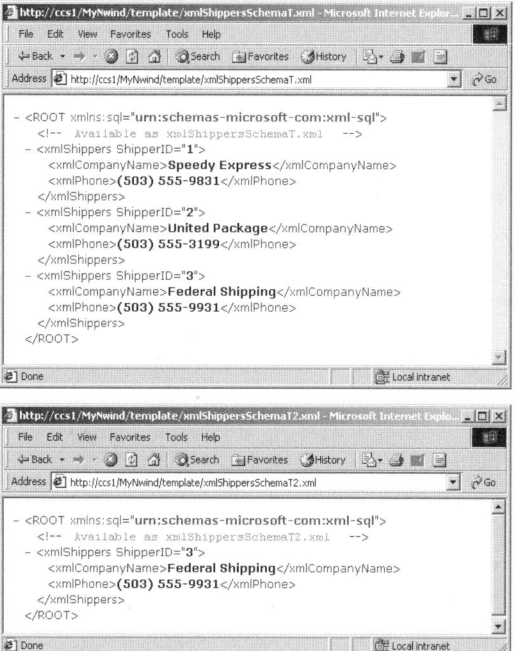

Figure 6-2. A pair of screen shots illustrating different result sets from the same annotated schema based on two templates with different XPath queries.

The lower screen shot in Figure 6-2 shows the result of an XPath query that asks for the return of just the row with *ShipperID* equal to 3. The syntax for the template with the query appears below. The parameter for *ShipperID* has a leading @. Notice that the Address box points to the file with the following template. By contrasting the following template with the preceding one, you can see how to reuse an annotated schema to derive different result sets. In a sense, the annotated schema serves as a parameterized view!

```
<ROOT xmlns:sql="urn:schemas-microsoft-com:xml-sql">
<!--xmlShippersSchemaT2.xml-->
  <sql:xpath-query mapping-schema="xmlShippersSchema.xml">
    /xmlShippers[@ShipperID=3]
  </sql:xpath-query>
</ROOT>
```

Recall that annotated schemas simulate views in SQL Server databases. Because views often join tables, the next annotated schema merges the *Orders* table with the *Shippers* table to make available the orders by *ShipperID*. The schema has to specify the join between the tables in the original SQL Server data source. The schema specifies the join with a *relationship* element (not to be confused with a *relation* element). The *relationship* element has five attributes.

- The *name* attribute assigns a name to the relationship for subsequent reference in the schema.
- The *parent* attribute denotes the parent row source, or *one* side, of the one-to-many relationship between *Shippers* and *Orders*. (Each shipper can have many orders.)
- The *parent-key* attribute denotes the field in the parent row source for linking the parent and child row sources.
- The *child* and *child-key* attributes point to the *many* side of the one-to-many relationship. The *Shipvia* field in the *Orders* table is a foreign key pointing to the *ShipperID* field in the *Shippers* table.

The *relationship* element is nested within the *appinfo* element, which in turn is nested in the *annotation* element.

After specifying the relationship in the SQL Server data source, the annotated schema focuses on specifying the layout of the XML document and linking that layout to the two source tables and the relationship between them. The schema defines a custom complex element named *ShipperType*. This custom type starts with a declaration for the *Order* complex type element. The *Order* complex element is based on the *Orders* table and the *ShipperOrders* relationship defined at the top of the schema. The *Order* element has two attributes, *OrderID* and *ShipVia*, that relate to *Orders* table columns with the same names. In addition to these attributes based on the *Orders* table, the *ShipperType* element has a parent with two additional attributes, *ShipperID* and *CompanyName*. As with the *Order* attributes, there is no need for the *sql:field* attribute to link these to columns in the *Shippers* table because the attribute names match the column names.

```
<xsd:schema xmlns:xsd="http://www.w3.org/2001/XMLSchema"
            xmlns:sql="urn:schemas-microsoft-com:mapping-schema">
<!--xmlShipperOrdersSchema.xml-->
<xsd:annotation>
    <xsd:appinfo>
    <sql:relationship name="ShipperOrders"
        parent="Shippers"
        parent-key="ShipperID"
        child="Orders"
        child-key="ShipVia" />
    </xsd:appinfo>
</xsd:annotation>
```

(continued)

```
<xsd:element name="Shipper" sql:relation="Shippers" type="ShipperType" />
    <xsd:complexType name="ShipperType" >
       <xsd:sequence>
        <xsd:element name="Order"
                   sql:relation="Orders"
                   sql:relationship="ShipperOrders" >
           <xsd:complexType>
              <xsd:attribute name="OrderID" type="xsd:integer" />
              <xsd:attribute name="ShipVia" type="xsd:integer" />
           </xsd:complexType>
        </xsd:element>
     </xsd:sequence>
        <xsd:attribute name="ShipperID"   type="xsd:string" />
        <xsd:attribute name="CompanyName"  type="xsd:string" />
    </xsd:complexType>

</xsd:schema>
```

The next XML document shows the template for referencing the preceding annotated schema in an XPath query. The query calls for the return of all rows from the joining of the *Shippers* table with the *Orders* table. An excerpt from the result set appears in Figure 6-3. The browser document window shows the transition from the last few rows for *ShipperID* 1 to the first few rows for *ShipperID* 2.

```
<ROOT xmlns:sql="urn:schemas-microsoft-com:xml-sql">
<!--xmlShipperOrdersSchemaT.xml-->
  <sql:xpath-query mapping-schema="xmlShipperOrdersSchema.xml">
    /Shipper
  </sql:xpath-query>
</ROOT>
```

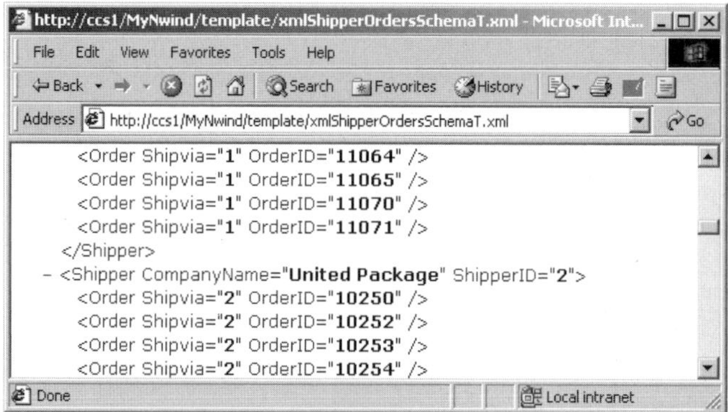

Figure 6-3. An excerpt from a result set based on the joining of the *Shippers* table with the *Orders* table.

URL Access to SQL Server

The preceding discussion of annotated schemas demonstrated URL access to a SQL Server database. You learned that by referencing an XPath query for an annotated schema in an XML file, a browser can return data based on its URL, the XPath query, and the annotated schema. In this section, I lay the foundation for a more comprehensive understanding of URL access for SQL Server databases. This section begins with a brief review of virtual directory management issues. The primary focus is how to set up a new virtual directory with the IIS Virtual Directory Management For SQLXML 2.0 utility in Web Release 2. You will also learn about why and when to upgrade a virtual directory created with the initial version of the utility for configuring IIS virtual directories to work with SQL Server. Next I demonstrate how to use the *FOR XML* clause for SQL Server *SELECT* statements in a browser's Address box. After an introduction to the *FOR XML* clause, I drill down on how to apply it with a collection of samples that highlight issues pertaining to its use and reveal workarounds for URL access problems with respect to SQL Server data sources. This closing material complements and extends the previous discussion of annotated schemas. Many database developers and administrators are likely to find the T-SQL approach illustrated in this section more familiar than the XPath queries of the preceding section.

Virtual Directory Management

Before users can gain URL access to a SQL Server database, an administrator must configure an IIS virtual directory that points to the database. This directory must reside on a computer running IIS server. This can be the same or a different computer from the one running SQL Server. You can have virtual directories on multiple IIS servers connecting to a single SQL Server database. Users gain URL access to the database through the virtual directory on a server that points to a SQL Server database.

The IIS Virtual Directory Management For SQLXML 2.0 utility lets you create and manage a virtual directory. This tool changed with the introduction of Web Release 2. This is because Web Release 2 is the first release to support client-side formatting of XML documents. Recall from earlier discussions of this topic that client-side XML formatting enhances scalability and reduces the load on a database server. As a result of the enhancement to the utility for Web Release 2, you cannot gain the benefits of client-side formatting without upgrading an old virtual directory or creating a new one with Web Release 2.

Launch the IIS Virtual Directory Management For SQLXML 2.0 utility by opening the Windows Start menu and choosing Programs, then SQLXML 2.0, and then Configure IIS Support. Select Default Web Site under the local IIS server. This exposes any previously created virtual directories in the right-hand pane of the management console for the utility. Double-click any existing directory to open a multitabbed Properties dialog box for that directory. From this dialog box, you can update the settings for the directory—just select the Version 2 tab and click Upgrade To Version 2. Right-click Default Web Site, choose New, and then choose Virtual Directory to start creating a new virtual directory. This opens the New Virtual Directory Properties dialog box, which has generally the same tabs as those for an existing virtual directory. You specify the new virtual directory by making selections on the dialog box's tabs and clicking OK.

Before starting to create a new virtual directory, pick an existing physical directory (a folder) or create a new one with Windows Explorer. The physical directory will be associated with the virtual directory you're creating. It is common to locate folders for a virtual directory in the wwwroot directory of the Inetpub folder. For instance, you can create a folder there named nwind. You will typically want to create two additional folders below the main folder for a virtual directory—one subfolder for storing templates and another for storing annotated schemas. The template folder is particularly flexible. Recall from the discussion of annotated schemas that you can store and use annotated schemas in the template folder.

> **Note** For more information about creating a virtual directory, see the "Creating the nwind Virtual Directory" topic in the SQLXML 2.0 documentation.

After creating folders for your virtual directory, open a New Virtual Directory Properties dialog box as just described. Next complete the information on the dialog box's tabs.

- On the General tab, enter a name for your virtual directory, such as MyNwind. Then use the Browse button to navigate to the root folder for your virtual directory.
- Next navigate to the Security tab. In the Credentials group, designate a login through which those browsing the virtual directory will log on to the database. For example, you can specify IUSR_CCS1 to designate anonymous Web users on a database server named CCS1. Make sure that you have a Windows account named IUSR_CCS1 as well as SQL Server login with user accounts in databases to which you want the IUSR_CCS1 user to have access. Give the user

accounts in a database whatever permissions your application requires. See Chapter 7 for a more comprehensive discussion of SQL Server security.

- On the Data Source tab, enter or select a SQL Server name and a database name on the server. These settings determine the database to which the virtual directory points.
- The Settings tab offers controls for determining how browsers can specify queries through the URL they show in the Address box. For example, you can enable and disable SQL queries, such as those demonstrated later in this section, directly from the Address box. You can also use this tab to specify XML formatting of a rowset returned by a query on the IIS client instead of the database server.
- With the Virtual Names tab, you can designate names and paths for the schema and template type folders. You can also create a virtual name as a dbobject type that facilitates users making direct references in a URL to database objects, such as a table or view.
- Use the Advanced tab to fine-tune performance and memory usage. When you complete all the specifications for a new virtual directory, click OK to create it.

Overview of *FOR XML* in *SELECT* Statements

SQL Server 2000 introduced a new clause for its *SELECT* statement that returns a rowset formatted as XML data. The clause causes the *SELECT* statement to return a text stream object formatted as XML instead of as a rowset. The rowset and the text stream contain the same information, but the *FOR XML* clause formats the information as an XML document. Using the *FOR XML* clause in combination with a virtual directory pointing to a SQL Server database permits your applications to return data from a SQL Server database via HTTP.

The *FOR XML* clause goes at the end of a *SELECT* statement for retrieving data. The clause requires one of four arguments. These arguments determine how to format the retrieved data as XML. In addition, three optional *FOR XML* arguments can further fine-tune the format for XML data from a *SELECT* statement. The operation of this clause depends in part on a virtual directory's setting for client-side formatting. As mentioned, the *FOR XML* clause appears at the end of a *SELECT* statement. Its general design is:

```
SELECT … FOR XML mode [, optional arguments]
```

The syntax requires a mode argument. This argument can take any of four values. (See Table 6-1.) The *RAW* mode argument provides the most basic XML representation of a row source. For example, this argument returns XML data with the same row identifier for all row sources, and a parent-child row source appears in a single collection of rows instead of in a nested format with the child data nested below the parent data to which it belongs. The *AUTO* mode argument provides more flexibility in the return and easier formatting for returning binary data. The *EXPLICIT* mode is a special mode for detailing the precise layout of an XML document from a *SELECT* statement. In return for the control over the layout, you must specially format the design of your *SELECT* statement. See the "Using *EXPLICIT* Mode" topic in Books Online for SQL Server 2000 for numerous samples illustrating this nonstandard approach to formatting XML documents.

The *NESTED* mode is a special mode that taps the features of client-side formatting. This is the only mode that supports the *GROUP BY* clause in a *SELECT* statement. For this mode to work, a virtual directory must enable client-side formatting. The check box for this feature is Run On The Client on the Settings tab of the Properties dialog box for a virtual directory. You can get to this dialog box from the IIS Virtual Directory Management For SQLXML 2.0 utility as described in the "Virtual Directory Management" section. The mode is available only for virtual directories created (or upgraded to become compatible) with Web Release 2.

Table 6-1 Mode Arguments in the *FOR XML* Clause

Name	Description
RAW	Formats rowset to XML with a generic row identifier. Non-null columns in a *SELECT* statement's rowset map to attributes within a row. Represents joined parent-child row sources in a flat format.
AUTO	Formats rowset to XML with a specific row source identifier based on the *SELECT* statement's *FROM* clause. Represents joined parent-child row sources in a hierarchical format.
NESTED	Formats similarly to *AUTO*, but it explicitly invokes client-side processing. Requires virtual directory to enable client-side formatting feature for valid operation. Enables *GROUP BY* clause and aggregate functions.
EXPLICIT	Allows explicit formatting of XML data, but it requires special *SELECT* statement syntax to accommodate the layout formatting flexibility.

The *FOR XML* clause optional arguments include *ELEMENTS*, *XMLDATA*, and *BINARY BASE64*. You can concurrently use more than one optional argument with the *FOR XML* clause for a *SELECT* statement. Delimit these arguments with commas from the mode argument and one another. The *FOR XML* clause returns column values from a *SELECT* statement as attributes by default. Specifying the *ELEMENTS* argument returns column values as elements instead of attributes. Referencing the *XMLDATA* argument in a *SELECT* statement inserts a schema for the XML formatted data at the beginning of the argument. This schema is in XDR (as opposed to XSD) format no matter what release you use. The *BINARY BASE64* argument facilitates the return of binary data when you're using either the *RAW* or *EXPLICIT* mode argument. Failing to use the *BINARY BASE64* argument for either of these modes when a result set has binary data generates an error.

RAW vs. *AUTO* Mode Samples

When using the *FOR XML* clause in the Address box of a browser, you will typically need to designate several items. Start with http://. Then follow this with the path to the server and virtual directory you are using. Next enter a question mark. This allows you to specify a parameter name and its value. Use sql as the parameter name followed by an equal sign (=). Then type a *SELECT* statement that terminates with a *FOR XML* clause, such as `SELECT * FROM Shippers FOR XML RAW`. There is no need to replace blank spaces with special characters, such as %20, because the Internet Explorer browser automatically inserts replacement characters for blank spaces. When the XML document for a *SELECT* statement returns more than a single row, you must specify a root element for the XML document to display the result set. You can do this by typing **&** and **root=root**. You can set the term *root* equal to any legitimate XML name, such as a or a1, but not 1a, which is an illegitimate name because it starts with a number.

Figure 6-4 shows in its top screen shot a sample *SELECT* statement to return all rows from the *Shippers* table in *RAW* mode:

```
http://ccs1/MyNwind?sql=SELECT * FROM Shippers FOR XML RAW&root=root
```

The browser submits the *SELECT* statement to the MyNwind virtual directory on the IIS server named ccs1. For this query statement to work, the MyNwind virtual directory must point to a SQL Server database with a *Shippers* row source, such as the *Shippers* table in the Northwind database. You can also use a view as the row source. Notice that the top screen shot includes an XML document in the browser window based on the *SELECT* statement in the Address box. All rows in the document have the same element—row. Column values appear as attributes after the row element. The attribute name matches the column name.

The bottom screen shot shows exactly the same *SELECT* statement except that the *FOR XML* mode argument is *AUTO* instead of *RAW*. The sole difference in the outcome for switching to *AUTO* is that the row element name changed from *row* to *Shippers*. When returning results, the *AUTO* argument always uses the table name, or its alias, as row identifiers.

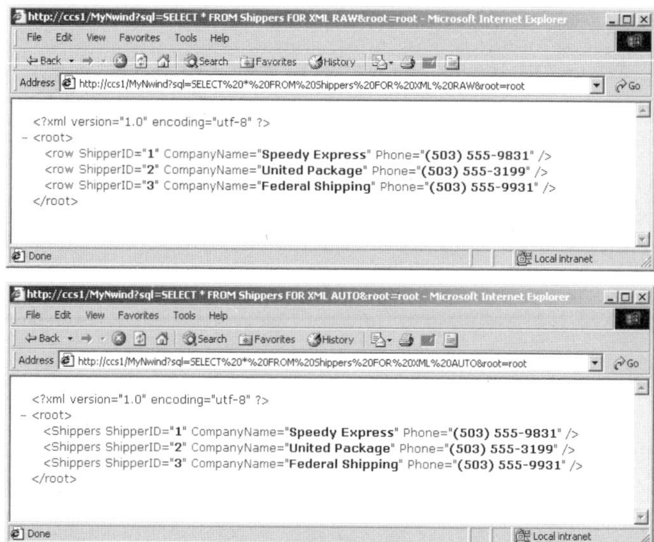

Figure 6-4. A pair of *SELECT* statements in browsers contrasting the impact of the *RAW* and *AUTO* mode arguments for a result set from a single table.

Using a *SELECT* statement that joins parent and child tables demonstrates another distinction between the *RAW* and *AUTO* mode arguments. Consider the following *SELECT* statement. It joins the *Orders* table to the *Shippers* table by *ShipperID* number, which has the name ShipVia in the *Orders* table. The *ORDER BY* clause arranges the rowset so that rows are sorted by *OrderID* within *ShipperID* instead of by *OrderID* without regard to *ShipperID*. *OrderID* is the default order for the result set. The *Orders* table rows relate hierarchically to the rows in the *Shippers* table because each shipper is responsible for transporting a mutually exclusive set of orders. Traditional relational database result sets appear as flat tables. However, XML can properly represent the hierarchical nature of the result set from the following *SELECT* statement. To display the return set hierarchically, use *AUTO* instead of *RAW* as the mode argument.

```
SELECT ShipperID, CompanyName,  ShipVia, OrderID, OrderDate
FROM Shippers JOIN Orders ON (Shippers.ShipperID=Orders.ShipVia)
ORDER BY ShipperID
```

Figure 6-5 shows an excerpt from the XML formatted result set for the preceding *SELECT* statement with both the *RAW* and *AUTO* mode arguments. The *RAW* mode argument outcome appears in the top pane. The document window for the browser in the top pane shows the last two rows for *ShipperID* 1 and the first two rows for *ShipperID* 2. The bottom pane shows the same results formatted based on *AUTO* mode. Notice that the first two *Order* rows for *ShipperID* 2 appear nested within a *Shippers* row. All the *Order* rows appear nested within whichever shipper transported them. This hierarchical display of the data is more meaningful than the flat table format in the top screen shot. However, in either case, you enjoy the benefit of capturing data directly from a SQL Server database over the Web.

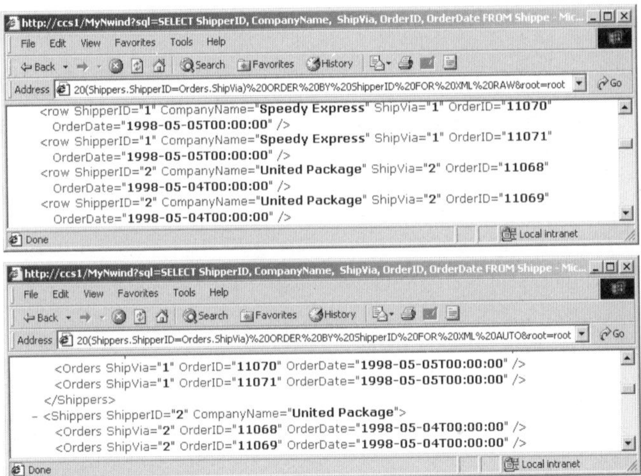

Figure 6-5. The top pane shows the format for a parent-child result set with *RAW* mode. The bottom pane shows the same result set formatted based on *AUTO* mode—notice it is hierarchical!

The default format for returning XML data is attribute-centric. That is, data values appear as attribute values. However, an element-centric format is popular with many developers. Using the *ELEMENTS* optional argument permits you to return values from a *SELECT* statement in an element-centric format. To specify the *ELEMENTS* option, you must use either *AUTO* or *NESTED* as the mode argument in the *FOR XML* clause. Notice that a comma delimits the *ELEMENTS* option from the *AUTO* mode designation:

```
http://ccs1/MyNwind?sql=SELECT * from Shippers →
for XML AUTO, ELEMENTS&root=root
```

Figure 6-6 demonstrates the use of this syntax for invoking the *ELEMENTS* option. To appreciate the impact of the *ELEMENTS* option, you can contrast the XML document in Figure 6-6 with the one in the bottom pane of Figure 6-4. The *SELECT* statement is identical in both cases except for the *ELEMENTS* clause.

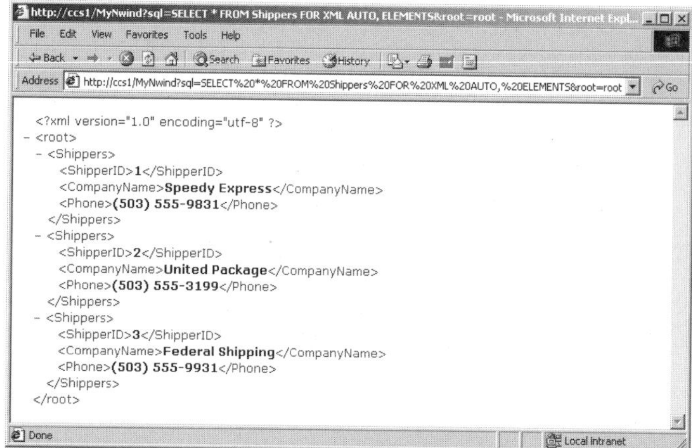

Figure 6-6. Format XML documents so they are element-centric, instead of the default attribute-centric layout, by specifying the optional *ELEMENTS* argument.

The samples in this chapter up to this point deal with result sets populated with characters. However, you sometimes have to deal with binary data. For example, the Northwind data populates two tables with binary data representing images. One of these is the *Categories* table that contains binary data for its *Picture* column values. The binary data in the *Picture* column represents images of the products in a category. When using *RAW* mode to return the columns of the *Categories* table, you must specify the *BINARY BASE64* optional argument in the *FOR XML* clause. The following URL shows the syntax for the Address box in the browser. The top screen shot in Figure 6-7 shows an excerpt from the XML document that the browser displays. Notice that the XML document shows an encoded representation of the image. Failing to specify the optional *BINARY BASE64* argument generates an error message in the browser window instead of an XML document.

```
http://ccs1/MyNwind?sql=SELECT * FROM Categories ¬
FOR XML RAW, BINARY BASE64&root=root
```

Specifying the *AUTO* mode passes back a path to the *Picture* column values in the XML document. (See the following URL and the middle screen shot in Figure 6-7.) You can open the *Picture* column value for any row in the browser as an image by appending the path to the Web server with the virtual directory pointing to the target database. The bottom screen shot in Figure 6-7 shows the XPath query statement comprising the Web server, the virtual directory name, and the first column value for *Picture* in the middle row. Notice that the bottom screen shot displays the picture for the binary object in the browser! To run the query in the bottom browser, your virtual directory must be able to run XPath queries, and you must have defined a dbobject virtual name. You can control these features with the IIS Virtual Directory Management For SQL Server utility.

```
http://ccs1/MyNwind?sql=SELECT * FROM Categories ➥
FOR XML auto &root=root
```

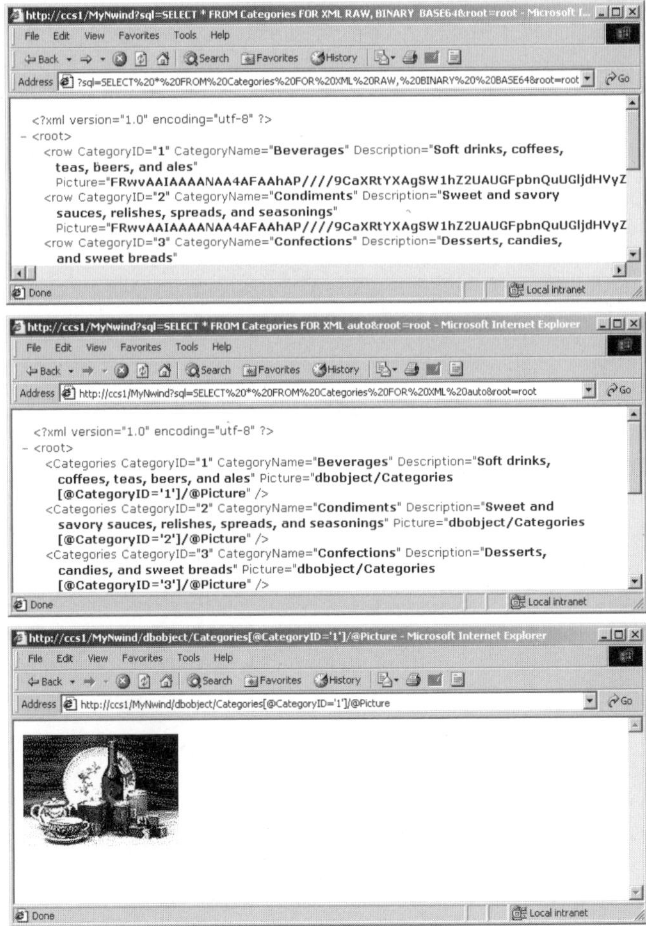

Figure 6-7. Working with binary image files can be straightforward when you use *AUTO* mode for the *FOR XML* clause and the XPath queries, but even *RAW* mode can return an encoded representation of an image to an XML document.

AUTO vs. *NESTED* Mode Samples

All the URL access samples to this point in the chapter worked with tables, but views can serve as the row source for a *SELECT* statement with a *FOR XML* clause as well. However, the resulting XML document varies slightly depending on whether you use *AUTO* or *NESTED* as the mode argument. With *AUTO* as the mode argument, the row identifier in the XML document is the name of the view. When you use *NESTED* as the mode for a *SELECT* statement based on a view, the row identifier in the XML document is the base table's name rather than the view's name.

Use Query Analyzer to create the *ShipperView* database object in the Northwind database. This view can serve as a row source for a *SELECT* statement. Notice that the view merely creates a set of aliases for the columns in the *Shippers* table.

```
--CreateShipperView.sql
USE Northwind
GO
CREATE VIEW ShipperView AS
SELECT ShipperID as SID, CompanyName as CName, Phone as PNo
FROM Shippers
GO
```

Executing a *SELECT* statement from the browser's Address box that selects all the columns from the *ShipperView* object formats an XML document showing the column aliases as attribute names. This outcome is true whether you use *AUTO* or *NESTED* as the mode argument for the *FOR XML* clause in the *SELECT* statement. However, with *AUTO* as the mode argument, the identifier element for each row in the document is the view's name, *ShipperView*. (See the top screen shot in Figure 6-8.) This outcome holds whether you enable client-side formatting for XML documents in the virtual directory or not. If your *SELECT* statement uses *NESTED* for its mode argument and you enabled client-side formatting for XML documents in the virtual directory, the row identifier refers to the base table for the view—namely, *Shippers* in the case of the view named *ShipperView*. (See the bottom screen shot in Figure 6-8.) If you run a *SELECT* statement with *NESTED* for the mode and the virtual directory doesn't enable client-side formatting, an error results.

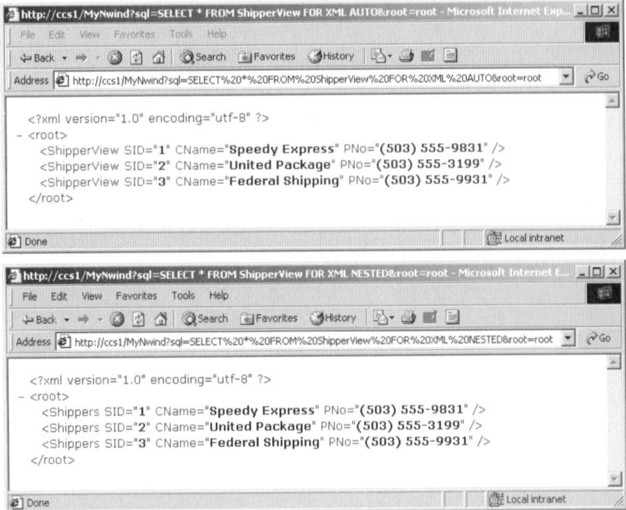

Figure 6-8. Using *NESTED* as the mode argument shows the base table for a view rather than the view's name.

Some developers might consider not showing a view's name a minor weakness for client-side processing. However, a major strength of client-side processing is its ability to use the *GROUP BY* clause and aggregate functions in *SELECT* statements that use *NESTED* as the mode in the *FOR XML* clause. Other mode arguments don't support the use of the *GROUP BY* clause. Because this clause is so common in *SELECT* statements, being able to specify the *GROUP BY* clause is a major advantage of client-side formatting for XML documents. Even if your virtual directory enables client-side formatting, you don't gain the ability to use the *GROUP BY* clause unless your *SELECT* statement explicitly designates *NESTED* as the mode argument in the *FOR XML* clause.

The *SELECT* statement in the following URL invokes the *GROUP BY* clause for *OrderID* in the *Invoices* view to compute total *ExtendedPrice* for each order. A *CAST* function formats total *ExtendedPrice* per order with two places after the decimal point. Figure 6-9 shows an excerpt from the XML document that the *SELECT* statement generates.

```
http://ccs1/MyNwind?sql=SELECT OrderID, ¬
CAST(SUM(ExtendedPrice) AS DEC(8,2)) AS [OrderTotal] ¬
FROM Invoices GROUP BY OrderID FOR XML NESTED&root=root
```

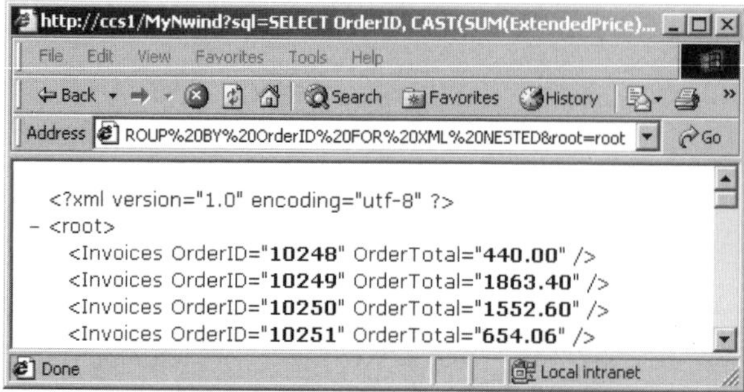

Figure 6-9. This excerpt from an XML document results from a *SELECT* statement that specifies the *NESTED* mode in the *FOR XML* clause so that the statement can specify a *GROUP BY* clause to sum *ExtendedPrice* column values by order.

> **Note** In the URL at the bottom of the previous page, notice that the alias for the total of *ExtendedPrice* per order is *OrderTotal*. Although this alias appears in brackets, they aren't strictly necessary. I could have used a *SELECT* statement with an alias of *[Order Total]* for total *ExtendedPrice*. However, because spaces are illegal in XML names, the parser would automatically convert the name when assigning it to an attribute for the aggregate column value. It is to avoid this renaming process that I reverted to a name without spaces. A slogan that I use in my seminars is "Real programmers do not use spaces."

Some applications group multiple *SELECT* statements in a single connection to a database server. This strategy returns multiple results without incurring the cost of a new connection for each result set. If your applications can benefit from this capability, avoid using *NESTED* as the mode setting for the *FOR XML* clause in your *SELECT* statements. The following code sample shows a URL with two *SELECT* statements. Notice that a semicolon delimits the two *SELECT* statements. Each *SELECT* statement designates *AUTO* as the mode argument for its *FOR XML* clause. This statement succeeds even if the virtual directory enables client-side formatting. (See Figure 6-10.) However, updating either of the *AUTO* keywords with *NESTED* generates an error.

```
http://ccs1/MyNwind?sql=SELECT * FROM Shippers →
WHERE ShipperID=1 FOR XML AUTO;SELECT OrderID, OrderDate →
FROM Orders WHERE ShipVia=1 FOR XML AUTO&root=root
```

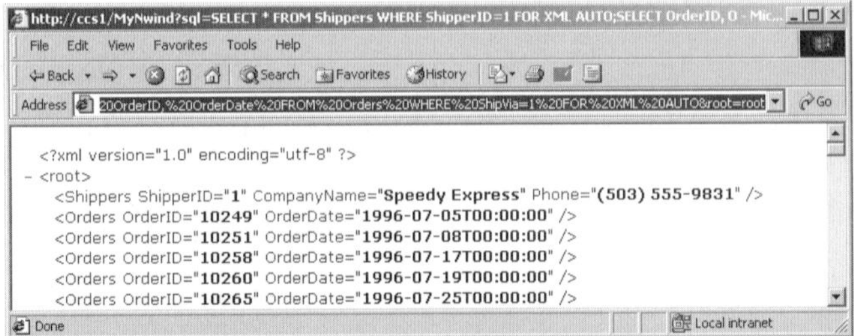

Figure 6-10. An XML document based on two distinct *SELECT* statements.

Template Access to SQL Server

Templates are XML files that reside in the template folder of a virtual directory pointing to a SQL Server database. Developers can create solutions that retrieve and manipulate the data in a database with the XML files in a template folder. By wrapping up the code to perform data retrieval and manipulation operations in an XML file, you can protect and secure your application's code and the database it references. Template-based solutions are as easy to run as entering a URL in a browser or navigating to a URL from a control on a form. The URL points to the XML file in the template folder. You can make your solutions dynamic at run time by passing parameters in the URL. To invoke template-based solutions for a database, the virtual directory pointing to the database must have a template folder. You can create a template folder reference when you initially create a virtual directory, or you can add a template folder or update the name and location of a template folder for an existing virtual directory.

XML files in a template folder can contain several types of contents to retrieve and manipulate the data in a database. In the "Annotated Schemas" section earlier in this chapter, you learned how to use XML files in a template folder containing annotated XSD schemas that are queried with the XPath language to retrieve the contents of a SQL Server data source. This section shows how to use XML files with T-SQL statements; SQL Server database objects, such as user-defined functions; and Updategrams. Updategrams are a special type of XML file for inserting, updating, and deleting data from SQL Server tables. Strictly speaking, Updategrams aren't template files, but you store them in the template folder. XML files in a template folder can contain other types of files, such as DiffGrams. Microsoft introduced DiffGrams for tight integrations with the .NET Framework, particularly the ADO.NET DataSet component. DiffGrams, like Updategrams, facilitate the manipulation of data source contents. I will revisit DiffGrams in Chapter 12.

Templates with T-SQL Statements

Using an XML file in a template folder is a two-step process. First you create the XML file. Second you invoke the file. If your template needs editing, you can pass through these steps as many times as necessary to fine-tune the design of your XML template file. The XML file must have a top-level tag, such as *ROOT*, with a reference to *urn:schemas-microsoft-com:xml-sql*. This namespace contains the elements and attributes for designing template files. After you've declared the namespace for the elements and attributes, the exact contents of a template file vary according to your objectives and how you go about implementing your template-based solution. For example, you can query a data source with either an XPath statement or a T-SQL statement. The elements that you use in your template file vary according to the language for expressing the query.

The following document illustrates the XML formatting for a simple T-SQL statement. The *ROOT* element designates sql as referencing the *urn:schemas-microsoft-com:xml-sql* namespace. Notice that you embed a T-SQL statement in a *sql:query* element. The T-SQL statement retrieves all rows and columns from the *Shippers* data source. The definition for this data source depends on the virtual directory holding the XML file in its template folder. In this chapter, I use the MyNwind virtual directory pointing to the Northwind database. If you run the same XML file from the template folder of a virtual directory pointing to a different database, you can obtain different results from the same XML template file.

```
<ROOT xmlns:sql="urn:schemas-microsoft-com:xml-sql">
<!--tmpSelectAllShippers.xml-->
    <sql:query>
        SELECT * FROM Shippers FOR XML RAW
    </sql:query>
</ROOT>
```

Figure 6-11 illustrates a URL pointing to the template file and the corresponding result set in the browser. The *FOR XML* clause determines the XML format for the result set. The browser's Address box in Figure 6-11 points to the ccs1 IIS server and the MyNwind virtual directory within the server. The template folder has the name template, but any other legitimate folder name will work as well so long as you adjust your settings for the virtual directory to point to it. The last item in the Address box specifically names the XML file with the *SELECT* statement.

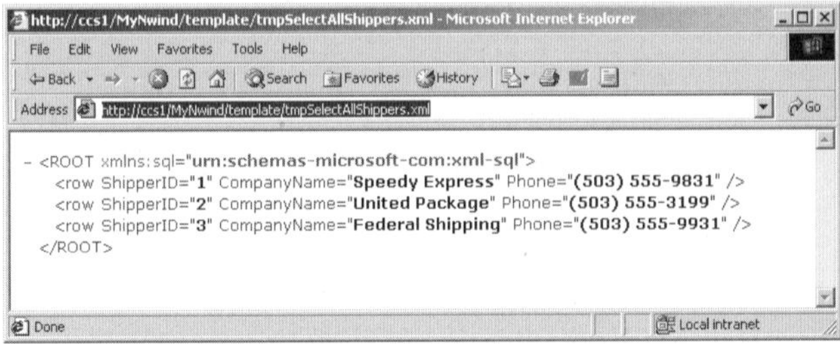

Figure 6-11. The Address box shows the format for referring to a template file that returns all the rows from the *Shippers* table.

The simple format for the Address box in Figure 6-11 enables you to readily create applications that allow users to tap the contents of your databases from anywhere in the world. Because the data returned is in XML format, the contents are readily usable by all applications compatible with XML data. Also, you can disable running queries directly from the URL and better secure your applications. Template files facilitate sanctioned retrievals from your database—namely, those that you preprogram for users.

It is frequently desirable to return a subset of records in a row source. This capability is even more powerful when you make it dynamic at run time so that an application can determine which subset to return according to user input. Enabling template files to return results based on parameters satisfies this requirement. Users can specify one or more parameters when they invoke the template file. The parameters can determine the result set from the template file.

Creating dynamic template files that accept run-time input requires an updated template design. In particular, you will need to add a minimum of two new elements to an XML template file. First, you need a *sql:header* element. You can define one or more parameters within this element. Second, you need the *sql:param* element. Use starting and ending *sql:param* tags for each parameter. Designate the parameter's name as the name attribute for the *sql:param* element. You can optionally specify a default value for the parameter. If the user fails to specify the parameter at run time, your application can execute its T-SQL statement with its default parameter value. Within a T-SQL statement, designate the parameter with a leading @ symbol. If your parameter name is *MyID* in the *sql:param* element, your T-SQL statement should refer to it as *@MyID*.

> **Note** One *sql:header* element can contain multiple parameter specifications. Reference more than one parameter in a template file by adding a *sql:param* element with a unique name attribute for each additional parameter.

The following XML document illustrates an extension of the preceding sample. A *WHERE* clause in the T-SQL uses a parameter to specify which row to retrieve from the *Shippers* table. Your application can specify this value at run time by including the parameter's name and value in the URL invoking the template file. Notice that the *sql:param* element names the parameter *MyID*, and the *WHERE* clause designates the parameter as *@MyID*. The parameter's default value is 1.

```
<ROOT xmlns:sql="urn:schemas-microsoft-com:xml-sql">
<!--tmpSelectShipperIDEquals.xml-->
    <sql:header>
        <sql:param name='MyID'>1</sql:param>
    </sql:header>
    <sql:query>
        SELECT * FROM Shippers WHERE ShipperID=@MyID FOR XML AUTO
    </sql:query>
</ROOT>
```

Figure 6-12 shows a browser invoking the template file with its result set. The URL trails the name for the template file with a question mark (?). Then the URL lists the parameter name, an equal sign (=), and the parameter value, 3. If you had additional parameters to specify, you could delimit them from one another with an ampersand (&). Each parameter designation follows the same format: parameter name, equal sign, parameter value. Failing to specify a parameter at run time returns the row with a *ShipperID* value of 1. If your template file didn't specify a default value, the result set would be empty. (No error message is returned.)

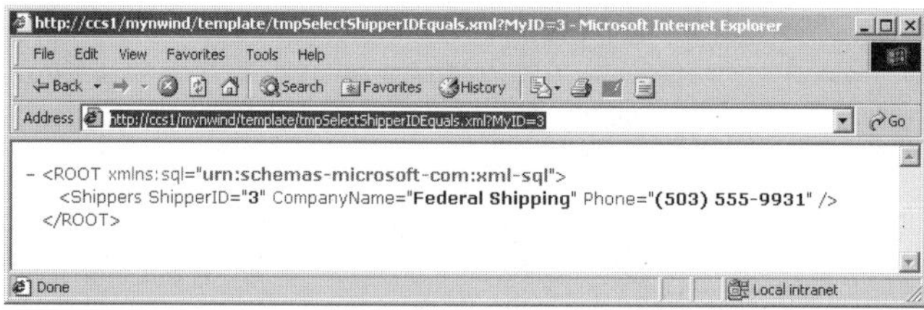

Figure 6-12. A sample demonstrating the specification of a parameter in a URL invoking a template file to return a row from the *Shippers* table.

XML template files with T-SQL don't restrict you to retrieving data. You can perform data manipulation and even other tasks. The trick is to use the proper T-SQL code and associate a login with the virtual directory that has permission to perform the tasks you program in the template file. (Chapter 7 examines SQL Server security.) For example, associating a login in the sysadmin fixed server role enables the execution of the next sample (as well as the updategram samples in the chapter's closing section). Using T-SQL in a template file is a very rich approach because you can accomplish anything that T-SQL performs (provided your login account has proper permission).

The next template file shows how to use the *INSERT* and *DELETE* statements to first add and then remove a record from the *Shippers* table. The template file monitors the starting, intermediate, and ending states of the *Shippers* table with a series of *SELECT* statements. In addition, the T-SQL script in the template file reseeds the *IDENTITY* property for the *Shippers* table so that the added record always appears with a *ShipperID* value of 4 instead of a progression of values, such as 4, 5, 6, on successive executions of the template file. This sample is instructive because it shows the use of the *DBCC CHECKIDENT* statement, which is neither a data retrieval nor a manipulation statement.

```
<ROOT xmlns:sql="urn:schemas-microsoft-com:xml-sql">
<!--tmpInsertAndDelete.xml-->
<sql:query>
    SELECT 'Shippers before an insert'
    SELECT *, 'Before Insert' as At FROM Shippers FOR XML AUTO

    INSERT INTO Shippers (CompanyName, Phone) VALUES ('foo','(123) 456-7890')
    SELECT 'Shippers after an insert'
    SELECT *, 'After Insert' as At FROM Shippers FOR XML AUTO

    DELETE FROM Shippers WHERE ShipperID > 3
    SELECT 'Shippers after deleting records with ShipperID > 3'
    SELECT *, 'After Delete' as At FROM Shippers FOR XML AUTO

    <!--Reseed Identity for Shippers table so it starts from 3-->
    DBCC CHECKIDENT (Shippers, RESEED, 3)
</sql:query>
</ROOT>
```

Figure 6-13 shows the result sets from the *SELECT* statements in the preceding XML template file—one before the insert, another after the insert, and a final one after the delete. Notice that the new record appears in the middle result set. No matter how many times you rerun the template file, the *ShipperID* value for the new record will always be 4. If you started with an initial *IDENTITY* value greater than 3, the first run of the template file will reflect the higher value, but all subsequent successive runs will act as if the last *IDENTITY* value were 3. This behavior reflects the impact of the *DBCC CHECKIDENT* statement at the close of the T-SQL script in the template file.

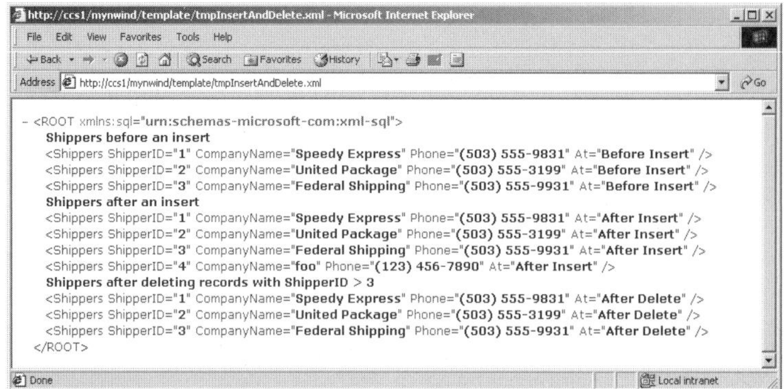

Figure 6-13. This browser shows the impact of a T-SQL script in an XML template file that adds and then removes a row from the *Shippers* table.

Templates Enhanced with Database Objects

The "*AUTO* vs. *NESTED* Mode Samples" section describes a T-SQL statement for a URL that computes a sum with a *GROUP BY* clause. Unfortunately, the same statement fails when executed from within an XML template file rather than a URL. However, you can still perform aggregates with *SELECT* statements that include *GROUP BY* clauses. The trick is to create a view with the *GROUP BY* clause and aggregate function. Then use the view as the source for a *SELECT* statement inside a template file. The template file returns rows with aggregated values based on the computations performed in the view that serves as its source.

The following script creates a view based on the T-SQL statement used to populate Figure 6-9. Recall that the figure excerpts the outcome from a T-SQL statement in a URL that groups and aggregates column values from a row source. The *SELECT* statement for the *OrderTotalView* view and the query generating the result set excerpted in Figure 6-9 are identical except for the *FOR XML* clause, which is missing from the view. This variance is because you want the view to return a traditional rowset. A second query in a template file can reference the *OrderTotalView* view as its source argument in the *FROM* clause. It is in the template file that your application can apply XML formatting to the rowset returned by the view.

```
--CreateOrderTotalView.sql
USE Northwind
GO
CREATE VIEW OrderTotalView AS
SELECT OrderID, CAST(SUM(ExtendedPrice) AS DEC(8,2)) OrderTotal
FROM Invoices
GROUP BY OrderID
GO
```

The XML template file can contain the following XML script. By using the *OrderTotalView* view as its source, the query in the template file draws on a rowset with aggregated extended price across the line items for each order in the *Invoices* view. An alias (*Invoices*) for the *OrderTotalView* view enables the *SELECT* statement to show *Invoices* as the ultimate source for the results. The XML formatted result set from running this template file looks identical to the one in Figure 6-9. However, the contents of the Address box are much more basic. The URL merely references the template file: `http://ccs1/MyNwind/template/tmpSelectFromAggregatingView.xml`.

```
<!--tmpSelectFromAggregatingView.xml-->
<ROOT xmlns:sql="urn:schemas-microsoft-com:xml-sql">
      <sql:query >
        SELECT *
        FROM OrderTotalView AS Invoices
        FOR XML AUTO
    </sql:query>
</ROOT>
```

The solution is desirable if you want a report with the totals for all the orders, but frequently applications require a result for just one item or some subset of items. To meet this requirement, you can aggregate by group and then filter based on the group values your application needs to return. By referencing a table-valued user-defined function from a query in a template file, you can enable a template file to dynamically filter a rowset with rows containing aggregated values at run time.

You can apply the logic in the preceding paragraph to extending the previous sample. The process requires two steps. First create a user-defined function named *OrderTotalFunction* that returns a table based on the *Invoices* view. The function's *SELECT* statement aggregates the *ExtendedPrice* column from the *Invoices* view by *OrderID*. The *@MyOrderID* parameter in the function permits a calling routine to determine for which order the function returns a table. In this case, the table consists of a single row. Second create an XML template file (tmpSelectFromAggregatingTableUDF.xml) that references the user-defined function. The template file can use the function as the source for a *SELECT* statement. In addition, the template file can pass a parameter to the function to designate which row the user-defined function should return. At run time for the template, users can dynamically specify the *OrderID* of the order for which they want a total.

Here's the script for creating the user-defined function. Its *SELECT* statement is identical to the *SELECT* statement in the view for the preceding sample except for the *HAVING* clause that filters the result set and the parameter, *@MyOrderID*, that facilitates the run-time designation of which order to return the sum for. See the "Creating and Invoking Table-Valued UDFs" section in Chapter 5 for a review of the syntax for user-defined functions.

```
--CreateOrderTotalFunction.sql
USE Northwind
GO
CREATE FUNCTION OrderTotalFunction(@MyOrderID int)
RETURNS TABLE
AS
RETURN(
    SELECT OrderID, CAST(SUM(ExtendedPrice) AS DEC(8,2)) OrderTotal
    FROM Invoices
    GROUP BY OrderID
    HAVING OrderID = @MyOrderID
)
GO
```

The following XML document invokes the *OrderTotalFunction* udf. This document fulfills the second step in the application development process. It defines a parameter named *MyOrderID* with a default value. Therefore, users can get a result set from running the template file whether or not they specify a parameter value. Figure 6-14 shows the XML formatted result set in the browser from a URL that specifies 10252 as the parameter value.

```
<ROOT xmlns:sql="urn:schemas-microsoft-com:xml-sql">
<!--tmpSelectFromAggregatingTableUDF.xml-->
    <sql:header>
        <sql:param name='MyOrderID'>10250</sql:param>
    </sql:header>
      <sql:query >
        Select * FROM OrderTotalFunction(@MyOrderID)
        FOR XML AUTO
    </sql:query>
</ROOT>
```

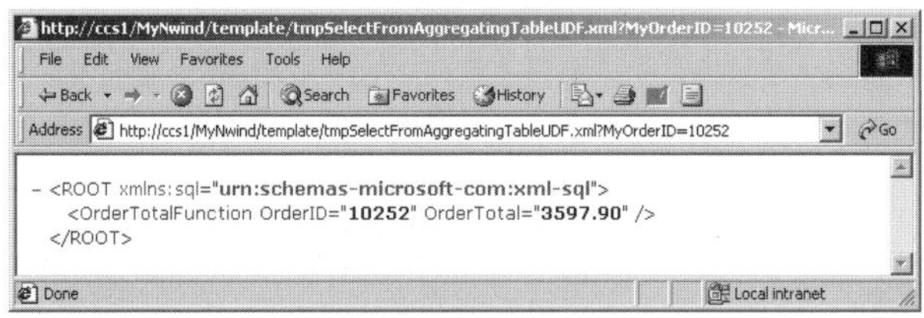

Figure 6-14. This browser shows the result set from an XML template file that invokes a user-defined function to return an aggregated value for the rows matching a specific *OrderID*.

Updategrams Are like Templates

Updategrams aren't templates, but you can invoke them in ways that are similar to how you run XML template files. Updategrams offer an XML-based way to insert, delete, and update rows in a SQL Server row source. Because Updategrams accept parameters, your applications can allow users to specify dynamically what rows to insert, delete, or update. A single Updategram can support multiple inserts, deletes, and updates. In addition, you can group your data manipulation tasks into transactions so that none will occur unless all tasks within the transaction complete. You can even compose an Updategram with multiple transactions so that the data manipulation tasks in one transaction occur even if those in another transaction roll back. Perhaps the best feature of Updategrams is that their syntax is easy to understand.

The following layout shows the overall design for most Updategrams. Notice that Updategrams have their own namespace. However, they follow standard XML syntax conventions. You can optionally designate an annotated schema for them to work against. If you don't specify an annotated schema, Updategrams operate against whatever row source you specify in the *updg:before* and *updg:after* elements. The *updg:sync* element allows you to group data manipulation tasks into transactions. You can have multiple *updg:sync* elements within a single Updategram, but every Updategram must have at least one *updg:sync* element. Before the first *updg:sync* element, you can optionally insert an *updg:header* element, and within this element you can insert one or more *updg:param* elements. You can use these *updg:param* elements in Updategrams in the same way that you do within XML template files to specify parameters. Within the body of the Updategram, you designate parameters with a leading $ (dollar sign) instead of the @ (at symbol) common in T-SQL code.

It is within the *updg:before* and *updg:after* elements that you specify much of the detail work that an Updategram performs. For example, you can insert a new row of column values into a row source by including a specification for the row within the *updg:before* element without referencing the row within the *updg:after* element. In contrast, you can delete a row by including a reference to it within the *updg:after* element without denoting the row in the *updg:before* element. To specify an update, reference the same row within the *updg:before* and *updg:after* elements. The column values in the *updg:before* element should identify the row (or rows) before the update, and the column values within the *updg:after* element should denote the new column values for the rows that require modification.

```
<ROOT xmlns:updg="urn:schemas-microsoft-com:xml-updategram">
<updg:sync [mapping-schema="SampleSchema.xml"] >
    <updg:before>
```

(continued)

```
    </updg:before>
    <updg:after>
    </updg:after>
</updg:sync>
</ROOT>
```

The next script denotes the contents of an Updategram to add a new row to the *Shippers* table. The entry inside the *updg:after* element denotes the column values for the new row. The new column values appear as attributes for the *Shippers* element. Don't specify values for columns with an *IDENTITY* property setting because SQL Server automatically adds values to columns with an *IDENTITY* property. It is for this reason that the Updategram assigns no value to *ShipperID*. The *updg:before* element is empty. It is the combination of an empty *updg:before* element and a populated *updg:after* element that causes the Updategram to add a new row to the *Shippers* table. You can save this Updategram with a name, such as updgInsertCABDelivers.xml, in the template folder of a virtual directory pointing to a database with a *Shippers* table. This convention lets you invoke Updategrams just as you do standard XML template files.

```
<ROOT xmlns:updg="urn:schemas-microsoft-com:xml-updategram">
<!--updgInsertCABDelivers.xml-->
<updg:sync >
    <updg:before>
    </updg:before>
    <updg:after>
         <Shippers CompanyName="CAB Delivers" Phone="(123) 456-7890" />
     </updg:after>
</updg:sync>
</ROOT>
```

Instead of specifying the new column values in a row as attributes of a single element in the Updategram, you can designate new values in an element-centric hierarchical format. The following excerpt from updgInsertCABDeliversElementsIn.xml illustrates how to lay out the preceding input data in a hierarchical format. All other design features of the updgInsertCABDeliversElementsIn.xml Updategram match those in updgInsertCABDelivers.xml. The attribute-centric and element-centric layouts generate XML documents with identical content, but the format of the generated document changes between the two files—namely, updgInsertCABDelivers.xml vs. updgInsertCABDeliversElementsIn.xml.

```
    <updg:after>
        <Shippers>
            <CompanyName>CAB Delivers</CompanyName>
            <Phone>(123) 456-7890</Phone>
        </Shippers>
```

You can run the element-centric version of the Updategram by entering **http://ccs1/mynwind/template/updgInsertCABDeliversElementsIn.xml** in the Address box of a browser. As with XML template files, you designate an IIS server name, a virtual directory name, a template folder name, and finally the Updategram filename. If the Updategram succeeds, your browser shows an XML file with a single root element containing the Updategram namespace designator. (See Figure 6-15.)

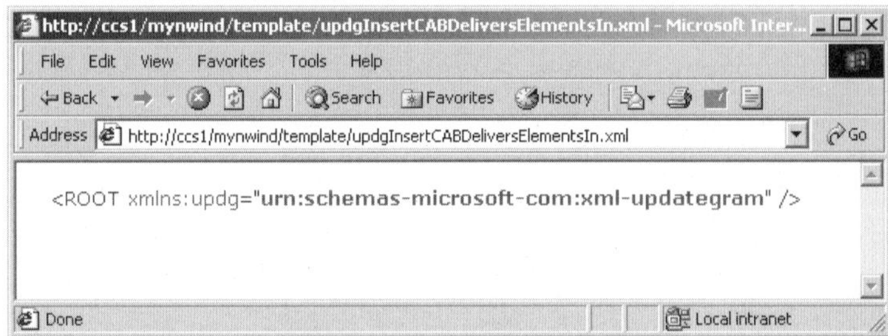

Figure 6-15. You invoke an Updategram similarly to the way you run an XML template file.

Running the tmpSelectAllShippers.xml template file can confirm the new row in the *Shippers* table with a *CompanyName* column value of CAB Delivers and a *Phone* column value of (123) 456-7890. The following Updategram modifies the Phone column value for the newly added row. It contains a single set of column values in both the *updg:before* and *updg:after* elements. The values in the *updg:before* element must reference a specific row in the *Shippers* table. If the values denote either more than one row or no row, the update fails with a message in the browser alerting the user to the problem. The values in the *updg:after* element include both the *CompanyName* to identify the row and a new *Phone* value to replace the existing one. You can invoke updgCABDeliversNewPhone.xml in the same way that you ran the first Updategram. Because the Updategram merely returns a single-lined document with the name of the Updategram namespace, you might want to rerun tmpSelectAllShippers.xml to confirm the update.

```
<ROOT xmlns:updg="urn:schemas-microsoft-com:xml-updategram">
<!--updgCABDeliversNewPhone.xml-->
<updg:sync >
    <updg:before>
        <Shippers CompanyName="CAB Delivers" Phone="(123) 456-7890" />
    </updg:before>
    <updg:after>
        <Shippers CompanyName="CAB Delivers" Phone="(234) 567-8901" />
    </updg:after>
</updg:sync>
</ROOT>
```

You can remove a row from a table by uniquely identifying it in the *updg:before* element and leaving the *updg:after* element empty. The identifying column values that you specify in the *updg:before* element must point to a unique row in a table. If the column values you use to denote a target row aren't unique, the Updategram returns an error message. For this reason, you should consider using primary key values when specifying rows for deletion. The sample below uses the *CompanyName* column value to identify the row to delete because the *ShipperID* value is set by SQL Server. You can revise the Updategram to delete a row based on *ShipperID* by running tmpSelectAllShippers.xml to discover the target *ShipperID* value and then using that value in the *updg:before* element. Finally, you can run the Updategram like either of the preceding two samples. The URL I entered was *http://ccs1/MyNwind/template/updgDeleteCABDelivers.xml*. You will need to revise the names for the IIS server, virtual directory, and template folder for your application's environment.

```
<ROOT xmlns:updg="urn:schemas-microsoft-com:xml-updategram">
<!--updgDeleteCABDelivers.xml-->
<updg:sync >
    <updg:before>
        <Shippers CompanyName="CAB Delivers"/>
    </updg:before>
     <updg:after>
     </updg:after>
</updg:sync>
</ROOT>
```

The next sample demonstrates the syntax for using parameters as you add a new row to a table. The Updategram declares the parameters with *updg:param* elements. The sample designates two parameters named *CompanyName* and *Phone*. The code doesn't assign default parameter values, so your application must specify values for the parameters at run time. The *updg:after* element demonstrates the syntax for referring back to the parameters as you specify a new row for a table. As you can see, the rule is to use the parameter name with a leading $.

```
<ROOT xmlns:updg="urn:schemas-microsoft-com:xml-updategram">
<!--updgInsertShippersParams.xml-->
<updg:header>
    <updg:param name="CompanyName" />
    <updg:param name="Phone" />
</updg:header>
<updg:sync >
    <updg:before>
    </updg:before>
    <updg:after>
        <Shippers CompanyName="$CompanyName" Phone="$Phone" />
```

```
    </updg:after>
</updg:sync>
</ROOT>
```

You can run a parametrically specified Updategram just as you would any XML template file with parameters. Enter a URL into a browser that starts with the path to the Updategram on the IIS server. Follow this with a question mark (?) and name-value pairs for each parameter that the Updategram requires. Figure 6-16 shows the syntax for adding a shipper with a *CompanyName* field of CAB Delivers and a *Phone* field of (123) 456-7890. The browser automatically replaces each blank space with %20.

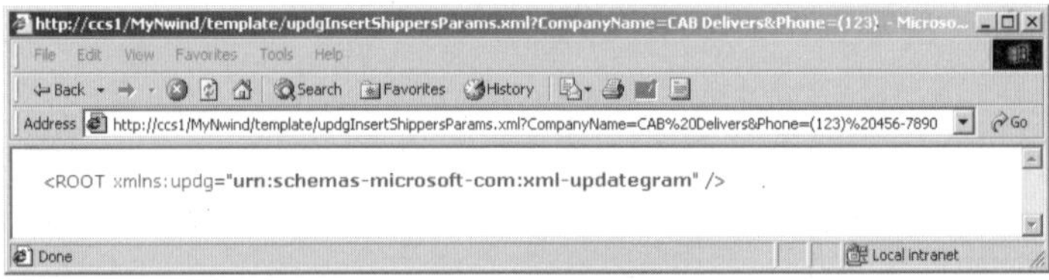

Figure 6-16. Designate parameter values at run time for an Updategram just as you do for an XML template file.

The approach demonstrated for adding a row based on run-time parameters applies to deleting and updating a row. The following Updategram shows the syntax for removing a row from the *Shippers* table based on *ShipperID* value. Users can run tmpSelectAllShippers.xml to determine the *ShipperID* value for the row they want to delete. For example, if the target row to delete had a *ShipperID* value of 5, you could remove it by entering **http://ccs1/MyNwind/template/updgDeleteShippersParams.xml?ShipperID=5** in the browser.

```
<ROOT xmlns:updg="urn:schemas-microsoft-com:xml-updategram">
<!--updgDeleteShippersParams.xml-->
<updg:header>
    <updg:param name="ShipperID"/>
</updg:header>
<updg:sync >
    <updg:before>
        <Shippers ShipperID="$ShipperID"/>
    </updg:before>
    <updg:after>
    </updg:after>
</updg:sync>
</ROOT>
```

7

SQL Server 2000 Security

In these times, all information technology professionals, including database developers, have a pressing need to protect their systems. There is no magic pill you can take to inoculate your systems against any kind of security attack that ever did, or will, exist. Securing systems is a matter of learning your applications and judiciously applying the security measures appropriate for your computing environment. This chapter exposes you to the security features available with Microsoft SQL Server 2000. Use the foundation you get from this chapter as a basis for drilling down deeper into selected topics that you feel a need to learn in greater depth.

Aside from general security concerns, SQL Server 2000 developers have specific reasons for needing to know about security. For example, the only way users can connect to a SQL Server instance is by specifying a login account. After gaining access to the database server with a login account, users cannot typically gain access to a database except by having a user account associated with the login account. Furthermore, login account and user account membership in various fixed and user-defined roles enable users to perform server and database functions, including managing security for a server and its databases or even for the databases on other servers.

The two resources for this chapter are similar to those for Chapter 2 through Chapter 5. The first resource is a set of T-SQL scripts with the samples in this chapter. These T-SQL scripts often reference the second resource, the Chapter07 database. In fact, there is a script among the samples files for this book to create the database, but the samples also include a copy of the database files themselves (Chapter07_dat.mdf and Chapter07_log.ldf) for your easy reference. The scripts in this chapter differ from those of preceding chapters in that the login for database connections varies between scripts. By using different logins, the samples enable you to evaluate the effects of different types of logins as well as understand how to create those logins.

Overview of SQL Server Security

SQL Server security centers on the database server, but the management of security extends upward to the operating system on which SQL Server runs and downward to client workstations that connect to a computer running SQL Server.

Security Accounts

SQL Server has two main kinds of security accounts. The first kind of security account grants access to a database server. SQL Server calls this first kind of security account a login security account or a login. The second kind of security account grants access to a database within a server. SQL Server applies the name user security account or user to this kind of security account. User accounts allow your application's users to gain access to the resources that you create for their use on a SQL Server instance. Any one login account can have multiple user security accounts associated with it—one for each database to which the login needs access.

Every SQL Server instance maintains a collection of logins. A login is like a key that lets a user open the door into a SQL Server instance. There are three types of logins. These types of logins relate to how SQL Server validates a user. The Windows User and Windows Group are two types of logins that relate to the Windows operating system. These are accounts validated by Windows. When you create a Windows User login type within a SQL Server instance for a Windows user, that user can gain access to the SQL Server instance without the need to revalidate her credentials. SQL Server accepts the Windows user account as valid for access to SQL Server. The same general notion applies to a Windows Group type login except that SQL Server accepts the Windows login as valid for any member of the Windows group.

SQL Server can also manage its own login accounts. These are standard logins. SQL Server must manage the login name and password in this case. While SQL Server security management features aren't as rich as those for Windows, there are times when standard security login accounts are especially useful. First, if SQL Server is running on an operating system other than Windows NT, Windows 2000, or Windows XP, such as Windows 98, you must use standard logins. Second, if your application has users who aren't registered with a Windows domain server, these users require SQL Server logins. Third, SQL Server logins are also necessary for compatibility with applications containing data imported from database vendors other than Microsoft.

No matter what type of security login a user presents, users also generally must have user security accounts for database access. The exceptions relate to login accounts with broad authority and databases with guest accounts for logins without a user account. User security accounts reside with each database. However, all user accounts except the guest account must relate to a specific login. The login type can be Windows User, Windows Group, or standard.

Authentication

As the previous section indicates, login security accounts are what clients present to a database server to gain access to the server. Authentication is the process by which a database server accepts the login security account and determines whether it is valid. SQL Server 2000 supports two authentication modes. These are Windows Authentication Mode, which is the default mode, and Mixed Mode. For servers running with Windows Authentication Mode, database users don't need to validate themselves when they attempt to gain access to a database server. For servers running Mixed Mode, only database users with a SQL Server login must submit their login name and password when attempting to gain access to a server. Database users with a Windows User or Windows Group login type on the SQL Server instance aren't prompted a second time to validate their credentials.

The default mode allows login to a SQL Server instance only via a Windows account. All database users must meet two criteria with Windows Authentication Mode. First, database users must have a valid Windows account with a domain server for either Windows NT or Windows 2000. Second, the SQL Server instance managing a database must authorize the individual user's Windows account or a Windows group to which the individual user belongs. Windows users without an account that SQL Server recognizes cannot enter the database.

When you install with the default mode, the Windows Administrator account on the computer running the SQL Server instance is the service account for SQL Server. The installation process automatically creates a login for the Administrator account that is a member of the sysadmin fixed server role. (You can override this selection of a service account.) As a result, the login for the Administrator account enjoys nearly all the privileges of the traditional sa security account. One critical difference is that you can delete the login for the Administrator account, but you cannot delete the sa login.

With Mixed Mode authentication, users can log in if they have an account with a Windows domain server or a SQL Server login maintained by a SQL Server instance. When you install the database server on a computer running Windows 98 or Windows Millennium Edition, SQL Server automatically runs with Mixed Mode authentication. If your SQL Server instance is an application server on a workgroup instead of a domain, and one or more of your client workstations run Windows 98, your server must support Mixed Mode authentication. This requirement exists whether or not SQL Server 2000 runs on a computer with either the Windows 2000 or the Windows NT operating system.

> **Note** When you choose Mixed Mode authentication during SQL Server 2000 installation, a reminder appears to assign a password to the sa login. Failing to properly respond to this reminder opens your computer to unwarranted entry.

Roles and Permissions

Getting into a SQL Server instance doesn't necessarily ensure that you can do anything once you get there. The role membership of login and user security accounts conveys permissions to perform various tasks—both for the server and for the databases maintained on a server. Some roles are fixed—that is, specified by SQL Server. Two collections of fixed roles are the fixed server roles and fixed database roles. SQL Server also permits the creation of user-defined roles. With user-defined roles, you can assign the precise permissions that an application requires. Permissions are of two general types. First, you can assign permissions for database objects, such as the ability to select rows from a table or view. These permissions are called object permissions. Second, you can grant the authority to exercise a subset of the T-SQL statements, such as *CREATE TABLE*. These permissions are called statement permissions.

The fixed server roles convey permissions for server tasks, such as creating, altering, and dropping databases or managing logins for other users and changing their passwords. SQL Server 2000 offers eight fixed server roles. (See Table 7-1.) The Bulk Insert role is new with SQL Server 2000. An individual login can belong to none, one, or more than one of these roles. Run the *sp_addsrvrolemember* system stored procedure to add a login to a fixed server role. Database users inherit the permissions for any fixed server roles to which their logins belong. You cannot directly assign a user account to a fixed server role. Use the *sp_helpsrvrole* system stored procedure to obtain a list of the fixed server role names along with brief descriptions. Invoke the *sp_srvrolepermission* system stored procedure for a detailed list of T-SQL statements and server functions for which each fixed server role grants permission.

Fixed database roles convey rights within a database, such as the ability to select or change data as well as the ability to add new database objects. There are nine fixed database roles. (See Table 7-2.) Use the *sp_addrolemember* system stored procedure to assign a user security account to a fixed database role in the current database. The security account used to designate membership in a fixed database role can be a user account in the current database based on a SQL Server login, a Windows User login, or a Windows Group login. Just as with the fixed server roles, there are two system stored procedures to help you discover more about the fixed database roles. Invoke *sp_helpdbfixedrole* for a listing of the roles with brief descriptions. Run *sp_dbfixedrolepermission* to view the complete list of permissions associated with each fixed database role.

Table 7-1 Fixed Server Roles

Role Name	Selected Tasks
Sysadmin	Can perform any task and gain unrestricted access to all databases
Serveradmin	Can perform *sp_configure* and *SHUTDOWN* operations
Setupadmin	Can designate a stored procedure to run at startup and manage linked server specifications
Securityadmin	Can perform *sp_grantlogin*, *sp_addlogin*, and *sp_denylogin* procedures; can also manage database creation permissions and password changes
Processadmin	Can perform *KILL* operations
Dbcreator	Can perform *CREATE DATABASE*, *ALTER DATABASE*, and *DROP DATABASE* operations
Diskadmin	Can perform *sp_addumpdevice* and *sp_dropdevice* procedures
Bulkadmin	Can perform *BULK INSERT* operations

Besides the nine fixed database roles in Table 7-2, another role exists within each database: the public role. All database users belong to the public role and can exercise whatever permissions the role allows. Each database has its own set of fixed database roles, including the public role. Membership in a role within one database doesn't convey membership in the same role for any other database. In addition, the public role in one database can possess different permissions than the public role in another database.

> **Note** It's often good practice to strip all permissions from the public role so that users in a database derive no permissions just from their ability to access a database. This practice is especially important when you have a guest user account in a database because the guest account, which allows database access by any login, is a member of the public role.

Table 7-2 Fixed Database Roles

Role Name	Selected Tasks
db_owner	Can perform any task in a database
db_accessadmin	Can perform *sp_grantdbaccess* and *sp_revokedbaccess* procedures
db_securityadmin	Can perform *sp_addrolemember* and *sp_droprolemember* procedures
db_ddladmin	Can execute *CREATE*, *ALTER*, and *DROP* statements for objects in a database
db_backupoperator	Can perform *BACKUP DATABASE* and *BACKUP LOG* operations
db_datareader	Can perform *SELECT* operations for any object in a database
db_datawriter	Can perform *INSERT*, *UPDATE*, and *DELETE* operations for any object in a database
db_denydatareader	Cannot perform *SELECT* operations for any objects in a database
db_denydatawriter	Cannot perform *INSERT*, *UPDATE*, or *DELETE* operations for any object in a database

In addition to the fixed roles listed in Tables 7-1 and 7-2, SQL Server permits the creation of user-defined roles. Create user-defined roles when your security needs are more granular than those accommodated by the fixed roles. Invoke the *sp_addrole* system stored procedure to create a new user-defined role. After creating a role, you can add members to it with the *sp_addrolemember* system stored procedure. You can assign members to user-defined roles from the same set of security accounts as for fixed database roles. Of course, you can manage permissions for a user-defined role so that membership has its privileges! Just as with fixed roles, user-defined roles exist within a database. Two user-defined roles in different databases with the same name can have different members and convey different permissions within each database. You can manage user-defined roles with any login that belongs to the sysadmin fixed server role or any user security account that is a member of the db_owner or db_securityadmin fixed database role.

You can assign two types of permissions to user-defined roles. The first kind of permissions grants authority for database objects. These permissions include *SELECT*, *INSERT*, *UPDATE*, *DELETE*, *REFERENCES*, and *EXECUTE*. You can apply *SELECT*, *INSERT*, *UPDATE*, and *DELETE* permissions to any entire table, view, or table-valued user-defined function. In addition, you can apply *SELECT* and *UPDATE* permissions to any subset of the columns in a table or view. *EXECUTE* permission pertains to both stored procedures and user-defined functions. *REFERENCES* allows two different types of permissions. First, you can use *REFERENCES* to designate permission to reference the primary key in one table as a match for the foreign key in another table. Second, you can also invoke the *REFERENCES* permission to enable a view or a user-defined function to specify its sources for *SCHEMABINDING*. The *REFERENCES* permission becomes necessary for these cases when the owner of the table with the primary key is different from the owner of the table with the foreign key or the owner of a view or user-defined function is different from its base tables or views.

The second kind of permissions that you can add to user-defined roles is T-SQL statement permissions. With these permissions, the members of your user-defined roles can perform tasks such as creating databases and creating tables, views, stored procedures, and user-defined functions within a database. The "Managing Permissions" topic in Books Online includes the full list of statements to which you can grant permissions.

T-SQL offers three statements for managing the permissions that a role can convey to its members. The *GRANT* statement gives a permission to a role. The *REVOKE* and *DENY* statements can both disable a permission in a role. When the same user belongs to multiple roles, conflicts with permissions can exist. A permission conveyed through a *GRANT* statement for one role overrides a *REVOKE* statement for the same permission in any other role. However, a *DENY* statement overrides any *GRANT* statement. Therefore, a user belonging to two different roles with a *GRANT* statement and a *DENY* statement for the same permission in both roles won't have the permission.

Introduction to Special Security Issues

A variety of special SQL Server security topics fall outside the scope of the preceding summary of security accounts, authentication, roles, and permissions. This section addresses three of these topics. First, you learn about application roles, which are a custom type of user-defined roles that can provide unique access to a database. Second, I explore techniques for working with linked servers, which let your users from one SQL Server instance readily connect with database resources on another SQL Server instance. Third, this section includes an examination of security issues relating to virtual directories, such as those reviewed in Chapter 6 for Web data access and manipulation via XML.

Application Roles

Application roles provide a database access route that complements those afforded by SQL Server security accounts. Instead of accessing a database with logins and user accounts, an application role provides access to a database via the application role's name and password. Any database user with permission to create a user-defined role can create an application role with the *sp_addapprole* system stored procedure. After creating an application role, assign permissions to it in the same way that you do for user-defined database roles. Users log in to an application role with the *sp_setapprole* system stored procedure. There are no role membership requirements to invoke *sp_setapprole*.

When a user invokes an application role, she loses all other security settings associated with a database connection. A user must disconnect and reconnect to regain standard security for her login and user security accounts. However, a user of an application role does enjoy any rights for the guest user in the current database or any other database. Therefore, you must be careful to administer permissions for the guest user to manage the permissions available through an application role.

One distinct advantage of an application role is that it can provide a single point of access for a database. All users must reference the same application role name and password with *sp_setapprole* to open an application role. Furthermore, with the standard SQL Server security features, you can restrict access to a database so that the only way for users to gain access to it is through the application role. In that case, you can uniformly define the permissions for all users of a database (except for sysadmin members, who have unrestricted access to all resources on a database server).

Linked Servers

Linked servers are an alternative technique to the *OPENROWSET* function for implementing remote server access and heterogeneous queries. See the "Views for Remote and Heterogeneous Sources" section in Chapter 4 for samples illustrating the use of the *OPENROWSET* function. As that section demonstrates, this capability facilitates performing queries for a data source on another computer, such as a SQL Server instance running on another computer, or queries against a different database, such as Oracle or Access. Linked servers readily support queries to any data source for which there is an OLE DB data provider with the proper feature set. Microsoft explicitly tested linked servers with five OLE DB providers: Microsoft OLE DB provider for SQL Server, Microsoft OLE DB provider for Jet, Microsoft OLE DB provider for Oracle, Microsoft OLE DB provider for ODBC, and Microsoft OLE DB provider for Indexing Service.

One advantage of the *OPENROWSET* function over a linked server is that the *OPENROWSET* function requires only your existing user credentials for the remote or heterogeneous data source. While the syntax for specifying distributed queries with linked servers is simpler than that for the *OPENROWSET* function, a member from either the sysadmin or setupadmin fixed server role must add the linked server before you can use it. With the *OPENROWSET* function, any user with the credentials to connect to a remote or heterogeneous data source can immediately make the query.

Your initial query from a linked server requires three steps. First you must create a linked server reference on the current computer running SQL Server 2000. Second you must map a login on the current computer to a login for the remote or heterogeneous data source. Third you must specify the query for the remote or heterogeneous data source with a four-part naming convention. The first part denotes the linked server reference. The second, third, and fourth parts complete the unique identification of the source; how you specify these parts can vary depending on the source. The fourth part typically specifies the table or view in the target data source. After the initial query, using a linked server is easier than using the *OPENROWSET* function because the linked server syntax is more straightforward, and you no longer have to perform the first two steps.

Create a linked server for a remote or heterogeneous data source with the *sp_addlinkedserver* system stored procedure. This procedure can take as many as seven arguments, but you can use as few as two arguments for creating a reference to a remote SQL Server source and as few as four arguments for a linked server pointing to an Access data source. After correctly initializing the linked server reference with the *sp_addlinkedserver* system stored procedure, invoke *sp_addlinkedsrvlogin* for mapping logins on the current SQL Server 2000 instance to logins for the remote or heterogeneous data source. When a user runs a query on the local server against the linked server, the local server logs in to the linked server with the credentials specified when the *sp_addlinkedsrvlogin* system stored procedure was last run for the linked server. You can invoke the *sp_linkedservers* system stored procedure to itemize in a result set the linked servers defined on a local server.

Security for Virtual Directories

Virtual directories are necessary for Web data access to SQL Server data sources via XML. Each database that requires Web access via XML must have a virtual directory pointing to it. As described in the "Virtual Directory Management" section of Chapter 6, you must designate a login for the virtual directory. All access to the database is mapped through the login that you specify on the Security tab of the Properties dialog for a directory.

Figure 7-1 shows the Properties dialog box used for the MyNwind virtual directory that served as the source for most of the samples in Chapter 6. Notice that the Security tab specifies IUSR_CCS1 in the User Name text box. The User Name text box contains the login name for the virtual directory. Selecting Windows as the Account Type automatically installs IUSR_servername as the login. Windows 2000 Server automatically installs the IUSR_servername user account. IIS automatically uses this Windows user account for anonymous login. Since the samples for Chapter 6 ran from a server named ccs1, the dialog replaced servername with CCS1.

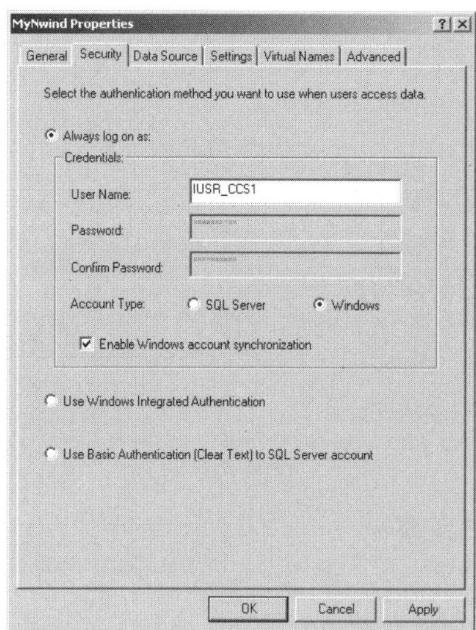

Figure 7-1. Use the Security tab for a virtual directory to specify the login by which users of the virtual directory will gain access to a SQL Server.

If you decide to allow access to your database through the IUSR_servername Windows account, you must manually create a login for the Windows user on your SQL Server instance. Then you must create a user security account in the database to which the virtual directory points. Finally you must assign permissions to the IUSR_servername security account appropriate to the needs of your application. For example, if you want to enable browsers to read from any row source in the database, you can assign the IUSR_servername user account to the db_datareader fixed database role. If you have more restrictive requirements, use the T-SQL *GRANT* statement to specify more granular permissions, such as the ability to view just one table or view. Make sure the database has permissions for the public role that don't allow the IUSR_servername account to access the database with a different set of permissions than the one you specify explicitly for the virtual directory user account.

When you decide to permit updates, inserts, and deletes to a database through a virtual server, the user security account for the virtual directory's login must enable these actions. My advice is to carefully restrict the row sources that you make available for updating over the Web. Avoid assigning the IUSR_servername account to the db_datawriter fixed database role. Instead, assign *INSERT*, *UPDATE*, or *DELETE* permissions with the T-SQL *GRANT* statement for whichever database objects require modification over the Web.

Samples for Logins and Users

Login and user security accounts complement one another. Recall that a login authorizes access to a server, but a user account grants access to a database on a server. The users of your applications typically need both types of security accounts to access a database on a SQL Server instance. In addition, there are two distinct types of logins. The samples in this section explore the different kinds of logins for SQL Server and how they relate to user security accounts. All the scripts in this section are in the LoginAndDropUsers.sql sample file.

Add a SQL Server Login and User

Recall that a login gets a user into a server but not necessarily into any databases on the server. This is because a login typically requires a matching security account for each database to which a user is to have access. However, there are two ways in which a user can access a database without a user account for the database. First, the database can have a guest account. The user will then enjoy any permissions assigned explicitly to the guest account or indirectly to the guest account through permissions for a database's public role. Second, if a login is a member of the sysadmin fixed server role, it can access any database on a server without any restrictions on its functionality. For this reason, you want to limit the number of logins with membership in the sysadmin role. If you need to carefully specify how the user of a login can interact with a database, you must create a user security account for the login in the database.

Invoke the *sp_addlogin* system stored procedure to create a new SQL Server login. With the *sp_addlogin* system stored procedure, you can create a login that SQL Server manages. When users attempt to gain access to a SQL Server instance with this login, they must explicitly designate both the login name and its associated password. To create a SQL Server login, you must be a member of either the sysadmin or securityadmin fixed server role. Any user can change her own password with the *sp_password* system stored procedure. Only members of the sysadmin and securityadmin fixed server roles can invoke *sp_password* to change the password for a login different from their own.

> **Note** While a SQL Server login enables a user to connect to a SQL Server instance by specifying a login name and password, it is the SID (security identifier) that SQL Server uses to identify and track the user. SQL Server internally generates a GUID to represent the SID for SQL Server logins.

Invoke the *sp_grantdbaccess* system stored procedure to create a user security account in a database for a login. Only members of the sysadmin fixed server role as well as the db_owner and db_accessadmin fixed database roles can run *sp_grantdbaccess*. Before running *sp_grantdbaccess*, make sure the database context is set to the database in which you want to create a user security account. For example, invoke the *USE* statement for a database name before running *sp_grantdbaccess*.

The following T-SQL script uses *sp_addlogin* to create a new SQL Server login. It is mandatory to specify the *@loginame* and *@passwd* arguments for the *sp_addlogin* system stored procedure. You can optionally specify several other arguments to change the default settings derived from your SQL Server configuration. For example, the script demonstrates the syntax for designating a default database of Chapter07, the sample database for this chapter. If the script didn't make this assignment for the *@defdb* argument, the default database would have been the master database. The master database is one of the built-in databases that SQL Server uses to administer itself. While all users require access to this database, you probably don't want to make it the default database for typical users.

Notice that the script explicitly references the master database before invoking *sp_addlogin*. This reference isn't strictly necessary since you can create a login security account from any database on a server. However, the sample script invokes the *USE* statement two more times, and these two references are necessary. You must invoke the *USE* statement before running the *sp_grantdbaccess* system stored procedure. Recall that this system stored procedure creates a user security account. Setting the database context before invoking *sp_grantdbaccess* determines the database for which the system stored procedure creates a user security account.

```
--LoginAndDropUsers
--Create a SQL Server login with access
--to the Chapter07 and Northwind databases.
USE master
EXEC sp_addlogin
    @loginame = 'vbdotnet1',
```

```
    @passwd= 'passvbdotnet1',
    @defdb = 'Chapter07'
USE Chapter07
EXEC sp_grantdbaccess 'vbdotnet1'
USE Northwind
EXEC sp_grantdbaccess 'vbdotnet1'
```

The vbdotnet1 login doesn't strictly require a user security account for the *Northwind* database because this sample database has a guest account, and the public role for the database grants permissions to all database objects in the initial version of the database. However, creating a user account for the vbdotnet1 login allows you to remove the guest account for the database and still maintain data access privileges. In addition, a user account for the vbdotnet1 login enables a database designer to fine-tune the permissions available to the login relative to other database users.

Remove a SQL Server Login and User

In the normal course of database management, it becomes necessary to remove as well as add database users. Since a SQL Server database user has two different security account types, you must remove both to flush a user completely from a database server. To prevent orphaned user accounts, SQL Server doesn't allow you to delete the login for a user without deleting the user accounts associated with that login. Removing the user accounts without eliminating their login still allows a user to access a database server, and the login can access any databases with a guest account.

> **Note** In addition to being unable to remove a login with one or more associated user accounts, you cannot remove a login that is currently in use, owns a database, or owns a job in the msdb database. A job is a sequence of steps for automating a task that is defined in the msdb database, one of the built-in databases that SQL Server uses to manage itself. As mentioned previously, you can never remove the sa login from a SQL Server instance.

Before you attempt to remove a login, it's useful to survey any associated user security accounts associated with the login. This permits you to make sure that you can remove all of the user security accounts associated with a login before attempting to remove the login. Invoke the *sp_helplogins* system stored procedure with the name of the login for which you're seeking information, as shown in the following code. The system stored procedure returns a result set comprising two recordsets. The first recordset contains a single row for the login that you specify. The second recordset contains a row for each user account associated with the login named as the argument for the *sp_helplogins* system stored procedure. If you don't specify a login name as an argument when you invoke *sp_helplogins*, the system stored procedure still returns two recordsets. However, these recordsets return information for all the logins on the current SQL Server instance.

```
--Return info about a login, including
--its database user accounts.
EXEC sp_helplogins @LoginNamePattern='vbdotnet1'
```

Figure 7-2 shows the two recordsets that result from running *sp_helplogins vbdotnet1* after first invoking the script in the preceding section. The first recordset starts with the login name followed by a partial display of the login's SID. The next two columns indicate the default database and language for the login. The next-to-last column, *AUser*, is *yes* when the login has at least one corresponding user account. The last column, *ARemote*, indicates whether the login specifies a remote login for a linked server. The second recordset provides information about each user account for the login. The first and third columns denote, respectively, the login name and the user name. By default, these are the same, but you can override this convention. The second column designates the database to which the user account belongs. The last column specifies whether the user account is for an individual user or a role.

	LoginName	SID	DefDBName	DefLangName	AUser	ARemote
1	vbdotnet1	0x17CD8AD6306AA04BBCC6252E7...	Chapter07	us_english	yes	no

	LoginName	DBName	UserName	UserOrAlias
1	vbdotnet1	Chapter07	vbdotnet1	User
2	vbdotnet1	Northwind	vbdotnet1	User

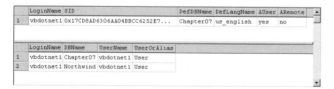

Figure 7-2. Use the *sp_helplogins* system stored procedure to learn about a login on a database server.

Armed with the information in Figure 7-2, you can construct a T-SQL script like the following to remove the vbdotnet1 security accounts from the server. Start by invoking the *sp_revokedbaccess* system stored procedure in each database with a user account for the vbdotnet1 login. Specify the user account name as the argument for the *sp_revokedbaccess* system stored procedure. Notice that the script invokes *sp_revokedbaccess* twice—once in each database for which the vbdotnet1 login has a user account. The script closes by running the *sp_droplogin* system stored procedure. This system stored procedure requires just one argument specifying the name of the login to remove. The permissions for removing user accounts and logins match those for adding them: a login attempting to remove a login must be a member of the sysadmin or securityadmin fixed server role to run *sp_droplogin*.

```
--Drop a SQL Server login,
--first revoking its user accounts.
USE Northwind
EXEC sp_revokedbaccess 'vbdotnet1'
USE Chapter07
EXEC sp_revokedbaccess 'vbdotnet1'
EXEC sp_droplogin @loginame = 'vbdotnet1'
```

Adding and Removing Logins for a Windows User

Managing a login based on a Windows user account for Windows NT, Windows 2000, or Windows XP is similar to managing a SQL Server login. By a Windows user account, I mean the account by which Windows validates a user. From a user perspective, the main difference is that a login based on a Windows user account doesn't have to specify a login and password when connecting to a SQL Server instance. For a database user with a login based on a Windows user account, all a user has to do is select the Windows Authentication option in the Connect To SQL Server dialog box of Query Analyzer. If the target SQL Server instance has a login for the Windows user account, the connection attempt succeeds. However, a member of the sysadmin group must first create a login for the Windows account in order for the attempt to succeed.

The process for creating login and user security accounts based on a Windows user account is similar to that for managing SQL Server logins. When creating a login for a Windows user account, invoke the *sp_grantlogin* system stored procedure to create a login for the Windows user. When you designate a login name for a Windows user account, the name must have two parts delimited by a backslash (\). The part before the backslash is the name of the Windows server. The part after the backslash is the name of the Windows user.

The *sp_grantlogin* system stored procedure is analogous to the *sp_addlogin* system stored procedure. Both of these system stored procedures create a new login. SQL Server saves both of the logins in the *syslogins* table. SQL Server also reports both types of logins in the same column of the result set from the *sp_helplogins* system stored procedure. However, the login created with *sp_grantlogin* is authenticated by a Windows 2000 or Windows NT server. When a Windows user attempts to connect, SQL Server stores the Windows security identifier for the Windows user. The Windows security identifier is analogous to the SQL Server SID. However, the Windows security identifier is managed by the Windows server, and the Windows security identifier is longer than the SQL Server SID (85 bytes for Windows and 16 bytes for SQL Server).

After you create a login for a Windows user account, the login cannot connect to any database without a user security account unless the database has a guest account. You can create a user security account for a login based on a Windows user account with the identical procedure for a SQL Server login. First set the database context for the user security account. For example, invoke the *USE* statement to specify the name of the database for which you want to create a user account. Second run *sp_grantdbaccess* with the name of the login as its argument.

The following short script demonstrates the syntax for creating a login based on a Windows user account. The Windows user account resides on a Windows 2000 Server named CCS1. The name of the account on the Windows server is winvbdotnet1. The last two lines of the script create a user security account in the Chapter07 database based on the login created with *sp_grantlogin*.

```
--Create a Windows login with
--access to Chapter07 database.
EXEC sp_grantlogin 'CCS1\winvbdotnet1'
USE Chapter07
EXEC sp_grantdbaccess 'CCS1\winvbdotnet1'
```

> **Note** If the Windows user account is for a Windows server that isn't a domain server but merely an application server, you must create a local account on a Windows NT Workstation or Windows 2000 Professional client computer with the same name and password as on the Windows server.

Removing the login is a two-step process because the login has a single user security account associated with it. First remove the user account for the Chapter07 database. The system stored procedure for eliminating a user security account based on a login for a Windows user account is the same as for deleting a user account based on a SQL Server login. Second revoke the login. When dropping a login, you use a different system stored procedure for one based on a Windows user account than for one created by SQL Server. Here is the T-SQL code for implementing the steps.

```
--Drop a Windows login with sp_revokelogin,
--but first revoke its user accounts.
USE Chapter07
EXEC sp_revokedbaccess 'CCS1\winvbdotnet1'
EXEC sp_revokelogin 'CCS1\winvbdotnet1'
```

Who's Using Your Application?

By now, you should feel comfortable with the idea that there are actually two reasonable answers to this question. The first answer is the login name. This name identifies a user as she enters a SQL Server instance. The second answer is the name of the user security account. This identifies a user within a database. If a login doesn't have a user security account assigned explicitly to it for a database and the database has a guest account, the login can enter the database with the guest user account.

SQL Server 2000 offers two built-in functions for telling you the login name and user account name of the user performing a task in your database. The *SYSTEM_USER* function returns the login name. The *CURRENT_USER* function returns the user account name. Before discussing a listing to clarify the operation of these functions, I want to mention the *DB_NAME* function. When you enter *DB_NAME()* in a *SELECT* statement, it returns the name of the current database.

The following short script invokes the *SYSTEM_USER* and *CURRENT_USER* functions in three different databases—master, Northwind, and Chapter07. If you run this script after connecting to a SQL Server instance with the CCS1\winvbdotnet1 login, you obtain an identical result set from each *SELECT* statement. However, two different values are displayed for the *CURRENT_USER* function. In the master and Northwind databases, the *CURRENT_USER* function returns *guest*. In the Chapter07 database, the *CURRENT_USER* function returns CCS1\winvbdotnet1. This is because the login has a user account named after it in the Chapter07 database.

```
--Demonstrate functions telling who's using a database.
USE master
SELECT DB_NAME(), SYSTEM_USER, CURRENT_USER
USE Northwind
SELECT DB_NAME(), SYSTEM_USER, CURRENT_USER
USE Chapter07
SELECT DB_NAME(), SYSTEM_USER, CURRENT_USER
```

Processing Logins Based on Windows Groups

In addition to basing a login on an individual Windows user account, you can also create a login for a Windows group account. The latter type of Windows account provides a single name for referencing more than one individual Windows account. When you create a login based on a Windows group, all the individual members of the group inherit the login assigned to the group. In addition, you can create separate logins for a subset of the individual members of a Windows group. These logins for individual Windows accounts complement the login based on the Windows group account by providing an alternative route into a SQL Server instance and the databases on it.

The sample for this section works with a Windows group named winvbdotnet. The group contains two individual Windows user accounts named winvbdotnet1 and winvbdotnet2. All the accounts reside on a CCS1 Windows 2000 server. The following T-SQL script shows the code for creating distinct logins for the Windows group and the individual Windows accounts that belong to the Windows group. After the execution of the script, both the winvbdotnet1 and winvbdotnet2 users connect to the SQL Server instance with their own logins as well as the login for the Windows group. In addition, both individual Windows user accounts have their own user accounts in the Chapter07 database, and the Windows user accounts map to the Chapter07 user account for the Windows group.

```
--Create login for winvbdotnet Windows group.
EXEC sp_grantlogin 'CCS1\winvbdotnet'
USE Chapter07
EXEC sp_grantdbaccess 'CCS1\winvbdotnet'

--Also create logins for group members individually.
EXEC sp_grantlogin 'CCS1\winvbdotnet1'
EXEC sp_grantdbaccess 'CCS1\winvbdotnet1'
EXEC sp_grantlogin 'CCS1\winvbdotnet2'
EXEC sp_grantdbaccess 'CCS1\winvbdotnet2'
GO
```

There are actually two ways to make a login unavailable for use. First, you can run the *sp_revokelogin* system stored procedure as demonstrated in the preceding section. This approach removes the login for the Windows user from the database server. With this approach in the current context, revoking the CCS1\winvbdotnet1 Windows user login still permits the winvbdotnet1 Windows member of the winvbdotnet group to connect to the database server. This capability is possible because the Windows user can access the database server through the login for the winvbdotnet Windows group.

The following script shows the syntax for a second approach. It denies login permission to an existing login—in this case, the one for the winvbdotnet1 Windows user. This approach still permits the winvbdotnet2 Windows user to access the database server. However, by denying the login permission for the CCS1\winvbdotnet1 login, the script overrides the ability of the winvbdotnet1 Windows user to access the database server through the CCS1\winvbdotnet login.

```
--This does not affect winvbdotnet2,
--which is a member in winvbdotnet group.
EXEC sp_denylogin 'CCS1\winvbdotnet1'
GO
```

The following one-line script blocks the winvbdotnet2 Windows user from accessing the database server. The logins for the winvbdotnet1 and winvbdotnet2 Windows users are still on the database server. In addition, the CCS1\winvbdotnet login still authorizes its members to log in to the server. A deny setting (instituted by the *sp_denylogin* system stored procedure) for the individual Windows accounts overrides the access granted by the *sp_grantlogin* system stored procedure for the CCS1\winvbdotnet Windows group account. This general rule is true for all permissions. A deny setting overrides a grant setting.

```
--This does affect winvbdotnet2,
--which is a member in winvbdotnet group.
EXEC sp_denylogin 'CCS1\winvbdotnet2'
GO
```

To remove the logins for the individual Windows users and the Windows group to which the users belong, you should revoke the database access to the user security accounts corresponding to logins. Then you can revoke the specific logins for the Windows users and Windows group. The following script shows the syntax for accomplishing these tasks. While the *sp_denylogin* system stored procedure disables a login from accessing a server, this system stored procedure doesn't remove the login from a SQL Server instance—instead, you need the *sp_revokelogin* system stored procedure to accomplish the task.

```
--Cleanup account settings.
USE Chapter07
EXEC sp_revokedbaccess 'CCS1\winvbdotnet'
EXEC sp_revokedbaccess 'CCS1\winvbdotnet1'
EXEC sp_revokedbaccess 'CCS1\winvbdotnet2'
EXEC sp_revokelogin 'CCS1\winvbdotnet'
EXEC sp_revokelogin 'CCS1\winvbdotnet1'
EXEC sp_revokelogin 'CCS1\winvbdotnet2'
GO
```

Samples for Assigning Permissions

This section demonstrates the essential T-SQL statements for organizing permissions within a database. Specific techniques exist for object and statement permissions. In addition, the final topic in the section reveals how to manage permissions when a user account can possess a permission directly as well as indirectly through its membership in one or more Windows accounts or SQL Server roles.

The samples in this section rely on a version of the *EmailContacts* table. The "Scripting Tables" section of Chapter 2 initially presented the T-SQL code for this table. For the purposes of this chapter, you can re-create this table in the Chapter07 database simply by changing the references to the Chapter02 database in Chapter 2 to the Chapter07 database. A copy of the modified code exists in the sample file CreateEmailContactsTable.sql for your easy reference. This section also relies on the existence of the four logins with their matching user security accounts created so far in this chapter. Recall that one login is a SQL Server login (vbdotnet1), another two are Windows user logins (CCS1\winvbdotnet1 and CCS1\winvbdotnet2), and a fourth login is a Windows group login (CCS1\winvbdotnet) comprising each of the two Windows user accounts. This section presents the T-SQL code for assigning permissions to the user accounts for the logins. The permissions relate to the *EmailContacts* table. Therefore, create the *EmailContacts* table with a member of the sysadmin fixed server role, such as the Windows Administrator user account or the SQL Server sa login.

Select, Insert, and Delete Permissions for a Table

To evaluate the effect of permission assignments, you will need two concurrent active connections to your database server. Connect once as a member of the sysadmin fixed server role, and connect a second time with a SQL Server login—namely, vbdotnet1. Note that if you ran the code shown earlier to drop the vbdotnet1 login account, you'll need to rerun the code that creates the account. To confirm that the user account for the vbdotnet1 login has no permissions in the Chapter07 database, attempt to run the following script with the user account for the login. Notice that the attempt returns an error message saying, in effect, that *SELECT* permission is denied on the *EmailContacts* object in the Chapter07 database.

```
--SelectInsertDeletePermission
--The SELECT succeeds if the user has
--SELECT permission.
USE Chapter07
SELECT * FROM EmailContacts
```

To remedy the error condition, you need to assign *SELECT* permission for the *EmailContacts* table to the vbdotnet1 user account. From your session initiated by a sysadmin member, run the following line of T-SQL. You must invoke this line of code from your session for the sysadmin role member. You can also always assign permissions from a session with any member of the db_owner fixed database roles. Sessions for selected other user accounts will work in special circumstances; see the "GRANT" topic in Books Online for details. Recall also that members of the sysadmin role have permission to perform all tasks on a database server.

```
--Assign SELECT permission for the EmailContacts
--table to the vbdotnet1 user account.
GRANT SELECT ON EmailContacts TO vbdotnet1
```

Notice that you can assign a *SELECT* permission with the *GRANT* T-SQL statement. The sample in the preceding T-SQL statement uses the *SELECT* keyword. This keyword denotes the permission to run a *SELECT* statement, such as the sample to select all columns for all rows from the *EmailContacts* table. You can optionally assign *INSERT*, *UPDATE*, *DELETE*, and *REFERENCES* permissions for a table. When concurrently assigning more than one permission, delimit the items in your list of permissions with commas. After the permissions, use the keyword *ON* and then specify the row source, which is the *EmailContacts* table in this demonstration. Conclude the *GRANT* statement with the *TO* keyword followed by the account to which you are granting permission. The preceding *GRANT* statement designates the user security account for the vbdotnet1 login. You can alternatively specify a SQL Server role for one or more user accounts or the user security accounts for a Windows user or a Windows group account.

After invoking the preceding *GRANT* statement, the session for the vbdotnet1 user can execute a *SELECT* statement against the *EmailContacts* table. However, the following attempts from the vbdotnet1 connection to insert a row and then delete the row fail with a pair of error messages about denied *INSERT* and *DELETE* permissions. Again, the problem is that the vbdotnet1 user doesn't have the proper permissions.

```
--Run from Chapter07 database context for vbdotnet1 user.
INSERT INTO EmailContacts
    VALUES(3,'Tony', 'Hill', 'thill@cabinc.net')
SELECT * FROM EmailContacts
GO

DELETE
FROM EmailContacts
WHERE Email1 = 'thill@cabinc.net'
SELECT * FROM EmailContacts
GO
```

Running the following statement from the sysadmin session enables the vbdotnet1 user account with the proper permissions to execute the preceding script. Notice that the syntax for adding multiple permissions is the same as for adding a single permission except that you delimit permissions with a comma. The following statement adds *INSERT* and *DELETE* permissions to the existing *SELECT* permission for the vbdotnet1 user account.

```
--Delimit more than one permission in a GRANT
--statement by using a comma.
GRANT INSERT, DELETE ON EmailContacts TO vbdotnet1
```

You can drop all permissions for the vbdotnet1 user account by revoking or denying them. When you are working with an individual user account that doesn't belong to any role, you can either revoke or deny existing permissions for the account. Use the *REVOKE* statement with the *ALL* keyword to remove any existing permissions from a user account. The following one-line script demonstrates the syntax for dropping the *SELECT*, *INSERT*, and *DELETE* permissions from vbdotnet1.

```
--Use the ALL keyword to concurrently
--drop all existing permissions.
REVOKE ALL ON EmailContacts TO vbdotnet1
```

Permission to Create a Table

When you assign the permission to create a table to user accounts for any login not in the sysadmin fixed server role, you complicate how an application must refer to tables. This is because all members of the sysadmin fixed server role are the dbo user. This dbo user belongs to all databases. You cannot drop the dbo user from a database—just as no one can drop the sa login from an instance of SQL Server. The rules for referencing tables created by the dbo user are different than those for tables created by any other database user.

Every user can refer implicitly to tables created by the dbo user. When the samples in the preceding section referenced *EmailContacts*, they implicitly referred to *dbo.EmailContacts* because the table was created by a member of the sysadmin fixed server role. SQL Server requires you to explicitly refer to tables created by other users.

When a user who doesn't qualify as a dbo user creates a table, other users can refer to the table by the name of the table's owner and the table's name. For example, if vbdotnet1, who isn't a dbo user, creates a table named *EmailContacts* in the Chapter07 database, other users must refer to the table as *vbdotnet1.EmailContacts*. The vbdotnet1 user can refer to the *EmailContacts* table that it created as either *vbdotnet1.EmailContacts* or just *EmailContacts*. However, if that user wants to reference the dbo *EmailContacts* table, he must specify *dbo.EmailContacts*. If any other user, who didn't herself create a table named *EmailContacts*, refers to a table with *EmailContacts*, SQL Server automatically interprets this as a reference to *dbo.EmailContacts*.

> **Note** When you permit non-dbo users to create tables, a best practice is always to use the owner qualifier when referring to a table. If a dbo user creates a table named *EmailContacts*, refer to it as *dbo.EmailContacts*. If a non-dbo user, such as vbdotnet1, creates a table named *EmailContacts*, refer to it as *vbdotnet1.EmailContacts*. Because users who write their own T-SQL statements can deviate from these rules and the rules lengthen T-SQL statements in any event, restrict the permission to create tables to the dbo user if at all possible.

The following line of script shows the syntax for enabling the vbdotnet1 user to create a table. Set the database context if it isn't already set to the database for which you want to grant the permission. Notice that the syntax for granting permission to execute a statement is slightly different than for an object permission. After the *GRANT* keyword, you list the statement for which you are granting permission, but there's no need to follow this statement with the *ON* keyword. In addition to *CREATE TABLE*, you can reference *CREATE DATABASE*, *CREATE VIEW*, *CREATE PROCEDURE*, *CREATE FUNCTION*, and selected other statements. (See the "GRANT" topic in Books Online for the complete list.) As with granting object permissions, you can use a comma delimiter when concurrently granting permission for more than one statement. Close the *GRANT* statement with the *TO* keyword followed by the name of the account that is to receive the statement permission.

```
--PermissionToCreateATable
--Set the database context before invoking.
GRANT CREATE TABLE TO vbdotnet1
```

After executing the preceding *GRANT* statement, the vbdotnet1 user can create a table, such as one named *EmailContacts*. Because vbdotnet1 owns *vbdotnet1.EmailContacts*, it can automatically insert and delete rows from the table—just like members of the sysadmin fixed server role and the db_owner fixed database role. However, owning an object doesn't automatically convey membership in any role. Since the vbdotnet1 login isn't a member of the sysadmin fixed database role, the vbdotnet1 user cannot be a dbo user. The following script shows the code for creating the *vbdotnet1.EmailContacts* table. Running the script from the session connection based on the vbdotnet1 login makes the vbdotnet1 user the table's owner.

```
--Invoke the DROP TABLE statement if the EmailContacts
--table already exists for the vbdotnet1 user.
CREATE TABLE EmailContacts
(
ContactID int Not Null PRIMARY KEY,
FirstName nvarchar(20) NULL,
LastName nvarchar(35) NULL,
Email1 nvarchar (255) NULL
)
```

Listing the tables from the sysadmin session now shows two tables with the name *EmailContacts*. Use the following script to display the list of tables with *EmailContacts* as their name located in the Chapter07 database. Figure 7-3 shows the result set from the script. One row in the result set is for the dbo user, and the other is for the vbdotnet1 user.

```
--List the EmailContacts tables after creating
--a second one with the vbdotnet1 user.
USE Chapter07
SELECT *
FROM INFORMATION_SCHEMA.TABLES
WHERE TABLE_NAME = 'EmailContacts'
```

	TABLE_CATALOG	TABLE_SCHEMA	TABLE_NAME	TABLE_TYPE
1	Chapter07	dbo	EmailContacts	BASE TABLE
2	Chapter07	vbdotnet1	EmailContacts	BASE TABLE

Figure 7-3. The *Table_Schema* column in the result set from the *INFORMATION_SCHEMA.TABLES* view denotes a table owner's user name.

Note You cannot drop a user and its corresponding login if the user owns an object, such as a table, in a database. If the objects for a user are no longer required, simply drop them and then drop the user and its login. If you require the objects that are owned by a user who must be dropped, invoke the *sp_changeobjectowner* system stored procedure to transfer object ownership to a user who will remain in the database. Then drop the user and login.

You can add rows to and delete rows from the *vbdotnet1.EmailContacts* table with a script such as the following. Because the script references the table with its owner qualifier, you can run the script from any connection based on a login with a user having permission to select, insert, and delete rows from the table—for example, the dbo user or the vbdotnet1 user. The script generates a result set with three recordsets. The first recordset is empty because the preceding script creating the table doesn't insert any rows. The second recordset shows the new row for Tony Hill. The third row shows the table empty again after the deletion of the row for Tony Hill.

```
--Run from Chapter07 database context.
SELECT * FROM vbdotnet1.EmailContacts
INSERT INTO vbdotnet1.EmailContacts
    VALUES(3,'Tony', 'Hill', 'thill@cabinc.net')
SELECT * FROM vbdotnet1.EmailContacts

DELETE
FROM vbdotnet1.EmailContacts
WHERE Email1 = 'thill@cabinc.net'
SELECT * FROM vbdotnet1.EmailContacts
```

Windows Users and Groups

Windows users that are part of Windows group accounts in SQL Server create special challenges for setting security. This is because an individual Windows user account can derive its permission for a task from multiple sources. Even if you revoke a permission from the user account for a Windows user, the Windows user may still be able to perform the task controlled by the permission. This can happen because the user account for a Windows group, to which a Windows user belongs, grants the same permission revoked for the individual Windows user account. In fact, this same scenario applies to SQL Server user-defined roles. A SQL Server account can belong to multiple roles and have permissions applied directly to it. Revoking one permission may not fully close all the routes by which a SQL Server user account can derive permission to perform the task.

> **Note** When working with a Windows user account that can belong to a Windows group or a SQL Server user account that can belong to one or more user-defined roles, consider using a *DENY* statement to remove a permission. This statement blocks the permission to perform a task even if the account is granted permission for the task by virtue of its membership in another Windows group or SQL Server role.

The *sp_helprotect* system stored procedure helps you monitor the permission assignments for user accounts. By default, *sp_helprotect* returns a result set with the object and statement permissions for all the user accounts in all databases on a database server. You can filter the result set by specifying selected arguments. For example, designating a database in the *@name* argument returns the permissions for just that database. You can also filter by type of permission (object or statement), by account to whom a permission is granted, and by who granted the permission. If you assign filters so that the result set from *sp_helprotect* is empty, the procedure returns an error message for the condition.

The following script tracks the assignment of permissions in the Chapter07 database. Before the execution of any *GRANT* statement in the script, a database connection to the Chapter07 database that is based on the login for CCS1\winvbdotnet1 cannot perform a *SELECT* statement on the *dbo.EmailContacts* table. After the first set of *GRANT* statements, the CCS1\winvbdotnet1 user account can perform a *SELECT* statement based on two distinct permissions. One permission is granted directly to the user in the second *GRANT* statement. The other permission is granted to the user account through the CCS1\winvbdotnet Windows group because CCS1\winvbdotnet1 is a member of this Windows group. The invocation of the *sp_helprotect* system stored procedure after the first three *GRANT* statements confirms these two permissions and one more for the CCS1\winvbdotnet2 Windows user account.

The next T-SQL statement in the script revokes the *SELECT* permission for the *dbo.EmailContacts* table for the CCS1\winvbdotnet1 Windows user. This removes the permission from the collection of permissions in the database. The execution of *sp_helprotect* in the next statement confirms that the permission is missing. However, removing the permission doesn't block the CCS1\winvbdotnet1 Windows user from performing a *SELECT* statement with the *dbo.EmailContacts* table as its source. This is because the CCS1\winvbdotnet1 Windows user derives *SELECT* permission for the table from its membership in the CCS1\winvbdotnet Windows group.

Revoking *SELECT* permission for the CCS1\winvbdotnet Windows group account in the database will block the CCS1\winvbdotnet1 Windows user from performing a *SELECT* statement on the *EmailContacts* table. However, this action will also remove *SELECT* permission for the CCS1\winvbdotnet2 Windows user. The script instead invokes a *DENY* statement for *SELECT* permission on the *dbo.EmailContacts* table for the CCS1\winvbdotnet1 user account. This statement restricts just the ability of the CCS1\winvbdotnet1 Windows user to perform a *SELECT* statement with *EmailContacts* as the source. Any other user in the CCS1\winvbdotnet Windows group still retains permission for a *SELECT* statement against the *dbo.EmailContacts* table. The final execution of *sp_helprotect* reveals an explicit permission denying the CCS1\winvbdotnet1 user account from performing a *SELECT* statement on the *dbo.EmailContacts* table.

```
--DenyPermission
--Before granting SELECT permissions, SELECT statements from
--either CCS1\winvbdotnet1 or CCS1\winvbdotnet2 were denied.

--Grant SELECT permission for dbo.EmailContacts for
--a Windows group and its two individual Windows accounts.
GRANT SELECT ON dbo.EmailContacts TO [CCS1\winvbdotnet]
GRANT SELECT ON dbo.EmailContacts TO [CCS1\winvbdotnet1]
GRANT SELECT ON dbo.EmailContacts TO [CCS1\winvbdotnet2]

EXEC sp_helprotect @name='dbo.EmailContacts'

--After granting SELECT permission, SELECT statements from
--either CCS1\winvbdotnet1 or CCS1\winvbdotnet2 were granted.

--Revoke SELECT permission for dbo.EmailContacts
--for CCS1\winvbdotnet1.
REVOKE SELECT ON dbo.EmailContacts TO [CCS1\winvbdotnet1]

EXEC sp_helprotect @name='dbo.EmailContacts'

--After revoking SELECT permission for CCS1\winvbdotnet1, the
--account could still perform a SELECT statement for EmailContacts.

--Deny SELECT permission for dbo.EmailContacts
--for CCS1\winvbdotnet1.
DENY SELECT ON dbo.EmailContacts TO [CCS1\winvbdotnet1]

EXEC sp_helprotect @name='dbo.EmailContacts'

--Denying SELECT permission makes it impossible
--for CCS1\winvbdotnet1 to SELECT from EmailContacts.

--Clean up permission assignments.
REVOKE SELECT ON dbo.EmailContacts TO [CCS1\winvbdotnet]
REVOKE SELECT ON dbo.EmailContacts TO [CCS1\winvbdotnet1]
REVOKE SELECT ON dbo.EmailContacts TO [CCS1\winvbdotnet2]
```

Part III

Using Visual Basic .NET and Related Technologies with SQL Server 2000

8

Overview of the .NET Framework

This book is aimed at professional developers who have an interest in programming SQL Server 2000 with Visual Basic .NET. Up to this point, the book's focus was primarily on SQL Server. I believe that you cannot optimally program SQL Server in any language without a firm understanding of its basic workings. Chapters 2 through 7 provide a foundation in SQL Server that will serve you especially well for data access and manipulation tasks, as well as related data definition tasks.

Chapter 1 introduces you to beginning Visual Basic .NET and ADO.NET techniques so that you have some context for understanding how to apply the SQL Server 2000 topics presented in Chapters 2 through 7. This chapter builds on the initial exposure to technologies for the .NET Framework that appears in Chapter 1. If you jumped to this chapter without any prior exposure to the .NET Framework, now is a great time to look over Chapter 1. To take maximum advantage of Visual Basic .NET for creating SQL Server solutions, you need this background. Chapter 1 starts to convey this background, and this chapter finishes the task so you are ready to dig into the .NET Framework code samples throughout the rest of the book.

Visual Basic .NET is one of the core programming languages for the .NET Framework, which Microsoft defines as "a new computing platform designed to simplify application development in the highly distributed environment of the Internet." Microsoft is taking a whole new initiative with the .NET Framework that radically redefines how businesses can program and deploy solutions as well as access resources over corporate intranets or the Internet. In many presentations on the beta versions, it was popular to hear that Microsoft was betting its business on the .NET Framework. Whether or not this is precisely true, it is clear that Microsoft has invested heavily in providing a comprehensive new structure for building solutions, and the firm has changed in a major way its most popular programming language—Visual Basic. The scope and magnitude of the changes provide Visual Basic database developers with challenges and opportunities.

This chapter attempts to familiarize you with the architecture of the .NET Framework and related technologies, including ASP.NET and XML Web services. See Chapter 1 for introductory material on Visual Basic .NET and ADO.NET. My goal in this chapter isn't to empower you as a programmer with these technologies. Instead, I aim to show how the technologies complement one another. In the process, I feel you will develop an appreciation of why it is important for you to adopt the .NET Framework and start programming it with Visual Basic .NET. This book's remaining chapters examine the programming you use for the topics introduced conceptually in this chapter and Chapter 1. This chapter contains a programming sample, but I put it there just for reference purposes. This chapter is about concepts—not code. ADO.NET, ASP.NET, and XML Web services each are covered in a separate chapter that drills down into techniques for developing solutions with them. Plus, there's another chapter—Chapter 12—on managing XML with Visual Basic .NET.

An Introduction to the .NET Framework

This section introduces you to core .NET Framework concepts. It starts with an overview of the .NET Framework architecture. Next it moves on to what's new about source code compilation. This is a natural entry point to discussing how you manage the referencing of solutions by clients and how to deploy solutions. The section closes with brief looks at selected .NET Framework features that build on material covered earlier in the section and are important to how you will use .NET Framework solutions.

.NET Framework Architecture

Perhaps the most dominant architectural element of the .NET Framework is its common language runtime. The *runtime* sits on top of the operating system. Programmers write to the runtime in any compliant language. The runtime eventually writes what is called *managed code* to the specific operating system on which it runs. As I write this chapter, the operating systems that support the common language runtime include those based on the 32-bit versions of Windows, including Windows 98, Windows Millennium, Windows NT, Windows 2000, and Windows XP. Microsoft has a Windows .NET Server operating system in beta that likely will include the .NET Framework. In addition, you can expect the runtime to produce code suitable for the forthcoming 64-bit version of Windows.

While the common language runtime runs on top of Windows systems, one of the great strengths of runtime-compliant solutions is their interoperability with other operating systems. This follows from runtime support for XML and XML Web services. The core technologies for XML and XML Web services rely on industrywide standards. Because other vendors are endorsing these standards along with Microsoft, you can be assured of a level of interoperability for the solutions that you create with the runtime. If vendors follow through on their endorsements for the standards and you build your solutions with code managed by the runtime, you can achieve levels of interoperability across operating systems not previously enjoyed by application developers.

> **Note** Learn more about XML in Chapter 6 and Chapter 12. XML Web services is the topic of the closing section in this chapter as well as the whole of Chapter 13.

When you develop solutions for SQL Server, you will benefit from the fact that the common language runtime can be hosted by SQL Server 7 and later versions and Microsoft Internet Information Services versions 4.0 and later; IIS is the Microsoft Web server for Windows NT and Windows 2000. This gives you a chance to integrate tightly your database and Web solutions with the managed code generated by the runtime. For example, the .NET Framework ships with managed providers for SQL Server and OLE DB data sources. The SQL Server provider offers substantial performance advantages because of its optimization for SQL Server 7 and SQL Server 2000. In addition, ASP.NET is a part of the .NET Framework that IIS hosts. ASP.NET is the next generation of development techniques for those creating solutions with ASP now. In order for ASP.NET pages to run, they must be compiled by the runtime. ASP.NET is an integral part of IIS 4, just as IIS 3 hosts the ASP object model. In addition, ASP.NET can interact with SQL Server through the .NET Framework data providers. (See Chapter 11.)

Figure 8-1 shows a simplified schematic of the path from source code in Visual Basic .NET (or another runtime-compliant language) through to interactions with SQL Server and browsers on a Web. The common language runtime translates the source code to managed code. This managed code can, in turn, interact with the Windows operating system, SQL Server, and browsers. With the aid of a managed provider, such as the one for SQL Server, your solutions can access and manipulate data. You can use the ASP.NET component of the .NET Framework to create ASP.NET pages that reside on an IIS server. These pages can serve dynamic elements to browsers on a Web. In addition, the pages can offer the browsers the opportunity to access and manipulate data on a SQL Server.

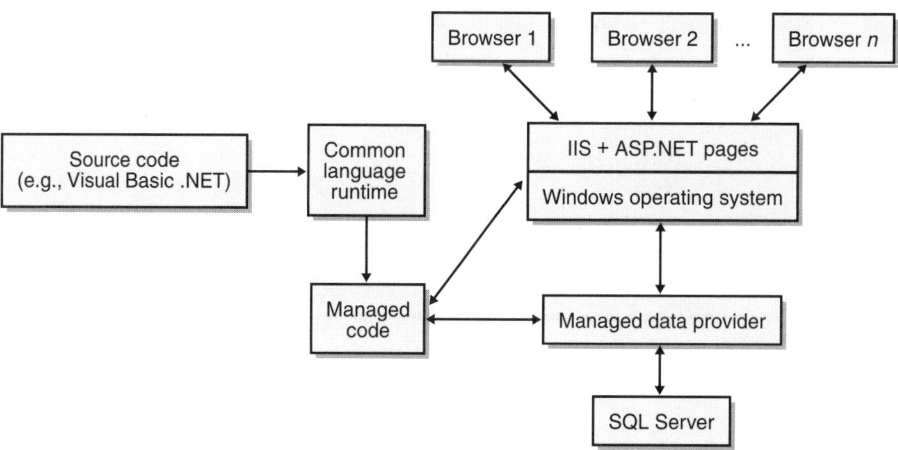

Figure 8-1. A schematic illustrating the role of the common language runtime and its managed code in interacting with the Windows operating system, SQL Server, and IIS.

Compiling Source Code

The .NET Framework supports multiple programming languages in a common way. In addition to Visual Basic .NET, Visual Studio .NET supports the preparation of source code in other languages, such as C# and Visual C++. Web developers who are used to building solutions in JScript will appreciate the fact that they can create ASP.NET solutions with JScript .NET. In fact, these developers can use JScript .NET to implement solutions across the full range of .NET Framework capabilities because JScript .NET is runtime-compliant. In addition, third-party vendors are readying other languages for runtime compliance. This proliferation of languages will offer developers a wide range of options in which they can program the .NET Framework.

> **Note** JScript .NET is an extension of the Microsoft JScript language, which was based on ECMAScript (ECMA-262). ECMA is the European Computer Manufacturers Association. JScript .NET is explicitly developed for use with the runtime. Since JScript .NET generally follows the ECMAScript conventions, it offers a standards-based route to creating .NET Framework solutions with a popular scripting language among Web developers.

A wonderful thing about the .NET Framework is that all languages can have the same capabilities if they are fully runtime-compliant. For example, Visual Basic .NET has the same capabilities as C# (and so does JScript .NET). In addition, developers in one language can freely use objects created by developers in other languages. This cross-language functionality wasn't always easy to implement before the .NET Framework because of slight incompatibilities in source code language compilation processing. The .NET Framework actually readies source code for execution through a series of two compilations. The first compilation converts the source code to Microsoft Intermediate Language (MSIL). The second compilation converts MSIL to CPU-specific code for the computer running the code.

The first compilation from source code to MSIL generates a representation of your program that captures its programming instructions and metadata about the program. The compilation stores its output in a portable execution (PE) file. MSIL is a language-independent way of expressing your programming logic. The metadata describes the types that your code creates as well as their members, such as methods, properties, and events. A type is an element, such as a class. Another important metadata element is the description of the assembly for an application. An assembly is the unit for storing a solution in the .NET Framework. The assembly description in the metadata includes an identity specification for the assembly, exported types, referenced types, and security permissions needed to run. A reference to a type is like a reference to a class in a type library. Because the metadata for an assembly includes internal types and externally referenced types, there is no need for references to type libraries in Visual Basic .NET and other runtime-compliant languages.

The second compilation from MSIL to machine code readies your code for execution on a specific processor. The .NET Framework can accomplish this with a Just-In-Time (JIT) compiler. JIT compilers are specific to each supported CPU architecture. JIT compilation compiles the contents of the PE file as a user references its elements during a session. PE file elements, such as a type member, aren't compiled until a user references them. After the initial compilation, the runtime automatically refers to the compiled version, thus reducing the time to execute the code. This process also saves compilation time by not compiling those elements that a user doesn't reference during a session. Unless an administrator explicitly designates otherwise, the compilation to machine code examines the MSIL and its metadata to determine whether it is type safe. The term *type safe* refers to the fact that a type accesses only memory locations for which it has access permission. This security check allows the .NET Framework to enforce security restrictions.

Assemblies and Manifests

Assemblies and their manifests are an exciting innovation introduced with the .NET Framework. They are exciting because they can clearly eliminate many opportunities for .dll conflicts—popularly referred to as "dll hell." A .dll conflict can emerge when a user installs a new application that writes over an existing .dll file with a new version that isn't fully backward compatible. If another, previously installed, application relies on a type member that is changed or eliminated in the new .dll, the previously installed application will fail. Assemblies and manifests offer a couple of workarounds to this problem for solutions based on COM components.

A .NET Framework solution exists as an assembly of one or more files. These files can include the MSIL as well as other resources, such as image files or other document files that a solution references. An assembly must include a manifest, which contains metadata about the assembly. This metadata describes the files in the assembly. In the case of a single-file assembly, the manifest resides within the solution's .dll file, but otherwise an assembly's manifest resides in a separate file. A solution's assembly can consist of up to four types of elements.

- The assembly's manifest
- The MSIL code for the solution
- The type metadata for the MSIL code
- Resource files required by the solution

The assembly is the deployment unit for solutions in the .NET Framework. Because all the elements for a solution can exist within a single assembly, you can deploy a solution by distributing the solution's assembly of files. Store the assembly as a directory or subdirectory on a target workstation. The common language runtime must be installed on the workstation in order to transform the MSIL to native machine code. This approach is particularly convenient where a solution performs tasks that you don't care to share with other solutions.

Some solutions are utilities. When these utility solutions are likely to be a part of many other solutions, you can store the utility solutions in the Global Assembly Cache (GAC). There is one GAC per computer. When you place an assembly in the GAC for sharing by one or more other solutions, the shared assembly in the GAC must have a strong name. The *strong name* uniquely identifies an assembly in the GAC to avoid conflicts from two assemblies that may have the same text for a name. Visual Studio .NET includes tools to simplify the creation of strong names that are based on the text for an assembly's name, its version number, culture information, public key, and a digital signature.

The .NET Framework SDK discourages locating assemblies in the GAC unless essential because it can complicate deployment and administration. For example, deploying a solution can require copying two directories—one for the main assembly and the other for the shared assembly in the GAC. In addition, the GAC resides in the system directory. This directory often has restricted access. These access restrictions may necessitate permissions for copying an assembly to the GAC that the user installing an application doesn't have.

Deploy a Solution—XCOPY a Folder

You can create .NET Framework solutions for Windows that are totally self-contained in a single folder. When you create a .NET Framework solution using the Windows Application template, Visual Studio .NET by default creates a folder for your solution in the last directory in which you saved a previous solution. This folder has a root folder and at least two subfolders—bin and obj. You can store the resources for your solutions, such as custom classes, image files, and XML schema files, anywhere you need in the root folder (or even outside the root). The advantage of storing all files for a solution in the root folder, or any of its subfolders, is that you can then deploy your solution with an XCOPY command, or any equivalent technique, that copies the solution's folder. All the Visual Basic .NET solutions included in this book's sample files are available as folders that you can copy to your computer. If you copy them to a machine with the proper configuration—for example, one with the common language runtime—you can run the solutions from the folder to which you copy them.

While I am talking about solution folders, it is probably worth mentioning a couple of special files within a solution folder. The solution's .exe file resides in the bin subfolder. You can launch the solution by invoking this file. By default, the .exe file has the same name as the solution. Therefore, if your solution has the name WindowsApplication1, the .exe file for starting the solution has the name WindowsApplication1.exe. To open the solution for editing in Visual Studio .NET, you can open a file with the solution's name and the extension .sln, such as WindowsApplication1.sln. This file resides in the root folder for the solution.

Note Whether you deploy an assembly in a directory or in the GAC, there is no need to add settings to the system registry in order to be able to use the solution based on the assembly. Just reference the solution assembly in the client application.

Selected .NET Framework Features

Even from the short introduction to the .NET Framework to this point, it should be clear that the .NET Framework is massive in scope. This section presents a few of the features that I find most worthy of brief mention and discussion. In order to manage the book's length, I leave out many that also are worthy of your consideration.

The runtime *garbage collector* can automatically manage the release of memory for an application, and it can cut back on the incidence of memory leaks for long-running applications. This is because the garbage collector can automatically recover memory for reference types—things such as classes and arrays—that consume memory when there are no longer pointers to them in memory.

The runtime garbage collector recovers unused memory based on several rules, one of which has to do with no more space available for recently created reference types. The good news is that you no longer have to worry about clearing memory for inactive reference types. The bad news is that you cannot tell precisely when the garbage collector will recover memory. In addition, the collector doesn't work for unmanaged resources, such as references to files. In this case, you can invoke the *Dispose* method, but you should also disable the garbage collector, checking for any objects explicitly disposed of. You can invoke the *System.GC.SuppressFinalize* method for the object disposed of to accomplish this task. Another approach is to use the *Close* method, which calls the *Dispose* method. You can also use the *Close* method to promptly remove selected managed objects, such as SQL Server database connection objects. Although the garbage collector will eventually remove such managed items as SQL Server connection objects, you can improve the responsiveness of your applications by eliminating them when you know they are no longer needed.

Namespaces are a means of organizing and referring to groups of elements in the runtime. In addition, your own custom applications have namespaces—by default, these namespaces bear the solution's name. The .NET Framework SDK lists the names of all the runtime namespaces. As a database developer, you are likely to have special interest in the *System.Data*, *System.Data.SqlClient*, *System.Data.SqlTypes*, and *System.Data.OleDb* namespaces.

Table 8-1 includes brief summaries of each of these namespaces. Notice that the names of the namespaces follow a hierarchical naming convention. The *System.Data* namespace represents the broadest grouping of elements in Table 8-1. The *Sytem.Data.SqlClient*, *System.Data.SqlTypes*, and *System.Data.OleDb* namespaces denote subsets of the broader *System.Data* namespace.

Table 8-1 Selected Runtime Namespaces for Database Developers

Name	Summary
System.Data	Represents mostly elements in the ADO.NET architecture.
System.Data.SqlClient	Represents elements in the SQL Server .NET data provider.
System.Data.SqlTypes	Represents elements for SQL Server native data types.
System.Data.OleDb	Represents elements in the OLE DB .NET data provider.

The namespaces parallel the kind of functionality that Visual Basic developers used to enable by adding references to type libraries. You can now accomplish the same thing by using the *Imports* statement for a namespace, where the elements in a namespace are analogous to the classes and members of a type library. Look in Chapter 10 for code samples illustrating the use of the *System.Data.SqlClient* namespace. As indicated in a note in the "Assemblies and Manifests" section, the way to reference a server solution assembly in a client solution is to reference the server solution assembly from the client assembly. An *Imports* statement in the client solution assembly permits you to reference the namespace for the server solution assembly. Chapter 9 demonstrates the syntax for this statement. You will find numerous code samples implementing the *Imports* statement throughout the rest of this book.

By now, you should understand that the .NET Framework is the way of the future for those developing solutions with Microsoft products. Nevertheless, it is likely that you either have built or are using solutions based on the previous Microsoft development framework—COM. Therefore, Microsoft introduced technology to help ease you through the transition period. For example, Visual Studio .NET offers graphical techniques for importing COM objects within .NET Framework solutions. Visual Studio .NET also offers graphical tools for exporting .NET Framework solutions so they can interoperate with your previously created COM solutions. Because there are fundamental incompatibilities between COM and the .NET Framework, these tools don't always work perfectly. See the "Troubleshooting Interoperability" topic in the Visual Studio .NET Help files for an enumeration of some issues that you may encounter along with suggested remedies.

An Overview of ASP.NET

ASP.NET is a specialized component of the .NET Framework. You can use ASP.NET to create Web applications that are accessible from browsers that can connect to the page. The same basic techniques (plus some more) apply to the creation of XML Web services solutions. This chapter aims to orient you to .NET Framework Web technologies.

How Does ASP.NET Relate to ASP?

ASP.NET is similar but not identical to ASP (Active Server Pages). Many professional Visual Basic developers found ASP a serviceable way to create Web solutions. One important reason for this is that ASP can create forms on Web pages that any browser can read. Nevertheless, ASP has drawbacks. For example, ASP mixes HTML page design code and programming logic in the same file. This leads to a type of spaghetti coding that is difficult to read and interpret. In addition, you can create your programming logic in any of a variety of languages, but pure Visual Basic isn't one of them. The closest you can get is VBScript. Furthermore, the Visual Basic development environment isn't suitable for creating ASP Web pages. Some Visual Basic developers adopted Visual InterDev, and these developers could use the Visual InterDev development environment. However, the Visual InterDev development environment had a different look and feel than the one for Visual Basic. As a consequence, many developers used Notepad or another favorite text editor to create ASP Web pages from scratch.

> **Note** What do you need to create solutions with ASP.NET? First, you need any Windows operating system that installs IIS automatically or allows you to install it optionally. This is because IIS is the Web server for ASP.NET solutions, and it contains the ASP.NET object model, just as it does the ASP object model. Second, you need the .NET Framework. If you installed Visual Studio .NET on your machine, your computer already has it. Visual Studio .NET provides a friendly, familiar development environment for creating ASP.NET solutions. Third, you need MDAC version 2.6 or later for data access and manipulation. Visual Studio .NET installs MDAC version 2.7, which is more than sufficient. However, you can download the latest MDAC version, free of charge, from the Microsoft site at *http://www.microsoft.com/data/download.htm.*

I believe ASP.NET will become immensely popular with Visual Basic developers because it solves the three problems described in the preceding paragraph.

- ASP.NET separates page design and program logic into two separate but related files. This ends the need to mingle HTML layout code and program logic code in the same file.
- You can create ASP.NET Web solutions with Visual Basic. No longer do you have to develop in another language that is almost like Visual Basic—namely, VBScript. In addition, the solutions you develop with Visual Basic .NET can interact with solutions created by Web developers creating solutions in JScript .NET because both languages are runtime-compliant.
- The Visual Studio .NET development environment has the same look and feel when you work with Web Forms as it does when you work with Windows Forms. For example, you have a Toolbox. You can drag and drop controls on a Web page just as you do with a Windows form. In addition, the Toolbox insulates you from the HTML syntax underlying the controls you use on Web Forms.

> **Note** Visual Basic developers migrating to ASP.NET from ASP may notice that a couple of familiar tools are gone. First, you no longer code solutions in VBScript—as indicated above, you can create both Windows and Web solutions with Visual Basic .NET. Second, Visual InterDev is gone too. Now you can use the same Visual Studio .NET development environment for Windows and Web solutions. If you are a Visual Basic developer who has been waiting until the time was right to do Web development, come on in—developing for the Web will feel familiar and be just as much fun to construct as Windows applications. If you are a Visual Basic developer who is experienced at Web development, there's no better time than right now to drastically speed up your Web development cycles by taking advantage of ASP.NET.

There is another critical difference between ASP.NET and ASP that merits your attention. ASP.NET is compiled, and ASP code is interpreted. Compiled code runs faster, so you are likely to enjoy performance benefits when you are running the compiled code. Of course, the first time ASP.NET uses a module, there is a delay associated with the compilation of the code. As a developer, you will likely encounter this compilation delay much more than your users simply because your job is to fine-tune the code for optimal performance. Each fine-tuning adjustment requires a new compilation.

In spite of all the differences between ASP and ASP.NET, there are many similarities. You can run ASP and ASP.NET pages side by side on the same Web server. Your ASP Web pages have an .asp extension. Your ASP.NET pages will typically have an .aspx extension. This side-by-side capability allows you to gradually introduce new functionality with ASP.NET into a previously existing solution initially created with ASP.

Selected objects, such as *Application* and *Session*, exist in both ASP and ASP.NET. *Application* objects serve as global variables across an application. When you need to make sure that some values are available to all users of an application, *Application* objects represent an option. ASP.NET also offers the ASP.NET cache as a means of sharing data across all the users of an application. As in the past, *Session* state variables allow the sharing of information between HTTP (Hypertext Transport Protocol) requests of a browser within a session. ASP.NET improves on the *Session* variables available in ASP by allowing you to share *Session* variables across a Web farm with multiple computers designed to offer the same Web application. If an application saves a *Session* variable in response to an HTTP request to one computer in a Web farm, a second request from the same user to a different computer in the Web farm can still gain access to that same *Session* variable.

Creating an ASP.NET Web Application

You can create a new ASP.NET solution by clicking the New Project link on the Visual Studio Start Page and choosing the ASP.NET Web Application template. When you do this, Visual Studio suggests a default location for the solution's assembly on the local IIS server, such as *http://localhost/WebApplication1*. You can choose any other solution name on any other IIS to which you can connect. (You need the .NET Framework installed on any computer from which you plan to run ASP.NET pages.) Clicking OK opens two folders—one on the Web server and another in the default location where Visual Studio stores its solution assembly folders. If the application has the name WebApplication1, launching a new ASP.NET Web application creates a new folder named WebApplication1 within the wwwroot directory of the inetpub directory.

> **Note** To remove an ASP.NET solution from your computer and eliminate it from appearing in the Visual Studio Start Page, you must delete both of its folders.

When Visual Studio .NET opens your application, you see a blank page. Solution Explorer shows that the page's title is WebForm1.aspx. You can assign a more meaningful name for the page's title property from the Properties window. The page initially opens with a *pageLayout* property setting of GridLayout. This setting lets you align controls on the Web page according to the grid marks. You can change the *pageLayout* property in the Properties window. The other possible *pageLayout* property setting is FlowLayout. In this mode, Visual Studio arranges your controls from top to bottom in classic Web page layout mode—like a word processor. Notice that the Solution Explorer and Properties windows serve the same kinds of functions for this Web application as they do for other, non-Web, applications.

Choosing the HTML tab at the bottom of the page exposes the empty Web page in HTML view. Between the *body* tags on the Web page, notice the *form* tags. The *form* tag has a *runat* setting of *server*. ASP.NET pages are designed to accept forms and controls that run on the server.

Adding Controls to an .aspx Page

Switch back to Design view by clicking the Design tab at the bottom of the page. Choose Toolbox from the View menu. If the Toolbox isn't open to the Web Forms section, click that section heading. This action permits you to add Web server controls to your .aspx Web page. Web server controls are highly abstracted for programming in your Visual Studio development environment. They insulate you from HTML conventions and provide richer functionality than is available through standard HTML form controls, such as *<input>* elements. In addition, the Web server controls offer a wider array of control options than is available with HTML form controls. For example, the Web server controls include a Calendar control and a configurable RadioButtonList control. In spite of the abstracting, Web server controls render HTML to a browser.

> **Note** In some cases, Web server controls require client-side scripting to perform properly. For this reason or performance reasons, you may care to switch to another type of Web control for selected applications.

You can add a control to a Web form by double-clicking the control in the Toolbox. Then you can drag the control to where you want it on the form. Add a button control and a label control from the Toolbox to the Web form, WebForm1.aspx.

Adding Code Behind an .aspx Web Page

Now you're ready to work with the code behind the Web form and its controls. On the form, double-click the button control. This opens the Code Editor for the file that contains the form code. The filename is WebForm1.aspx.vb, which appears on a tab at the top of the Code Editor. You should be able to see WebForm1.aspx.vb in Solution Explorer. If not, click the Show All Files icon on the Solution Explorer toolbar and then click the + next to WebForm1.aspx. (Recall that Windows displays the name of a toolbar icon when you hold the mouse pointer over it.)

Enter the code in Figure 8-2 in the Code Editor for WebForm1.aspx.vb. When the page opens initially, there is no code in either the *Page_Load* or *Button1_Click* event procedure. The *Page_Load* event procedure initializes the page by assigning a caption to the button and inserting an empty string for the label control. The *Button1_Click* event procedure assigns the text Hello World to the label when the user clicks the button. This page works in very old browsers. For example, I used Internet Explorer 4 to view the WebForm1.aspx page, and it worked perfectly. The computer running the browser didn't have the .NET Framework installed either.

```
Public Class WebForm1
    Inherits System.Web.UI.Page
    Protected WithEvents Button1 As System.Web.UI.WebControls.Button
    Protected WithEvents Label1 As System.Web.UI.WebControls.Label

 Web Form Designer Generated Code 

    Private Sub Page_Load(ByVal sender As System.Object, _
        ByVal e As System.EventArgs) Handles MyBase.Load
        'Put user code to initialize the page here
        Button1.Text = "Click me"
        Label1.Text = ""
    End Sub

    Private Sub Button1_Click(ByVal sender As System.Object, _
        ByVal e As System.EventArgs) Handles Button1.Click
        Label1.Text = "Hello World"
    End Sub
End Class
```

Figure 8-2. A pair of event procedures for an ASP.NET Web application with a version of the classic Hello World sample.

XML Web Services

XML Web services facilitate computer-to-computer interaction in the same general way as ASP.NET facilitates computer-to-human interaction through an .aspx Web page. This section tries to acquaint you with why XML Web services are a part of the .NET Framework. The content in this section provides an overview of the technologies used to implement XML Web services. See Chapter 13 for more coverage of XML Web services, with specific attention to how you create, test, and deploy XML Web services as well as how clients use an XML Web service.

What Can XML Web Services Do for Me?

As a professional developer, you should be very interested in XML Web services. This is because XML Web services can expand the reach of your existing solutions. The more folks your applications serve, the more those applications are worth (and the more money you can make from them).

In the preceding section on ASP.NET, you gained some exposure on how to create classic Web solutions with the .NET Framework, or more specifically ASP.NET. In ASP.NET, you create a Web-based solution for an individual to read and interact with through a browser. Whether users access your Web page for solving a problem over an intranet or an extranet, the end result is that it appears in a browser. A user, which is another name for a person, has to do something with it. XML Web services provide an environment for creating solutions that machines—not people—consume. However, both classic Web pages and solutions created with XML Web services work over the Web. To be more specific, XML Web services let machines interact with each other and share information across the Web. The beauty of the underlying XML Web services architecture is that the machines can be using different operating systems (Windows vs. Unix, for example), and the programming language used to create a solution on one machine can be different from the programming language in which a client solution accepts results from a server (Java vs. Visual Basic .NET).

So again, how are XML Web services going to help you? XML Web services promise to deliver universal access to your software solutions no matter what the operating system or programming language on client and server machines. In addition, this isn't just a Microsoft initiative. It is an open initiative with sponsors from leading software firms. For example, one of the technologies underlying XML Web services is UDDI (Universal Description, Discovery, and Integration). I'll describe this technology in a moment, but I mention it here because its developers include IBM, Intel, SAP, Ariba, and Microsoft. In addition, the technology rests on industry standards, such as those published by the W3C (World Wide Web Consortium). By building new solutions that take advantage of XML Web services or retrofitting XML Web services to existing solutions, you are positioning your efforts to support the leading information technology firms and the most widely accepted computing industry standards.

Overview of the XML Web Services Infrastructure

XML Web services permit client and server machines to interact with each other as if they were two machines on the same LAN with all compatible systems—except that the machines can be connected over a Web with incompatible systems. The client machine can request the server machine to perform a transaction, such as move money from one account to another. In this scenario, the client passes the parameters for the transaction. In return, the server can perform the transaction and return an outcome to the client workstation. Alternatively, a client can request some information from a server, such as a document. The server can retrieve the document from its archives and return it to the client over popular transport protocols as a self-describing, text-based message (think XML documents described by XSD schemas). XML Web services support a couple of popular protocols—namely HTTP (both *PUT* and *GET* methods) as well as SOAP (Simple Object Access Protocol), which is a W3C standard. If I were a different kind of author and this were a different kind of book, I would say XML Web services developers can use SOAP to clean up their applications.

A couple of other really cool features about XML Web services deserve mention. One of these is that the technology helps you find XML Web services; UDDI implements this feature. The other bit of technology is a language that enables an XML Web service running on a server to describe itself so that a client machine can determine how to interact with it. This language has the name Web Services Description Language (WSDL).

A Closer Look at the Underlying Technologies

The preceding overview confirms that XML Web services rely on three main technologies.

- UDDI can provide a way of discovering what's available as a Web service.
- WSDL is an XML-based grammar for describing XML Web services.
- SOAP is another XML-based standard, but this standard targets the exchange of information between two loosely coupled computers.

UDDI

UDDI offers a directory service capability. The UDDI online directory service allows firms to publish contact information for their organization, summaries of XML Web services offered, and standards with which clients must comply to access their XML Web services. You can discover more about the UDDI implementation from its organization site at *http://www.uddi.org*. Those who want to make their XML Web services available for use can register with a UDDI directory service. Those searching for an XML Web service can go to the UDDI site to discover XML Web services that meet their search criteria. The UDDI returns URLs for learning more about XML Web services. A searcher can use the URLs to discover the location of one or more documents in WSDL describing each XML Web service.

> **Note** At the time that I write this chapter, you can register your business and its XML Web services at *http://www.uddi.org/register.html.*

WSDL

A WSDL document describes the things that an XML Web service does. Such a document also declares where and how to get the XML Web service to make those things happen. A WSDL document is expressed in XML. The W3C formal specification is available at *http://www.w3c.org/tr/wsdl*. This document describes and demonstrates the objectives of WSDL as well as specifying the XML syntax, elements, and attributes for a WSDL document. A WSDL document describes an XML Web service in terms of six elements, as shown in Table 8-2.

Table 8-2 WSDL Elements

Element	Description
types	Encloses data type definitions used in messages exchanged between the XML Web service and its clients.
message	Specifies an abstract definition of the message exchanged between the XML Web service and its clients.
portType	Refers to an abstract set of operations—each operation has an associated input message and one or more output messages.
binding	Designates a concrete protocol and data format specification for operations and their messages relating to a specific *portType*. The binding can be to HTTP, SMTP (Simple Mail Transport Protocol), or some other communication protocol or medium.
port	Designates a single communication endpoint, namely, the combination of a binding and an address, for an operation.
service	Refers to a collection of related ports.

SOAP

SOAP (version 1.1) is the third main technology underpinning XML Web services. Go to *http://www.w3c.org/tr/soap* for the standard's specification. The SOAP standard is an XML-based mechanism for exchanging messages between two computers. SOAP is a one-way messaging format for remote procedure calls, but you can adapt it for a request/response message paradigm as well as a request/multiresponse paradigm.

The SOAP specification has three parts, but only the first is mandatory. This part designates what's in a message, who the message is for, and whether the message is optional or mandatory. The SOAP specification refers to this first part as the SOAP *Envelope* element.

The second and third parts aren't mandatory. In its second part, the SOAP specification designates a serialization scheme for exchanging application-specific data types that are outside the scope of native XML data types. The third part of the specification denotes techniques for representing remote procedure calls and their responses. The client for an XML Web service is likely to call some method for the XML Web service. This method can optionally require a response.

Visual Studio .NET permits you to create XML Web services and clients without working intimately with the UDDI, WSDL, and SOAP standards. Nevertheless, having a basic grasp of the issues that accompany these underlying standards will equip you to understand better how XML Web services work and how to create them.

9

Creating Windows Applications

Windows applications in the .NET Framework are applications based on one or more Windows Forms. These applications target computers that can run code behind a form and provide a rich environment to the user. Each form in a Windows application is an instance of the Windows *Form* class. This class behaves similarly to the forms in prior versions of Visual Basic (and other Microsoft development environments such as Microsoft Access forms), but the Windows *Form* class in the .NET Framework is distinct and independent of forms in earlier Microsoft development environments. It is convenient to think of the *Form* class as a die or a mold from which you derive specific instances of a form. Like other classes, the *Form* class is a collection of properties, methods, and events. The forms in your Windows applications inherit the *Form* class properties, methods, and events.

This chapter covers creating solutions with Windows applications and managing the Windows Forms in those applications with Visual Basic .NET code. The focus of the chapter is on intermediate to advanced topics, such as creating and using classes, inheritance, event programming, and handling run-time errors with structured exception handling. For each topic covered, I identify what's new for the topic with Visual Basic .NET. In some cases, such as inheritance and structured exception handling, the emphasis is wholly on what's new because Visual Basic .NET introduces these capabilities to Visual Basic programmers.

Getting Started with Windows Forms

Windows Forms exist within Windows applications. You can create the shell for a Windows application from a template within Visual Studio .NET. Windows applications are for environments that find it efficient to take advantage of the local processing power of client workstations. When developing solutions based on the Windows Applications template, you will often use Windows Forms to manage interaction with users and display information to users. This section introduces you to the basics of creating and managing solutions based on Windows Forms.

Start with *Form1* in a Windows Application

You can create a Windows application from the Visual Studio .NET Start Page. If you followed the instructions in Chapter 1 for configuring Visual Studio .NET and the Start Page, you can open the Start Page by clicking the Windows Start button, choosing Programs, selecting the Microsoft Visual Studio .NET folder, and then selecting Microsoft Visual Studio. Begin a new Windows application by clicking New Project on the Start Page and selecting the Windows Application template in the New Project dialog box. Next enter a project name, such as **StartWithForm1**. Visual Studio assigns a default folder for your project's assembly of files, but you can override the default location for a solution's assembly folder by either typing the path to the alternate folder or browsing to it. Figure 9-1 illustrates the New Project dialog box set to create a new Windows application named StartWithForm1 in the VisualStudioProjects folder of the C:\Documents and Settings\Administrator\MyDocuments path.

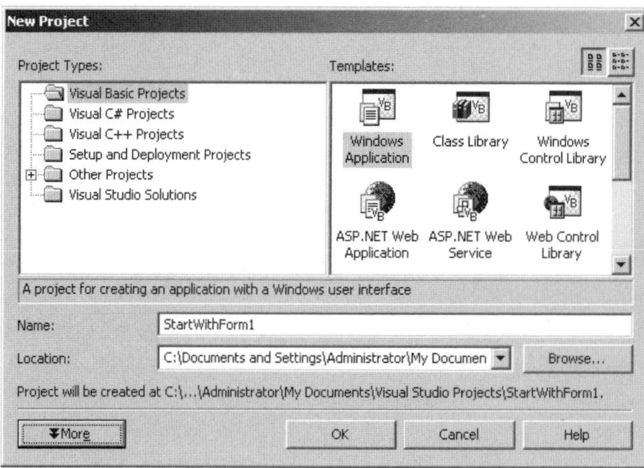

Figure 9-1. Start a Windows application by selecting Windows Application in the New Project dialog box.

Click OK in the New Project dialog box to create a new project for a Windows application. Visual Studio opens the Windows Forms Designer environment. The Windows Forms Designer window, Form1.vb[Design], enables you to graphically manipulate the form for an application. For example, you can use the Toolbox to add controls to a form, and you can add code behind the overall form as well as the controls on a form in the Windows Forms Designer. The overall Visual Studio .NET development environment should show three windows at this point. In addition to the Windows Forms Designer, you should see to the right Solution Explorer and the Properties window. Solution Explorer provides a tree view, much like Windows Explorer, of the items in the project for a solution. The Properties window provides an interface for manually viewing and updating the settings for selected items in Solution Explorer or the items on a form.

Figure 9-2 shows a blank form—*Form1*—in the Windows Forms Designer. Solution Explorer displays the Form1.vb file. This file contains your graphical design changes as well as any code behind the form. The Assembly.vb file in the Visual Studio .NET development environment enables you to view assembly attributes, such as version numbers for a solution. I expanded the References folder in Solution Explorer so you can see selected references available to *Form1*, including the *System.Windows.Forms* namespace. The Properties window below Solution Explorer shows that the *Text* property setting for the form is Form1. You can type over the *Text* property setting to assign a more meaningful caption to your form.

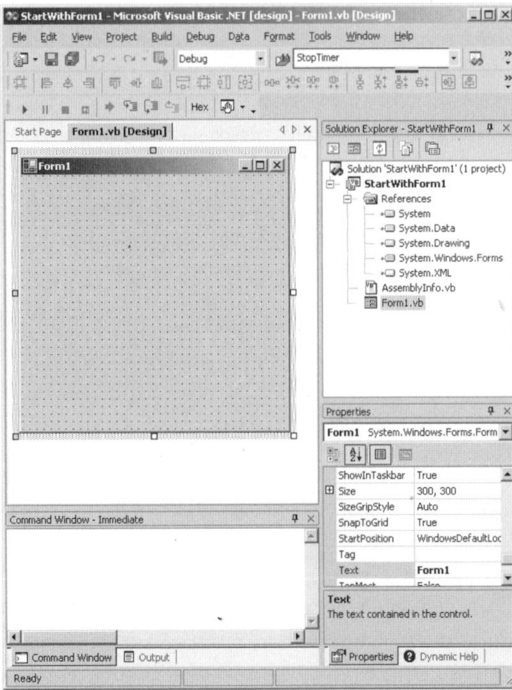

Figure 9-2. The initial layout for a Windows application includes a blank form and a few references to selected namespaces.

Managing Windows Forms

You can manage Windows Forms in at least three standard ways. First, manipulate the properties of the form. Second, add controls to a form that facilitates common tasks, such as user input. Third, add code behind a form.

The form in Figure 9-2 inherits its initial properties, methods, and events from the *Form* class in the *System.Windows.Forms* namespace. Use a form's *Text* property to set its caption, for example, from Form1 to My First Form. You can position a form with the *DesktopLocation* and *Location* properties. *Form* class methods let you manipulate form instances. Use the *ShowDialog* method to open a modal form instance. When you open a form with this method, you must close the form (with the *Close* method) before you can navigate to another open form. By opening a form with the *Show* method, you enable users to navigate to another form without closing the modeless form opened with the *Show* method.

Note A namespace can serve as a reference to a type library in Visual Basic 6. It is the reference to *System.Windows.Forms* that provides the properties, methods, and events for a Windows form, such as the one in Figure 9-2.

To make a form part of a Windows application, you can add controls to the form. In addition, you can write code for the form and the controls on it. Choose Toolbox from the View Menu in Visual Studio .NET to open a window with multiple sections, or tabs, from which you can drag controls and other object classes onto your forms. In the Windows Forms section of the Toolbox, you can select from several different types of controls.

- A wide variety of familiar controls facilitate the input and output of information and user interactivity. These familiar controls include button, text box, combo box, slider or trackbar, label, tab, radio button, check box, two different list box controls, and data grid.
- Another set of items in the Windows Forms section of the Toolbox includes controls that aren't typical, but they still help you manage the way a form displays information and operates. For example, use the *Tooltip* class to provide help to a user about the purpose of controls on a form when a mouse hovers over a control. Other special Toolbox items facilitate the creation and management of menus, the highlighting of controls with invalid data, and the provision of Help.

- A final set of elements in the Windows Forms section of the Toolbox includes a number of common dialog boxes. Application developers can use these Toolbox elements to give their custom applications the look and feel of a standard Windows application. There are seven of these control items: OpenFileDialog, SaveFileDialog, FontDialog, ColorDialog, PrintDialog, PrintPreviewDialog, and PageSetupDialog.

The Toolbox makes other sets of selections available from its Components and Data sections. You can use the Components section of the Toolbox to insert built-in components that ship with the .NET Framework. You can also add to this Toolbox section components that you acquire from third-party sources or develop internally. I will demonstrate the use of one of these components, the system timer, later in this chapter. The Toolbox's Data section offers components that facilitate ADO.NET tasks, such as making a connection with a data source, passing a SQL command to a data source, and returning a result set from a data source. The items in the Data section of the Toolbox are covered in Chapter 11.

You can initialize selected form properties and respond to user actions with form controls through event procedures. For example, in a *Load* event procedure for a form, you can set the form's *DesktopLocation* property. With the *Click* event procedure for a button, you can run Visual Basic .NET code to perform common actions, such as opening a message box. Double-click a form's caption or a control on a form to open the Code Editor window and display the shell, or stub, for an event procedure. The event is the default one for the form or control. When you double-click a form, Visual Studio .NET opens the shell for the *Load* event procedure. You can place any code your application requires in the shell. The next time the form opens, it runs that code. Double-clicking a button creates the shell for the button's *Click* event.

As with the Start Page and the Windows Form Designer, Visual Studio .NET opens the Code Editor on a tab, which in the case of *Form1* is labeled *Form1.vb*. In most ways, the Code Editor is like a standard code window. You can enter code into event procedure shells. You can also add sub procedures and function procedures to the code behind a form. You can use the Project menu to add other items to a Windows application, such as more forms or new custom classes. Use the drop-down lists at the top of the Code Editor to select a class, such as a button, and then see all the events for the class. Selecting an event from the list on the right opens an event procedure shell for that event. Visual Basic .NET uses the familiar naming convention of a class name followed by an underscore and the event name for event procedure shells. Therefore, the *Click* event procedure for *Button1* has the name *Button1_Click*.

A Windows Form with Two Button Controls

Developers often place buttons on forms to let users interact with an application. This section presents a Windows application with two buttons—one for saying hello and a second for moving the form around on the desktop. When the application opens, the *Form1_Load* event procedure positions *Form1* on the desktop and sets a caption for the form. *Form1* is the default startup object for a Windows application. The sample for this section completes the StartWithForm1 application initially launched in the commentary for Figures 9-1 and 9-2.

Figure 9-3 shows three event procedures for the StartWithForm1 application. The event procedures appear in the Code Editor, on the Form1.vb tab. Recall that you don't have to write the shell—just the contents—of an event procedure. I did insert a line continuation character (_) in the shell so you could see all the code generated automatically. Notice a rectangle around *Windows Forms Designer generated code.* You can expand the section by clicking the "+" next to it; click the "–" next to the top line of the expanded code to hide the section. This region contains code necessary for a form. For example, the code instantiates an instance of the *Form* class. The section also persists, or saves, your manual changes to the form and control property settings. Visual Studio manages the code in this section. Don't make your changes to the form from this section. Instead, use the Properties window for a selected class, such as the form or any of its controls, or use code in event procedures to assign property settings at run time.

> **Note** The *Windows Forms Designer generated code* region can be a convenient way for learning the syntax and naming conventions for manipulating form and control properties. Make changes graphically in the Windows Forms Designer and the Properties window. Then expand the *Windows Forms Designer generated code* region to view how Visual Studio creates the setting programmatically.

The *Form1_Load* event procedure uses two lines to set the initial location of *Form1* on the desktop. These lines set the form's top left edge in 450 pixels from the desktop's left border and down 450 pixels from the desktop's top border. The syntax relies on the *DesktopLocation* property for *Form1* (referred to by its *Me* keyword) and the *Point* structure. The *Form1_Load* event procedure assigns the string *Caption for Hello World* to the form.

> **Note** The *Point* structure represents values for a pair of xy-coordinates in a two-dimensional plane. A structure is like a data primitive in that it contains values and you can assign variables to those values (for example, *MyStartPoint* in Figure 9-3).

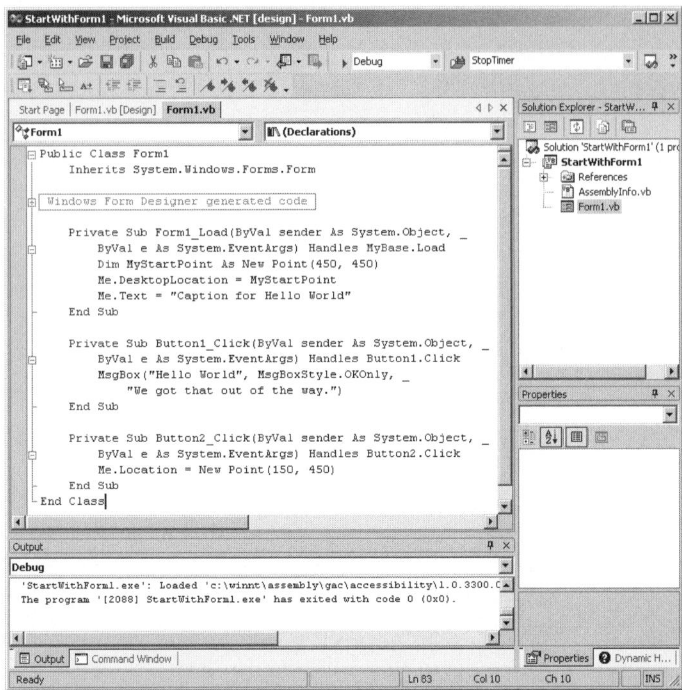

Figure 9-3. Three event procedures for managing the initial display of a form and how an application responds to clicks for each button on the form.

The *Click* event procedure for *Button1* displays a message box. The *MsgBox* statement in the event procedure takes three parameters. The first assigns a string for the message box to display, namely, *Hello World*. The second parameter specifies the types of buttons that will be displayed in the message box. The statement designates a single OK button. The closing parameter indicates a caption for the message box. As with Visual Basic 6, the IntelliSense feature in Visual Basic .NET helps you specify the *MsgBox* statement. For example, as you type the *MsgBox* statement you can choose from an array of button specifications for the message box.

The *Button2_Click* event procedure repositions the form on the screen from its initial point of (450, 450) to a new point of (150, 450). The event procedure moves the form 300 pixels to the left. You will find this capability useful when you need to actively manage where forms appear on your desktop. The event procedure's syntax uses a *Point* structure to specify the new location for the form. However, this event procedure specifies the position for the form with the *Location* property instead of the *DesktopLocation* property used in the *Form1_Load* event procedure. If a user docks the Windows taskbar (with the Start button) on the top, *DesktopLocation* will yield superior performance, but the two properties otherwise let you set a position anywhere on the desktop. If the taskbar is at the screen's top or left border, positioning a form with a *Location* property setting of (0, 0) can obscure part of the form. However, the *DesktopLocation* property setting assigns position relative to the taskbar. Therefore, a *DesktopLocation* property setting of (0, 0) positions a form flush with the taskbar.

After populating a form with controls and code behind the form, you will want to test your application. There are a couple of ways to do this. First, you can choose Start from the Debug menu. This will compile your application and launch its start object. In this case, that object is *Form1*. If the code compiles without error, your application launches. You can then start to test it. Second, you can choose to compile your application without attempting to run it immediately. You can compile a program into Microsoft Intermediate Language (MSIL) by choosing Build Solution from the Build menu. In this case, that process returns a file named StartWithForm1.exe in the bin folder of the solution's assembly folder. The assembly folder has the name StartWithForm1. You can run the solution's .exe file by double-clicking it in Windows Explorer or by typing the file's name and path in the Run dialog box and then clicking OK. The Run dialog box is available by choosing Run from the Windows Start menu.

Deploying a solution can be as simple as copying the StartWithForm1.exe to another computer running the .NET Framework. You don't need Visual Studio .NET installed on the other computer. The .NET Framework is available as a separate download for computers without Visual Studio .NET. See *msdn.microsoft.com/netframework/prodinfo/getdotnet.asp* for information on how to download the framework from MSDN or order it on CD.

Opening One Windows Form with Another

A form can open another form as a modal form or a modeless form. A *modal* form doesn't allow the user to activate another form until the modal form is closed. A message box is an example of a modal form. Users have to respond to the message box before they can proceed to any other form. A *modeless* form does allow users to activate another form before they close the modeless form. A toolbar is an example of a modeless form. The Find dialog box that you can open by choosing Find And Replace and then Find from the Edit menu in Visual Studio is an example of a modeless form. You can search for a string, switch the focus away from the Find dialog box, and then transfer the focus back to the Find dialog box to search for another incidence of a string.

A form doesn't have a modal or modeless property. Instead, you can open a form with methods that expose it as either a modal or a modeless form. Invoke the *ShowDialog* method for a form to open it as a modal form. To open a form as a modeless form, invoke its *Show* method.

Figure 9-4 shows a pair of forms with the captions Form1 and Form2. These forms belong to a Windows application named CallOneFormFromAnother. When a user clicks the button on *Form1*, the button's *Click* event procedure invokes a procedure named *OpenForm2*. This procedure can open *Form2* as either a modal or a modeless form. *Form1* also has a label control. This label control accentuates the form's name beyond the information in the form caption. *Form2* contains three controls: a label, a text box, and a button. The label in *Form2* serves the same purpose as the one in *Form1*. The text box in *Form2* is for displaying whether the form is open as a modal or a modeless form. The application assigns the *Text* property of *TextBox1* at run time. *Button1* closes *Form2* in response to a click.

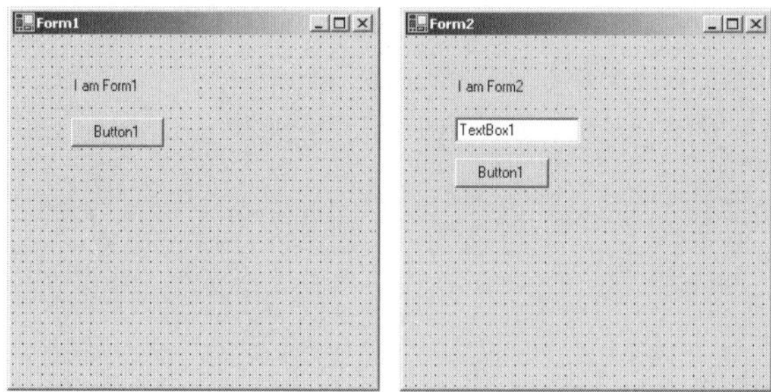

Figure 9-4. A design view of a pair of forms used in the CallOneForm-FromAnother sample.

Some of the form controls for the Windows application have static property settings that don't change at run time. When you have controls like this, you can assign the property settings at design time. For example, you can change the *Text* property of *Label1* in either form in the Properties window.

When a form or its controls have dynamic property settings that can change at run time in response to user actions, your application's code makes the property settings. The following listing contains two event procedures and a sub procedure. These procedures, which make up the custom code behind *Form1*, make dynamic property settings and handle interaction with the user.

The *Form1_Load* event procedure makes three dynamic property settings. First it positions the form toward the upper left corner of the desktop with a setting that is 100 pixels down and 100 pixels to the left from the upper left corner. Next the procedure widens the width of *Button1* from its default setting of 75 pixels to a new setting of 85 pixels. This extra width permits the display of the full *Text* property setting for *Button1*, which the procedure's last line assigns.

The *Button1_Click* event procedure contains a single line of code that invokes the *OpenForm2* procedure. This standard sub procedure presents as many as two message boxes. The first message box asks whether to open *Form2* as a modal form. If the user clicks the Yes button, the procedure executes a block of code to achieve that purpose. Notice the use of the *ShowDialog* method to open the form in this code block. Otherwise, the second message box appears with a prompt to open *Form2* as a modeless form. If the user clicks the OK button, the application opens *Form2* as a modeless form with the *Show* method. The user can close the message box without opening *Form2* by clicking the Cancel button. Recall that a message box is a modal form. Therefore, you must offer an opportunity to close a message box for an application to proceed.

```
Private Sub Form1_Load(ByVal sender As System.Object, _
    ByVal e As System.EventArgs) Handles MyBase.Load

    'Position the form toward top left area of desktop,
    'widen Button1's width from its default setting of 75 pixels
    'and assign a caption for Button1 as its Text property.
    Me.DesktopLocation = New Point(100, 100)
    Button1.Width = 85
    Button1.Text = "Open Form 2"

End Sub

Private Sub Button1_Click(ByVal sender As System.Object, _
    ByVal e As System.EventArgs) Handles Button1.Click

    'Invoke the OpenForm2 procedure.
    OpenForm2()

End Sub

Sub OpenForm2()

    'Declare a pointer reference for Form2.
    Dim MyFormPointer As New Form2()
```

```
    'Assign Text property for Button1 in Form2.
    MyFormPointer.Button1.Text = "Close"

    'Open a new instance of Form2 as a modal form or a modeless form.
    'When opening Form2 as a modal form,
    '   1. Assign a value to the Text property of TextBox1.
    '   2. Assign a start position 400 pixels down the page.
    '   3. Use the ShowDialog method for the object reference.
    '      pointing at Form2
    'When opening Form2 as a modeless form,
    '   1. Assign a start position 200 pixels down the page
    '   2. Use the Show method for the object reference
    '      pointing at Form2.
    '   3. Assign a value to the Text property of TextBox1.
    If MsgBox("Open Form2 as Modal", MsgBoxStyle.YesNo) = _
        MsgBoxResult.Yes Then
        MyFormPointer.TextBox1.Text = "I am modal."
        MyFormPointer.Downpix = 400
        MyFormPointer.ShowDialog()
    ElseIf MsgBox("OK, I am opening Form2 as a Modeless form.", _
        MsgBoxStyle.OKCancel) = MsgBoxResult.OK Then
        MyFormPointer.Downpix = 200
        MyFormPointer.Show()
        MyFormPointer.TextBox1.Text = "I am modeless."
    End If

End Sub
```

The code blocks for opening *Form2* as a modal or modeless form vary in more ways than just the use of the method to open the form. For the block that opens *Form2* as a modal form, the block starts by setting the *Text* property of *TextBox1* on *Form2*. Visual Basic doesn't allow you to dynamically set the *Text* property of *TextBox1* when *Form2* is open as a modal form. Therefore, the application makes the setting before opening the form. In the case of a modeless form, the application sets the *Text* property for *TextBox1* after the form opens. *Downpix* is the custom *Form2* property that determines how far down on the desktop *Form2* appears. By varying the value of *Downpix* depending on whether *Form2* opens as a modal or modeless form, the application makes it easier to identify how *Form2* is open. Because the *Downpix* property determines where the form opens on the desktop, you naturally have to specify the property's value before opening the form.

The custom code behind *Form2* consists of the two event procedures in the following code sample along with a *Public* variable declaration. The *Public* declaration is for the *Downpix* variable. The *Form2_Load* event procedure uses the value of this variable to specify the position for opening *Form2* on the desktop. The event procedure also dynamically sets the *Text* property for *Button1*. The *Button1_Click* event procedure demonstrates the syntax for closing a form programmatically without using the standard Close button on forms. Using the *Close* method is appropriate for situations in which you have to perform some special functions at the time that a form closes.

> **Note** You can suppress the display of the standard Close button on a Windows form by setting the form's *FormBorderStyle* property to None in the Properties window.

```
Public Downpix As Integer
Private Sub Form2_Load(ByVal sender As System.Object, _
    ByVal e As System.EventArgs) Handles MyBase.Load

    'Position the form 450 pixels from the desktop's left border,
    'and Downpix units from the desktop's top border.
    Dim MyStartPoint As New Point(450, Downpix)
    Me.DesktopLocation = MyStartPoint
    Button1.Text = "Close"

End Sub

Private Sub Button1_Click(ByVal sender As System.Object, _
    ByVal e As System.EventArgs) Handles Button1.Click

    'Close the current form (Form2).
    Me.Close()

End Sub
```

Creating and Using Class References

A firm grasp of class development principles is more important when creating solutions with Visual Basic .NET than for prior versions of Visual Basic. In addition, through namespace designations you can refer with a common syntax to both custom classes and built-in .NET Framework classes. Built-in classes are more prominent than in any prior version. For example, even data types behave as classes in that you can instantiate a data type when you declare a variable based on it. Namespaces and classes underpin one another, so a good grasp of either requires a working knowledge of both. This section contains a mix of commentary on class and namespace issues along with samples especially designed to jump-start your use of classes with Visual Basic .NET.

Creating a Class to Perform Calculations

A typical reason for using classes is to ensure that selected calculations are always performed exactly the same way throughout an organization. A calculation can be for taxing authorities, accounting reports, or scientific applications. Rather than have every application that needs the calculations separately code the expression for a calculation, your applications can reference a class with the calculations accurately performed. This application for classes eliminates possible errors by junior programmers who may not have the experience to code the calculation properly. In addition, the practice of coding calculations in classes makes for easy updating of the computations because there is a single point to modify when an update is necessary (for example, because of a new tax rate).

Although you can create a computational class as part of a Windows application, you will typically derive more value from the class by creating a stand-alone .dll file for it. Then any project can create a reference to the class through its .dll. This section demonstrates the overall process of creating a .dll for a class that performs calculations.

> **Note** To create a Class project, choose the Class Library template from the New Project dialog box (which, as you'll recall, opens when you click the New Project button on the Visual Studio Start page). Assign a name for your class. Visual Studio .NET creates an assembly folder for the class. The .dll file in the assembly folder with the same filename as the project for the Class Library contains the compiled code for the class.

To keep the focus on the construction of the class .dll file, I construct a simple sample class named *Class1* with its compiled code in ArithmeticClass.dll. (See the following code for the class, which is available for viewing in Class1.vb.) *Class1* exposes two properties and four methods. The properties represent two numbers that serve as input for one of four calculations also defined in the class. The properties are designated as *WriteOnly* because applications referencing the class merely need to copy values to the properties, which is another way of saying assign values to the properties. The class returns values through its four function procedures, which implement the four methods for the class. The functions, respectively, add, subtract, multiply, and divide the two numbers represented by the class property values.

Because the class calls for *WriteOnly* properties, we cannot use a *Public* variable declaration. Instead, the class uses a property procedure to enforce write-only access to each property. When you use only the *Get* clause or only the *Set* clause in a property procedure, you must also declare the property with either the *ReadOnly* keyword or the *WriteOnly* keyword. The sample demonstrates the syntax for using the *WriteOnly* keyword with the *Set* clause for the *dblFirst* and *dblSecond* properties of *Class1*. These property names are for external communication with the *Class1* in the ArithmeticClass project. The class internally manipulates *dbl1* and *dbl2*, which correspond to *dblFirst* and *dblSecond*. The *Set* clauses for each property accept values through their *dblValue* input argument.

After the property procedures for *dblFirst* and *dblSecond*, the listing shows the four function procedures for implementing the add, subtract, multiply, and divide operations between the two property values. Visual Basic .NET permits you to return a value from a function procedure in either of two ways. First, you can assign a value to the function name, as you did in previous versions of Visual Basic. Second, you can designate the function's value with an expression serving as the argument for a *Return* statement. The syntax for both approaches appears in the *Add2dbls* function procedure. I commented out the traditional approach that assigns a value based on the function's name. The other three function procedures demonstrate use of the traditional approach for specifying a return value.

```
Public Class Class1
    Private dbl1 As Double
    Private dbl2 As Double

    'WriteOnly property named dblFirst.
    Public WriteOnly Property dblFirst() As Double
    Set(ByVal dblValue As Double)
        dbl1 = dblValue
    End Set
    End Property

    'WriteOnly property named dblSecond.
    Public WriteOnly Property dblSecond() As Double
    Set(ByVal dblValue As Double)
        dbl2 = dblValue
    End Set
    End Property
```

```
    'Add dbls.
    Function Add2dbls() As Double
    'Add2dbls = dbl1 + dbl2
    Return (dbl1 + dbl2)
    End Function

    'Subtract dbls.
    Function Diff2dbls() As Double
    Diff2dbls = dbl1 - dbl2
    End Function

    'Multiply dbls.
    Function Mult2dbls() As Double
    Mult2dbls = dbl1 * dbl2
    End Function

    'Divide dbls.
    Function Div2dbls() As Double
    Div2dbls = dbl1 / dbl2
    End Function

End Class
```

Referencing a Class from a Windows Application

The class constructed in the preceding section has no visual interface. In order to use the class in an interactive application, you need to team the class project with another type of project, such as a Windows application. When a Windows application refers to the project, you get the best of both. The Windows application offers a rich graphical environment for gathering input and displaying results to users. The class project offers an environment that can efficiently perform calculations and share its computational engine with many clients concurrently. Each client can simply make an instance of the class to gain access to its properties and methods.

Figure 9-5 shows a Windows application with one form that uses *Class1* in the ArithmeticClass project. The form that appears in Figure 9-5 resides in the ArithmeticForm project. When the user clicks one of the four buttons on the form, the Windows application takes the values in the top two text boxes and passes them to the *dblFirst* and *dblSecond* properties in the class. Then it invokes a class method that corresponds to the clicked button. For example, Figure 9-5 shows that the + button was selected last. Therefore, the application invoked the *Add2dbls* function procedure and inserted the return value from the procedure in the bottom text box on the form.

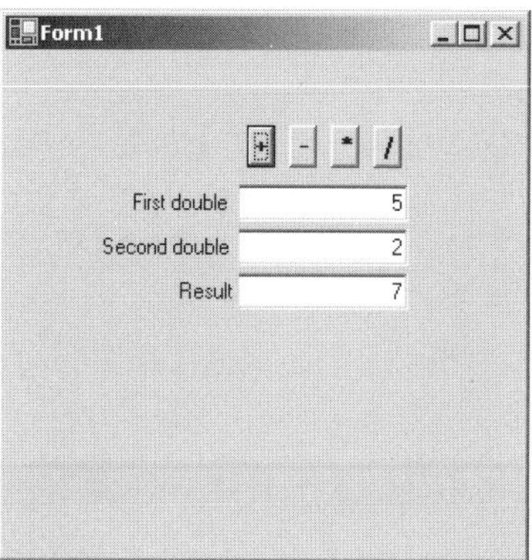

Figure 9-5. A Windows application for using the ArithmeticClass class library project.

The controls on the form in Figure 9-5 have property settings to make the application's user interface visually appealing. Many developers might prefer to make more refinements while using those here as a base. The buttons, for example, have a slightly enlarged font over the default size that appears in boldface. Of course, the button size is reduced to accommodate the side-by-side display of all four buttons above the text boxes. The *TextAlign* property of the text boxes is set to Right. This setting displays the text box contents with an alignment that is typical for numbers as opposed to strings, which is the default *TextAlign* property value.

Because the class in the preceding section resides in a standalone .dll file, the Windows application whose form appears in Figure 9-5 must have a reference to that .dll file. This reference permits the form to interface with the class properties and methods defined in the Visual Basic .NET code for the class. (See the preceding section.) There are two techniques to help you manage a reference to a .dll file within a Windows application. First, you can choose to add a reference to the .dll file. After you add the reference, you can refine how your application refers to the referenced .dll file with the *Imports* statement, which defines the second technique. The *Imports* statement groups the class elements as items in a namespace similar to the way the *System.Windows.Forms* namespace groups the elements underlying the functionality in a Windows form. Instead of using the full project name and class name to designate a collection of items, you can define an alias as a more familiar nickname for the class. If the names of elements in your class conflict with those in your project or another referenced namespace, using the nickname resolves conflicts.

> **Note** Visual Basic doesn't strictly require the use of an alias defined by an *Imports* statement to resolve naming conflicts between different namespaces. However, the ability to help resolve conflicts combined with the opportunity to define a custom familiar name defined by the alias is a very attractive pair of features.

To add a reference for a project, choose Add Reference from the Project menu in the Code Editor. For example, if you are working with a Windows application, you can choose Project and then Add Reference from the Form1.vb tab. Next select the Projects tab. Then click Browse and navigate to the .dll to which you want to form a reference. For this example, you can navigate to the bin folder of the ArithmeticClass project assembly. Select the .dll file, which has the name ArithmeticClass.dll in our example, and click Open in the Select Component dialog box. Then click OK to close the Add Reference dialog box.

After creating a reference to the .dll file, you must still instantiate the class in the code behind a form before you can refer to its elements. Use the *Imports* statement's alias for the class library in the *Dim* statement that instantiates the class. You must position the *Imports* statement immediately after the *Option* statement, which is the first statement within the code module behind a form. The following sample listing shows an *Imports* statement that creates an alias named *clsArith* for the *Class1* class in the ArithmeticClass project.

> **Note** Although the *Option* statement isn't strictly required, its use can help you manage your code. For example, the *Option Strict On* declaration embraces and extends the *Option Explicit* statement. With an *Option Strict On* declaration, you must declare variables with a type before using them. In addition, this *Option* statement prohibits data type conversions that can lead to data loss. Although a run-time error accompanies these conversions, the *Option Strict On* declaration flags these conversions at compile time. The *Option Strict On* statement also prohibits most references to the *Object* type, which serves as a catchall type, much like the *Variant* data type in earlier versions of Visual Basic.

After the *Dim* statement, the code behind the form relies on four *Click* event procedures and one sub procedure, *PassTextBoxValues*, called by each event procedure. The *PassTextBoxValues* procedure passes the values from the text boxes on the form to the properties for the *clsArith* class. As the procedure passes the contents of the text boxes, it transforms them from string values into numeric values with the *CDbl* function. All the event procedures for the four buttons have the same general structure. They differ by function name and the class method invoked. For example, the first event procedure is for *Button1* with its *Text* property set to +. This event procedure invokes the *Add2dbls* method for the *clsArith* class. Before inserting the return value from the method into the bottom text box on the form, the procedure transforms the *Double* data type into a *String* data type for compliance with the *Text* property of a text box.

Note The application in the following listing is a bare-bones demonstration of how to reference a class. For example, the form fails if you don't enter values in both of the text boxes for input before clicking an arithmetic function button. You can remedy this situation by assigning default values for the input boxes or prompts in the input boxes with the *Load* event procedure for *Form1*.

```
Option Strict On
Imports clsArith = ArithmeticClass.Class1
Public Class Form1
    Inherits System.Windows.Forms.Form

'Windows Form Designer generated code goes here.

    'Instantiate Class1 from ArithmeticClass for use
    'with all the code behind Form1.
    Dim MyClass1 As New clsArith()

    Private Sub Button1_Click(ByVal sender As System.Object, _
    ByVal e As System.EventArgs) Handles Button1.Click

    'Pass text box values to class.
    PassTextBoxValues()

    'Convert Add2dbls function to a string in TextBox3.
    Me.TextBox3.Text = MyClass1.Add2dbls.ToString()

    End Sub
```

```
    Private Sub Button2_Click(ByVal sender As System.Object, _
       ByVal e As System.EventArgs) Handles Button2.Click

    'Pass text box values to class.
    PassTextBoxValues()

    'Convert Diff2dbls function to a string in TextBox3.
    Me.TextBox3.Text = MyClass1.Diff2dbls.ToString()

    End Sub

    Private Sub Button3_Click(ByVal sender As System.Object, _
       ByVal e As System.EventArgs) Handles Button3.Click

    'Pass text box values to class.
    PassTextBoxValues()

    'Convert Mult2dbls function to a string in TextBox3.
    Me.TextBox3.Text = MyClass1.Mult2dbls.ToString()

    End Sub

    Private Sub Button4_Click(ByVal sender As System.Object, _
       ByVal e As System.EventArgs) Handles Button4.Click

    'Pass text box values to class.
    PassTextBoxValues()

    'Convert Div2dbls function to a string in TextBox3.
    Me.TextBox3.Text = MyClass1.Div2dbls.ToString()

    End Sub

    Sub PassTextBoxValues()

    'Pass text box values to class.
    MyClass1.dblFirst = CDbl(Me.TextBox1.Text)
    MyClass1.dblSecond = CDbl(Me.TextBox2.Text)

    End Sub

End Class
```

.NET Namespace Architecture

Namespaces are the means by which the .NET Framework carves up and makes available its fundamental functionality. Namespaces correspond to types. In the preceding two sections, *Class1* in the ArithmeticClass project was a type. However, this type was a user-defined type. The .NET Framework includes its own built-in namespace architecture. This architecture includes two general categories of types.

The first of these general categories is value types. *Value types* contain values as well as the description for a value. For example, a string is a value type. The *String* value is a sequence of Unicode character codes for representing the characters that make up the string. The contents in a text box are represented as a *String* value type. A *Double* value type is a 64-bit floating-point number. There is a core set of these .NET Framework value types. Visual Basic .NET has data types that correspond to many of the .NET Framework data types.

The second general category of types is reference types. A *reference type* can be your custom class, such as *ArithmeticClass.Class1* or any of the built-in .NET Framework namespaces. The *System* namespace contains nearly 100 classes that facilitate core .NET Framework functionality, such as the garbage collector and exception handling. The .NET Framework offers exception handling for the processing of run-time errors; I dwell on this more deeply in this chapter's last major section. The *System* namespace contains many second-level and third-level namespaces that handle important functionality. For example, *System.Windows.Forms* is a third-level namespace that supports the instantiation and manipulation of form classes within a Windows application. The *System.Web* namespace enables the ASP.NET infrastructure. The *System.Data* namespace performs corresponding functions for ADO.NET.

Table 9-1 lists the main value types for the *System* namespace. This table includes a *System* namespace class name, a matching Visual Basic data type when there is one, and a brief description of the value type.

One important difference between value types and reference types is that value types retain values with them, but reference types point to values. This simple statement can lead to some significant differences in the behavior of variables declared as value vs. reference types. An equality assignment statement between two variables pointing to value types sets the values of the variables equal. If you subsequently assign a new value for one of these variables, it's no longer equal to the other variable. With reference types, the rules are different. When you assign two variables pointing to reference types equal to one another, you set their object references to the same object. Subsequently, setting one variable equal to a quantity assigns that quantity to both variables. This is because the variables point to the same object. Although the behavior of these variable references is substantially different, the syntax for manipulating them is similar. Just remember, value types store actual values, but reference types store pointers to objects. The reference types don't store values. Instead, the reference types derive value from the objects to which they point.

Table 9-1 Summary of Selected .NET Framework Value Types

System Namespace Class Name	Visual Basic Data Type	Description
Byte	*Byte*	8-bit unsigned integer
Int16	*Short*	16-bit signed integer
Int32	*Integer*	32-bit signed integer
Int64	*Long*	64-bit signed integer
Single	*Single*	32-bit floating point number
Double	*Double*	64-bit floating point number
Boolean	*Boolean*	A value that can be either *True* or *False*
Char	*Char*	Unicode characters with hexadecimal values ranging from 0x0000 through 0xFFFF
Decimal	*Decimal*	A signed integer number with a maximum of 96 bits of precision and up to 28 digits after the decimal point
IntPtr	No built-in type	A signed integer whose size depends on the platform; for example, it can be a 32-bit value on a 32-bit platform or a 64-bit value on a 64-bit platform
DateTime	*Date*	Dates and times in the range from 0:00:00 January 1, 0001, through 11:59:59 December 31, 9999
String	*String*	An immutable fixed-length sequence of Unicode characters
Object	*Object*	Root of the type hierarchy; all other classes in the .NET Framework derive from this one

To highlight this distinction, I constructed the TypeTests Windows application. It contains a Windows form with a button that invokes a procedure when you click it. The procedure demonstrates the potential variable references pitfalls as well as a remedy. The TypeTests project also contains a built-in class. This class is a reference type. The class definition includes a custom constructor function for initializing the class's property value as well as a property procedure with both *Get* and *Set* clauses for reading and writing to its sole property.

The following Visual Basic code sample shows the syntax for the class definition. *TypeRef* is the class name. Its only property has the name *Value*.

The *Sub New* constructor initializes *Value* to *myInput* whenever an application instantiates a new instance of the *TypeRef* class. The syntax for the *Value* property procedure demonstrates how to specify a read/write property for a function.

```
Public Class TypeRef
    Private intLocal

    'Intialize Value to myInput.
    Public Sub New(ByVal myInput As Integer)
    Dim Value As Integer = myInput
    End Sub

    'Read/Write property named Value.
    Public Property Value() As Integer
    Get
        Return intLocal
    End Get
    Set(ByVal Value As Integer)
        intLocal = Value
    End Set
    End Property

End Class
```

The next code excerpt from the TypeTests project shows the code for demonstrating the problem as well as a workaround to the problem. The code excerpt invokes the *ValueReferenceTypeTest* procedure when a user clicks *Button1*. The procedure has three sections. Each section pauses by presenting a message box that shows the result of variable assignments for either value or reference types.

```
    Private Sub Button1_Click(ByVal sender As System.Object, _
        ByVal e As System.EventArgs) Handles Button1.Click
    ValueReferenceTypeTest()
    End Sub

    Sub ValueReferenceTypeTest()
    'Declare and assign values to a type instance (Integer).
    Dim val1 As New Integer()
    Dim val2 As Integer = val1
    val2 = 123
    MsgBox("val1 = " & CStr(val1) & vbCrLf & _
        "val2 = " & CStr(val2), _
        MsgBoxStyle.DefaultButton1, _
        "Type Assignments Test")
```

```
    'Declare and assign values to a class reference.
    Dim ref1 As New TypeRef(0)
    Dim ref2 As TypeRef = ref1
    ref2.Value = 123
    MsgBox("ref1 = " & CStr(ref1.Value) & vbCrLf & _
               "ref2 = " & CStr(ref2.Value), _
               MsgBoxStyle.DefaultButton1, _
               "Reference Assignments Test1")

    'Declare and assign values to two different class references.
    Dim ref3 As New TypeRef(0)
    Dim ref4 As New TypeRef(0)
    ref4.Value = 123
    MsgBox("ref3 = " & CStr(ref3.Value) & vbCrLf & _
           "ref4 = " & CStr(ref4.Value), _
               MsgBoxStyle.DefaultButton1, _
               "Reference Assignments Test2")
End Sub
```

The results in each message box reveal the outcome of the assignment statements. Figure 9-6 shows each message box. Because the boxes have unique titles, you can map the outcomes to the different syntactic constructions.

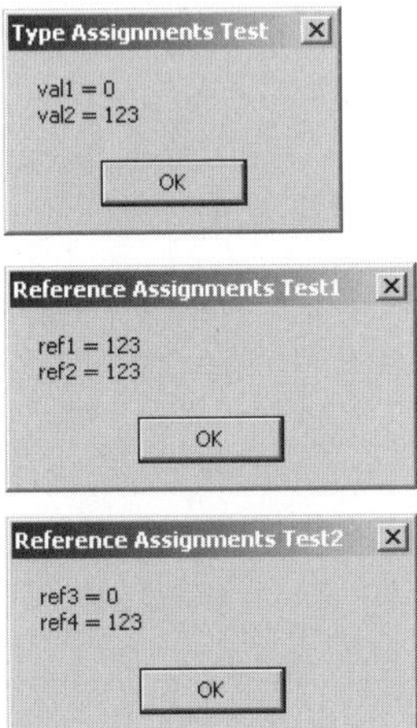

Figure 9-6. Similar assignment statements can yield different outcomes for value and reference type variable declarations.

The first message box in Figure 9-6 presents the contents of two variables pointing to value references. Both *val1* and *val2* point to *Integer* data types, which are value types. The .NET Framework initializes an *Integer* value to 0. Therefore, the *Dim* statement for *val1* sets the variable to 0. The *Dim* statement for *val2* sets the *val2* variable equal to the current value of *val1*, which is 0 from the preceding statement. Next the procedure assigns the value 123 to *val2* and then prints the values of *val1* and *val2* in a message box. As you can see, *val1* equals 0, but *val2* equals 123. This is because the value goes with the variable for variable assignments to value types.

The second message box in Figure 9-6 shows the outcome for the next block of statements. These begin by defining a new variable reference to the *TypeRef* class. This statement explicitly initializes the variable to 0. (See the *New* constructor for *TypeRef*.) Next the procedure uses a *Dim* statement to set *ref2* equal to *ref1*. Because *ref1* equals 0, *ref2* also equals 0 after the statement. Then the procedure assigns 123 to the *Value* property of the *ref2* variable reference. The statement assigns 123 to the *Value* property of *ref1* as well. This is because the preceding statement sets the two variables, *ref1* and *ref2*, equal to the same object instance of the *TypeRef* class. Because there is just one instance, it can have just one *Value* property. Therefore, the message box for the second section shows both variables equal to the same value. This is so even though the second *Dim* statement has the same syntax in the first and second sections. When working with variables pointing to reference types, you must separately instantiate a class object for each variable if you want to make distinct assignments to each of them. The final section in the *ValueReferenceTypeTest* procedure demonstrates the syntax for achieving this outcome. The final message box in Figure 9-6 confirms the result.

Converting Between Value Types

The value types denoted in Table 9-1 have fundamentally different ways of representing values within a computer. Nevertheless, applications frequently need to pass values back and forth between different value types. Any text box has a *Text* property, which relies on a *String* value type for representing its contents. However, applications will sometimes need to gather numeric input or display numeric output via a text box. The numeric representation of a number in a text box can require a translation from a *String* type to another type, such as *Double* or *Integer*. The translation is necessary because it is only in a numeric representation that a computer can perform arithmetic calculations with value types. If you don't explicitly perform the translation, the .NET Framework will perform it implicitly. You should understand that you might not always be able to work perfect translations between all value types. This section and the next one include some samples to acquaint you with the kinds of issues that affect translations between data types.

Visual Basic offers a rich array of functions for converting between value types. A series of inline conversion functions can transform any appropriate expression into a corresponding value type. For example, `CInt(63.4)` returns an integer equal to 63. The *CInt* function rounds fractions. The full set of inline conversion functions comprises *CBool*, *CByte*, *CChar*, *CDate*, *CDbl*, *CDec*, *CInt*, *CLng*, *CObj*, *CShort*, *CSng*, and *CStr*. For these functions to work properly, their argument must be suitable for the value they return. Attempting to return a value from `CByte(256)` raises an exception, or run-time error, because 256 is outside the range of legitimate byte values. The *CType* function can explicitly convert an expression (or constant) to a value type. For example, you can use `CType(63.4, Integer)` to convert a value with a decimal point to one without a decimal point. A convenient approach for converting a number to a string is to append the *ToString* function name to the end of the numeric value, such as `45.ToString`. Additional transformation functions in the style of *ToString* are available for other value types.

I updated *Form1* in the TypeTests project by adding another button, *Button2*, and a text box, *TextBox1*. In addition, this sample relies on *Option Strict On* being the first statement in the module behind *Form1* for the project. The code involves two event procedures. (See the following listing.) The *Form1_Load* event procedure labels the button *Add 1* because clicking it adds 1 to the text box value. The procedure also assigns the string *1* to the *Text* property of the text box. The *Click* event procedure for *Button2* adds 1 to the value in the text box. Without two conversions, the arithmetic for the conversion will fail. First the *Click* event procedure transforms the string property of the value in the text box into an integer. Second the expression in the event procedure uses the *ToString* function to convert the numeric value in the addition expression to a string. Without both of these conversions, you will generate a compilation error when *Option Strict On* is the first statement in the module.

```
Private Sub Form1_Load(ByVal sender As System.Object, _
    ByVal e As System.EventArgs) Handles MyBase.Load

    'Initialize button and text box text settings.
    Button2.Text = "Add 1"
    TextBox1.Text = "1"

End Sub

Private Sub Button2_Click(ByVal sender As System.Object, _
    ByVal e As System.EventArgs) Handles Button2.Click

    'Transformations required by Option Strict On.
    TextBox1.Text = (CInt(TextBox1.Text) + 1).ToString
End Sub
```

From *Long* to Hexadecimal and Back Again

Visual Basic has long had the *Hex* function for converting integer numeric values to hexadecimal strings that represent the numeric value of the *Hex* function argument. The .NET documentation explicitly states that the function will work for *Byte*, *Short*, *Integer*, *Long*, and *Object* data types. As it turns out, the maximum value that the *Hex* function will convert is 9,223,372,036,854,775,807, which is the maximum *Long* value type. Values above this raise an exception.

> **Note** If you aren't familiar with conversions between hexadecimal numbers and base 10, you can use the Windows Calculator to help verify the operation of the samples in this section.

The following pair of procedures demonstrates how to use the *Hex* function to convert the *Long* value in the text box from the preceding sample to a *Hex* value that appears in a message box. Clicking *Button3* on the form in the TypeTests project launches the *ConvertLngToHex* procedure. This procedure's listing demonstrates the syntax for specifying a conditional compilation, which includes the # before keywords. The value of *BoundCheck* is True, so the compiler inserts the optional code that performs a bound check to abort the conversion if the *Hex* function argument is greater than the maximum value that the built-in function can convert. Conditional compilation was initially introduced into Visual Basic with version 5. The conversion procedure concludes by displaying the return value of the *Hex* function (unless the procedure aborts because the argument is too large).

> **Note** Setting the *BoundCheck* compiler constant to False permits you to generate an exception for values greater than the maximum conversion value—for example, 9,223,372,036,854,775,808.

```
Private Sub Button3_Click(ByVal sender As System.Object, _
    ByVal e As System.EventArgs) Handles Button3.Click

    'Call procedure to convert text box value
    'from long to hexadecimal.
    ConvertLngToHex()

End Sub
```

```
Sub ConvertLngToHex()
    #Const BoundCheck = True

    #If BoundCheck Then
        'Bound check on input; use CDec to accommodate values
        'beyond bound check.
        If CDec(TextBox1.Text) > 9223372036854775807 Then
            MsgBox("Number too large for Hex function.")
            Exit Sub
        End If
    #End If

    'Convert from string representation of Long number to
    'hex character representation of number.
    MsgBox("Hex value of text box equals:" & vbCrLf & _
        Hex(CLng(TextBox1.Text)))

End Sub
```

Going from a hexadecimal value to a *Long* value is more complicated for a couple of reasons. First, there is no built-in function. Second, hexadecimal numbers need to be converted on a character-by-character basis that reflects the character's position in the hexadecimal number. This task is further complicated by that fact that characters go outside the decimal range of 0 through 9 to the hexadecimal range of 0 through F. The following sample performs a check to verify that the hexadecimal string value doesn't exceed the maximum *Long* value. The hex representation for the maximum *Long* value is 7FFFFFFFFFFFFFFF.

After performing a bound check for the maximum hexadecimal value, the *ConvertHexToLng* procedure starts a loop that iterates through successive characters in the hexadecimal number. Starting at the far right character, the loop evaluates each character. The evaluation multiplies the hex character's decimal value by a power of 16. The powers range in value from 0 for the far right character to up to 15 for the sixteenth hex character (if there is one). When the *ConvertHexToLng* procedure finishes looping through the characters in the hexadecimal number, the procedure presents a message box with the decimal value of the hexadecimal number in *TextBox1*.

```
Private Sub Button4_Click(ByVal sender As System.Object, _
    ByVal e As System.EventArgs) Handles Button4.Click

    'Call program to convert a hexadecimal number to
    'a Long number.
    ConvertHexToLng()
End Sub
```

(continued)

```
Sub ConvertHexToLng()

    'Assign TextBox1 contents to hexStr.
    'Dim strValue As String = TextBox1.Text
    Dim hexStr As String = TextBox1.Text

    'If hexStr greater than 7FFFFFFFFFFFFFFF, then abort.
    Dim hexchars As Integer = Len(hexStr)
    If (hexchars = 16 And hexStr.Chars(0) > "7") Or _
        hexchars > 16 Then
        MsgBox("Hex values beyond 7FFFFFFFFFFFFFFF " & _
        "generate an exception. Enter a smaller " & _
        "hex value.")
        Exit Sub
    End If

    'Variable lnghexstr stores long of hex string in TextBox1,
    'and i is a loop counter value.
    Dim lnghexstr As Long
    Dim i As Integer

    'Loop through characters to compute decimal equivalent
    'of hex string.
    lnghexstr = 0
    For i = 0 To hexchars - 1
        Select Case Mid(UCase(hexStr), hexchars - i, 1)
        Case "0"
            lnghexstr += CLng(0 * (16 ^ i))
        Case "1"
            lnghexstr += CLng(1 * (16 ^ i))
        Case "2"
            lnghexstr += CLng(2 * (16 ^ i))
        Case "3"
            lnghexstr += CLng(3 * (16 ^ i))
        Case "4"
            lnghexstr += CLng(4 * (16 ^ i))
        Case "5"
            lnghexstr += CLng(5 * (16 ^ i))
        Case "6"
            lnghexstr += CLng(6 * (16 ^ i))
        Case "7"
            lnghexstr += CLng(7 * (16 ^ i))
        Case "8"
            lnghexstr += CLng(8 * (16 ^ i))
        Case "9"
            lnghexstr += CLng(9 * (16 ^ i))
        Case "A"
            lnghexstr += CLng(10 * (16 ^ i))
```

```
            Case "B "
                lnghexstr += CLng(11 * (16 ^ i))
            Case "C"
                lnghexstr += CLng(12 * (16 ^ i))
            Case "D"
                lnghexstr += CLng(13 * (16 ^ i))
            Case "E"

                lnghexstr += CLng(14 * (16 ^ i))
            Case "F"
                lnghexstr += CLng(15 * (16 ^ i))
            End Select
        Next i

        'Display long value for hex string.
        MsgBox("Long value for text box equals:" & vbCrLf & _
            lnghexstr.ToString)
    End Sub
```

Inheriting Classes

Classes are great because they package blocks of Visual Basic code for easy reuse. Class inheritance multiplies that core benefit of classes by letting one class inherit the properties, methods, and events of another class. Inheritance for custom classes is new to Visual Basic programmers with Visual Basic .NET. This section begins with an overview of design issues and keywords for implementing class inheritance. Next I cover a couple of samples that demonstrate the syntax for implementing inheritance with different keywords. At the section's close, you will discover a discussion of overloading. This feature can make one method or property within a class easily accept many different types of value inputs. Instead of building capabilities into applications by layering one class on top of another or manually coding a class to test multiple value types and then respond appropriately to the input value type, the *Overloads* keyword expands the capabilities of a single class. I cover the *Overloads* keyword in this section because of its resemblance to the *Overriding* keyword—one of the keywords for managing inheritance—and because *Overloads* widens the capabilities of a class much as inheritance can.

Overview of Inheritance

Inheritance is for classes. It lets one class inherit the properties, methods, and events of another class. My discussion of inheritance focuses on properties and methods to simplify the presentation. (See the "Programming Events" section later in this chapter for more on managing class events.) When Class B inherits Class A, Class B can offer the same methods, properties, and events of Class A.

In addition, Class B can offer new properties and methods as well as modified versions of the properties and methods in Class A. Visual Basic developers didn't have this capability for custom stand-alone classes with versions of Visual Basic prior to the .NET version. Therefore, it is natural that you need to learn some new concepts and syntax to take advantage of inheritance. We can start our new inheritance vocabulary by referring to the inherited class as the base class. The class that inherits a base class is a derived class.

When one class inherits from another class, the derived class must contain a declaration stating from which class it inherits properties and methods. Visual Basic .NET uses an *Inherits* statement to make the declaration. The *Inherits* statement takes as its argument the name of the base class. You can have just one class name as the argument for *Inherits*. Therefore, a class can inherit from at most one other class at a time. If the derived class adds any new methods, it can offer the methods of the base class along with its own new methods. In addition to offering new methods, the derived class can offer modified implementations of one or more methods from the base class. Another new inheritance term in Visual Basic .NET is *polymorphism*. It describes the ability of a derived class to change the implementation of a base class member, such as a property or a method. An application can instantiate instances for a derived class and its base class. In this way, the application can invoke an unmodified method from a base class and an updated method with the same name from a derived class.

In order for Visual Basic .NET to modify a base class method in a derived class, your class methods require special keywords. First, the base class must mark the method name with the *Overridable* keyword, such as in the following code:

```
Class MyBaseClass
    Overridable Function One () As Double
        'Code for returning a value.
    End Function
End Class
```

In addition to a keyword in the base class, you need a corresponding keyword, *Overrides*, in the derived class. This keyword must be applied to a method in the derived class with the same name as the one in the base class whose implementation you want to change. For example

```
Class MyDerivedClass
    Inherits MyBaseClass
    Overrides Function One () As Double
        'New code for returning a value.
    End Function
End Class
```

As you can see, implementing polymorphism requires planning. That is, you must mark the base class that you want overridden in derived classes with the *Overridable* keyword. You must also synchronize method names between the base and derived classes. The method names within a class—either base or derived—should generally be distinct. In general, you should also keep the method and property names distinct between base and derived classes. Using the same name for a method or a property in both base and derived classes has a special meaning that we will consider shortly.

In order for a derived class to refer back to a method or property in a base class, you need to use the special *MyBase* keyword. You will typically use the *MyBase* keyword within a function in a derived class that overrides an identically named function in a base class. You can also use the *MyBase* keyword to set and get property values for a base class from a derived class. Then you can use the *MyBase* keyword to invoke a method with the values that you passed to the base class. For example, `MyBase.One()` in a derived class invokes the *One* method in the base class.

The *Shadows* keyword can apply to properties and methods in a derived class. This keyword essentially blocks the availability of identically named properties and methods in a base class. In a sense, the *Shadows* keyword for a property or method in a derived class casts a shadow over an identically named property or method in a base class. The *Shadows* keyword is more flexible and powerful than the *Overridable/Overrides* keywords. For example, the *Overridable/Overrides* keywords apply only to methods implemented with sub procedures or function procedures. The *Shadows* keyword apples to methods as well as properties. In addition, you can shadow a method in a base class with a property in a derived class. The *Shadows* keyword removes the dependence of a derived class on an identically named object in a base class. This insulates the derived class from any changes to the base class that could inadvertently cause an error in the derived class. The *Overridable/Overrides* keywords don't offer this protection for a derived class from changes made in a base class.

The *Overloads* keyword isn't strictly an inheritance topic, but this keyword pertains to classes, and its name is similar to *Overrides*. In addition, using the *Overloads* keyword on a function procedure, sub procedure, or property procedure can alter the behavior of the procedure. However, the *Overloads* keyword can apply to methods or properties within the same class. A common use of the *Overloads* keyword is to enable multiple versions of a function procedure to operate as one. Each function procedure in a set of overloaded function procedures has the same name. However, the argument types change for each function procedure within a set. Therefore, one version of a method can accept a string argument, but another version can accept a double data type as an argument. The .NET Framework will automatically invoke the right function procedure based on an input's data type! That's the power of the *Overloads* keyword.

An Inheriting and Overriding Sample

Any Windows application applying class inheritance will contain at least three units of code. You need two units of code for the classes: one for the base class and a second for the derived class. A third unit of code is necessary to instantiate one or more classes and invoke the methods or manipulate the procedures in the derived class or its base class. In a Windows application, you can instantiate classes and manipulate the instances from event procedures for buttons on a form. One or more text boxes on a form can provide vehicles for users to specify input values as arguments for methods and properties.

The sample for this section is a Windows application that includes a form (*Form1*) with multiple buttons and text boxes for users to manipulate. The first sample uses *Button1* along with *TextBox1* and *TextBox2*. Clicking *Button1* launches an event procedure that instantiates a base class, *ArithmeticClass1*, and a derived class, *Class1*. The procedure manipulates these class instances in various ways with input from the entries in *TextBox1* and *TextBox2*. I will detail the manipulations by describing the *Button1_Click* event procedure after discussing the code in the *ArithmeticClass1* and *Class1* classes.

> **Note** The sample for this section and the next two sections demonstrating inheritance with Visual Basic .NET all use the same solution, InheritingSample. You can double-click InheritingSample.sln in Windows Explorer to open the solution in Visual Studio. To run the application from Windows Explorer, invoke the InheritingSample1.exe file. The filename for the .exe file retains the original name for the solution.

ArithmeticClass1 is a variation of the stand-alone class in the ArithmeticClass project discussed in the "Creating and Using Class References" section. This base class resides in the InheritingSample solution. The code for the base class follows. It begins by specifying two write-only properties.

ArithmeticClass1 also specifies two methods—both based on function procedures. The *Add2dbls* method follows directly from the ArithmeticClass presented earlier in this chapter; the method adds two values with a *Double* value type. A sub procedure implements this method. The input for the function procedure is from the *WriteOnly* properties, which specify the double values to add. A function procedure implements the second method, *Add2dbls2*, in *ArithmeticClass1*. Using arguments for the function procedure eliminates the need to rely on properties to specify the values to add. The *Overridable* keyword appears at the start of the *Add2dbls2* method specification. This means that another class inheriting *ArithmeticClass1* can override the code for the method that appears below.

```
Public Class ArithmeticClass1
    Private dbl1 As Double
    Private dbl2 As Double

    'WriteOnly property named dblFirst.
    Public WriteOnly Property dblFirst() As Double
        Set(ByVal dblValue As Double)
            dbl1 = dblValue
        End Set
    End Property

    'WriteOnly property named dblSecond.
    Public WriteOnly Property dblSecond() As Double
        Set(ByVal dblValue As Double)
            dbl2 = dblValue
        End Set
    End Property

    'Add dbls.
    Function Add2dbls() As Double
        Return (dbl1 + dbl2)
    End Function

    'Overridable version of Add dbls.
    Overridable Function Add2dbls2(ByVal MyNum1 As Double, _
          ByVal MyNum2 As Double) As Double
        Add2dbls2 = MyNum1 + MyNum2
    End Function

End Class
```

The code for *Class1* has three major sections; the full listing for the class appears next. The first section inherits *ArithmeticClass1*. The *Inherits* statement makes *Class1* a derived class with *ArithmeticClass1* as its base class. *Class1* can reference all the properties and methods of *ArithmeticClass1* through the *MyBase* keyword.

The next section in *Class1* adds a new method with the *NthPower* function. The function computes the value of the *base* value to a power, such as 2^3 equaling 8. This function accepts arguments for the *base* and *power* variable values.

The final section of code in *Class1* defines a new implementation for the *Add2dbls2* method initially specified in the base class. (See the preceding code for *ArithmeticClass1*.) The *Overrides* keyword at the beginning of the method specification in *Class1* along with the matching *Overridable* keyword for the same method name in *ArithmeticClass1* permits the override. The new implementation for the *Add2dbls2* method doubles the value computed in the base class. The *MyBase* keyword facilitates the reference back to the base class. The arguments passed to the *Add2dbls2* method in *Class1* transfer to the base class through the arguments in the expression containing the *MyBase* keyword.

```
Public Class Class1
    'Class1 class inherits from ArithmeticClass1.
    Inherits ArithmeticClass1

    'Added method to complement inherited method
    'from ArithmeticClass1.
    Public Function NthPower(ByVal base As Double, _
        ByVal power As Double) As Double
        NthPower = (base ^ power)
    End Function

    'The Add2dbls2 method in Class1 overrides the
    'overridable Add2dbls2 method in ArithmeticClass1.
    Overrides Function Add2dbls2(ByVal MyNum1 As Double, _
         ByVal MyNum2 As Double) As Double
        'The following code calls the original method in the base
        'class, and then modifies the returned value.
        Add2dbls2 = MyBase.Add2dbls2(MyNum1, MyNum2) * 2
    End Function

End Class
```

The *Click* event for *Button1*, which appears next, begins by hiding some controls that aren't necessary for this use of the form. Then the event procedure instantiates *ArithmeticClass1* as the *arclass1* variable and *Class1* as the *c1* variable. The procedure uses two text boxes on the form so that users can specify double values for the methods in the classes. Because the text box values require conversion to make them *Double* values for the procedures implementing the methods, the sample computes the conversion once and stores the results in two variables with a *Double* value specification.

After concluding the preceding preliminary steps, the event procedure starts computing and displaying results. Initially the procedure passes the *Double* values saved in *num1* and *num2* to the property procedures assigning values to the *dblFirst* and *dblSecond* properties in *ArithmeticClass1*. Next the procedure invokes the *Add2dbls* method within the *ArithmeticClass1* and converts the outcome to a string with the *ToString* method for display in a message box. After a user clears the message box from the screen, the event procedure invokes the *NthPower* method in *Class1*. Again, the message box argument converts the number to a string for display. The last pair of *MsgBox* functions in the event procedure invokes the *Add2dbls2* method. The first message box displays the *Add2dbls2* method outcome from its base class implementation (in *ArithmeticClass1*). The procedure concludes by invoking the same method from *Class1*. This result appearing in the second message box will be twice as large as its predecessor. This is because different function procedures implement the method in each class. (Contrast the code for *Add2dbls2* in the two preceding class listings.)

```
'Sample to demonstrate basic inheritance to add a
 'new method or override an existing one.
Private Sub Button1_Click(ByVal sender As System.Object, _
    ByVal e As System.EventArgs) Handles Button1.Click

    'Hide unnecessary text controls.
    Button2.Visible = False
    Button3.Visible = False

    'Instantiate objects based on the ArithmeticClass1
    'and Class1 classes.
    Dim arclass1 As New ArithmeticClass1()
    Dim c1 As New Class1()

    'Declare num1 and num2 variables and assign values
    'to the variables based on text box entries.
    Dim num1 As Double
    Dim num2 As Double

    num1 = CDbl(TextBox1.Text)
    num2 = CDbl(TextBox2.Text)

    'Set properties and invoke the Add2dbls method from
    'the ArithmeticClass1 class.
    arclass1.dblFirst = num1
    arclass1.dblSecond = num2
    MsgBox(arclass1.Add2dbls.ToString, , _
        "Return from Add2dbls in ArithmeticClass1")

    'Invoke the NthPower method in Class1, which is a
    'new method not in ArithmeticClass1.
    MsgBox(c1.NthPower(num1, num2).ToString, , _
        "Return from NthPower in Class1")
```

(continued)

```
        'Invoke the Add2dbls2 method for the ArithmeticClass1
        'and Class1 classes; the Add2dbls2 method in Class1
        'overrides the Add2dbls2 method in ArithmeticClass1.
        MsgBox(arclass1.Add2dbls2(num1, num2).ToString, , _
            "Return from Add2dbls2 in ArithmeticClass1")
        MsgBox(c1.Add2dbls2(num1, num2).ToString, , _
            "Return from Add2dbls2 in Class1")

    End Sub
```

Figure 9-7 summarizes the results. On the left is the form after I entered values in both text boxes and clicked *Button1*. Notice that *Button2* and *Button3* aren't there; that's because the *Button1_Click* event procedure made them invisible on the form by setting their *Visible* property to False. The four message boxes on the right display the results in the order that the *Button1_Click* event procedure computes them. The caption for each message box specifies the source, including the method and the class, for the displayed result. Notice in particular the last two message boxes. These results in coordination with the listing for the *Button1_Click* event procedure document and confirm how you can override a method in a base class with a different implementation in a derived class.

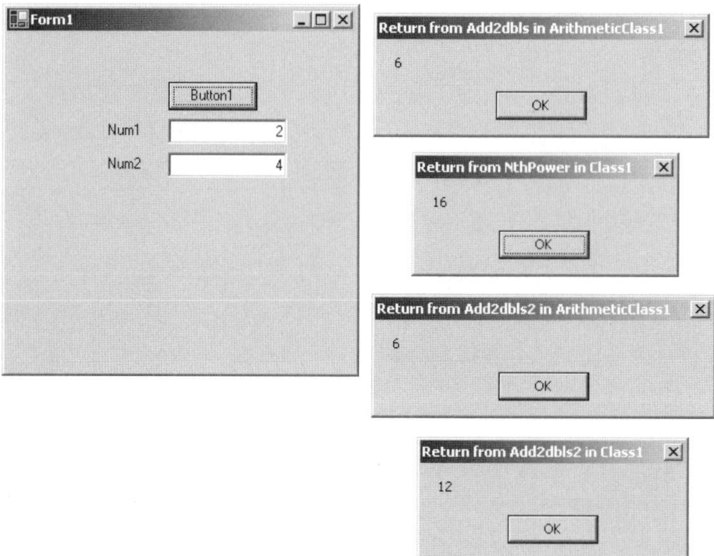

Figure 9-7. By creating instances for both a base class and a derived class, you can invoke methods for both classes, and some of your method references in a derived class can override those in a base class.

A Shadowing Sample

As indicated in the "Overview of Inheritance" section, shadowing acts similarly to overriding but is more flexible. The sample for this section demonstrates the use of the *Shadows* keyword. You can use the *Shadows* keyword in a derived class; doing so doesn't require any corresponding changes to a base class. The sample in the preceding section required the *Overridable* keyword in the base class for the *Overrides* keyword in the derived class to function properly.

The sample in this section uses the *TypeRef1* class that follows as the base class. Notice that the listing for *TypeRef1* includes a property procedure for a property named *Value*. The procedure includes both *Get* and *Set* clauses. This class is similar to the *TypeRef* sample presented earlier in this chapter. The sole distinction between *TypeRef1* and *TypeRef* is that *TypeRef1* commented out the *New* method. Recall that in the prior sample using *TypeRef*, the *New* method was helpful in setting an initial value for a variable instantiated on the class. However, when you use a class as the base class for an *Inherits* statement, the base class cannot include a method named *New*. The inability to specify a *New* method within the class isn't major because an application can assign a value to a variable based on the class immediately after instantiating the variable.

```
Public Class TypeRef1
    Private intLocal

    'Intialize Value to myInput -- not permissible in
    'inherited class.
    'Public Sub New(ByVal myInput As Integer)
    '    Dim Value As Integer = myInput
    '    MsgBox(Value.ToString, , "in new")
    'End Sub

    'Read/Write property named Value.
    Public Property Value() As Integer
        Get
            Return intLocal
        End Get
        Set(ByVal Value As Integer)
            intLocal = Value
        End Set
    End Property

End Class
```

The shadowing sample also relies on a second sample named Class2. This class inherits *TypeRef1*, so *Class2* is a derived class with *TypeRef1* as its base class. Because *TypeRef1* has just one property, *Class2* must have a member by the same name if it is to shadow the property procedure in *TypeRef1*. I specifically used the term *member*. This leaves open the possibility of the shadowing element being either a property or a method. The *only* requirement is that the shadowing element have the same name as the member that it shadows. Although the following listing for *Class2* demonstrates the use of the *Shadows* keyword, the use of this keyword is optional for implementing shadowing. As you can see from the following listing, the shadowing version of the property procedure for *Value* in *TypeRef1* adds 2 to the input. The original version of the property procedure for the *Value* property in *TypeRef* merely echoes the input.

```
Public Class Class2
    'Class2 inherits from TypeRef1
    Inherits TypeRef1

    Private intLocal

    'Read/Write property named Value in Class2
    'shadows property with the same name in TypeRef1.
    Public Shadows Property Value() As Integer
        Get
            Return intLocal
        End Get
        'New version adds 2 to initial input.
        Set(ByVal Value As Integer)
            intLocal = Value + 2
        End Set
    End Property

End Class
```

Clicking *Button2* on *Form1* in the InheritingSample solution launches an event procedure, which appears next. The procedure uses *Button2* and *TextBox1* (along with its label). Therefore, the event procedure starts by hiding the other controls on the form. Next the procedure converts and copies the contents of *TextBox1* to *num1*, which the procedure declares as an *Integer* variable. This value type specification for *num1* is consistent with the *Value* property in *TypeRef1* and *Class2*. After storing the converted text box entry in a variable for the event procedure, the procedure assigns the value saved in *num1* to the *Value* property in *TypeRef1* and *Class2*. Finally, a pair of *MsgBox* functions echoes the quantity in the property.

```
    'Sample to demonstrate shadowing with inheritance.
    Private Sub Button2_Click(ByVal sender As System.Object, _
        ByVal e As System.EventArgs) Handles Button2.Click

        'Hide unnecessary text controls.
        TextBox2.Visible = False
```

```
        Label2.Visible = False
        Button1.Visible = False
        Button3.Visible = False

        'Instantiate objects based on the TypeRef1
        'and Class2 classes.
        Dim trclass1 As New TypeRef1()
        Dim c2 As New Class2()

        'Declare num1 variable and assign a value
        'to the variable based on the text box's entry.
        Dim num1 As Integer

        num1 = CInt(TextBox1.Text)

        trclass1.Value = num1
        c2.Value = num1

        MsgBox(trclass1.Value.ToString, , _
            "Return from Value property in TypeRef1")
        MsgBox(c2.Value.ToString, , _
            "Return from Value property in Class2")

    End Sub
```

Figure 9-8 shows the shadowing sample. On the left panel, you see the text box and button for launching the event procedure. Notice that the text box contains the value 3. On the right side, you see the two message boxes containing the echoed *Value* properties from *TypeRef1* and *Class2*. Although the input to both properties was the same, the output is different because the one expression in *Class2* is distinct from its counterpart for a shadowed property in *TypeRef1*.

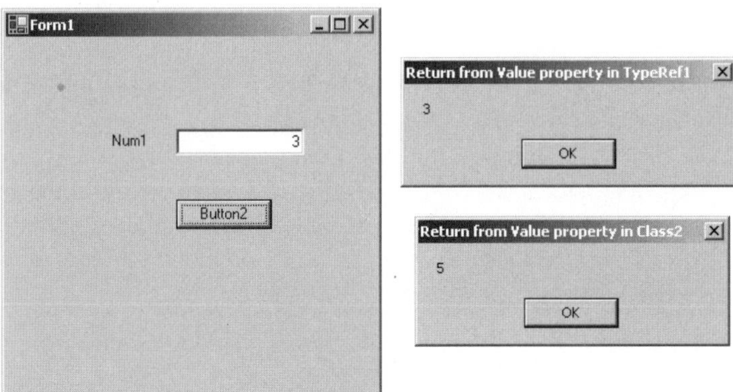

Figure 9-8. Shadowing makes it easier for a derived class to return a different result than a property with the same name in a base class.

An Overloading Sample

Both overriding and shadowing are about doing more things with the same methods and properties. The *Overloads* keyword is one more example of a keyword that simplifies how you can do more with the code in your samples. In essence, it allows you to construct a set of procedures all of which have the same name but with different argument type specifications. When a user invokes a method based on the set of procedures, the .NET Framework automatically detects the specific procedure that matches the input data type. You don't have to use the *Overloads* keyword in an inheritance context, but it can work with inheritance. For simplicity, this section demonstrates the use of the *Overloads* keyword without involving inheritance.

> **Note** You can also achieve overloading without the *Overloads* keyword. Just make sure all the procedure names are identical, with different value type specifications for the arguments in each member within the set of procedures. However, if you use the *Overloads* keyword for at least one member in the set, you must use it for all members.

The Class3 listing shows a simple overloading sample. The class contains two instances of the *TenPercentOfIt* function procedure. These instances collectively implement the *TenPercentOfIt* method for *Class3*. If a user enters an argument with a *Double* value type, such as 55.5, in the *TenPercentOfIt* method, *Class3* responds by invoking the first function procedure. This might happen if the user invokes the method from a database with a column of *Double* values. On the other hand, when the input for the *TenPercentOfIt* function is a string, such as *55.5*, *Class3* automatically invokes the second function procedure. This might happen if an application passes a value directly from a text box to the class method. By using the *Overloads* keyword in front of both versions of the function, the developer can leave it to the .NET Framework to figure out with which specific function procedure to implement the method. As more potential data sources become available, it is easy to add a new copy of the function procedure with different value type declarations for the arguments.

```
Public Class Class3
    Overloads Function TenPercentOfIt(ByVal It As Double) As Double
        Return (It * 0.1)
    End Function

    Overloads Function TenPercentOfIt(ByVal It As String) As Double
        Return (CDbl(It) * 0.1)
    End Function
End Class
```

The following *Click* event procedure for *Button3* demonstrates a test of the overloading feature implemented in *Class3*. After hiding the unnecessary controls on the form, the application instantiates *c3* as an instance of *Class3*. Next it assigns a *Double* value of 55.5 to *num1*. The final pair of *MsgBox* functions invokes the *TenPercentOfIt* method in *Class3* with the *num1 Double* value type or a *String* value type based on the contents of *TextBox1*. Because the return from the method is a *Double* value, the argument for the *MsgBox* functions invokes the *ToString* method on the return value. The important point to note is that even though the two *MsgBox* functions invoke the *TenPercentOfIt* method with different value types, they both invoke exactly the same method with exactly the same syntax.

```
'Sample to demonstrate overloading within a class.
Private Sub Button3_Click(ByVal sender As System.Object, _
    ByVal e As System.EventArgs) Handles Button3.Click

    'Hide unnecessary text controls.
    TextBox2.Visible = False
    Label2.Visible = False
    Button1.Visible = False
    Button2.Visible = False

    'Instantiate Class3 with overloaded functions and declare
    'a variable with a Double type for one of the functions.
    Dim c3 As New Class3()
    Dim num1 As Double

    'Assign a value to the Double variable type and
    'invoke one version of the overloaded function.
    num1 = 55.5
    MsgBox(c3.TenPercentOfIt(num1).ToString, , _
        "Return based on a double input")

    'Invoke another version of the overloaded function with
    'string input instead of numerical input.
    MsgBox(c3.TenPercentOfIt(TextBox1.Text).ToString, , _
        "Return based on a string input")

End Sub
```

Figure 9-9 confirms that you can obtain identical results from the *TenPercentOfIt* overloaded set of functions based on two different input value types. The form on the left shows *55.5* in a text box. This text box contains a *String* value. The two message boxes on the right show identical return values. However, their captions confirm that they have different input value types, and all our code did to get this result was to use the *Overloads* keyword. Sometimes Microsoft can make life so sweet!

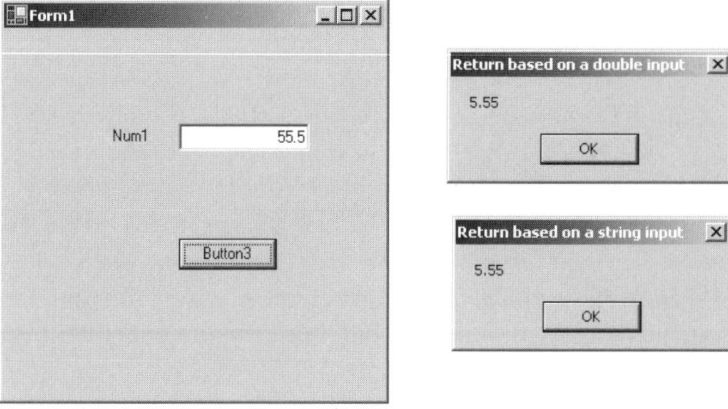

Figure 9-9. Overloading automatically matches the procedure invoked to the data type of the argument in a statement calling a set of overloaded procedures.

Programming Events

An *event* is a notification that something happened. As Visual Basic programmers, you are well aware of events from built-in objects, such as forms and buttons. Many intermediate and advanced programmers regularly create custom classes that generate custom events with prior versions of Visual Basic. Adding events to custom classes allows objects based on the classes to convey information back to the applications that instantiate the objects.

Visual Basic .NET retains the event functionality from earlier versions while it adds new capabilities as well, related to defining custom event handlers and working with new sources for events. This section reviews the basics of event programming to provide a standard background for more advanced topics, including the ability to dynamically define event handlers and new components that can raise events.

Event Programming Concepts

Even when working with built-in events for forms and their controls, it helps to have a basic understanding of event programming concepts, but a knowledge of this topic is essential when you develop events for custom classes. Happily, a few core concepts that are easy to grasp can enable you to declare and manage custom events.

Events have a source or a sender. This *source* is the element that sends out the notification that an event happened. A class that you create can be a source. A form class can be a source. For example, Visual Basic raises the *Load* event when it opens a form instance. Similarly, when a user clicks a button on a form instance, this raises the *Click* event for the button. For a source to raise an event, two things must happen. First, the event must be declared for the object. You can declare an *Event* statement. Second, some code inside the class for the object instance must invoke the *RaiseEvent* statement. The *RaiseEvent* statement triggers an event declared with the *Event* statement. You can raise an event only from the class in which it occurs. Therefore, a button cannot raise a *Load* event for a form on which it resides. Similarly, a derived class cannot use the *RaiseEvent* statement to trigger an event declared in its base class.

Event handlers process an event. Just because a class instance raises an event doesn't mean that an application has to acknowledge the event. Clicking a button before you add a sub procedure to process the click has no effect. The sub procedure is an event handler. Event handlers allow applications to respond to events raised by class instances. Visual Basic can automatically create empty event handlers for the Windows Forms and their controls. These empty event handlers are called stubs. A *stub* includes the sub procedure declaration with a name for the procedure, a list of arguments, and a terminating statement for the procedure (namely, *End Sub*). Stubs also include a *Handles* clause that associates them with a class instance and an event name. You can determine how your application responds to an event by placing your own code inside the sub procedure.

When you write event handlers for custom classes, you may need to create your own stub. If you use the *WithEvents* keyword when you instantiate an object based on a class, you can use the Visual Studio development environment to create a stub for you automatically. When using the *WithEvents* keyword, you must instantiate your object at the module level. Without the *WithEvents* keyword, events don't propagate from a class to an object instance based on it. Establishing an association between an event handler and an event with the *WithEvents* keyword requires you to specify the event handler at design time.

The *AddHandler* and *RemoveHandler* statements allow you to dynamically add and remove a handler for an event at run time. You can also use these statements at design time. With these two statements, you don't have to instantiate an object using the *WithEvents* keyword in order to process events raised by the object. In turn, this means that you can instantiate within a procedure or at the module level. Recall that the *WithEvents* keyword requires instantiation at the module level. When using the *AddHandler* statement to associate an event with an event handler, you must write your own stub for the event handler. I will demonstrate how to do this in a sample that illustrates the use of the *AddHandler* statement.

Using Built-In Form Events

There are a couple of ways of managing built-in events with Windows Forms and their controls from the Windows Forms Designer. Double-clicking a form's caption in the Windows Forms Designer opens the stub for the form's default event, the *Load* event, in the Code Editor. This same technique works for the controls on a form. For example, double-clicking a button on a form opens the stub for the button's default event, a *Click* event. After adding one or more controls on a form, you can select any event for any control in the Code Editor. Choose the control name from the Class Name drop-down list at the upper left of the Code Editor, and choose the event name from the Method Name list at the right. After you click an event for the control, a stub for the event procedure appears automatically. To display a nondefault event for the form, select (Base Class Events) from the Class Name list and then choose a desired event from the Method Name list.

If you search through the events for a form or any of the controls on a form, you will quickly discover an exceedingly large array of events. Although the large number of events is useful for fine-grained control over the operation of an application, it may be difficult for some programmers to discern the order of the events so they can know which one to use. The following excerpt from the Code Editor for *Form4* in the EventsSamples solution demonstrates a stratergy for tracking events. Within each event procedure is a *MsgBox* function indicating which event generated the current message box in an application. For example, the message box for the form *Load* event fires before *Form4* is displayed. When you click the form's Close button, you will notice that the *Closing* event fires prior to the *Closed* event. See the following note for detailed instructions on making *Form4* the startup object for the EventsSamples solution.

> **Note** A Windows application starts by default with *Form1*, which is the object that Visual Studio .NET makes after opening a Windows application for design. By default, the Windows application opens to this object when you run the solution. However, you can choose another object for a Windows application to open when it starts to run. Right-click the solution's name in Solution Explorer, and choose Properties to open the Property Pages dialog box for the solution. Use the Startup Object drop-down list to select another object. For example, selecting *Form4* will cause this form to open initially when a user chooses to run the solution.

Events sometimes fire so quickly that message boxes can pile up and make discovering their order confusing. In cases like this, you can sometimes set a property for an object on the form—and thus change its appearance—to help indicate the order of events. The procedures for the *MouseEnter*, *MouseHover*, and *MouseLeave* events from *Button1* demonstrate this approach. These event procedures change the *BackColor* property for *Button1*. Initially positioning the mouse over *Button1* changes the *BackColor* property from its default setting to System.Drawing.Color.Cyan. Because Visual Studio automatically creates a reference to the *System.Drawing* namespace when it initializes a Windows application, you can abbreviate the setting to Color.Cyan. Leaving the mouse over a button eventually invokes the *MouseHover* event, which changes the *BackColor* setting to System.Drawing.Color.Red. Removing the mouse from over the button restores the default *BackColor* setting of System.Drawing.SystemColors.Control. Clicking *Button1* displays a message box and shifts the focus from *Form4* to the message box. This *Button1_Click* event is orthogonal to the *MouseEnter* and *MouseHover* events in that clicking the button can interrupt the transition from the *MouseEnter* event to the *MouseHover* event.

```
Private Sub Form4_Load(ByVal sender As Object, _
    ByVal e As System.EventArgs) Handles MyBase.Load
    MsgBox("Just before I load.")
End Sub

Private Sub Form4_Closing(ByVal sender As Object, _
    ByVal e As System.ComponentModel.CancelEventArgs) _
    Handles MyBase.Closing
    MsgBox("From Closing event.")
End Sub

Private Sub Form4_Closed(ByVal sender As Object, _
    ByVal e As System.EventArgs) Handles MyBase.Closed
    MsgBox("From Closed event.")
End Sub

Private Sub Button1_MouseEnter(ByVal sender As Object, _
    ByVal e As System.EventArgs) Handles Button1.MouseEnter
    Me.Button1.BackColor = System.Drawing.Color.Cyan
End Sub

Private Sub Button1_MouseHover(ByVal sender As Object, _
    ByVal e As System.EventArgs) Handles Button1.MouseHover
    Me.Button1.BackColor = System.Drawing.Color.Red
End Sub

Private Sub Button1_MouseLeave(ByVal sender As Object, _
    ByVal e As System.EventArgs) Handles Button1.MouseLeave
```

(continued)

```
    Me.Button1.BackColor = System.Drawing.SystemColors.Control
End Sub

Private Sub Button1_Click(ByVal sender As System.Object, _
    ByVal e As System.EventArgs) Handles Button1.Click
    MsgBox("You clicked Button1")
End Sub
```

Before proceeding to a second sample, it may be useful to review the syntax for an event procedure. Notice that they are sub procedures meant for operation in the current module, as specified by the use of the *Private* keyword. *Private* marks the event procedure for exclusive use in the current module. The arguments list can offer you a way of changing the operation of the event procedure. The next sample demonstrates the use of an event argument to control the behavior of the *Closing* event. After the argument list, the *Handles* clause specifies the object and event that the sub procedure handles. You control the operation of the event procedure by placing custom code between the *Sub* and *End Sub* statements.

The next selection of event procedures shows a pair of procedures for controlling how a user can close a form. When a user chooses to close a form by clicking the form's Close button, the application fires the *Closing* event. This event occurs before the form closes. By setting the *Cancel* event argument to True in the *Closing* event, you can block the *Close* event from occurring (namely, the form will remain open). The default value for the *Cancel* event argument is False. You can use this feature to perform other actions just before closing a form. For example, you can display a message blocking the operation of the form's Close button and instructing the user to click a button that launches the other actions you want done before invoking the form's *Close* method. Because the *Close* method raises the *Closing* event, you must construct the form's *Closing* event procedure to optionally bypass setting the *Cancel* argument to True.

The following code excerpt for *Form5* demonstrates how to disable a form's Close button and redirect the user to a button on the form. The solution uses two events. First the *Form5_Closing* event procedure blocks the *Close* event from occurring by setting the *Cancel* event argument to *bolDisableClose*. The module-level declaration for *bolDisableClose* sets the variable's default value to True. The *If...Then...Else* statement in the procedure displays a message box directing the user to click *Button1* to close the form. The *Click* event procedure for *Button1* sets *bolDisableClose* to False before invoking the *Close* method for the *Me* keyword that refers back to the current form, which is *Form5* in this case. The invocation of the *Close* method, in turn, launches the

Form5_Closing event procedure, but this time the procedure takes a different path through its *If...Then...Else* statement because of the new value for the *bolDisableClose* variable.

```
'bolDisableClose controls Cancel argument.
Dim bolDisableClose As Boolean = True

'Conditionally block close of form.
Private Sub Form5_Closing(ByVal sender As Object, _
    ByVal e As System.ComponentModel.CancelEventArgs) _
    Handles MyBase.Closing
    If bolDisableClose Then
        e.Cancel = bolDisableClose
        MsgBox("Click Button1 to close form.", , _
        "After clicking Close button")
    Else
        MsgBox("From form's Closing event.", , _
        "After clicking Button1")
    End If
End Sub

'Enable form close by setting bolDisableClose to False.
Private Sub Button1_Click(ByVal sender As System.Object, _
    ByVal e As System.EventArgs) Handles Button1.Click
    'Perform any other necessary actions before closing Form5.
    bolDisableClose = False
    Me.Close()
End Sub
```

Processing Events Using the *WithEvents* Keyword

The event processing techniques for this sample and the next two all emanate from *Form1* in the EventsSample solution. Figure 9-10 shows this form two different ways. At left is the form as it looks in the Windows Form Designer—in design view. At right is the form as it appears when you run the EventsSample.exe file. The differences between the two views of the form are the result of the *Form1_Load* event procedure. (See the following sample.) This procedure adds text to some controls and clears it from other controls. In addition, it formats the alignment for the label and text controls as well as resizes the default *Width* property setting for the button controls. This transformation demonstrates a use for the form *Load* event that makes it easy to spot changes to the default settings for the controls on a form. If you need to duplicate form settings across multiple forms or systematically change settings across multiple forms, this kind of procedure can prove especially convenient.

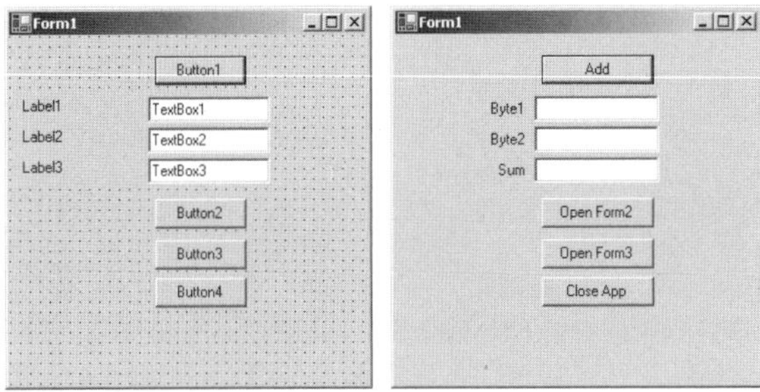

Figure 9-10. Using a form *Load* event procedure to document your format settings for a form can help in documenting those settings and applying those settings in a uniform way to multiple forms in an application.

```
Private Sub Form1_Load(ByVal sender As System.Object, _
    ByVal e As System.EventArgs) Handles MyBase.Load
    'Set selected properties for form controls at load time.

    'Set Text and Width properties for Button1.
    Button1.Text = "Add"
    Button1.Width = 90

    'Set TextAlign property for text boxes.
    TextBox1.TextAlign = HorizontalAlignment.Right
    TextBox2.TextAlign = HorizontalAlignment.Right
    TextBox3.TextAlign = HorizontalAlignment.Right

    'Set Text property for labels.
    TextBox1.Text = ""
    TextBox2.Text = ""
    TextBox3.Text = ""

    'Set TextAlign align property for labels.
    Label1.TextAlign = ContentAlignment.MiddleRight
    Label2.TextAlign = ContentAlignment.MiddleRight
    Label3.TextAlign = ContentAlignment.MiddleRight

    'Set Text property for text boxes.
    Label1.Text = "Byte1"
    Label2.Text = "Byte2"
    Label3.Text = "Sum"

    'Set Text and Width properties for Button2.
    Button2.Text = "Open Form2"
    Button2.Width = 90
```

```
    'Set Text and Width properties for Button3.
    Button3.Text = "Open Form3"
    Button3.Width = 90

    'Set Text and Width properties for Button4.
    Button4.Text = "Close App"
    Button4.Width = 90

End Sub
```

The form at right in Figure 9-10 permits a user to enter two *Byte* value type quantities in the Byte1 and Byte2 text boxes. When a user clicks the Add button, the form returns the total of the two quantities in the Sum text box. If the sum happens to exceed 255, which is the maximum legitimate *Byte* value, the application displays a message box with a reminder of the problem. Because the application computes the sum as a *Decimal* value type, return values greater than the maximum don't generate a run-time error. However, you can raise an event that identifies sums greater than 255. If a user enters a value greater than 255 in either the *Byte1* or *Byte2* text box, Visual Basic raises an error because the Add button's *Click* event procedure uses the *CByte* function to convert the text box values to *Byte* data types.

Before reviewing the code behind *Form1* that manages the operation of the form, it will be useful to examine the code listing for the *ByteArithmetic* class. *Form1* relies on the class to save the values in the two input text boxes, compute the sum, and raise the event. The class listing includes an event declaration, a *Private* statement for declaring two internal variables, two property procedures, and a function procedure. The *Public* accessibility qualifier for the event declaration at the top of the listing makes the event available throughout the EventsSample solution assembly. If *ByteArithmetic* existed as a stand-alone class project with a .dll extension, the *Public* declaration would permit the accessibility of the event in other projects that reference the .dll file.

The property procedures named *Byte1* and *Byte2* can accept converted data from text boxes on *Form1*. The class represents these property settings internally with the *byt1* and *byt2* variables, which are declared directly below the event declaration. A function procedure, *Add2byte*, in *ByteArithmetic* computes the sum and conditionally raises an error. This procedure computes the sum of the two types as a *Decimal* value type, which it saves in the *mysum* variable. This design feature avoids the potential of a run-time error from a sum that exceeds the *Byte* value limit. However, *Add2byte* also checks for sums that exceed 255. When it finds a sum that exceeds the maximum *Byte* value, it raises the *TooHigh* event and returns as an event argument the *mysum* variable value. The *Add2byte* procedure listing concludes with a

Return statement that passes back the value of *mysum* to the procedure that invoked the *ByteArithmetic* class instance.

```
Public Class ByteArithmetic
    'You need to declare an event before you can raise it.
    Public Event TooHigh(ByVal ReturnValue As Decimal)

    'Local variables for property values.
    Private byt1, byt2 As Decimal

    'Property procedures for Byte1 and Byte2.
    Public Property Byte1() As Byte
        Get
            Return byt1
        End Get
        Set(ByVal Value As Byte)
            byt1 = Value
        End Set
    End Property

    Public Property Byte2() As Byte
        Get
            Return byt2
        End Get
        Set(ByVal Value As Byte)
            byt2 = Value
        End Set
    End Property

    'Function procedure for the Add2byte method.
    Function Add2byte() As Decimal
        Dim mysum As Decimal

        'Compute mysum.
        mysum = byt1 + byt2

        'Raise event if sum is too high.
        If mysum > 255 Then RaiseEvent TooHigh(mysum)

        Return mysum

    End Function

End Class
```

The next code excerpt shows the code behind *Form1* that works with the *ByteArithmetic* class. The listing starts with a declaration of an instance named *ba* for the *ByteArithmetic* class. There are two especially important features of this declaration. First, the declaration includes the *WithEvents* keyword. This allows *Form1* to process events raised by *ba*. Second, the declaration occurs at the module level. This is mandatory when you use the *WithEvents* keyword in the declaration for a class instance.

I generated the stub for the *Button1_Click* event procedure by double-clicking the control in the Windows Forms Designer. The event procedure is generated by the double click on the control because *Click* is the button's default event. Within the *Click* event are two blocks of code. First the procedure converts the text box entries with the *CByte* function to *Byte* value types from their native *String* value types. Second the procedure invokes the *Add2byte* method for the *ba* class instance and stores the return value as a string in *TextBox3*.

The second procedure is the event handler for the *TooHigh* event from the *ba* class instance. In the Code Editor for *Form1*, you can create the stub for the event procedure automatically by choosing *ba* in the Class Name box and clicking TooHigh in the Method Name box to its right. After Visual Studio created the stub, I had to add just one line of code, which presents a message box reminding the user that the sum is too large for a legitimate *Byte* value. The message box also contains the value returned as the sum.

```
'WithEvents keyword must apply to module-level declaration;
'the keyword permits events to pass from event source (ByteArithmetic).
    Private WithEvents ba As New ByteArithmetic()

    Private Sub Button1_Click(ByVal sender As System.Object, _
        ByVal e As System.EventArgs) Handles Button1.Click

        'Copy converted text box entries to Byte1 and
        'Byte2 properties in ByteArithmetic class.
        ba.Byte1 = CByte(TextBox1.Text)
        ba.Byte2 = CByte(TextBox2.Text)

        'Display result of addition in TextBox3.
        TextBox3.Text = (ba.Add2byte).ToString()

    End Sub


    'Handles clause in event sub stub requires a WithEvents keyword
    'in variable declaration for event source (ByteArithmetic).
    Private Sub ba_TooHigh(ByVal ReturnValue _
        As Decimal) Handles ba.TooHigh

        'Display event message.
        MsgBox("Sum of " & ReturnValue & " too large for byte value.")

    End Sub
```

Figure 9-11 shows the outcome of trying to add 4 and 252 with the application detailed in the preceding two code segments. Each quantity alone is a legitimate *Byte* value. However, their sum exceeds the maximum *Byte* value. Therefore, the application displays the message box shown at the left of Figure 9-11 before populating *TextBox3* with the return value from the *ByteArithmetic* instance. *Form1* appears on the right side of Figure 9-11, with the two input values and their sum. To properly close the solution, a user must click the Close App button.

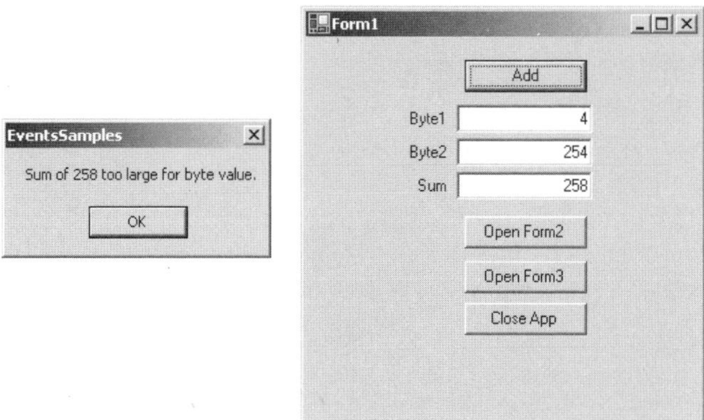

Figure 9-11. You can use a custom event to display a message box.

Processing Events with the *AddHandler* Statement

Below the third text box in Figure 9-11 is the Open Form2 button. Clicking this button opens a second form that demonstrates how to use the *AddHandler* statement to process a raised event. *Form2* has just two buttons. That's because this form uses the text boxes on *Form1* to display input and output from the instance of *ByteArithmetic* that it declares. Therefore, another benefit of this sample is that it reveals how to pass values back and forth between two forms.

The only way that the application will open *Form2* is by a click to the Open Form2 button on *Form1*. The application's logic requires that there be numeric entries in the Byte1 and Byte2 text boxes before the click. Failing to populate the text boxes with appropriate values before the click will generate a run-time error. The *Click* event procedure for *Button2* on *Form1* follows. Notice that the *Button2_Click* event procedure commences by instantiating an instance of *Form2* and referencing it with the *frmForm2* variable. With the *frmForm2* variable, the event procedure can then access elements in the code behind *Form2*. As a subsequent listing shows, two of these elements are variables named *frm2byte1* and *frm2byte2*. The assignment statements in the *Click* event procedure demonstrate the syntax for copying converted text box values from one form (*Form1*) to variables in the module behind another form (*Form2*). The event procedure concludes by showing *Form2* and hiding *Form1*.

```
Private Sub Button2_Click(ByVal sender As System.Object, _
    ByVal e As System.EventArgs) Handles Button2.Click

    'Instantiate a new instance of Form2 class.
    Dim frmForm2 As New Form2()

    'Populate variables in module behind Form2 with
    'Text property settings of text boxes in Form1.
    frmForm2.frm2byte1 = CByte(TextBox1.Text)
    frmForm2.frm2byte2 = CByte(TextBox2.Text)

    'Show Form2 in a modeless window and
    'hide currently open form (Form1).
    frmForm2.Show()
    Me.Hide()

End Sub
```

For ease in grasping how the programming elements behind *Form2* work among themselves and interplay with *Form1*, the following listing includes the whole module behind *Form2*. The paragraphs after the listing selectively highlight different aspects of the code.

```
Public Class Form2
    Inherits System.Windows.Forms.Form

'Region for " Windows Form Designer generated code "

    'You can instantiate variables for classes within a procedure
    'when you specify event handler with AddHandler statement. However,
    'to make ba class instance available in two procedures, this
    'sample declares ba variable at the module level.
    Dim ba As New ByteArithmetic()

    'Declare variables.
    Public frm2byte1, frm2byte2 As String
    Private temp As Decimal

    Private Sub Form2_Load(ByVal sender As System.Object, _
        ByVal e As System.EventArgs) Handles MyBase.Load

        'Set Text and Width properties for Button1.
        Button1.Text = "Add"
        Button1.Width = 90
```

(continued)

```
    'Set Text and Width properties for Button2.
    Button2.Text = "Open Form1"
    Button2.Width = 90

    'Assign values to Byte1 and Byte2 properties.
    ba.Byte1 = frm2byte1
    ba.Byte2 = frm2byte2

End Sub

Private Sub Button1_Click(ByVal sender As System.Object, _
    ByVal e As System.EventArgs) Handles Button1.Click

    'Designate ba_TooHigh sub procedure to process ba.TooHigh event
    AddHandler ba.TooHigh, AddressOf ba_TooHigh

    'Assign the return value from Add2byte to temp and display the
    'method inputs and outputs if the Add2byte method return value
    'is less than or equal to 255.
    temp = ba.Add2byte
    If temp <= 255 Then
        MsgBox("Sum of " & frm2byte1 & " and " & frm2byte2 & _
        " is " & temp & ".", MsgBoxStyle.OKOnly, _
        "Result from Form2")

End Sub

Private Sub ba_TooHigh(ByVal ReturnValue As Decimal)

    'Process event.
    MsgBox("Result of " & ReturnValue & " is too high. " & _
        "Returning to new Form1.")

    'Exit to Form1
    MyForm2Exit()

End Sub

Private Sub Button2_Click(ByVal sender As System.Object, _
    ByVal e As System.EventArgs) Handles Button2.Click

    'Exit to Form1.
    MyForm2Exit()

End Sub

Sub MyForm2Exit()
```

```
        'Declare an instance of Form1 and show it.
        Dim frmForm1 As New Form1()
        frmForm1.Show()

        'Pass local variables from Form2 module to
        'text boxes on Form1.
        frmForm1.TextBox1.Text = frm2byte1.ToString
        frmForm1.TextBox2.Text = frm2byte2.ToString
        frmForm1.TextBox3.Text = temp.ToString

        'Close the current form (Form2).
        Me.Close()

    End Sub

End Class
```

Form2 has just two buttons on it with the default *Text* property settings. The form's *Load* event procedure assigns more meaningful *Text* property settings than the default one: *Button1* becomes the Add button, and *Button2* becomes Open Form1. In addition, the *Form2_Load* event procedure sends the values transferred from the text boxes on *Form1* to an instance of *ByteArithmetic* named *ba*. This populates the *Byte1* and *Byte2* properties in *ByteArithmetic*. In order to facilitate referencing the *ba* variable from several different procedures within the module behind *Form2*, the sample instantiates *ByteArithmetic* at the module level. Notice that the statement performing the instantiation doesn't include a *WithEvents* keyword. Therefore, unless the procedure takes other measures, the code behind *Form2* won't be able to handle events raised by the *ba* instance of *ByteArithmetic*.

As mentioned, the *Text* property for *Button1* is set to Add. True to this setting, the *Button1_Click* event procedure invokes the *Add2byte* method for the *ba* variable. The event procedure stores the return value from *Add2byte* in a *Decimal* variable named *temp*. However, before invoking the method, the *Button1_Click* event procedure specifies an *AddHandler* statement. By placing this statement before the invocation of the *Add2byte* method, the procedure enables the code behind *Form2* to respond to an event raised by the *ba* class instance of *ByteArithmetic*. The *AddHandler* statement has two clauses. The *AddHandler* keyword denotes the start of the first clause. The argument for this clause is the concatenation (with a dot [.] delimiter) of the object name and the name of the event to process. In this sample, these are *ba* for the object and *TooHigh* for the event. In the *AddressOf* clause, you designate the name of the procedure that handles the event named in the first clause. The preceding listing follows conventional naming standards for an event procedure by specifying *ba_TooHigh* as the name of the procedure for handling the event. If the return value from the *Add2byte* method in the *temp* variable is less than or equal to 255, the *Button1_Click* event procedure invokes a *MsgBox* function to display the result.

The *ba_TooHigh* event procedure fires conditionally when the *Add2byte* procedure for the *ba* object returns control to the *Form2* module. It is the *Button1_Click* event procedure that invokes the method. However, depending on whether the method raises the *TooHigh* event, control can return to either the *Button1_Click* event procedure or the *ba_TooHigh* event procedure. The condition for firing the event procedure is that the *ba* object raises the *TooHigh* event. When the *ba* object raises the event, the *ba_TooHigh* event procedure in the *Form2* module takes control before control returns to the *Button1_Click* event. The *ba_TooHigh* event procedure displays a message box alerting the user that the sum is too large and calls the *MyForm2Exit* procedure. Within the *MyForm2Exit* procedure, the application copies the *frm2byte1*, *frm2byte2*, and *temp* values back to the text boxes in *Form1* and shows *Form1* as it closes *Form2*. Because *temp* doesn't yet receive an assignment with the value of the sum when control passes to the *ba_TooHigh* procedure, the value of *temp* is its default value, 0, instead of the sum of *frm2byte1* and *frm2byte2*.

> **Note** At the cost of a couple of lines of code, you can modify the application to differentiate between a true value of 0, such as the sum of 0 plus 0, and a value of 0 to signify an illegitimate *Byte* value. I leave this as a problem for you because it is outside the scope of the sample's main objectives, which are to demonstrate the operation of the *AddHandler* statement and to illustrate event processing techniques generally.

The *Text* property for *Button2* on *Form2* is set to Open Form1 in the *Form2_Load* event procedure. A click to *Button2* actually does more than its label suggests. The *Button2_Click* event procedure has just a single line, but that line calls the *MyForm2Exit* procedure. Recall from the discussion in the preceding paragraph that this procedure copies values from the module behind *Form2* to the text boxes in *Form1* as it opens *Form1* and closes *Form2*. If a user clicks *Button2* after computing a sum with a value less than or equal to 255, the procedure has a computed *temp* variable value to pass back from *Form2* to *Form1*.

There are basically two paths from *Form1* to *Form2* and back to *Form1*—one path for a sum that is a legitimate *Byte* value and another for a sum that exceeds a legitimate *Byte* value. The three screen shots at the left of Figure 9-12 show the path for text box entries of 2 and 25 on *Form1*. Clicking the Open Form2 button transfers control to *Form2* and conveys the *Byte* value type equivalents of the text box entries in *Form1* into the *frm2byte1* and *frm2byte2* variables in the module behind *Form2*. Clicking the Add button on *Form2* computes the result and generates a message box describing the inputs and the legitimate return value. Clicking the Open Form1 button (*Button2*) copies the two *Byte* operands and their sum to the text boxes on *Form1* as it closes *Form2* and opens *Form1*.

The right side of Figure 9-12 shows the path for the text box entries *2* and *255* on *Form1*. Because these two numbers add up to more than 255, *Form2* displays a message to that effect when a user clicks the Add button. In this case, control passes back to *Form1* without the need to click *Button2*. When *Form1* opens, it shows 0 as the sum to signify a result that is too large to display as a *Byte* value.

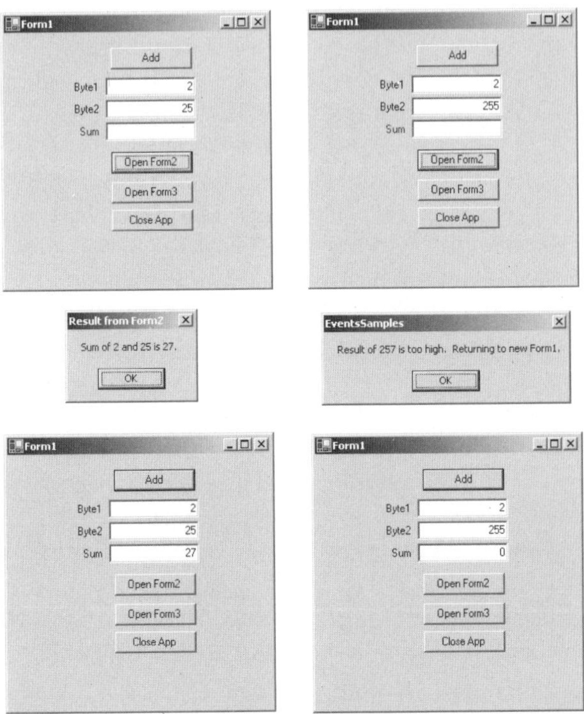

Figure 9-12. Event procedures can redirect the path of applications and result in different feedback to users. (Notice particularly the middle message boxes and the bottom dialog boxes.)

Processing Events from Server-Based Timers

In addition to Windows Forms, their controls, and the outcome of computations, timers represent another typical source for events. The .NET Framework offers two types of timers—Windows timers and Server timers. Windows timers target applications inside Windows Forms. You can add them to your forms either from the Windows Forms control section of the Toolbox in the Windows Forms Designer or programmatically. Instantiate timer instances from the *System.Windows.Forms* namespace. Microsoft initially introduced Windows timers with Visual Basic 1.0. Although Server timers can run in Windows Forms, they target tasks that don't require a visual interface. Nevertheless, Visual Studio .NET lets you add Server timers to forms from the Components section of the Toolbox. You can also add Server timers programmatically. Instantiate Server timers from the *System.Timers* namespace.

When your applications require a robust timer, you should consider a Server timer, which is more accurate than a Windows timer. You can specify the interval of a Server timer between elapsed time events down to the level of milliseconds. The Windows timer is limited to a minimum interval of 55 milliseconds. In addition, a Windows timer runs on a single thread within a Windows form. A Server timer is designed to work with multiple threads—not just one like the Windows timer. Therefore, Server timers are less likely to degrade the accuracy of their timing behavior as the load on a computer becomes heavy from database access, intensive calculations, or other tasks that can heavily consume computer resources.

When you drag a Server timer to a Windows form, the timer appears in the Component tray below the form. All nonvisual components appear in this tray. Figure 9-13 shows a Windows Forms Designer for the EventsSample solution just after I dragged a Server timer from the Toolbox to *Form6*. The Properties window shows the default settings for the Server timer component. To use the timer, you must set its *Interval* property to a value in milliseconds and its *Enabled* property to True. For example, to set a 3-second interval for a timer, set its *Interval* property to 3000. The Server timer raises an *Elapsed* event at the end of every interval. Without any intervention, the Server timer runs continuously after you initialize it by setting its *Enabled* property to True. You can stop and restart the timer with the *Stop* and *Start* methods. To perform actions associated with the *Elapsed* events, your application must have an *Elapsed* event handler for the timer component.

> **Note** The .NET Framework routinely calls a thread from its system-thread pool for processing *Elapsed* events associated with Server timers. By using any available thread, the Server timer's *Elapsed* event can be missed by the thread associated with a Windows form. Therefore, when you add a Server timer to a Windows form, Visual Studio .NET automatically sets the timer's *SynchronizingObject* property to the form's name. This feature ensures that the event for processing the timer's *Elapsed* event is available to the Windows form.

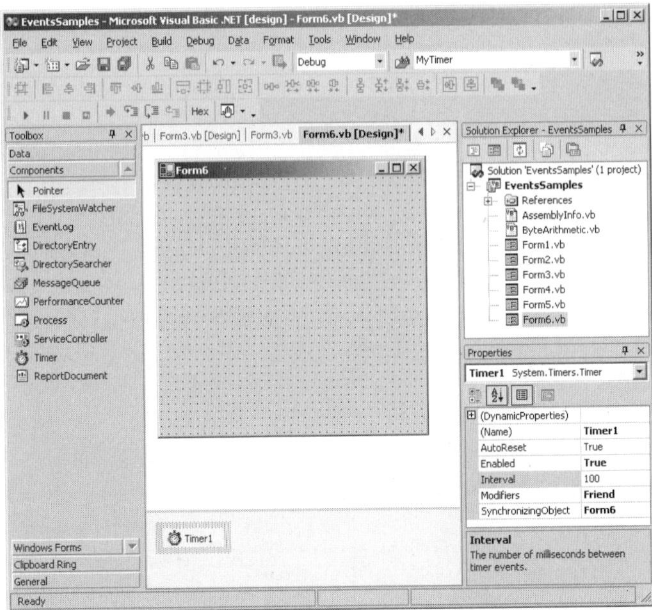

Figure 9-13. Add a Server timer control to a form from the Components tab or section of the Toolbox.

One advantage of adding a Server timer from the Toolbox instead of programmatically is that you can select the timer's name from the Class Name box and the *Elapsed* event from the Method Name box to automatically create a stub for the timer's *Elapsed* event procedure. The arguments for the *Elapsed* event procedure are *sender As Object* and *e As System.Timers.ElapsedEventArgs*. If you programmatically create a Server timer object, you should start your form module with an *Imports* statement that references *System.Timers*. With this convention, you can specify the type in the *Elapsed* event procedure as *ElapsedEventArgs* instead of *System.Timers.ElapsedEventArgs*.

The left side of Figure 9-14 shows the raw layout of a form that manages Server timer *Elapsed* events. The form's caption is *Form3*; you can get to *Form3* by clicking the Open Form3 button (*Button3*) on *Form1* of the EventsSample solution. You must return to *Form1* by clicking the Open Form1 button (*Button2*) on *Form3* and exit the EventsSamples application by clicking the Close App button (*Button4*) on *Form1*. A form *Load* event in the module behind *Form3* assigns *Text* property settings and selected other settings to the controls on *Form3*; see the following code excerpt. The right side of Figure 9-14 shows the form immediately after formatting by the *Form3_Load* event procedure.

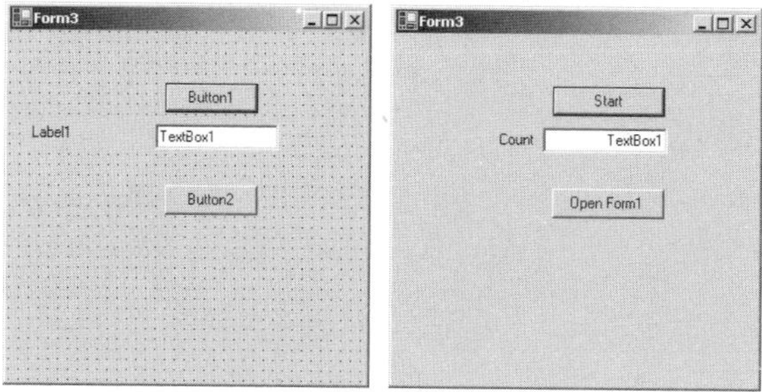

Figure 9-14. A design view of *Form3*, which demonstrates techniques for managing Server timer events.

```
Private Sub Form3_Load(ByVal sender As System.Object, _
    ByVal e As System.EventArgs) Handles MyBase.Load

    'Set selected control properties.
    Button1.Text = "Start"
    Button2.Text = "Open Form1"
    Button1.Width = 90
    Button2.Width = 90
    Label1.Text = "Count"
    Label1.TextAlign = ContentAlignment.MiddleRight
    TextBox1.TextAlign = HorizontalAlignment.Right

End Sub
```

At the top of the module are two statements that set up the whole application. First an *Imports* statement declares a link to the *System.Timers* namespace. Its syntax is `Imports System.Timers`. The statement appears as the top line in the *Form3* module. The next critical statement toward the top of the module is a *Dim* statement that instantiates a Server timer with the *MyTimer* variable. The syntax for this statement is:

```
Dim MyTimer as New System.Timers.Timer
```

After the project starts with the form *Load* event and the preceding two statements, two procedures combine to manage the Server timer and its *Elapsed* events. The *Button1_Click* event procedure assigns the value 0 to *TextBox1*. Next the *Button1_Click* event procedure sets up an event handler for the Server timer's *Elapsed* events. The procedure closes by setting three properties for the *MyTimer* object. Setting *SynchronizingObject* to Nothing enables the timer to respond correctly to very short *Interval* property settings. For example, the following listing shows an *Interval* property of only 3 milliseconds that performs correctly. With this short *Interval* setting, you cannot see screen updates associated with individual *Elapsed* events, but the setting makes the point that the Server timer can work with exceedingly short intervals. By setting the *Enabled* property to True, the code starts the timer.

The *MyTimer_Elapsed* event procedure actually responds to the events raised by the timer. In this sample, the *Elapsed* event procedure for the timer successively adds 1 to the quantity displayed by *TextBox1* for each elapsed event. To actually view the individual increments, assign a larger value to the timer's *Interval* property. By using the built-in *Mod* function, the procedure detects values in *TextBox1* that are evenly divisible by 3, such as 3, 6, and 9. Whenever the value in the text box is evenly divisible by 3, the procedure stops the timer and in a message box asks whether the user wants to continue. Clicking No in the message box restarts the timer for another three elapsed timer events. When the user clicks Yes in the message box, the timer remains stalled.

```
Private Sub Button1_Click(ByVal sender As System.Object, _
    ByVal e As System.EventArgs) Handles Button1.Click

    'This procedure and the next one require an
    'Imports System.Timer statement and a module-level
    'declaration for the Server timer.

    'Initialize TextBox1 to 0, if text box has default name.
    If TextBox1.Text = "TextBox1" Then
        TextBox1.Text = "0"
    End If
```

(continued)

```
    'Declare handler (MyTimer_Elapsed) for the elapsed event
    'for MyTimer.
    AddHandler MyTimer.Elapsed, AddressOf MyTimer_Elapsed

    'Enable MyTimer to fire an elapsed event every 3 milliseconds.
    MyTimer.SynchronizingObject = Nothing
    MyTimer.Enabled = True
    MyTimer.Interval = 3
End Sub


Sub MyTimer_Elapsed(ByVal source As Object, _
    ByVal e As ElapsedEventArgs)

    'Specify what should happen when MyTimer fires its
    'Elapsed event.

    'Start incrementing quantity in TextBox1.
    TextBox1.Text = (CInt(TextBox1.Text) + 1).ToString

    'After adding three units, check whether to stop MyTimer
    'permanently; initial stop is to suspend incrementing
    'while waiting for user input.
    If (CInt(TextBox1.Text) Mod 3 = 0) Then
        MyTimer.Stop()
        If MsgBoxResult.No = MsgBox("Want to stop?", _
        MsgBoxStyle.YesNo) Then
        MyTimer.Start()
        End If
    End If

End Sub
```

If the user clicks the Open Form1 button, the procedure shows *Form1* and closes *Form3*. The code for this *Click* event follows the same pattern of earlier samples.

```
Private Sub Button2_Click(ByVal sender As System.Object, _
    ByVal e As System.EventArgs) Handles Button2.Click

    'Close current form and open Form1.
    Dim frmForm1 As New Form1()
    frmForm1.Show()
    Me.Close()

End Sub
```

Exception Handling for Run-Time Errors

Visual Basic .NET introduces an attractive new way of handling run-time errors based on structured exception handling. Run-time errors are errors that occur because a computer isn't ready to process a request from your application or an end user fails to enter values correctly. For example, if your application attempts to connect to a SQL Server instance that is temporarily off line, a run-time error might be generated. Your applications can suffer from run-time errors even if your code is syntactically perfect and your logic is impeccable. All applications have a susceptibility to run-time errors, and it is therefore imperative to handle them efficiently. That's why Microsoft upgraded its support for handling run-time errors with Visual Basic .NET.

Visual Basic 6 and earlier versions of Visual Basic offered unstructured error handling with the *On Error* statement. This statement type transfers control within a procedure to another point with the *GoTo* keyword. Most modern Visual Basic programs avoid the use of the *GoTo* statement for everything except run-time error processing. Now you can avoid applying the *GoTo* statement even for this purpose. Visual Basic .NET still supports the *On Error GoTo* statement for backward compatibility. However, structured exception handling is built into the .NET Framework. The new run-time error processing capability is therefore more efficient. This section begins with a brief overview of the new features. Two samples demonstrate selected features of structured exception handling in Windows applications. The samples for this section are in the ExceptionsSamples solution. This section closes with best practices recommendations for structured exception handling.

Overview of Structured Exception Handling

Structured exception handling is built on a system for tracking run-time errors that the .NET Framework introduces. Run-time errors *throw*, or *raise*, built-in exceptions. In fact, one of the especially attractive features of structured exception handling is that all run-time errors raise a .NET Framework exception. You can view the full list of exceptions by choosing Exceptions from the Debug menu in Visual Studio .NET. The Exceptions dialog box that opens organizes all possible exceptions with a tree control. Expand the tree branches to find end nodes listing individual exception names. Controls on the Exceptions dialog box facilitate searching for exceptions by name and adding your own custom exceptions to those already built into the system.

From a syntax perspective, the primary innovation of structured exception handling is the introduction of the *Try...Catch...Finally* statement. You can place a block of code vulnerable to run-time errors in the *Try* clause. Then you can catch various exceptions in one or more *Catch* clauses. Each *Catch* clause contains its own block of code for recovering from a run-time error or at least gracefully exiting from a run-time error. For example, you can tell the user what problem caused the error and what to do about the problem. Any given *Try* clause can have multiple *Catch* clauses after it. You can design each *Catch* clause for a *Try* clause to trap one or more errors. For example, one *Catch* clause can route control to its code block for a specific kind of error, but a second *Catch* clause can route all remaining exceptions to its code block.

While the *Try* clause and at least one *Catch* clause are mandatory for each *Try…Catch…Finally* statement, the *Finally* clause is optional. The code block in the *Finally* clause always executes—even if one of the code blocks for a *Catch* clause invokes an *Exit Sub* statement or an unhandled exception occurs. The *Finally* clause is useful for releasing resources, such as closing database connections or open files.

Use the *Throw* statement to create programmatically a custom exception. This enables your applications to create exceptions that you can catch just like those that are built into the .NET Framework. The last sample in this chapter demonstrates the syntax.

Catching Errors

The first exception handling sample uses *Form1* in the ExceptionsSamples solution. This sample solution contains two forms, *Form1* and *Form2*, each of which is designed to serve, in turn, as the startup object for the application. If *Form1* isn't the startup object, right-click ExceptionsSamples in Solution Explorer. Select Properties in the context menu. Then choose *Form1* from the Startup Object drop-down list in the ExceptionsSamples Property Pages dialog box. Confirm your selection by clicking OK.

Like many of the previous samples, this sample performs formatting for the form in a form *Load* event procedure. Figure 9-15 shows *Form1* before and after formatting by the *Form1_Load* event procedure in the following listing. *Form1* is the first form in this chapter to use RadioButton controls. You can drag these to your form from the Windows Forms tab of the Toolbox. By default, the RadioButton controls that you drag use the Windows form as their container. Clicking one RadioButton control deselects all remaining RadioButton controls on the form. The *Checked* property for a RadioButton control indicates whether the control is selected.

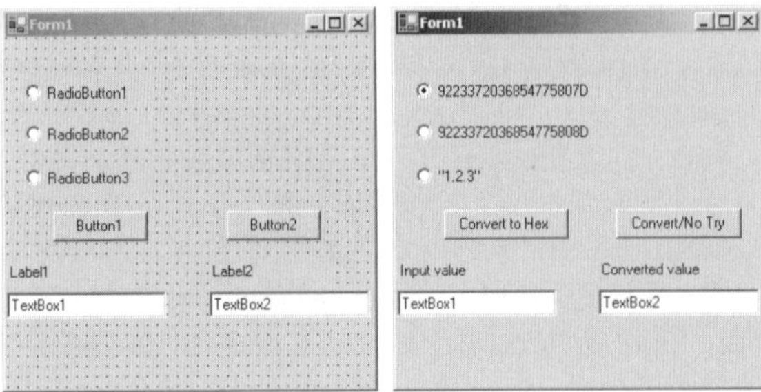

Figure 9-15. A design view of *Form1* and its startup appearance from the ExceptionsSamples solution that reveals the formatting effects in the *Form1_Load* event procedure.

```
Private Sub Form1_Load(ByVal sender As System.Object, _
    ByVal e As System.EventArgs) Handles MyBase.Load

    RadioButton1.Text = "9223372036854775807D"
    RadioButton2.Text = "9223372036854775808D"
    RadioButton3.Text = """" & "1.2.3" & """"

    RadioButton1.Width = 200
    RadioButton2.Width = 200
    RadioButton3.Width = 200

    RadioButton1.Checked = True

    Button1.Text = "Convert to Hex"
    Button1.Width = 100

    Button2.Text = "Convert/No Try"
    Button2.Width = 100

    Label1.Text = "Input value"
    Label2.Text = "Converted value"

End Sub
```

The sample attempts to convert one of three items to a hexadecimal format using the *Hex* function. A previous sample in this chapter introduced the *Hex* function. It converts a *Long* integer value to a corresponding hexadecimal representation. Users can select a value to convert by picking one of the three radio buttons on *Form1* and then clicking the Convert To Hex button (*Button1*). The first RadioButton control is for the maximum value the *Hex* function will convert. The second RadioButton control is for 1 larger than the maximum value. The third button is for a string that doesn't convert to a number, and it cannot therefore be converted by the *Hex* function. The *Button1_Click* event procedure copies either a *Decimal* value or a *String* value to a local variable, either *dec1* or *str1*, and invokes the *ConvertDecToHexTryCatch* procedure. There are actually two versions of the *ConvertDecToHexTryCatch* procedure that implicitly overload one another. I say *implicitly* overload because the procedure declarations don't begin with the *Overloads* keyword. See the section "An Overloading Sample" for a review of overloading.

Both of the *ConvertDecToHexTryCatch* procedures demonstrate basic syntax for the *Try...Catch...Finally* statement. Each procedure has just a single *Catch* clause. In addition, the *Catch* clause traps any possible exception. The code blocks for the *Catch* clause in each overloaded procedure have two lines. The first line just echoes the standard error message. The second line displays a custom message instead of the default message for the exception. You can craft these custom messages to convey special information in terms of the context of your application. For example, you can suggest actions for the user to take to eliminate the problem. Notice that the second line in each overloaded function displays a different message that reflects the custom circumstances causing the exception.

```
Private Sub Button1_Click(ByVal sender As System.Object, _
    ByVal e As System.EventArgs) Handles Button1.Click
    Dim dec1 As Decimal
    Dim str1 As String

    If RadioButton1.Checked Then
        'Verify normal operation with valid input
        dec1 = 9223372036854775807D
        ConvertDecToHexTryCatch(dec1)
    ElseIf RadioButton2.Checked Then
        'Confirm processing for number too large
        dec1 = 9223372036854775808D
        ConvertDecToHexTryCatch(dec1)
    Else
        'Confirm processing for invalid format
        str1 = "1.2.3"
        ConvertDecToHexTryCatch(str1)
    End If

End Sub

Sub ConvertDecToHexTryCatch(ByVal dec1 As Decimal)

    'Convert from string representation of decimal number to
    'hex character representation of number.
```

```
    TextBox1.Text = dec1.ToString
    Try
        TextBox2.Text = Hex(TextBox1.Text)
    Catch er As System.OverflowException
        MsgBox(er.Message & vbCrLf & er.ToString)
        MsgBox("Custom message for number too large.")
    End Try

End Sub

Sub ConvertDecToHexTryCatch(ByVal str1 As String)

    'Store the string representation of number in
    'TextBox1 for conversion to hex characters.
    TextBox1.Text = str1
    Try
        TextBox2.Text = Hex(TextBox1.Text)
    Catch er As System.InvalidCastException
        MsgBox(er.Message & vbCrLf & er.ToString)
        MsgBox("Custom message for string representing " & _
        "number in wrong format.")
    End Try

End Sub
```

Figure 9-16 contrasts the built-in error message (top) with the custom one (bottom) prepared in the sample. I don't think users ever like to see any kind of error messages. However, which error message would get you the least amount of grief from your clients? Remember, you add value to the solution by your understanding of the client's needs and the problem context. Craft your custom error messages so they provide the most useful information to your community of users.

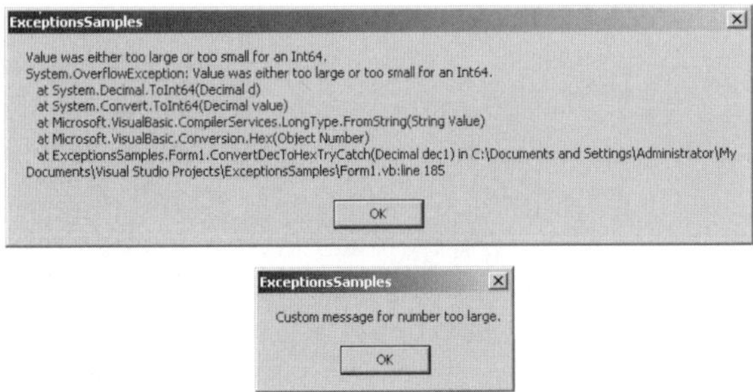

Figure 9-16. You can craft custom error messages that are shorter and more helpful than the built-in error messages.

The errors generated by the second and third radio buttons aren't fatal. If you run the application's .exe file outside Visual Studio .NET without a *Try...Catch...Finally* statement and either the second or third radio button selected, a dialog box is displayed with a summary of the error and a Continue button. Clicking the Continue button returns control to *Form1*. With a *Try...Catch...Finally* statement, you can bypass the pause for the error altogether. For example, comment out both lines within the *Catch* clause of the *ConvertDecToHexTryCatch* procedure. The procedure will catch the error, but it won't perform any action after catching the exception raised by the error. Coding a solution like this is equivalent to *On Error Resume Next* in unstructured run-time error processing.

> **Note** The Convert/No Try button allows you to attempt to convert the values denoted by the second or third radio button without any processing via a *Try...Catch...Finally* statement. For brevity, I include the code for the button and its related procedures exclusively with this book's sample files.

Catching and Fixing Run-Time Errors

The main point of the preceding sample is that you can catch errors. However, after catching the error, the sample merely displays the error message—either a standard one or a custom one. The preceding section also discusses how to bypass the display of a message altogether. However, neither of these options does what users really want—namely, to fix the error automatically. Just as you could achieve that result with unstructured error processing, you can achieve the same outcome with structured exception handling.

The sample for this section uses *Form2* as the startup object in the ExceptionsSamples solution. Make this form the startup object to run the sample in this section. See the instructions at the beginning of the preceding section for changing an application's startup object. The code behind *Form2* enables the multiplication of two *Byte* values. The form contains three text boxes. The first two text boxes display the values to multiply. You should enter a number between 0 and 255 in each of those two boxes. The third text box displays the result of the multiplication as a *Byte* value. A variable declared with a *Byte* value type stores the product. Therefore, any products greater than 255 raise a *System.OverflowException* exception. The application catches this exception and then automatically enters a value in the third text box reminding the user that the value is too large. This is a fix of sorts in the sense that the application doesn't just stop and leave it up to the user to change something for the application to conclude. The conclusion is the automatic entry of a reminder message in the third text box.

Clicking the Multiply button (*Button1*) launches the *InvokeByteProduct* procedure. This procedure begins by rounding off any places after the decimal point for the values in the first and second text boxes, *TextBox1* and *TextBox2*. The procedure uses the *Round* function, which is a part of the *System.Math* namespace. Because the procedure doesn't import the *System.Math* namespace, it must use the *Math* qualifier before the name of the *Round* function.

After rounding the *Byte* equivalents of the numbers that appear in *TextBox1* and *TextBox2* if necessary, the procedure passes the numbers to the *ByteProduct* function. This function includes a *Try…Catch…Finally* statement that explicitly traps for the *System.OverflowException* exception. If the *Try…Catch…Finally* statement detects such an exception, the *Catch* clause for the overflow assigns True to the *bolByteOverflow* module-level variable behind *Form2*. When the *ByteProduct* function returns control, the *InvokeByteProduct* uses the *bolByteOverflow* variable as the condition for an *If…Then…Else* statement. When *bolByteOverflow* is False, which is its default value, the procedure transfers the string equivalent of the *Byte* product to *TextBox3*. If *bolByteOverflow* is True, the code in the *Else* clause block copies *value too large* into *TextBox3* and resets *bolByteOverflow* to its default value.

```
Dim bolByteOverflow As Boolean

Private Sub Button1_Click(ByVal sender As System.Object, _
    ByVal e As System.EventArgs) Handles Button1.Click
    InvokeByteProduct()
End Sub

Sub InvokeByteProduct()

    Dim byte1 As Byte = CByte(TextBox1.Text)
    Dim byte2 As Byte = CByte(TextBox2.Text)
    Dim byte3 As Byte
    Dim bol1 As Boolean
    Dim strPrompt As String

    'Round to drop values after decimal points.
    If Math.Round(CDec(TextBox1.Text), 0) <> CDec(TextBox1.Text) Then
        TextBox1.Text = Math.Round(CDec(TextBox1.Text), 0).ToString
        bol1 = True
    End If
```

(continued)

```
    If Math.Round(CDec(TextBox2.Text), 0) <> CDec(TextBox2.Text) Then
        TextBox2.Text = Math.Round(CDec(TextBox2.Text), 0).ToString
        bol1 = True
    End If

    If bol1 = True Then
        MsgBox("Truncated any values after decimal points to " & _
        "provide whole number inputs.")
    End If

    'Compute product and save it along with base message.
    'for summarizing the result
    byte3 = ByteProduct(byte1, byte2)

    'Show product or "too large" message in TextBox3.
    If bolByteOverflow = False Then
        TextBox3.Text = byte3.ToString
    Else
        TextBox3.Text = "value too large"
        bolByteOverflow = False
    End If

End Sub


Function ByteProduct(ByVal byte1 As Byte, _
    ByVal byte2 As Byte) As Byte

#Const ThrowCustomException = False

    'Test for specific error or any other error.
    'Conditionally Throw custom test error.
    Try
        'Conditionally throw custom exception.
#If ThrowCustomException = True Then
        Throw New Exception("Custom error for testing.")
#End If

        Return (byte1 * byte2)
    Catch er As System.OverflowException
        bolByteOverflow = True
    Catch er As Exception
        MsgBox(er.Message)
        Application.Exit()
    End Try
End Function
```

Notice that the *ByteProduct* function includes some compilation directives that can force the function procedure to raise a custom exception each time it opens. The default setting for the *ThrowCustomException* compiler constant is

False. If you change the value of this constant to True and recompile the application, you will raise an exception on each pass through the *ByteProduct* function. Because this exception doesn't have the name *System.OverflowException*, the second *Catch* clause in the *ByteProduct* function catches it. The code block for this second *Catch* clause prints the *Message* declared for the exception when the procedure raised it with the first line inside the *Try* clause. Then the application closes. (You can, of course, do anything else Visual Basic permits you to program.)

Best Practices for Exception Handling

Many developers prefer to eliminate run-time errors before they happen. Others prefer to let run-time errors happen that they can fix with a little data validation or some other minor bit of programming. I believe that any real-world solutions are likely to have lots of opportunities for run-time errors no matter how heroic the efforts of a programming team to eliminate them.

When it is highly likely that users will respond inappropriately to a form, it makes sense to program a solution in your regular programming logic. The same considerations apply to hardware-based external factors, such as files not being in a folder or database servers not being available for a connection. However, there are many external factors that can negatively impact your program. Some of these have a low probability of occurrence. For these rare cases, it is probably not worth the programming effort to develop detailed solutions in your standard program logic. Routine exception handling makes great sense for these cases.

I also want to point out that exception handling is an integral part of Visual Basic .NET. This means that your programming teams will gradually achieve high levels of proficiency with the approach. Therefore, placing your code in *Try*, *Catch*, and *Finally* blocks will improve its clarity to others who know the programming paradigm as opposed to some ad hoc programming solution one of your programming team members concocts.

Although the *On Error GoTo* statement is familiar from earlier versions of Visual Basic and still available in Visual Basic .NET, I recommend that you migrate away from it in your new application development efforts. The *GoTo* statement leads to unstructured ("spaghetti") code. This code design style is widely recognized to be difficult to debug and maintain. In addition, you can have only one active *On Error GoTo* statement at a time. You can nest multiple *Try...Catch...Finally* statements within one another.

Finally, I leave you with two parting recommendations. First, replace the built-in error messages with custom ones that maximize the amount of contextual help your applications get. Second, try to fix problems rather than just let a user know that a problem exists. For example, if your application cannot connect to a database server, attempt to connect to a backup database server when one is available.

10

Programming Windows Solutions with ADO.NET

Chapter 1 introduces you to ADO.NET conceptually and shows you how to create a simple ADO.NET application using Visual Studio .NET graphical design tools. This chapter builds on the ADO.NET introduction in Chapter 1 and the intervening chapters that enhance your SQL Server and Visual Basic .NET skills. Think of this chapter as a "how to" guide for solutions to typical database problems with ADO.NET. The focus is on programming solutions for Windows applications. Chapter 11 delves into creating solutions with ASP.NET, and Chapter 12 puts the spotlight on XML issues as they relate to ADO.NET and SQL Server.

The chapter has five major sections.

- The chapter begins with a brief overview of ADO.NET design issues. This section drills down into the data set object model. This material will help you to programmatically coordinate data set objects with SQL Server database objects.
- Next the chapter presents programming samples for making a connection to a SQL Server database. This presentation also demonstrates how to secure access to your SQL Server databases. (See Chapter 7 for more on SQL Server security.)
- Coverage moves from making a connection to forward-only, read-only data access. Several samples reveal the flexibility you can achieve with this form of data access for displaying data. In addition, you learn how to dynamically configure the source that a *DataReader* object contains at run time.

- The next section introduces how to display data set objects with Windows Forms. It covers how to programmatically bind Windows Forms controls—such as text boxes, combo boxes, and data grids—to data set objects. You'll also learn how to display parent-child data relationships so that users can control the display of child data by manipulating a control for the parent data.
- The chapter concludes with a section that demonstrates how to update, insert, and delete rows in a SQL Server database from a Windows form.

All the samples throughout this chapter use the MyADODOTNETSamples solution. You can open the solution file (MyADODOTNETSamples.sln) in Visual Studio .NET. This chapter provides specific instructions for launching each sample from the solution. By following the instructions, you'll gain familiarity with how to start a Windows application from an element within a solution other than *Form1*—the default startup object.

An Overview of ADO.NET Objects

ADO.NET lets you use any of three data providers. These providers can link your Visual Basic .NET application to a remote data source. As a developer concerned with solutions for SQL Server databases, you'll be pleased to know that one of the data providers is exclusively for SQL Server—in particular, SQL Server 7 and SQL Server 2000. You can take advantage of the SQL Server provider through the *System.Data.SqlClient* namespace. You can place an *Imports* statement at the top of any module needing access to the ADO.NET objects available through the SQL Server data provider. The syntax for this statement is:

```
Imports System.Data.SqlClient
```

There are six basic ADO.NET object classes. These classes are the *Connection* class, the *Command* class, the *DataReader* class, the *DataAdapter* class, the *DataSet* class, and the *DataView* class. This section provides a brief orientation to each of these classes that focuses on selected properties and methods for each class that you are likely to find useful in your work. Much of this material specifically equips you to understand the samples that appear later in this chapter.

The *Connection* Class

The *Connection* class enables your application to read from, and optionally write to, a remote data source. Instantiate *Connection* objects with the SQL Server data provider as a *SqlConnection* object. You can use this object to connect to a server with either Windows NT or SQL Server authentication. The connection string syntax is very similar to that for ADO. In addition, you can open and close connections with the *Open* and *Close* methods. You can catch exceptions during an attempt to connect to a server and respond appropriately. For example, if you have a backup server available for data access, you can attempt to connect to the backup server when the primary server is unavailable. Your applications should explicitly close *Connection* objects after there is no longer a need for them.

> **Note** When used with a *SqlCommand* object, a *SqlConnection* object can even permit a client to administer a SQL Server instance. For example, you can add and remove database objects, such as logins, user-defined functions, and stored procedures.

The *SqlConnection* object's *ConnectionString* property lets you get or set the connection string for a *Connection* object. The *DataSource* property returns the SQL Server instance to which a *SqlConnection* object links, and the *Database* property denotes the specific database on the server to which the *Connection* object provides access. The *ConnectionTimeout* property allows you to fine-tune how long an application waits for a connection from a server before raising an exception because the server is unavailable.

The *Command* Class

The *Command* class encapsulates SQL instructions for a remote database server. These instructions can be simple *SELECT* statements, data manipulation statements, or statements that create and manipulate objects on the database server. Code your instructions to a remote SQL Server instance with T-SQL. See Chapters 2 through 6 for examples of the kinds of statements that you can encapsulate in a *Command* object. Apply objects based on the *Command* class with another object based on either the *DataReader* class or the *DataAdapter* class.

Instantiate a *SqlCommand* object to represent a *Command* object with the SQL Server data provider. Three especially critical *SqlCommand* properties are *CommandText*, *CommandType*, and *Parameters*. The *CommandText* property holds a T-SQL statement, a stored procedure name, or a table name. By default, ADO.NET interprets the *CommandText* property as a T-SQL string. The *CommandType* property settings are *Text*, *StoredProcedure*, and *TableDirect*. *Text* is the default setting. Use a *StoredProcedure* setting for *CommandType* when the *CommandText* property designates a stored procedure. When you are selecting all the rows and columns from one or more tables, the *TableDirect* property setting is especially useful. With the *TableDirect* property setting, you can name one or more tables in the *CommandText* property. Delimit multiple table names from one another with a comma.

The *Parameters* property for a *SqlCommand* object returns the *Parameters* collection. Use parameters to dynamically set arguments for stored procedures, other database objects, and even T-SQL strings at run time. Parameters are especially useful when you're performing database manipulation tasks, such as modifying records, inserting new records, and deleting rows from a SQL Server data source. In this context, you add the parameters to a *Command* property of a *DataAdapter* object. You can also use the *Parameters* collection to retrieve output parameters and return values from stored procedures.

> **Note** When working with the SQL Server data provider, you must designate parameters by name instead of using a question mark place marker as you can with the OLE DB .NET data provider.

Several methods facilitate the ability of a *Command* object to implement a T-SQL statement in its *CommandText* property. Use the *ExecuteReader* method to populate a *DataReader* object based on a *SELECT* statement. The *ExecuteNonQuery* method signals that a T-SQL statement doesn't return values. This method is particularly appropriate for T-SQL statements that create and manipulate objects, such as those that add logins or manipulate permissions. The *ExecuteScalar* method returns a single value, instead of a set of rows, from a T-SQL statement. The value corresponds to the first column value in the first row of the result set from the T-SQL statement on the server.

The *DataReader* Class

The *DataReader* class enables read-only, forward-only access to a remote data source. Objects based on this class maintain an open connection with the remote data source. *DataReader* objects let clients read data, but they don't provide editing capability or bidirectional navigational features. Objects based on the *DataReader* class are especially well suited when client performance times are more critical than scalability issues. This is because each *DataReader* object requires its own exclusive database *Connection* object. When the number of active *DataReader* objects from clients exceeds the number of connections available from a server, clients must wait for another *DataReader* object to release a connection (or return at a time when there is less demand for connections).

Instantiate *DataReader* objects as instances of the *SqlDataReader* class for the SQL Server data provider. You populate *SqlDataReader* objects by invoking the *ExecuteReader* method for a *SqlCommand* object that returns a rowset. You can free the connection associated with a *DataReader* object by invoking the *Close* method for either the *Connection* or *DataReader* object. Although the *RecordsAffected* property reports the number of records that a *DataReader* selects, this property returns accurate results only after you close the *DataReader*. If a query fails to return rows, the *FieldCount* property of a *DataReader* will equal 0.

Immediately after a *DataReader* is populated, its position is just prior to the first row. You can access the first row by invoking the *Read* method. Repeatedly invoking the *Read* method allows an application to pass through successive rows in the result set for a *DataReader*. A return value of *False* from the *Read* method indicates that no more rows remain in a result set. Retrieve the column values within a row with any of a series of *Get* methods, such as *GetInt32*, *GetString*, or *GetSqlDateTime*. The methods allow you to represent column values with data type formats. *Get* methods with SQL in their names, such as *GetSqlDateTime*, return SQL Server data type values, such as those discussed in Chapter 2. *Get* methods without SQL in their names return values in .NET Framework value types, such as those discussed in Chapter 9. Reference individual column values within a row by ordinal number. For example, `drd1.GetString(0)` returns the first column value as a string for the current row in the *drd1 DataReader*.

The *DataAdapter* Class

The *DataAdapter* class serves as a bridge for connecting a SQL Server data source to a *DataSet* class instance. You can use a *DataAdapter* object to initially populate a data set, and you can also use a *DataAdapter* object to synchronize a local data set with matching data in a SQL Server instance. The *DataAdapter* class is fundamental to ADO.NET, and it is a major design feature enabling the high scalability of ADO.NET applications. The *DataSet* class, together with its hierarchically dependent objects, represents a disconnected data source. Therefore, the *DataAdapter* class doesn't require a constant connection to a remote data source. *DataAdapter* objects can link to SQL Server data sources only when necessary, freeing the server in intervening periods to service other clients.

Instantiate *DataAdapter* objects with the SQL Server data provider as instances of the *SqlDataAdapter* class. You must use a *SqlDataAdapter* object in concert with a *SqlConnection* object. The *SqlConnection* object that a *SqlDataAdapter* object references is the conduit the *DataAdapter* object uses to link a local data source, represented by a *DataSet* object, to a remote data source on a server. You can instantiate a *SqlDataAdapter* object with an embedded T-SQL statement or with a reference to a *SqlCommand* object. The T-SQL statement, whether it is embedded or available in a *SqlCommand* object, determines which remote database objects get tapped to populate a local data set.

Use the *SqlDataAdapter Fill* method to populate a local data set. Before you can invoke the method, the *SqlDataAdapter* must have an open connection to a remote data source. After initially invoking the *Fill* method, your application can close the connection and work with the local data set version.

The *SqlDataAdapter* class facilitates data manipulation for SQL Server objects through its *Update* method and its related *UpdateCommand*, *InsertCommand*, and *DeleteCommand* properties. By specifying these three properties, you can designate data manipulation instructions, such as T-SQL syntax for an update, an insert, or a delete task. You can specify the T-SQL property directly as part of the property specification or indirectly by referencing a stored procedure. In either case, you will map columns in the local data set to columns in a remote data source by adding parameters to the commands designated by the *UpdateCommand*, *InsertCommand*, and *DeleteCommand DataAdapter* properties. Invoke the *Update* method to transfer changes to a remote data source from a local data set. The *Update* method—in concert with the *Command* objects *UpdateCommand*, *InsertCommand*, and *DeleteCommand*—accommodates update, insert, and delete data manipulation tasks.

The *SqlDataAdapter* object supports optimistic concurrency between the remote data source and the local data set. This follows from the disconnected status of the local data set from the remote data source. In fact, ADO.NET doesn't enable pessimistic concurrency. Keyset cursors and connected recordsets aren't a part of ADO.NET as they are of ADO. While optimistic concurrency helps to enhance scalability, it requires an extra measure of care to match the changes in a local data set back to the remote server. For example, attempting to update a row in a remote data source from a local data set that changed since you last populated the data set raises an optimistic concurrency violation. This violation raises an exception.

> **Note** Optimistic and pessimistic concurrency are two contrasting ways of managing data manipulation in a multiuser environment. With *pessimistic* concurrency, a lock applies to a row as soon as a user signals the start of a data manipulation task for a row. This lock doesn't release until the completion of the task. With *optimistic* concurrency, no locks go on a row after the start of a data manipulation task. Therefore, another user can change data before the current user commits a change. If the data does change before the commitment of a change by the current user, the database server raises a concurrency violation when the current user attempts to commit the change. Optimistic concurrency scales better than pessimistic concurrency. Therefore, optimistic concurrency is more suitable for multiuser applications—particularly if the applications serve many users.

ADO.NET provides two techniques for handling exceptions resulting from optimistic concurrency violations. First, you can create an event procedure for the *RowUpdated* event. ADO.NET raises this event after each attempt to change a remote data source based on a modified row from a local data set. With a *RowUpdated* event procedure, you can process exceptions as they occur for each row. Second, you can set the *ContinueUpdateOnError* property of the *SqlDataAdapter* object to *True* before invoking the *Update* method. This causes ADO.NET to complete all valid updates and write any error messages to the local data set so that you can respond to them after the *Update* method terminates.

The *DataSet* Class

The *DataSet* is a memory-resident object that can contain one or more tables and relationships between tables. This memory-resident object and its child objects make up the disconnected data source that is the centerpiece of the ADO.NET architecture. Figure 10-1 presents an overview of the *DataSet* object model. The balance of this section describes selected components within that model.

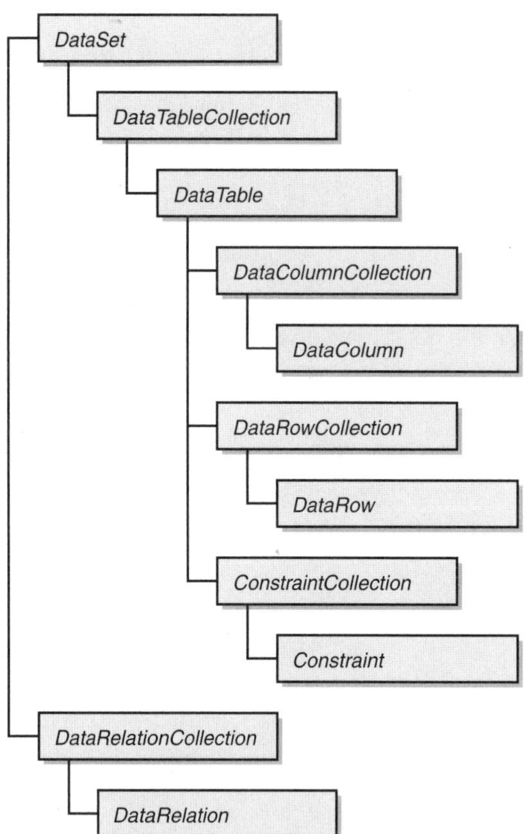

Figure 10-1. The *DataSet* object model.

ADO.NET refers to each individual table within a data set as a *DataTable* object. The collection of all tables within a data set is the *DataTableCollection* class. The tables within a data set can relate hierarchically to one another. This makes it possible for you to represent the schema for the tables in the Northwind database within a data set. The *Recordset* object from classic ADO doesn't directly represent hierarchical relationships. Instead, classic ADO flattens the relationships between tables into a single rowset.

DataTable objects consist of *DataColumn* and *DataRow* objects. The set of data columns within a *DataTable* object is the *DataColumnCollection* object. The *DataColumnCollection* class defines the schema for a *DataTable* object. For example, the individual *DataColumn* objects specify a data type that each column can contain. *DataTable* objects can have a *PrimaryKey* property. You can define this property with a *DataColumn* array that can contain one or more *DataColumn* objects. The *DataRowCollection* class represents all rows within a

DataTable. Column values for a local table reside within the *DataRow* objects that make up the *DataRowCollection* object for a *DataTable* object. Invoke the *NewRow* method for a *DataTable* to create a new row. You can then assign column values to the row and add the new *DataRow* object to the *DataRowCollection* object for a *DataTable* object.

ADO.NET specifies the relationship between tables in a data set with a *DataRelation* object. The set of all *DataRelation* objects within a data set is a *DataRelationCollection* object. Additionally, you can specify constraints for tables with the *Constraint* class. With a *Constraint* object, you can specify unique or foreign key constraints. A *DataRelation* object between two tables denotes a parent-child relationship between the tables. When you create a *DataRelation* object between two tables, ADO.NET automatically creates a foreign key constraint in the child table and a unique constraint on the primary key in the parent table. A *DataRelationCollection* class for a *DataSet* object contains each of the *DataRelation* objects in a data set. You can access *DataRelation* object members through the *ChildRelations* and *ParentRelations* properties of individual *DataTable* objects.

There are two techniques for eliminating a *DataRow* object from the *DataRowCollection* of a *DataTable* object. The first of these techniques is the *Delete* method, which applies to individual *DataRow* objects within a *DataTable*. This technique assigns *Deleted* to the *RowState* property for a *DataRow*, but it doesn't actually remove the row from the local table. (Your application can restore a deleted row with the *RejectChanges* method for a *DataRow* object.) Alternatively, you can commit the application of a *Delete* method to a row so that it isn't recoverable by invoking the *AcceptChanges* method for the row.

The second technique for eliminating a row from a local table is to invoke the *Remove* method for the *DataRowCollection* object within a *DataTable* object. This method requires that you specify the index for the row that you want to eliminate. Index values start with 0 and progress by 1 for each *DataRow* object within a *DataTable* until 1 minus the count of rows within the *DataTable*. This second technique doesn't allow you to restore a row.

> **Note** Use the *Delete* method when you plan to invoke the *Update* method to synchronize local changes with a remote data source. The *Update* method will apply the *AcceptChanges* method to the row after synchronization with the remote data source. Eliminating a row with the *Remove* method will raise an error based on a concurrency violation between the data set and the remote data source when you invoke the *Update* method.

The *DataView* Class

A *DataView* object is to a *DataTable* as a view is to a table in SQL Server. You base a *DataView* object on a single *DataTable* object. The *DataView* object for a table supports filtering, sorting, and enhanced searching capabilities not directly available from *DataTable* objects. Any given *DataTable* object can have multiple *DataView* objects specified for it with different property settings for filtering and sorting. You can filter the rows for a *DataView* with either the *RowFilter* or *RowStateFilter* property. *RowFilter* property settings have the same form as a *WHERE* clause for a single column in a table. Enclose *RowFilter* expressions in double quotation marks. If the expression contains a string constant, enclose the constant in single quotation marks. The *RowStateFilter* property allows you to filter the rows in a *DataTable* object by the *DataViewRowState* property setting for each row in a table. By filtering on this property, you can detect rows eliminated with the *Delete* property as well as inserted rows and rows with modified values.

The *Sort* property for a *DataView* object denotes a sort order for the rows of a *DataView* object. You designate the *Sort* property as a series of column names that are comma delimited if you specify more than one column for sorting a *DataView* object. By default, ADO.NET sorts in ascending order. However, you can explicitly specify an ascending sort order by following a column name with *ASC*. Follow a column name with *DESC* to designate a descending sort order for a column. The *DataView* object sorts its rows in the order of the columns listed for its *Sort* property.

Although you can return a single row or a subset of rows with the *RowFilter* property, doing so isn't an efficient use of it. In general, you should try to set the *RowFilter* property just once to save on the cost of indexing a *DataView* object. If you need to find a single row or a subset of rows, invoke either the *Find* or *FindRows* method. For either of these methods to work, you must first assign a *Sort* property setting for the criteria that you use to find rows. The *FindRows* method returns an array of *DataRowView* objects. The *Find* method returns the row index for a row matching the *Find* argument. You can then use the row index value to display a row from the *DataView* or its underlying *DataTable*.

Making Connections

Making a connection is sometimes thought of as a mundane task, but it's at the core of projects that process data from a remote database server. When you're building SQL Server solutions, your applications will nearly always start with the making of a connection to a SQL Server instance. This section illustrates the syntax for making connections to a SQL Server instance based on either a Windows login or a SQL Server login. It also shows you how to trap errors that can arise as you attempt to open a connection. Finally, the section concludes with a Windows Forms sample that lets users pick the style of login they want for their connection attempt as well as the database to which they want to connect.

Logging In with Integrated Security

The sample in this section shows the syntax for logging in to the Northwind database with Windows NT security. The syntax for the connection string refers to the designation of Windows NT security as Integrated Security. Recall from Chapter 7 that this type of login relies on the Windows login account for access to a database on a SQL Server instance. The sample makes a connection to the Northwind database, which is a SQL Server sample database that is installed with a guest user account. Therefore, anyone who can log in to a SQL Server instance can connect to the database.

The sample runs from *Module1* within the MyADODOTNETSamples solution. After opening the solution in Visual Studio .NET, right-click the solution's name in Solution Explorer and choose Properties from the context menu. Select *Module1* as the startup object. Then double-click *Module1* in Solution Explorer to open it in the Code Editor with the tab label Module1.vb. Finally, remove the comment marker (') from `IntegratedCnnToNorthwind()` in the *main* sub procedure at the top of the module, and make sure all other procedure calls in the *main* procedure have comment markers in front of them. You can launch the procedure to run its lines in one step by pressing the F5 key. Step through the procedure one line at a time by pressing F8 once for each successive line. These steps actually start the *main* procedure. Then continue pressing F8 for each step through the *main* and *IntegratedCnnToNorthwind* procedures. I often use F8 to help debug procedures or even just to clarify the flow of control through a procedure.

> **Note** Notice the *Imports* statement at the top of *Module1* that references the *System.Data.SqlClient* namespace. This is necessary for the abbreviated style used by the sample to refer to the *SqlConnection* class. The sample in the "Connecting from a Windows Form" section later in this chapter illustrates another convention for referencing the *SqlConnection* class that doesn't require the *Imports* statement.

The sample code for the *IntegratedCnnToNorthwind* procedure appears next. It begins with a declaration for *cnn1* as a *SqlConnection* class instance. The statement both declares and instantiates the *cnn1* object reference in a single statement. The *New* keyword instantiates a *SqlConnection* object. The argument for the *Connection* object specifies the connection string for the current Windows user to connect to the Northwind database on the local default instance of SQL Server on the current computer. When referring to the local default instance, you can designate the *Data Source* as either "(local)" or "localhost". You can also designate a server's name instead of the local one. For example, you could enter **cab2000** as the argument for *Data Source* if you could physically connect to a SQL Server instance named cab2000. The server need not have the .NET Framework installed—just the workstation running your .NET application. The *Initial Catalog* element of the *ConnectionString* argument specifies the database to which you want to open a connection. By setting the *Integrated Security* element of the *ConnectionString* argument to SSPI, you can designate a connection based on the current Windows account.

After declaring and instantiating *cnn1*, the sample invokes the *Open* method for the *SqlConnection* object. Provided the Northwind database is available on the local SQL Server instance and the current local user has permission to access the Northwind database, the *Open* method succeeds. If you are the administrator of the local server and you performed a standard installation of a regular SQL Server edition, the *Open* method will work. After making the connection, the sample echoes the connection string. The syntax for returning the connection string either to the Debug window in Visual Studio .NET or to a message box is in the sample. (The message box way is commented out.) Before terminating, the sample closes the *cnn1 SqlConnection* object. You should always explicitly close *SqlConnection* objects in your applications when you no longer need them.

> **Note** MSDE 2000 (Microsoft SQL Server 2000 Desktop Engine) doesn't ship with the Northwind database. Therefore, when using this database server, you must use another database on the MSDE 2000 server instance or create a Northwind database with appropriate objects within it.

```
Sub IntegratedCnnToNorthwind()
    'Specify connection string for connection via user's
    'Windows login; make sure user's Windows login has access
    'to the Northwind database or the Northwind database has
```

```
    'a guest user account.
    Dim cnn1 As SqlConnection = _
        New SqlConnection("Data Source=(local);" & _
        "Initial Catalog=northwind;Integrated Security=SSPI")

    'Attempt to open Northwind database with user's Windows login.
    cnn1.Open()

    'Echo connection string to either Debug window
    'or a message box.
    Debug.WriteLine(cnn1.ConnectionString)
    'MsgBox(cnn1.ConnectionString)

    'Close connection object to dispose of it.
    cnn1.Close()

End Sub
```

Logging In with SQL Server Security

Although Windows NT security is the preferred way to connect to a SQL Server database, there are times when SQL Server security is necessary or convenient. In any event, your applications frequently need to accommodate users who connect to your application with a SQL Server login. This section presents a sample that illustrates the syntax for creating a *Connection* object based on a SQL Server login.

Before reviewing the code for the procedure that illustrates the *ConnectionString* syntax for a SQL Server login, you need to make sure that a SQL Server login is available. If you have one available, feel free to replace our sample login. However, the following T-SQL script builds on the earlier work conducted in Chapter 7. It begins by dropping the vbdotnet1 SQL Server login. This is a two-step process. First you must drop user accounts associated with the login, and then you can drop the account. After dropping the account, the script re-creates it. However, the new version explicitly grants the vbdotnet1 login access to the Northwind database. By running this script in Query Analyzer, you ensure the availability of vbdotnet1 as a valid SQL Server login for the Northwind database with passvbdotnet1 as a password.

```
--vbdotnet1LoginScripts.sql
--Drop vbdotnet1 login, if it exists.
--Ignore message that login doesn't exist
--or user doesn't exist in current database.

USE Chapter07
EXEC sp_revokedbaccess 'vbdotnet1'
EXEC sp_droplogin 'vbdotnet1'
```

(continued)

```
--Add vbdotnet1 login with database access
--for the Northwind database.
USE Northwind
EXEC sp_addlogin
    @loginame = 'vbdotnet1',
    @passwd = 'passvbdotnet1',
    @defdb = 'Northwind'
EXEC sp_grantdbaccess 'vbdotnet1'
```

The connection sample for this section runs from the *SqlServerCnnToNorthwind* procedure in *Module1* of the MyADODOTNETSamples solution. In the *main* procedure for *Module1*, comment out all procedure calls except the one for the *SqlServerCnnToNorthwind* procedure. Make sure that *Module1* is the startup object for the solution (as described in the preceding section). Then press F5 to run the sample.

The *SqlServerCnnToNorthwind* procedure has the same general format as the one in the preceding section. The most important distinction between the two procedures is the syntax for the *ConnectionString* argument. The *ConnectionString* argument for this sample replaces the *Integrated Security* element from the preceding sample with userid and password elements. When connecting with a SQL Server login, you must specify a login name and a password if there is one. It's common practice to refer to the login as a userid. The following sample uses the vbdotnet1 login and password created by the preceding T-SQL script. After you run the procedure in the following sample, the Debug window will display a line that echoes the *ConnectionString* argument.

```
Sub SQLServerCnnToNorthwind()
    'Specify connection string for connection via vbdotnet1
    'SQL Server login; make sure vbdotnet1 login has access
    'to the Northwind database via its own account or guest account.
    Dim str1 As String = "Data Source=(local);" & _
        "Initial Catalog=northwind;" & _
        "user id = vbdotnet1; password=passvbdotnet1"
    Dim cnn1 As SqlConnection = _
        New SqlConnection(str1)

    'Attempt to open Northwind database with vbdotnet1 login.
    cnn1.Open()

    'Echo connection string.
    Debug.WriteLine(cnn1.ConnectionString)

    'Close connection object to dispose of it.
    cnn1.Close()

End Sub
```

Catching *SqlConnection* Exceptions

When you're performing database work, there are lots of opportunities for run-time errors. You can catch the exceptions associated with these errors and respond appropriately (even if only to convey the exception message to the user and avoid an abnormal end of your application). One way to generate a run-time error with the preceding sample is to drop the login for vbdotnet1. The following T-SQL script performs this action. The script also removes the guest user account from the Northwind database. Therefore, a user with login rights to a SQL Server instance but no special data access permission to the Northwind database will not be able to connect to the Northwind database.

```
--Remove access to Northwind database by
--vbdotnet1 through own or guest account,
--then drop vbdotnet1 login.
EXEC sp_revokedbaccess 'vbdotnet1'
EXEC sp_revokedbaccess guest
EXEC sp_droplogin @loginame = 'vbdotnet1'
```

After you run the preceding T-SQL script, the *SqlServerCnnToNorthwind* procedure that ran successfully in the preceding section will fail. In fact, it ends abnormally with an exception dialog like the one in Figure 10-2. Interestingly, the additional information in the dialog about the exception is singularly uninformative—"System error." Choose Continue on the dialog to recover from the exception.

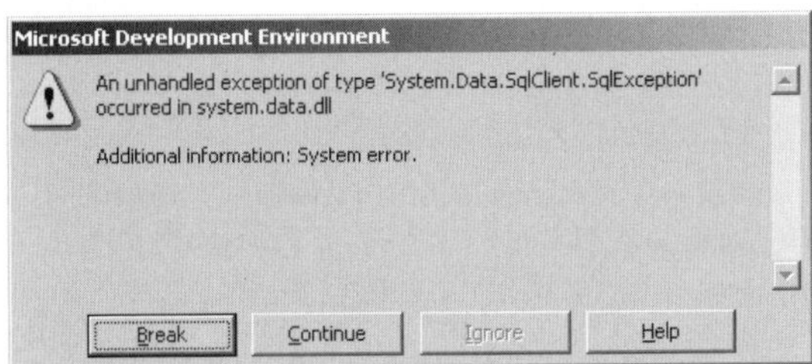

Figure 10-2. Default exception dialog from attempt to connect to the Northwind database with an invalid SQL Server login.

There is a single *SqlClient* exception for all the run-time errors that could happen. Happily, this exception automatically returns distinct messages for different kinds of errors. The *CatchSQLClientException* procedure shows an adaptation of the *SQLServerCnnToNorthwind* procedure. The adaptation is to place the *Open* and *Close* methods from the *SQLServerCnnToNorthwind* procedure in the *Try* clause of a *Try...Catch...Finally* statement; the sample omits the optional

Finally clause. The *Catch* clause demonstrates the syntax for explicitly referencing the *SqlClient* exception and printing the associated message.

```
Sub CatchSQLClientException()
    'Specify connection string for connection via vbdotnet1
    'SQL Server login; make sure vbdotnet1 login doesn't have
    'access to the Northwind database if you want to test
    'Try...Catch...Finally statement.
    Dim str1 As String = "Data Source=(local);" & _
        "Initial Catalog=northwind;" & _
        "user id = vbdotnet1; password=passvbdotnet1"
    Dim cnn1 As SqlConnection = _
        New SqlConnection(str1)
    'Start looking for exceptions.
    Try
        'Attempt to open Northwind database with vbdotnet1 login.
        cnn1.Open()

        'Echo connection string.
        Debug.WriteLine(cnn1.ConnectionString)

        'Close connection object to dispose of it.
        cnn1.Close()

        'Print default error message because it is
        'so short and informative.
    Catch er As System.Data.SqlClient.SqlException
        MsgBox(er.Message)
    End Try

End Sub
```

The *CatchSQLClientException* procedure resides in *Module1*. You can run it like the preceding samples. Namely, comment out the calls to other procedures and remove the comment marker for the *CatchSQLClientException* procedure in the *main* procedure within *Module1*. Then press F5. Figure 10-3 shows the resulting error message—an exception for an invalid vbdotnet1 login. Contrast this error message with the one that appears in Figure 10-2. Notice how much more informative the second message is compared with the first one. It pays to trap the *SqlClient* exception! In addition, if your server were down, the same *CatchSQLClientException* procedure would detect it and display a message that indicates this. There is no need to tweak the code. The procedure automatically traps the error and displays an appropriate message. By the way, the message for an unavailable server is, "SQL Server does not exist or access denied."

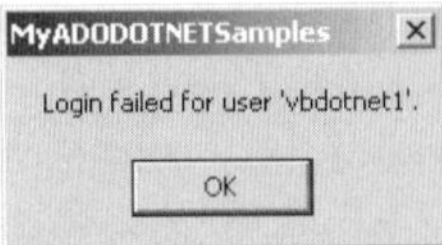

Figure 10-3. *SqlClient* exception dialog from attempt to connect to the Northwind database with an invalid SQL Server login.

Connecting from a Windows Form

Now that you have experience making a connection to a SQL Server database with the approaches described in the preceding three sections, you're probably wondering how to integrate these approaches with a Windows form. With a form, users can name the database to which they want to connect and select either a Windows NT account or a SQL Server account for making the connection. Because it is so easy to do, the form should be smart enough to include controls for a userid and password only when the user chooses to use a SQL Server account for making a connection to a SQL Server instance.

The sample for this section is available as *Form3* in the MyADODOTNET-Samples solution. In Solution Explorer, right-click the solution's name and choose Properties. From the Startup Object drop-down list, select *Form3* and click OK. Then double-click *Form3.vb* in Solution Explorer. This opens *Form3* in Design view. You can start the application by pressing F5.

Figure 10-4 shows the sample's Windows form instance in Design view and at run time in either of two different configurations. The Design view appears on the left. It shows *Form3* with three text boxes, each with matching label controls. The top text box is for the database name, and the next two text boxes are for the userid and password when a user decides to make a connection with a SQL Server login. I assigned * to the *PasswordChar* property for the bottom text box so that asterisks would mask characters typed in the box. The two radio buttons on the lower left portion of *Form3* allow users to specify whether they want to make a connection based on their Windows login account or use a SQL Server login account to make the connection. Finally, the *Click* event procedure of the Login button (*Button1*) makes a connection to a SQL Server instance according to what the user specifies in the form's other controls.

The top right form in Figure 10-4 shows *Form3* when it initially opens. Notice that the default setting is for making a connection with a Windows login. The *Checked* property of the Windows NT radio button is set to *True*, and just one text box appears with the Login button below. All a user has to do is type the database name in the sole text box on the form. If the login attempt succeeds, the sample displays a message confirming that the connection was made. A failed attempt might result because the Windows login account isn't valid for the SQL Server instance. For example, perhaps there is no corresponding SQL Server login for the Windows login. Alternatively, the Windows login might not have permission to access the database named in the top text box. In any event, the application returns the *SqlClient* exception message associated with the error that blocked the connection from succeeding.

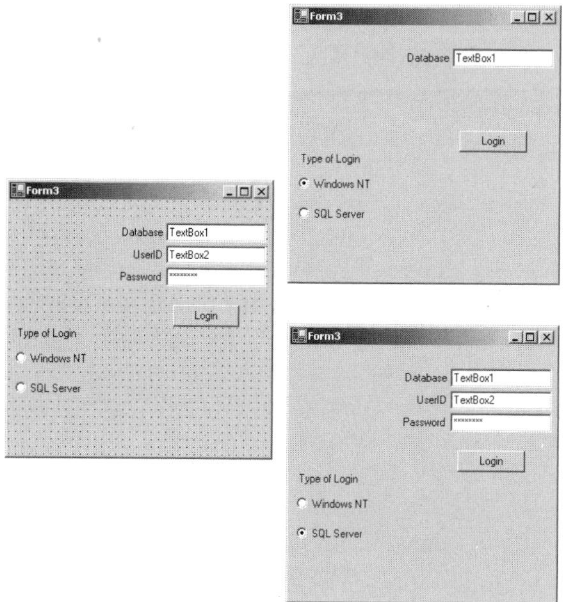

Figure 10-4. Design view and run-time views of a form that accepts user input and makes a connection to a SQL Server database based on either a Windows login or a SQL Server login.

The bottom right of Figure 10-4 shows *Form3* ready to accept SQL Server login credentials, including a SQL Server login and its password. A user can display the text boxes for the login and password by clicking the SQL Server radio button (*RadioButton2*). After the user clicks the Login button, the application attempts to make the connection to the database named in the top text box with the credentials specified in the second two text boxes.

Right-clicking *Form3* in Design view and choosing View Code opens the module behind *Form3*. This module handles both form management issues, such as controlling the visibility of the second and third text boxes, and ADO.NET issues, such as handling the attempt to connect to a database.

Three event procedures and a regular sub procedure (*ShowLabelsBoxes*) control the form's appearance. Users can invoke these procedures by running *Form3* or by clicking controls on *Form3*. For example, the *Form3_Load* event procedure checks *RadioButton1*, the one labeled Windows NT, and calls the *ShowLabelsBoxes* procedure while passing it a value of *False*. This argument causes the procedure to make the second two text boxes and their corresponding labels invisible. This appearance for the form is consistent with the default Windows login offered by *Form3*.

Clicking the SQL Server radio button invokes the *RadioButton2_CheckedChanged* event procedure. This procedure makes the second and third text boxes and their labels visible by passing the argument *True* to *ShowLabelsBoxes*. As a result, a user can enter a SQL Server login and password so that the form can attempt to make a connection based on a SQL Server instead of a Windows login.

Finally, by clicking the Windows NT radio button, the user invokes the *RadioButton1_CheckedChanged* event procedure. This procedure makes the controls for SQL Server login credentials invisible if they are showing. When the user clicks this *RadioButton1*, it indicates he or she wants to make a connection with a Windows login. Therefore, *Form3* doesn't need to show the controls for a SQL Server login.

```
Private Sub Form3_Load(ByVal sender As System.Object, _
    ByVal e As System.EventArgs) Handles MyBase.Load

    'Set RadioButton1 to Checked for connection via
    'Windows NT login.
    RadioButton1.Checked = True

    'Hide login and password controls because they
    'aren't necessary with Windows NT login.
    ShowLabelsBoxes(False)

End Sub

Private Sub RadioButton1_CheckedChanged _
    (ByVal sender As System.Object, _
    ByVal e As System.EventArgs) _
    Handles RadioButton1.CheckedChanged

    'Hide login and password controls because they
    'aren't necessary with Windows NT login.
    ShowLabelsBoxes(False)

End Sub
```

(continued)

```
Private Sub RadioButton2_CheckedChanged _
    (ByVal sender As System.Object, _
    ByVal e As System.EventArgs) _
    Handles RadioButton2.CheckedChanged

    'Show login and password controls because they
    'are necessary for a SQL Server login.
    ShowLabelsBoxes(True)

End Sub

Sub ShowLabelsBoxes(ByVal bolShowEm As Boolean)

    'Set the visibility of the second and third text
    'boxes and their labels according to the value
    'of bolShowEm.
    Label2.Visible = bolShowEm
    TextBox2.Visible = bolShowEm
    Label3.Visible = bolShowEm
    TextBox3.Visible = bolShowEm

End Sub
```

The following excerpt from the *Form3* module shows the code devoted to making the connection based on the radio button selection and text box entries. The excerpt starts with a module-level declaration of the *cnn1* object reference as a *SqlConnection* object. A module-level declaration isn't strictly necessary in the context of this sample, but this type of declaration makes the *SqlConnection* object available to other procedures that could use it. In any event, notice that the declaration specifies the full name for the namespace containing the *SqlConnection* object reference. This is because the module doesn't include an *Imports* statement for the *System.Data.SqlClient* namespace. By not using the *Imports* statement at the top of the *Form3* module, the *Catch* clause in the excerpt must reference a *System* exception instead of the more specific *SqlClient* exception. In spite of this deviation from the sample in the "Catching *SqlConnection* Exceptions" section, *SqlClient* exceptions still percolate up through the more general *System* exception specification.

Aside from the declaration issues for *cnn1*, the balance of the code excerpt is a straightforward mixture of the code samples developed previously in this chapter. Based on whether *RadioButton1* is checked, the *Button1_Click* event procedure composes a connection string for either a Windows or a SQL Server login. Then the procedure instantiates a connection based on the connection string. Within a *Try...Catch...Finally* statement, the procedure attempts to open the connection. If the attempt succeeds, the procedure displays a message confirming the attempt was successful and naming the database. Otherwise, control flows to the *Catch* clause, and the procedure displays the error message associated with the exception. Because *SqlClient* exceptions percolate up through the *System* exception, the message is likely to be specific and helpful for diagnosing any problems.

```
'Using the full namespace name removes the need to
'start module with Imports System.Data.SqlClient.
Dim cnn1 As System.Data.SqlClient.SqlConnection

Private Sub Button1_Click(ByVal sender As System.Object, _
    ByVal e As System.EventArgs) Handles Button1.Click

    'Make local variable declarations.
    Dim strDBName As String = TextBox1.Text
    Dim strConnect As String

    'Compose a connection string for either a Windows
    'or a SQL Server login.
    If RadioButton1.Checked = True Then
        strConnect = "Data Source=(local);" & _
                    "Initial Catalog=" & strDBName & _
                    ";Integrated Security=SSPI"
    Else
        Dim strLogin As String = TextBox2.Text
        Dim strPassword As String = TextBox3.Text
        strConnect = "Data Source=(local);" & _
            "Initial Catalog=" & strDBName & ";" & _
            "user id=" & strLogin & _
            "; password=" & strPassword
    End If

    'Instantiate a SqlConnection object based on the
    'connection string.
    cnn1 = _
        New System.Data.SqlClient.SqlConnection(strConnect)

    'Embed the attempt to open the cnn1 object inside a
    'Try...Catch...Finally statement, and display a
    'message for the exception if there is one.
    Try
        cnn1.Open()
        MsgBox("Successfully connected to " & cnn1.Database & _
            " database on local server.")
    Catch er As System.Exception
        MsgBox(er.Message)
    End Try

End Sub
```

Working with *Command* and *DataReader* Objects

One of the most common uses for *Command* objects is to contain the SQL string that defines the values contained in a *DataReader* object. Therefore, this section drills down on that use for *Command* objects. In this section, you learn how to format the display of values in a *DataReader* object as well as how to populate a *DataReader* with either a SQL string or a stored procedure. Beyond these typical applications for *Command* objects with *DataReader* objects, the section also includes a sample that demonstrates how to use the *Command* object for data definition tasks, such as creating a user-defined function. The presentation of the topic covers a special method for *Command* objects that is appropriate when the *CommandText* property for a *Command* object doesn't return any values.

Displaying Results in a Message Box or the Output Window

It's easy to put *SqlCommand* and *SqlDataReader* objects to use for reporting results from a SQL Server database. Start by connecting to the remote data source from which you want to display results. Next declare a *Command* object as a *SqlCommand* type. The *Command* object requires two inputs: a database connection and a source of SQL statements to execute. You can link a *Command* object to a *Connection* object when you instantiate the *Command* object. Specify a data source for the *Command* object to return with either a SQL string or a stored procedure. This capability of commands to take SQL statements and stored procedures allows you to draw on all data access topics covered in Chapters 3 through 5.

DataReader objects read the result set returned by *Command* objects. Use the *ExecuteReader* method on a *Command* object to convey its result set to a *DataReader* object. After the invocation of the *ExecuteReader* method, you can extract sequential rows from a result set with the *Read* method for the *DataReader* object. Use one of the *DataReader Get* methods to extract the value for a specific column into a data type designated by the *Get* method. Columns are designated with index numbers of 0 through 1 less than the number of columns in a result set.

The *EnumerateCategories* procedure, which appears next, demonstrates the application of these guidelines for using *Command* and *DataReader* objects. You can invoke this procedure from *Module1* in the MyADODOTNET-Samples solution by adapting the instructions for running other procedures from *Module1*. The procedure enumerates *CategoryID* and *CategoryName* values from the *Categories* table in the Northwind database. A compiler constant, *bolOutputWindow*, permits you to direct the contents of a *DataReader* object to either a message box or the Output window in the Visual Studio .NET design environment. The default value for *bolOutputWindow* directs the *DataReader* contents to a message box.

After assigning a value to the compiler constant, the *EnumerateCategories* listing begins by declaring and instantiating *cnn1* as a *Connection* object before invoking the object's *Open* method. Next the procedure declares *cmd1* as a *Command* object and specifies *cnn1* as its *Connection* property with the *CreateCommand* method for *cnn1*. The listing proceeds to assign a SQL string to the *CommandText* property for *cmd1*. With an *ExecuteReader* method in a declaration for the *drd1 DataReader*, the procedure generates a result set for *drd1* based on the SQL string used to define *cmd1*.

> **Note** Throughout this chapter, and elsewhere in the book, I use generic terms interchangeably when referencing specific classes in the *System.Data.SqlClient* namespace. For example, I use the term *DataReader* to reference the more specific class name *SqlDataReader*. Using the generic term reminds you that *SqlClient* classes have parallel classes in other .NET data providers, namely the OLE DB .NET data provider and the ODBC .NET data provider.

After the conclusion of the *ExecuteReader* method, the *DataReader* object is ready to expose its contents to a Visual Basic .NET application. The balance of the procedure introduces you to two different strategies for achieving this. A compiler *If...Then...Else* statement based on a compiler constant adds one of two statements to the compiled version of the procedure. Either statement returns a row from the *DataReader* object, but they display the row in different ways. Although the listing shows both the *Then* and *Else* clauses, the compiled procedure contains only one or the other clause based on the compiler constant value for *bolOutputWindow*. Before encountering the compiler *If...Then...Else* statement, the procedure declares a string constant that can serve as a title for the enumerated values in a message box. The constant ends with a *StrDup* function that can duplicate a string constant any number of times. In this case, the function appends two carriage returns to the end of the text for the title. The intrinsic constant, *vbCr*, denotes the string equivalent of a carriage return.

Next the procedure starts a *Do...While* statement with the condition `drd1.Read()`. This condition will return the value *True* as long as there are remaining rows in the *DataReader*. After the *Read* method passes through all the rows from the *drd1* object, the condition returns the value *False*, which causes control to pass to the first statement after the *Loop* statement for the *Do…While* statement. The compiler *If…Then…Else* statement compiles one of two possible statements depending on the value of *bolOutputWindow*. When *bolOutputWindow* equals its default value (*False*), the statement appends *CategoryID* and *CategoryName* values for the current row to a string value. The values for each row end with a carriage return (*vbCr*). If *bolOutputWindow* equals *True*, Visual Basic .NET compiles a different statement that simply echoes the row values to the Output window with the *WriteLine* method for a Console object. Notice that the two compiled statements use slightly different techniques for capturing the first column value for *CategoryID*. Both statements use a *GetInt32* method because the SQL Server data type of *int* for *CategoryID* is consistent with the .NET value type of *Int32*, a 32-bit signed integer. However, the path for adding the values to a string for display in a message box invokes the *ToString* method to convert explicitly the *Int32* number to a string. This kind of conversion is preferred because it saves the time for a run-time determination of how to finally represent a returned value.

```
Sub EnumerateCategories()
    'Compiler constant directing output to Output window
    'or a message box. Default value is False.
    #Const bolOutputWindow = False

    'Declare and open connection to Northwind.
    Dim cnn1 As SqlConnection = New _
        SqlConnection("Data Source=(local);" & _
        "Integrated Security=SSPI;Initial Catalog=northwind")
    cnn1.Open()

    'Declare a command and assign a SQL string to it.
    Dim cmd1 As SqlCommand = cnn1.CreateCommand()
    cmd1.CommandText = _
        "SELECT CategoryID, CategoryName FROM Categories"

    'Declare a data reader and copy result set from SQL string
    'for cmd1 to drd1.
    Dim drd1 As SqlDataReader = cmd1.ExecuteReader()

    'Loop through data reader and display in Output
    'window or message box.
    Dim str1 As String = _
        "Summary of CategoryID and Category Names" _
            & StrDup(2, vbCr)
```

```
    Do While drd1.Read()
    #If bolOutputWindow = True Then
        Console.WriteLine("Category " & drd1.GetInt32(0) & _
            " is " & drd1.GetString(1))
    #Else
        str1 = str1 & "Category " & _
            drd1.GetInt32(0).ToString & _
            " is " & drd1.GetString(1) & vbCr
    #End If
    Loop

    'Conditionally display results in a message box.
    #If bolOutputWindow = False Then
    MsgBox(str1)
    #End If

    'Close data reader and connection object references.
    drd1.Close()
    cnn1.Close()

End Sub
```

After control passes from the *Do…While* statement, control can flow optionally to a *MsgBox* function statement for displaying the string computed in the loop. A compiler *If…Then* statement inserts the *MsgBox* function into the compiled procedure if *bolOutputWindow* equals *False*. Figure 10-5 shows the outcome from the procedure when the value of *bolOutputWindow* is *False*, and Figure 10-6 is an excerpt from the Output window generated when *bolOutputWindow* is *True*. No matter which path the procedure takes to generate results, it ends by closing the *drd1* and *cnn1* object references. You should always perform these tasks when you no longer need a *DataReader* object so that SQL Server can make the connection available for other requirements.

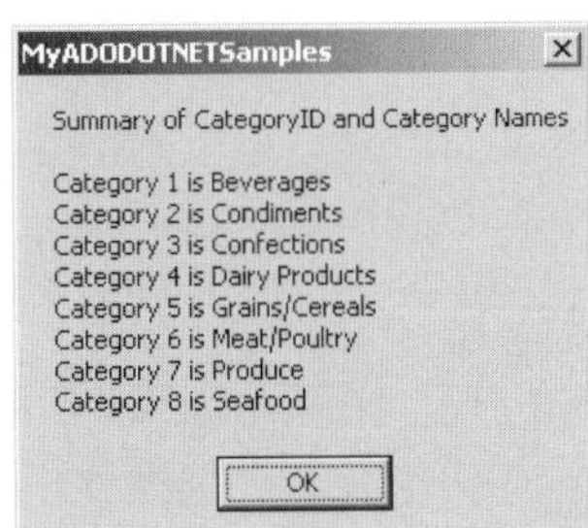

Figure 10-5. Return for the *EnumerateCategories* procedure when *bolOutputWindow* equals *False*.

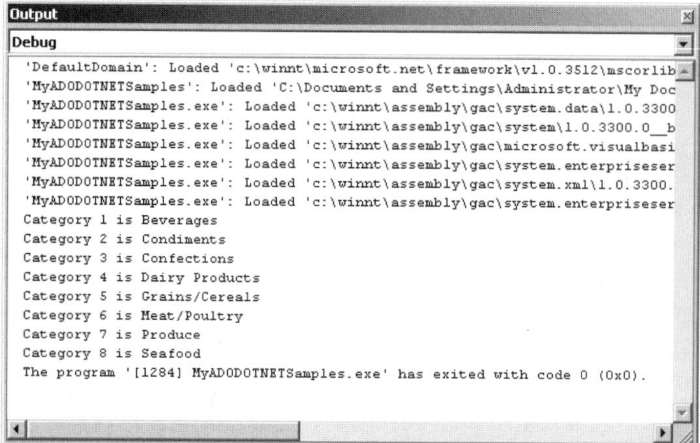

Figure 10-6. An excerpt from the return for the *EnumerateCategories* procedure when *bolOutputWindow* equals *True*.

Displaying Rows in Blocks from a *DataReader*

The preceding sample demonstrates how convenient a message box can be for displaying the contents of a *DataReader* object. However, a single message box can be filled to its character limit before it completes displaying results from a *DataReader* object. A workaround to this situation is to display your results from the *DataReader* objects in blocks of *x* rows at a time. When your application displays rows in blocks, users can sequentially page through a result set to find an item, or items, of interest. Because the *DataReader* provides forward-only data access, you cannot page back, but you can provide your users a forward-only look at some data.

The *EnumerateCustomerIDNames* procedure allows a user to specify the number of rows to show in a message box. The procedure returns the *CustomerID* and *CompanyName* column values from the *Customers* table in the Northwind database. You can invoke the *EnumerateCustomerIDNames* procedure from the *main* procedure in *Module1*. Launching this procedure is slightly different than with preceding samples from *Module1*. In this case, you must pass along an argument value as you invoke the procedure. The argument is for the maximum number of rows to show in a text box. The result set from the *Command* object for a *DataReader* object may extend over several blocks and require multiple message boxes. Each message box, except the final one, must hold the maximum number of rows per block passed as an argument to the *EnumerateCustomerIDNames* procedure. The final message box will display from one row up to the maximum number of rows.

The *EnumerateCustomerIDNames* procedure starts in the same general fashion as the preceding one in that it makes a connection to the Northwind database and then populates a *DataReader*, *drd1*, with the results of a *Command* object, *cmd1*. The sole distinction in how the two procedures start is that this one has a different SQL string for the *Command* object that returns more rows than the one in the earlier sample. This larger number of rows in the *DataReader* for this sample calls for special treatment because a single message box cannot display all its rows.

The balance of the procedure demonstrates one solution for the problem of too many rows to display in a message box. Two code blocks facilitate the solution. The first block iterates through the rows in *drd1* in blocks of *intSize*. The procedure obtains a value for *intSize* as a passed argument from the procedure that calls the *EnumerateCustomerIDNames* procedure. A user can specify a block size that does fit within a single message box no matter how many rows are in the *DataReader*. By clicking OK on each message box, the user can view successive blocks of rows from the *DataReader*. The second code block captures any remaining rows at the end of a *DataReader* object that don't fill a complete block.

The first code block uses *int1* as a variable to count the cumulative number of rows read from the *drd1 DataReader*. A string variable, *str1*, accumulates rows in successive blocks of size *intSize*. The first code block uses a *Do…While* statement with a condition of `drd1.Read()` to pass successively through all the rows in the *drd1 DataReader*. As the code block reads each new row, it recomputes *str1* so that the new row appears at the bottom of the string variable. When the remainder of *int1* divided by *intSize* equals 0, the procedure accumulates a new block of rows (of size *intSize*) to display in a message box. The expression `int1 mod intSize` returns the remainder of *int1* divided by *intSize*. When the first code block detects the end of a block of rows, the string variable storing row values is passed to a *MsgBox* function as the message argument. After printing the message, the procedure resets the string variable *str1* to start a new block of rows. Then the whole process starts over again.

When no more rows remain in the *DataReader*, the procedure passes control to the second code block. This second block starts by testing to see whether any rows remain that didn't appear since the display of the last message box. Any remainder of *int1* divided by *intSize* signals undisplayed rows. If there are any of these rows, the second code block passes the value of *str1* to a *MsgBox* function as the message argument to show them. The procedure concludes in the standard way by closing the *DataReader* object and its *Connection* object.

```
Sub EnumerateCustomerIDNames(ByVal intSize As Integer)
    'Declare and open connection to Northwind.
    Dim cnn1 As SqlConnection = _
```

(continued)

```
        New SqlConnection("Data Source=(local);" & _
            "Integrated Security=SSPI;Initial Catalog=northwind")
    cnn1.Open()

    'Declare command and assign a SQL string to it, and then
    'declare a data reader and copy result set from cmd1 to drd1.
    Dim cmd1 As SqlCommand = cnn1.CreateCommand()
    cmd1.CommandText = _
        "SELECT CustomerID, CompanyName FROM Customers"
    Dim drd1 As SqlDataReader = cmd1.ExecuteReader()

    'Loop through data reader in blocks of intSize and sequentially
    'display the contents of successive blocks.
    Dim int1 As New Integer()
    Dim str1 As String = _
        "CustomerID and matching CompanyName column values" _
            & StrDup(2, vbCr)
    Do While drd1.Read()
        str1 = str1 & drd1.GetString(0) & vbTab & _
            drd1.GetString(1) & vbCrLf
        int1 += 1
        If (int1 Mod intSize) = 0 Then
            str1 = str1 & StrDup(2, vbCr) & _
                "Click OK for next " & _
                intSize.ToString & " customers."
            MsgBox(str1, , "CustomerID and Customer Name")
            str1 = _
                "CustomerID and matching CompanyName " & _
                "column values" & StrDup(2, vbCr)
        End If
    Loop

    'If a partial block remains at end of data reader contents,
    'display partial block.
    If (int1 Mod intSize) > 0 Then
        str1 = str1 & StrDup(2, vbCr) _
            & "Click OK to close message box."
        MsgBox(str1, , "CustomerID and Customer Name")
    End If

    'Close data reader and connection object references.
    drd1.Close()
    cnn1.Close()

End Sub
```

Figure 10-7 shows the first and last message boxes that result from running the *EnumerateCustomerIDNames* procedure with an *intSize* argument value of 25. The first message box contains 25 rows, as do all the intervening message boxes up until the last one. The last message box shows the rows remaining at the end that don't fill an entire block of 25 rows.

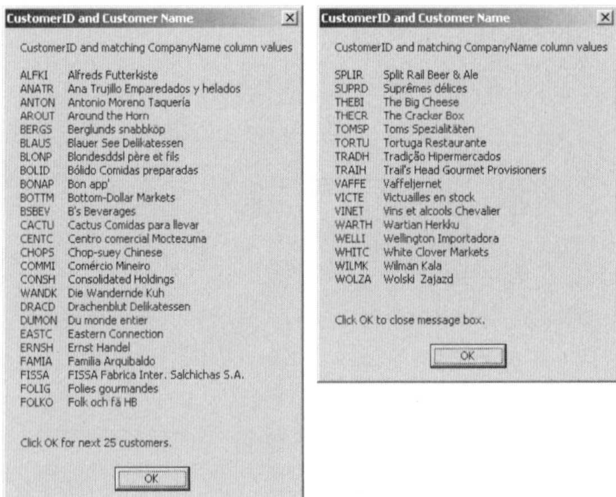

Figure 10-7. The first and last message boxes displayed by the *EnumerateCustomerIDNames* procedure.

Invoking a Stored Procedure with a Parameter by a SQL String

In addition to using SQL strings to designate the data for the *Command* objects that populate *DataReader* objects, you can also specify a stored procedure as the source for a *Command* object. There are two main advantages to using stored procedures. First, stored procedures are compiled. This saves the server the time of compiling a SQL string before it can start to return data for your *DataReader* object. Second, stored procedures accept parameters. This allows the users of your applications to change the result set returned at run time.

There are two approaches to setting parameter values for stored procedures. Many developers prefer to specify a SQL string that invokes the stored procedure and passes the value. Chapter 4 illustrates the syntax for accomplishing this, and we demonstrate the use of the technique in a .NET Framework application with the sample for this section. A second approach is to add parameters with the .NET Framework syntax. This approach allows you to explicitly specify the data type as you pass a parameter. I will demonstrate this second approach in the next section.

The sample for this section and the next one depends on the *CustOrderHist* stored procedure in the Northwind database. This procedure returns the quantity of each product ordered by a customer. The procedure takes a five-character string parameter to designate the *CustomerID* value. The result set contains a single row for each product ever ordered by a customer. Each row contains the product name and quantity ordered by the customer specified in the parameter when you invoke the stored procedure. For your convenience in understanding the logic of the *CustOrderHist* stored procedure, here's the T-SQL code for the stored procedure:

```
CREATE PROCEDURE CustOrderHist @CustomerID nchar(5)
AS
SELECT ProductName, Total=SUM(Quantity)
FROM Products P, [Order Details] OD, Orders O, Customers C
WHERE C.CustomerID = @CustomerID
AND C.CustomerID = O.CustomerID AND
O.OrderID = OD.OrderID AND OD.ProductID = P.ProductID
GROUP BY ProductName
```

Two sub procedures make up the solution for displaying the results from running the *CustOrderHist* stored procedure with a SQL string. The first sub procedure, *RunCustOrderHistWithString*, invokes the SQL string for the stored procedure and creates a *DataReader* object based on its result set. *RunCustOrderHistWithString* takes two arguments—one for the *CustomerID* value and a second for specifying the maximum number of rows to display as a block in a message box. This initial Visual Basic .NET procedure:

- Creates a *Connection* object.
- Instantiates a *Command* object that executes the *CustOrderHist* stored procedure while passing a *CustomerID* value as a parameter.
- Populates a *DataReader* based on the result set from *CustOrderHist*.

Because the sample uses a SQL string to invoke the stored procedure and pass a parameter, the process of running a stored procedure with a parameter is similar to just specifying a SQL string as the source for the *Command* object. This similarity is the chief advantage of using the SQL string to invoke the stored procedure. One disadvantage of the approach is that the server has to compile the T-SQL statement in the string to invoke the stored procedure. Another disadvantage is that you don't get the benefit of explicit data typing for the parameter value at the client end of the solution. This explicit typing can allow you to catch inappropriate parameter values earlier in the solution and save server time devoted to detecting erroneous parameter values as well as passing back feedback on the error to the client.

The solution's second sub procedure, *drdToMessageBox*, displays the rows in the *DataReader* created by *RunCustOrderHistWithString*. The *drdToMessageBox* procedure requires four arguments. The first two are passed by reference instead of in the normal Visual Basic .NET way of by value. These arguments are for the *DataReader* object and its associated *Connection* object. The second two arguments are passed by value. These are the *CustomerID* parameter value and the value for the maximum number of rows to display in a message box. The design of this second sub procedure is a direct extension of prior samples with specific adjustments, such as for the title within a message box. A specific benefit of dividing the solution across two sub procedures is that we will be able to reuse this second sub procedure in the next section's sample.

```
Sub RunCustOrderHistWithString(ByVal CustomerID As String, _
    ByVal intSize As Integer)

    'Declare and open connection to Northwind.
    Dim cnn1 As SqlConnection = _
        New SqlConnection("Data Source=(local);" & _
            "Integrated Security=SSPI;Initial Catalog=northwind")
    cnn1.Open()

    'Declare command with T-SQL for a stored proc with a parameter.
    Dim cmd1 As SqlCommand = _
        New SqlCommand("EXEC CustOrderHist " & CustomerID, cnn1)

    'Declare data reader and populate with result set
    'from stored procedure.
    Dim drd1 As SqlDataReader = cmd1.ExecuteReader()

    'Display result set.
    drdToMessageBox(drd1, cnn1, CustomerID, intSize)

End Sub

Sub drdToMessageBox(ByRef drd1 As SqlClient.SqlDataReader, _
    ByRef cnn1 As SqlClient.SqlConnection, _
    ByVal CustomerID As String, _
    ByVal intSize As Integer)

    'Declare header for report in message box and counter for rows
    'showing within a message box.
    Dim str1 As String = _
        "Quantities for Products Ordered by " & _
            CustomerID & StrDup(2, vbCr)
    Dim int1 As Integer

    'Loop through data reader in blocks of intSize and
    'sequentially display the contents of successive blocks.
    Do While drd1.Read()
        str1 = str1 & drd1.GetInt32(1) & vbTab _
            & drd1.GetString(0).ToString & vbCrLf
        int1 += 1
        If (int1 Mod intSize) = 0 Then
            str1 = str1 & StrDup(2, vbCr) _
```

(continued)

```
                & "Click OK for next " & _
                intSize.ToString & " customers."
            MsgBox(str1, , "From CustOrderHist Stored Proc")
            str1 = _
                "Quantities for Products Ordered by " & _
        CustomerID & StrDup(2, vbCr)
        End If
    Loop

    'If a partial block remains at end of data reader contents,
    'display partial block.
    If (int1 Mod intSize) <> 0 Then
        str1 = str1 & StrDup(2, vbCr) _
            & "Click OK to close message box."
        MsgBox(str1, , "From CustOrderHist Stored Proc")
    End If

    'Close data reader and connection object references.
    drd1.Close()
    cnn1.Close()

End Sub
```

You can run the sample defined by the preceding two sub procedures from *Module1* in the MyADODOTNETSamples solution. The sample procedure call in the *main* procedure for invoking the first procedure follows. It passes two arguments to the *RunCustOrderHistWithString* procedure. The first argument is a *CustomerID* value, and the second argument designates the maximum number of rows to display in a message box. You can obtain a result set to display for any *CustomerID* in the *Customers* table that has orders associated with it. (Two *CustomerID* values don't have any orders.) The solution automatically populates the argument list for the second sub procedure that prints the rows in the *DataReader* created by the *RunCustOrderHistWithString* procedure.

```
RunCustOrderHistWithString("TORTU", 10)
```

Invoking a Stored Procedure with a Parameter by Its Name

It is possible to invoke a stored procedure and pass it parameter values without using a SQL string. Some developers would count this as an advantage. The approach has the extra advantage of strong data typing for parameter values on the client side of a database solution. Therefore, illegitimate values can be detected before encountering time for a round-trip to the server and without diverting any valuable server time to error processing. As the scale of an application grows relative to server processing power and network throughput, these considerations gain significance.

The solution to invoke a stored procedure without a SQL string requires you to assign the name of the stored procedure as the *CommandText* property for a *Command* object. You must also designate *CommandType.StoredProcedure* as the *CommandType* property setting for the *Command* object. If the stored procedure requires parameters, you can invoke the *Add* method for the *Parameters* collection of the *Command* object to declare the parameters. As with many Visual Basic .NET methods, the specification for the *Add* method of the *Parameters* collection has multiple overloaded specifications. The one used in the sample for this section uses *@CustomerID* to designate the parameter's name. The second and third arguments for the *Add* method designate the *@CustomerID* parameter as a Unicode fixed length text field of 5 characters. The sample follows the parameter declaration with the syntax for assigning an actual value to the parameter. As you can see, you use the parameter's *Value* property to perform this task.

Aside from the exceptions noted previously, the solution for running the *CustOrderHist* stored procedure with or without a SQL string is the same. You create the *Connection* object identically, and you pass the return set from the *Command* object to the *DataReader* object in the same way. Furthermore, this second-solution approach uses exactly the same second sub procedure, *drdToMessageBox*, to display the result set from the *CustOrderHist* stored procedure in a series of message boxes.

```
Sub RunCustOrderHistWithParameter(ByVal CustomerID As String, _
    ByVal intSize As Integer)

    'Declare and open connection to Northwind.
    Dim cnn1 As SqlConnection = _
        New SqlConnection("Data Source=(local);" & _
            "Integrated Security=SSPI;Initial Catalog=northwind")
    cnn1.Open()

    'Instantiate a command reference pointing at the
    'CustOrderHist stored proc.
    Dim cmd1 As SqlCommand = _
        New SqlCommand("CustOrderHist", cnn1)
    cmd1.CommandType = CommandType.StoredProcedure

    'Declare the parameter with a SqlDbType to eliminate
    'the need for conversion, then assign the parameter a value.
    Dim prm1 As SqlParameter = _
        cmd1.Parameters.Add("@CustomerID", SqlDbType.NChar, 5)
    prm1.Value = CustomerID

    'Declare data reader and populate with its result
    'set from the stored proc.
```

(continued)

```
    Dim drd1 As SqlDataReader = cmd1.ExecuteReader()

    'Display result set.
    drdToMessageBox(drd1, cnn1, CustomerID, intSize)

End Sub
```

You can invoke the *RunCustOrderHistWithParameter* procedure from the *main* procedure in *Module1* for the MyADODOTNETSamples solution. Simply remove its comment marker and ensure that all other procedure calls have a comment marker preceding them.

Creating a *Database* Object with a *Command* Object

The *Command* object provides more flexibility than just returning result sets. For example, you can use a *Command* object to administer a database object on a SQL Server instance. This section demonstrates the capability by adding a new user-defined function to the Northwind database, using it, and then removing the user-defined function. For this demonstration to work, your connection must be based on a login with permission to create whatever user-defined objects you attempt to create or drop. See Chapter 5 for the T-SQL syntax on adding and removing user-defined functions and Chapter 7 for a discussion of the security associated with logins to a SQL Server instance. If your login is the administrator for your local instance of SQL Server, you have appropriate permission to run the sample.

The user-defined function *udfDaysDiffLessx* in this sample computes the difference between two dates minus an offset. You can use the function to report how many days late an event occurred. For example, if the standard for shipping an order is within 3 days of the order date, you can use this user-defined function to report how many days after the standard an order ships.

The *CreateAndInvokeUDF* procedure in *Module1* illustrates the Visual Basic .NET syntax for creating, using, and finally dropping a user-defined function like the one described. The *CreateAndInvokeUDF* procedure connects to the Northwind database. The procedure takes two optional arguments. (If the user doesn't supply values for the arguments when calling the procedure, the procedure assigns default values to the arguments.) The *intOrderNo* argument denotes the *OrderID* value for the order about which you seek shipping information, and the *strx* argument is a string representing the offset in days between two *datetime* values.

While somewhat lengthy, the *CreateAndInvokeUDF* procedure design is straightforward. In actual practice, you are likely to extract the code for creating a user-defined function into a separate sub procedure. The procedure begins by making a connection to the Northwind database. Next the procedure defines a SQL string for dropping any prior version of the *udfDaysDiffLessx* user-defined function. The procedure runs this string from a *Command* object with the *ExecuteNonQuery* method. In the next code block, the procedure runs with the *ExecuteNonQuery* method a second SQL string to create a new version of the *udfDaysDiffLessx* user-defined function. Notice that the user-defined function includes a parameter to specify the offset for the difference between two dates.

After ensuring that the code for the user-defined function is the second SQL string, the procedure runs a third SQL string that invokes the user-defined function within a query statement. The design of the SQL string for the query uses the *strx* argument as a variable so that a procedure calling the *CreateAndInvokeUDF* procedure can dynamically set the offset between two dates. In addition, the *intOrderNo* argument is a variable in the SQL string so that a calling procedure can specify the order via an *OrderID* value on which to report. The procedure uses the *ExecuteReader* method to run the SQL string in a *Command* object and passes the result to a *DataReader*. After executing the *Read* method for the *DataReader*, a message box displays the shipping information for the order. The procedure concludes by performing various cleanup chores, including restoring the Northwind database so that the database no longer has a user-defined function named *udfDaysDiffLessx*. In practice, you may very well decide to keep a user-defined function after creating it, but the sample runs this step to restore your initial copy of the Northwind database.

```
Sub CreateAndInvokeUDF( _s
    Optional ByVal intOrderNo As Integer = 10248, _
    Optional ByVal strx As String = "1")

    'Declare and open connection to Northwind.
    Dim cnn1 As SqlConnection = _
        New SqlConnection("Data Source=(local);" & _
            "Integrated Security=SSPI;Initial Catalog=northwind")
    cnn1.Open()

    'Define SQL string to drop prior version of user-defined
    'function, then run the T-SQL batch with ExecuteNonQuery
    'method for a command.
    Dim str1 As String = _
        "IF EXISTS " & _
        "(SELECT * " & _
        "FROM INFORMATION_SCHEMA.ROUTINES " & _
        "WHERE ROUTINE_NAME = 'udfDaysDiffLessx') " & _
        "DROP FUNCTION udfDaysDiffLessx"
    Dim cmd1 As SqlCommand = New SqlCommand(str1, cnn1)
    cmd1.ExecuteNonQuery()
```

(continued)

```
'Define SQL string to create a new user-defined function,
'then run the T-SQL batch with ExecuteNonQuery method
'for a command.
str1 = "CREATE FUNCTION udfDaysDiffLessx" & _
    "(@date1 as datetime, @date2 as datetime, " & _
    "@x as Integer) " & _
    "RETURNS int " & _
    "AS " & _
    "BEGIN " & _
    "Return(DATEDIFF(day,@date1,@date2)-@x) " & _
    "END"
cmd1.CommandText = str1
cmd1.ExecuteNonQuery()

'Define a SQL string to use the preceding user-defined
'function and accept variables for SQL string
'(strx and intOrderNo), then assign SQL string to
'CommandText property of command(cmd1).
Dim strSQL As String
strSQL = "SELECT LEFT(OrderDate,11) AS 'Order Date', " & _
    "LEFT(ShippedDate,11) AS 'Shipped Date',  " & _
    "dbo.udfDaysDiffLessx(OrderDate, ShippedDate, " & _
    strx & ") AS 'Days Late' " & _
    "FROM Orders " & _
    "WHERE OrderID = " & intOrderNo.ToString
cmd1.CommandText = strSQL

'Store result set from SQL string in a data reader and
'format its contents for display via a MsgBox function.
Dim drd1 As SqlDataReader = cmd1.ExecuteReader()
drd1.Read()
str1 = "For Order " & intOrderNo.ToString & vbCr & _
    "OrderDate is " & drd1.GetString(0) & vbCr & _
    "ShippedDate is " & drd1.GetString(1) & vbCr & _
    "Days to ship after " & strx & " days is " _
        & drd1.GetInt32(2).ToString
MsgBox(str1, , _
    "SQL string with a scalar user-defined function")

'Restore the Northwind database by removing the udf.
str1 = _
    "IF EXISTS " & _
    "(SELECT * " & _
    "FROM INFORMATION_SCHEMA.ROUTINES " & _
    "WHERE ROUTINE_NAME = 'udfDaysDiffLessx') " & _
    "DROP FUNCTION udfDaysDiffLessx"
cmd1.CommandText = str1

'Close the data reader so the command can use it.
drd1.Close()
```

```
    'Execute the SQL string to drop the user-defined function.
    cmd1.Connection = cnn1
    cmd1.ExecuteNonQuery()

    'Finally, close the connection to the Northwind database.
    cnn1.Close()

End Sub
```

The line in the *main* procedure of *Module1* invoking the *CreateAndInvokeUDF* procedure specifies an *OrderID* of 10249 with *intOrderNo* and an offset of 3 days with *strx*. In response to invoking the *CreateAndInvokeUDF* procedure with this line, the procedure presents a message box like the one in Figure 10-8. If you were interested in tracking performance on a next-day delivery promise, you could replace the value 3 in the calling procedure with 1.

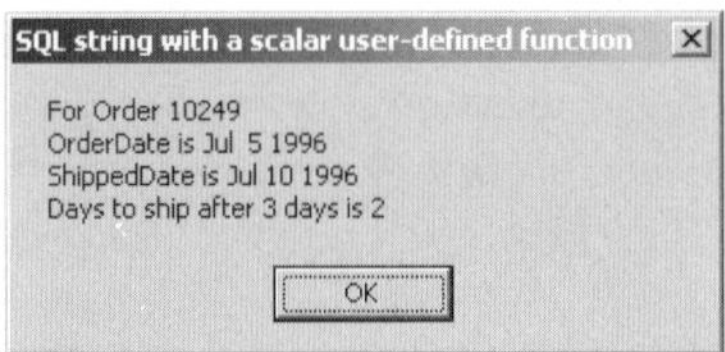

Figure 10-8. The message box displayed for running the *CreateAndInvokeUDF* procedure with the arguments specified for it in the *main* procedure of *Module1*.

DataAdapters, Data Sets, Forms, and Form Controls

This section covers how to place a data set behind a Windows form and allow users to interact with the data set through form controls. You will learn how to bind SQL Server data to the controls on a Windows form. This section covers several typical design applications such as attaching data to text boxes, combo boxes, and data grids. The code samples and form designs illustrate how to manage parent-child relationships programmatically in the data set behind a form as well as interactively for a user through form controls. The section closes with a sample that demonstrates how to dynamically configure a Windows form based on the data that it has to show.

Adding a Data Set to a Form

A typical way of interacting with data from Visual Basic .NET will be from Windows Forms. While you can readily present message boxes that show the *DataReader* contents, many applications will require a richer form of data interactivity than the forward-only, read-only model supported by the *DataReader*. The key to getting to a richer model of data interactivity is to place one or more data sets in the module behind a form. The data set object lets users navigate backward and forward in a data set. In addition, users can update the data for local use only or at a remote data source. Any one data set can contain multiple tables, and the data set object permits the existence of hierarchical relationships between the tables within it.

The key to populating a data set behind a form with data from a SQL Server instance is to create a *DataAdapter* object that points to a data source on a SQL Server instance. You can represent the data source on the server with a SQL string, a table name, a view, or a stored procedure. As with the *DataReader* object, you can represent a SQL string for the *DataAdapter* object with a *Command* object. The *DataAdapter* object has two main roles. First, it can fill a data set behind a form. That's the focus of this section. Second, you can use a *DataAdapter* to update a remote data source from the data set behind a form. That's the focus of the last major section in this chapter.

Use the *DataAdapter* object's *SelectCommand* property to reference the *Command* object specifying the remote data source for a *DataAdapter*. Recall that one important role for a *DataAdapter* is to copy to the data set behind a form. Make the remote data source available through the *DataAdapter* by opening the connection for the *Command* object. Copy the data from the remote data source to the data set by invoking the *Fill* method of the *DataAdapter*. In this type of application, the *DataAdapter* requires two arguments—one referencing the name of the data set behind the form and the other naming the table in the data set. You can designate the tables within a data set either by an index number indicating the order in which you added them to the data set or by the name that you specify as an argument to the *Fill* method.

The *Populate* procedure that follows illustrates the syntax for copying a remote data source to the data set behind a form. This procedure is in the module behind *Form4*, which I will discuss in more detail in the next sample discussion. For now, just understand that the *Populate* procedure is in a module behind a Windows form. I'll be using several samples throughout the balance of this chapter that are variations of this procedure, so I decided to give the procedure a section of its own to help you focus on it.

> **Note** The code for the *Populate* procedure assumes the existence of an *Imports* statement at the top of the module for the *System.Data.SqlClient* namespace.

It's common to describe the *DataAdapter* as a bridge between a remote data source and the data set behind a form. Therefore, the *Populate* procedure starts by declaring a *Connection* object, *cnn1*. The *cnn1* object reference points to the Northwind database on the local instance of SQL Server. Next the procedure declares and instantiates a *Command* object, *cmd1*. A SQL string specifies the *CategoryID*, *CategoryName*, and *Description* columns from the *Categories* tables to designate the result set from *cmd1*. The *Command* object *cmd1* links to the *Categories* table through the *Connection* object *cnn1*. After indirectly specifying the *CommandText* property for a *Command* object, the procedure instantiates a *DataAdapter* object and uses the *dap1* object reference to point to it.

In order for the *dap1 DataAdapter* to fill the data set behind the form, two conditions must hold. First, the *DataAdapter* needs a *Command* object assigned to its *SelectCommand* property. Assigning *cmd1* to the *SelectCommand* property of *dap1* satisfies this condition. Second, the *DataAdapter* requires an open connection to the *Categories* table in the Northwind database. Invoking the *Open* method for the *cnn1* object meets this requirement. After meeting these two conditions, the procedure invokes the *Fill* method for *dap1*. The arguments for the method in the procedure designate *Categories* as the name of the *DataTable* object that holds the result set from *cmd1* in the *das1* data set. The module behind *Form4* declares and instantiates *das1* as a data set at the module level. This makes the *das1* data set available for use in all the procedures behind a form. Of course, it also means that you cannot see the declaration in the listing for the *Populate* procedure. For your easy reference, I include the statement declaring and instantiating *das1* just before the listing for the *Populate* procedure.

Notice that the *Populate* procedure concludes by closing the *Connection* object *cnn1*. In contrast to the *DataReader* object, the data set object operates while disconnected from a remote data source. Recall that this ability to operate while disconnected adds to the scalability of Visual Basic .NET applications for SQL Server.

```
'Module-level declaration of data set object.
Dim das1 As DataSet = New DataSet()

Sub Populate()
    'Specify a connection for a data adapter that
    'fills the data set used on the form.
    Dim cnn1 As SqlConnection = _
        New SqlConnection _
        ("Data Source=(local);" & _
        "Integrated Security=SSPI;" & _
        "Initial Catalog=northwind")
```

(continued)

```
        'Specify the command and data adapter that serves
        'as the source for the data set on the form.
        Dim cmd1 As SqlCommand = _
            New SqlCommand _
            ("SELECT CategoryID, CategoryName, Description " & _
            "FROM Categories", _
            cnn1)
        Dim dap1 As SqlDataAdapter = New SqlDataAdapter()
        dap1.SelectCommand = cmd1
        cnn1.Open()

        'Fill the data set (das1) with the data adapter dap1;
        'the Fill method populates the data set with a table
        'named Categories.
        dap1.Fill(das1, "Categories")

        'Close the connection because a data set is a
        'disconnected data source.
        cnn1.Close()

    End Sub
```

Binding Controls on a Form to Data

After populating the data set behind a form, you'll want to reference the data set with the controls on the form. One way to accomplish this is to bind the controls to the data set. There are two styles of data binding for controls. Simple data binding maps a column in a local data source, such as a *DataTable* in a data set, to a property of a control, such as the *Text* property of a text box. Use the *DataBindings* collection of a control to bind control properties to a column of values in a local data source. Complex data binding is a second way of binding a control to data. For this style of data binding, a control—such as a combo box, list box, or data grid—binds to a collection of columns, such as a *DataTable* in a data set. The sample in this section demonstrates both approaches for binding controls to the *Categories DataTable*. The preceding section described the code that created the *Categories DataTable* in the *das1* data set for *Form4*.

> **Note** One interesting new development with Visual Basic .NET is the ability to bind any property of a visible control, such as its *BackColor* or *ForeColor* property, to a column of data. This feature opens the possibility for a local data source dynamically controlling the formatting of a form as well as the data the form shows.

Figure 10-9 shows *Form4*. At the left is the form in Design view. At the top right of the figure is the form after it initially opens. The bottom right of the figure shows the form after I selected Confections from the combo box. Open *Form4* in Design view by double-clicking *Form4.vb* in Solution Explorer for the MyADODOTNETSamples solution. Right-click the solution's name in Solution Explorer, choose Properties, and select *Form4* as the startup object to make the form easy to launch (for example, by pressing the F5 key).

The Design view of *Form4* reveals that the form contains a combo box with a label, two text boxes with labels, and a button. As shown in Chapter 1, you can graphically bind controls at design time. However, *Form4* programmatically sets the data binding for the combo box and the two text boxes. On the other hand, I set several control features at design time. For example, the *Multiline* property of *TextBox2* is set to *True*, while the same property for *TextBox1* has the default setting, *False*. The *Multiline* property setting facilitates *TextBox2* showing Description column values that extend over more than one line.

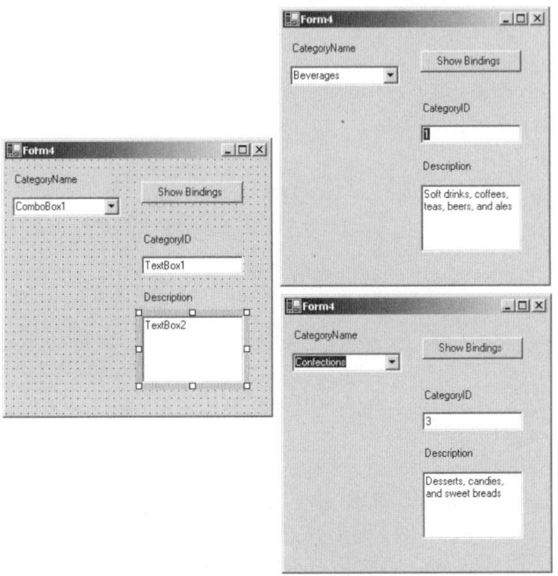

Figure 10-9. A design-time view and two run-time views of *Form4*. The two text boxes are programmed to update their contents based on the selection from the combo box.

The initial view of *Form4* shows that when it opens it displays the first category. Beverages appears in the combo box, and the two text boxes show 1 as the *CategoryID* and the description for the beverages product category. There is nothing mandatory about opening the form for the first category—any other category will work equally well. The form synchronizes the two text boxes with the combo box. For example, selecting Confections from the combo box revises the content displayed in the two text boxes to 3 and the description for the confections category.

To bind the form controls to data set columns and make the text boxes dependent on the combo box selection takes just a few lines of code. I used five lines of code to bind the controls to data set column values and set the category that appears when the form opens. This code appears in a form *Load* event procedure for *Form4* that starts by calling *Populate* to create the *das1* data set described in the preceding section.

The event procedure puts *das1* to use by binding the *Text* property of *TextBox1* to the *CategoryID* column in the *Categories DataTable*. You bind a column of values to a text box property by invoking the *Add* method for the *DataBindings* collection of a control. The *Add* method takes a *Binding* object as an argument. The arguments for the *Binding* object specify the *TextBox* property to bind (*Text*) and the column of values to bind to the property. This sample requires two arguments to specify the data source that binds to the text box property. First designate the data set name—*das1*. Second indicate the table name and column name within the data set that you want to bind to the property. Use a period delimiter to separate the two names, as in *Categories.CategoryID*. The *Load* event procedure uses the same syntax to bind the *Description* column in the *Categories DataTable* to the *Text* property of *TextBox2*. Both data bindings demonstrate the approach for simple data binding.

It takes a couple of lines to bind the combo box to the *Categories DataTable*. Actually, one line does the binding, but a second line specifies the values that the combo box displays for the user to make a selection. Assign a *DataTable* to the *DataSource* property of a combo box to bind the combo box to the *DataTable*. The syntax for specifying the *Categories* table used a named argument for denoting the table in the data set. I could also have indicated the *Categories* table by indicating its table index value, such as `das1.Tables(0)`. This syntax depends on the table index values not changing. After setting the *DataSource* property for the combo box, the procedure assigns the *CategoryName* column from the *Categories DataTable* as the value for the combo box to display when the user clicks the control to make a selection.

The final line of the form *Load* event procedure designates the position in a column that the controls on *Form4* bound to the first table in the *das1* data set are to show when the form initially opens. Position 0 points to the first row in a *DataTable* (for example, the *Categories DataTable* in this sample). The *Position* property belongs to the *BindingContext* object associated with a form. The keyword *Me* denotes *Form4* in the last line of the form *Load* event procedure.

```
Private Sub Form4_Load(ByVal sender As Object, _
    ByVal e As System.EventArgs) Handles MyBase.Load

    'Call the routine for creating the data set
    'for the form.
    Populate()

    'Bind each text box to a different column in the
    'Categories table of the data set (das1)on the form.
    TextBox1.DataBindings.Add _
       (New Binding("Text", das1, "Categories.CategoryID"))
    TextBox2.DataBindings.Add _
       (New Binding("Text", das1, "Categories.Description"))

    'Bind combo box to Categories table in the
    'data set (das1) on the form. Because the data set
    'includes just one table, its index is 0.
    ComboBox1.DataSource = das1.Tables("Categories")
    ComboBox1.DisplayMember = "CategoryName"
    Me.BindingContext(das1.Tables(0)).Position = 0

End Sub
```

The *SelectedIndexChanged* event procedure for the combo box takes just one line to synchronize the contents of the text boxes with the category name a user selects from the combo box. The index values for a combo box start at 0 for the first item in the list for a combo box. By setting the combo box's *SelectedIndex* property to the *Position* property of the form's *BindingContext* object, the line positions all controls on the form to the same row a user selected indirectly when picking a category name from the combo box.

```
Private Sub ComboBox1_SelectedIndexChanged _
    (ByVal sender As System.Object, _
    ByVal e As System.EventArgs) _
    Handles ComboBox1.SelectedIndexChanged

    'Use selected combo item as basis for text boxes.
    Me.BindingContext(das1, "Categories").Position _
        = Me.ComboBox1.SelectedIndex

End Sub
```

Reporting *DataBindings*

When working with a complex form with many controls with simple data bindings or a form that you didn't develop, you may find it convenient to print a report on the *DataBindings* collections for the controls on a form. A button on

Form4 invokes a procedure that generates such a report. The *Click* event for this button invokes a procedure named *PrintBindingMemberInfo* in *Module1*. You can also run this procedure from outside a form to report on the *DataBindings* collections for the controls on a form.

As you can see from the following listing, the *Click* event for the button merely calls the *PrintBindingMemberInfo* procedure. However, the call also passes a reference to *Form4* by using the keyword *Me* as an argument. The *PrintBindingMemberInfo* procedure in this sample is adapted from an example in the Visual Basic .NET Help file. While the adaptation is subtle, it substantially enhances the applicability of the procedure. First, the adaptation works for any form reference passed to it. The sample in the Help file had to be copied into the module for any form on which you sought a report. Second, you can run the adapted procedure even if you aren't in the form for which you seek a report. The sample in the Help file works only from a form that a user has open with the focus.

The *PrintBindingMemberInfo* procedure accepts a form reference as an argument. For the referenced form, the procedure starts a loop to pass through all the controls on the form. Within the loop for the controls on a form, the procedure runs a second loop to report any data binding for the currently selected control in the loop through the controls. If there are no data bindings for a control, the inner loop merely returns control to the outer loop for the controls. When all the controls on a form are looped through, the *PrintBindingMemberInfo* procedure returns control to its calling procedure, which is the *Click* event for *Button1* on *Form4* in the following listing.

```
'From module for Form4.
Private Sub Button1_Click(ByVal sender As System.Object, _
    ByVal e As System.EventArgs) Handles Button1.Click

    'Display run-time binding settings specified in this module.
    Module1.PrintBindingMemberInfo(Me)

End Sub

'From Module1.
'Adapted from Visual Basic .NET Help; the adaptation accommodates
'any form as a passed argument and facilitates displaying run-time
'bindings from outside a form.
Sub PrintBindingMemberInfo(ByRef MyForm As Form)
    Dim thisControl As Control
    For Each thisControl In MyForm.Controls
        Dim thisBinding As Binding
        For Each thisBinding In thisControl.DataBindings
            'Print the control's name and Binding information.
            Console.WriteLine(ControlChars.Cr + thisControl.ToString())
            Dim bInfo As BindingMemberInfo = thisBinding.BindingMemberInfo
```

```
            Console.WriteLine("Binding Path " + ControlChars.Tab _
                             + bInfo.BindingPath)
            Console.WriteLine("Binding Field " + ControlChars.Tab _
                             + bInfo.BindingField)
            Console.WriteLine("Binding Member " + ControlChars.Tab _
                             + bInfo.BindingMember)
        Next thisBinding
    Next thisControl

End Sub
```

Figure 10-10 shows an excerpt from the Output window showing the outcome generated by clicking the Show Bindings button in *Form4* just after the form opens. The output shows feedback for the two text boxes. The text box reporting descriptions appears above the one that displays the *CategoryID* value. Recall that the form initially shows data for *CategoryID* 1 when it opens. The contents for each text box reflect the value for this category. You can also see that the procedure returns information about the *DataTable* name and the column within a table to which each text box on the form binds.

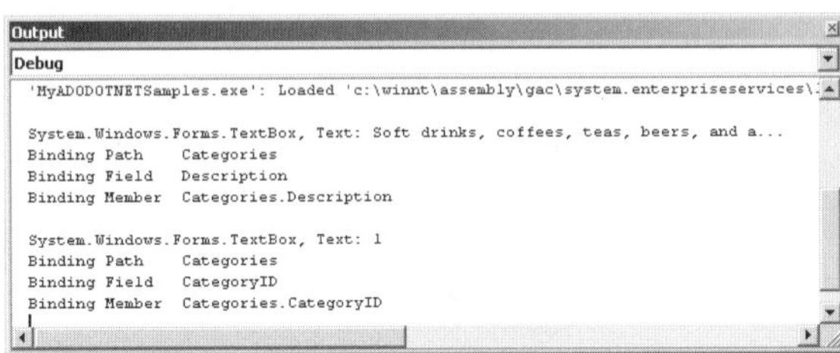

Figure 10-10. A report generated by clicking the Show Bindings button on *Form4*.

The *PrintBindingMemberInfo* procedure also works for forms that don't have the focus. For example, you can instantiate an instance of a form and then pass the reference for that form instance to the *PrintBindingMemberInfo* procedure. If the referenced form has data bindings set at design time, the procedure will generate a report for them. However, the procedure won't generate a report for a form that sets its data bindings at run time, such as in a form *Load* event procedure. Chapter 1 contains a sample with data bindings set at design time. I reproduced that form in the MyADODOTNETSamples solution as *Form2*. Figure 10-11 shows on its left *Form2* in Design view with *TextBox1* selected. On the right of Figure 10-11 is the Properties window for the selected text box control on the left. You can see that the *Text* property for the text box binds to the *CategoryID* column in the *Categories DataTable* of a data set named *DsCategories1*. The *Text* property for *TextBox2* binds to the *CategoryName* column of the *Categories DataTable* in the data set.

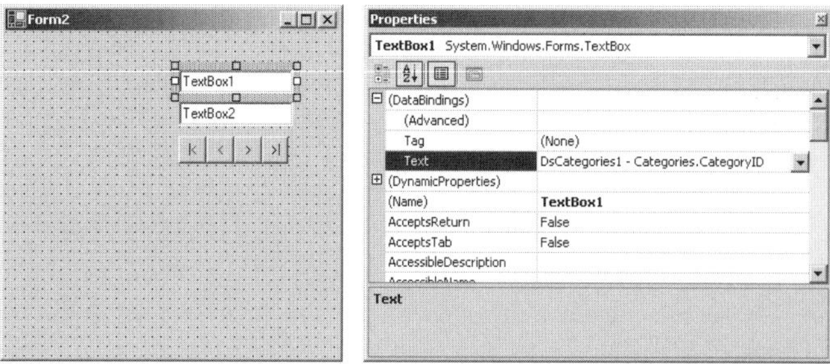

Figure 10-11. *Form2* depicting a data binding set at design time.

The following listing is a short procedure named *ShowForm2Bindings* that demonstrates the syntax for generating a report on the data bindings in *Form2* with the *PrintBindingMemberInfo* procedure. As you can see, the procedure declares and instantiates an instance of *Form2* with the reference variable *MyForm*. Then the procedure passes that reference name to the *PrintBindingMemberInfo* procedure when invoking the reporting procedure. The report generated by the *PrintBindingMemberInfo* procedure in the Output window correctly reflects the data bindings for the two text boxes on *Form2*.

```
Sub ShowForm2Bindings()
    Dim MyForm As New Form2()
    PrintBindingMemberInfo(MyForm)

End Sub
```

Using a Data Set with Tables in a Parent-Child Relationship

In addition to working with one database object, such as a table, you can populate a data set with rows from two or more database objects. Each remote database object contributes rows to a distinct *DataTable* within the data set. Instead of forcing you to join one *DataTable* to another to represent relationships as with ADO recordset objects, data sets let you hierarchically represent the relationship between two tables. We commonly refer to hierarchical relationships as parent-child relationships. The sample in this section illustrates techniques for working with two *DataTable* objects in a data set. In addition, it shows how to use a combo box to control the records that are displayed in a data grid control. This operation depends on filtering the rows for a *DataView* object on the selected item in a combo box. The *DataView* object, in turn, serves as the data source for the data grid.

The sample for this section relies on *Form5* in the MyADODOTNETSamples solution. Set up to use it in the normal way. First make *Form5* the startup object for the solution. Second double-click *Form5* in Solution Explorer to open *Form5* in Design view. Third right-click *Form5* and choose View Code to expose the module behind the form in the Code Editor on a tab labeled Form5.vb.

Figure 10-12 shows two views of *Form5*. At the top is the form when it initially opens, showing the Beverages *CategoryName* value in the combo box and selected columns of information for products in the beverages category in the data grid. When a user selects a new item from the combo box, the products appearing in the data grid change to reflect the most recently selected item. For example, the bottom of Figure 10-12 shows how the data grid contents changed when I changed the combo box from Beverages to Produce.

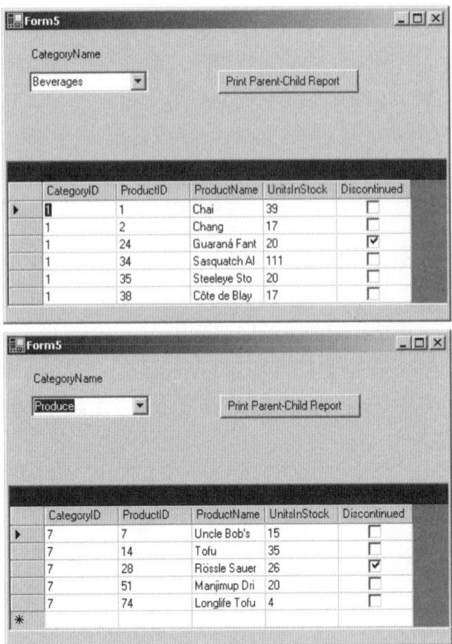

Figure 10-12. The combo box filters the rows from the *Produce* table that appear in the data grid.

The data set for *Form5* defines a relationship between the *Categories* and *Products DataTable* objects. This relationship facilitates expressing the product items that belong to each category. Instead of having to filter rows for a *DataView*, you can explicitly refer to rows in a child table that refer to the currently selected row in a parent table. The button labeled Print Parent-Child Report generates a table based on a hierarchical relationship between the *Categories* and *Products DataTable* objects. Figure 10-13 shows an excerpt from the report that a click of the button generates in the Output window. The excerpt reveals the *CategoryID* and *CategoryName* values for categories 6 through 8. Within each category, the report lists the *ProductID* and *ProductName* values that belong to the category.

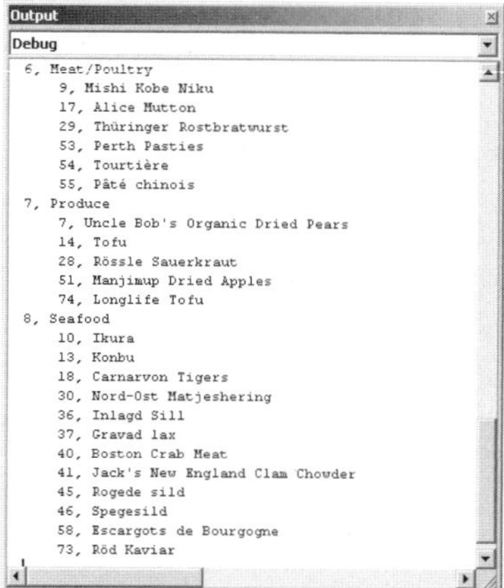

Figure 10-13. A report based on the parent-child relationship between the *Categories* and *Products DataTable* objects.

The *Form5_Load* event procedure populates the two *DataTable* objects, creates a relationship between them, and binds the combo box and data grid to local data sources. However, in order to keep the logic easy to follow, I divided the logic for populating the data set and creating a relationship between the two *DataTable* objects into two separate procedures that the form *Load* event procedure calls. The listing for all three of these procedures appears next.

The listing starts with three module-level declarations for a *DataSet* object, a *DataView* object, and a *Relation* object. I declare these objects at the module level because two or more separate procedures in the module need to refer to them.

The *Populate* procedure fills the data set with excerpts from the *Categories* and *Products* tables in the Northwind database. The code for filling the data set with the excerpt from the *Categories* table exactly follows the sample code in *Form4*. However, when the *Products* table is added to the data set, the code is shorter because *Connection* and *DataAdapter* objects are already instantiated and suitable for reuse. In addition, the code for the Products *DataTable* object follows the same general logic for specifying the *Command* object that defines the *SelectCommand* property and invoking the *Fill* method that was used for the *Categories DataTable* object.

The *RelateProductsToCategories* procedure relates the *Products DataTable* to the *Categories DataTable* in a parent-child hierarchy. The procedure achieves this by adding a new *DataRelation* object to the collection of all relationships in the data set. The code for the procedure starts by declaring the matching columns in the parent and child tables. Next the procedure instantiates a new relationship object based on the matching columns. Figure 10-1 shows that the *DataRelationCollection* is directly dependent on the data set object. The procedure uses the *Add* method for the *Relations* collection of the *das1* data set to insert the new relationship instantiated in the preceding line into the *DataRelationCollection* object within the *das1* data set.

The *Form5_Load* event procedure starts by invoking the *Populate* and *RelateProductsToCategories* procedures. These steps properly populate and configure the data set for *Form5*. The event procedure next binds the combo box to the *Categories* table and sets the position to the first row in the *Categories* table. The procedure uses a *DataView* object with a filter based on the index for the combo box. To implement this, the procedure declares and instantiates the *dav1 DataView* object based on the *Products DataTable* object. Next it defines a string with the filter expression. The expression designates all rows from the *Products DataTable* that correspond to the index for the currently selected item in the combo box. There is an offset of 1 between the index for a combo box and the *CategoryID* values for which the filter expression accounts. By assigning the expression in the string variable (*strFilter*) to the *RowFilter* property of *dav1*, the procedure populates the *dav1 DataView* object with the rows matching the category name showing in the combo box. The event procedure concludes by assigning the *dav1 DataView* object to the *DataSource* property of the data grid.

```
'Module-level declaration of data set,dataview, and datarelation objects.
Dim das1 As DataSet
Dim dav1 As DataView
Dim rel1 As DataRelation

Sub Populate()

    'Specify a connection for a data adapter that
    'fills the data set used on the form.
    Dim cnn1 As SqlConnection = _
        New SqlConnection _
        ("Data Source=(local);" & _
        "Integrated Security=SSPI;" & _
        "Initial Catalog=northwind")

    'Specify an extract from the Categories table as the source
    'for a command  that supplies a data adapter which serves
    'as the source for the data set on the form.
    Dim cmd1 As SqlCommand = _
        New SqlCommand _
        ("SELECT CategoryID, CategoryName, Description " & _
            "FROM Categories", _
            cnn1)
    Dim dap1 As SqlDataAdapter = New SqlDataAdapter()
    dap1.SelectCommand = cmd1
    cnn1.Open()
```

(continued)

```
        'Fill the data set (das1) with the data adapter dap1;
        'the Fill method populates the data set with a datatable
        'named Categories  -- notice that the datatable Categories
        'isn't the same as the Categories table in the
        'Northwind database.
        das1 = New DataSet()
        dap1.Fill(das1, "Categories")

        'Re-specify the SQL string for the command and the data
        'adapter to extract columns from the Products table.
        cmd1.CommandText = "SELECT CategoryID, ProductID, " & _
            "ProductName, UnitsInStock, Discontinued " & _
            "FROM Products"
        dap1.SelectCommand = cmd1

        'Create a datatable named Products in the das1 data set
        'based on an extract from the Products table in the
        'Northwind database.
        dap1.Fill(das1, "Products")

        'Close the connection because a data set only requires
        'a connection while it is being populated from or
        'writing updates to a SQL Server data source.
        cnn1.Close()

    End Sub

    Sub RelateProductsToCategories()

        'Declare and assign parent and child columns for
        'relating the Products datatable to the Categories
        'datatable in the das1 data set.
        Dim parentcol As DataColumn
        Dim childcol As DataColumn
        parentcol = das1.Tables("Categories").Columns("CategoryID")
        childcol = das1.Tables("Products").Columns("CategoryID")

        'Instantiate a datarelation between the
        'Products and Categories datatables.
        rel1 = New DataRelation _
            ("CategoriesProducts", parentcol, childcol)
        das1.Relations.Add(rel1)

    End Sub

    Private Sub Form5_Load(ByVal sender As System.Object, _
        ByVal e As System.EventArgs) Handles MyBase.Load
        'Run the Populate procedure to download extracts from
        'the Categories and Products table to a data set for
        'this form instance.
        Populate()
```

```
    'Form a datarelation between the Categories and Products
    'datatables in the das1 data set on this form.
    RelateProductsToCategories()

    'Bind combobox to table 0 (the Categories datatable)
    'in the das1 data set.
    ComboBox1.DataSource = das1.Tables(0)
    ComboBox1.DisplayMember = "CategoryName"
    Me.BindingContext(das1.Tables(0)).Position = 0

    'Instantiate a dataview based on the Products datatable
    'in the das1 data set and filter the view on the basis of
    'selectedindex value for a combo box.
    dav1 = New DataView(das1.Tables("Products"))
    Dim strFilter = "CategoryID = " & _
        (ComboBox1.SelectedIndex + 1).ToString
    dav1.RowFilter = strFilter

    'Assign the view as the data source for a data grid control.
    DataGrid1.DataSource = dav1

End Sub
```

The *SelectedIndexChanged* event procedure for the combo box keeps the data grid synchronized whenever a user changes the category name displayed in the combo box. To accomplish this, the event procedure recomputes the string filter for the new combo box selection. Then it assigns the new string filter to the *RowFilter* property of the *dav1 DataView*. This step updates the data grid to show new rows that match the most recent selection from the combo box.

```
Private Sub ComboBox1_SelectedIndexChanged _
    (ByVal sender As System.Object, _
    ByVal e As System.EventArgs) _
    Handles ComboBox1.SelectedIndexChanged

    'Assign filter based on selected item, and
    'apply the filter to the dataview for the data grid control.
    Dim strFilter = "CategoryID = " & _
        (ComboBox1.SelectedIndex + 1).ToString
    dav1.RowFilter = strFilter

End Sub
```

The final unit of code for this sample generates the parent-child report between categories and products in Figure 10-13. The code to generate the report fires when a user clicks the sole button on the form. The *Click* event procedure for the button begins by declaring *DataRow* objects for the parent (*pRow*) and child (*cRow*) *DataTable* objects as well as two strings for lines from the parent and row data sources. Next the procedure opens a loop to pass through successive rows in the parent data source, the *Categories DataTable* object. After printing the *CategoryID* and *CategoryName* for the parent row, the procedure starts a loop through the child rows of the parent that match the current parent row. The *GetChildRows* method returns the appropriate rows. With the loop for child rows, the procedure prints the *ProductID* and *ProductName* values for all products matching the current parent row.

```
Private Sub Button1_Click(ByVal sender As System.Object, _
    ByVal e As System.EventArgs) Handles Button1.Click

    Dim pRow, cRow As DataRow
    Dim strParentLine, strChildLIne As String

    'Loop through rows in parent DataTable.
    For Each pRow In das1.Tables("Categories").Rows
        strParentLine = pRow("CategoryID") & ", " & _
            pRow("CategoryName")
        Console.WriteLine(strParentLine)

        'Loop through matching rows in child DataTable.
        For Each cRow In pRow.GetChildRows(rel1)
            strChildLIne = vbTab & cRow("ProductID") & _
                ", " & cRow("ProductName")
            Console.WriteLine(strChildLIne)
        Next

    Next

End Sub
```

Creating Data-Aware Forms

All forms that display data are data-aware at one level or another. However, the more a form automatically configures itself to the data set behind it, the more aware of data that form is. A form can even change the data behind it in response to the form's environment. I refer to this kind of interaction between a form and its associated data as the data awareness of a form. This section presents a sample that demonstrates a higher degree of data awareness than the previous ones. In addition, the sample illustrates how to use a stored procedure that accepts a parameter to dynamically control the data that a form displays.

The sample has two forms—*Form1* and *Form6* in the MyADODOTNET-Samples solutions. *Form1* collects a value designating a country and passes the value on to *Form6* while opening it. When *Form6* opens, it populates two *DataTable* objects in a data set behind it. Both *DataTable* objects vary based on the value passed to the form. In the first *DataTable* object, the code behind the form uses the passed value as the parameter value for a stored procedure. This code behind *Form6* assigns this *DataTable* object to the Data-

Source property of a combo box. A second *DataTable* object relies on a SQL string expression that relies on the passed value. This table doesn't directly populate three data-bound text boxes on *Form6*. Instead, the text boxes bind to a *DataView* object based on the second *DataTable* but filtered based on the value in the combo box.

As I said, this sample actually configures *Form6* based on the data. The combo box lists the cities in a country, which is based on a value passed to *Form6* from *Form1*. The three text boxes display the *CustomerID*, *ContactName*, and *Phone* for one or more customers within the city displayed in the combo box. *Form6* conditionally shows navigation buttons for moving among the rows of contact data within a country. If there aren't at least two customers in a city, the form hides the navigation buttons. Incidentally, this sample also demonstrates how to construct navigation buttons for moving through the rows behind a set of data-bound text boxes.

Because the sample for this section uses two forms, you'll probably want to open both *Form1* and *Form6* in Design view. You'll also likely want to view the code behind each form. The sample begins with a user responding to *Form1*, so make that form your startup object in the MyADODOTNETSamples solution. However, before launching the application successfully, you must add the *udpCitiesInCustomersCountry* stored procedure to the Northwind database. The procedure returns from the *Customers* table all the cities within a country specified by a parameter supplied at run time. As is standard practice, the following T-SQL script for Query Analyzer drops any prior version of the stored procedure before creating a new version of it. You can run the script most easily from Query Analyzer.

```
--Work with Northwind database.
USE Northwind
GO

--Remove any prior version of
--udpCitiesInCustomersCountry.
IF EXISTS (SELECT ROUTINE_NAME
    FROM INFORMATION_SCHEMA.ROUTINES
    WHERE ROUTINE_TYPE = 'PROCEDURE' AND
    ROUTINE_NAME = 'udpCitiesInCustomersCountry')
    DROP PROCEDURE udpCitiesInCustomersCountry
GO

--Create new version of udpCitiesInCustomersCountry.
CREATE PROC udpCitiesInCustomersCountry
@country nvarchar (15) = 'USA'
AS
SELECT DISTINCT City
FROM Customers
WHERE Country = @country
GO
```

After running the sample in this section, you can rerun the portion of the preceding script to drop the *udpCitiesInCustomersCountry* stored procedure from the Northwind database. This action will allow you to preserve the initial design of the Northwind database.

Figure 10-14 shows *Form1* on the left with Brazil entered as the country. Clicking the Open Form6 button opens *Form6* as shown in the upper right of the figure. Initially, the city Campinas appears in the combo box. Notice that no navigational buttons appear below the text boxes. This is because there is just one customer located in Campinas. The combo box in *Form6* is open to make São Paulo the selected city. The view of *Form6* in the lower right of Figure 10-14 shows São Paulo selected in the combo box, with navigational buttons below the text boxes because the *Customers* table has four customers situated in São Paulo.

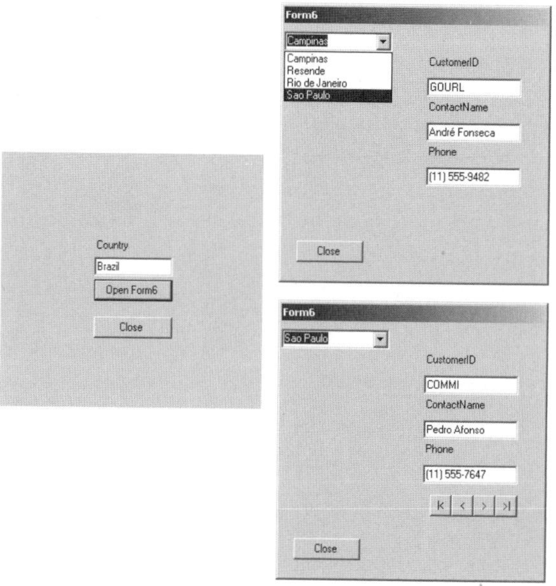

Figure 10-14. This example of a data-aware form displays navigational buttons only when there is more than one customer in a city to view. Combo box selections change the set of cities that the text boxes can show.

Notice also the form borders in Figure 10-14. *Form1* appears with no border. *Form6* appears with a caption, but it has no built-in Minimize, Maximize, or Close button. Both forms require users to close a form through the custom control on the form that enables the form close function. This feature is especially appropriate in this design because using the standard buttons can fail to close the application properly. I will describe briefly the two techniques for managing the look of the forms in reviewing the code behind each form.

The Code Behind *Form1*

The code behind *Form1* consists of three short event procedures. The form *Load* event sets the *FormBorderStyle* property to *None*. This removes any sign of a standard window border. In the process, it removes the built-in Close button, which was the main objective of the property assignment for this application. Users can still close the form with the custom button labeled Close. This removes the form in a way that clears any trace of the application.

Button1 is labeled Open Form6. Clicking this button actually does a little more. First it instantiates an instance of *Form6* so that it can assign a value to a public variable named *Country* in the *Form6* class instance. The event procedure copies the contents of the *Text* property for *TextBox1* to the *Country* variable in the *Form6* instance. After assigning a value to the *Country* variable, the event procedure opens the application's second form by invoking the *Show* method for the *frm6* instance. Just before the event procedure concludes, it hides the current form.

The event procedure for the Close button exits the entire application with the *Exit* method for the *Application* object. An *Application* object's *Exit* method closes all windows for an application, but it doesn't invoke any special code associated with the *Close* event or the *Closing* event for a form instance. Therefore, if you have explicit termination code associated with those events, run the *Close* method for any form that requires the code to run before invoking the *Exit* method for the *Application* object.

```
Private Sub Form1_Load(ByVal sender As System.Object, _
    ByVal e As System.EventArgs) Handles MyBase.Load

    'Reset border to remove Close button.
    Me.FormBorderStyle = FormBorderStyle.None

End Sub

Private Sub Button1_Click(ByVal sender As System.Object, _
    ByVal e As System.EventArgs) Handles Button1.Click

    Dim frm6 As New Form6()

    'Open Form6 and hide Form1.
    frm6.Country = TextBox1.Text
    frm6.Show()
    Me.Hide()

End Sub
```

(continued)

```
Private Sub Button2_Click(ByVal sender As System.Object, _
    ByVal e As System.EventArgs) Handles Button2.Click

    'Exit application.
    Application.Exit()

End Sub
```

The Code Behind *Form6*

The code behind *Form6* starts with some module-level declarations and an adaptation of the *Populate* procedure for adding *DataTable* objects to the data set behind the form. The module-level declarations, with one exception, are for objects and values used in more than one procedure in the module behind *Form6*. The exception is for the *Country* variable. Notice that a *Public* keyword declares this variable so that it is available for reference outside the module. Recall that the *Click* event for *Button1* in *Form1* assigns a value to this important variable.

> **Note** It's necessary to both declare and instantiate the *dav1 DataView* object at the module level to make it available across multiple procedures. This requirement doesn't exist for the *das1* data set object.

The *Populate* procedure for the *Form6* module uses the *udpCitiesInCustomersCountry* stored procedure as the remote data source for the *CitiesInCountries DataTable* object. This stored procedure requires an input parameter. Therefore, the syntax for the sample confirms the syntax for using a stored procedure with a parameter as the source for a *DataTable* object. The *Populate* procedure generates another *DataTable* object named *CustomersInCountry*. This *DataTable* object relies on a SQL string expression that combines a string constant with the *Country* variable. Because the code for the second *DataTable* reuses elements used to create the first *DataTable* object, some modifications are necessary. In particular, the procedure respecifies the *CommandType* as text and drops the *prm1* parameter.

```
'Module-level declaration of data set and 'dataview objects.
Dim das1 As DataSet
Dim dav1 As DataView = New DataView()

'Boolean for tracking manipulation ComboBox1
'in form load event.
Dim bolViewSetInFormLoad As Boolean
```

```
'Declare Country publicly so that the variable
'is available for assignment from another module.
Public Country As String

Sub Populate()

    'Connect to Northwind database on local server.
    Dim cnn1 As SqlConnection = _
        New SqlConnection("Data Source=(local);" & _
            "Integrated Security=SSPI;" & _
            "Initial Catalog=northwind")

    'Instantiate a command reference pointing at the
    'udpCitiesInCustomersCountry stored proc; the stored
    'proc enumerates the cities in countries from the
    'Customers table.
    Dim cmd1 As SqlCommand = _
        New SqlCommand("udpCitiesInCustomersCountry", cnn1)
    cmd1.CommandType = CommandType.StoredProcedure

    'Declare the parameter with a SqlDbType, then assign
    'the parameter a value based on a public variable
    'whose value is passed from another form.
    Dim prm1 As SqlParameter = _
        cmd1.Parameters.Add("@country", SqlDbType.NVarChar, 15)
    prm1.Value() = Country

    'Assign cmd1 to the SelectCommand property of dap1, then
    'open dap1.
    Dim dap1 As SqlDataAdapter = New SqlDataAdapter()
    dap1.SelectCommand = cmd1
    cnn1.Open()

    'Fill the data set das1 with the data adapter dap1;
    'the Fill method populates the data set with the
    'udpCitiesInCustomersCountry result set and names
    'the resulting datatable CitiesInCountry.
    das1 As DataSet = New DataSet()
    dap1.Fill(das1, "CitiesInCountry")

    'Specify a second cmd1 CommandText property and
    'reset cmd1 properties for use with a SQL string
    'instead of a stored proc with a parameter.
    cmd1.CommandText = "SELECT CustomerID, " & _
        "ContactName, Phone, City " & _
        "FROM Customers " & _
        "WHERE Country = '" & Country & "'"
    cmd1.Parameters.Remove(prm1)
    cmd1.CommandType = CommandType.Text
    dap1.SelectCommand = cmd1
```

(continued)

```
        'Fill a datatable with the SQL string's
        'result set.
        dap1.Fill(das1, "CustomersInCountry")

        'Close the connection because a data set is a
        'disconnected data source.
        cnn1.Close()

    End Sub
```

The form *Load* event procedure along with two other sub procedures that it calls performs basic setup for *Form6*. One of these sub procedures is the *Populate* procedure, which creates a data set for the form to use. The other called sub procedure is the *ShowNavButtons* procedure, which controls the visibility of the navigation buttons that can appear below the text boxes. The *SelectedIndexChanged* event procedure for the combo box also calls the *ShowNavButtons* procedure whenever a user makes a selection from the combo box.

After calling *Populate* to create the *das1* data set, the form *Load* event procedure starts to put the data set to use by binding the combo box to the first table in the data set with an index of 0. This is the *CitiesInCountries DataTable* object. Notice also that the code explicitly assigns both the *DisplayMember* and *ValueMember* properties of the combo box to the only column in the *CitiesInCountries DataTable* object. By setting the *ValueMember* property, the module can subsequently use the *SelectedValue* property for the combo box as an indicator of the most recent selection from the combo box.

The form *Load* event procedure next moves its focus to creating the *dav1 DataView* object that the three text boxes bind to. The *dav1* object relies on the *CustomersInCountry DataTable* object. The reason the code binds the text boxes to the *DataView* object (instead of the *DataTable* object) is that you can readily filter a *DataView*. In this case, the filter is for the city appearing in the combo box. The statements binding the *Text* property of each text box to the *DataView* columns don't use a two-part naming convention (tablename.columnname), as is the case when you bind a text box to a *DataTable* object in a data set. Because a *DataView* holds just one source of rows, a *DataView* object name uniquely identifies a source of rows. Recall, however, that data set objects can contain multiple *DataTable* objects.

The last two blocks of code in the form *Load* event procedure address formatting issues. The first of these blocks calls the *ShowNavButtons* procedure with the count of rows in *dav1* as an argument. If there is only one row in *dav1*, there is no need for navigator buttons (because there is only one row to display). Any count value greater than 1 will cause the *ShowNavButtons* procedure to set the *Visible* property of the navigator buttons to *True* so that users can browse the data for the different customers in a city. The final block of code shows a second technique (from the one used in the module for *Form1*) to make the built-in Close button unavailable. This approach leaves the caption area at the top of the form so that you can show the form's *Text* property assignment. Setting the form's *ControlBox* property to *False* hides the built-in Close button. However, I found through trial and error that I also needed to have either the *MinimizeBox* or *MaximizeBox* property set to *False*. The sample clears all three built-in controls from the form.

```
Private Sub Form6_Load(ByVal sender As System.Object, _
    ByVal e As System.EventArgs) Handles MyBase.Load

    'Call the routine for creating the data set
    'for the form.
    Populate()

    'Bind combo box to the first datatable in das1
    'on the form. Assign both the displaymember and
    'valuemember combobox properties to the sole
    'column in the first datatable.
    ComboBox1.DataSource = das1.Tables(0)
    ComboBox1.DisplayMember = _
        das1.Tables(0).Columns(0).ColumnName
    ComboBox1.ValueMember = _
        das1.Tables(0).Columns(0).ColumnName

    'Specify a dataview (dav1) based on the
    'CustomersInCountry dataTable that filters
    'the datatable based on the selected value
    'in the combobox when the form opens.
    dav1 = New DataView(das1.Tables("CustomersInCountry"))
    Dim strFilter = "City = '" & ComboBox1.SelectedValue & "'"
    dav1.RowFilter = strFilter

    'After the form load event sets the dataview's
    'filter, reset the Boolean from its default
    'value of False.
    bolViewSetInFormLoad = True

    'Bind each text box to a different column in dav1.
    TextBox1.DataBindings.Add _
       (New Binding("Text", dav1, "CustomerID"))
    TextBox2.DataBindings.Add _
       (New Binding("Text", dav1, "ContactName"))
    TextBox3.DataBindings.Add _
       (New Binding("Text", dav1, "Phone"))

    'Control visibility of navigation buttons.
    ShowNavButtons(dav1.Count)
```

(continued)

```
    'Reset the form's ControlBox property
    'to False (should also set either MinimizeBox
    'or MaximizeBox to False).
    Me.MinimizeBox = False
    Me.MaximizeBox = False
    Me.ControlBox = False

End Sub

Sub ShowNavButtons(ByVal NavNum As Integer)

    'Sub procedure to make nav buttons visible
    'if there is more than one customer in the
    'selected city.
    If NavNum > 1 Then
        cmdFirst.Visible = True
        cmdPrevious.Visible = True
        cmdNext.Visible = True
        cmdLast.Visible = True
    Else
        cmdFirst.Visible = False
        cmdPrevious.Visible = False
        cmdNext.Visible = False
        cmdLast.Visible = False
    End If

End Sub
```

Six event procedures complete the application. One procedure is for a selection from the combo box, four more are for clicks of the navigation buttons, and the last one is for the button labeled Close. The *SelectedIndexChanged* event procedure for the combo box revises the row filter for the *dav1 DataView* object if the value of *bolViewSetInFormLoad* is *True*. This updates the data bindings for the text boxes so they match the last city selected in the combo box. The conditional execution of the row filter revision avoids performing the calculation when the *Form6_Load* event procedure is initially populating the combo box with values. The event procedure also calls the *ShowNavButtons* procedure to show or hide the navigation buttons depending on the number of rows in the *dav1* object.

The *Click* event procedures for the four navigation buttons assign a different value to the *Position* property of the *BindingContext* object for each text box control relying on a simple data binding in *Form6*. The *Click* event procedures for the Previous (<) and Next (>) buttons merely subtract 1 from, or add 1 to, the current position. This moves the row displayed in the text boxes backward or forward one row. Visual Basic .NET is smart enough not to raise an exception if a user clicks the Next button when the *Position* property is already at its maximum setting. In this case, the *Position* property value stays unchanged. The same principle applies to clicks of the Previous button when the *Position* property is already at its minimum setting. Clicks of the First (|<) and Last (>|) buttons assign the minimum and maximum values, respectively, to the *Position* property for the *BindingContext* object of the text box controls.

The *Click* event procedure for the Close button (*Button1*) eventually closes *Form6* by applying the *Close* method to the *Me* keyword. However, before doing this, the event procedure for *Button1* opens an instance of *Form1*. Recall that *Form1* includes a button that exits the application. In addition, it is common in a hierarchy of forms to return to the top-level form before exiting an application.

```
Private Sub ComboBox1_SelectedIndexChanged _
    (ByVal sender As System.Object, _
    ByVal e As System.EventArgs) _
    Handles ComboBox1.SelectedIndexChanged

    'Update dataview filter for combobox selection.
    If bolViewSetInFormLoad = True Then
        Dim strFilter = "City = '" & _
        ComboBox1.SelectedValue & "'"
        dav1.RowFilter = strFilter
    End If

    'Control visibility of navigation buttons based
    'on the outcome of the filter.
    ShowNavButtons(dav1.Count)

End Sub

Private Sub cmdFirst_Click(ByVal sender As System.Object, _
    ByVal e As System.EventArgs) Handles cmdFirst.Click

    'Move to first record.
    Me.BindingContext(dav1).Position _
        = Me.BindingContext(dav1).Position.MinValue

End Sub

Private Sub cmdPrevious_Click(ByVal sender As System.Object, _
    ByVal e As System.EventArgs) Handles cmdPrevious.Click

    'Move to previous record.
    Me.BindingContext(dav1).Position -= 1

End Sub
```

(continued)

```
Private Sub cmdNext_Click(ByVal sender As System.Object, _
    ByVal e As System.EventArgs) Handles cmdNext.Click

    'Move to next record.
    Me.BindingContext(dav1).Position += 1

End Sub

Private Sub cmdLast_Click(ByVal sender As System.Object, _
    ByVal e As System.EventArgs) Handles cmdLast.Click

    'Move to last record.
    Me.BindingContext(dav1).Position _
        = Me.BindingContext(dav1).Position.MaxValue

End Sub

Private Sub Button1_Click(ByVal sender As System.Object, _
    ByVal e As System.EventArgs) Handles Button1.Click

    'Return control to calling form (Form1).
     Dim frm1 As New Form1()
    frm1.Show()
    Me.Close()

End Sub
```

Modifying, Inserting, and Deleting Rows

This concluding section of this chapter takes you through a sample application for updating, inserting, and deleting rows in a SQL Server database based on actions you take in a Windows form bound to a local *DataTable*.

The Data Manipulation Sample in Action

The sample application for this section illustrates how to modify, insert, and delete rows in a SQL Server data source. The application uses *Form7* in the MyADODOTNETSamples solution. This form connects to the Northwind database on the local SQL Server instance. Follow the instructions from prior samples for making *Form7* the startup object, and open *Form7* in Design view.

Before you can run the sample code behind *Form7*, you will also need the *udpInsertANewShipper* stored procedure on your local SQL Server instance. By invoking the following T-SQL script in Query Analyzer, you can create *udpInsertANewShipper* on the SQL Server instance to which you connect. The first two

T-SQL batches connect to the Northwind database and eliminate any prior version of the stored procedure. The last T-SQL batch in the script is a *CREATE PROCEDURE* statement that defines the stored procedure. The *udpInsertANewShipper* stored procedure contains an *INSERT INTO* statement for adding the *CompanyName* and *Phone* column values to a new row in the *Shippers* table.

The stored procedure has two input parameters. The *@CompanyName* parameter passes in the name of the new shipper, and the *@Phone* parameter performs the same function for the telephone number. The procedure returns the *ShipperID* value generated by the *IDENTITY* property for the *Shippers* table in the Northwind database with the *@Identity* output parameter. By using the built-in *SCOPE_IDENTITY* function instead of *@@IDENTITY*, the procedure ensures that the *@Identity* parameter value is the *IDENTITY* property value generated by the *INSERT INTO* statement in the current instance of the *udpInsertANewShipper* stored procedure.

```
--ShippersTableScripts
--Connect to the Northwind database.
USE Northwind
GO

--Remove any prior version of udpInsertANewShipper.
IF EXISTS (SELECT ROUTINE_NAME
    FROM INFORMATION_SCHEMA.ROUTINES
    WHERE ROUTINE_TYPE = 'PROCEDURE' AND
    ROUTINE_NAME = 'udpInsertANewShipper')
    DROP PROCEDURE udpInsertANewShipper
GO

--Create a new version of udpInsertANewShipper.
CREATE PROCEDURE udpInsertANewShipper
    @CompanyName nchar(40),
    @Phone nvarchar (24),
    @Identity int OUT
AS
INSERT INTO Shippers (CompanyName, Phone)
    VALUES(@CompanyName, @Phone)
SET @Identity = SCOPE_IDENTITY()
GO
```

Figure 10-15 shows the Design view of *Form7*. Three text boxes are bound to the *ShipperID*, *CompanyName*, and *Phone* column values in a local data set with a *Shippers DataTable* based on the *Shippers* table in the Northwind database. Below the text boxes are four buttons for navigating through the rows to which the text boxes are bound. From left to right, the buttons navigate to the first row, the previous row, the next row, and the last row.

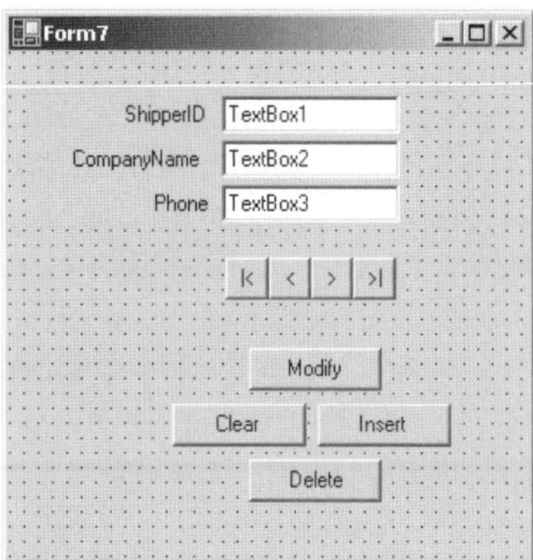

Figure 10-15. A Windows form for performing update, insert, and delete tasks for a local *DataTable* and its synchronized table on a SQL Server instance.

The four buttons below the navigator buttons implement the main new feature associated with the sample. The Modify button updates the *Shippers* table in the Northwind database with any changed values from the *Shippers DataTable* in the data set behind *Form7*. You can accumulate more than one change locally by navigating between rows with the navigator buttons and changing multiple records. Then you can convey all updates to a server since the last time you clicked the Modify button.

The Clear and Insert buttons work together to accommodate the insertion of a single new record at a time. Click the Clear button to erase any data on the form. Clicking the button doesn't alter any existing data. Then enter new values in the CompanyName and Phone text boxes. (These have the names *TextBox2* and *TextBox3* in the code behind the form.) Finish the insert task by clicking the Insert button. This adds the new *CompanyName* and *Phone* column values as a row in the *Shippers* table within the Northwind database. It also adds the *Text* property settings for *TextBox2* and *TextBox3* to the *Shippers DataTable* within the data set along with the *Identity* value created for the new row on the SQL Server instance.

The Delete button operates on one record at a time. Navigate to the record that you want to remove, and then click the Delete button. Repeat the process for as many additional rows as you need to remove. The Delete button removes the row from the *DataTable* supplying values to the current record appearing in a form as well as the same row in the table on the SQL Server instance with which the local *DataTable* synchronizes.

Figure 10-16 shows an update task in progress through *Form7*. On the left side of the figure are three form windows on the first, second, and third rows of the *Shippers DataTable*. The top window shows the addition of 1 to the *CompanyName* entry on the form for the row with the *ShipperID* value 1. The second and third windows in the left column show the addition of 2 and 3 to the *CompanyName* entries for the rows with the *ShipperID* values 2 and 3. After navigation off a row, any changes made to a text box value on a form automatically update the corresponding local *DataTable* row. However, those changes don't propagate to the SQL Server instance until the code behind the form invokes the *Update* method. Clicking the Modify button performs this task for any rows changed since the last time a user clicked the button.

The two windows on the right of Figure 10-16 show a Query Analyzer session that can select all the column values for all the rows from the *Shippers* table in the Northwind database. The top window shows the result set from the *SELECT* statement before a click of the Modify button but after all three records were updated in the local *DataTable*. Although the local user can view and navigate between the records after changing them, those changes don't propagate to the server until after the user clicks the Modify button. The bottom window on the right shows the result set from the same *SELECT* statement as the one on top, but this one reflects the changes to the *DataTable* to which the form text box controls bind. The *DataTable* values were updated for the top and bottom result sets. The only difference is that the bottom result was generated after I clicked the Modify button on *Form7*.

Figure 10-17 demonstrates how to perform insert and delete tasks with the sample application. The sample application expects users to click the Clear button when they want to add a new row. This not only clears the form but also unbinds the text boxes temporarily from the *Shippers DataTable*. Users can then enter new values in the text boxes for *CompanyName* and *Phone* column values. To commit the new column values locally and on a SQL Server instance, the sample application expects the user to click the Insert button. The window on the left in Figure 10-17 shows the form after I entered New Mover1 for CompanyName and (123) 456-7890 for Phone. Clicking the Insert button creates a new row with those values in both the local *Shippers DataTable* and the *Shippers* table in a SQL Server instance.

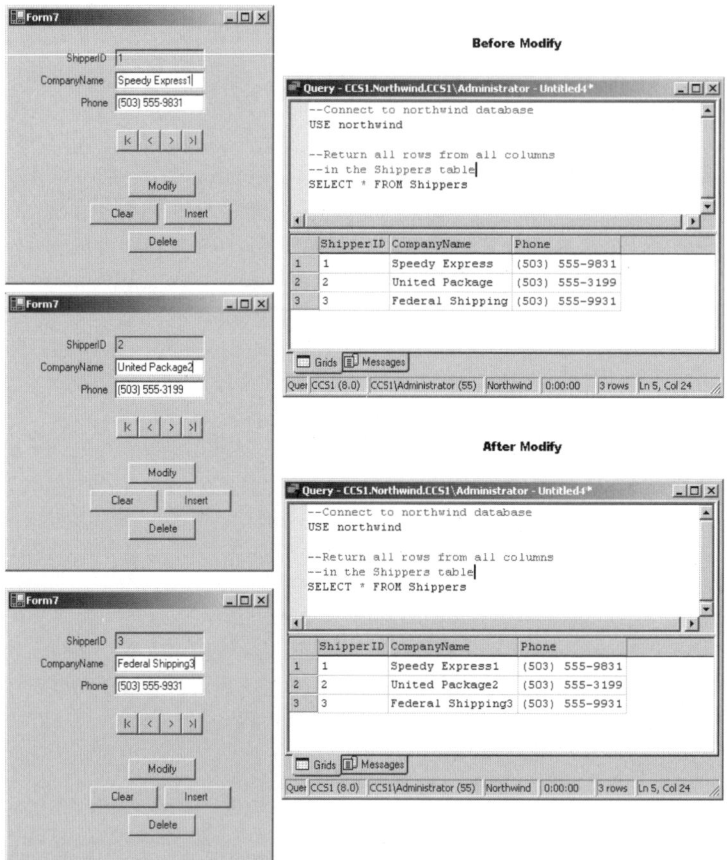

Figure 10-16. The three windows in the column on the left show changes made to a local *DataTable*. The two windows on the right contrast the impact on a synchronized SQL Server version of the table before and after a click of the Modify button.

The window on the right in Figure 10-17 shows the form after I clicked the Insert button. The application automatically navigates to the inserted record after a user clicks Insert. In addition, it shows the *ShipperID* value for the row that was generated on the SQL Server instance. Clicking the Delete button at this point can remove the new row from both the *Shippers DataTable* in the data set behind the form and the *Shippers* table in the SQL Server instance. Alternatively, you can navigate to another row that you want to delete.

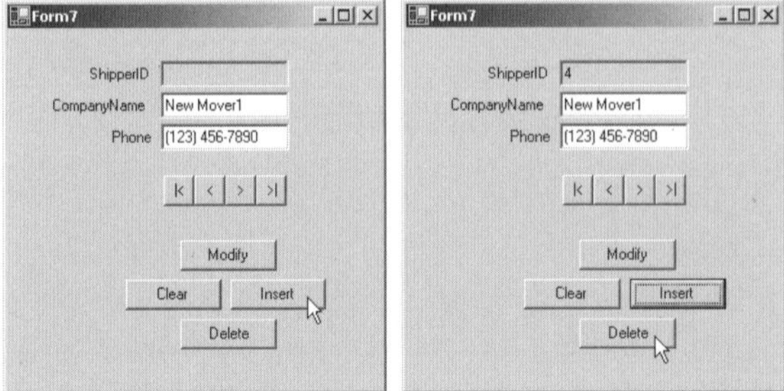

Figure 10-17. Two windows that show column values just before and after their insertion into a local *DataTable* and a synchronized SQL Server table. The window on the right also shows the cursor on the button to remove the newly added row.

Code Associated with the Form *Load* Event

The *Load* event for *Form7* handles setting up for the update, insert, and delete tasks described in the discussions of Figures 10-16 and 10-17. The major setup issue for forms enabling data manipulation tasks is to specify *UpdateCommand*, *InsertCommand*, and *DeleteCommand* properties for the *DataAdapter* that populates the data set behind the form. The *UpdateCommand* property enables update tasks. The *InsertCommand* property permits the insertion of new rows into a SQL Server data source. The *DeleteCommand* property facilitates the removal of rows from a SQL Server data source. As usual, the sample code places the setup code for the *DataAdapter* and data set in a procedure named *Populate* that the form *Load* event procedure calls. I'll start by reviewing the *Populate* procedure, and I'll follow that with a review of the form *Load* event procedure.

Because the sample uses the *DataAdapter* and data set in more than one procedure behind *Form7*, the sample code declares the references for these objects at the module level. After these declarations, the *Populate* procedure instantiates *Connection* (*cnn1*) and *DataAdapter* (*dap1*) objects in the normal way. The *cnn1* object designates a connection to the Northwind database on the local SQL Server instance. The SQL string that is the argument for the *dap1* *SqlDataAdapter* reference specifies the SQL Server source used to populate the data set. Because ADO.NET enables updates, inserts, and deletes through the *DataAdapter*, the SQL string is especially important when you are performing data manipulation tasks. All data manipulation tasks operate on the source specified when you instantiate the *DataAdapter*. You can optionally create a

Command object with its own SQL string and then set the *SelectCommand* property of the *DataAdapter* to the *Command* object. Either technique achieves the same result of specifying a source for the data manipulation tasks through a *DataAdapter* object.

After designating a data source for the *DataAdapter*, the *Populate* procedure specifies the *UpdateCommand* property for the *dap1 DataAdapter*. The *UpdateCommand* property assignment instantiates a new *Command* object and references the *Connection* object *cnn1*, instantiated earlier in the procedure. The SQL string for the *Command* object is a T-SQL *UPDATE* statement. The syntax specifies the *Shippers* table as the target. In the statement's *SET* clause, you'll notice the *@CompanyName*, *@Phone*, and *@ShipperID* parameters. These parameters let the sample application pass changed values from the data set that the *DataAdapter* fills to the *Shippers* table in the Northwind database.

> **Note** The T-SQL *UPDATE* statement uses a primary key, *ShipperID*, in its *WHERE* clause. This is a useful technique for precisely specifying the rows that you want to change on a server.

The sample must explicitly add parameter objects to the *Parameters* collection for the *Command* object to which the *UpdateCommand* property points. The *Populate* procedure shows one syntax for using the *Add* method as it adds the *@CompanyName* and *@Phone* parameters. The sample code specifies each of these parameters with four arguments. The first argument is the parameter name. The second and third arguments designate the data type for the parameter. Because the *@CompanyName* and *@Phone* parameters update columns in a table within a SQL Server database, you should assign SQL Server data types that match the columns they are updating, namely `nvarchar(40)` and `nvarchar(24)`. When you're using a numeric format, you can designate the third argument as *0*. The fourth argument is the column name in the local *DataTable* that serves as the source for the parameter. This is the column from which the *DataAdapter Update* method will derive the changed values to pass along to the SQL Server instance according to the *UPDATE* statement in the *UpdateCommand* property setting of the *DataAdapter*.

Following the addition of the *@CompanyName* and *@Phone* parameters, the *Populate* procedure demonstrates another syntax while adding the *@ShipperID* parameter. For the *@ShipperID* parameter, the procedure uses just two arguments for the *Add* method—one for the parameter's name and another for its numeric data type. Instead of specifying the local source for the parameter in the argument string for the *Add* method, the code uses the parameter's *SourceColumn* property to designate the source column in the *Shippers DataTable*. The last statement for the *@ShipperID* parameter specification assigns a value to the parameter's *SourceVersion* property. This value is *Current* by default—meaning that it is the current value in the local *DataTable* serving as the source for updating a SQL Server data source. This is why we didn't need to specify the property for the *@CompanyName* and *@Phone* parameters. For those two parameters, we wanted to specify the current column values from the local *DataTable*. However, the *@ShipperID* parameter is an argument in the *WHERE* clause for the *UPDATE* statement, which specifies which SQL Server table rows to update. Designating *Original* for the *SourceVersion* property ensures that we are using the initial values that the *DataAdapter* uses to fill the *Shippers DataTable*.

The next block of code in the *Populate* procedure specifies the *InsertCommand* property for *dap1* and adds parameters for the *Command* object assigned to the property. The sample uses the *udpInsertANewShipper* stored procedure instead of a SQL string. Recall that the code for the T-SQL script for the stored procedure is available in the preceding section. Using a SQL string makes the ADO.NET code more transparent, but invoking a stored procedure supports faster performance. When you designate a stored procedure name as the source for an *InsertCommand*, *UpdateCommand*, or *DeleteCommand* property, you must also set the corresponding *CommandType* property to *StoredProcedure*. The *Populate* procedure demonstrates the syntax for this in the line following the *InsertCommand* property assignment.

The *Add* method statements for the *@CompanyName* and *@Phone* parameters with the *Command* object *InsertCommand* follow the same syntax as for the *UpdateCommand* command parameters. Notice that you are adding these parameters to *InsertCommand* instead of the *Command* object *UpdateCommand*. There is no *@ShipperID* parameter for *InsertCommand* because SQL Server generates that value on the SQL Server instance. However, the procedure declares *prm2* as an output parameter for getting the value of *@Identity*. This parameter allows the local copy of the *Shippers DataTable* to recover the value that the SQL Server instance assigns as the value of *ShipperID* in the *Shippers* table when it inserts a new row into the table.

The next code block shows the syntax for setting the *DeleteCommand* property of *dap1*. In this case, the *Populate* procedure uses a SQL string to specify the T-SQL for the *DELETE* statement on a SQL Server instance. As with the *UPDATE* statement, you must be careful to designate the specific rows that you want to manipulate. Using a primary key in the *WHERE* clause is one way to specify a unique row in a SQL Server data source. The code for specifying the *@ShipperID* parameter for the *DeleteCommand* property of *dap1* is the same as that used for *UpdateCommand* except for the *Command* object reference.

Once the *Populate* procedure completes specifying the *UpdateCommand*, *InsertCommand*, and *DeleteCommand* properties for the *DataAdapter*, the procedure concludes in the normal fashion. First it opens the *Connection* object so that the *dap1 DataAdapter* can connect with a SQL Server instance. Second it fills a table. Third it closes the *Connection* object.

```
'Module-level declaration of data adapter and data set.
Dim dap1 As SqlDataAdapter
Dim das1 As DataSet

Sub Populate()

    'Connect to Northwind database on local server.
    Dim cnn1 As SqlClient.SqlConnection = _
    New SqlConnection("Data Source=(local);" & _
        "Integrated Security=SSPI;" & _
        "Initial Catalog=northwind")

    'Instantiate a data adapter based on a SQL string.
    dap1 = New SqlDataAdapter _
        ("SELECT ShipperID, CompanyName, Phone " & _
        "FROM Shippers", _
        cnn1)

    'Set the UpdateCommand property for dap1.
    dap1.UpdateCommand = _
        New SqlCommand _
            ("UPDATE Shippers " & _
            "SET CompanyName = @CompanyName, " & _
            "Phone = @Phone " & _
            "WHERE ShipperID = @ShipperID", _
            cnn1)

    'Add two parameters that take source columns
    'from the Shippers table in the data set for the
    'dap1 adapter and feed the parameters in the SQL
    'string for the UpdateCommand property.
    dap1.UpdateCommand.Parameters.Add _
        ("@CompanyName", SqlDbType.NVarChar, 40, _
        "CompanyName")
    dap1.UpdateCommand.Parameters.Add _
        ("@Phone", SqlDbType.NVarChar, 24, _
        "Phone")

    'Specify matching criterion values based on the
    'original version of the ShipperID column in the
    'local Shippers table.
```

```
Dim prm1 As SqlParameter = _
    dap1.UpdateCommand.Parameters.Add _
    ("@ShipperID", SqlDbType.Int)
prm1.SourceColumn = "ShipperID"
prm1.SourceVersion = DataRowVersion.Original

'Point InsertCommand at a SQL Server stored procedure;
'you must have the stored procedure on the server.
dap1.InsertCommand = New SqlCommand("udpInsertANewShipper", cnn1)
dap1.InsertCommand.CommandType = CommandType.StoredProcedure

'Specify input parameters for the stored procedure.
dap1.InsertCommand.Parameters.Add _
    ("@CompanyName", SqlDbType.NVarChar, 40, _
    "CompanyName")
dap1.InsertCommand.Parameters.Add _
    ("@Phone", SqlDbType.NVarChar, 24, _
    "Phone")

'Designate an output parameter for the identity
'value assigned within SQL Server so that your
'local Shippers table can have a matching ShipperID
'column value.
Dim prm2 As SqlParameter = _
    dap1.InsertCommand.Parameters.Add _
     ("@Identity", SqlDbType.Int, 0, "ShipperID")
prm2.Direction = ParameterDirection.Output

'Specify the SQL string for the DeleteCommand
'property of dap1.
dap1.DeleteCommand = _
    New SqlCommand("DELETE " & _
    "FROM Shippers " & _
    "WHERE ShipperID = @ShipperID", cnn1)

'Specify matching criterion values based on the
'Original version of the ShipperID column in the
'local Shippers table.
Dim prm3 As SqlParameter = _
    dap1.DeleteCommand.Parameters.Add _
    ("@ShipperID", SqlDbType.Int)
prm3.SourceColumn = "ShipperID"
prm3.SourceVersion = DataRowVersion.Original

cnn1.Open()

'Instantiate a data set object and fill it with
'a table based on the SQL string for the dap1
'data source
```

(continued)

```
    das1 = New DataSet()
    dap1.Fill(das1, "Shippers")

    'Close the connection because a data set
    'functions as a disconnected data source.
    cnn1.Close()

End Sub
```

The *Form7_Load* event procedure performs three types of tasks. First it calls the *Populate* procedure. This creates the data set for the form and readies the data set for data manipulation tasks through the *dap1 DataAdapter*. The data set, in turn, contains the *Shippers DataTable*. Second the event procedure binds the *Text* property of *TextBox1*, *TextBox2*, and *TextBox3* to the *ShipperID*, *CompanyName*, and *Phone* columns in the *Shippers DataTable*. Third the form *Load* event procedure sets the *ReadOnly* property to *True* for *TextBox1*—the text box that displays *ShipperID*. This is because users aren't supposed to edit *ShipperID* values. The SQL Server instance managing the *Shippers* table is responsible for managing values of *ShipperID*.

```
Private Sub Form7_Load(ByVal sender As System.Object, _
    ByVal e As System.EventArgs) Handles MyBase.Load

    'Populate the das1 data set.
    Populate()

    'Bind each text box to a different column in the
    'Shippers table within das1.
    TextBox1.DataBindings.Add _
       (New Binding("Text", das1, "Shippers.ShipperID"))
    TextBox2.DataBindings.Add _
       (New Binding("Text", das1, "Shippers.CompanyName"))
    TextBox3.DataBindings.Add _
       (New Binding("Text", das1, "Shippers.Phone"))

    'Make TextBox1 read-only.
    TextBox1.ReadOnly = True

End Sub
```

Code for the Navigation Buttons

The *Click* event procedures for the navigation buttons appear next. The basic syntax for the navigation buttons in this sample follows those in the "Creating Data-Aware Forms" section. The main difference in this instance is that we need to specify the data source for the *BindingContext* object with a data set name and a *DataTable* name within the data set. The button name denotes the role of each button. For example, clicking *cmdFirst* shows the first row in the *Shippers DataTable* within the form.

```
Private Sub cmdFirst_Click(ByVal sender As System.Object, _
    ByVal e As System.EventArgs) Handles cmdFirst.Click

    'Move to first record.
    Me.BindingContext(das1, "Shippers").Position _
        = Me.BindingContext(das1, "Shippers").Position.MinValue

End Sub

Private Sub cmdPrevious_Click(ByVal sender As System.Object, _
    ByVal e As System.EventArgs) Handles cmdPrevious.Click

    'Move to previous record.
    Me.BindingContext(das1, "Shippers").Position -= 1

End Sub

Private Sub cmdNext_Click(ByVal sender As System.Object, _
    ByVal e As System.EventArgs) Handles cmdNext.Click

    'Move to next record.
    Me.BindingContext(das1, "Shippers").Position += 1

End Sub

Private Sub cmdLast_Click(ByVal sender As System.Object, _
    ByVal e As System.EventArgs) Handles cmdLast.Click

    'Move to last record.
    Me.BindingContext(das1, "Shippers").Position _
        = Me.BindingContext(das1, "Shippers").Position.MaxValue

End Sub
```

Code for the Modify Button

The *Click* event procedure for the Modify button (*cmdModify*) performs just two tasks. First it commits the current edit if there is one in progress. Second it invokes the *Update* method for the *dap1 DataAdapter*.

The procedure commits the current edit in one of two ways depending on the position of the *Shippers DataTable* row showing in the form. If the position is any other than the first row (position 0), the procedure moves to the previous row and then the next row. The move to the previous row commits the current form values to the *Shippers DataTable* by moving off the current row. Then the move to the next row returns the form's focus to the row before the move to the previous row. If the form is showing the first row in the *Shippers DataTable*, the procedure just issues a command to move to the previous record. This commits the form's values to the *Shippers DataTable* without changing the row that appears in the form.

The *Update* method invokes the *Command* objects associated with the *UpdateCommand*, *InsertCommand*, and *DeleteCommand* properties of *dap1*. Because the sample application immediately synchronizes individual insert and delete actions, the *Update* method behind the Modify button synchronizes just rows with changed values in the *Shippers DataTable* with the *Shippers* table in the Northwind database on the local SQL Server instance. However, all changed rows since the last click of the Modify button attempt to update corresponding *Shippers* table rows on the SQL Server instance. The syntax for the *Update* method in the sample specifies the names for the data set and the *DataTable* within it. Failing to explicitly generate the *DataTable* name can generate an error in this context.

```
Private Sub cmdModify_Click(ByVal sender As System.Object, _
    ByVal e As System.EventArgs) Handles Button1.Click

    'Commit the current edit by moving off and returning to
    'the current row in the DataTable.
    If Me.BindingContext(das1, "Shippers").Position = 0 _
        Then
        Me.BindingContext(das1, "Shippers").Position -= 1
    Else
        Me.BindingContext(das1, "Shippers").Position -= 1
        Me.BindingContext(das1, "Shippers").Position += 1
    End If

    'Invoke the Update method to copy the change
    'to the SQL Server data source.
    dap1.Update(das1, "Shippers")

End Sub
```

Code for the Clear and Insert Buttons

Recall that the form *Load* event procedure binds the text boxes to columns in the *Shippers DataTable*. Therefore, letting a user mark over text box values and invoke the *Update* method with a click of the Insert button won't add a new record. Instead, it will modify an existing row in the *Shippers DataTable*. To add a new row to the *DataTable* (and eventually to the *Shippers* table on a SQL Server instance), you need to start with an unbound form. If this form is empty, it reminds the user that it is for data entry. Next add the text box values as a new row to the local *DataTable*, and finally invoke the *Update* method to propagate the new row from the local *DataTable* to the corresponding table on the SQL Server database.

The *cmdClear_Click* event procedure performs three tasks. The preceding paragraph mentioned two of these functions: remove the data bindings for the text boxes and clear the contents of the text boxes. You can remove all data bindings for a control with the *Clear* method for the *DataBindings* collection. (Recall that you can have multiple data bindings for different properties on a control.) You can clear the contents of a text box by assigning an empty string ("") to its *Text* property. There is also an explicit *Clear* method for the text box control. The sample demonstrates the approach using an empty string.

> **Note** The *cmdClear_Click* event procedure starts with an assignment that moves the text box to the first row before clearing the data bindings. This step is necessary to ensure that the first row in the local *DataTable* will be editable through the form after a new row is inserted with the Insert button.

The user is supposed to click the Insert button (*cmdInsert*) after entering values for a new shipper. The *Click* event procedure for *cmdInsert* starts by adding a new row to the local *DataTable* based on the text box *Text* property settings. Next the procedure invokes the *Update* method for the *dap1 DataAdapter* to synchronize the local *DataTable* with its corresponding table on the SQL Server instance to which the *DataAdapter* connects. Then the procedure restores the data binding settings for the three text boxes. The last action the *Click* event procedure performs is to assign the *Position* property for the *BindingContext* object of *Form7* to the last row in the local *DataTable*. This exposes the newly entered row on the form that was inserted into the last row of the local *DataTable*.

It's helpful to review the steps for adding a new row to the local *DataTable* to get a feel for the object model associated with the *DataTable* object. (See Figure 10-1 as well.) The steps start at the top of the *cmdInsert_Click* event procedure by declaring and instantiating a new *DataRow* object based on the *Shippers DataTable*. Assign the *Text* property values for *TextBox2* and *TextBox3* to the *CompanyName* and *Phone* columns of the new *DataRow* object. Then invoke the *Add* method for the *Shippers DataTableRows* collection to add the new row object as the last row in the *DataTable*.

```
Private Sub cmdClear_Click(ByVal sender As System.Object, _
    ByVal e As System.EventArgs) Handles cmdClear.Click

    'Always insert from first row to enable
    'updating that row later.
    Me.BindingContext(das1, "Shippers").Position _
        = Me.BindingContext(das1, "Shippers").Position.MinValue

    'Disconnect the form's textboxes from any
    'data bindings.
    TextBox1.DataBindings.Clear()
    TextBox2.DataBindings.Clear()
    TextBox3.DataBindings.Clear()

    'Clear text box contents.
    TextBox1.Text = ""
    TextBox2.Text = ""
    TextBox3.Text = ""

End Sub

Private Sub cmdInsert_Click(ByVal sender As System.Object, _
    ByVal e As System.EventArgs) Handles cmdInsert.Click

    'Add text box values to new row in data set Shippers table.
    Dim newRow As DataRow = das1.Tables("Shippers").NewRow()
    newRow("CompanyName") = TextBox2.Text
    newRow("Phone") = TextBox3.Text
    das1.Tables("Shippers").Rows.Add(newRow)

    'Update for insert ADO.NET automatically passes data source
    'identity value to current row for Shippers table in data set.
    dap1.Update(das1, "Shippers")

    'Re-bind each text box to a different Shipper's
    'column in the das1 data set.
    TextBox1.DataBindings.Add _
       (New Binding("Text", das1, "Shippers.ShipperID"))
    TextBox2.DataBindings.Add _
       (New Binding("Text", das1, "Shippers.CompanyName"))
    TextBox3.DataBindings.Add _
       (New Binding("Text", das1, "Shippers.Phone"))

    'Move to last row to show inserted row.
    Me.BindingContext(das1, "Shippers").Position _
        = Me.BindingContext(das1, "Shippers").Position.MaxValue

End Sub
```

Code for the Delete Button

When a user clicks the Delete button (*cmdDelete*), they launch its *Click* event procedure, which appears next. Before the procedure can drop the row from the local *Shippers* table, it must locate the row corresponding to the values that appear on the form. There is a *Find* method for the *Rows* collection of a *DataTable*, but the method can search only by a primary key column. When the *DataAdapter* fills the data set with the *Shippers* table column values from the local SQL Server instance, it doesn't also create a primary key for the *ShipperID* column. As a result, you cannot use the *Find* method for the *Rows* collection of a *DataTable*. However, the *Find* method for a *DataView* object based on the local *Shippers DataTable* doesn't require a primary key. Therefore, the procedure can use this method to find the row to delete.

The *cmdDelete_Click* event procedure starts by declaring and instantiating a *DataView* based on the local *Shippers DataTable*. Next the procedure sets the *Sort* property of the *DataView* so that its rows are sorted in ascending order based on *ShipperID* value. This step is necessary so that the *Find* method can return the row index value for the first *ShipperID* matching a value. Row index values start at 0 for the first row and progress by 1 for each row.

After finding the row to delete, the procedure performs two tasks. First it invokes the *Delete* method for the row in the local *Shippers DataTable* matching the discovered row index value. Second it invokes the *Update* method to synchronize the local *Shippers DataTable* with the *Shippers* table in the SQL Server database.

> **Note** Recall that the *DataTable* model lets developers remove rows with either the *Delete* or *Remove* method. When deleting a row for use with the *Update* method, *never* use the *Remove* method because the *Remove* method doesn't leave the row available for use by the *Update* method. See "The *DataSet* Class" section for more background on this topic.

```
Private Sub cmdDelete_Click(ByVal sender As System.Object, _
    ByVal e As System.EventArgs) Handles cmdDelete.Click

    'Create a dataview based on the Shippers table in
    'the data set and find the row index that matches
    'the current ShipperID.
    Dim dav1 As DataView = _
        New DataView(das1.Tables("Shippers"))
```

(continued)

```
        dav1.Sort = "ShipperID"
        Dim rowIndex As Integer = _
        dav1.Find(TextBox1.Text)

        'Mark the row for deletion in the data set.
        das1.Tables("Shippers").Rows(rowIndex).Delete()

        'Invoke the Update method to complete the deletion
        'in both the SQL Server and data set Shippers tables.
        dap1.Update(das1, "Shippers")

    End Sub
```

11

Programming ASP.NET Solutions

ASP.NET is the Web development environment for building Web solutions in the .NET Framework. Like ADO.NET, the .NET Framework data component, ASP.NET works with any .NET language, including Visual Basic .NET. In other words, you can build Web applications directly with Visual Basic .NET. Building Web applications with Visual Basic is highly similar to creating Windows applications in Visual Basic. This simple fact (now Visual Basic can build Web solutions) promises to open up Web development to millions of Visual Basic developers. In the past, a large segment of Visual Basic developers avoided creating Web solutions because of the many differences between Windows development techniques and traditional Web development techniques. If you are a Visual Basic developer who has been waiting for the right time to start creating Web solutions, now is the time, and ASP.NET is the way.

So what if you already know ASP development? Can ASP.NET help? Maybe even more to the point, will ASP.NET hurt your existing Web solutions? ASP.NET compiles your code so that the compiled version of your pages will always run faster than interpreted ASP pages. In addition, ASP.NET splits the graphical layout of Web pages from the programmatic logic controlling Web pages into two separate files. This promises to greatly expedite your development efforts by removing the need for interspersing HTML and some scripting code, such as VBScript or JScript. Because ASP.NET Web pages can run side by side with older ASP pages, they don't hurt or break existing applications. Instead, ASP.NET solutions can complement ASP applications by expediting the development of new features for previously existing Web solutions.

This chapter introduces Visual Basic developers to building Web solutions with ASP.NET. I start the chapter with an overview of conceptual and hands-on design issues that can make you more productive when you get around to writing code. Next I introduce code development techniques with ASP.NET even while I continue to highlight special Web issues, such as dynamically adapting to the browser on which your solution runs. Communicating between Web pages is different than with traditional Windows applications because the HTTP protocol used in nearly all Web applications is stateless. That is, the protocol by itself doesn't convey anything about the history of visits to a Web server by a browser in a session. An entire section goes into clarifying session management and offering a mix of remedies optimized for different situations. Perhaps this chapter's most important section discusses and demonstrates how to use SQL Server databases in ASP.NET solutions. You will learn about classic data issues, such as browsing a data source, creating parent-child forms, and performing update, insert, and delete operations. The final section highlights how to graphically and programmatically manage the validity of data on Web pages in ASP.NET.

The resources for this chapter include a series of samples. The discussion of each sample describes the key files and folders for running the samples from Visual Studio .NET and from within a browser.

Review of ASP.NET Design Issues

ASP.NET is the collection of tools available in the .NET Framework for creating Web applications. This section orients you to Web development issues and introduces design interfaces for creating solutions. Understanding the material in this section is a vital stepping-stone for the next section, which gets you started creating and running ASP.NET solutions.

Round-Trips

ASP.NET is the collection of .NET tools that explicitly target Web application development. The defining element of Web applications is that browsers communicate with a Web server in a call-and-response dynamic. The browser sends a page of content as a file to the Web server, and the server can respond with a new page of information to the browser. You can think of this exchange of information between the browser and the Web server as a round-trip.

While browsers can run programs locally without exchanging information with the Web server, it's the round-trip feature that distinguishes Web applications from classic Windows applications. One aspect of Web security is that the ability of browsers to run programs locally is restricted. Windows applications, in contrast, specifically exploit the resources of a local workstation to provide a rich computing environment. Chapter 10 described how to deliver data access and manipulation capabilities via a data set residing on a local workstation. In ASP.NET applications, the data set typically resides with the Web page that a browser and a Web server exchange with one another. Any updates resulting from the communication of a Web server with a database server result in a refreshed data set for return to a Web browser. Because the page moves back and forth between the browser and the Web server, you should scale the size of data sets residing on the page so that the data sets don't significantly add to the exchange time between a browser and a Web server.

Figure 11-1 graphically portrays how ASP.NET facilitates the communication among a browser, a Web server, and a database server, such as a SQL Server instance. Notice in the figure that a cylinder representing a data set resides on a page. The page is passed from a browser to a Web server and back again. The exchange between a browser and a Web server takes place through a Web. This can be the Internet, a companywide intranet, or your HTTP connection to a local Web server running on your machine. In fact, many of the samples in this chapter are configured so you can test them with a local Web server on your computer. Notice that the browser doesn't directly interface with the database server. Instead, the Web server communicates with the database server and exchanges data with the browser; the Web server stands between the browser and the database server. This process enables the browser to view data on the database server and synchronize its updates with those of other database users.

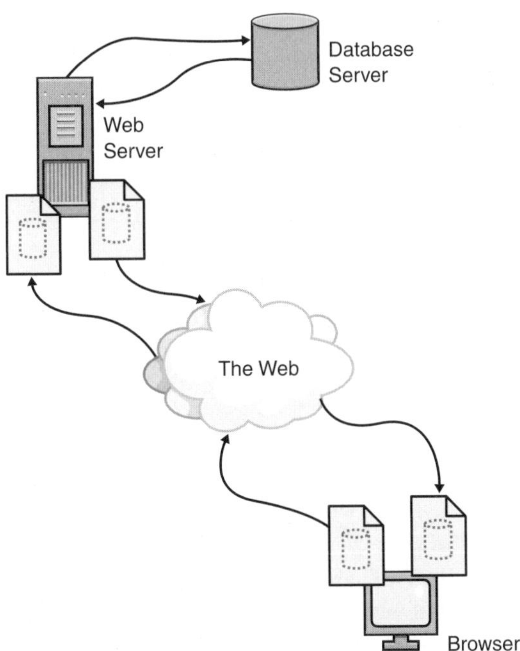

Figure 11-1. A schematic illustrating the round-trip process for data on a Web page in ASP.NET.

A typical ASP.NET application will be run in an environment in which many browsers are connected to a single Web server or a farm of Web servers. For simplicity, I discuss the case of the single Web server, but the same general principles apply to a farm of Web servers. The asynchronous nature of communication between a Web server and browsers facilitates the maintenance of a large number of concurrent browser sessions with a single Web server. Each of these browsers can have a different session state with the Web server. In other words, the same page can show different contents to different users depending on the interactions of each user with the Web server. At the same time, a database server can provide a consistent set of information across multiple browser sessions.

Another defining characteristic of Web applications is that a Web server can serve pages to many different kinds of browsers. Although all browser types render HTML code in pages served from a Web server, the rendering isn't necessarily invariant from one browser type to the next. Some browsers handle client-side scripting in one language but not another. Different browser versions target different HTML versions (3.2 and 4.0 are two common HTML versions). Some support absolute positioning, but support isn't universal for this feature. For differences such as those noted, it's not uncommon for Web applications to have to "sniff" the browser type to determine its characteristics and then send a page that is rendered and behaves well on that browser.

ASP.NET offers a couple of approaches to handling Web application development issues. First, ASP.NET can elicit HTML from Web servers in an attempt to minimize the impact of different browser types on the way that a page appears in a browser. Second, ASP.NET has built-in capabilities for detecting browser types and their capabilities. Your applications can tap these capabilities to direct browsers to pages that are rendered well within them.

> **Note** It's a big drain on limited Web application development resources to detect browsers and prepare multiple pages that are rendered well in different browsers. As a business employing talented Web developers, wouldn't you rather those developers spend their time creating more useful content in different pages than creating multiple copies of a smaller number of less useful pages so as to optimize for different browsers? Because ASP.NET is free with the IIS 5.0 Web server, and the Internet Explorer browser is free with most Microsoft products and from Microsoft's Internet site, I recommend you use the Internet Explorer browser for your ASP.NET applications. Note that Microsoft didn't encourage me to make this statement. Instead, I make the statement on the basis of my observations about how taxing it is on organizations to create Web solutions that work well with multiple browsers.

Pages and the *Page* Class

As indicated in Chapter 8, ASP.NET builds on ASP. For example, Web servers can discern an ASP.NET page based on its extension, .aspx. The extension for an ASP.NET page is the same as the extension of ASP pages with an *x* appended to it. For example, an ASP.NET page will have a name like mypage.aspx.

Any ASP.NET solution can have multiple pages within it. You can designate one page as the start page for an application. (There is no startup object as there is with Windows applications.) An ASP.NET solution can contain multiple pages, and users can navigate within and between the pages of a solution. In addition, you can navigate to old .asp page files or even other types of files, such as .htm or .html files.

When an ASP.NET application opens an .aspx file, the application launches the *Page_Load* event procedure (unless you remove it). The *Page* class is a programming abstraction of an .aspx file. This *Page* class provides many valuable services. For example, you can use a page's *IsPostBack* property to determine whether a page is being displayed for the first time in a session or is the result of a browser posting a page back to a Web server. A page's *Session* property enables your application to manage variables across multiple asynchronous connections to a Web server from a browser within a session. A page's *Application* property points to an *Application* object for sharing variable values across an application's users. One of the most exciting features of the *Page* class is the way that it automates the management of formatting and content between round-trips; I'll discuss this topic more fully in the "Session State Management" section. With the *Response* and *Request* properties for a page, you can explicitly manage the exchange of information between a Web server and a browser. The *Response* property enables you to echo content to Web pages so that you can monitor the ingoing and outgoing values for controls and variable values on Web pages. Developers will recognize this capability as particularly handy for debugging.

My personal favorite feature of ASP.NET is the way that it separates page layout issues from program logic. Those of you familiar with ASP will recall how you had the opportunity (indeed it was a requirement) to mix HTML layout with your script for managing the logic on a page. Although you can still do this, Visual Studio supports a two-file structure for the Web page class. The file with the .aspx extension contains the HTML layout code. A new, second, file contains the program logic. This file's extension depends on the programming language. For example, if your Web page file has the name yourpage.aspx, its code file in Visual Basic will have the name yourpage.aspx.vb. The page with the .aspx extension contains controls, such as labels, text boxes, and list boxes. The code file (with the aspx.vb extension) includes page initialization code, event procedures for the objects on the page, and other routines and declarations to manage the behavior of a page.

An ASP.NET application that you develop with Visual Studio has two folders for managing a solution. Your .aspx and .aspx.vb files reside in a folder on the Web server. The project folder's default location is in the wwwroot subdirectory of the Inetpub folder of the IIS server hosting your application. You can have multiple files within the Web folder for a solution, including other Web pages and graphic files. You open a Web solution by invoking any .aspx file within the folder on the Web server. A second folder in your Visual Studio solution directory contains the solution file (.sln) for an ASP.NET project. This second folder is the same one Visual Studio uses to store the files for your Windows application solutions. Use the .sln file to open your solution in Visual Studio when you want to edit the design of a solution. Both the Web folder and the regular Windows folder can have the same name to facilitate their coordination.

Controls on Pages

You start an ASP.NET project in Visual Studio .NET by clicking New Project on the Visual Studio .NET Start Page and then highlighting the ASP.NET Web Application template. Designate a folder name for your new project. The default location is on the localhost IIS server. See the overview of ASP.NET in Chapter 8 for the three elements that you need to create ASP.NET solutions. As Visual Studio .NET starts the project, it creates a Web site for the solution on the Web server.

When the project opens, you will view an empty Web page (with the .aspx extension). The default name for the page is WebForm1.aspx. You can assign a new name that is more meaningful in terms of your application by right-clicking the file's name in Solution Explorer and choosing Rename to assign a new name.

Use the Toolbox to add controls to a blank page. You can display the Toolbox by choosing Toolbox from the View menu from within Design view for the startup page. There are three categories of native controls that you are likely to add to an .aspx page. These reside in three separate tabs within the Toolbox.

- First, you can click the HTML tab in the Toolbox to expose classic HTML controls. These controls can operate as HTML elements or as a new type of HTML server control. If you are used to building Web solutions with ASP or some other Web development language (such as Perl), you probably already have a working knowledge of HTML controls. One key distinction between classic HTML form controls and HTML server controls is that server controls offer an object model for programming on a Web server.

- Second, you can click the Web Forms tab in the Toolbox to expose Web server form controls designed explicitly for use with ASP.NET. These controls are rendered as HTML on Web pages, but they have properties, methods, and events associated with them. You can use Web server controls on the ASP.NET *Page* class instances similarly to the way you use Windows form controls on forms in Windows applications.
- Third, you can use the items on the Data tab in the Toolbox to invoke wizards for declaring and instantiating ADO.NET objects, such as a data adapter for SQL Server or a data set. These ADO.NET objects reside on a page at design time, and they can thus simplify your code by reducing the need to declare and instantiate objects. See Chapter 1 for the discussion of an example that demonstrates the use of these forms in a Windows application. This chapter contains supplementary ASP.NET applications that illustrate the use of Data controls on Web pages.

HTML controls and Web server controls both represent text boxes, buttons, and similar kinds of controls. The list of HTML control items maps to the classic HTML form controls, such as a label, a text field, a submit button, and a reset button. HTML controls can run either as classic HTML form controls or as HTML server controls. You need to designate a special attribute (*runat="server"*) in order for the items on the Toolbox's HTML tab to be available for programming on a Web server. HTML controls with the special attribute setting are often designated HTML server controls in the ASP.NET documentation. You must give HTML server controls a name at design time by assigning a value to their *ID* attribute in order to reference them programmatically on a Web server. Without the special *runat* attribute setting, HTML controls pass their values along in either of the two traditional ways: in the HTTP header or in the body of a form on an .aspx Web page. If you use the special attribute setting, you can manipulate HTML control properties similarly to the way you manage controls on a Windows form.

> **Note** The HTML form's *method* attribute tells a Web server where to look for values with a form on a Web page. The "get" setting for a method attribute says to look in the HTTP header. This is a query string appearing after the URL to which a Web page navigates. The "post" setting designates the storage of values in the body of a Web page.

Web server controls convey HTML to browsers. However, the HTML syntax for these controls doesn't map in a one-to-one way to HTML form controls. For example, the RadioButtonList Web server control contains text inside an HTML *table* element. This control doesn't map to the HTML Radio Button control, although both controls can have a similar look on a Web page. Selected Web server controls include Button, Label, ListBox, DataGrid, HyperLink, and about 25 more. You can see the full list of Web server controls with links for drilling down further into the properties, methods, and events for each one in the "Web Server Controls" topic of the Visual Studio .NET documentation.

> **Note** You can open the Visual Studio .NET documentation from the Programs menu on the Windows Start button. Choose Microsoft Visual Studio .NET Documentation from the Microsoft Visual Studio .NET item on the Programs menu. Use the Search tab to return a list of items matching a search criterion, such as *Web Server Controls*. If you have difficulty finding a particular topic because too many items return, sort by Title by clicking the Title header in the Search results window. Then scroll through the items, which are now listed in alphabetical order, to the item you want.

Web server controls and HTML server controls share selected features in common. For example, one killer feature is the ability for form controls to maintain their values on round-trips to a Web server. This maintenance of form field values can require a lot of programming with traditional HTML controls on HTML forms. However, Web server controls and HTML server controls provide this feature without any programming. Another significant feature shared by Web server controls and HTML server controls is the ability to use the validation controls to assess the content of controls on a form. Validation controls enable certain validity tests, such as whether the control contains an entry, whether the control has a value in a specified format, and whether the value is in a specified range. Again, no programming is necessary for base functionality. However, learning a few programming tricks for the validation controls can enable you to refine the user experience.

I strongly urge you to use Web server controls instead of HTML server controls in all your ASP.NET applications. As their names imply, Web server controls run automatically on the Web server. There is no special attribute for you to set in order to use the controls on a Web server. Web server controls are much more extensive in their variety than HTML server controls. In addition to the standard HTML control types, Web server controls offer a variety of specialized controls to facilitate your display and manipulation of data, including a DataGrid control for displaying data as a table. Developers who build solutions for entering or showing dates are likely to find the Web server Calendar control of special value. This control enables entering and displaying dates on a standard monthly calendar display. The general HTML format for a Web server control appears here. The *asp* prefix denotes the control as a Web server control. The *controlname* parameter specifies the type of control (for example, label). The *attributes* parameter corresponds to a list of property settings.

```
<asp:controlname attributes runat="server">
```

ASP.NET Design Interfaces

I have been developing Web solutions primarily with Microsoft technology since approximately 1995, and the ASP.NET design interface is by far my favorite over that time span. This is because the ASP.NET design interface offers you the flexibility of developing a Web application very much as you create Windows solutions with Visual Basic .NET. It leaves me free to focus on my solution instead of being distracted by Web layout development issues. In other words, ASP.NET provides a design environment that makes me feel as though I'm creating a typical Windows solution—except it's for the Web. (See Chapter 8 for more coverage on this point.) Nonetheless, the ASP.NET design environment still has some unique features, which will be covered in this section.

After initially creating a new ASP.NET project (as described in the preceding section), you are confronted with the HTML Designer, which displays a blank Web layout page. By default, this page will have the filename WebForm1.aspx. The first point to note is that the tab for the page has two controls at its bottom. The page opens with the Design control selected (unless you change the default setting), which presents a graphical view of the page. Clicking the HTML control displays the HTML code behind the page. In other words, the HTML Designer offers two views for each page—a Design view for graphical development of a page and an HTML code view for programmatic design of a page.

When you look at the page in HTML view, you'll see that it starts with an *@Page* directive. In this directive are setting assignments that you should typically not edit. Next there is a document declaration declaring the page to be an HTML 4.0 document.

After the two preliminary declaration statements, the HTML code window displays an *html* tag. A matching */html* tag ends the document. Other HTML tags nest between these beginning and ending tags for the HTML content within a document. Two sets of matching tags nest directly beneath the *html* and */html* tags. The content between the *head* and */head* tags is mostly boilerplate material routinely prepared by Visual Studio for all .aspx page files that it generates. However, the *title* and */title* tags contain the title that appears in the title bar of a Web browser window when the browser displays the page. You can edit a page's title either from the HTML code window or the Properties window for the document. Changes in either location update the other location automatically.

The next pair of nested tags within the *html* and */html* tags are the *body* and */body* tags. Unless you change the default settings, the *body* tag will have an *MS_POSITIONING* attribute setting of GridLayout. This handy setting lets you drag and drop controls around a Web page just as on a Windows form. The *MS_POSITIONING* attribute setting corresponds to the *pageLayout* property setting in the Properties window for the document. The default setting for the *pageLayout* setting matches the *MS_POSITIONING* attribute setting of GridLayout. Choosing the other property setting of FlowLayout for the *pageLayout* property removes the *MS_POSITIONING* attribute from the HTML code window. This alternative layout setting allows you to position controls on a Web page as you do content on a typical word processing document. This is the traditional HTML way of positioning controls on a page, and it provides your greatest compatibility with browser types—especially older browser types that don't support absolute positioning. However, you give up the convenience of being able to drag and drop controls on a Web page. The *form* and */form* tags reside within the *body* tags. All the controls on a Web page appear within the *form* and */form* tags. I will discuss these tags next as I review the page design for our WebApplication1 project, which was initially discussed in Chapter 8.

> **Note** The WebApplication1 sample, like most of the samples in this chapter, exists as two folders. Both folders have the name WebApplication1. One contains just two files in its root. One of these files is WebApplication1.sln. The folder containing this file belongs in the directory that your computer uses for storing Visual Basic .NET Windows solutions. You can open the WebApplication1 solution in Visual Studio by choosing Open Solution from the File menu and selecting WebApplication1.sln. You may need to browse to the folder containing WebApplication1.sln before being able to select it. The second folder contains WebForm1.aspx in its root. This folder belongs in the wwwroot directory of the Inetpub folder on the computer from which you will be running the application. You can open the Web page by browsing *http://<webserver>/WebApplication1/WebForm1.aspx.*

Recall that the WebApplication1 project from Chapter 8 contains two controls: a button and a label. Clicking the button causes the label to show "Hello World." Figure 11-2 reveals the button control above the label control in Design view for WebApplication1's WebForm1.aspx file. Both controls are Web server controls. I selected them from the Web Forms tab of the Toolbox. When you add a control from the Toolbox to a Web page, you can select it in the Toolbox and then size the control by dragging it out on your Web page. Alternatively, you can right-click the control type in the Toolbox and choose Copy. Then right-click in Design view for the Web page, and choose Paste. This adds the control with preconfigured size settings in the upper left corner of the page. If your document has a GridLayout setting for its *pageLayout* property, you can then just drag the control to its desired location. Figure 11-2 shows the label and button controls with their preconfigured size settings.

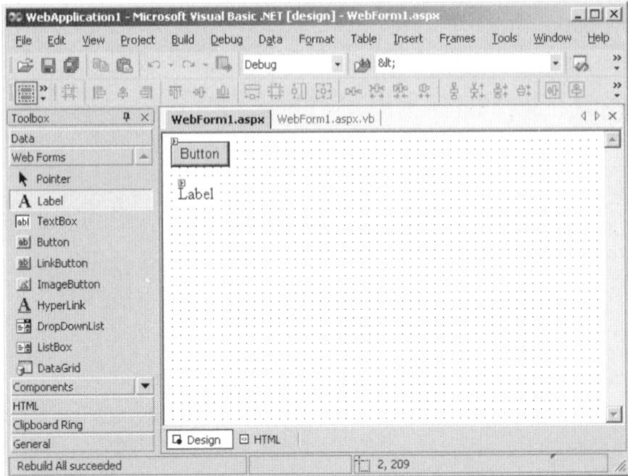

Figure 11-2. The ASP.NET Design view for WebForm1.aspx in the WebApplication1 project.

Figure 11-2 shows several toolbars. All the controls on the bottom row, after the first two, belong to the Layout toolbar. If this toolbar isn't visible, you can make it appear in the usual way for Windows applications—right-click any toolbar, and select the one you want (Layout) from the context menu. (You can also select Toolbars from the View menu and select the appropriate toolbar from the list.) The controls on this toolbar can make fast work of typical form layout design tasks, such as aligning, sizing, and spacing controls. Notice also in the figure that the Web page appears with a grid. The default setting is for controls to snap to the grid marks as you move controls around the form. If you prefer more granular positioning or you don't want to show a grid, you can achieve these results by choosing Options from the Tools menu. In the Options dialog box, Open the HTML Designer folder and select Display. The right portion of the dialog box then reveals controls for setting the Snap To Grid and Show Grid options. This portion of the Options dialog box also includes text boxes for you to specify the spacing between grid marks in Design view. You can also control the appearance of the grid by right-clicking any blank area of a page in Design view and choosing Properties. If the *pageLayout* property for a page is GridLayout, the General tab of the DOCUMENT Property Pages dialog box exposes the Show Grid check box. Clearing the check box stops the grid from appearing, but controls still snap to the grid when you move them.

If you switch from Design view to HTML view, you can see the *form* and */form* tags inside bounding *body* and */body* tags. Just as the *form* and */form* tags are within *body* and */body* tags, so are the tags for the button and label controls within the tags for the form. You can see from the following HTML excerpt for the WebForm1.aspx page that the button and label controls are Web server controls because their initial tag begins with the *asp* prefix (*asp:Button* and *asp:Label*). After the tag designation initiating a control, a series of attribute settings defines the control features. The attribute settings are so numerous that they cause the control tag to wrap to a second line. The *id* attribute indicates the name by which your program can refer to the control. The *TOP* attribute designates how far down, in pixels, a control is from the top page border. Notice that the label control is 40 pixels farther down the page than the button. The button control is 7 pixels closer to the page's left border than the label control.

```
<body MS_POSITIONING="GridLayout">
    <form id="Form1" method="post" runat="server">
        <asp:Button id="Button1" style="Z-INDEX: 101; LEFT: 8px;
         POSITION: absolute; TOP: 8px" runat="server" Text="Button">
        </asp:Button>
        <asp:Label id="Label1" style="Z-INDEX: 102; LEFT: 15px;
         POSITION: absolute; TOP: 48px" runat="server">Label
        </asp:Label>
    </form>
</body>
```

Right-clicking any blank area in the Design view that appears in Figure 11-2 opens a context menu from which you can choose View Code. This exposes the Visual Basic code behind the form. (See Figure 11-3.) The tab displaying the code behind the form has the name WebForm1.aspx.vb. This is also the name of the file containing the code behind the form. The Solution Explorer window to the right of the code window shows the WebForm1.aspx.vb file selected. You won't see this file unless you've selected Show All Files on the Solution Explorer toolbar. The declarations at the top of the module window indicate that the code resides in a class instance named *WebForm1*, which inherits properties, methods, and events from the *Page* namespace in the *System.Web.UI* hierarchy. In addition, the *Button1* and *Label1* controls on the Web page are instances of the *Button* and *Label* classes. The definitions for the *Button* and *Label* classes reside in the *System.Web.UI.WebControls* namespace.

Note Recall that you can discover the function of controls on a toolbar, such as the Show All Files control, by hovering your cursor over the control until a descriptive phrase appears.

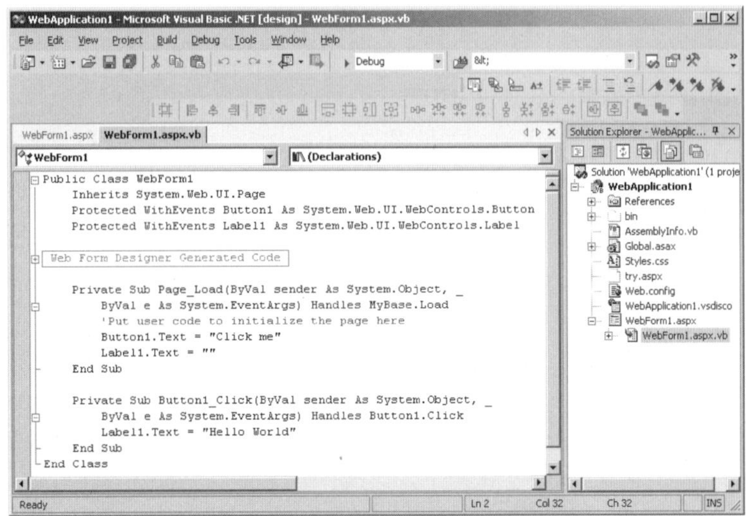

Figure 11-3. The code window for the WebApplications1 sample with the WebForm1.aspx.vb file selected in Solution Explorer.

When you choose to view the code for an empty Web page, you will see just one procedure, the *Page_Load* event procedure. This procedure will contain a comment that reads, "Put user code to initialize the page here." I retained this comment in Figure 11-3 for your reference. The *Page_Load* event procedure works much like the *Form_Load* event procedure for Windows applications. You can make assignments that need to take place before a user interacts with a Web page. In the WebApplication1 sample, the *Page_Load* event procedure assigns "Click me" to the *Text* property for *Button1* and clears the *Text* property for *Label1*. The *Button1_Click* event procedure can be included because of the *Protected WithEvents* declaration at the top of the module.

Creating and Running ASP.NET Solutions

Building Web solutions with ASP.NET can be very straightforward for Visual Basic developers. This section includes several samples to illustrate basic Web design issues. You start with a review of techniques for compiling and viewing Web pages. This review leads to a sample that drills down on techniques for managing the appearance of controls on a Web page. In the process, you learn syntax issues for the *Page_Load* event procedure as well as event procedures for controls on a Web page. Another pair of samples demonstrates how to construct a multifunction calculator. These samples illustrate techniques for working with text boxes on a Web page as well as how to optimize pages for different types of browsers. The section concludes with a sample that automatically detects the type of the browser requesting a page and transfers control to a page optimized for that browser type.

Compiling and Viewing Web Pages

If you install the folder with the WebForm1.aspx file for WebApplication1 in the wwwroot folder for the Web server on your local computer, you can open the solution in a browser with the following URL:

http://localhost/WebApplication1/WebForm1.aspx

This URL designates the local Web server by specifying localhost. If you have the WebApplication1 folder containing WebForm1.aspx installed on a different computer running IIS and the .NET Framework, you can open the Web page in a browser with the following URL. *Servername* typically specifies the name of the computer running the Web server.

http://<servername>*/WebApplication1/WebForm1.aspx*

I recommend running pages from a browser. In fact, if you are sure that your application will have to be run by users with different browser types, you should test your Web pages with as many of these browser types as possible. You might even consider trying out your Web pages with different settings. Some settings can affect how the page works in a browser—particularly if the page taps any client-side (this means browser) functionality. I will cover examples of these issues later in this chapter.

You must compile any changes to a page before you can view those changes in a browser. Therefore, for initial testing purposes, you might care to open your Web pages from within Visual Studio so you can more easily debug your solutions. You can right-click a page that you want to open in Solution Explorer and choose one of two menu items to view the page. If you haven't made any changes to the page since the last build, you can select View In Browser. This opens a Browse window within Visual Studio that simulates the appearance of the page as if it were in a browser. If you edited the page's layout or code behind the page since the last time the page was viewed, choose Build And Browse from the context menu when you right-click the page in Solution Explorer. This recompiles the solution with any changes that you made before displaying the page within the Visual Studio Browse window. No matter which approach you use to open a Browse window, the window appears on a separate tab like the ones for the Web page's layout and the code behind the page. Right-click within the Browse window for a selection of common browser commands, such as Back, Forward, and Refresh Browser.

Figure 11-4 shows WebForm1.aspx from WebApplication1 when it initially opens in Internet Explorer and after a click of the button labeled Click Me. One click of the button causes a label below the button to show Hello World. Repeatedly clicking the button seems to have no effect, although the *Page_Load* and *Button1_Click* event procedures operate for each click. This is because each click returns the Web page back to the server for processing. The reason nothing appears to change is that the label's *Text* property gets set to the same value on each return to the server as a result of a click of *Button1*.

Figure 11-4. The top window shows how WebForm1.aspx from WebApplication1 appears when it initially loads. The bottom window shows the Web page after a click of the button.

Remembering the State of a Page

One way to improve on the operation of the page in WebApplication1 is to keep track of whether a browser opens a page for the first time or whether a browser sends a page back to the server that is already open within that browser. You can additionally coordinate this knowledge with the appearance of the page. This will give users fresh information that reflects the state of the page—not just the same information on every click.

The PostbackSample project has a Web page named WebForm1.aspx that reflects four separate states. Furthermore, although the page address, WebForm1.aspx in the PostbackSample folder, stays the same, the appearance of the page's form changes with each successive click. The page's appearance indicates the state of the form on the page. When there are no more states to show, the page makes all buttons invisible so that a user cannot repeatedly click a button without anything happening.

> **Note** Like the WebApplication1 sample, the PostbackSample exists as two separate folders. Place the folder that contains WebForm1.aspx in the wwwroot directory of the Inetpub folder for the computer serving as a Web server. Place the folder with PostbackSample.sln in the directory storing your Visual Studio projects.

Figure 11-5 shows how the WebForm1.aspx page appears for each successive state. The top window shows the page when a user initially navigates to the page. This initial state for the PostbackSample application has the same appearance as the initial page for the WebApplication1 solution. After a user clicks the button labeled Click Me, the page returns saying, "Hello World", but the page changes its look in other ways as well. Specifically, the PostbackSample application makes *Button1* invisible. In addition, the application shows a new button, *Button2*, with a *Text* property of "Hello Showed". By clicking this second button, the user causes the Web page to travel to the server and back to the browser. While at the Web server, the layout of the page changes again. This time, the button with a label of Hello Showed changes its label to "Click for advice". In addition, *Label1* appears with a new *Text* property of "Get busy." Clicking the button one more time changes the appearance to the window at the bottom of Figure 11-5. In this final state, no buttons are visible for a user to click. In addition, the code behind the page has no more distinct appearances left to present. In addition to making both buttons invisible, the *Text* property for *Label1* changes to "Stay busy."

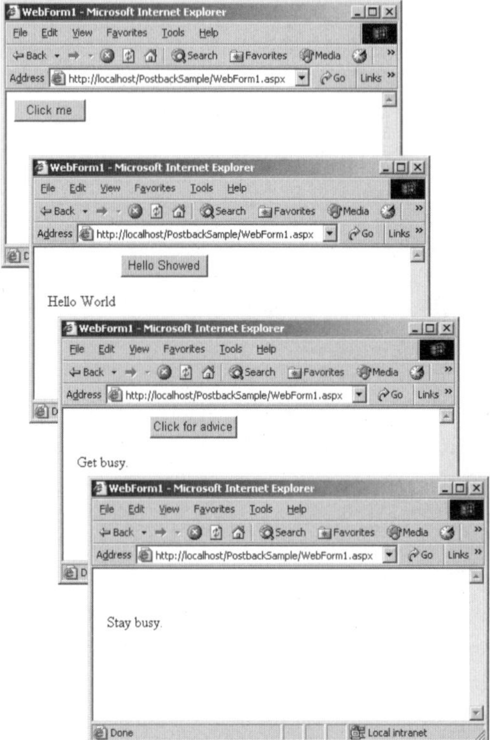

Figure 11-5. A single Web page, WebForm1.aspx in the PostbackSample project, presents four different appearances depending on the state of the Web page and the controls on it.

Figure 11-6 shows the Design view of WebForm1.aspx in the PostbackSample project. Notice that it contains two buttons and a label (*Label1*). I dragged the size of *Button2* so that it is slightly wider than *Button1*. If you ever programmed with ASP, you'll appreciate how remarkable the simplicity of the page is. Notice specifically that no code is mixed in with the page.

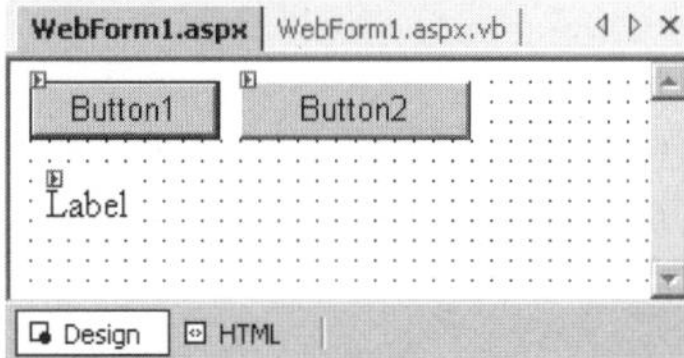

Figure 11-6. The Design view of the Web page that appears in the four different states shown in Figure 11-5.

Because the layout for the Web page is so basic, the control of the page's appearance must be in the logic of the code behind the page. Before focusing on the specific code behind the page, I want to introduce the *IsPostback* property for a page. This property tells the server whether the page is loading initially or as the result of the user clicking a control on the page that sends the page back to the server. If the *IsPostback* property is *False*, the page is opening initially. If the *IsPostback* property is *True*, the page is being sent back to the server by the user clicking on a control. The logic of the PostbackSample application takes advantage of the *IsPostback* property to help control the appearance of the Web page.

The following listing shows the three event procedures managing the appearance of WebForm1.aspx in the PostbackSample project. The listing commences with the *Page_Load* event procedure. This procedure fires each time the page opens—whether initially or otherwise. However, within the *Page_Load* event, different code executes depending on the value of the *IsPostback* property and the *Text* property setting for *Button2*. If the *IsPostback* property is *False*, the procedure makes three property assignments that make the page appear like the top window in Figure 11-5. The *ElseIf* and *Else* clauses for the *If* statement handle cases in which the Web page returns to the server after opening initially. The *ElseIf* clause specifically handles the case in which a page returns to the server with the *Button2 Text* property equal to "Hello Showed". If the page returns to the server with a different value for the Button2 *Text* property, the *If* statement routes control to the *Else* clause.

The *Button1_Click* event fires when the user clicks *Button1*. There is only one chance to do this because the *Click* event procedure makes the button invisible. In addition, the procedure assigns "Hello World" and "Hello Showed" as values to the *Text* property for *Label1* and *Button2*, respectively.

The *Button2_Click* event procedure can fire in either of two circumstances, and it needs to respond differently to each case. Therefore, it uses an *If...Then...ElseIf* statement to control which statement to execute. When *Label1* shows "Get busy.", the procedure changes the *Text* property for *Button2* to "Click for advice". If the label shows "Stay busy.", the *ElseIf* clause operates to make *Button2* invisible.

```
Private Sub Page_Load(ByVal sender As System.Object, _
    ByVal e As System.EventArgs) Handles MyBase.Load
    'If it is a first-time presentation, then
    'set like WebApplication1, or
    'if it is a postback with Hello Showed button,
    'then change message to Get busy, or else
    'change message to Stay busy.
    If IsPostBack = False Then
        Button1.Text = "Click me"
```

```
        Button2.Visible = False
        Label1.Text = ""
    ElseIf IsPostBack = True And _
        Button2.Text = "Hello Showed" Then
        Label1.Text = "Get busy."
    Else
        Label1.Text = "Stay busy."
    End If
End Sub


Private Sub Button1_Click(ByVal sender As System.Object, _
    ByVal e As System.EventArgs) Handles Button1.Click

    'Make label say Hello World.
    Label1.Text = "Hello World"

    'Make Text for Button2 read Hello Showed and
    'make Button2 visible.
    Button2.Text = "Hello Showed"
    Button2.Visible = True

    'Make Button1 invisible.
    Button1.Visible = False

End Sub


Private Sub Button2_Click(ByVal sender As System.Object, _
    ByVal e As System.EventArgs) Handles Button2.Click
    'If Label1 says Get busy, show Button2
    'with a Text property of Click for advice,
    'else make Button2 invisible.
    If Label1.Text = "Get busy." Then
        Button2.Text = "Click for advice"
    ElseIf Label1.Text = "Stay busy." Then
        Button2.Visible = False
    End If

End Sub
```

A Multifunction Calculator Web Page

One of the truly cool features of forms on pages in ASP.NET is that the property values for controls persist between round-trips to the servers. The preceding sample didn't highlight this feature because the whole point of that sample was to show how to change the values of controls on successive round-trips to the server. This sample, the WebCalculator project, takes advantage of automatic persistence of control property values during the round-trip from a browser to a Web server and back again. If you did much ASP coding, you may recall that it was necessary to write code if you wanted controls to display the same values on the way back from a server as on the way up to a server.

The WebCalculator project highlights the automatic persistence of control values by letting users enter values in two text boxes. When the user clicks one of four buttons for a type of arithmetic between the values appearing in the text boxes, the page goes off to the server. The procedures for performing the arithmetic work directly with the *Text* property for the text box controls on the Web page. In other words, the values pass to the server via the text box controls. With traditional HTML forms, the values pass to the server as name and value pairs. The name represents the control name, and the value represents the entry in the control. If values need to appear in a page when it returns to a browser from a server on a traditional HTML form, you must write code to reassign the values to controls on the page the server sends back to the browser.

The WebCalculator project is a four-function calculator. Each function has its own button with a *Text* property setting representing the type of calculation it performs—namely, +, –, *, and /. Users enter values in the first two text boxes on the Web page. Users access this project by navigating to WebCalculator.aspx in the WebCalculator project. When I first created the project, ASP.NET assigned WebForm1.aspx as the stat page name for the project. However, I revised the name to WebCalculator.aspx in Solution Explorer using the technique described previously. When the page goes to the server, it performs the calculation denoted by the button a user clicks. A simple event procedure for each button handles this. Each of the event procedures for the four buttons calls another procedure that formats the value returned to the browser in the third text box on the page. This formatting procedure assigns a color to the text box *ForeColor* property based on the value returned and makes the font bold.

Figure 11-7 shows the WebCalculator project working for a pair of values in the first and second text boxes. The top window shows the WebCalculator.aspx page before a user clicks one of the four function buttons. Notice that the user entered values in the first and second text boxes (–2.2 and 3.3). The third text box is empty. The bottom window shows the page that returns from the Web server after the user clicked the bottom button on the form with a *Text* property equal to /. In the bottom window, the application populates the third text box with the quotient of –2.2 divided by 3.3. The text box displays the result to single-precision accuracy. Because the value is negative, it appears in red within the browser window. In addition, the value in the third text box appears in a bold font.

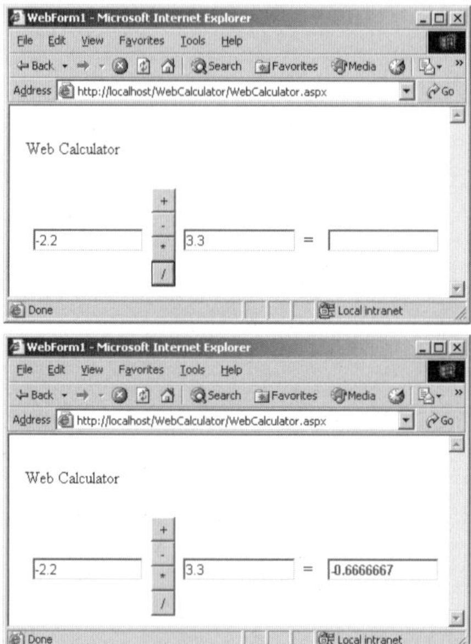

Figure 11-7. The WebCalculator.aspx page before and after a trip to the Web server. The user invoked the round-trip to the server by clicking the bottom button (/).

The buttons on the page have *ID* property settings of Button1 through Button4 from the top button to the bottom button. The core of the application is the event procedures behind each of these buttons. The module for the page starts by declaring a single-precision variable named *sgn1*. This variable stores the result of the calculation performed on the contents of *TextBox1* and *TextBox2*. Because the module declares *sgn1* as a *Single* data type and its input values are converted from a *String* data type to a *Single* data type, the result of the arithmetic computation has a single data type. However, the *Text* property of *TextBox3* requires a *String* data type. Therefore, the assignment of *sgn1* to a *Text* property invokes the *ToString* method to convert a numeric value to a string.

Each of the *Click* event procedures for the buttons invokes the *ColorTextInTextBox3* procedure. This procedure has an *If* statement with *Then*, *ElseIf*, and *Else* clauses. The *If* statement assigns one of three colors to *TextBox3* based on the value in *sgn1*. Positive values result in a *ForeColor* property assignment for *TextBox3* of green. Negative values lead to a red *ForeColor* property assignment. If the *sgn1* value is 0, the procedure assigns black as the foreground color for *TextBox3*. No matter what color the procedure assigns to the *ForeColor* property for *TextBox3*, the procedure concludes by making the font bold.

```
Dim sgn1 As Single
Private Sub Button1_Click(ByVal sender As System.Object, _
    ByVal e As System.EventArgs) Handles Button1.Click

    'Add text boxes.
    sgn1 = CSng(TextBox1.Text) + CSng(TextBox2.Text)
    TextBox3.Text = sgn1.ToString
    ColorTextInTextBox3()

End Sub


Private Sub Button2_Click(ByVal sender As System.Object, _
    ByVal e As System.EventArgs) Handles Button2.Click

    'Subtract text boxes.
    sgn1 = CSng(TextBox1.Text) - CSng(TextBox2.Text)
    TextBox3.Text = sgn1.ToString
    ColorTextInTextBox3()

End Sub


Private Sub Button3_Click(ByVal sender As System.Object, _
    ByVal e As System.EventArgs) Handles Button3.Click

    'Multiply text boxes.
    sgn1 = CSng(TextBox1.Text) * CSng(TextBox2.Text)
    TextBox3.Text = sgn1.ToString
    ColorTextInTextBox3()

End Sub


Private Sub Button4_Click(ByVal sender As System.Object, _
    ByVal e As System.EventArgs) Handles Button4.Click

    'Divide text boxes.
    sgn1 = CSng(TextBox1.Text) / CSng(TextBox2.Text)
    TextBox3.Text = sgn1.ToString
    ColorTextInTextBox3()

End Sub


Sub ColorTextInTextBox3()
```

```
    'Assign forecolor to TextBox3 based on result value.
    If sgnl > 0 Then
        TextBox3.ForeColor = Drawing.Color.Green
    ElseIf sgnl < 0 Then
        TextBox3.ForeColor = Drawing.Color.Red
    Else
        TextBox3.ForeColor = Drawing.Color.Black
    End If

    'Make font bold to highlight assignment.
    TextBox3.Font.Bold = True

End Sub
```

A Multifunction Calculator in a Table

All the samples in this chapter to this point display Web pages in a Microsoft Internet Explorer browser. I tested the pages with the Internet Explorer 5 and Internet Explorer 6 browsers. However, many visitors browse Internet sites with non–Internet Explorer browsers. I am the Webmaster at *www.ProgrammingMSAccess.com*, a site that caters to the interests of Microsoft Access, Microsoft SQL Server, and Visual Basic developers. This site explicitly targets the interests of those loyal to Microsoft products, and it has done this for about four years as I write this chapter. Nevertheless, about 15 percent of the visitors to the site browse pages with a Netscape browser. The overwhelming majority of the Netscape browser sessions are conducted with a Netscape 4.x browser.

As stated previously, I fully believe in supporting one browser. My personal preference is for the most recent version of the Internet Explorer browser because it provides the latest features from a proven software leader—Microsoft. When developing intranet and extranet solutions, you can mandate a single browser for the solution. When developing Internet solutions, the guidelines for deciding which browser (or how many browsers) to support can be more complex because you cannot mandate that users browse your site with a specific browser. Therefore, for Internet solutions, you have at least a couple of options. First, you can prominently state in browser-neutral text that a page is optimized for one browser. If users want to view the page, they can install the browser for which the page is optimized. Second, you can develop different pages for different browsers. This section illustrates the second approach with the sample from the preceding section.

In deciding whether to prepare multiple versions of a page for different browser types, the first step is to view the page in all the target browsers that you plan to support. For example, Figure 11-8 shows the WebCalculator.aspx page in a Netscape 4.01 browser. Notice that the page doesn't look like the windows in Figure 11-7. The primary reason for the divergence in appearance is that the Netscape browser doesn't support absolute positioning. ASP.NET uses this feature to enable the positioning of controls on a Web page with drag-and-drop techniques.

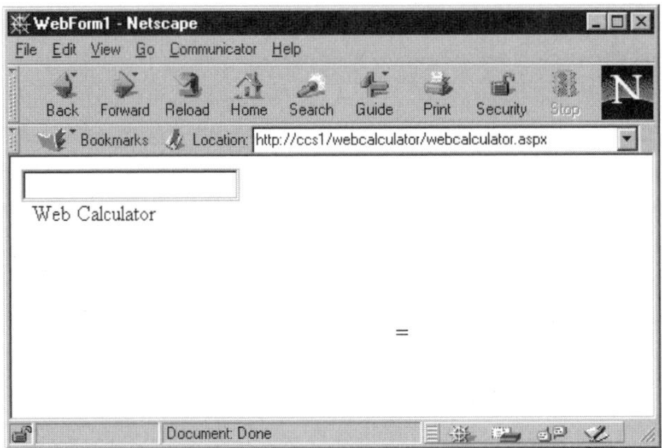

Figure 11-8. The WebCalculator.aspx page in a Netscape 4.01 browser.

Many traditional Web developers have experience using tables to position controls on a Web page. When you position controls by placing them inside table cells, you don't need to rely on absolute positioning control property settings to designate the location of a control on a form. By using a table instead of absolute position control settings, you can develop a page that is much more likely to appear similar in both Internet Explorer and Netscape browsers. The trick to achieving similar results in different browsers by positioning controls in tables is to set the *pageLayout* property to FlowLayout. Recall that this setting causes content to appear on a Web page in the flow pattern of a word processor instead of the classic Visual Basic drag-and-drop style.

I built another version of the WebCalculator.aspx page in the WebCalculator project to demonstrate the steps for creating a calculator in a table. Start by creating a new Web page in the WebCalculator project. Choose Project, Add Web Form from the Visual Studio main menu in Design view. In the Add New Item dialog, choose the Web Form template, name the new Web page WebCalculatorInTable.aspx, and click Open. If you are using the same project and you want to duplicate my steps, name the new Web page something else, for example, MyWebCalculatorInTable.aspx. Set the *pageLayout* property for the document to FlowLayout (as described in the "ASP.NET Design Interfaces" section).

Add a table with four columns and three rows to the WebCalculatorInTable.aspx Web page. Start by choosing Insert and then Table from the Table menu. Set the Columns box to 4 and click OK on the Insert Table dialog box, leaving the default setting of 3 for the Rows box. Next embed a new table in the second column of the original table's third row. The embedded table should have one column of four rows with a width of 27 pixels. After positioning the cursor where you want the embedded table, choose Table, Insert, Table. Set the Rows box to 4 and the Columns box to 1. Assign 27 to the Width box. Then click OK.

Next copy the text box and button controls from the WebCalculator.aspx page to the WebCalculatorInTable.aspx page. You can also copy the label with a *Text* property of "Web Calculator". Arrange the layout so that it looks like Figure 11-9. I achieved this look with a sequence of copy-and-paste operations from the WebCalculator.aspx page to the WebCalculatorInTable.aspx page. No other operations were necessary.

> **Note** I purposely excluded the equal sign (=) before the third text box to simplify the steps and eliminate the possibility of an invisible character causing alignment problems. If you are reasonably experienced at editing HTML code, you can add the equal sign in the HTML view.

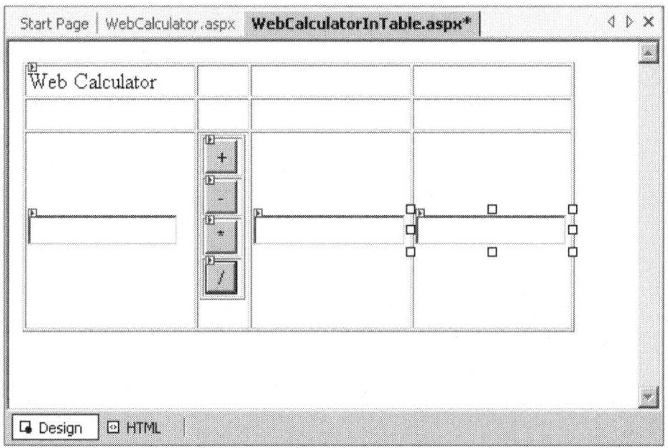

Figure 11-9. The WebCalculatorInTable.aspx page in Design view after adding the third text box to the table on the page.

Next add the code behind the WebCalculator.aspx page to the module behind the WebCalculatorInTable.aspx page. Start by copying the *sgn1* variable declaration, the four event procedures, and the sub procedure that appear in the preceding sample from the module behind the WebCalculator.aspx page. See the "ASP.NET Design Interfaces" section for how to open the module behind a Web page. Then open the module behind the WebCalculatorInTable.aspx page. Paste the copied code over the default version of the *Page_Load* event procedure because this procedure isn't necessary for the current sample. Now that you have composed the page, compile and view it from Visual Studio by right-clicking the page in Solution Explorer and choosing Build And Browse. This will allow you to verify the look and test the operation of the calculator.

Figure 11-10 shows WebCalculatorInTable.aspx in both Internet Explorer and a Netscape browser. The Internet Explorer browser appears in the top window. As you can see, the WebCalculatorInTable.aspx page looks about the same as its predecessor, WebCalculator.aspx, in the Internet Explorer browser. The major difference is that you can see the overall table border and the border for all populated cells.

The Netscape browser view of the WebCalculatorInTable.aspx page appears in the bottom window of Figure 11-10. This version of a calculator page in the Netscape browser is a huge improvement from the result with the WebCalculator.aspx page. First, you can see the calculator. Second, the calculator generates numeric results that are identical to those from the calculator in Internet Explorer. However, there are some formatting differences. Notice that the calculator buttons vary in size depending on the width of the arithmetic symbol on the button. For example, the plus sign (+) is wider than the division sign (/). As a consequence, the control for the plus sign is wider. The Internet Explorer browser view of the page recognizes the width setting (24 pixels) for the buttons so that all buttons have the same width. In addition, the Netscape browser doesn't modify the color of the third text box based on the value appearing within it. This is because the code used to manipulate the color depends on proprietary ASP.NET property settings.

Experienced Web developers will argue that I could have worked around both of the distinctions between the two browsers using more elaborate HTML coding. While this may be so, one major benefit of ASP.NET is that it insulates Visual Basic developers from doing much HTML coding when they are building their Web solutions. Taking away this benefit in the interest of browser-neutral applications can regress Web application code development to the spaghetti-coding styles common in some ASP application code. At the very least, achieving browser-neutral code will drive down the efficiency of the Visual Basic developers on a project as they ramp up the HTML learning curve. If the coding efficiency of your development team and powerful solutions are important, you should definitely consider adopting a browser that helps your developers code Web solutions efficiently. As I said before, I recommend the latest version of the Internet Explorer browser.

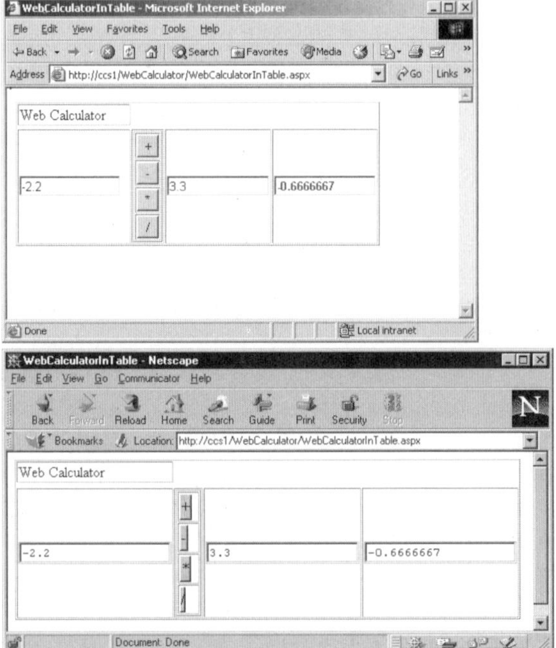

Figure 11-10. The WebCalculatorInTable.aspx page appearing in an Internet Explorer browser (top window) and a Netscape browser (bottom window).

Sniffing the Browser

For very high priority projects, such as e-commerce sites and sites that need to serve hundreds of thousands of visitors a day, it may be necessary to detect browsers so that the site can return pages optimized for the specific browser type making a request. In such situations, ASP.NET developers can use the *Browser* property of the *Request* object. The *Browser* property returns the *Browser* object, which, in turn, has a series of properties that enable your applications to "sniff," or detect, the browser type as well as its capabilities. Search for the "HttpBrowserCapabilities Class" topic in Visual Studio .NET Help for detailed documentation on the properties of the *Browser* object.

When you design a program to detect the browser in the code behind a Web page, there is typically no need to provide a user interface on the Web page. The whole point of the code behind the page is to direct the user to another page, which is optimized for a specific kind of browser. This redirection should happen almost instantaneously. The page doing the detecting directs a user to a page that has an interface optimized for the user's browser. You can use the *Redirect* method of the ASP.NET *Response* object to transfer control to another page. The *Redirect* method takes a string containing a URL for its argument.

The sample for this section demonstrates the syntax for detecting the browser type. It is likely that you will need a more complex program if your needs necessitate browser detection (for example, a program that can detect more than two broad categories of browser brands), but this sample illustrates how to get started with browser detection. The sample transfers control to either of the two pages, both of which are in the WebCalculator project. (See the preceding two sections.) The Web page performing the detecting has the name MyWebCalculator.aspx in the SniffBrowser project. This Web page can be blank. The page executes on the server, and it doesn't appear in browsers. The code behind the page presents the URL that is the argument of a *Redirect* method for a *Response* object.

The following listing shows the sole procedure behind the MyWebCalculator.aspx page. When a user navigates to the page, the *Page_Load* event procedure looks at the first two characters of the browser name. The *Type* property for the *Browser* object returns the name and major version number of the browser type originating a request. If the browser's name begins with *IE*, control transfers to the WebCalculator.aspx page in the WebCalculator project on the ccs1 Web server. Otherwise, control goes to the WebCalculatorInTable.aspx page in the WebCalculator project on the ccs1 Web server. Therefore, a Netscape browser and an Internet Explorer browser both navigating to the MyWebCalculator.aspx page in the SniffBrowser project will navigate ultimately to different pages.

> **Note** You will need to replace the ccs1 Web server name in the code for the MyWebCalculator.aspx page. Replace ccs1 with the name of a Web server hosting the application in your computing environment.

```
Private Sub Page_Load(ByVal sender As System.Object, _
    ByVal e As System.EventArgs) Handles MyBase.Load

    If Left(Request.Browser.Type, 2) = "IE" Then
        Response.Redirect _
            ("http://ccs1/WebCalculator/WebCalculator.aspx")
    Else
        Response.Redirect _
```

```
            ("http://ccs1/WebCalculator/" & _
            "WebCalculatorInTable.aspx")
    End If
End Sub
```

Session State Management

The HTTP protocol on which you build ASP.NET solutions doesn't retain information about Web pages between successive round-trips from the browser to the server. Therefore, ASP.NET offers various solutions for conveying information about prior visits to a Web server. Microsoft uses the term *session state management* to describe the context of a visit by a Web page to a Web server. This context can include such items as information about the last visit, the sum of all previous visits, and the identity of the visitor. This section introduces a collection of samples that demonstrates selected session state management techniques with a general overview of session state management solutions strategies.

Overview of Session State Management Issues

In Web applications, Web servers don't typically retain data on a page between round-trips; this is because of the servers' use of the HTTP protocol. Therefore, on two separate round-trips from a browser to a server, the server has no built-in way to determine whether the page is from the same user. This stateless characteristic of Web pages is one important reason why a single Web server can handle a large number of requests from many different users. On the other hand, your Web applications will typically need to work around the stateless characteristic of Web pages so that Web servers can "remember" information about a session with a user from one request to the next.

There are two basic approaches to maintaining the state of a session between round-trips of a page to a Web server. First, you can store information on the browser's computer and pass it on a Web page to the Web server. This approach improves scalability by relieving the Web server of handling this session state data. The drawback of this approach is that information that you pass on a Web page is available to be read by unauthorized individuals while the page is in transit between a browser workstation and the Web server. Second, you can store information on a Web server or another computer to which the Web server has access. You can normally specify variables and maintain values associated with them over the life of a session or an application. There are advantages to each approach (Session or Application variables), but Session variables are more commonly used in many practical Web development projects.

Server-Side Session State Management

You can think of Application variables as global variables that permit multiple users of an application to share access to data on a single Web server. While multiple users can access an Application variable, these variables are visible only to users running that application on the server used to create the variable. Use Application variables for frequently used values that don't change often. Application variables have a lifetime associated with the duration of an application. When an application shuts down, the variable values, which reside in memory, are lost. If you need to persist the values beyond the lifetime of an application, consider saving the variables to a storage medium at periodic intervals. Because multiple users have access to Application variables, it is important to minimize conflicts between users. Such conflicts can slow an application.

Session variables allow the tracking of variable values within a session for an application on a Web server. With these variables, your applications can maintain separate sets of values for each user of an application. Because your applications maintain separate values for each user, there is no issue of conflicts between users. Therefore, you can use Session variables in situations that require frequent updates for individual users.

You can store Session variables in process on a Web server as in ASP. In addition, you can store Session variables out of process on a stand-alone remote Windows server, such as Windows 2000 Server, or on a SQL Server instance. These latter two options are an ASP.NET innovation. The ability to store Session variables out of process allows Session variables to have a scope that extends across multiple Web servers running an application or even restarts of a Web server. See the "SessionStateMode Enumeration" topic in the Visual Studio .NET documentation for details on setting the mode for a Session variable in the code behind a Web page. By default, Session variables are in process. This in-process setting yields superior performance, although it doesn't extend the scope in the same way that out-of-process storage does.

Client-Side Session State Management

There are four approaches to session state management with client-side tools. These are cookies, hidden variables, query strings, and view state. View state is a new option introduced with ASP.NET.

Cookies are primarily an identification technology. Web applications can read cookies residing on a browser's workstation to determine who the user is and customize the interface based on a knowledge of the user's identity or membership in a group. For example, you can expose users to IT books instead of electronics products if the users previously implicitly or explicitly expressed a preference for seeing IT books. Cookies are versatile because they can contain information specific to a user, session, or client. One especially significant weakness of cookies is that users can configure their browsers not to store them. Therefore, your application cannot count on their availability. Another weakness of cookies is their susceptibility to tampering because they reside on a user's hard drive.

Query strings are name and value pairs appended to the end of a URL. These name-value pairs can contain information about anything, including the state of a session, such as a userid value. You must specifically assign the "get" setting to the *method* attribute for a form on a Web page to pass variables via a query string. Query strings are particularly useful for exchanging information between Web pages—even if the Web pages belong to different applications. Because query strings reside at the end of a URL, they offer no security. Query strings are available to the originating and destination computers as well as to anyone who can view the HTTP header for a page as it hops between computers from an originating computer to a destination computer. In addition, the maximum number of characters is often restricted to 255. However, query strings are a fast and easy technique to implement for situations in which you need to exchange a relatively small amount of session state information across multiple applications and where security isn't a critical issue.

Hidden fields offer a traditional technique for exchanging data between a Web page and a Web server so that the field value isn't rendered on the Web page. You must specifically assign the "post" setting for the *method* attribute of a Web page's form to pass variables via a hidden field. Although a hidden field isn't rendered on a Web page, it is still readily available if you view the HTML for the page in a text editor. The term *hidden* merely reflects the fact that the field doesn't appear on a Web page in a browser.

View state is an innovation introduced with ASP.NET for exchanging information between a Web page and a Web server. ASP.NET applications routinely store information about the controls on a Web page in a view state field for the page. Microsoft enables ASP.NET developers to take advantage of this built-in field. The view state field on a Web page updates at both the browser and Web-server sides of a page's round-trip. View state variables, including the built-in ones and your custom ones, are converted to strings, hashed, and stored in a hidden field on the Web page. Therefore, values have some encrypting, but the data is available for tampering (and decrypting). As with the other client-side techniques for maintaining state, this technique doesn't consume any server-side resources. In addition, the syntax is similar to the syntax for specifying Session variables. Therefore, ASP developers who are familiar with techniques for using Session variables can apply similar techniques for taking advantage of custom view state variables.

Using a Session Variable

The first session state management sample illustrates the use of Session variables. This sample is also interesting because it reveals how to use a ListBox control to create a simple shopping cart application. The sample exists as WebForm1.aspx and WebForm1.aspx.vb in the SessionVariableSample project. As is normal with ASP.NET applications, there is another folder with the SessionVariableSample.sln file. Open the .sln file in its folder to examine the solution with Visual Studio .NET.

Web Page Layout and Operation

The WebForm1.aspx layout consists of three buttons, a pair of text boxes, a list box, and three labels—one label for each text box and a third label for the Web page. Figure 11-11 shows the Design view of WebForm1.aspx.

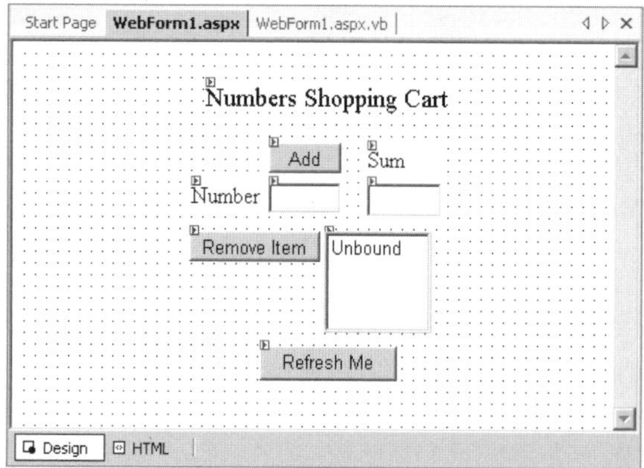

Figure 11-11. Design view of WebForm1.aspx in the SessionVariable-Sample project.

Button1, *Button2*, and *Button3* have text property settings of "Add", "Remove Item", and "Refresh Me", respectively. Each of these buttons has a *Click* event procedure in the code behind the Web page. The operation of these event procedures interacts with the entries in the two text boxes and the list box on the Web page. The text box next to the label showing "Number" is *TextBox1*, and the other text box on the page is *TextBox2*. The *ID* property setting for the ListBox control is *ListBox1*.

Entering a number in *TextBox1* and clicking *Button1* (Add) transfers the value from *TextBox1* to the bottom entry in *ListBox1*. In addition, clicking *Button1* updates the value in *TextBox2*, which shows a running sum of the values in *ListBox1*. Repeatedly entering values in *TextBox1* and clicking *Button1* populates a "shopping cart" of numbers in the list box. The list box shows up to four numbers at a time. If the user adds a fifth number to the bottom of the list box control, a scroll bar appears. This lets users expose any contiguous four numbers in the list.

The *Click* event procedure for *Button2* (Remove Item) allows a user to drop an item from the list. The user starts to remove an item by selecting the item in the list box. Next she clicks *Button2*. After removing the selected item, the procedure also updates the running sum of the values in the ListBox control.

Clicking the Refresh button on a browser (not the Refresh Me button on the page) doesn't generate the typical result of a blank form you might expect. Instead, Internet Explorer displays a dialog box that says, in part, that the page cannot be refreshed without resending the information. When the browser sends the information, the server repeats the last operation, which can be either an addition to or a subtraction from the running sum showing in *TextBox2*. However, the entries in *ListBox1* don't change in a corresponding way. As a result, *ListBox1* and *TextBox2* come out of synchronization. In contrast, clicking *Button3* (Refresh Me) clears all control values. It is for this reason that *Button3* is on the form. Clicking this button clears all the controls on the form as well as the running sum that the application maintains with a Session variable.

Figure 11-12 shows the SessionVariableSample application in operation just before a click of *Button1* in the top window and before a click of Button2 in the bottom window. In the top window, two items are in the list box. A third item, with the value 6, is ready for entry just as soon as the user clicks *Button1*. The bottom window shows the Web page just before an item is removed from the shopping cart that the list box shows. *ListBox1* contains five items, four of which appear in the window. The fifth can be viewed by scrolling to it. The sum of all the items is 81 (see the value in *TextBox2*), and the sum of the items appearing in the ListBox control is 80 (2 + 6 + 18 + 54). Therefore, the ListBox control value not displayed must be 1. In any event, clicking Button2 with 6 selected in the list box drops this value from the list box so that just four numbers are in the list and reduces the quantity appearing in *TextBox2* to 75.

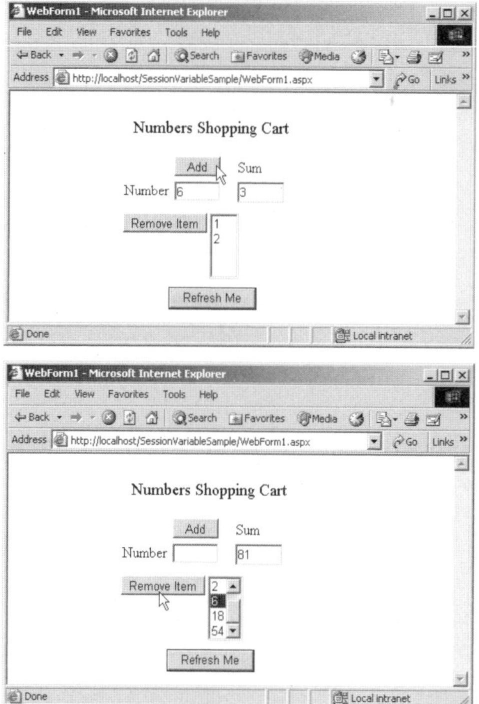

Figure 11-12. WebForm1.aspx in the SessionVariableSample project in operation just before adding and dropping a number from the list box.

Program Listing for the SessionVariableSample Project

The code behind the Web page in Figure 11-11 consists of four event procedures and a module-level variable declaration (*str1*). The variable declared at the module level appears in a couple of event procedures. In addition, the sample shows the syntax for managing a Session variable named *sum*. Because the value for the *sum* Session variable appears on the form as the *Text* property, you don't strictly need the Session variable to manage the behavior for the Web page. However, using a Session variable to control the value in a text box makes it easy to visualize how the Session variable behaves in the application.

The *Page_Load* event procedure appears first in the code listing, and it fires before any of the other three event procedures in the listing. Within the *Page_Load* event procedure is an *If…Then…Else* statement. The condition for the *If* statement is an expression that is *True* when the page loads for the first time in a session. In this case, the statement executes the statements in the *Then* clause. These statements initialize the form for first-time use. For the majority of the times that the event procedure fires, the *Page_Load* event procedure will pass control to the statements in the *Else* clause. The two statements in this path save the *Text* property setting of *TextBox1* in *str1* and clear the contents of the text box for the next time that it appears in the browser.

After executing the *Page_Load* event procedure, the code behind the page will typically execute one of the remaining three event procedures. That's because clicking any button on the Web page automatically sends the page back to the server. The only time that the *Page_Load* event procedure fires without a user clicking a button is on the first time that a user navigates to the WebForm1.aspx page in the SessionVariableSample project.

When the user clicks *Button1*, three actions take place. First, the *Button1_Click* event procedure adds the value in *str1* to the end of the list of items in *ListBox1*. Recall that the *Else* clause in the *Page_Load* event procedure copies the *Text* property value of *TextBox1* into the *str1* variable. Next the procedure adds to the *sum* Session variable the single value representing the string that was in *TextBox1* when it came to the server. This creates a new running sum. The *Click* event procedure for *Button1* concludes by saving the *sum* Session variable value as a string in the *Text* property of *TextBox2*.

The *Button2_Click* event procedure handles the removal of an item from the list box. As you can see, this is a slightly more complex process. First the procedure saves the selected item from the list box into *sng1*, a *Single* variable. Then the procedure updates the running sum, but this time it reduces the running sum instead of increasing it. Before concluding, the event procedure needs to perform two related tasks. The first of these is the removal of the item that the user selected from the list in the list box. The procedure uses the *RemoveAt* method for *ListBox1* with an integer value argument (*int1*) pointing to the selected item. The second task is the clearing of the selected item from the list box. Assigning –1 to the *SelectedIndex* property of *ListBox1* accomplishes this task.

I mentioned during the review of how the SessionVariableSample operates that the browser's Refresh button generates undesired results. Therefore, the application includes its own refresh button, labeled Refresh Me, as *Button3*. The *Button3_Click* event procedure blanks both text boxes, clears the list box, and sets the *sum* Session variable to 0. This event procedure truly refreshes the Web page for a new start—just as if the page had initially loaded.

```
Dim str1 As String
Private Sub Page_Load(ByVal sender As System.Object, _
    ByVal e As System.EventArgs) Handles MyBase.Load

    If Not IsPostBack Then
        'If new page, initialize text boxes and
        'sum Session variable (optional step that is
        'not strictly necessary since these are
```

(continued)

```
            'default startup values).
            TextBox1.Text = ""
            TextBox2.Text = ""
            Session("sum") = 0
        Else
            'If postback, save value showing in
            'TextBox1 and clear the control.
            str1 = TextBox1.Text
            TextBox1.Text = ""
        End If
    End Sub


    Private Sub Button1_Click(ByVal sender As System.Object, _
        ByVal e As System.EventArgs) Handles Button1.Click

        'Add number that was in TextBox1 into ListBox1,
        'compute a new sum of items in ListBox1 in a
        'Session variable and show variable value
        'in TextBox2.
        ListBox1.Items.Add(str1)
        Session("sum") += CSng(str1)
        TextBox2.Text = CStr(Session("sum"))

    End Sub


    Private Sub Button2_Click(ByVal sender As System.Object, _
        ByVal e As System.EventArgs) Handles Button2.Click

        Dim int1 As Integer
        Dim sng1 As Single

        'Identify value for item marked for removal.
        int1 = ListBox1.SelectedIndex
        sng1 = CSng(ListBox1.Items(int1).Value)

        'Reduce Session variable sum by item value
        'and display new sum in TextBox2.
        Session("sum") -= sng1
        TextBox2.Text = CStr(Session("sum"))

        'Remove item marked for removal.
        ListBox1.Items.RemoveAt(int1)

        'Clear ListBox1 selected item.
        ListBox1.SelectedIndex = -1

    End Sub
```

```
Private Sub Button3_Click(ByVal sender As System.Object, _
    ByVal e As System.EventArgs) Handles Button3.Click

    'Refresh form with blank field and session values.
    If TextBox1.Text <> "" Then TextBox1.Text = ""
    TextBox2.Text = ""
    ListBox1.Items.Clear()
    Session("sum") = 0

End Sub
```

Using a View State Variable

Using a view state variable is similar from a coding perspective to using a Session variable. However, conceptually and operationally there are some very significant differences. This section will explore all three areas (coding, conceptual, operational) so that you know how to use view state variables as well as what happens when you use them.

The major conceptual difference between using a view state variable and a Session variable is that the view state variable resides on the Web page, while the Session variable typically resides in the memory of the Web server. While the view state variable is an example of client-side technology, the Session variable is a server-based variable. The view state variable is on the Web page for each round-trip of a Web page between a browser and a Web server. The Session variable resides on the Web server (or even another server, such as a Windows server or SQL Server instance). This means that you must keep the amount of data that you pass with a view state variable to a manageable size because passing a large amount of data can lengthen the duration of a round-trip. Because a Session variable exists on a Web server, you can have a relatively large Session variable on the server and copy only a small portion of it to a Web page on successive round-trips. For example, the server can hold all orders or all products in a Session variable representing a data set. However, any given round-trip of a page between a browser and server can show just the orders for one customer or the products in one category. Because a view state variable doesn't have this flexibility, it will have to send all the data back and forth on each round-trip or draw a fresh collection of data from a database server on each round-trip. However, when you have a small amount of data for which to maintain the state, the view state variable places lower demands on a Web server and can increase the number of users that a Web server can service effectively.

The sample for the view state variable resides in the WebForm1.aspx and WebForm1.aspx.vb files of the ViewStateSample project. WebForm1.aspx has a layout that is identical to that of the file of the same name in the SessionVariableSample project. When you have a form layout that is the same in two projects, you can copy an excerpt from the HTML view for the project created first to the HTML view for the second project. This speeds development time, and it ensures that the two forms will be exactly the same in both projects. In this case (and indeed most cases), the appropriate excerpt is the HTML between the *form* and */form* tags.

Because the syntax for using view state variables is so similar to the syntax for Session variables, you can start to create the code behind the form for the ViewStateSample project by copying the code behind the Web page in the SessionVariableSample project. Then all you have to do is to perform an edit that transforms all instances of `Session("sum")` to `ViewState("sum")`. This results in a change to just a few lines, which I made boldface in the following listing to make them easy to detect. Notice that the syntax for using *ViewState* to designate a view state variable directly parallels the syntax for using *Session* to denote a Session variable.

```
Dim str1 As String
Private Sub Page_Load(ByVal sender As System.Object, _
    ByVal e As System.EventArgs) Handles MyBase.Load

    If Not IsPostBack Then
        'If new page, initialize text boxes and
        'sum ViewState variable (optional step that is
        'not strictly necessary since these are
        'default startup values).
        TextBox1.Text = ""
        TextBox2.Text = ""
        ViewState("sum") = 0
    Else
        'If postback, save value showing in
        'TextBox1 and clear the control.
        str1 = TextBox1.Text
        TextBox1.Text = ""
    End If
End Sub


Private Sub Button1_Click(ByVal sender As System.Object, _
    ByVal e As System.EventArgs) Handles Button1.Click

    'Add number that was in TextBox1 into ListBox1,
    'compute a new sum of items in ListBox1 in a
    'ViewState variable and show variable value
    'in TextBox2.
    ListBox1.Items.Add(str1)
    ViewState("sum") += CSng(str1)
    TextBox2.Text = CStr(ViewState("sum"))

End Sub
```

```
Private Sub Button2_Click(ByVal sender As System.Object, _
    ByVal e As System.EventArgs) Handles Button2.Click
    Dim int1 As Integer
    Dim sng1 As Single

    'Identify value for item marked for removal.
    int1 = ListBox1.SelectedIndex
    sng1 = CSng(ListBox1.Items(int1).Value)

    'Reduce ViewState variable sum by item value
    'and display new sum in TextBox2.
    ViewState("sum") -= sng1
    TextBox2.Text = CStr(ViewState("sum"))

    'Remove item marked for removal.
    ListBox1.Items.RemoveAt(int1)

    'Clear ListBox1 selected item.
    ListBox1.SelectedIndex = -1

End Sub


Private Sub Button3_Click(ByVal sender As System.Object, _
    ByVal e As System.EventArgs) Handles Button3.Click

    'Refresh form with blank field and state values.
    If TextBox1.Text <> "" Then TextBox1.Text = ""
    TextBox2.Text = ""
    ListBox1.Items.Clear()
    ViewState("sum") = 0
End Sub
```

Just as the syntax of using a view state variable is similar to that of using a Session variable, so is the result of running WebForm1.aspx in ViewStateSample similar to that of running WebForm1.aspx in SessionVariableSample. Both versions of WebForm1.aspx add items to and remove items from *ListBox1* in the same way during normal operation. In addition, clicking the browser's Refresh button while viewing WebForm1.aspx in the ViewStateSample project raises the same dialog box about how the page cannot be refreshed without resending the information. However, with the view state variable, the *Text* property for *TextBox2* doesn't come out of synchronization with the items in *ListBox1*. The running sum text box display remains unchanged after the refresh, as do the items in the list box. This is an improvement over the Session variable that generates an error in response to a click of the browser's Refresh button. On the other hand, the browser's Refresh button doesn't cause the Web page to revert to values as if the page had opened initially. Therefore, there is still a need for

Button3 with a *Text* property of "Refresh Me" because this button restores the initial values to the Web page.

Using the *QueryString* Property to Identify a User

A query string is a name and a matching value pair that appears at the end of a URL. A question mark delimiter separates the end of the URL and the first query string name-value pair. An equal sign (=) divides the name from its matching value within a query string. The URL, the ? delimiter, and the query string appear in the HTTP header. You can see the HTTP header in the Address box of the Internet Explorer browser. ASP.NET will automatically generate a collection of query strings for a Web page that it sends to a Web server if you set the *method* attribute for the page's form to "get". You make this attribute assignment from the HTML view for the page in the .aspx file.

When you send a page to a Web server with a *method* attribute of "get" for the page's form, controls on the form with a single value, such as text boxes and buttons, will appear as individual members of the query string collection after the URL. Each member appears in the query string with a name equal to the *ID* property for the control and a value equal to the *Text* property for the control. For example, if you have a text box with an *ID* property of UserID and a *Text* property of MyUserID, the UserID text box appears in the collection string for the URL header as UserID=MyUserID. In addition, ASP.NET sends a *__VIEWSTATE* member in the query string collection to the Web server. The *__VIEWSTATE* member is the accumulation of all the property values for all controls on a page. This query string collection member corresponds to the view state for a form. Recall that property values in the view state are encrypted with a hashing algorithm.

On a Web server, your applications can recover the members of the query string collection with the *QueryString* property for the ASP.NET *Request* object. Before accessing the query string members, you will typically deposit the collection into a *NameValueCollection* object. This object is explicitly designed to store structures in the form of a query string collection. You can access individual elements within a *NameValueCollection* object by member name or index value. The ASP.NET documentation refers to the member names for a query string collection as key names. The collection of all member names is the return value from the *AllKeys* property of the *NameValueCollection* object storing a query string collection.

Sample Layout Design and Operation

Now that you have a grasp of the principles for using a query string collection with ASP.NET, let's look at a specific sample to demonstrate the application of query strings. Figure 11-13 shows a form in Design view with three text boxes, a button, and some labels. The form is on the WebForm1.aspx page in the QueryStringSample project. The page's form contains the elements for a typical login form. The top two text boxes have the *ID* property values UserID and Password. The *TextMode* setting for the Password text box control is Password. This setting creates a single-line text box that masks user input. In addition, the Password setting for the *TextMode* property clears the *Text* property of a text box on return from a Web server. The form for WebForm1.aspx in the QueryStringSample project has the *method* attribute "get". As mentioned previously, this attribute setting sends the control names and values to the Web server as a query string collection in the HTTP header for the Web page.

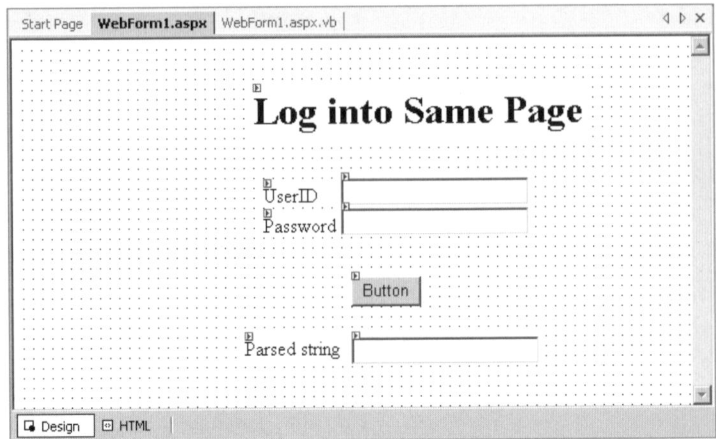

Figure 11-13. A Design view of WebForm1.aspx in the QueryStringSample project.

When the user clicks the button, which has the name *Button1*, the page with its form goes to the Web server. The combination of the *Page_Load* event procedure and the *Button1_Click* event procedure extracts and displays the values for the UserID and Password text boxes in the query string collection for the page's HTTP header. On the initial load, both text boxes are empty. If a user populates these text boxes and clicks *Button1*, the event procedure for the button's *Click* event concatenates the values from the UserID and Password text boxes with a comma delimiter and displays the result in the third text box at the bottom of the form.

Figure 11-14 displays WebForm1.aspx from the QueryStringSample project in operation. In the top window, you see a value in the UserID text box and asterisks across the Password text box to indicate a masked entry. Also, notice that the Address box in the browser shows just the URL for the page in the QueryStringSample project on the local Web server. After the user clicks the button in WebForm1.aspx, the page returns the UserID and Password text box entries in the text box at the bottom of the form. The bottom window shows that the password for a UserID value of MyUserID is MyPassword.

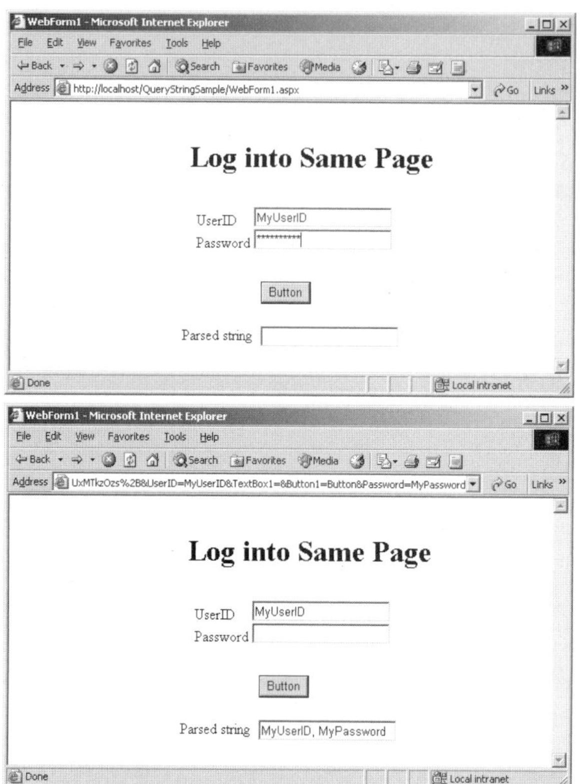

Figure 11-14. The WebForm1.aspx page from the QueryStringSample project in operation.

If you look at the Address box in the bottom window within Figure 11-14, you see an excerpt from the HTTP header that WebForm1.aspx sends to the Web server when a user clicks the button on the Web page. The following HTTP header value shows the full entry in the Address box. I broke the line at each major divider. For example, the HTTP header starts with the URL for WebForm1.aspx in the QueryStringSample project. A ? signals that a query string collection follows the URL. The first query string that appears is the name and value for the *__VIEWSTATE* member. In order, the HTTP header shows the member names and values for UserID, TextBox1, Button1, and Password. UserID and Password are the key names for the top two text boxes on the form. TextBox1 is the name for the third text box at the bottom of the page. Notice that there is no value for this query string member. This is because the HTTP header shows the control values as they travel from the browser to the Web server, and the Web server assigns a value to TextBox1 based on the UserID and Password query string member values.

```
http://localhost/QueryStringSample/WebForm1.aspx?
__VIEWSTATE=dDwxNTM3ODQyNzc7Oz4%3D&
UserID=MyUserID&
TextBox1=&
Button1=Button&
Password=MyPassword
```

Code Behind the Page

The following listing shows the code behind WebForm1.aspx in the QueryStringSample project. The listing begins with module-level declarations for *struserid* and *strpassword*. These two string values are populated in the *Page_Load* event procedure and displayed by the *Button1_Click* event procedure.

The *Page_Load* event procedure starts with a declaration for *col1* as a *NameValueCollection* object. The object belongs to the *System.Collections.Specialized* namespace. By using the namespace as a prefix to the *NameValueCollection* item in the namespace, I eliminate the need for an *Imports* statement at the top of the module. Next the procedure declares two variable-length string arrays: one for the query string key names (*passedkeys*) and another for the query string values (*passedvalues*). Actually, the procedure will use the *passedvalues* array as a scalar, that is, an array with a count of one element. The last declaration in the *Page_Load* event procedure is for an integer value (*int1*) that serves as an index value for the array members in the *passedkeys* array.

After the declarations, the procedure starts working on the query string collection. The first step is to pass the query string collection to *col1*. Next the procedure takes the collection of key names in *col1* and saves it in *passedkeys*. Then the procedure performs a loop from 0 through 1 less than the count of elements in the *passedkeys* arrays. The *GetUpperBound* method with an argument of 0 automatically returns the count of array elements less 1. This loop enumerates the members of the *passedkeys* array. When the loop detects a *passedkeys* array value with a name of either UserID or Password, the code saves the corresponding value from *col1* in the first element of the *passedvalues* array. Then a *Select Case* statement sorts out whether the key is a userid or a password and assigns the *passedvalues* element to an appropriately named string value. At the conclusion of the *Page_Load* event procedure, the *struserid* and *strpassword* strings contain the *Text* property settings for the UserID and Password text boxes at the time the page left the browser. If the user clicked *Button1*, the *Button1_Click* event procedure concatenates these two strings and assigns them to the *Text* property of *TextBox1*.

```
Dim struserid As StringDim strpassword As String

Private Sub Page_Load(ByVal sender As System.Object, _
    ByVal e As System.EventArgs) Handles MyBase.Load

    'Declare query string parsing variables.
    Dim coll As _
        System.Collections.Specialized.NameValueCollection
    Dim passedkeys(), passedvalues() As String
    Dim int1 As Integer

    'Use QueryString property of Request object to pass
    'query string to coll, a NameValueCollection variable, and
    'return all key names to passedkeys string array.
    coll = Request.QueryString
    passedkeys = coll.AllKeys

    'Loop through keys and get value for
    'UserID and Password keys.
    For int1 = 0 To passedkeys.GetUpperBound(0)
        If passedkeys(int1) = "UserID" Or _
            passedkeys(int1) = "Password" Then
            passedvalues = coll.GetValues(int1)
            Select Case passedkeys(int1)
                Case "UserID"
                    struserid = passedvalues(0)
                Case "Password"
                    strpassword = passedvalues(0)
            End Select
        End If
    Next int1
End Sub


Private Sub Button1_Click(ByVal sender As System.Object, _
    ByVal e As System.EventArgs) Handles Button1.Click

    'Populate TextBox1 with UserID and Password text values.
    TextBox1.Text = struserid & ", " & strpassword

End Sub
```

Using Query Strings Across Pages

The preceding sample showed how to use a page's query string collection to pass information to that page. You can use this sample to track and selectively show information on a page depending on the state of the userid. You can use the preceding sample as a starting point for an application that returns with a form showing orders for a customer or 401(k) distributions by an employee. Another common use for query strings is to pass information between pages. The sample in this section (based on the Page1QSPage2 project) shows how you can accomplish this as a simple extension of the logic from the preceding sample.

Figure 11-15 shows the Page1QSPage2 sample in operation. This sample starts with the WebForm1.aspx page in the Page1QSPage2 project. You can see the page in the top window of Figure 11-15. As you can see, the page includes a pair of text boxes, a button, and three labels. The two text boxes and the button are excerpted from the HTML for the preceding sample. However, in this case control doesn't return to the same page when the user clicks the button. Instead, control passes to WebForm1.aspx in the Page2 project. The bottom window in Figure 11-15 shows the second page.

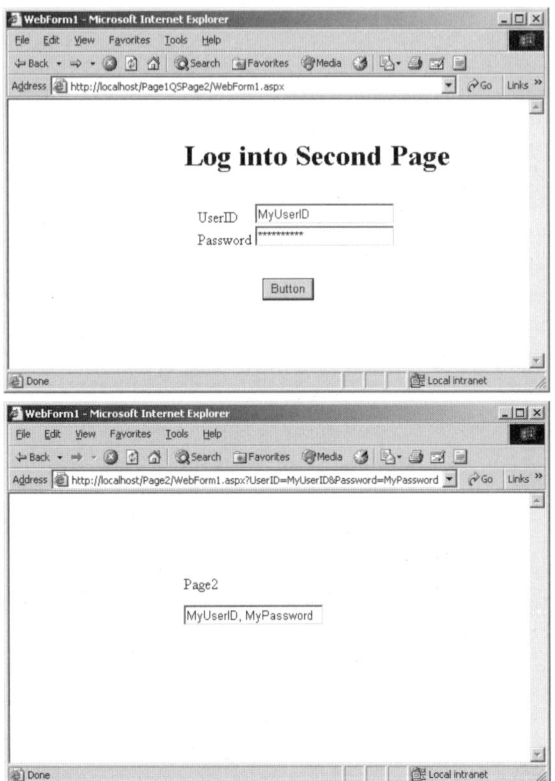

Figure 11-15. The Page1QSPage sample lets a user pass values from WebForm1.aspx in the Page1QSPage2 project to WebForm1.aspx in the Page2 project.

The sample uses a query string appended to the end of the URL for WebForm1.aspx in the Page2 project. By selecting name-value pairs for specific controls into the query string collection, you make the HTTP header shorter. This reduces the transport time. It also shortens the enumeration time through the query string collection because the only items in the query string are those you put there for the task.

Two techniques are especially critical to making this sample work. First, your application must construct a string based on a URL and a query string collection. Second, your application must navigate to the URL in the string so that the query string members can pass to the other page designated by the URL.

Before reviewing the code, you may benefit from a quick review of the string syntax for a URL with an appended query string collection. Start with *http://*. Follow this with the URL for the target page. For example, you might enter localhost/Page2/WebForm1.aspx. Append a question mark (?) to the end of the URL. Then follow the first query string member name with an equal sign (=). Conclude the query string definition by adding the value for the query string member. If the query string collection has another member, trail the query string value with an ampersand (&). Repeat the process for as many additional query string members as necessary.

The next listing shows the code behind WebForm1.aspx in the Page1QSPage2 project. It consists of two event procedures: *Page_Load* and *Button1_Click*. All the *Button1_Click* event procedure does is send the page to the Web server from the browser. The *Page_Load* event procedure constructs the string with the URL and the appended query string collection. As you can see, the code implements the rules for constructing a query string at the end of a URL. Once the string is available as *str1*, the *Page_Load* event procedure invokes the *Redirect* method for the *Response* object to navigate to the URL and pass the appended query string collection to another page (the one designated in the URL).

```
Private Sub Page_Load(ByVal sender As System.Object, _
    ByVal e As System.EventArgs) Handles MyBase.Load
    'Put user code to initialize the page here.
    If IsPostBack Then
        Dim str1 As String = _
            "http://localhost/Page2/WebForm1.aspx" & _
            "?UserID=" & UserID.Text & _
            "&Password=" & Password.Text
        Response.Redirect(str1)
    End If
End Sub
```

```
Private Sub Button1_Click(ByVal sender As System.Object, _
    ByVal e As System.EventArgs) Handles Button1.Click
    'Just causes a postback to the server.
End Sub
```

The code behind WebForm1.aspx in the Page2 project is a simple adaptation of the code from the preceding sample. The *Page_Load* event procedure does all the work in this case because it the sole purpose of WebForm1.aspx in the Page2 project to display the query string member values passed to it—namely, a userid and password. However, you can readily adapt the sample to do something with the userid and password passed to the page.

```
Dim struserid As StringDim strpassword As String

Private Sub Page_Load(ByVal sender As System.Object, _
    ByVal e As System.EventArgs) Handles MyBase.Load

    'Declare query string parsing variables.
    Dim coll As _
        System.Collections.Specialized.NameValueCollection
    Dim passedkeys(), passedvalues() As String
    Dim int1 As Integer

    'Use QueryString property of Request object to pass
    'query string to coll, a NameValueCollection variable, and
    'return all key names to passedkeys string array.
    coll = Request.QueryString
    passedkeys = coll.AllKeys

    For int1 = 0 To passedkeys.GetUpperBound(0)
        If passedkeys(int1) = "UserID" Or _
            passedkeys(int1) = "Password" Then
            passedvalues = coll.GetValues(int1)
            Select Case passedkeys(int1)
                Case "UserID"
                    struserid = passedvalues(0)
                Case "Password"
                    strpassword = passedvalues(0)
            End Select
        End If
    Next int1

    'Populate TextBox1 with UserID and Password text values.
    TextBox1.Text = struserid & ", " & strpassword

End Sub
```

Data on Web Pages

Although working with data on a Web page with ASP.NET is more involved than in a Windows form, the process is still vastly simpler than with classic ASP methods. Your database development projects will still gain the ASP.NET benefits derived from isolating code from page layout. In addition, once you master the ADO.NET techniques for managing data in Windows forms, it's just a slight extrapolation to extend those techniques for use with Web pages. This section starts with an overview of some defining issues for using data on Web pages. The section then moves on to cover four sample applications that illustrate typical kinds of problems that you may want to include in your Web/database applications. First you learn how to create and program a parent-child form. Next the focus shifts to techniques for browsing through data on a Web page. The third sample presents two procedures for creating database objects on a SQL Server instance from a Web page. The section closes with a sample that reveals how to perform all three classic data manipulation tasks from a Web page.

Managing Database Solutions with ASP.NET

Using a SQL Server database with ASP.NET introduces a special set of issues that build on your core understanding of ADO.NET and SQL Server. Web pages in an ASP.NET solution travel back and forth regularly between a browser and a Web server. This simple fact raises the question of where you store the data for your ASP.NET solution—on the Web server, the Web page, or the browser workstation. A related question is how much of a SQL Server database at any one instant do you store in your ASP.NET solution—possible answers are one row, a whole table, or several related tables. Figure 11-1 in this chapter's first section illustrates some of these issues graphically by portraying the flow of data on a Web page.

The samples that I present all store their data on the Web page. This is suitable for cases in which there is a relatively small amount of data to transport between the browser and the Web server. If a solution needs more data, there are several strategies for handling this. For example, you may be able to implement a strategy that successively works with small subsets of a larger data source. You can then create these small subsets as your application needs them from the SQL Server database. If a solution requires a large data store locally, you must store it on the Web server or browser workstation. This introduces a need for special data access and retrieval techniques as well as security procedures for the local data store.

Another kind of special issue pertaining to the use of data in ASP.NET solutions follows from the fact that you are likely to use Web server controls on a Web page instead of Windows Forms controls on a Windows form. Displaying data through these two different sets of controls in distinct containers doesn't work identically, just as ADO.NET data binding doesn't work identically for all controls on a Windows form.

Before closing this introduction, I want to remind you that using Web solution strategies doesn't magically relieve the developer of needing to know about ADO.NET and SQL Server. For example, if you want to update data, you will likely need a data adapter and a data set on the Web page. In addition, you can improve the performance of your solutions by using stored procedures instead of uncompiled SQL statements. Also, you may find that your solutions can benefit from designing and populating custom tables. It may even be useful to enable this functionality dynamically from within your ASP.NET solution. The following samples in this section will illustrate how to dynamically create database objects from within your ASP.NET solutions.

Populating ListBox and DataGrid Controls

One of the most common data applications lets users choose from one control so that they determine the data appearing in one or more other controls. The sample in this section lets a user choose from a list box to determine the subset of data that appears in a data grid. The list box value has a parent relationship with the values appearing in the data grid. Both the list box and the data grid derive their values from a SQL Server database through *SqlConnection* and *SqlDataAdapter* objects. This sample also describes the *AutoPostBack* property, which is a special ListBox control property for ASP.NET applications.

Web Page Layout and Operation

The sample exists as WebForm1.aspx in the ListToGrid project. Figure 11-16 shows the Design view of WebForm1.aspx. Four controls appear on the page. These are a list box, a text box, a button, and a data grid. In addition, two ADO.NET controls, a *SqlConnection* object and a *SqlDataAdapter* object, appear in the system tray at the bottom of the page. These latter two controls don't appear on the Web page, but they are available for use by the code behind the page. By graphically creating the two ADO.NET controls on the page, you save having to write the code to declare and instantiate the objects.

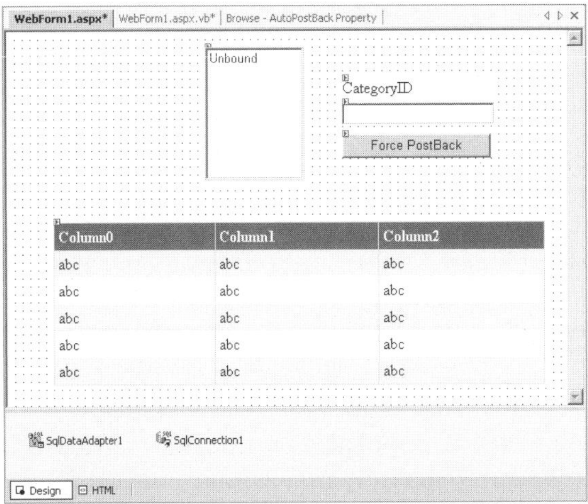

Figure 11-16. A Design view of WebForm1.aspx in the ListToGrid project.

Use the Data tab on the Toolbox to drag the *SqlDataAdapter* to the Web page. After you finish interacting with its wizard, Visual Studio .NET will automatically create a *SqlConnection* object. This sample connects to the Northwind database. See Chapter 1 for more details of the steps for adding *SqlDataAdapter* and *SqlConnection* objects graphically. The sample in this section uses the following SQL string to specify the rowset that the data adapter will eventually load into a data set. The sample application ultimately assigns the data set to the *DataSource* property of the DataGrid control.

```
SELECT ProductID, ProductName, CategoryID, UnitPrice, UnitsInStock,
UnitsOnOrder, Discontinued FROM Products
```

The names for all the controls on the page end with a 1 appended to the name of the type of control. For example, the list box, button, and *SqlDataAdapter* controls are respectively *ListBox1*, *Button1*, and *SqlDataAdapter1*. Because there is just one item for each type of control, the sample discussion refers to individual controls by the control's type name.

Notice that no data appears in any of the controls. The *DataSource* properties for the ListBox and DataGrid controls don't have design-time assignments. You can set the *DataSource* properties for these controls either at design time or at run time. One advantage to assigning the *DataSource* property at run time is that you can make the assignment dynamic depending on other factors. For example, the sample sets the *DataSource* property for the DataGrid control based on the selection in the ListBox control. You can also use a Session state variable, determined by any of the techniques described earlier in this chapter, to contribute to the specification of the *DataSource* property for the ListBox and DataGrid controls.

The ListBox control has its *AutoPostBack* property set to *True* in the Properties dialog box. The property allows selections from a list box to post back immediately to the Web server. In many Web applications, immediately posting a selection from a list box to a Web server isn't necessary. Therefore, the default setting for this property is *False*. In addition, the property doesn't work unless Active Scripting is enabled for a browser. Because enabling the Active Scripting feature can expose a browser to a security violation, some browser users may elect to disable the feature (Active Scripting). For this reason, the sample offers a button. By clicking the button, users can force a postback of the Web page to the Web server. By posting back the selection from the list box one way or the other, the Web server is able to dynamically set the *DataSource* property for the DataGrid control based on the most recent selection from the ListBox control.

> **Note** You can manually control the operation of the Active Scripting feature from the Internet Options dialog box in an Internet Explorer 5 or later browser. Select Internet Options from the Tools menu, and then select the Security tab. Click Custom Level to bring up the Security Settings dialog box. Scroll down to Active Scripting under Scripting. Then select Disable, Enable, or Prompt depending on your preference for how you want the feature to operate. Click OK twice to exit the Security Settings and Internet Options dialog boxes.

The list box displays the category names and stores the *CategoryID* values from the *Categories* table in the Northwind database. When a user selects a category name, the list box highlights the selection. The text box displays the corresponding *CategoryID* value for the selected category name in the list box. The list box doesn't draw on the same data source as the DataGrid. The sample programmatically creates a *SqlCommand* object and then uses the *ExecuteReader* method to populate the list box based on the *SqlCommand* object's *CommandText* property.

Figure 11-17 shows the WebForm1.aspx Web page in operation immediately after the selection of the Produce category. Because I ran this sample on a computer with its Active Scripting feature disabled, it was necessary to click the button to update the DataGrid control so that it showed products for the Produce category. A user can change the products appearing in the DataGrid control by selecting another category in the list box and clicking the button. If the browser's Active Scripting feature is enabled, changing the selection in the list box will automatically cause the products in the data grid to be revised without a need to click the button.

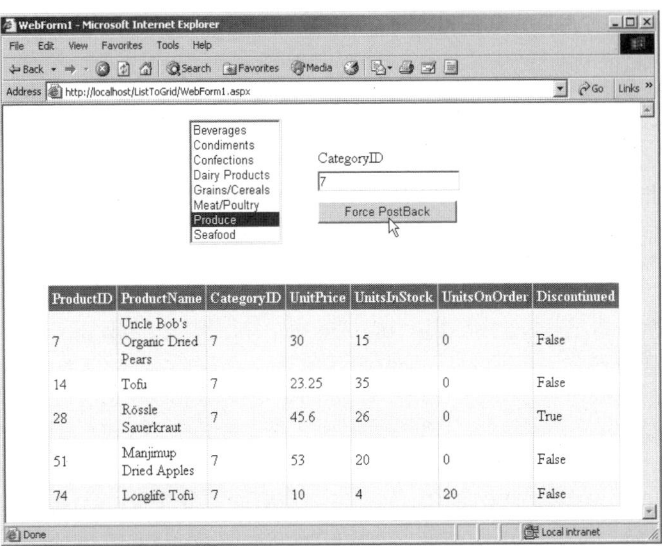

Figure 11-17. WebForm1.aspx in the ListToGrid project immediately after a selection and click of the button.

Code Behind the Web Page

The code behind the Web page handles the management of the database connectivity for the controls on the page. The code achieves this task by complementing and extending the ADO.NET objects in the system tray as well as by creating ADO.NET objects. All the code behind the page resides in the *Page_Load* event procedure, but two other event procedures play pivotal roles in the application, although they contain no code.

The *Button1_Click* event procedure is a backup procedure for sending the Web page to a Web server. The primary vehicle for sending the Web page to a Web server after the user makes a selection from the list box is the *ListBox1_SelectedIndexChanged* procedure. Recall that I set the *AutoPostBack* property for the list box to *True* at design time. Therefore, the page goes to the server after each selection from the list box, provided the user's browser enables the Active Scripting feature. If this feature is turned off (or not available because a browser doesn't support it), a user can still send the page to the Web server by clicking the button. Neither procedure has any code within it. The only function of the procedures is to send the page to the Web server.

The *Page_Load* event procedure is triggered the first time a user opens WebForm1.aspx in the ListToGrid project. The *Page_Load* event procedure also fires on each subsequent visit to the Web server no matter which of the other two event procedures initiates the visit. The code inside the *Page_Load* event procedure includes an *If...Then* statement that executes one block of code during only the first visit to the Web server within a session—that is, when *Not (Me.IsPostBack)* is *True*—as well as another code block that fires on each subsequent page visit.

The code block that executes only when *Not (Me.IsPostBack)* is *True* populates the ListBox control with two columns from the *Categories* table. This block begins by declaring and instantiating the *SqlCommand1* object and assigning to a *CommandText* property setting a SQL query that returns all the columns from all the rows in the *Categories* table. The use of the *ExecuteReader* method in an assignment statement designates the *Category* table as the *DataSource* property for *ListBox1*. The assignment of *CategoryName* to the *DataTextField* property determines the column of values *ListBox1* shows. When a user selects a category name, *ListBox1* saves a matching value from its *DataValueField* property setting. Therefore, the assignment of *CategoryID* to the *DataValueField* property designates that *ListBox1* save a *CategoryID* value that matches whatever category name a user selected. Invoking the *DataBind* method ties the *DataSource* setting to *ListBox1* for the duration of the setting. Before exiting the *Then* clause, the *If...Then* statement selects the first item appearing in *ListBox1*, which corresponds to the category name Beverages and the *CategoryID* value 1.

Immediately after exiting the *Then* clause or even if the clause doesn't execute, the procedure assigns a value to *TextBox1* that equals *ListBox1*'s *SelectedIndex* property value plus 1, which is the same as *SelectedItem* (the selected *CategoryID* value). On the initial page load for a session, *TextBox1* will show the value 1 because the *Then* clause sets the *SelectedIndex* property to 0. Otherwise, the computed value appearing in *TextBox1* will match the *CategoryID* for whatever item a user selected most recently from *ListBox1*.

The balance of the *Page_Load* event procedure aims to populate DataGrid1. The process of populating the DataGrid control starts by declaring and instantiating a new *DataSet* object (*ds1*) and filling it with the data source specified by the SQL statement for *SqlDataAdapter1*. This data source includes a subset of the columns from the Products table, but it includes all the rows. Because the application calls for the DataGrid control showing just a subset of the rows that depends on the most recently selected item from *ListBox1*, *ds1* isn't an appropriate data source for *DataGrid1*. This is the reason that the procedure declares and instantiates a *DataView* object (*dav1*). The filter for *dav1* is the set of rows from *ds1* that have a *CategoryID* column value matching

(ListBox1.SelectedIndex + 1).ToString, which is an expression that returns the *CategoryID* for the most recently selected item in the list box. After computing *dav1*, the procedure concludes by assigning it to the *DataSource* property for DataGrid1. Finally the procedure concludes by invoking the *DataBind* method for DataGrid1. Without this step, the *DataSource* property for DataGrid1 would not update to show the most recently selected item from *ListBox1*.

```
'This procedure depends on drag-and-drop instantiation
'of SqlConnection1 and SqlDataAdapter1 for selected
'columns from the Products tables in the northwind database.
Private Sub Page_Load(ByVal sender As System.Object, _
    ByVal e As System.EventArgs) Handles MyBase.Load

    If Not (Me.IsPostBack) Then

        'Setup SqlCommand1 with SqlConnection1 for ListBox1.
        Dim SqlCommand1 As New SqlClient.SqlCommand()
        SqlCommand1.CommandText = "SELECT * FROM Categories"
        SqlCommand1.Connection = SqlConnection1
        SqlConnection1.Open()

        'Assign CategoryName and CategoryID to ListBox1.
        ListBox1.DataSource = SqlCommand1.ExecuteReader()
        ListBox1.DataTextField = "CategoryName"
        ListBox1.DataValueField = "CategoryID"
        ListBox1.DataBind()
        SqlConnection1.Close()

        'Select first item in ListBox1.
        ListBox1.SelectedIndex = 0
    End If

    'Assign to ListBox1 Selected item + 1,
    'which is the same as CategoryID value.
    TextBox1.Text = (ListBox1.SelectedItem).ToString

    'Fill Products data table from northwind database.
    Dim ds1 As New DataSet()
    SqlDataAdapter1.Fill(ds1, "Products")

    'Specify filter for dav1 based on selected
    'item in ListBox1.
    Dim dav1 As New DataView(ds1.Tables("Products"))
    Dim strFilter As String
    strFilter = "CategoryID = " & _
        (ListBox1.SelectedIndex + 1).ToString
    dav1.RowFilter = strFilter
```

```
    'Assign dav1 as data source for DataGrid1 and
    'bind source to data grid.
    DataGrid1.DataSource = dav1
    DataGrid1.DataBind()

End Sub


Private Sub ListBox1_SelectedIndexChanged( _
    ByVal sender As System.Object, _
    ByVal e As System.EventArgs) _
    Handles ListBox1.SelectedIndexChanged
    'AutoPostBack setting of True will generate event
    'if Active Scripting is enabled.
End Sub


Private Sub Button1_Click( _
    ByVal sender As System.Object, _
    ByVal e As System.EventArgs) _
    Handles Button1.Click
    'Force postback if AutoPostBack setting of True
    'does not operate.
End Sub
```

Navigating Text Boxes Through a Data Set

Another popular database application enables browsing of a set of records with a set of navigator buttons that let users move to the next or previous row as well as the first and last row. The sample for this section (WebForm1.aspx in the NavTextBoxes project) demonstrates how to build that kind of functionality into a Web page while taking advantage of the *SqlConnection* and *SqlDataAdapter* objects from the previous sample.

One special addition to the design of this sample is another ADO.NET object, the *Ds1* data set, in the system tray. See Figure 11-18 for the appearance of the *Ds1* data set object in the Design view of the Web page for the sample. Recall that you can graphically create ADO.NET objects at design time. Then your code can refer to them. If you don't need the dynamic functionality associated with programmatically declaring and instantiating objects or you just feel uncomfortable with coding the objects, consider adding the objects at design time. Creating objects at design time can also benefit Web applications by reducing the programming in the *Page_Load* event procedure. This reduction can cause pages to load faster. To create a data set after you have a *SqlDataAdapter* already on a Web page is straightforward. Select the *SqlDataAdapter* in the system tray. In the Properties window, click the Generate Dataset hyperlink below the list of *SqlDataAdapter* properties. Select the New radio button in the Generate Dataset dialog box if it isn't already selected. Then type a name for the data set. Click OK to complete the creation of the data set.

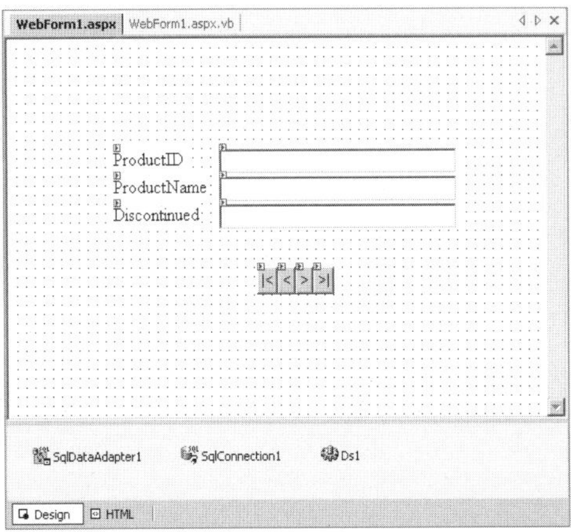

Figure 11-18. A Design view of WebForm1.aspx in the NavTextBoxes project. Notice that it shows a data set object (*Ds1*) as well as two other ADO.NET objects (*SqlDataAdapter1* and *SqlConnection1*).

> **Note** Creating a data set graphically displays it in the system tray for the Design view of a Web page. However, the data set isn't populated with values. You must programmatically fill the data set just as if you had created it in a program.

The operation of this sample is straightforward. Figure 11-19 shows the Web page layout. The page has three text boxes, one for each of the column values from the Products table that the page shows. Recall that the *SqlDataAdapter* object for the prior sample uses a SQL statement that extracts selected columns from the Products table in the Northwind database, including the three that appear in Figure 11-19. The four buttons below the text boxes enable navigation. From left to right, the buttons move to the first row, the previous row, the next row, and the last row. When the page opens initially, it shows the first row in the Products table. The *ProductID* column contains values 1 through 77, which run successively from the first row to the last row. I navigated to the 74th row by clicking the last row button and then clicking the previous row button three times.

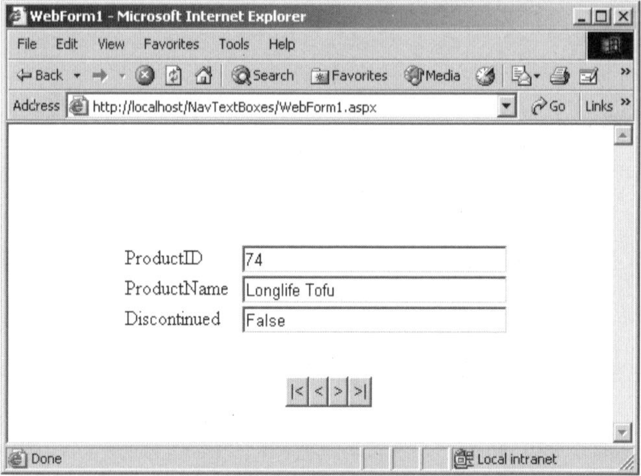

Figure 11-19. WebForm1.aspx in the NavTextBoxes project after opening the page, clicking the last row button (>|), and then clicking the previous row button (<) three times.

I didn't set the *ReadOnly* property for the text boxes to *True*. (The default setting is *False*.) As a consequence, users can edit the value in a text box. However, the change doesn't persist between round-trips to the Web server, for at least a couple of reasons. First, the text boxes don't bind to the values that they show. The text box controls work as controls on an unbound form. Therefore, a change to a value in a text box is just that. The value in the text box doesn't tie directly to an underlying source of rows. Even if the text boxes did bind to the data set on the Web page, there is a second reason why the changes won't persist between round-trips to the server. The Web server refreshes the data set on each round-trip. This unbound characteristic of text boxes and the volatile nature of a data set on Web pages is an important difference between text boxes on Windows forms and text boxes on Web pages. Recall from Chapter 10 that on Windows forms it is common to bind text boxes to a local, persistent data set.

The code behind WebForm1.aspx in the NavTextBoxes project appears next. You can see that the *Page_Load* event procedure starts by filling the *Ds1* data set. This repopulates the *Products* data table in the *Ds1* data set on each round-trip to the server. Therefore, users get a fresh look at any changes to the *Products* table in the Northwind database made by other users or a central updating program. Next the *Page_Load* event procedure checks to see whether the page is loading initially. For the first-time load of the Web page in a session, the event procedure sets *Session("MyRowID") = 0* and calls the *MoveToRow* sub procedure. The *MyRowID* Session variable maintains the state for the last row viewed in the *Products DataTable.* Initially, this row should be 0 for the first row in the *Products DataTable.*

The call to the *MoveToRow* procedure populates the text boxes with values from the row specified by the *MyRowID* Session variable. First the procedure declares and instantiates a *DataRow* object (*MyRow*) based on the row in the *Products DataTable* specified by the *MyRowID* Session variable. Next the procedure selects and converts, if appropriate, a column value from *MyRow* for each of the text boxes on the Web page.

The *Click* event procedures for *Button1* through *Button4* enable navigation through the rows of the *Products* data table. *Button1* corresponds to the leftmost button on the Web page, and *Button2* through *Button4* match each successive button on the page. Each *Click* event procedure calls the *MoveToRow* procedure but first updates the value of the *MyRowID* Session variable according to the function of the button clicked, as described here:

- *Button1*, which navigates to the first row, sets the *MyRowID* Session variable to 0.
- *Button2* moves to the previous row in the *Products DataTable.* The event procedure for this button checks to see whether the current value of the *MyRowID* Session variable is greater than 0. If so, the procedure reduces the *MyRowID* Session variable value by 1. Otherwise, the procedure leaves the *MyRowID* Session variable at the value 0, which corresponds to the first row in the *Products DataTable.*
- *Button3*, which moves to the next row, checks to see whether the current value of the *MyRowID* Session variable corresponds to less than the last row in the *Products DataTable.* If the current value is less, the procedure adds 1. Otherwise, the procedure leaves the *MyRowID* Session variable pointing to the last row in the *Products DataTable.*
- *Button4* sets the *MyRowID* Session variable to point to the last row in the *Products DataTable.*

```
Private Sub Page_Load(ByVal sender As System.Object, _
    ByVal e As System.EventArgs) Handles MyBase.Load

    'Fill Ds1 Products data table in Ds1.
    SqlDataAdapter1.Fill(Ds1, "Products")

    'On initial page load move to first row and
    'populate text boxes.
```

```
    If Not Me.IsPostBack Then
        Session("MyRowID") = 0
        MoveToRow()
    End If

End Sub


Sub MoveToRow()
    'Specify selected row based on Session("MyRowID").
    Dim MyRow As DataRow
    MyRow = Ds1.Tables("Products").Rows(Session("MyRowID"))

    'Assign value from selected row to TextBox1.
    Dim str1 As String = CStr(MyRow(0))
    TextBox1.Text = str1

    'Assign value from selected row to TextBox2.
    str1 = MyRow(1)
    TextBox2.Text = str1

    'Assign value from selected row to TextBox3.
    str1 = CStr(MyRow(6))
    TextBox3.Text = str1

End Sub


Private Sub Button1_Click(ByVal sender As System.Object, _
    ByVal e As System.EventArgs) Handles Button1.Click

    'Move to first row and populate text boxes.
    Session("MyRowID") = 0
    MoveToRow()

End Sub

Private Sub Button2_Click(ByVal sender As System.Object, _
    ByVal e As System.EventArgs) Handles Button2.Click

    'Move to previous row and populate text boxes.
    If Session("MyRowID") > 0 Then
        Session("MyRowID") -= 1
    End If
    MoveToRow()

End Sub
```

(continued)

```
Private Sub Button3_Click(ByVal sender As System.Object, _
    ByVal e As System.EventArgs) Handles Button3.Click

    'Move to next row and populate text boxes.
    If Session("MyRowID") < _
        Ds1.Tables("Products").Rows.Count - 1 Then
        Session("MyRowID") += 1
    End If
    MoveToRow()

End Sub


Private Sub Button4_Click(ByVal sender As System.Object, _
    ByVal e As System.EventArgs) Handles Button4.Click

    'Move to last row and populate text boxes.
    Session("MyRowID") = Ds1.Tables("Products").Rows.Count - 1
    MoveToRow()

End Sub
```

Creating Database Objects from Web Pages

Your applications will sometimes need the availability of custom database objects. For example, stored procedures, which store precompiled, optimized SQL code, are great for managing data manipulation tasks, such as inserting new records into a table, and data definition tasks, such as dynamically creating a new table. If you happen to create a custom table for your application, your application can probably also benefit from one or more stored procedures performing data manipulation tasks for the table. For example, your application can pass the stored procedure parameters specifying the column values for a new row, and the stored procedure can execute the *INSERT INTO* statement. If your application needs the value for a column with an *Identity* property created on the SQL Server instance, the stored procedure can return it as an output parameter.

The sample for this section demonstrates the creation of a table and a stored procedure. The sample is the setup program for the next section that demonstrates how to program data manipulation tasks. Specifically, you will learn how to create a table and a stored procedure on a SQL Server instance from an ASP.NET application. Figure 11-20 shows the Web page for the sample. The page's name is WebFrom1.aspx, and it resides in the SetupForWebUpdate-Sample project. The page includes two buttons and a hyperlink. The buttons have *Text* property settings reflecting the text they show. The button *ID* property settings are Button1 for the top button and Button2 for the one below it.

The hyperlink control has two design-time property settings. First, its *Text* property specifies the message to display when rendered on a Web page. Second, the *NavigateUrl* property designates the URL of the page to which to pass control when a user clicks the hyperlink. If you are running the application against another Web server besides the local one on your workstation, you will need to update the *NavigateUrl* property for the hyperlink control.

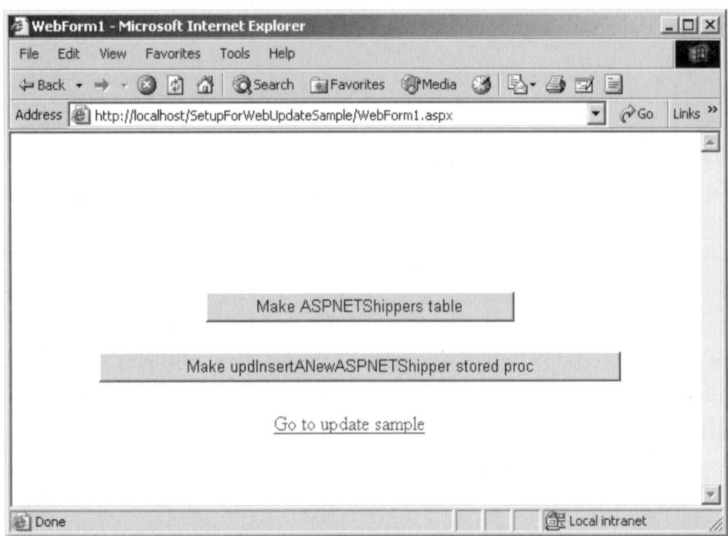

Figure 11-20. WebForm1.aspx in the SetupForWebUpdateSample project.

The sample's new table is essentially a scratch copy of the *Shippers* table in the Northwind database. By creating a scratch copy of the table, you will be able to make changes against the new sample table without destroying the original data in the sample database. The *Button1_Click* event procedure performs three subtasks as it creates a new table named *ASPNETShippers*. First it removes the *ASPNETShippers* table if it already exists in the database. Next it creates the *ASPNETShippers* table. Third it populates the rows of the *ASPNETShippers* table with rows from the *Shippers* table.

The listing that follows starts by declaring and instantiating a *SqlConnection* object (*cnn1*) and a *SqlCommand* object (*cmd1*). By declaring the objects at the module level, I can use them in event procedures for each button in Figure 11-20. The *Button1_Click* event procedure starts by specifying the connection string for *cnn1* and opening the object. Next the procedure assigns *cnn1* to the *Connection* property for *cmd1*, the *SqlCommand* object. After these preliminary steps, the procedure successively repeats two statements for assigning a

CommandText property to *cmd1* and then invoking the *ExecuteNonQuery* method for *cmd1*. Apply the *ExecuteNonQuery* method of a *SqlCommand* object when the object's *CommandText* property doesn't return a result set. The three *CommandText* property settings remove any prior version of the *ASPNETShippers* table, create a new *ASPNETShippers* table, and populate the *ASPNETShippers* table with rows from the *Shippers* table in the Northwind database. The *Button1_Click* event procedure concludes by closing *cnn1*.

The logic for the *Button2_Click* event procedure follows the same basic design as that in the *Button1_Click* event procedure. The overall process is: (1) make a connection, (2) run one or more SQL statements with a *SqlCommand* object, and (3) close the connection. The objective of the *Button2_Click* event procedure is to create a new stored procedure named udpInsertANewASPNETShipper. The event procedure executes two SQL statements to achieve this objective. First it runs one statement to remove any prior version of the connection in the Northwind database. Second it runs a procedure to create a new version of the udpInsertANewASPNETShipper stored procedure. We discussed the logic for this stored procedure in Chapter 10. That chapter demonstrated how to create the stored procedure in Query Analyzer and discussed the logic that the SQL statements express. This chapter extends the earlier treatment of the topic by demonstrating how to create the stored procedure programmatically from within ASP.NET.

> **Note** For data definition SQL statements to function properly, such as those in the *Button1_Click* and *Button2_Click* event procedures, you must run them from a login with appropriate permission to create database objects on the SQL Server instance to which you connect. See Chapter 7 for detailed coverage of SQL Server security, including logins and permissions. Alternatively, you can use the SQL Server sa login. However, this is poor application design because it allows users unrestricted authority on a SQL Server.

```
Dim cnn1 As New SqlClient.SqlConnection()Dim cmd1 As New SqlClient.SqlCommand()

Private Sub Button1_Click(ByVal sender As System.Object, _
    ByVal e As System.EventArgs) Handles Button1.Click

    'Make connection to northwind database.
    cnn1.ConnectionString = "Data Source=(local);" & _
```

```
        "Initial Catalog=northwind;" & _
        "Integrated Security=SSPI"
    cnn1.Open()

    'Assign connection to cmd1.
    cmd1.Connection = cnn1

    'Execute query to drop prior version of table.
    cmd1.CommandText = "IF EXISTS (" & _
        "SELECT * FROM INFORMATION_SCHEMA.TABLES " & _
        "WHERE TABLE_NAME = 'ASPNETShippers') " & _
        "DROP TABLE dbo.ASPNETShippers"
    cmd1.ExecuteNonQuery()

    'Execute query to create new version of table.
    cmd1.CommandText = "CREATE TABLE dbo.ASPNETShippers " & _
        "(" & _
        "ShipperID int IDENTITY (1, 1) NOT NULL, " & _
        "CompanyName nvarchar (40) NOT NULL, " & _
        "Phone nvarchar (24) NULL, " & _
        "CONSTRAINT PK_ASPNETShippers " & _
        "PRIMARY KEY  CLUSTERED (ShipperID)" & _
        ")"
    cmd1.ExecuteNonQuery()

    'Populate table based on Shippers.
    cmd1.CommandText = _
        "SET IDENTITY_INSERT dbo.ASPNETShippers ON " & _
        "INSERT INTO ASPNETShippers " & _
        "(ShipperID, CompanyName, Phone) " & _
        "SELECT * FROM Shippers " & _
        "SET IDENTITY_INSERT dbo.ASPNETShippers OFF"
    cmd1.ExecuteNonQuery()

    cnn1.Close()

End Sub


Private Sub Button2_Click(ByVal sender As System.Object, _
    ByVal e As System.EventArgs) Handles Button2.Click

    'Make connection to northwind database.
    cnn1.ConnectionString = "Data Source=(local);" & _
        "Initial Catalog=northwind;" & _
        "Integrated Security=SSPI"
    cnn1.Open()
```

(continued)

```
        'Assign connection to cmd1.
        cmd1.Connection = cnn1

        'Drop any prior version of udpInsertANewASPNETShipper.
        cmd1.CommandText = "IF EXISTS (" & _
            "SELECT ROUTINE_NAME " & _
            "FROM INFORMATION_SCHEMA.ROUTINES " & _
            "WHERE ROUTINE_TYPE = 'PROCEDURE' AND " & _
            "ROUTINE_NAME = 'udpInsertANewASPNETShipper') " & _
            "DROP PROCEDURE dbo.udpInsertANewASPNETShipper"
        cmd1.ExecuteNonQuery()

        'Create a new version of udpInsertANewASPNETShipper.
        cmd1.CommandText = _
            "CREATE PROCEDURE udpInsertANewASPNETShipper " & _
            "@CompanyName nchar(40), " & _
            "@Phone nvarchar (24), " & _
            "@Identity int OUT " & _
            "AS " & _
            "INSERT INTO ASPNETShippers " & _
            "(CompanyName, Phone) " & _
            "VALUES(@CompanyName, @Phone) " & _
            "SET @Identity = SCOPE_IDENTITY()"
        cmd1.ExecuteNonQuery()

        cnn1.Close()

    End Sub
```

Data Manipulation from ASP.NET

After running the application in the preceding section, you will have a new copy of the *ASPNETShippers* table in the Northwind database as well as a stored procedure, *udpInsertANewASPNETShipper*, to facilitate inserting new rows into the *ASPNETShippers* table. The sample application in this section illustrates how to modify, insert, and delete rows in the *ASPNETShippers* table from an ASP.NET application. The application builds on the browsing sample illustrated by the WebForm1.aspx page in the NavTextBoxes project. The addition of data manipulation to that earlier application is particularly interesting because that application used an unbound form to display column values from the *Shippers* table. In other words, the form field values don't bind to any data source. Therefore, all data manipulation tasks must be performed in code. The sample in this section is important for another reason. The application enables users to update a SQL Server database over the Web.

> **Note** As with the sample in the preceding section, users of this application must have permission to perform a task before the application automating that task will work. In this section, the tasks are the classic three data manipulation ones of modifying, inserting, and deleting records.

Web Page Layout and Operation

Figure 11-21 shows the Web page layout for this application. The page's name is WebForm1.aspx in the UpdateWithWebForm project. Except for four new buttons at the bottom of the page, the page layout looks similar to the one in Figure 11-18 for browsing records with text box controls. The four new buttons facilitate changes to the row currently appearing on the Web page, delete the row currently appearing, and clear the fields and insert a new row into the database based on new form field values. The Web page in Figure 11-21 connects to the *ASPNETShippers*, instead of the *Shippers*, table in the Northwind database. This distinction enables application users of the sample in this section to manipulate the data appearing on the Web page without changing the original data in the sample database. By contrasting the Design views of the two pages, you will also notice that the new Web page has no ADO.NET objects created at design time. You can tell this because the system tray doesn't appear in Figure 11-21.

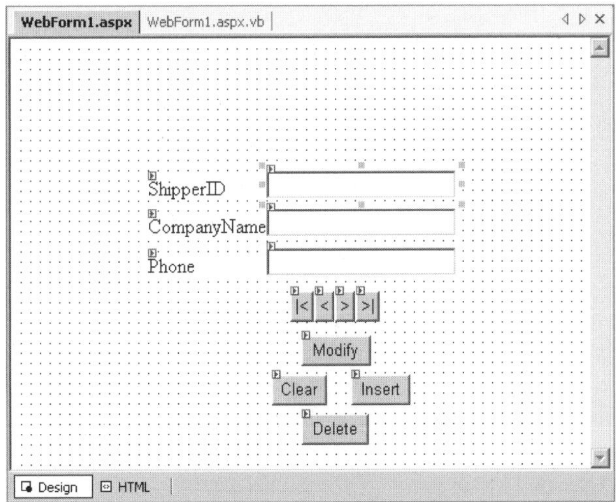

Figure 11-21. WebForm1.aspx in the UpdateWithWebForm project.

The entire reason for this sample is to demonstrate that you can enable data manipulation tasks from a Web page with ASP.NET. Figure 11-22 starts to demonstrate this capability by showing two views of the Web page in operation. The top window shows the Web page after a click of the Clear button (its name is *cmdClear*) and then the addition of new text in two of the text boxes. The *cmdClear* button clears the form on the Web page so the user can enter a new row of data. In this top window, you can see that the *CompanyName* and *Phone* values for a new shipper have been entered but that the top text box for *ShipperID* is empty. That's because the SQL Server instance assigns a value to this field. Clicking the Insert button (its name is *cmdInsert*) changes the browser to look like the window in the bottom portion of Figure 11-22. Notice that the CompanyName and Phone text boxes are the same. However, you now have a ShipperID text box value. SQL Server generated this value on the server, and the UpdateWithWebForm application retrieved the value by capturing the return parameter value from the *udpInsertANewASPNETShipper* stored procedure.

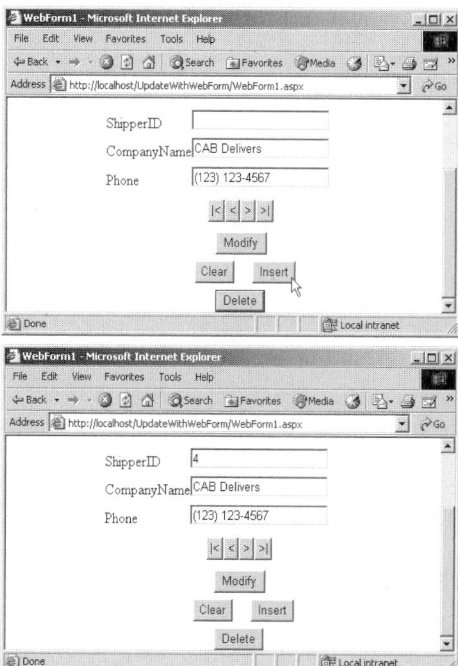

Figure 11-22. WebForm1.aspx in the UpdateWithWebForm project before and after committing an insert to the *ASPNETShippers* table.

Figure 11-23 shows the row entered in the preceding sample in the process of being modified. Notice that the user changed the last digit in the telephone number from 7 to 8. The application doesn't commit this change until the user clicks the Modify button. (Its name is *cmdModify*.) After the user clicks *cmdModify*, the application conveys the new value to the SQL Server instance and refreshes the local copy of the data set on the Web page with the table of values from the SQL Server instance.

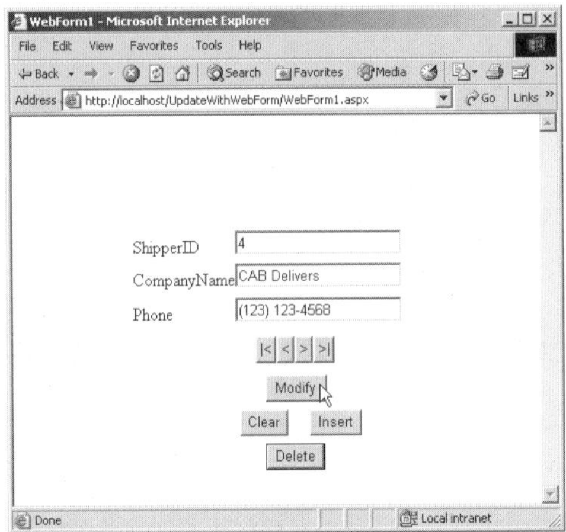

Figure 11-23. WebForm1.aspx in the UpdateWithWebForm project just before a modification to the telephone number for the row added in Figure 11-22.

Figure 11-24 shows the Delete button (its name is *cmdDelete*) in operation. In the top window, you can see the new row with its edited *Phone* value. The cursor rests on the *cmdDelete* button. Clicking this button removes the row appearing on the Web page from the *ASPNETShippers* table in the SQL Server instance and updates the data set on the Web page to reflect this result. Because the click to the *cmdDelete* button removed the former last row in the *Shippers* data set, the Web page shows the new last row with a *ShipperID* column value of 3. The *Click* event procedure behind the *cmdDelete* button manages the display of which row appears on the page after the removal of a row. For example, if a user removed the first row (with a *ShipperID* column value of 1), the row appearing on the Web page would be the new first row in the data set with a *ShipperID* value of 2.

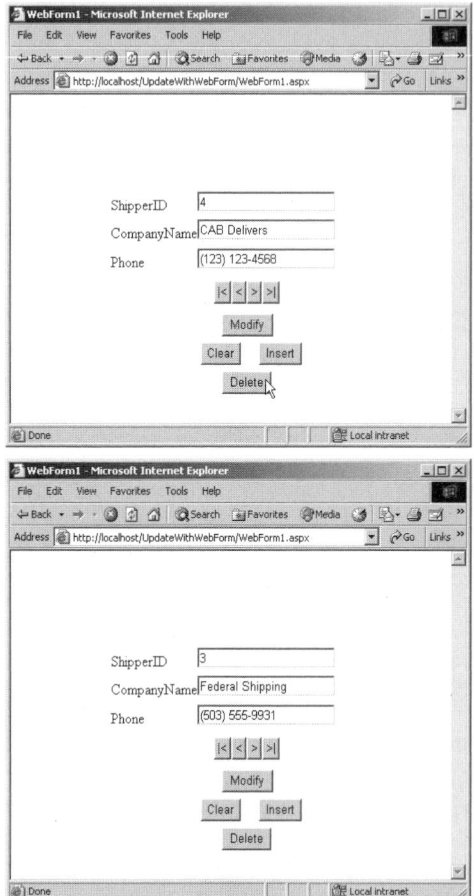

Figure 11-24. WebForm1.aspx in the UpdateWithWebForm project just before and just after the removal of the row that had its *Phone* value edited in Figure 11-23.

Code Behind the Web Page

The code for performing data manipulation on a Web page parallels that for performing data manipulation in a Windows form. However, one important difference is that in a Windows form, your code has to create most of the ADO.NET objects, such as a *SqlDataAdapter* and a data set, just once. In the case of a Web application, your code will typically have to re-create these objects each time a Web page does a round-trip between a browser and a Web server—for example, every time the user clicks a button on the Web page. As mentioned previously, you should keep the size of the data set on a Web page small for this reason. In our case, the *ASPNETShippers* table is already a small table of just three original rows. If your original data source is large, consider pulling down just a small portion of it on successive round-trips by using a stored procedure or a user-defined function that returns a customizable result set based on input that you pass it through a parameter.

The following listing includes those parts of the code behind the Web page that pertain directly to the data manipulation part of the sample. The data display and navigation code closely follow the code appearing in the section titled "Navigating Text Boxes Through a Data Set". In order to conserve space in this book for fresh information, I direct you to the code samples for this book, where the complete listing is available for the code behind the Web page.

The listing starts by declaring and instantiating at the module level four ADO.NET objects: a *SqlConnection* object (*cnn1*), a *SqlCommand* object (*cmd1*), a *SqlDataAdapter* object (*dap1*), and a *DataSet* object (*das1*). The *Page_Load* event procedure uses each of these objects, and the objects find selective use in other event procedures throughout the code behind the page.

After making a connection to the Northwind database, the *Page_Load* event procedure declares the *dap1* data adapter dependent on all the columns from all the rows of the *ASPNETShippers* table. Next the procedure defines the *UpdateCommand* property for the data adapter. A SQL *UPDATE* statement with parameters specifies the items to update. After the SQL statement for the *UpdateCommand* property, two additional statements add parameters to the command for the *UpdateCommand* property. These parameters allow the Web page to pass values from the entries in its text boxes. The next parameter is for the text box holding a *ShipperID* value on the Web page. Whereas the parameter ties to the *ShipperID* value in the data set behind the Web page, it uses the row currently appearing in the first text box on the Web page.

The next several lines of code in the *Page_Load* event procedure define the *InsertCommand* property for the *dap1* data adapter and its associated parameters. In this case, the procedure designates the performance of the insert via the *udpInsertANewASPNETShipper* stored procedure. Recall that the preceding section demonstrated how to create this stored procedure in the code behind a separate stand-alone Web page. The statements adding parameters illustrate the syntax for passing parameters to a stored procedure and capturing a return value from a stored procedure. Notice that you designate a *Direction* property for *prm2* with the *ParameterDirection.Output* enumeration value. This parameter (*prm2*) returns the *Identity* value for the inserted row by the SQL Server instance.

The next block of code in the *Page_Load* event procedure defines the *DeleteCommand* property and its parameter for the *dap1* object. This block of code uses a SQL *DELETE* statement to designate which row to drop from the *ASPNETShippers* table along with the row's copy in the data set behind the Web page. Because the *ShipperID* value is the primary key of the *ASPNETShippers* table, the code uniquely identifies a row to remove from the table by specifying a value for this column.

After defining the *dap1* data adapter and its data manipulation properties, the *Page_Load* event procedure performs two more essential tasks. First the procedure fills the *das1* data set with the values from the *ASPNETShippers* table. Second the procedure populates the text boxes on the page with values from the first row of the *das1* data set.

Users make a change by modifying the CompanyName or Phone text box values on the Web page and then clicking the *cmdModify* button. In the *Click* event for this button, the procedure declares and instantiates a data view (*dav1*) based on the *ASPNETShippers DataTable* in the *das1* data set. The procedure defines a sort key for *dav1* based on the *ShipperID* column. Then the procedure uses the data view's *Find* method to return the *rowindex* for the row with a *ShipperID* column value matching the current *ShipperID* value displayed on the Web page. Defining the sort key is a necessary step for using the *Find* method (because the *ASPNETShippers DataTable* in *das1* doesn't have a primary key constraint). With the index reflecting the row displayed on the Web page, the procedure creates a *DataRow* based on the data table's schema and data that points to the row from the data table displayed on the Web page. Then the procedure updates the row's column values with those from the Web page. This modifies the data table. Finally the procedure closes by invoking the *Update* method for the *dap1* data adapter. This method transfers the changes from the local table to the matching one on the SQL Server instance.

The cmdClear and cmdInsert buttons work together. In general, a user should click the cmdClear button before clicking the cmdInsert button. The cmdClear button's *Click* event procedure blanks the text box controls on the Web page. Next the user should insert values in those blank controls. The *Click* event procedure for the cmdInsert button declares a new row to add to the *ASPNETShippers* data table and then populates the row with values from text boxes on the Web page. At this point, updating the local data table is as easy as invoking the *Add* method. This step appends the new row to the end of the *ASPNETShippers* data table. Next the procedure invokes the *Update* method to upload the new row to the *ASPNETShippers* table in the SQL Server instance and to download the *ShipperID* value created on the SQL Server instance. The output parameter statements for the *dap1 InsertCommand* property in the *Page_Load* event procedure automatically assure the proper handling of the return value from the *udpInsertANewASPNETShipper* stored procedure. Finally the procedure updates the *MyRowID* Session variable to point to the last row in the data table and shows this row (where ADO.NET performs the insert) on the Web page.

> **Note** The *cmdModify* button *Click* event procedure doesn't update the *MyRowID* Session variable or the values on the Web page. At the end of the modify update, the correct row already appears on the Web page. Therefore, there is no need to show another record.

The *cmdDelete_Click* event procedure borrows from the logic of the two preceding event procedures and adds a new wrinkle or two. First the procedure defines a data view to find an index value for the row displayed on the Web page, which is the row a user wants to delete. The second step is new. In this step, the procedure invokes the *Delete* method for the row in the data table that matches the row displayed on the Web page. This method doesn't physically remove the row from the local data table. Instead, it marks the row for deletion. When the procedure invokes the *Update* method in the third step, it finds all rows marked for deletion and removes them from the SQL Server version of the *ASPNETShippers* table. In this application, there will always be just one such row. After removing the row on the server, the *Update* method automatically removes the row locally. This time the procedure physically removes the row from the local data table. After completing the deletion, the procedure displays on the Web page the previous row before the one just deleted. If that row (the one just deleted) was the first row, the procedure shows the old second row, which is the new first row.

```
Dim cnn1 As New SqlClient.SqlConnection()Dim cmd1 As New SqlClient.SqlCommand()
Dim dap1 As New SqlClient.SqlDataAdapter()
Dim das1 As New DataSet()

Private Sub Page_Load(ByVal sender As System.Object, _
    ByVal e As System.EventArgs) Handles MyBase.Load

    'Make connection to northwind database and
    'point data adapter (dap1) at it
    cnn1.ConnectionString = "Data Source=(local);" & _
        "Initial Catalog=northwind;" & _
        "Integrated Security=SSPI"
    dap1 = _
        New SqlClient.SqlDataAdapter( _
        "SELECT * FROM ASPNETShippers", cnn1)

    'Set the UpdateCommand property for dap1.
    dap1.UpdateCommand = _
        New SqlClient.SqlCommand _
            ("UPDATE ASPNETShippers " & _
```

(continued)

```
        "SET CompanyName = @CompanyName, " & _
        "Phone = @Phone " & _
        "WHERE ShipperID = @ShipperID", _
        cnn1)

'Add two parameters that take source columns
'from the ASPNETShippers table in the dataset for the
'dap1 adapter and feed the parameters in the SQL
'string for the UpdateCommand property.
dap1.UpdateCommand.Parameters.Add _
    ("@CompanyName", SqlDbType.NVarChar, 40, _
    "CompanyName")
dap1.UpdateCommand.Parameters.Add _
    ("@Phone", SqlDbType.NVarChar, 24, _
    "Phone")

'Specify matching criterion values based on the
'original version of the ShipperID column in the
'local ASPNETShippers table.
Dim prm1 As SqlClient.SqlParameter = _
    dap1.UpdateCommand.Parameters.Add _
   ("@ShipperID", SqlDbType.Int)
prm1.SourceColumn = "ShipperID"
prm1.SourceVersion = DataRowVersion.Original

'Point InsertCommand at a SQL Server stored procedure;
'you must have the stored procedure on the server.
dap1.InsertCommand = New _
    SqlClient.SqlCommand("udpInsertANewASPNETShipper", cnn1)
dap1.InsertCommand.CommandType = CommandType.StoredProcedure

'Specify input parameters for the stored procedure.
dap1.InsertCommand.Parameters.Add _
    ("@CompanyName", SqlDbType.NVarChar, 40, _
    "CompanyName")
dap1.InsertCommand.Parameters.Add _
    ("@Phone", SqlDbType.NVarChar, 24, _
    "Phone")

'Designate an output parameter for the identity
'value assigned within SQL Server so that your
'local ASPNETShippers table can have a matching
'ShipperID column value.
Dim prm2 As SqlClient.SqlParameter = _
    dap1.InsertCommand.Parameters.Add _
    ("@Identity", SqlDbType.Int, 0, "ShipperID")
prm2.Direction = ParameterDirection.Output
```

```
    'Specify the SQL string for the DeleteCommand
    'property of dap1.
    dap1.DeleteCommand = _
        New SqlClient.SqlCommand("DELETE " & _
        "FROM ASPNETShippers " & _
        "WHERE ShipperID = @ShipperID", cnn1)

    'Specify matching criterion values based on the
    'original version of the ShipperID column in the
    'local ASPNETShippers table.
    Dim prm3 As SqlClient.SqlParameter = _
        dap1.DeleteCommand.Parameters.Add _
        ("@ShipperID", SqlDbType.Int)
    prm3.SourceColumn = "ShipperID"
    prm3.SourceVersion = DataRowVersion.Original

    'Fill dataset.
    das1 = New DataSet()
    dap1.Fill(das1, "ASPNETShippers")

    'On initial page load move to first row and
    'populate text boxes; this code segment must
    'appear after you create the local ASPNETShippers
    'table.
    If Not Me.IsPostBack Then
        Session("MyRowID") = 0
        MoveToRow()
    End If

End Sub


Private Sub cmdModify_Click(ByVal sender As System.Object, _
    ByVal e As System.EventArgs) Handles cmdModify.Click

    'Use dav1 to find the row in ASPNETShippers
    'that appears in the text boxes from the local
    'ASPNETShippers table.
    Dim dav1 As DataView = _
        New DataView(das1.Tables("ASPNETShippers"))
    dav1.Sort = "ShipperID"
    Dim rowindex As Integer = _
        dav1.Find(TextBox1.Text)

    'Create a DataRow object pointing at the row
    'to update in the local table.
    Dim IndexedRow As DataRow = _
        das1.Tables("ASPNETShippers").Rows(rowindex)
```

(continued)

```
        'Update the local table with the text boxes.
        IndexedRow("CompanyName") = TextBox2.Text
        IndexedRow("Phone") = TextBox3.Text

        'Invoke Update method for dap1 to synchronize
        'the local table with the one in northwind.
        dap1.Update(das1, "ASPNETShippers")

    End Sub


    Private Sub cmdClear_Click(ByVal sender As System.Object, _
        ByVal e As System.EventArgs) Handles cmdClear.Click

        'Clear text boxes for data entry.
        TextBox1.Text = ""
        TextBox2.Text = ""
        TextBox3.Text = ""

    End Sub


    Private Sub cmdInsert_Click(ByVal sender As System.Object, _
        ByVal e As System.EventArgs) Handles cmdInsert.Click

        'Add text box values to new row in dataset Shippers table.
        Dim newRow As DataRow = das1.Tables("ASPNETShippers").NewRow()
        newRow("CompanyName") = TextBox2.Text
        newRow("Phone") = TextBox3.Text
        das1.Tables("ASPNETShippers").Rows.Add(newRow)

        'Update method synchronizes inserted local row
        'with its copy in northwind and returns the identity
        'column value added by the northwind database.
        dap1.Update(das1, "ASPNETShippers")

        'Move to last row and populate text boxes.
        Session("MyRowID") = das1.Tables("ASPNETShippers").Rows.Count - 1
        MoveToRow()

    End Sub


    Private Sub cmdDelete_Click(ByVal sender As System.Object, _
        ByVal e As System.EventArgs) Handles cmdDelete.Click

        'Create a dataview based on the ASPNETShippers table
        'in the dataset and find the row index that matches
        'the current ShipperID.
```

```
    Dim dav1 As DataView = _
        New DataView(das1.Tables("ASPNETShippers"))
    dav1.Sort = "ShipperID"
    Dim rowIndex As Integer = _
        dav1.Find(TextBox1.Text)

    'Mark the row for deletion in the dataset.
    das1.Tables("ASPNETShippers").Rows(rowIndex).Delete()

    'Invoke the Update method to complete the deletion
    'in both the SQL Server and dataset Shippers tables.
    dap1.Update(das1, "ASPNETShippers")

    'Move to previous row and populate textboxes.
    If Session("MyRowID") > 0 Then
        Session("MyRowID") -= 1
    End If
    MoveToRow()

End Sub
```

Validating the Data on a Web Page

ASP.NET introduces some powerful controls for facilitating validation of the data in controls on Web pages. You can use these powerful controls graphically or both graphically and programmatically. This section introduces you to the controls overall and then presents a series of three samples to demonstrate how to apply validator controls in your Web applications.

Built-In Data Validation Tools

ASP.NET offers five special Web server controls to facilitate validating the data users enter into other controls on a Web page. You can use these special Web server controls without any programming, or you can use the *Page* object model for programmatically responding to the validation controls individually or collectively. In addition, the five validation controls enable you to dictate how to display errors. Basically, there are two display options with some variations in between. First, you can show error messages individually near the controls to which the messages apply. Second, you can choose to display error messages collectively in a central area.

You can drag to a Web page any of the five types of validator Web server controls from the Web Forms tab on the Toolbar. For each control, you must specify the *ControlToValidate* property, which designates the control to which the Web server validator control applies. You can optionally specify a custom error message or accept the default error message associated with the validator control, and selected validator controls may have other mandatory or optional properties to set. Brief summaries of the five types of validator controls appear below.

- The RequiredFieldValidator control detects a missing value for a validated control. This is the only validator control that checks for empty controls, and you might therefore want to use RequiredFieldValidator controls with other Web server validator controls.
- The CompareValidator control uses a comparison operator, such as less than, equal to, or greater than, to determine how a property for a target control compares with another value. You can also use CompareValidator to check the data type of an entry.
- The RangeValidator control can check to ensure that a target control's property is in a specified range. This validator control lets you set lower and upper boundary values for validating a control.
- The RegularExpressionValidator control enables you to check that entries follow a pattern, such as for telephone numbers or social security numbers. The *ValidationExpression* property in the Properties window for this validator control offers a selection of prespecified regular expressions for such entries as phone number, postal code, e-mail address, and social security number. In addition, you can program custom regular expressions.
- With the CustomValidator control, you can develop custom checks for data that aren't covered by the preceding controls.

You have several display options for showing error messages associated with the Web server validator controls. Assign a string to the *ErrorMessage* property for a validator control to specify a custom error message, such as "Enter a company," instead of a default message, which happens to be "RequiredFieldValidator," the same text as the name of the control type. The error messages associated with a validator control will always appear where you place the control on a Web page unless you also add a ValidationSummary control to the page. With a ValidationSummary control on a page, you can have error messages appear collectively in the ValidationSummary control by assigning an HTML character, such as an asterisk, to the *Text* property for a validator control. In this scenario, the HTML character appears where you have the validator control and the error message appears in the ValidationSummary control. By setting the *Display* property for the validator control to None, you can cause no error indicator to appear where the validator control is on a page. The only indication of an error for the validator will be the message in the ValidationSummary control. If you prefer to have the error message for a validator control appear at the control and in the ValidationSummary control, leave the *Text* property for the validator control empty.

With Internet Explorer 4 and later browsers, the validation controls verify the data on the client workstation and at the server unless you explicitly specify otherwise. In cases in which you want to send an improperly validated Web page to a Web server, client-side validation can cause a problem. Some validator controls might be on a Web page to encourage compliance with data entry forms, but you might not want to decline a form from a user just because they fail to comply with all the validator controls on a Web page. This is especially the case in e-commerce applications or any situation in which the user is doing your organization a favor by returning the form. In such situations, you can explicitly disable client-side script validation by setting the *EnableClientScript* property for the validator control to *False*.

One of the great features of validator controls is that they provide a lot of functionality without any programming. However, you can also program the validator controls and derive even more functionality from them. If the data for any validator control on a page doesn't satisfy the validator, the page's *IsValid* property becomes *False*. As a consequence, you can use the page's *IsValid* property to execute blocks of code conditionally. In addition, ASP.NET supports a *ValidatorCollection* object for each page. With this object, you can iterate through the validator controls on a page and check each member's *IsValid* property. This capability enables you to respond selectively to errors from individual validator controls on a page.

Using Validator Controls on Web Pages

Adding validator controls to a Web page is a simple matter of dragging them to a Web page in Design view from the Web Forms tab of the Toolbox. Figure 11-25 shows a Web page with three validator controls. The basic Web page design is an adaptation of the one used in the preceding sample. Aside from the validator controls, the main distinction is the omission of the button for modifying text box values. The Web page is WebForm1.aspx in the Validator-UISample project.

Figure 11-25 shows a selected validator control next to the CompanyName text box. The right panel in Figure 11-25 displays the Properties window for the selected control. The Properties window for the selected validator control shows the default *ID* name RequiredFieldValidator1. The *ControlToValidate* property reads TextBox2. You must always set the *ControlToValidate* property for a validator control because the sole purpose of a validator control is to check the validity of another control. The validator control *ID* and *ControlToValidate* settings indicate that the form isn't valid without an entry for the CompanyName text box, which is *TextBox2*. Instead of the default error message returned by the RequiredFieldValidator control, the Properties window shows the setting "Enter a company name" for the *ErrorMessage* property.

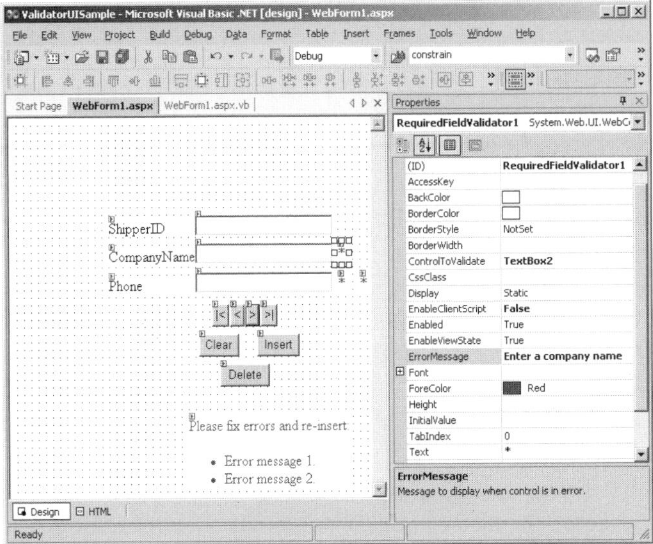

Figure 11-25. See the validator control indicators (*) and the Validation-Summary control in Design view for the WebForm1.aspx page in the ValidatorUISample project.

Turn your attention again to the Design view of the Web page. You can see two additional validator controls next to the text box for Phone text box values. One of these, a RequiredFieldValidator, necessitates a Phone text box entry, and the other, a RegularExpressionValidator, specifies a format for the telephone number. By using both of these validator controls together, the application specifies not only that the user input a phone number but that he input it in a designated format. If you specified a format for the phone number by using a RegularExpressionValidator control without also designating a RequiredFieldValidator, users could submit a valid form without entering anything in the Phone text box. I specified a designated format by using the *ValidatedExpression* property in the Properties window for the RegularExpressionValidator control. Clicking the Build button for this property opens a window of prespecified regular expressions, from which I chose U.S. Phone Number. The regular expression for this designation accepts numbers in these two formats: (123) 123-1234 and 123-1234.

A ValidationSummary control appears below the buttons on the Web page. Because the *Text* property settings for all the validator controls equal *, all the error messages appear in the ValidationSummary control. The only indicator of an error next to the control is an * at the location where the validator control appears on the page. The default format for listing error messages in a ValidationSummary control is with bullets. You can select from either of two other prespecified formats or program your own custom layout for showing error messages in the ValidationSummary control.

Figure 11-26 shows the validator controls depicted in Figure 11-25 operating for some sample input. Notice that the CompanyName text box is blank and that the Phone text box has an improper value for a phone number. (It ends in the letter *r* instead of a number.) The ValidationSummary control area of the Web page properly reports both errors, and asterisks next to the text boxes further signal the need to fix the entries for the text boxes.

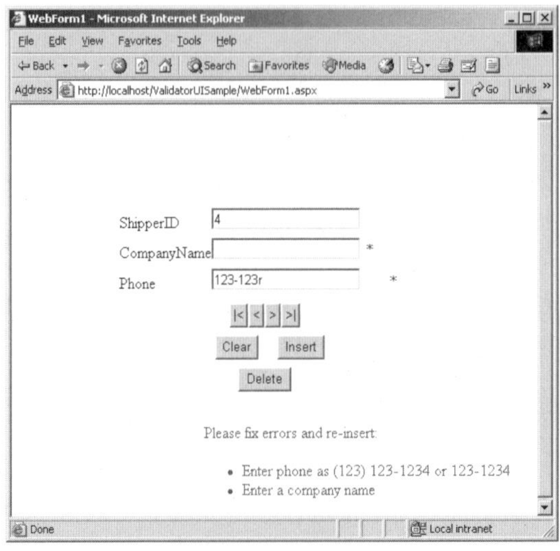

Figure 11-26. Error messages and indicators from the WebForm1.aspx page in the ValidatorUISample project based on improper input in the CompanyName and Phone text boxes.

Note There's a second problem with the Web page shown in Figure 11-26 besides the fact that the text box entries are invalid. We'll highlight this second issue in the next section when we refer back to the figure.

Programming the Page *IsValid* Property

Validator controls will pass a Web page to the browser if you set the *EnableClientScript* property to *False*, even if one or more controls on a page make the page invalid. The same action also takes place if the client workstation disables client-side scripting or if the client-side scripting capability for a browser is incompatible with ECMAScript 1.2, a subset of Microsoft JScript. Although the validator controls do operate on a Web server when client-side validation doesn't take place, event procedures for the page also operate. The operation of these event procedures, such as for a procedure to insert a new row in a table, can enter invalid data in a database.

Despite the issues highlighted in the preceding paragraph, using server-side validation is cleaner than client-side validation because it doesn't depend on the capabilities of a browser (or even whether client-side scripting is disabled in a browser that has the capability). However, to take advantage of server-side validation, you need the Web server to be able to detect whether a page has valid controls and then conditionally execute data manipulation or data access tasks based on the validity of the controls.

> **Note** If you use server-side validation without making data manipulation tasks, such as inserts and updates, conditional on the validity of the controls on a page, you run the risk of entering invalid data in your database. When you combine server-side validation with invalid data, a related problem emerges. The error messages for data will be one row out of synchrony with the invalid data. As a result, error messages will appear on pages with valid data, and pages with invalid data will appear without error messages.

You can use the *IsValid* property for a *Page* object to detect on a Web server whether the page to which a *Page* object points has any invalid controls before committing an insert or an update to a database. If any controls are invalid, you can bypass the code to insert a new row or update an existing row with the data from the invalid controls. WebForm1.aspx in the IsValidSample project demonstrates the syntax for using the *IsValid* property for a *Page* object. The IsValidSample project is identical to the ValidatorUISample project in the preceding section except for the following Visual Basic code to implement the *cmdInsert_Click* event procedure. Both projects assign *False* to the *EnableClientScript* property for all validator controls, which forces server-side validation. The ValidatorUISample project uses the logic from the "Data Manipulation from ASP.NET" section to implement the *cmdInsert_Click* event procedure.

The IsValidSample project inserts a new row with the following adaptation of the code from the ValidatorUISample project. Notice the use of the *Me* name to point to the current page. If any control on the page is invalid, the *IsValid* property is *False*, and the procedure doesn't invoke the *Update* method. Instead, the page returns to the browser with the error message or messages showing. If the page's *IsValid* property is *True*, the procedure executes the *Update* method and the browser shows the last row in the local *ASPNETShippers DataTable*, which contains the most recently inserted row.

```
Private Sub cmdInsert_Click(ByVal sender As System.Object, _
    ByVal e As System.EventArgs) Handles cmdInsert.Click

    'Add text box values to new row in dataset Shippers table.
    Dim newRow As DataRow = das1.Tables("ASPNETShippers").NewRow()
    newRow("CompanyName") = TextBox2.Text
    newRow("Phone") = TextBox3.Text
    das1.Tables("ASPNETShippers").Rows.Add(newRow)

    'Update method synchronizes inserted local row
    'with its copy in northwind and returns the identity
    'column value added by the northwind database.
    If Me.IsValid Then
        dap1.Update(das1, "ASPNETShippers")
        'Move to last row and populate text boxes
        Session("MyRowID") = _
            das1.Tables("ASPNETShippers").Rows.Count - 1
        MoveToRow()
    End If

End Sub
```

Figures 11-27 and 11-28 show the WebForm1.aspx page from the IsValidSample project in operation. Figure 11-27 shows the result from an attempt to insert a new row with an invalid *Phone* field value. (It ends with the letter *r* instead of a number.) Notice that the error message at the bottom of the screen and the asterisk highlight the problem and instruct the user what to do (fix the error and reinsert). Also, notice that the ShipperID text box is empty. This is because the procedure didn't attempt to execute the *Insert* statement with invalid data according to the Web page validator controls. Figure 11-28 shows the Web page returned by the Web server after the user changes the last character in the Phone text box from *r* to *4*. Notice that this version includes a *ShipperID* value, indicating that the Web server submitted the new row to the SQL Server instance and received a new column value as an output parameter value from the stored procedure that performed the insert.

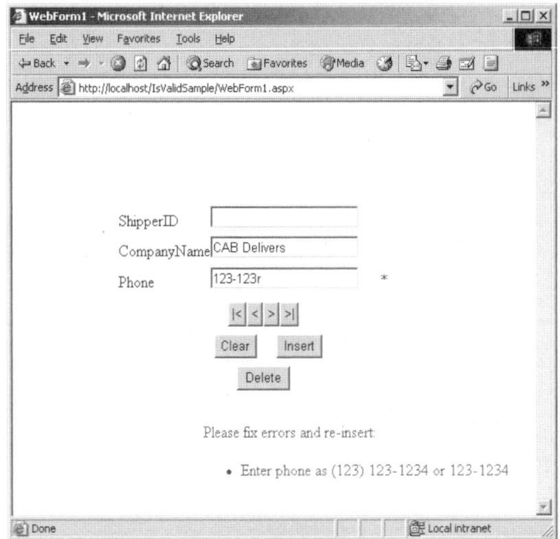

Figure 11-27. WebForm1.aspx from the IsValidSample project with an invalid value in the Phone text box.

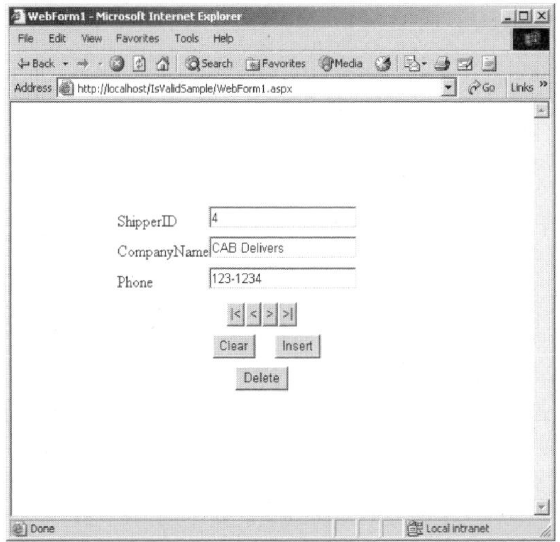

Figure 11-28. WebForm1.aspx from the IsValidSample project after its fix.

Now's a good time to focus on the second problem with Figure 11-26. Notice that it committed the row with invalid *CompanyName* and *Phone* column values to the *ASPNETShippers* table. The reason you can tell is that the

Web page shows a *ShipperID* value, which SQL Server assigns only after it inserts a record into a table. Unless the user deletes the faulty row, the error messages can come out of sync with the data showing on a Web page. The user can get rid of the faulty row by clicking the Delete button on the Web page. However, this action requires the user to start entering the new row over again from scratch. If the Web page had a Modify button, which I removed to simplify the sample, the user could use that button to fix the page. However, the real problem with WebForm1.aspx in the ValidatorUISample project is that the Web page inserts the new row unconditionally (whether or not the data on the page is invalid). It is this problem that the IsValidSample project corrects.

Dynamically Disabling a Validator Control

Sometimes you may want the option to disable a validator control dynamically. This situation can arise in cases in which a user can't figure out the right format for all the fields but she has filled out enough of the form on a Web page for your organization to contact her and resolve any inconsistent data. For example, if you have a valid phone number, you may be willing to accept an invalid e-mail address or URL. To be able to perform a task like this, you need the ability to reference programmatically the individual validators on a form. The sample in this section demonstrates how to disable a validator control at run time.

Figures 11-29 and 11-30 show a pair of windows that illustrates the disabling of a validator control at run time. Figure 11-29 shows WebForm1.aspx in the ValidatorCollectionSample project after an attempt to insert a new row into the *ASPNETShippers* table with a faulty *Phone* value. (It ends with an *r* instead of a number.) Businesses use validators to obtain clean data. On the other hand, some transactions may benefit a business more if they accept partially faulty data. This example offers the user a button for entering a row even if the *Phone* value is in the wrong format. Figure 11-30 shows the Web page after a click of the Insert Bad Phone button. Notice that the record enters the table (because it shows a *ShipperID* value), even though the record has invalid data in the Phone text box.

While the sample shown in Figures 11-29 and 11-30 isn't very compelling, selected high-priority Web applications, such as e-commerce and gathering contact data, can benefit from accepting partially faulty data more than losing a site visitor or potential customer because they get frustrated by the data validation process. For example, your code might give visitors one or two attempts to enter an e-mail address in a valid format and then accept the row so long as the phone number and URL values are in a valid format.

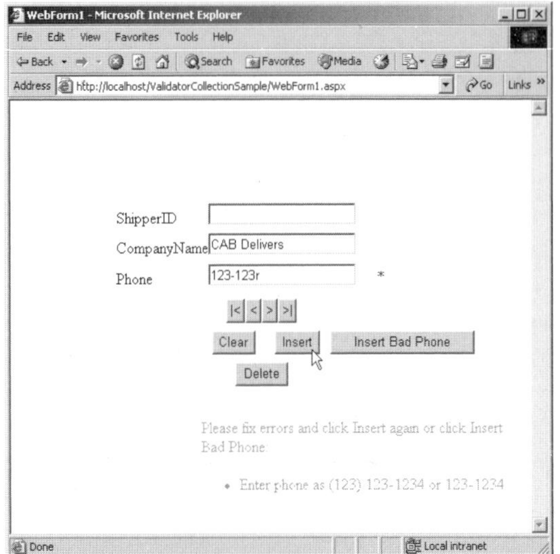

Figure 11-29. The RegularExpressionValidator control for *Phone* values blocking the entry of a row.

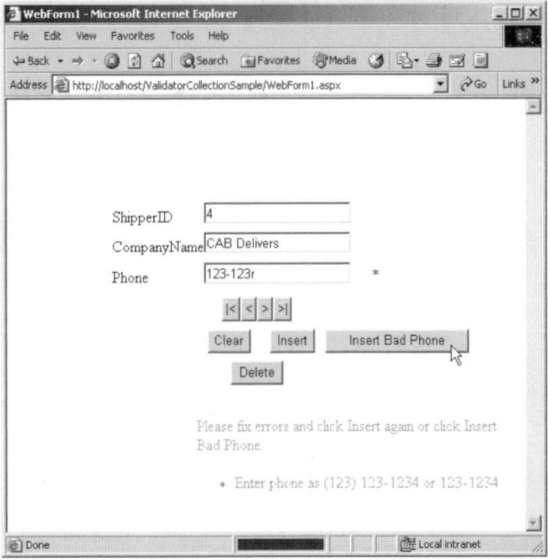

Figure 11-30. The RegularExpressionValidator control disabled so that the same row can enter a table in a SQL Server database.

The following listing shows the *Click* event procedure behind the button (its name is *cmdInsertAnyway*) that allows the insertion of a row with an invalidly formatted *Phone* value. Recall that the objective of this application is to disable a selected validator control. Therefore, you need to be able to address the validator controls individually. Happily, the *Validators* property in the *Page* object contains objects pointing to all the validator controls on a page. ASP.NET permits the declaration of an object based on the *ValidatorCollection* class that contains the items in the *Page.Validators* property. A *Dim* statement toward the top of the program listing illustrates the syntax for declaring an object pointer, *myCollection*, for the validators on the page. You can reference the objects within *myCollection* by an index value. The commented code block immediately after the *Dim* statement for *myCollection* shows one approach to enumerating the members of the collection. It displays the item number, which serves as an index value, and the *ErrorMessage* property for the objects in the *myCollection* object. From running code like this, I was able to determine that the RegularExpressionValidator for the *Phone* value was *myCollection(0)*.

After adding a row to the local data table with the text box values and declaring the *myCollection* object, the procedure opens an *If...Then...ElseIf* statement. The procedure takes the *Then* clause if the user successfully fixed the *Phone* value on the Web page. If the *Phone* value isn't in the correct format, the procedure still enters the record in the *ElseIf* clause. The condition for the *ElseIf* clause is *True* when the *IsValid* property for *myCollection(0)* is *False*, but the other two members of the *myCollection* object have *IsValid* property values of *True*. This syntax shows how to disable temporarily just the RegularExpressionValidator control for the Phone text box. The next time the user tries to enter a new row, the validator for the Phone text box will operate (unless the user disables it again).

```
Private Sub cmdInsertAnyway_Click(ByVal sender As System.Object, _
    ByVal e As System.EventArgs) Handles cmdInsertAnyway.Click

    'Add text box values to new row in dataset Shippers table.
    Dim newRow As DataRow = das1.Tables("ASPNETShippers").NewRow()
    newRow("CompanyName") = TextBox2.Text
    newRow("Phone") = TextBox3.Text
    das1.Tables("ASPNETShippers").Rows.Add(newRow)

    ' Get 'Validators' of the page to myCollection.
    Dim myCollection As ValidatorCollection = Page.Validators

    'Uncomment from next Dim to the Next statement
    'in the For loop to match ValidatorCollection index
    'numbers to validator controls.
    'Dim int1 As Integer
    'Dim str1 As String
    'For int1 = 0 To myCollection.Count - 1
    'str1 = CStr(int1) & ", " & _
    '    myCollection.Item(int1).ErrorMessage & "<br>"
    'Response.Write(str1)
    'Next
```

(continued)

```
        'Update method synchronizes inserted local row
        'with its copy in northwind and returns the identity
        'column value added by the northwind database.
        If Me.IsValid Then
            'Do normal Insert if Phone OK
            dap1.Update(das1, "ASPNETShippers")
            'Move to last row and populate text boxes
            Session("MyRowID") = _
                das1.Tables("ASPNETShippers").Rows.Count - 1
            MoveToRow()
        ElseIf (Not (myCollection.Item(0).IsValid) _
            And (myCollection.Item(1).IsValid)) _
            And (myCollection.Item(2).IsValid) Then
            'Do insert anyway if just phone format bad
            dap1.Update(das1, "ASPNETShippers")
            'Move to last row and populate text boxes
            Session("MyRowID") = _
                das1.Tables("ASPNETShippers").Rows.Count - 1
            MoveToRow()
        End If

    End Sub
```

12

Managing XML with Visual Basic .NET

The main objective of this chapter is to convey an understanding of XML documents for use with Visual Basic .NET. This chapter assumes a basic grasp of XML data formats, schemas, and related technologies, such as XPath (XML Path Language) and XSLT (Extensible Stylesheet Language Transformation). If you have basic questions about any of these topics, now is a great time to review Chapter 6; that chapter includes material on XML document formatting, samples illustrating the use of XML documents for Web development, and references for additional research.

Two other features characterize this chapter's XML coverage. The second major feature is the special emphasis on using XML with SQL Server 2000 databases. Although some of the techniques demonstrated in this chapter, particularly those involving ADO.NET data sets, are appropriate for other database sources, all samples are tested and evaluated for their specific usefulness with SQL Server 2000. The third feature characterizing this chapter is the focus on SQL Server 2000 Web releases. Chapter 6 included coverage of Web releases 1 and 2, but this chapter positions Web Release 3 relative to the two earlier releases. In addition, I drill down on two innovations (SQLXML managed classes and DiffGrams) introduced with Web Release 2 that have a special relevance for .NET developers. Microsoft's stated policy is to keep SQL Server 2000 current with the latest XML developments through a sequence of Web releases. Innovations introduced with the Web releases materially affect your ability to use Visual Basic .NET to process SQL Server data sources with XML.

After overviews of the Web releases and the XML technologies in the .NET Framework, this chapter presents a series of samples in four sections. The first set of samples targets creating XML documents with SQL queries and annotated

XML schemas. The second set of samples expands the functionality available with the first set of samples by imparting the ability to generate XML documents based on run-time input. In addition, this second section demonstrates the use of XPath queries to return XML documents and reveals alternative means to produce equivalent results with SQL queries. The third section particularly examines the interplay between ADO.NET data sets and XML documents. It also examines ways of performing advanced XPath queries. A couple of samples in this section demonstrate how to process XML documents with hierarchical data sets as well as how to manage changes to a remote SQL Server database. The chapter's closing section drills down on how to use XSLT to prepare Web pages with HTML tables based on XML documents that you create with Visual Basic .NET from a SQL Server data source.

All except one of the samples for this chapter reside in *Module1* of the XMLSamples solution. These samples highlight the Visual Basic .NET code for managing XML documents when working with SQL Server data sources. Examine other chapters for more general coverage of Visual Basic .NET development. (For example, see Chapter 9 for coverage of Windows forms and controls.) You can invoke this chapter's samples by removing the comment character from the main procedure line that specifies the procedure to run. In several cases, you need to remove the comment character from more than one line. The text describing these samples explicitly specifies the lines that need to have their comment markers removed. The one sample not in the XMLSamples solution folder has the name XMLWebSample. This ASP.NET project has two folders, one for the wwwroot folder within the Inetpub directory on your Web server, and a second one for inclusion in the normal place where you hold your Visual Basic .NET solution folders. Both folders for the ASP.NET solution have the name XMLWebSample.

SQL Server Web Releases

If you're going to use XML with SQL Server 2000, you should definitely evaluate the most recent Web release. As I write this chapter, that release is Web Release 3. Microsoft continues to fully support all Web releases. This section builds on your prior exposure to Web releases and general XML functionality availability from SQL Server 2000. (See Chapter 6.) In addition, this section introduces Web Release 3, which wasn't discussed in Chapter 6. I also present in this section two important XML technologies for .NET development (SQLXML managed classes and DiffGrams) that were introduced with Web Release 2 but haven't gained focus in the book to this point.

Overview of First and Second Web Releases

Review Chapter 6 for a more thorough description of the first and second Web releases for SQL Server 2000. The first Web release for SQL Server 2000, which shipped February 15, 2001, featured the introduction of Updategrams. This XML-based technology enables developers to manipulate a SQL Server database programmatically through HTTP protocol via a Web connection. Although data manipulation is possible via a Web connection, the capability is still subject to standard security administration rules. In addition, Web Release 1 introduced the capability to bulk-load XML documents into a SQL Server database.

Web Release 2 shipped on October 15, 2001. This update to SQL Server 2000 added more general XML features, such as client-side formatting, as well as a couple of capabilities that explicitly targeted .NET developers—SQLXML Managed Classes and DiffGrams. With SQLXML Managed Classes, developers can take advantage of Web release features directly from the .NET environment. You use these classes instead of selected ADO.NET classes. For example, replace the *SqlDataAdapter* ADO.NET class with the *SqlXmlAdapter* SQLXML Managed Class. In addition to offering more functionality, the syntax for SQLXML Managed Classes is easier to master. The second new feature with special interest for .NET developers is the DiffGram. This XML document type facilitates the updating of a SQL Server database directly from within the .NET Framework. See Chapter 6 for coverage of the full set of enhancements introduced with Web Release 2.

Overview of Web Release 3

Web Release 3 is part of the Microsoft SQL Server 2000 Web Services Toolkit. Web Release 3 became available as a stand-alone product on February 9, 2002. The toolkit shipped slightly later (February 14, 2002). The headline capability of the Microsoft SQL Server 2000 Web Services Toolkit is its ability to expose SQL Server stored procedures as XML Web services. Chapter 13 will explore this aspect of the toolkit because that chapter covers how to program XML Web services. There are two URLs for downloading Web Release 3. If you want the core capabilities of Web Release 3 without the special features introduced by the Microsoft SQL Server 2000 Web Services Toolkit, you can download them from *http://msdn.microsoft.com/downloads/default.asp?URL=/downloads/sample.asp?url=/MSDN-FILES/027/001/824/msdncompositedoc.xml.*

If you want the full features of the toolkit, you can go to the Web site at the following URL. This site offers a much larger file for download than the basic Web Release 3 (12.3 MB vs. 2.7 MB) as well as a link for the Microsoft SOAP Toolkit, which you will need in order to publish an XML Web service. The site also includes links for Webcasts and white papers that you may find of value: *http://msdn.microsoft.com/downloads/default.asp?url=/downloads/sample.asp?url=/MSDN-FILES/027/001/872/msdncompositedoc.xml&frame=true*.

> **Note** I developed the samples in this chapter with the release containing the full features of the toolkit. Although you are downloading this version of Web Release 3, I urge you to download the Microsoft SOAP Toolkit 2.0, which is available from a link on the same page for the download of Web Release 3. Samples in Chapter 13 require SOAP (so you might as well clean up your act now).

Aside from the capability of publishing XML Web services, Web Release 3 features the same major capabilities of earlier Web releases with a variety of subtle improvements and bug fixes. For example, Web Release 3 introduces the *parentID* annotation for DiffGrams. The *SqlXmlAdapter* managed class uses this annotation as it performs data manipulation tasks for a SQL Server database from a Visual Basic .NET solution. Many of the enhancements are available through the IIS virtual directory for SQL Server. Web Release 3 includes the capability of upgrading virtual directories created with prior Web releases.

I recommend you deploy Web Release 3 if you don't have any solutions running with either of the prior two Web releases. This is because Web Release 3 includes the earlier two Web releases (along with the improvements introduced by Web Release 3). As is typical of new software, Web Release 3 isn't fully backward compatible with prior Web releases because of minor functional enhancements and bug fixes. Therefore, if you do have solutions running with earlier Web releases, you should test these solutions before deploying Web Release 3. One attractive option for those with solutions built for earlier Web releases is the ability to run Web Release 3 in a side-by-side mode with these earlier Web releases. This feature is possible because installing Web Release 3 (referred to as SQLXML 3.0) doesn't write over the files for prior Web releases. See caveats and special issues in the "Understanding the Side-by-Side Installation Issues" section (and the three subsequent ones) in the "About This Release" topic for the Web Release 3 documentation. You can open this documentation from the SQLXML 3.0 program group from the Windows Start menu.

> **Note** If you have only test solutions running, you may care to upgrade IIS virtual directories from Web Release 1 and Web Release 2 through the IIS Virtual Directory Management For SQLXML 3.0 utility. Double click the root of the old virtual directory in the IIS Virtual Directory Management For SQLXML 3.0 utility. Then select the Version 3 tab and click Upgrade To Version 3. Complete the upgrade by choosing Yes and then OK.

SQLXML Managed Classes

SQLXML Managed Classes enable you write Visual Basic .NET programs to tap the features from the second and third Web releases. There are three SQLXML managed classes. Their names are *SqlXmlCommand*, *SqlXmlParameter*, and *SqlXmlAdapter*. You use these classes within Visual Basic .NET procedures to create objects and then gain programmatic control of their properties and methods. The SQLXML Managed Classes propagate no events.

Although you use the SQLXML Managed Classes from within .NET Framework programs, there is no documentation on the classes available from within either Visual Studio .NET Help or Visual Basic .NET Help. Web Release 3 Help details the properties and methods exposed by the SQLXML Managed Classes. In addition, this Help system includes several code samples that you are likely to find useful. One of the white papers (titled "SQLXML Managed Classes") available as part of the Microsoft SQL Server 2000 Web Services Toolkit includes more background that I found helpful in understanding how to use these valuable classes.

> **Note** All the sources of help for the SQLXML Managed Classes mentioned previously explicitly specify how to use the classes with C# programs and include code samples for using them with C#. Because the .NET Framework Help generally provides code samples in Visual Basic .NET as well C#, you may be misled to believe that the SQLXML Managed Classes work only with C#. You can translate all the C# samples into Visual Basic .NET syntax. This chapter includes several Visual Basic .NET samples that you can use as a guide for translating C# samples.

SqlXmlCommand Class

You instantiate a *SqlXmlCommand* object by designating the connection string for the object as part of an expression with the *New* operator. There is no explicit connection class in the SQLXML Managed Classes. The connection string must designate the sqloledb data provider as well as the classic ADO and ADO.NET features of a server, database, and security identification. For example,

```
Dim cmd1 As SqlXmlCommand = New SqlXmlCommand(provider=sqloledb; _
    server=servername;database=databasename;user id=userlogin; _
    password=userpassword)
```

Before you can use (or instantiate) any SQLXML managed class, your Visual Basic .NET module must have a reference to the *Microsoft.Data.SqlXml* namespace. You can add this reference from within Visual Studio .NET by opening the Code Editor and choosing Add Reference from the Project menu. On the .NET tab of the Add Reference dialog box, choose Microsoft.Data.SqlXml from the Component Name column. If your workstation has both Web Release 2 and Web Release 3, select the appropriate version of Microsoft.Data.Sql.Xml for the Web release you're using. Web Release 3 has the version number of 3.0.1523.0; the version number for Web Release 2 is 2.0.1125.0. After adding the reference to a solution, you need to specify an *Imports* statement in any module you'll be using the managed class in unless you want to precede individual references to class entities with the *Microsoft.Data.SqlXml* namespace identifier.

> **Note** It should be obvious by this point in the book that I don't rigidly adhere to programming conventions. This is because I believe specific contexts—both technical and business—should have strong bearing on programming conventions. For example, the demands for code samples designed to illustrate design features aren't necessarily the same as those for production software, which are also different from those for prototype software. Nevertheless, many readers may want a starting point for guidelines on whether to use namespace prefixes or *Imports* statements. Consider using namespace prefixes when you want to draw explicit attention to the namespace source for a particular object.

***SqlXmlCommand* Methods** As its name implies, a *SqlXmlCommand* object can perform a SQL statement against a database on a SQL Server and return the result set in XML format. For example, the *ExecuteStream* method generates the result set for a SQL statement and creates a new *Stream* object for the result set in XML format. A *Stream* object represents a byte sequence, such as the byte sequence for an XML document. Before you can work with the contents of a *Stream* object, you will typically pass it to a reader and the reader will pass its output to an XML document that you can view or process as text characters. There are several varieties of *Stream* objects. The samples within this chapter demonstrate how to work with *FileStream* and *MemoryStream* objects, which are both defined in the *Sytem.IO* namespace. A *FileStream* object points to a file in your file system. A *MemoryStream* object is a memory variable that you can reference as long as it has scope. The *ExecuteToStream* method for a *SqlXmlCommand* object passes its result set to an existing *Stream* object instead of creating a new *Stream* object.

You can use a *SqlXmlCommand* object to pass back an *XmlReader* object with the *ExecuteXmlReader* method. An *XmlReader* object is an element in the *System.Xml* namespace. Procedures using *XmlReader* objects gain fast, noncached, forward-only access to a stream containing XML. One common reason for generating an *XmlReader* object is to select a subset of the nodes in the XML document associated with the *XmlReader* object. A *node* can correspond to a row in the data that an XML document comprises. In this context, selecting a subset of the nodes is equivalent to using a *WHERE* clause in a *SELECT* statement to specify a subset of the rows in a table or a view.

You can also invoke the *CreateParameter* and *ClearParameters* methods with instances of the *SqlXmlCommand* class. The *CreateParameter* method lets you add a parameter to a *SqlXmlCommand* object so that you can specify values at run time. This capability enables your procedures to dynamically set values for commands based on user input or other aspects of the operating environment. If you want to reuse a *SqlXmlCommand* object with other parameters or no parameters, invoke the *ClearParameters* method to remove any existing parameters.

One last method completes the functionality offered by the *SqlXmlCommand* class. The *ExecuteNonQuery* method is suitable for commands that don't return a result set, such as DiffGrams.

***SqlXmlCommand* Properties** The possible settings for the *CommandType* property of a *SqlXmlCommand* object point to the special kind of roles that a *SqlXmlCommand* object can play. The following enumeration of *CommandType* settings designates all the possible sources for a *SqlXmlCommand* object.

- *SqlXmlCommandType.Sql* indicates that the command specifies a SQL source, such as a *SELECT* statement with a *FOR XML* clause, for the command.
- *SqlXmlCommandType.XPath* is appropriate when you designate a query command with an XPath expression.

- *SqlXmlCommandType.TemplateFile* permits the execution of a template file, containing either SQL or XPath syntax, in a path named by the *CommandText* property. The *CommandText* property points specifically to the template file. These template files have the same design as those reviewed in Chapter 6, but they don't have to reside in an IIS virtual directory.
- *SqlXmlCommandType.Template* enables the command to execute the contents of a template file, containing either SQL or XPath syntax, in a path specified by the *CommandStream* property. The *CommandStream* property designates the parameters for opening a file stream object with the template. The *SqlXmlCommandType.TemplateFile* parameter merely points to the path and filename for the template file—not its actual contents.
- *SqlXmlCommandType.UpdateGram* specifies an Updategram object for a command to execute.
- *SqlXmlCommandType.Diffgram* designates a DiffGram as the command's argument.

Use the *CommandText* property to designate the source for a *SqlXmlCommand* object. For example, a *CommandType* setting of *SqlXmlCommandType.TemplateFile* enables you to use the *CommandText* property to point to the path and filename for the template file. In Visual Basic .NET applications, you don't have the same need to shield the text for a query statement as with Web applications and IIS virtual directories; this is because users run Visual Basic .NET solutions from compiled .exe files. You will typically use either SQL or XPath syntax to specify the *CommandText* property with a matching *CommandType* property setting.

Selected other *SqlXmlCommand* properties appear in the samples throughout this chapter. When your result set doesn't include a single top-level or root element, you can designate one with the *RootTag* property. If you use an XPath query, you can specify the path for the mapping schema file associated with a query through the *SqlXmlCommand* object's *SchemaPath* property. A mapping schema can denote with special annotations correspondences between the elements and attributes of a schema representing an XML document and a SQL Server data source. The *XslPath* property enables you to designate the filename and path for a file that transforms the raw XML output specified by a *CommandText* property into another format, such as an HTML table. See the "SqlXmlCommand Object" topic in the Web Release 3 documentation for summaries of a few *SqlXmlCommand* properties that this chapter doesn't cover.

SqlXmlParameter Class

SqlXmlCommand objects can have hierarchically dependent parameters represented by *SqlXmlParameter* objects. Use the *CreateParameter* method for a *SqlXmlCommand* object to instantiate a parameter object. After its instantiation, you can assign values to the parameter's *Name* and *Value* properties. The *Name* property gives you a convenient handle for referencing the parameter object, and the *Value* property enables you to assign a value to a parameter at run time.

SqlXmlAdapter Class

SqlXmlAdapter objects serve a purpose that generally corresponds to that for the *SqlDataAdapter* object in the *System.Data.SqlClient* namespace. After declaring a variable as a *SqlXmlAdapter* object, you can instantiate the variable with an expression containing the *New* operator for the *SqlXmlAdapter* class. The *SqlXmlAdapter* object can take a variable pointing to a *SqlXmlCommand* object as its argument. The syntax for this construction appears here, where *cmd1* represents a previously instantiated *SqlXmlCommand* object. The *cmd1* argument designates the data source to which a *SqlXmlAdapter* connects.

```
Dim dap1 as SqlXmlAdapter
Dap1 = New SqlXmlAdapter (cmd1)
```

SqlXmlAdapter objects have two methods, *Fill* and *Update*. Use the *Fill* method to populate a data set. Invoke the *Update* method to insert, modify, or delete rows in the data source to which a *SqlXmlAdapter* object points. For either method, all you have to do is specify a data set as the argument. There is no need to designate a specific table within the data set. I like the *SqlXmlAdapter* object because of the easy way in which it permits me to specify data manipulation tasks relative to the *SqlDataAdapter* object in the *System.Data.SqlClient* namespace. A pair of samples later in this chapter demonstrates the new syntax that eliminates the need for an *UpdateCommand* property (and, by extension, *InsertCommand* and *DeleteCommand* properties).

DiffGrams Let You Modify Data

A DiffGram is an XML format for representing the data values in a data set. The .NET Framework automatically uses this XML format for passing data between a client and a SQL Server database. In addition, you can use the DiffGram format directly with SQL Server databases similarly to the way that you use Updategrams. See Chapter 6 for examples of how to use Updategrams for data manipulation tasks with a SQL Server 2000 database as a guideline for the kinds of ways in which you can use DiffGrams in Web applications with SQL Server.

The following code shows the general layout for a DiffGram. Notice that it starts with a declaration stating that it is an XML document. Then it references several namespaces. For data manipulation tasks, the core of the document is the *DataInstance* and *before* sections. The *DataInstance* section denotes the current value of all rows in a data source. For example, this section contains any rows with modified column values, any inserted rows, and any unmodified rows that aren't deleted from the data source. The *before* section conveys the before values for modified rows. Deleted rows also appear in the *before* section but not in the *DataInstance* section. The *errors* section is optional; it contains error messages for rows from the *DataInstance* section. A collection of attributes facilitate selected objectives, such as matching rows in the *DataInstance* section with corresponding rows in the *before* and *errors* sections as well as highlighting rows participating in insert, update, and delete tasks.

```
<?xml version="1.0"?>
<diffgr:diffgram
        xmlns:msdata="urn:schemas-microsoft-com:xml-msdata"
        xmlns:diffgr="urn:schemas-microsoft-com:xml-diffgram-v1"
        xmlns:xsd="http://www.w3.org/2001/XMLSchema">

    <DataInstance>
    </DataInstance>

    <diffgr:before>
    </diffgr:before>

    <diffgr:errors>
    </diffgr:errors>

</diffgr:diffgram>
```

If you are a Visual Basic developer migrating to the .NET Framework, it may please you to learn that you can benefit from DiffGrams without really learning their format. For example, Chapter 10 and Chapter 11 illustrate how to perform data manipulation tasks with Windows Forms and ASP.NET pages. In both cases, ADO.NET uses DiffGrams in the background. I find that understanding the format and layout of DiffGrams helps me to understand the reason for the syntax to designate data manipulation tasks in the .NET Framework. I have two favorite resources for developing the understanding.

- The "DiffGrams" topic in the Visual Studio .NET documentation; you can get to this documentation from the Windows Start menu.
- The "Using DiffGrams to Modify Data" topic in the Web Release 3 documentation; this ships and installs with the standard version of Web Release 3, and you can get to the documentation from the Windows Start menu.

This chapter includes a couple of samples manipulating ADO.NET data sets with SQLXML managed classes. One of these samples highlights how the .NET Framework uses DiffGrams during data manipulation tasks. The second sample illustrates how easy it is to convert this ADO.NET application for a Windows application to an ASP.NET application. Both samples confirm that you can perform data manipulation tasks that take advantage of DiffGrams without manipulating them in your code.

The fact that you can use DiffGrams without actually coding them raises an interesting question about the general role of XML for typical .NET developers. There is no doubt that for intermediate and advanced .NET developers a firm grasp of XML will be mandatory. However, it remains to be seen to what degree typical developers will need to master all (or even most of) the details of all XML programming languages. (See the next section for an overview of some of these languages.) For example, it may be that much of the XML syntax is unnecessary because you can indirectly manipulate XML with Visual Basic .NET or with *SELECT* statements containing a *FOR XML* clause. If this trend continues, XML could underlie a broad range of functions, but typical developers will be able to use another, more familiar, language to manipulate XML constructs. This is similar to the way Visual Basic developers used to employ ADO as a way to program OLE DB data providers. On the other hand, XML may emerge as the must-know syntax for all "real" developers. Indeed, if you measure the amount of space devoted to XML in computer publications, you could easily come to this conclusion. I am not sure where you will end up on this continuum. However, it is clear that not learning XML is a risky way to manage your future as a developer.

Overview of XML Technologies

There's a lot more to XML than the basic design of an XML document that contains data. This section is designed to work in concert with the coverage of XML document formats and related technologies introduced in Chapter 6. In addition, the section provides an overview of the kinds of XML-related tasks that you can perform from the .NET Framework.

XML Data Formats

There are several distinguishing features of XML formats.

- Tags can be customized for particular documents.
- You can represent data with either elements or attributes.
- All XML documents start with a declaration stating the version of XML in the document.

These and other syntax features are discussed in Chapter 6 at a level sufficient for grasping the material in this chapter. Scan the sections on XML formats and schemas to make sure that you have an adequate background for the material in this chapter. Visit the World Wide Web Consortium site (*http://www.w3c.org* or *http://www.w3.org*) for definitive information on the latest XML standards in the public domain.

XML Documents

The XML data format wins praise for many reasons. One of the most prominent for database developers is the ability of XML data to represent hierarchical relationships. The style for representing hierarchical relationships in XML documents is a distinct departure from relational data models that depict hierarchical relationships with a join between two or more tables. For example, an XML document can portray a collection of orders with the line items, or order details, physically within each order. In the hierarchical representation popular in XML formats, each row from the *Orders* table appears once no matter how many line items are within an order. A relational model portrays the collection of orders as a single flat virtual table with data from the *Order Details* table matching corresponding data from the *Orders* table. In the relational representation, identical column values from the *Orders* table repeat in the virtual table for each line item within an order.

Another very important characteristic of XML formatting is that it represents data as text. This means you (and other humans) can read it without any special translations. Prior data formats typically used some kind of binary format that made the data in the document less immediately accessible and also less transportable through corporate firewalls. Although a rich programming model is available for processing XML data documents, it is important to understand that an XML document is just text. Therefore, it is possible to devise traditional text parsing techniques to extract selected data items from an XML document. I will demonstrate a custom parsing technique later in this chapter.

XML Schemas

In addition to data in XML documents, you will often work with schemas for XML documents. Schemas for XML documents serve similar roles to schemas for databases. Namely, a schema describes data elements and relationships between collections of data elements. You can use the .NET Framework both to help you construct new schemas and to write schemas for existing documents. This chapter focuses exclusively on schemas in XSD format. XSD is the current standard for representing the structure of a document. When Microsoft first shipped SQL Server 2000, it adopted an XDR format for designating the structure of documents. This is because when the XDR format was specified, there was no universally adopted standard, such as XSD, for representing the structure of an XML document. Microsoft published an XSLT style sheet for transforming schemas in XDR format to corresponding XSD schemas. You can find this style sheet at *http://msdn.microsoft.com/downloads/default.asp?url=/downloads/sample.asp?url=/MSDN-FILES/027/001/539/msdncompositedoc.xml.*

As a .NET developer working with SQL Server, you will most often base your XML documents on SQL Server data sources. In this case, the .NET Framework can infer a schema for an XML document from the schema for the SQL Server data source supplying values to the XML document. Indeed, you can manipulate ADO.NET objects and build indirectly a DiffGram or XSD schema from within the .NET Framework.

One reason for manually creating your own schema is to create a strongly typed data set. This kind of data set can act as a custom class except that it inherits the properties, methods, and events for an ADO.NET data set. You designate a schema at design time for the class that defines the structure for the strongly typed data set. Then you can instantiate an instance of the data set at any time with the same *New* operator that you use for instantiating other objects. You can populate the typed data set instance with a *SqlDataAdapter* object. Strongly typed data sets offer distinct advantages over standard data sets that .NET builds for you. For example, you can explicitly refer to columns by name instead of by their column position within a data table in a data set. See the "Working with a Typed DataSet" topic and its links in the Visual Studio .NET documentation for more detail on this type of data set, instructions on how to create one, and a code sample for using one.

Annotated schemas are a special type of schema for designating the structure of an XML document while you concurrently specify an external source for the structure. Instead of having the .NET Framework implicitly build a schema, you can explicitly create one. The "Using Annotations in XSD Schemas" topic in the documentation for Web Release 3 includes many helpful links for drilling down further on manual techniques that you can use to build annotated schemas. A general grasp of this material combined with numerous samples throughout the .NET Framework documentation and in this book can help you read annotated schemas and adapt them for custom extensions in your work. Two common uses for annotated schemas in the .NET Framework include basing an XML document on a database and facilitating the naming of column names differently in an XML document from its underlying data source.

XPath Queries

XPath is a language that permits you to address the parts of an XML document. You can use XPath to query an XML document much as you use SQL to query a database. An XPath query expression can select on document parts, or types, such as the document's elements, attributes, and text. You can select nodes for ancestors, descendants, and siblings of a specified document type. An ancestor is a type that contains the current type. For example, an order is the ancestor of an order detail item. Conversely, a descendant is contained within the current type. Each type that you use for selection in an XPath query can return a set of nodes. These nodes correspond generally to the rows in the result set from a SQL statement, but the syntax for designating XML document types with an XPath query is entirely different from traditional SQL syntax.

You can use SQLXML Managed Classes to formulate and execute XPath queries. You can even make the query statements dynamic at run time. The set of nodes returned by an XPath query is contained in an *XmlNodeList* object. The .NET Framework enables Visual Basic developers to iterate through the nodes within a node list to examine the result from an XPath query expression. Several samples throughout the balance of this chapter demonstrate the syntax for performing this kind of task. See Chapter 6 for additional coverage of the XPath language and additional resources for learning more about it.

XSLT Formatting

XSLT permits the programmatic transformation of files in XML format to various other formats. XSLT has many potential applications, but this book drills down on the capability of XSLT to transform raw XML files into HTML tables on Web pages. You can specify an XSLT transformation with SQLXML Managed Classes from within a .NET application. The .xslt file exists as a separate file, and the .NET application can refer to the .xslt file as a property setting for the *SqlXml-Command* object.

An .xslt file can contain style sheet elements, HTML code, and processing instructions for extracting content from an XML document. An .xslt file is the kind of file that a Web developer is more likely to construct than a typical Visual Basic developer. With sufficient forethought and collaboration, the Web developer can prepare a set of standard .xslt files for reuse by Visual Basic developers. Given the existence of an .xslt file, a Visual Basic developer can readily reference it to format data for a Web page. That is, a Visual Basic program can directly create an HTML file with the help of an .xslt file. A Visual Basic developer can use the *SqlXmlCommand* class to extract rows in XML format from a SQL Server data source and then assign a property setting to the *SqlXmlCommand* class instance that enables the formatting of rows for display on a Web page as an HTML table. The Web page will be static. However, by letting users invoke the program to create the static page, the .NET Framework can permit the creation of content in Web format on demand.

Generating XML Documents with the .NET Framework

This section demonstrates techniques for creating and persisting XML documents based on SQL Server data sources. Mastering the concepts for achieving this kind of task introduces you to techniques for working with XML content within a Visual Basic .NET application. Because XML is important for so many purposes, including publishing content as HTML, it is important for you to learn these techniques.

For many of the samples throughout this chapter, you will need to add a reference to the *Microsoft.Data.SqlXml* namespace. See the section titled "SQLXML Managed Classes" for detailed instructions on adding a reference to the *Microsoft.Data.SqlXml* namespace. In addition, some samples also assume an *Imports* statement for this namespace and selected other namespaces. I developed all the samples in this chapter, except one, with the following *Imports* statements above the start of the module. I issue special instructions for setting up the environment for the exception as I describe it.

```
Imports Microsoft.Data.SqlXml
Imports System.Data.SqlClient
Imports System.Xml
Imports System.IO
```

Creating an XML Document with T-SQL

One of the most natural ways for a SQL Server developer to create an XML document is with a SQL statement. Recall from Chapter 6 that SQL will generate XML fragments with the *FOR XML* clause (if the result set includes more than a single row). Actually, the fragments are nearly complete XML documents except for a root-level element. Therefore, one approach to creating a result set as an XML document is to execute a SQL statement with a *FOR XML* clause and to declare a root-level element. Because a SQL statement is a command to a SQL Server instance, you can use a *SqlXmlCommand* object to execute the command and return an XML document.

The *SqlXmlCommand* object has several features that make it particularly appropriate for connecting to a SQL Server data source and returning an XML document. The constructor for a *SqlXmlCommand* object takes a connection string directly. This means there is no need to instantiate a separate connection object when all you want to do is execute a command. Next, the *RootTag* property for a *SqlXmlCommand* object lets you specify a root-level element to transform the XML fragment returned by a SQL statement with the *FOR XML* clause into a complete XML document. Two more properties let you complete the SQL specification for the *SqlXmlCommand* object. Designate *SqlXmlCommandType.Sql* as the *CommandType* property to indicate that your command is to execute a SQL statement. Then assign the SQL statement to the *CommandText* property. Finally, the *ExecuteToStream* method for a *SqlXmlCommand* object can return the XML document as a sequence of bytes.

The *SaveDBQueryAsXmlToFile* procedure that follows illustrates the syntax for creating a file containing an XML document based on a SQL statement. The procedure begins by specifying a connection string for a *SqlXmlCommand* object. Because this object is an instance of the SQLXML Managed Class with the same name, the connection string must specify the SQLOLEDB data provider. The constructor for the *SqlXmlCommand* object then references this connection string to instantiate the object. The next block of code in the sample sets the *SqlXmlCommand* object properties for returning an XML document. In particular, the *CommandText* property indicates that the document will contain all rows from the *Shippers* table. The *RootTag* property designates the string "Shippers" to serve as a root-level element for the document.

As you can see, transferring the output to the *SqlXmlCommand* object to a file is a multistep process. Before invoking the *ExecuteToStream* method for the *SqlXmlCommand* object, you need to specify a name and a path for the file that will hold the XML document generated by the *SqlXmlCommand* object. The procedure completes this requirement with an assignment statement for a string named *myXMLfile*; the assigned value is the path and filename for the document. (You should specify a different path to the file if that path doesn't exist on your computer.) Next the procedure instantiates a *FileStream* object to store the XML document. The constructor takes two arguments. One is the string variable, *myXMLfile*, denoting the name and path for the file. The second argument indicates that the file should always be created—even if a file already exists with the name and path specified. Finally the *ExecuteToStream* method takes the *FileStream* object as an argument so that the *SqlXmlCommand* object knows where to deposit the XML document that it generates. The procedure concludes by closing the *FileStream* object. This step returns control to the application from the file.

```
Sub SaveDBQueryAsXmlToFile()
    'Specify connection string for SqlXmlCommand.
    Dim cnn1String As String = _
      "Provider=SQLOLEDB;Server=(local);" & _
      "database=Northwind;" & _
      "Integrated Security=SSPI"

    'Specify connection for cmd1 SqlXmlCommand object.
    Dim cmd1 As SqlXmlCommand = _
        New Microsoft.Data.SqlXml.SqlXmlCommand(cnn1String)

    'Designate data source for cmd1.
    cmd1.RootTag = "Shippers"
    cmd1.CommandType = SqlXmlCommandType.Sql
    cmd1.CommandText = "SELECT * FROM Shippers " & _
        "FOR XML AUTO"

    'Name the path and file for the XML result set, then
    'instantiate a Stream object for the file's contents.
    Dim myXMLfile As String = _
```

```
        "c:\SQL Server Development with VBDotNet\" & _
        "Chapter12\myShippersFromFORXML.xml"
    Dim myFileStream As New System.IO.FileStream _
        (myXMLfile, System.IO.FileMode.Create)

    'Execute cmd1 and store the result set in the stream.
    cmd1.ExecuteToStream(myFileStream)

    'Close the file stream to recover the resource.
    myFileStream.Close()

End Sub
```

Figure 12-1 shows the XML document generated by the *SaveDBQuery-AsXmlToFile* procedure. I navigated to the file designated by the value assigned to *myXMLfile* and opened it from Windows Explorer. Its root-level element is Shippers, the value assigned to the *RootTag* property for the *SqlXmlCommand* object. The row values from the *Shippers* table appear as attributes with each row corresponding to the element. Each row has the same element name because of the way the *FOR XML* clause formats the result set; the element's name is the name of the row source for the *SELECT* statement—namely, *Shippers* for the *Shippers* table.

> **Note** Although it is good practice to name the root-level element differently from other elements within an XML document, you can see from the *SaveDBQueryAsXmlToFile* procedure and its output in Figure 12-1 that *SqlXmlCommand* permits you to generate an XML document with the root tag name matching the name of other elements.

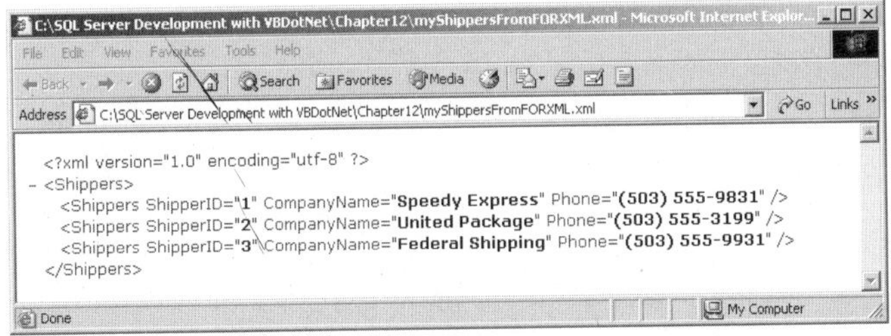

Figure 12-1. The output from the *SaveDBQueryAsXmlToFile* procedure opened in a browser from Windows Explorer.

Creating an XML Document with an Annotated Schema

Annotated schemas make it possible for you to specify the format for a result set. With the typical way of specifying a *FOR XML* clause in a *SELECT* statement, the column values in a result set always appear as attributes.

The following XML script shows an annotated schema for the *Shippers* table. The schema is named Shippers1.xsd and is located in the root folder for the XMLSamples solution. After the initial XML document declaration (remember, an XSD schema is an XML document), the listing specifies two namespaces for defining the terms in the schema. The first namespace points to the World Wide Web Consortium site for the XML schema specification. The second namespace points to a Microsoft universal resource name (*urn*) for mapping or annotated schemas.

The body of the schema starts by declaring an element named *Shipper*. This element has the annotation attribute *sql:relation,* which ties it to a data source named *Shippers*. When an application with a connection to the Northwind database references this schema, the application can extract rows from the *Shippers* table according to the format of the schema. This schema specifies the formatting of *ShipperID* column values as an attribute and *CompanyName* and *Phone* as elements. The use of the *sequence* element specifies that the *CompanyName* element must appear before the *Phone* element for each shipper.

```
<?xml version="1.0" encoding="utf-8" ?>
<xs:schema xmlns:xs="http://www.w3.org/2001/XMLSchema"
xmlns:sql="urn:schemas-microsoft-com:mapping-schema">
     <xs:element name="Shipper" sql:relation="Shippers">
        <xs:complexType>
            <xs:sequence>
                <xs:element name="CompanyName" type="xs:string" />
                <xs:element name="Phone" type="xs:string" />
            </xs:sequence>
            <xs:attribute name="ShipperID" type="xs:int" />
        </xs:complexType>
    </xs:element>
</xs:schema>
```

You can use an annotated schema along with a *SqlXmlCommand* object to return a result set from the *Shippers* table in the Northwind database, and you can persist that result set locally by saving the XML document as a file. When you use an annotated schema to format the XML document returned by a *SqlXmlCommand*, you must specify the location of the schema file as one of the *SqlXmlCommand* properties. Designate the path to the schema with the *SchemaPath* property. You can specify the path either as an absolute address or as a relative address. If you use a relative address, the address is relative to the .exe file for the .NET solution, which resides in the Bin subfolder of a solution's root folder. Therefore, if you save your schema in the root folder for a solution, the *SchemaPath* property should be ../Schemaname.xsd. The ../ designates the folder one up from the Bin subfolder, which is the root folder for a solution.

When you use a *SchemaPath* property, you must specify the *CommandText* property for a *SqlXmlCommand* with an XPath expression. When you want to return a single table and the schema denotes just one table, the XPath expression is very simple. Just list the outermost element in the schema, which in this case is *Shipper*.

The *RunAnnotatedSchemaXPathQuery* procedure shows the syntax for generating an XML document based on the Shippers1.xsd annotated schema. Despite many similarities with the preceding sample, this one differs in several respects. The most important differences appear in bold type. Notice that the *SqlXmlCommand* object in this sample has a *SchemaPath* property. You assign the property a string value that points to the location of the annotated schema. Next, the *CommandType* property designates an XPath query. The *CommandText* property specifies the query as an XPath expression.

Aside from these differences, all the other changes are cosmetic or at least not essential. The most important of these minor changes is the path and filename for persisting the XML document created by the *SqlXmlCommand* object. For this sample, the file's name is myShippersFROMANNOTATEDSCHEMA.xml. By using a different name from the preceding sample, you can more readily contrast the output from the two samples.

```
Sub RunAnnotatedSchemaXPathQuery()
    'Specify connection string for SqlXmlCommand.
    Dim cnn1String As String = _
      "Provider=SQLOLEDB;Server=(local);" & _
      "database=Northwind;" & _
      "Integrated Security=SSPI"

    'Specify connection for cmd1 SqlXmlCommand object.
    Dim cmd1 As SqlXmlCommand = _
        New Microsoft.Data.SqlXml.SqlXmlCommand(cnn1String)

    'Specify root tag for XML file.
    cmd1.RootTag = "Shippers"

    'Designate an XPath query based on an
    'annotated schema using the Shipper element
    'in the Shippers1.xsd schema one directory
    'above .exe file for application.
    cmd1.SchemaPath = ("..\Shippers1.xsd")
    cmd1.CommandType = SqlXmlCommandType.XPath
    cmd1.CommandText = "Shipper"
```

(continued)

```
        'Name the file for the XML result set, then
        'instantiate a Stream object for the file's contents.
        Dim myXMLfile As String = _
            "c:\SQL Server Development with VBDotNet\" & _
            "Chapter12\myShippersFROMANNOTATEDSCHEMA.xml"
        Dim myFileStream As New System.IO.FileStream _
            (myXMLfile, System.IO.FileMode.Create)

        'Execute cmd1 and store the result set in the stream
        'before closing the stream file.
        cmd1.ExecuteToStream(myFileStream)
        myFileStream.Close()

End Sub
```

Figure 12-2 shows the XML document saved by the *RunAnnotatedSchemaXPathQuery* procedure. Notice that this document has a different format from the one based on the *SELECT* statement with a *FOR XML* clause. In fact, the document in Figure 12-2 has the format specified by the preceding annotated schema. You can adjust the schema to show just a subset of column values or arrange the elements differently or switch the column values that appear as elements vs. attributes. Therefore, using an XPath query with an annotated schema enables you to specify the format for the XML document.

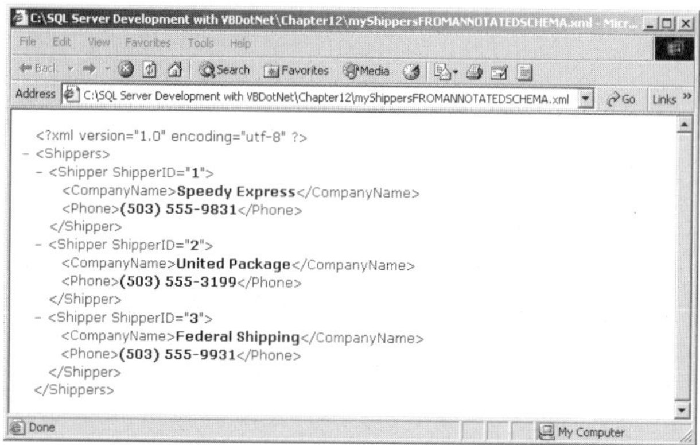

Figure 12-2. The output from the *RunAnnotatedSchemaXPathQuery* procedure opened in a browser from Windows Explorer.

Designing Annotated Schemas

Now that you see how flexible annotated schemas are, you may be wondering if there is any easy way to create them from within Visual Studio .NET. Developers have their choice of at least a couple of techniques for building annotated schemas and incorporating them into their solutions.

Creating a Schema with Code

Let's say you already have a schema, such as Shippers1.xsd, already developed in another text editor. You may want to copy the text for the annotated schema to Visual Studio .NET for more fine-tuning and saving within the solution's folder. Visual Studio .NET offers the XML Designer for this purpose. To open a new window in the XML Designer, choose Add New Item from the Project menu in Visual Studio .NET, select the XML Schema template from the Add New Item dialog, and then either accept the default name or specify a new name such as Shippers2. By default, the designer automatically appends the .xsd extension and saves the schema file in the root folder for the current solution. You can override these defaults if your prefer.

> **Note** Storing an annotated schema file, and other resource files, within a solution's folder simplifies deployment. This is because all the files reside within a single folder that you can deploy to another computer.

The XML Designer offers two views of a schema—a graphical one in its Schema view and a text-based one in its XML view. You can select a view by selecting tabs at the bottom of the window. To enter a new schema from scratch, switch to the XML view. The template automatically enters a document type declaration as well as several other namespace and related settings. You can amend or edit these as your needs dictate. For example, you can add a declaration for a custom namespace to define special attribute or element names. Start typing the new schema after the last namespace declaration and before the ending schema tag (*</xs:schema>*).

If you want to copy the text of a previously existing schema into the designer, copy that text to the Windows Clipboard, and then switch to Visual Studio .NET. Show the XML view of a new designer window. Depending on the source of the original schema, you may need to edit the copied schema. For example, opening and closing angle brackets (< and >) may appear with the special XML escape representations < and >. I noticed this requirement for schemas copied from the Visual Studio .NET documentation. You can use the Edit, Find And Replace, Replace menu option in Visual Studio .NET to change all the escape representations to < and >. Figure 12-3 shows an XML view of a copied schema with an edit in progress.

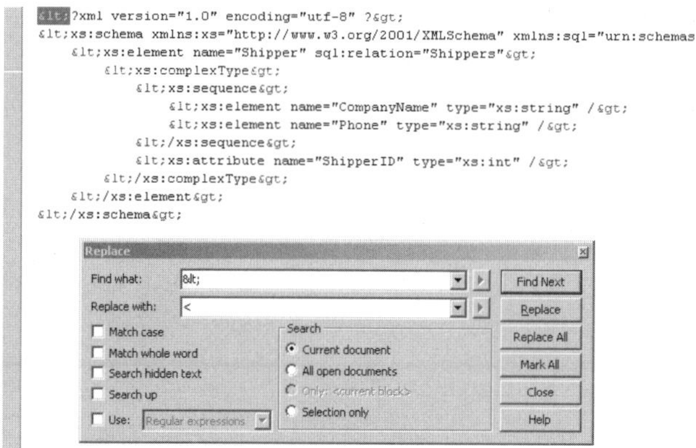

Figure 12-3. The XML view of a copied schema just before the editing of the < escape representation to <.

Creating a Schema Graphically

Some may welcome the fact that Visual Studio .NET can build annotated schemas with graphical techniques. Again, you'll start with a new template. Unless you define a custom name, the first schema you create in a project will have the name XMLSchema1.xsd. The number will increment by one for each subsequent schema you add to the project with the default naming conventions.

With your new XML Designer window open in Schema view, choose Server Explorer from the View menu. From the Server Explorer window, expand Servers and the server you are using, then SQL Servers and the SQL Server instance you want, and then a database on that server instance. To use the Tables collection within the database as the source for a schema, expand Tables. Then drag one or more tables from the Server Explorer window to the Schema view of your new schema, XMLSchema1.xsd. Figure 12-4 shows the XMLSchema1.xsd schema just after dragging the *Shippers* table from the Northwind database on a SQL Server instance named CCS1. The graphical view shows the definition of a *Shippers* entity within a document. The primary key definition comes across—notice the key icon next to the *ShipperID* element in the *Shippers* entity definition.

Although close to what you need, this graphically created schema requires a little fine-tuning for use with the *SqlXmlCommand* object. You can perform the final editing in XML view. The following listing is the schema from Figure 12-4 in XML view. The element lines for *ShipperID*, *CompanyName*, and *Phone* wrap onto a second line. Within the designer, each of these elements appears as one long line. The lines shown here in bold require removal; the lines to remove don't appear as bold within the XML view of the designer. Deleting the lines with bold text and saving the schema as XMLSchema1.xsd creates a schema that you can use just like the Shippers1.xsd schema that was created manually. This schema editing plan removes the Document box and the primary key designation from *ShipperID* in Schema view of XMLSchema1.xsd.

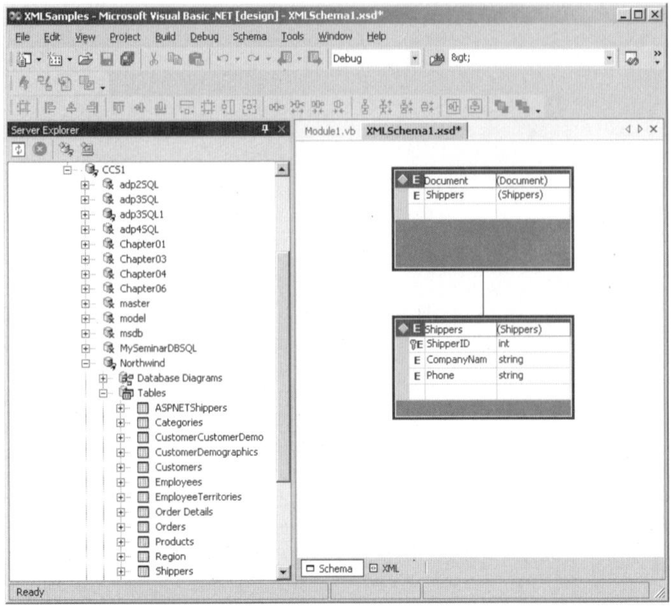

Figure 12-4. The initial graphical view of the *Shippers* table dragged from the Northwind database to XMLSchema1.xsd.

Note The graphically generated schema doesn't use any special SQLXML XSD annotation attributes, such as *sql:relation*. This is because graphically generated annotated schemas can make their connection through the *SqlXmlCommand* object connection and synchronize their element and attribute names with those in a source database object. For example, the element name *Shippers* corresponds to the *Shippers* table in the Northwind database. Similarly, the element names *ShipperID*, *CompanyName*, and *Phone* correspond to column names in the *Shippers* table.

```
<?xml version="1.0" encoding="utf-8" ?>

<xs:schema id="XMLSchema1" targetNamespace="http://tempuri.org/XMLSchema1.xsd"
elementFormDefault="qualified"
xmlns="http://tempuri.org/XMLSchema1.xsd"
xmlns:mstns="http://tempuri.org/XMLSchema1.xsd"
xmlns:xs="http://www.w3.org/2001/XMLSchema"
xmlns:msdata="urn:schemas-microsoft-com:xml-msdata">
<xs:element name="Document">
    <xs:complexType>
        <xs:choice maxOccurs="unbounded">
            <xs:element name="Shippers">
                <xs:complexType>
                    <xs:sequence>
                        <xs:element name="ShipperID" msdata:ReadOnly="true"_
                        msdata:AutoIncrement="true" type="xs:int" />
                        <xs:element name="CompanyName" type="xs:string" />
                        <xs:element name="Phone"_
                        type="xs:string" minOccurs="0" />
                    </xs:sequence>
                </xs:complexType>
            </xs:element>
        </xs:choice>
    </xs:complexType>
    <xs:unique name="DocumentKey1" msdata:PrimaryKey="true">
        <xs:selector xpath=".//mstns:Shippers" />
        <xs:field xpath="mstns:ShipperID" />
    </xs:unique>
</xs:element>
</xs:schema>
```

I created a procedure named *RunNETGeneratedSchemaXPathQuery* for generating an XML document based on the content in the *Shippers* table within the Northwind database. This procedure is identical to the *RunAnnotatedSchemaXPathQuery* schema shown previously except for two lines. The two replacement lines appear here. Notice that the new sample uses a different schema than in the earlier case. Also, the *CommandText* property changes from *Shipper* to *Shippers*. This is because the XMLSchema1.xsd schema uses *Shippers* to denote the element name for a shipper, while the Shipper1.xsd schema used the name *Shipper*. If we didn't change the *CommandText* property for the *SqlXmlCommand* property, the XPath query in the sample would fail.

```
cmd1.SchemaPath = ("..\XMLSchema1.xsd")
cmd1.CommandText = "Shippers"
```

For your convenience, a complete listing for the *RunNETGeneratedSchemaXPathQuery* procedure is available among this book's sample files.

Dynamically Setting an XML Result Set

The preceding section focused on creating XML results from a fixed source, such as all the rows and columns from the *Shippers* table. This general approach has the advantage of persisting remote database resources locally. The samples in this section enhance the functionality provided by those in the preceding section to work with data sources defined dynamically at run time. You can query a local XML document that you create either on the fly with the current procedure or previously with another procedure. The first sample in this section creates a specific XML document and saves it locally before querying it with a specific XPath expression. The second sample in this section illustrates creating any XML document on the fly and then querying it any way that you choose.

Using an XML document as the source for your queries relieves you of depending on a connection to a database server. However, there are times when your applications require the most recent data (and therefore, a local XML document won't be appropriate). The closing samples in this section demonstrate two progressively more flexible approaches to querying a remote SQL Server database and displaying the results as XML.

Running an XPath Query for a Specific XML Document

In addition to just saving a result set as an XML document, you can use the document and query the document directly. When working with an XML document, you cannot query the document with a SQL statement. In this situation, XPath is the ideal solution for deriving a result set that meets some criterion.

The sample procedure in this section, *RunXPathQueryWithArgumentForALocalDocument*, queries a local document. The procedure creates the document based on the *Products* table in the Northwind database. Then the procedure extracts document nodes that have a *Discontinued* attribute value equal to 1. This value signals that the corresponding product is no longer available for sale.

The procedure starts by using a *SELECT* statement with a *FOR XML* clause to extract all rows from the *Products* table in the Northwind database. Instead of using an *ExecuteToStream* method as in the samples from the preceding section, this sample invokes the *SqlXmlCommand* object's *ExecuteXmlReader* method. Recall that this method returns an *XMLReader* object (*xrd1*), which provides a fast forward-only non-cached stream containing XML. Instead of storing its XML document in a *FileStream* object as in the samples from the preceding section, this sample makes the XML available through a reader. The next step is to create an XML document based on the contents of the reader. The procedure does this in two steps. First it declares an *XMLDocument* object, *xdc1*. Second the procedure invokes the *Load* method for the document with the *XMLReader* object as an argument. After filling the XML document through the *XMLReader* object, the procedure immediately closes the reader to recover its resource as soon as possible.

Loading the XML document through the *XMLReader* object makes the XML from the *SELECT* statement available in memory. If the currency of the data were an issue (because the data doesn't change often or at all), we could have loaded the *xdc1* object with a previously saved copy of an XML document. (A subsequent sample demonstrates the syntax to accomplish this.) The samples in the preceding section demonstrate how to persist XML locally from a remote server.

With the aid of an XPath expression, the procedure generates an *XmlNodeList* object (*xnl1*), which you will recall is a collection of nodes from a document. The collection in this case satisfies the XPath expression in the *RunXPathQueryWithArgumentForALocalDocument* procedure. A node is an XPath item in a document. These items can include elements, attributes, and other features of an XML document. Recall that the XML document in this case is the result set from the *SELECT* statement with a *FOR XML* clause in the procedure. The XPath expression returns any element that contains a *Discontinued* attribute value of 1. The XPath expression applies to all nodes in the XML document because it selects nodes from the *DocumentElement* property, which contains the root element of an XML document. After creating the *XmlNodeList* object, the procedure reports on the list of nodes in two ways. First it reports the number of nodes in *xnl1*. Second the procedure enumerates the XML for the individual nodes within *xnl1*.

```
Sub RunXPathQueryWithArgumentForALocalDocument()
    'Specify connection string for SqlXmlCommand.
    Dim cnn1String As String = _
      "Provider=SQLOLEDB;Server=(local);" & _
      "database=Northwind;" & _
      "Integrated Security=SSPI"

    'Specify connection for cmd1 SqlXmlCommand object.
    Dim cmd1 As SqlXmlCommand = _
        New Microsoft.Data.SqlXml.SqlXmlCommand(cnn1String)

    'Designate data source for cmd1 with result set
    'in XML format.
    cmd1.RootTag = "Products"
    cmd1.CommandType = SqlXmlCommandType.Sql
    cmd1.CommandText = "SELECT * FROM Products FOR XML AUTO"

    'Pass the cmd1 result set to an XmlReader, and load
    'an XmlDocument with the contents of the XmlReader.
```

```
    Dim xrd1 As System.Xml.XmlReader = cmd1.ExecuteXmlReader()
    Dim xdc1 As New System.Xml.XmlDocument()
    xdc1.Load(xrd1)

    'Close the reader.
    xrd1.Close()

    'Specify an XPath query for nodes from the xdc1
    'XmlDocument with a Discontinued value of 1.
    Dim xnl1 As System.Xml.XmlNodeList = _
         xdc1.DocumentElement.SelectNodes _
         ("//Products[@Discontinued=1]")

    'Declare a node and a string.
    Dim xnd1 As System.Xml.XmlNode
    Dim str1 As String

    'For each node display a message with the contents,
    'including the XML tags.
    Debug.WriteLine( _
        "The record count for the result set is " & _
        xnl1.Count.ToString & ".")
    For Each xnd1 In xnl1
        str1 = xnd1.OuterXml
        Debug.WriteLine(str1)
    Next

End Sub
```

Figure 12-5 shows an excerpt from the Output window with results generated by the *RunXPathQueryWithArgumentForALocalDocument* procedure. It shows there are 8 products in the XML document based on the *Products* table with a *Discontinued* value of 1. The *ProductID* column values for discontinued products are 5, 9, 17, 24, 28, 29, 42, and 53. Notice the *ProductID* column values appear as XML attribute values. This is because the procedure invokes the *OuterXML* method to return the actual XML for each individual node within *xnl1*.

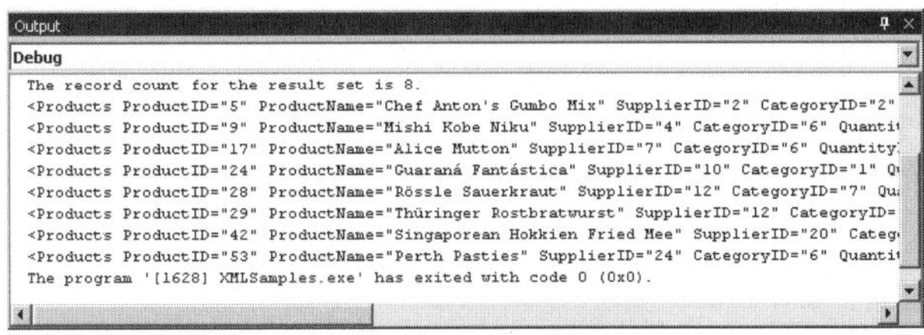

Figure 12-5. The *RunXPathQueryWithArgumentForALocalDocument* procedure returns XML content for discontinued products.

Running an XPath Query for Any XML Document

The preceding sample is interesting because it shows a practical use for an XML document based on a database object. Namely, you can process database contents through a local copy in an XML document. However, the preceding section's sample works for just one XML document. To make the sample work for another XML document, you need to get into the internals of the procedure and change specific lines of code. This is awkward. It would be much better if you could pass parameters that define the XML document and query and then have a procedure generate an appropriate result set. The sample in this section demonstrates how to code such a solution.

I developed two code blocks to call the sample procedure for this section. The first code block executes the same XPath query against the same XML document as in the preceding sample. What's different is that this sample passes the SQL for defining the document and the XPath query for the document as arguments. Unsurprisingly, this invocation of the procedure for this section generates the same results as for the sample in the preceding section. The second code block uses the same procedure to generate a different XPath query against a different XML document. Although it is clearly not surprising that we obtain a different result from the same procedure, the sample is interesting because it demonstrates how easy it is to accomplish this feat with an XPath query and an XML document—both of which are unfamiliar to typical Visual Basic developers.

The first code block contains three lines of code. The first line assigns a value to the *strSQL* string variable. This memory variable contains the SQL string for a result set that the *RunXPathQueryWithArgumentForAnyLocalDocument* procedure uses to populate an XML document. The second line of code assigns a value to the *strXPath* string variable, which stores an XPath query for the XML document generated by the procedure. It is the application of the XPath query to the XML document that generates a result set, such as the one in Figure 12-5. The final line of code in the first code block passes the *strSQL* and *strXPath* variables to the *RunXPathQueryWithArgumentForAnyLocalDocument* procedure. The procedure, in turn, executes the SQL query and populates an XML document with the result set. In the end, the procedure lists a set of nodes in the Output window.

```
Dim strSQL As String = "SELECT * FROM Products FOR XML AUTO"
Dim strXPath As String = "//Products[@Discontinued=1]"
RunXPathQueryWithArgumentForAnyLocalDocument(strSQL, strXPath)
```

The second block of code for invoking the *RunXPathQueryWithArgumentForAnyLocalDocument* procedure appears next. Because this block uses the same variable names as the preceding block, you should always comment out at least one of these blocks in order to avoid a compilation error for declaring the same variable more than once; this comment assumes both code blocks reside within the same procedure as they do in the main procedure for Module1 of the XMLSamples solution. This second block defines a different XML document through its SQL string than the first code block. The XML document from the first block contains a list of products, but the second block's XML document is a list of employees. In addition, the XPath query changes to extract a specific subset of employees. The main point of the second block is that you can use any SQL string to generate an XML document and then query it with an appropriate XPath query. You achieve this flexibility without having to modify any internal code in the *RunXPathQueryWithArgumentForAnyLocalDocument* procedure. You could readily extend this application by offering a list of previously formulated SQL query statements with matching XPath query statements. In this way, you can dramatically simplify the task of generating and using XML documents for those just gaining familiarity with the topic.

```
Dim strSQL As String = "SELECT * FROM Employees FOR XML AUTO"
Dim strXPath As String = "//Employees[@EmployeeID>4]"
RunXPathQueryWithArgumentForAnyLocalDocument(strSQL, strXPath)
```

Despite its substantially enhanced generality, the procedure in this section is nearly identical to the one in the preceding section. The major modification is the using of the two passed string variables—*strSQL* and *strXPath*. In addition, this procedure changes the assignment for the *RootTag* so that it isn't tied to a list of products but rather to a list of any type of entity. The application always uses a connection to the Northwind database, but you can parameterize the connection string as well to obtain even greater generality. At the very least, you will want to change the connection string so that it refers to a database in your application.

```
Sub RunXPathQueryWithArgumentForAnyLocalDocument( _
    ByVal strSQL As String, ByVal strXPath As String)
    'Specify connection string for SqlXmlCommand.
    Dim cnn1String As String = _
      "Provider=SQLOLEDB;Server=(local);" & _
      "database=Northwind;" & _
      "Integrated Security=SSPI"

    'Specify connection for cmd1 SqlXmlCommand object.
    Dim cmd1 As SqlXmlCommand = _
        New Microsoft.Data.SqlXml.SqlXmlCommand(cnn1String)

    'Designate data source for cmd1 with result set
    'in XML format.
    cmd1.RootTag = "MyRoot"
    cmd1.CommandType = SqlXmlCommandType.Sql
```

(continued)

```
        cmd1.CommandText = strSQL
        'Pass the cmd1 result set to an XmlReader, and load
        'an XmlDocument with the contents of the XmlReader.
        Dim xrd1 As System.Xml.XmlReader = cmd1.ExecuteXmlReader()
        Dim xdc1 As New System.Xml.XmlDocument()
        xdc1.Load(xrd1)

        'Close the reader.
        xrd1.Close()

        'Specify an XPath query based on the strXPath argument
        'for nodes from the xdc1 XmlDocument.
        Dim xnl1 As System.Xml.XmlNodeList = _
             xdc1.DocumentElement. _
             SelectNodes(strXPath)

        'Declare a node and a string.
        Dim xnd1 As System.Xml.XmlNode
        Dim str1 As String

        'For each node display a message with the contents,
        'including the XML tags.
        Debug.WriteLine( _
            "The record count for the result set is " & _
            xnl1.Count.ToString & ".")
        For Each xnd1 In xnl1
            str1 = xnd1.OuterXml
            Debug.WriteLine(str1)
        Next

    End Sub
```

Running Parameterized SQL Server Queries

Sometimes your applications won't be able to use an XML document as a data source because of a need for the most recent data. In this case, you can run a parameterized SQL Server query. The parameter in the query statement will still enable your users to specify a result set for a specific query at run time. The SQLXML Managed Classes in Web Release 2 and Web Release 3 facilitate this kind of query. The sample in this section demonstrates the application of the *SqlXmlParameter* class. Using a parameter with a SQL statement is useful for prototyping the SQL code for a stored procedure or for cases in which you don't have a stored procedure available with the parameter you need to perform a task. Two other features of the sample for this section are that it reminds you of a technique for specifying parameters in SQL statements, and it illustrates how to use a *StreamReader* object to capture the result set from a query.

The sample, *RunSQLParameterQuery*, begins by specifying a connection string and instantiating a *SqlXmlCommand* object based on the string. Next the sample assigns selected *SqlXmlCommand* properties for defining a query to execute. For example, the *CommandText* property is a SQL string that designates a parameter with a question mark (?). Users can execute the *SqlXmlCommand* object to return the information denoted in the list for the *SELECT* statement. The value for the *Country* parameter designates for which country the *SqlXmlCommand* returns results. In the listing, the procedure hard codes the value Brazil for the *Country* parameter. The syntax for the parameter assignment requires the declaration of a *SqlXmlParameter* object, the invocation of the *CreateParameter* method for the *SqlXmlCommand* object, and the assignment statement for the *Value* property of the *SqlXmlCommand* object's parameter.

This sample demonstrates yet another way of capturing the XML that a *SqlXmlCommand* object can return. In this case, the sample ultimately passes the result set from the query for the *SqlXmlCommand* object to a message box for display. The *ExecuteStream* method for the *SqlXmlCommand* object creates a *MemoryStream* object with the XML created by the query specified in the *CommandText* property. Using this *MemoryStream* object as the argument for instantiating a *StreamReader* object enables the procedure to capture the XML generated by the *SqlXmlCommand* object as a string. The *ReadToEnd* method for the *StreamReader* object returns a string with all the XML created by the *SqlXmlCommand* object. By using *srd1.ReadToEnd* as the argument for a *MsgBox* function, the procedure displays the XML the *SqlXmlCommand* object creates.

```
Sub RunSQLParameterQuery()
    'Specify connection string for SqlXmlCommand.
    Dim cnn1String As String = _
      "Provider=SQLOLEDB;Server=(local);" & _
      "database=Northwind;" & _
      "Integrated Security=SSPI"

    'Specify connection for cmd1 SqlXmlCommand object.
    Dim cmd1 As SqlXmlCommand = _
        New Microsoft.Data.SqlXml.SqlXmlCommand(cnn1String)

    'Designate data source for cmd1 with a parameter.
    cmd1.RootTag = "Customers"
    cmd1.CommandType = SqlXmlCommandType.Sql
    cmd1.CommandText = "SELECT ContactName, " & _
        "CompanyName, City " & _
        "FROM Customers " & _
        "WHERE Country = ? For XML Auto"
```

(continued)

```
    'Create a parameter for cmd1 and assign it a value.
    Dim prm1 As SqlXmlParameter
    prm1 = (cmd1.CreateParameter())
    prm1.Value = "Brazil"

    'Declare and instantiate a stream in memory and
    'populate it with the XML result set from cmd1.
    Dim stm1 As New System.IO.MemoryStream()
    stm1 = cmd1.ExecuteStream()

    'Copy result set in stream to a stream reader
    'to display stream contents in a message box.
    Dim srd1 As New System.IO.StreamReader(stm1)
    MsgBox(srd1.ReadToEnd)
    srd1.Close()

End Sub
```

Parameterizing Any SQL Query

Just as you can parameterize which XML document you process, you can also extend the preceding sample to parameterize any query instead of just one specific query. The trick to this task is to pass both the query and the parameter value to the procedure that performs the query. In turn, the procedure performing the query must be adapted from the preceding sample to accept these parameters and use them to generate a string for the message box that displays results at the procedure's conclusion.

The following code block shows the setup code that's required before calling the procedure to run the query and display its results in a message box. Notice that the setup code designates a different query than the sample in the preceding section. The query for this section is for the *Shippers* table, but the one in the preceding section is for the *Customers* table. Nevertheless, the code to execute the query is nearly the same in both sections. More important, you can execute a query for any table or combination of tables without changing the *RunSQLParameterQueryWithPassedParams* procedure. All your application needs to do is to make two assignments—one for the string variable designating the query (*strSQL*) and the other for the string designating a parameter value (*strPrm1Value*).

```
Dim strSQL As String = "SELECT * FROM Shippers " & _
    "WHERE ShipperID = ? For XML Auto"
Dim strPrm1Value As String = "1"
RunSQLParameterQueryWithPassedParams( _
    strSQL, strPrm1Value)
```

The following shows the code for the *RunSQLParameterQueryWithPassedParams* procedure. The lines that change from the *RunSQLParameter-*

Query procedure in the preceding section appear in bold. Notice just four lines change. These are mostly for receiving and using the passed string variables that specify the query syntax and the parameter value. The *RootTag* property assignment changes to make it appropriate for any SQL query string. Aside from these minor changes, there is nothing more to updating the earlier procedure so that it can accommodate any SQL query string.

```
Sub RunSQLParameterQueryWithPassedParams( _
    ByVal strSQL As String, _
        ByVal strPrm1Value As String)
    'Specify connection string for SqlXmlCommand.
    Dim cnn1String As String = _
        "Provider=SQLOLEDB;Server=(local);" & _
        "database=Northwind;" & _
        "Integrated Security=SSPI"

    'Specify connection for cmd1 SqlXmlCommand object
    Dim cmd1 As SqlXmlCommand = _
        New Microsoft.Data.SqlXml.SqlXmlCommand(cnn1String)

    'Designate data source for cmd1 with a parameter.
    cmd1.RootTag = "MyRoot"
    cmd1.CommandType = SqlXmlCommandType.Sql
    cmd1.CommandText = strSQL
    'Create a parameter for cmd1 and assign it a value.
    Dim prm1 As SqlXmlParameter
    prm1 = (cmd1.CreateParameter())
    prm1.Value = strPrm1Value
    'Declare and instantiate a stream in memory and
    'populate it with the XML result set from cmd1.
    Dim stm1 As New System.IO.MemoryStream()
    stm1 = cmd1.ExecuteStream()

    'Copy result set in stream to a stream reader
    'to display stream contents in a message box.
    Dim srd1 As New System.IO.StreamReader(stm1)
    MsgBox(srd1.ReadToEnd)
    srd1.Close()

End Sub
```

The Interplay Between XML and Data Sets

XML documents and ADO.NET data sets interact with one another in multiple ways. Understanding these interactions and knowing how to put them to use can help you query and manipulate data both locally on a client's workstation and on a database server. This section provides a selection of samples to show how to use XML documents with data sets for these purposes. As with many topics addressed by this book, the presentation isn't meant to provide exhaustive coverage of every possible feature on a topic. Instead, the section aims to provide a firm foundation that will equip you to go on and learn more in whatever directions your needs dictate.

Creating Hierarchical XML Documents

One of the really valuable aspects of the *DataSet* object in ADO.NET is that it is XML-based. What this means is that you can manipulate the elements within a data set and indirectly modify XML structures. This feature is particularly beneficial when working with multitable row sources that have parent-child relationships because it relieves developers from representing these complex relationships in XSD schemas. Although ADO.NET and XML are relatively new to many Visual Basic developers, the object model for data sets in ADO.NET makes it relatively more familiar to those with any background in manipulating objects. See Chapter 10 for a general review of ADO.NET objects. Figure 10-1 provides an overview of the *DataSet* object model, and numerous code samples throughout Chapter 10 demonstrate ADO.NET programming topics, including the *DataSet* object and its hierarchically dependent objects.

A *DataSet* object and its associated XML document are like two sides of the same coin. With the *WriteXml* method for a *DataSet* object, you can persist both the contents of an XML document and the underlying schema for the document. In addition, when a data set has changes not committed to a remote database, you can generate via the *WriteXml* method the DiffGram representing the data set with its uncommitted changes. Recall that a DiffGram contains current values as well as previous values. The DiffGram is readily available because ADO.NET conveys changes from a client to a SQL Server instance via DiffGrams.

The sample in this section demonstrates how to create a three-tiered data set based on three tables from the Northwind database. These tables are the *Customers*, *Orders*, and *Order Details* tables. Individual customers are parents of individual orders, and orders, in turn, are parents of order details, or line items within an order. This pair of nested relations is the kind of structure that XML documents represent especially well because the document shows the actual nesting instead of a single flat rowset.

The sample relies on two procedures. The first procedure, *SaveThreeTierDasAsXmlDocument*, calls a second procedure that generates a data set and then persists the data set as an XML document. By using the *WriteXml* method, the *SaveThreeTierDasAsXmlDocument* procedure avoids a reliance on SQLXML Managed Classes. This means the techniques demonstrated in this chapter are relatively robust in that they can work with any data source to which ADO.NET can connect. In addition, the procedures demonstrated for the *DataSet* object don't require the installation of either Web Release 2 or Web Release 3, as is necessary for the use of Managed Classes. The second procedure, *CreateThreeTierDataSet*, is a function procedure that returns a *DataSet* object to the procedure that calls it. It is this returned data set that the first procedure persists as an XML document in a file.

The *SaveThreeTierDasAsXmlDocument* procedure starts by instantiating a *DataSet* object and populating it with the data set returned by the *CreateThreeTierDataSet* function procedure. After populating the data set, the procedure prepares to persist it as a file with Unicode characters. These actions take several steps. The procedure starts the process by assigning the name of the XML document to a string variable (*str1*). Next the procedure instantiates a *FileStream* object (*fst1*) to hold the file containing the XML document. Then the procedure instantiates an *XmlTextWriter* object (*txw1*) to copy the XML within the data set to the *FileStream* object. The *WriteXml* method uses *txw1* as one of its two arguments for copying the XML from the data set to the file. The other argument, which is *XmlWriteMode.WriteSchema* in this case, determines how the *WriteXml* method conveys content from the data set to the file. The *XmlWriteMode.WriteSchema* argument directs the *WriteXml* method to start by copying the schema for the document and then follow the schema with the contents of the XML document. After writing the document, the procedure frees resources and returns control to the procedure by closing both the *XmlTextWriter* and *FileStream* objects.

The *CreateThreeTierDataSet* procedure starts by instantiating a connection object and opening it so that the connection points to the Northwind database. The procedure next instantiates a *DataSet* object (*das1*) and uses the connection object to connect a *SqlDataAdapter* object (*dap1*) with the *Customers* table in the Northwind database. Then the procedure copies the *Customers* table rows into a data table named *Customers* within *das1* by invoking the *Fill* method for the *dap1* object. After adding the *Customers* table from the Northwind database to the *das1* data set, the procedure points *dap1* to the *Orders* table in the Northwind database. Then it adds the *Orders* table to *das1*. It repeats the process a third and final time to create an *OrderDetails* data table in *das1* with the column values from the *Order Details* table in the Northwind database.

At the end of these three invocations of the *Fill* method, the *das1* data set contains three unrelated tables. However, we need *DataRelation* objects to specify the hierarchical relationship between tables. In fact, *das1* needs two *DataRelation* objects. One *DataRelation* object expresses the relationship between the *Customers* and *Orders* data tables. A second *DataRelation* object represents the relationship between the *Orders* and *OrderDetails* data tables. The procedure builds the first *DataRelation* object by invoking the *Add* method for the *Relations* collection of the *das1* data set. The first argument, which is a string with the value "CustOrders", names the *DataRelation* object. The next two arguments identify the columns used to join the two data tables. By setting the *Nested* property for the *DataRelation* object to *True*, you cause the XML document to show orders nested within customers. The default value for the *Nested* property is *False*. In this case, the *WriteXml* method shows two sets of column values without any nesting of column values from one data table within those of another data table. By invoking the *Add* method a second time for the *Relations* collection in the *das1* data set, the procedure creates a second data relationship expressing the parent-child structure between the *Orders* and *OrderDetails* data tables. Finally the *CreateThreeTierDataSet* procedure concludes by invoking the *Return* statement to pass the *das1* data set back to the procedure that called it.

```
Sub SaveThreeTierDasAsXmlDocument()
    'Declare and instantiate the das1 data set and
    'populate it with the return data set from
    'the CreateThreeTierDataSet function procedure.
    Dim das1 As New DataSet()
    das1 = CreateThreeTierDataSet()

    'Declare string for filename to hold file stream
    'based on XmlTextWriter with contents of das1 data set.
    Dim str1 As String = _
        "c:\SQL Server Development with VBDotNet\" & _
        "Chapter12\myCustomersSchema.xml"
    Dim fst1 As New System.IO.FileStream _
       (str1, System.IO.FileMode.Create)
    Dim txw1 As New System.Xml.XmlTextWriter _
       (fst1, System.Text.Encoding.Unicode)

    'Write from das1 the XML along with schema.
    das1.WriteXml(txw1, XmlWriteMode.WriteSchema)

    'Close TextWriter and FileStream.
    txw1.Close()
    fst1.Close()

End Sub

Function CreateThreeTierDataSet()

    'Open connection to northwind database.
    Dim cnn1 As SqlConnection = _
        New SqlConnection( _
```

```
        "Data Source=localhost;" & _
        "Initial Catalog=northwind;" & _
        "Integrated Security=SSPI")
    cnn1.Open()

    'Declare and instantiate a data set (das1)
    Dim das1 As DataSet = New DataSet("CustomerOrders")

    'Declare and instantiate a data adapter (dap1) to fill
    'the Customers data table in das1.
    Dim dap1 As SqlDataAdapter = _
        New SqlDataAdapter( _
        "SELECT CustomerID, CompanyName, ContactName, Phone " & _
        "FROM Customers", cnn1)
    dap1.Fill(das1, "Customers")

    'Re-use dap1 to fill the Orders data table in das1.
    dap1.SelectCommand.CommandText = _
        "SELECT OrderID, OrderDate, CustomerID FROM Orders"
    dap1.Fill(das1, "Orders")

    'Re-use dap1 to fill the OrderDetails data table in das1.
    dap1.SelectCommand.CommandText = _
        "SELECT * FROM [Order Details]"
    dap1.Fill(das1, "OrderDetails")

    'Close the connection.
    cnn1.Close()

    'Specify a relationship between Customers and Orders
    'data tables with orders elements nesting within
    'customers elements.
    das1.Relations.Add("CustOrders", _
        das1.Tables("Customers").Columns("CustomerID"), _
        das1.Tables("Orders").Columns("CustomerID")). _
        Nested = True

    'Specify a relationship between Orders and
    'OrderDetails data tables with OrderDetails elements
    'nesting within orders elements.
    das1.Relations.Add("OrderDetail", _
        das1.Tables("Orders").Columns("OrderID"), _
        das1.Tables("OrderDetails").Columns("OrderID"), _
        False).Nested = True

    Return das1

End Function
```

When the *SaveThreeTierDasAsXmlDocument* procedure invokes the *WrileXxml* method with its second argument equal to *XmlWriteMode.WriteSchema*, the method actually writes two documents in one. The XSD schema for the XML argument appears before the actual data. The .NET documentation refers to this kind of schema as an inline schema because it appears in line with the XML data that follows it. The schema for the XML document corresponding to *das1* is reasonably complex because it specifies columns from three tables, two data relationship specifications, and supporting elements, such as constraints to enable the *DataRelation* objects. Figures 12-6 and 12-7 show portions of the schema in browser windows; the schema is too long to fit in one window. This schema appears at the beginning of the XML document named in the *SaveThreeTierDasAsXmlDocument* procedure. The XML document's filename is myCustomersSchema.xml in the c:\SQL Server Development with VBDotNet\Chapter12 folder. In testing the application on your system, you may care to change the destination folder for the XML document to a folder that you already have on your workstation.

```
- <CustomerOrders>
  - <xs:schema id="CustomerOrders" xmlns=""
      xmlns:xs="http://www.w3.org/2001/XMLSchema" xmlns:msdata="urn:schemas-
      microsoft-com:xml-msdata">
    - <xs:element name="CustomerOrders" msdata:IsDataSet="true">
      - <xs:complexType>
        - <xs:choice maxOccurs="unbounded">
          - <xs:element name="Customers">
            - <xs:complexType>
              - <xs:sequence>
                  <xs:element name="CustomerID" type="xs:string"
                    minOccurs="0" />
                  <xs:element name="CompanyName" type="xs:string"
                    minOccurs="0" />
                  <xs:element name="ContactName" type="xs:string"
                    minOccurs="0" />
                  <xs:element name="Phone" type="xs:string"
                    minOccurs="0" />
                - <xs:element name="Orders" minOccurs="0"
                    maxOccurs="unbounded">
                  - <xs:complexType>
                    - <xs:sequence>
                        <xs:element name="OrderID" type="xs:int"
                          minOccurs="0" />
                        <xs:element name="OrderDate"
                          type="xs:dateTime" minOccurs="0" />
                        <xs:element name="CustomerID"
                          type="xs:string" minOccurs="0" />
                      - <xs:element name="OrderDetails"
                          minOccurs="0" maxOccurs="unbounded">
                        - <xs:annotation>
                          - <xs:appinfo>
                              <msdata:Relationship
                                name="OrderDetail"
                                msdata:parent="Orders"
                                msdata:child="OrderDetails"
                                msdata:parentkey="OrderID"
                                msdata:childkey="OrderID" />
                            </xs:appinfo>
```

Figure 12-6. The first part of the inline schema for the XML document in the myCustomersSchema.xml file.

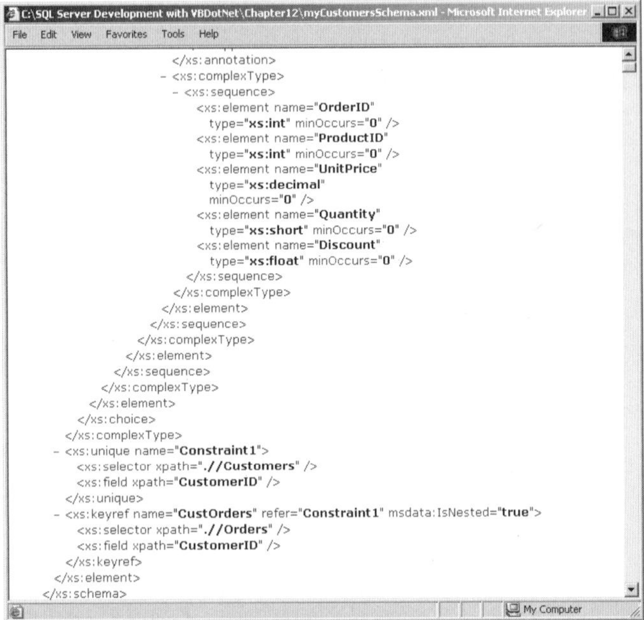

```
</xs:annotation>
- <xs:complexType>
- <xs:sequence>
<xs:element name="OrderID" type="xs:int" minOccurs="0" />
<xs:element name="ProductID" type="xs:int" minOccurs="0" />
<xs:element name="UnitPrice" type="xs:decimal" minOccurs="0" />
<xs:element name="Quantity" type="xs:short" minOccurs="0" />
<xs:element name="Discount" type="xs:float" minOccurs="0" />
</xs:sequence>
</xs:complexType>
</xs:element>
</xs:sequence>
</xs:complexType>
</xs:element>
</xs:sequence>
</xs:complexType>
</xs:element>
</xs:choice>
</xs:complexType>
- <xs:unique name="Constraint1">
<xs:selector xpath=".//Customers" />
<xs:field xpath="CustomerID" />
</xs:unique>
- <xs:keyref name="CustOrders" refer="Constraint1" msdata:IsNested="true">
<xs:selector xpath=".//Orders" />
<xs:field xpath="CustomerID" />
</xs:keyref>
</xs:element>
</xs:schema>
```

Figure 12-7. The second part of the inline schema for the XML document in the myCustomersSchema.xml file.

As you can see from the schema's length and complexity, it is of value to be able to write the schema automatically. Creating a data set in code should be fairly straightforward by this point in the book. In any event, if you are building solutions with ADO.NET, it is highly likely that you will gain a comfort level with building data sets programmatically. Therefore, using a programmatically created data set as the basis for a schema may be a useful process if you aren't handy at specifying XSD schemas from scratch. In fact, writing out the schemas and correlating them with the design of your data sets may be a way to have Visual Basic .NET teach you XSD syntax so that you can eventually write your own complex schemas from scratch. Figure 12-8 shows an excerpt from the beginning of the XML data in myCustomersSchema.xml. You can see all of the first order (*OrderID* 10643) and the beginning of the second order (*OrderID* 10692) for the customer with a *CustomerID* value of ALFKI. Notice how orders nest within customers. Also, the line items, or order details, for an order nest within an order.

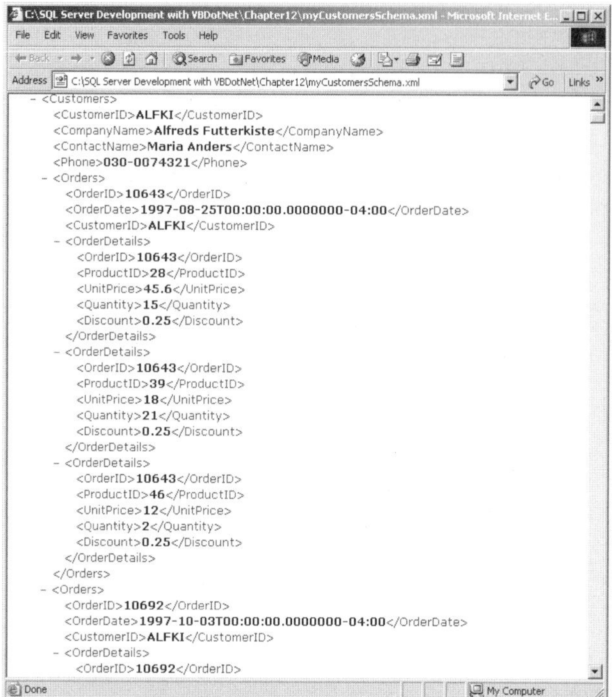

Figure 12-8. An excerpt from the beginning of the XML data in the myCustomersSchema.xml file.

Querying Descendants in a Data Set with XPath

The hierarchical design of the *das1* data set in the preceding sample provides a source that is suitable for demonstrating how to query descendants with XPath query syntax. Recall that the data set has order details that are the children of orders that in turn are the children of customers. In Figure 12-8, the first *UnitPrice* value of 45.6 is a descendant of the first order with an *OrderID* value of 10643. This *OrderID* is a child of the customer with the *CustomerID* value ALFKI. XPath query syntax permits you to create a result set of customers based on any of their descendant values, such as *UnitPrice*. The sample in this section illustrates how to construct such an XPath query, and the sample also reveals how to enumerate the nodes of the result set. Although XPath queries return a collection of nodes in an *XmlNodeList* object, the enumeration reports individual values without the clutter of the XML tags that delimit values in an XML document.

The *RunXPathQueryForThreeTierXmlDocument* procedure, which implements the sample for this section, starts by instantiating a new data set named *das1* and then populating it with the three-tiered data set created by the *CreateThreeTierDataSet* function. (See the preceding section for the listing with this function procedure.) Because ADO.NET automatically creates an XML document behind each data set, you can query either the data set or its underlying XML document and obtain identical result sets.

The *RunXPathQueryForThreeTierXmlDocument* procedure presents one approach to processing the XML document behind a data set. After populating the data set, the procedure instantiates a new *XmlDataDocument* object (*xdc1*) based on the *das1* data set. The *XmlDataDocument* class is an extension of the *XmlDocument* class that enables .NET applications to load the XML behind a data set into an XML document. *XmlDataDocument* objects permit the application W3C processing techniques for XML documents, such as XPath queries. The procedure demonstrates this capability by specifying an XPath query that selects all customer nodes that contain any descendants with a *UnitPrice* value of more than 100.

The XPath expression creates an *XmlNodeList* object (*xnl1*) based on the structure of the associated data set for the *XmlDataDocument* object that it queries. The association between the *XmlDataDocument* object and the *das1* data set makes it possible to select individual values from each node in the *XmlNodeList* object as column values in a *DataRow* object from the *DataSet* object model. The procedure prepares to implement this approach by declaring a *DataRow* object (*myRow*). Before starting a loop, the procedure returns a count of the number of nodes within the *xnl1* node list. The loop uses a *For Each* statement to successively pass through each node within *xnl1*. The *GetRowFromElement* method transfers individual values from the current node to the *myRow DataRow* object. The method transfers values stripped of any XML tags. Once the values of a node are available as column values within the *myRow* object, the procedure constructs a string for the first four column values. The schema in Figure 12-6 confirms that these columns correspond to *CustomerID*, *CompanyName*, *ContactName*, and *Phone*. The last statement within the loop prints the four column values to the Output window.

```
Sub RunXPathQueryForThreeTierXmlDocument()
    'Declare and instantiate the das1 data set and
    'populate it with the return data set from
    'the CreateThreeTierDataSet function procedure.
    Dim das1 As New DataSet()
    das1 = CreateThreeTierDataSet()

    'Declare and instantiate an XmlDataDocument based
    'on the contents of das1.
    Dim xdc1 As System.Xml.XmlDataDocument = _
        New XmlDataDocument(das1)
```

```
    'Generate a result set with all Customers ordering
    'products with a UnitPrice greater than 100.
    Dim xnl1 As XmlNodeList = _
        xdc1.DocumentElement.SelectNodes( _
        "descendant::Customers" & _
        "[Orders/OrderDetails/UnitPrice>100]")

    'Declare objects for a loop through result set.
    Dim myRow As DataRow
    Dim xnd1 As XmlNode
    Dim str1 As String

    'Loop through result set and print values
    'in Output window.
    Debug.WriteLine("There are " & _
        xnl1.Count.ToString & " in the result set.")
    For Each xnd1 In xnl1
        myRow = xdc1.GetRowFromElement(CType(xnd1, XmlElement))
        str1 = myRow(0) & ", " & myRow(1) & _
            ", " & myRow(2) & ", " & myRow(3)
        Debug.WriteLine(str1)
    Next

End Sub
```

Figure 12-9 presents an excerpt from the Output window showing values generated by the *RunXPathQueryForThreeTierXmlDocument* procedure. The first line in the excerpt reports the number of customers purchasing any item with a *UnitPrice* value of more than 100. Then the window shows a list of the individual customers meeting this criterion. For each customer, the list shows the associated *CustomerID*, *CompanyName*, *ContactName*, and *Phone* values.

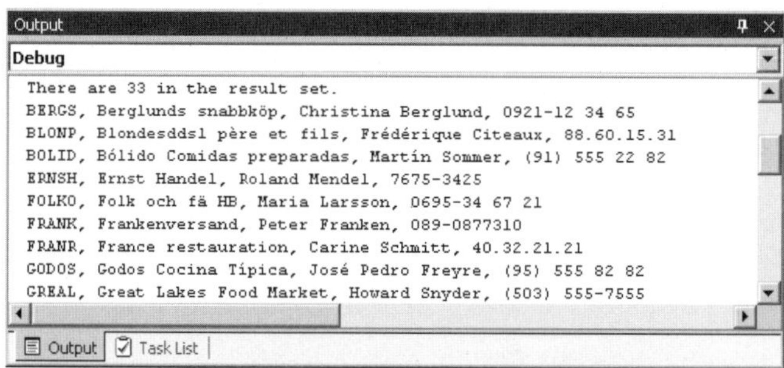

Figure 12-9. An excerpt displaying the initial output from the *RunXPathQueryForThreeTierXmlDocument* procedure.

Querying Descendants in an XML Document with XPath

The sample in the preceding section created a fresh data set by calling the *CreateThreeTierDataSet* procedure to generate a new data set. For applications in which the data changes slowly or at regular intervals, you may be able to improve performance by using a previously saved copy of the XML document behind a data set. Using a previously saved XML document can reduce the load on a database server and improve application responsiveness. The *SaveThreeTierDasAsXmlDocument* procedure, described previously, saves an XML document based on the same three-tied data structure generated by the *CreateThreeTierDataSet* procedure. The file containing the XML document is myCustomersSchema.xml, and its path is c:\SQL Server Development with VBDotNet\Chapter12. If you updated either the document's filename or its path for testing on your system, you will need to revise them for the sample in this section as well.

The sample for this section relies on two procedures. The first procedure, *RunXPathQueryForSavedThreeTierXmlDocument*, processes the saved XML document in myCustomersSchema.xml. The second procedure, *MyTagValue*, extracts tag values from a string containing values delimited by XML tags. The string values passed to the *MyTagValue* procedure are the nodes returned from an XPath query.

The *RunXPathQueryForSavedThreeTierXmlDocument* procedure starts by instantiating an XML document, *xdc1*, and then loading the previously saved myCustomersSchema.xml. The procedure uses an *XmlTextReader* to connect with the XML document in myCustomersSchema.xml, navigate to the root node, and load the data from the file into *xdc1*.

After loading the previously saved XML document, the sample executes the same XPath query as in the preceding sample. Although the syntax for the XPath query is identical in this sample and the preceding one, the source for the query is different in a couple of important ways. First, the source for this sample doesn't require a trip to the database server because it works with a locally saved file containing an XML document. If the database server or the connection to it is down temporarily, this local resource can substantially improve the robustness of an application. Second, there is no data set underlying the XML document. This means the XML nodes returned by the XPath query are strings with no associated row structure. As a consequence, this procedure processes elements in nodes differently than in the preceding sample.

This procedure generates identical output to that which appears in Figure 12-9, but it arrives at that output via a different path than the preceding sample.

The alternative approach to extracting tag values is necessary because there is no underlying row structure from a data set to facilitate the extraction of values. Each node in the XPath query's result set for this sample is a string. Tags delimit tag values within each string. From Figure 12-8, you can see that the *<CustomerID>* and *</CustomerID>* tags bound the ALFKI tag value. Therefore, you can extract any tag value by specifying its opening and closing tags. With the *Mid* function, you can extract the tag value contained within any tag. The *RunXPathQueryForSavedThreeTierXmlDocument* and *MyTagValue* procedures work together to extract the first four tag values for each successive node in the XPath query's result set. The *RunXPathQueryForSavedThreeTierXmlDocument* procedure passes the tag name for each of the first four tags in a node, and the *MyTagValue* function procedure returns a string with the corresponding tag's value. Then the *RunXPathQueryForSavedThreeTierXmlDocument* procedure concatenates the tag values and writes them to the Output window.

```
Sub RunXPathQueryForSavedThreeTierXmlDocument()
    'Procedure works from saved document instead of
    're-creating the document from a new data set.

    'Declare and instantiate an XML document.
    Dim xdc1 As New System.Xml.XmlDocument()

    'Declare and instantiate reader based on
    'previously saved XML document; move to root
    'node of document and load into xdc1.
    Dim xrd1 As XmlTextReader = _
        New XmlTextReader _
        ("c:\SQL Server Development with VBDotNet\" & _
        "Chapter12\myCustomersSchema.xml")
    xrd1.MoveToContent()
    xdc1.Load(xrd1)

       'Close the XmlTextReader.
        xrd1.Close()
    'Generate a result set with all Customers ordering
    'products with a UnitPrice greater than 100.
    Dim xnl1 As XmlNodeList = _
        xdc1.DocumentElement.SelectNodes( _
        "descendant::Customers" & _
        "[Orders/OrderDetails/UnitPrice>100]")

    'Declare objects for a loop through result set.
    Dim xnd1 As XmlNode
    Dim str1, str2 As String

    'Loop through result set and print values
    'in Output window.
```

```
    Debug.WriteLine("There are " & _
        xnl1.Count.ToString & " in the result set.")
    For Each xnd1 In xnl1

        'Saver node's inner XML.
        str1 = xnd1.OuterXml

        'Get CustomerID tag value.
        str2 = MyTagValue("CustomerID", str1)

        'Get CompanyName tag value.
        str2 = str2 & ", " & MyTagValue("CompanyName", str1)

        'Get ContactName tag value.
        str2 = str2 & ", " & MyTagValue("ContactName", str1)

        'Get Phone tag value.
        str2 = str2 & ", " & MyTagValue("Phone", str1)

        'Write first four tag values.
        Debug.WriteLine(str2)

    Next

End Sub

Function MyTagValue(ByVal TagName As String, _
    ByVal strXML As String)

    'Declare and compute constants for this tag.
    Dim str1 = "<" & TagName & ">"
    Dim str2 = "</" & TagName & ">"
    Dim int1, int2 As Integer
    int1 = InStr(strXML, str1) + Len(str1)
    int2 = InStr(strXML, str2)

    'Compute tag value and return it;
    'strXML is string with XML to parse,
    'int1 is start position,
    'int2 - int1 is number of characters.
    Dim TagValue As String = Mid(strXML, _
        int1, int2 - int1)
    Return TagValue

End Function
```

Using Data Sets to Update Databases via DiffGrams

By now you should be getting the idea that you can perform database operations to obtain identical results with data sets or the XML documents associated with them. This general rule applies to database updates as well. Recall from earlier in this chapter that ADO.NET updates a database via a DiffGram, which is an XML document that can separately specify current values and prior column values in a data table within a data set. When an ADO.NET application invokes the *Update* method for a data adapter and specifies a data set, the application sends the DiffGram to the .NET Framework running on a server. The .NET Framework, in turn, attempts to perform the update with the database server and passes back any necessary feedback to the client, such as an identity value or a message that the database rejects the updates because the prior value changed from the time the data set was initially populated.

The sample in this section interacts with XML in two different ways. First, it uses an annotated schema to specify which column values to return from a remote data source. After retrieving values from a remote data source, the sample fills a data table in a data set on the client. Second the sample updates a column value in the local data table. Then the procedure writes the DiffGram that contains the change before calling the *Update* method for a data adapter to send the DiffGram to a database server. Although it is possible to work with DiffGrams directly, just like Updategrams (see Chapter 6), Visual Basic developers might generally find it more convenient to manipulate the ADO.NET object model to update values both locally and on a remote server.

The following schema listing shows the contents of an EmployeesFirstLastNames.xsd file used by the sample within this section. The file resides in the root folder of the XMLSamples solution. (The lines for the *Fname* and *LName* elements wrap onto a second line because they are too long to fit on one line.) After the namespace declarations for a W3C xsd schema and Microsoft mapping attributes, the listing declares *Emp* as the name for the *Employees* object in a database connection. The *sql:relation* attribute sets the correspondence between *Emp* and *Employees*. Because the sample connects to the Northwind database, *Emp* is the name for the collection of retrieved values from the *Employees* table. The schema designates *FName* and *LName* as matching names within the local data set for the *FirstName* and *LastName* column values in the *Employees* table on the database server. The *sql:field* attribute indicates the server-based columns to which the local data set columns point.

```
<xsd:schema xmlns:xsd="http://www.w3.org/2001/XMLSchema"
xmlns:sql="urn:schemas-microsoft-com:mapping-schema">
    <xsd:element name="Emp" sql:relation="Employees">
        <xsd:complexType>
```

```
            <xsd:sequence>
                <xsd:element name="FName" _
                            sql:field="FirstName" type="xsd:string" />
                <xsd:element name="LName" _
                            sql:field="LastName" type="xsd:string" />
            </xsd:sequence>
            <xsd:attribute name="EmployeeID" type="xsd:integer" />
        </xsd:complexType>
    </xsd:element>
</xsd:schema>
```

The following *PopulateModifyUpdateWithDiffGram* procedure starts by specifying a connection string and then using the string to construct a *SqlXmlCommand* object. The contents of the string point to the Northwind database on the default local SQL Server instance. Next the procedure creates a local data set (*das1*) with a data table named *Emp* based on the EmployeesFirstLastNames.xsd schema file. This data set completes the setup for the sample's data environment.

```
Sub PopulateModifyUpdateWithDiffGram()
    'Specify connection for cmd1 SqlXmlCommand object;
    'connection specification must include
    'provider designation (sqloledb).
    Dim cmd1 As New SqlXmlCommand("Provider=sqloledb;" & _
        "Data Source=(local);" & _
        "Initial Catalog=northwind;Integrated Security=SSPI")

    'Specify SQLXmlCommand to return first and last
    'names based on an XPath query.
    cmd1.RootTag = "ROOT"
    cmd1.CommandText = "Emp"
    cmd1.CommandType = SqlXmlCommandType.XPath
    cmd1.SchemaPath = "..\EmployeesFirstLastNames.xsd"

    'Instantiate a SqlXmlAdapter object using the
    'SqlXmlCommand object .
    Dim dap1 As SqlXmlAdapter
    dap1 = New SqlXmlAdapter(cmd1)

    'Instantiate a new DataSet object (das1) and
    'fill via dap1.
    Dim das1 As DataSet = New DataSet()
    dap1.Fill(das1)

    'Edit the value in the first row's first column
    'of Emp data table.
    das1.Tables("Emp").Rows(0)(0) = "Nancie"
```

(continued)

```
        'Write the XML as a DiffGram before committing
        'change to server.
        Dim str1 As String = _
            "c:\SQL Server Development with VBDotNet\" & _
            "Chapter12\myDiffGram.xml"
        Dim myFileStream As New System.IO.FileStream _
            (str1, System.IO.FileMode.Create)
        Dim xtw1 As New System.Xml.XmlTextWriter _
            (myFileStream, System.Text.Encoding.Unicode)
        das1.WriteXml(xtw1, XmlWriteMode.DiffGram)

        'Perform update to server-based data source for
        'the das1 data set; don't specify a specific
        'data table within the data set.
        dap1.Update(das1)

End Sub
```

After setting up the data environment, the procedure assigns a new value, "Nancie", to the first column in the first row of the *Emp* data table. The *Rows* collection for the *Emp* data table exposes the column values for individual rows within the data table. In the following line,

```
das1.Tables("Emp").Rows(0)(0) = "Nancie"
```

the first number in parentheses after *Rows* designates the row and the second number in parentheses points to a column within a row. (The *Rows* collection is zero-based; the first column and row are both numbered *0*.)

Before transferring the update to the Northwind database with the *Update* method for a data adapter, the procedure copies the data set in DiffGram format to a file named C:\SQL Server Development With VBDotNet\Chapter12\MyDiffGram.xml on the local computer's C drive. Change the name and destination to fit your computer environment.

Figures 12-10 and 12-11 show the DiffGram created in myDiffGram.xml by the sample for this section. Figure 12-10 is a browser window displaying the top half of the DiffGram, and Figure 12-11 presents the bottom half of the DiffGram in a browser window. As Figure 12-10 reveals, the employee whose *EmployeeID* value is 1 has the *FName* tag value Nancie. (See toward the top of the window.) In Figure 12-11, the before section of the DiffGram (see toward the bottom of the browser window) shows the initial value for any changes in the data set uncommitted on the remote database source. In this instance, you can see that the initial value for the *FName* tag is Nancy for the employee whose *EmployeeID* value is 1. Immediately after invoking the *Update* method in the final line of the *PopulateModifyUpdateWithDiffGram* procedure, the DiffGram for *das1* will change. In particular, the before section will drop because the data set will contain only current values until there is a modification of the local *Emp* data table.

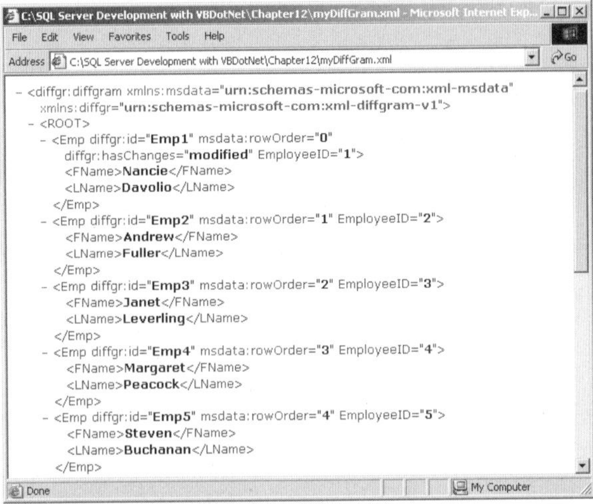

Figure 12-10. The beginning part of the myDiffGram.xml file generated by the *PopulateModifyUpdateWithDiffGram* procedure.

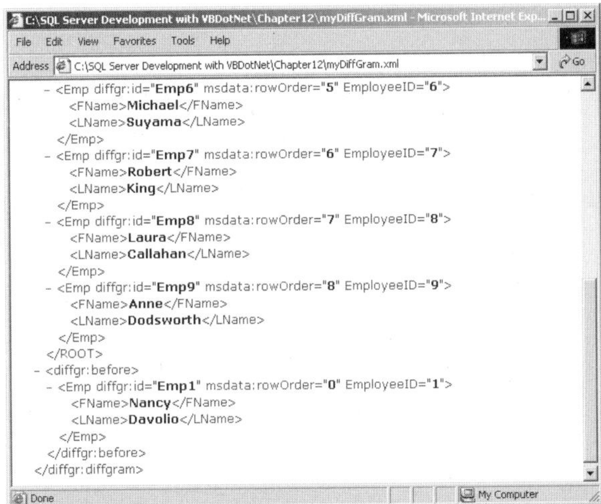

Figure 12-11. The ending part of the myDiffGram.xml file generated by the *PopulateModifyUpdateWithDiffGram* procedure.

You probably want to restore your *Employees* table in the Northwind database so that the first name for *EmployeeID* 1 is *Nancy* instead of *Nancie*. You can do that by changing *Nancie* to *Nancy* in the *PopulateModifyUpdateWithDiffGram* procedure and re-running the procedure.

> **Note** As I mentioned, many Visual Basic .NET developers might find it more convenient to enable data manipulation through *DataSet* objects than by directly coding DiffGrams or Updategrams. This book's sample files include an additional sample procedure, *ListAndEditWithDataset*, to further illustrate the flexibility and ease of this approach. For the sake of brevity, the procedure's listing doesn't appear in the book.

Using DiffGrams on the Web Without Virtual Directories

One of the best features about the preceding sample is how robust it is. For example, very nearly the identical code works in an ASP.NET application. Furthermore, that ASP.NET application permits updates to the Web without the necessity of a virtual directory for a database. This simplifies administration of your Web solutions.

The following five steps build an ASP.NET Web Application solution named XMLWebSample. These steps adapt the sample from the preceding section to run in an ASP.NET solution.

1. Start a new ASP.NET solution named XMLWebSample, and add a reference to the *Microsoft.Data.SqlXml* namespace as described earlier in this chapter.
2. Select the default WebForm1.aspx file in Design view, and open the module behind the Web page by right-clicking the page and choosing View Code. At the top of the module for the page, insert **Imports Microsoft.Data.SqlXml**.
3. Copy the code from the *PopulateModifyUpdateWithDiffGram* procedure in the preceding solution to the *Page_Load* event for the XMLWebSample solution.
4. Create in the root Web folder of the XMLWebSolution a schema just like EmployeesFirstLastNames.xsd. You can use the XML Designer for this task as described earlier in the chapter. (It's probably easiest to open the schema in XML Source view and replace the existing XML with the XML from the EmployeesFirstLastNames.xsd in this book's sample files.) Name the schema EmployeesFirstLastNames.xsd.

5. Change the setting for the *SchemaPath* property setting of the *SqlXmlCommand* object in the *Page_Load* event code from *"..\EmployeesFirstLastNames.xsd"* to *MapPath("EmployeesFirstLastNames.xsd")*.

After completing the above steps, you can right-click the WebForm1.aspx page in the Solution Explorer window and choose Build And Browse. This process will set the *FirstName* field for the row in the *Employees* table with the *EmployeeID* value 1 to *Nancie*. You can restore the original first name by changing *Nancie* to *Nancy* in the *Page_Load* event procedure and choosing Build And Browse a second time.

For your easy reference, the *Page_Load* event procedure listing appears here. The two lines that changed from the *PopulateModifyUpdateWithDiffGram* procedure appear in bold. The important point to grasp is that although the following listing is for ASP.NET, it works nearly identically to the prior Windows application solution. The *MapPath* function returns the full path to a file that serves as its argument. This Web technique enables developers to reference the path to a file without explicitly including it in their application. In addition, the *MapPath* function improves your code's portability because the function dynamically computes the path to the file even if you change the folder for the solution.

```
Private Sub Page_Load(ByVal sender As System.Object, _
    ByVal e As System.EventArgs) Handles MyBase.Load
    'Put user code to initialize the page here.

    'Specify connection for cmd1 SqlXmlCommand object;
    'connection specification must include
    'provider designation (sqloledb).
    Dim cmd1 As New SqlXmlCommand("Provider=sqloledb;" & _
            "Data Source=(local);" & _
            "Initial Catalog=northwind;Integrated Security=SSPI")

    'Specify SQLXmlCommand to return first and last
    'names based on an XPath query.
    cmd1.RootTag = "ROOT"
    cmd1.CommandText = "Emp"
    cmd1.CommandType = SqlXmlCommandType.XPath
    cmd1.SchemaPath = MapPath("EmployeesFirstLastNames.xsd")
    'Instantiate a SqlXmlAdapter object using the
    'SqlXmlCommand object.
    Dim dap1 As SqlXmlAdapter
    dap1 = New SqlXmlAdapter(cmd1)

    'Instantiate a new DataSet object (das1) and
    'fill via dap1.
```

(continued)

```
    Dim das1 As DataSet = New DataSet()
    dap1.Fill(das1)

    'Edit the value in the first row's first column
    'of Emp data table.
    das1.Tables("Emp").Rows(0)(0) = "Nancie"

    'Write the XML as a DiffGram before committing
    'change to server.
    Dim str1 As String = _
            "c:\SQL Server Development with VBDotNet\" & _
            "Chapter12\myDiffGram.xml"
    Dim myFileStream As New System.IO.FileStream _
           (str1, System.IO.FileMode.Create)
    Dim xtw1 As New System.Xml.XmlTextWriter _
           (myFileStream, System.Text.Encoding.Unicode)
    das1.WriteXml(xtw1, XmlWriteMode.DiffGram)

    'Perform update to server-based data source for
    'the das1 data set; don't specify a specific
    'data table within the data set.
    dap1.Update(das1)

End Sub
```

Creating HTML Pages with XSLT

As you start to work with Visual Basic .NET, most of your Web development work should focus around ASP.NET. (See Chapter 11.) This technology is especially crafted to make Visual Basic developers feel right at home when building Web solutions. As you can see from the preceding pair of samples, it's easy to adapt Visual Basic code is to ASP.NET. However, you might occasionally want to generate output for a Web environment using XSLT. In my experience, one of the most popular uses for XSLT is the transformation of XML documents into tables on HTML pages. The chapter up until this point aimed to convey a working knowledge of how to create and consume XML documents in .NET solutions. The remainder of this chapter helps you prepare XML documents for display on HTML pages via XSLT.

When you're using XSLT to transform XML documents into HTML pages, it's useful to have a working knowledge of HTML formatting syntax as well as cascading style sheets. You, of course, also need some familiarity with how to select tags from XML documents to display in your HTML pages. Many Visual Basic developers have little or no HTML programming experience. If this is your situation, I recommend a couple of strategies. First, use a graphic Web page designer, such as the one built into .NET or the one in FrontPage. With a graphic Web page designer, you can graphically create pages and then look at the HTML behind the code. You can then incorporate that code into your XSLT transformation file. Second, if you belong to a project team that includes Web specialists, plan the project so that the Web specialists create general XSLT files that can fit many situations or be easily adapted. Then the Visual Basic developers can reference the XSLT transformation files as is or with minor editing.

The Visual Studio .NET documentation includes several samples illustrating how to load XML documents and transform them with XSLT. (For example, see the "XslTransform.Load Method (XmlReader)" topic in the Visual Basic .NET documentation.) This section in the book includes a couple of samples to complement those from the Visual Basic .NET documentation that work with the *SqlXmlCommand* class. Recall that you can use this SQLXML Managed Class to generate XML documents from SQL statements. The SQLXML Managed Classes are there to make life simple for SQL Server developers. For example, the *SchemaPath* property facilitates referencing annotated schema for filtering the return set from a database object. Similarly, the *XslPath* property for a *SqlXmlCommand* object references an XSLT file. When you specify this attribute, your procedures can return HTML pages instead of raw, unformatted XML tags and values in a document file. The referenced XSLT transform file must synchronize with the XML document that would have returned from the *SqlXmlCommand* object. Two sample XSLT transformation files illustrate how to implement this synchronization.

Formatting Two Columns from the *Employees* Table

When you use the *XslPath* property with a *SqlXmlCommand* object, you don't get to see the underlying XML document. The internal code in the *SqlXmlCommand* class automatically converts its XML document to HTML code according to the instructions in the file to which the *XslPath* property points. The following sample transforms an XML document based on the *Employees* table in the Northwind database. Instead of just saving the final HTML page, the procedure first saves the XML document without setting the *XslPath* property. Then the procedure assigns a string value to the *XslPath* property that points to an XSLT file and saves a second document in HTML format.

The *SQLToXMLToHTMLForEmployees* procedure starts creating an XML document with a *SqlXmlCommand* object pointing to the Northwind database. The SQL string for the object extracts the *EmployeeID*, *FirstName*, and *LastName* columns from the *Employees* table by using a *SELECT* statement with a *FOR XML* clause. Recall that this process returns an XML fragment without a unique outer tag for the document. Therefore, the procedure assigns a string value ("MyRoot") to the *RootTag* property for the *SqlXmlCommand* object. Next the procedure sets up to save the XML document in a file named UnformattedEmployees.xml before invoking the *ExecuteToStream* method to save the XML document. The setup process enables the *ExecuteToStream* method to pass the document directly from the *SqlXmlCommand* object to a file.

After saving the XML document, the procedure assigns the *XslPath* property for the *SqlXmlCommand* object. The property points to the MyXSL.xslt file in the root folder of the XMLSamples solution folder. Then, the procedure invokes the *ExecuteStream* method for the *SqlXmlCommand* object to represent the HTML page with an in-memory stream object. After capturing the HTML as a stream object, the procedure moves on to read the stream and then write it to an external file named FormattedEmployees.html.

```
Sub SQLToXMLToHTMLForEmployees()
    'Specify SqlXmlCommand.
    Dim cmd1 As New SqlXmlCommand("Provider=sqloledb;" & _
        "Data Source=(local);" & _
        "Initial Catalog=northwind;Integrated Security=SSPI")
    cmd1.CommandText = _
        "SELECT EmployeeID, FirstName, LastName " & _
        "FROM Employees FOR XML AUTO"
    cmd1.CommandType = SqlXmlCommandType.Sql
    cmd1.RootTag = "MyRoot"

    'Name the path and file for the Xml result set, then
    'instantiate a Stream object for the file's contents.
    Dim myXMLfile As String = _
        "c:\SQL Server Development with VBDotNet\" & _
        "Chapter12\UnFormattedEmployees.xml"
    Dim myFileStream As New System.IO.FileStream _
        (myXMLfile, System.IO.FileMode.Create)

    'Execute cmd1 and store the result set in the stream.
    cmd1.ExecuteToStream(myFileStream)

    'Close the file stream to recover the resource.
    myFileStream.Close()

    'Set the XslPath property to specify the name of
    'the XSLT style sheet.
    cmd1.XslPath = "..\MyXSL.xslt"

    'Return the HTML from cmd1 as an in-memory stream
    'object; then, create a stream reader to read the
    'contents of the stream.
    Dim stm1 As Stream
    stm1 = cmd1.ExecuteStream
    Dim srd1 As New StreamReader(stm1)
```

```
    'Declare and instantiate a string for the name of
    'the file pointing at the FileStream with the
    'HTML content.
    Dim str1 As String = _
        "c:\SQL Server Development with VBDotNet\" & _
        "Chapter12\FormattedEmployees.html"
    Dim fst1 As New FileStream(str1, FileMode.OpenOrCreate)

    'Declare and instantiate a StreamWriter to populate
    'the file holding the HTML content; then, read the
    'StreamReader's contents into a string and write the
    'string to fst1.
    Dim swt1 As New StreamWriter(fst1)
    Dim str2 As String = srd1.ReadToEnd
    swt1.Write(str2)

    'Close the file.
    swt1.Close()

End Sub
```

Figure 12-12 shows the UnFormattedEmployees.xml file. Notice that it contains nine Employees elements. Each element has three attributes with values for *EmployeeID*, *FirstName*, and *LastName*. The content and layout follow directly from the *CommandText* property setting for the *SqlXmlCommand* object in the *SQLToXMLToHTMLForEmployees* procedure. It is the UnFormatted-Employees.xml file that the MyXSL.xslt file transforms.

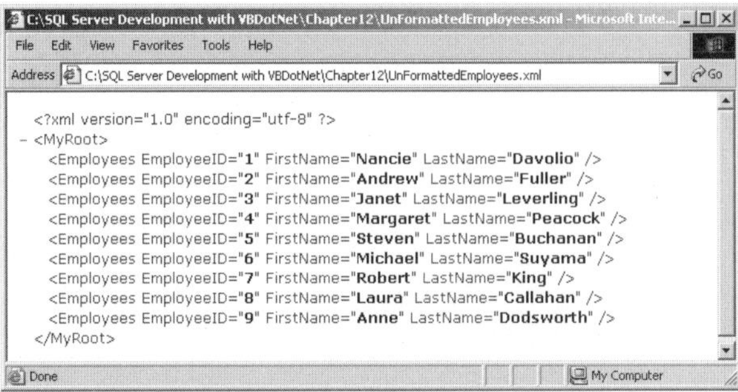

Figure 12-12. The UnformattedEmployees.xml file contents generated by the *SQLToXMLToHTMLForEmployees* procedure.

Figure 12-13 shows the transformed XML document saved as Formatted-Employees.html. The file in Figure 12-13 appears as a table instead of a raw listing of elements. In addition, the second column displaying last name appears in italics and bold. There's additional formatting as well, such as a table header with a background color. The MyXSL.xslt file facilitated all the layout and formatting changes between Figure 12-12 and Figure 12-13. There's one more difference between the two figures. Figure 12-13 has only two columns, but the initial XML document has three attributes for every *Employees* element within the document. This difference results from the fact that the MyXSL.xslt file selects only two of the three attributes for display.

Figure 12-13. The FormattedEmployees.html file contents generated by the *SQLToXMLToHTMLForEmployees* procedure.

The listing for MyXSL.xslt appears next. It commences with its declaration as an XML document and a reference to the World Wide Web Consortium namespace for XSLT files. The design of the transform has two main parts denoted within two *xsl:template* elements. The first element matches the *Employees* element in the source XML document, namely UnformattedEmployees.xml. For each *Employees* element within the source document, the transform file selects two attributes—*FirstName* and *LastName*. The *LastName* selection is embedded within tags that render the attribute values in bold and italic. This initial segment of the file also defines a row layout for the result with beginning and ending <*TR*> tags. Each selected value appears within beginning and ending <*TD*> tags to indicate that the values occupy different cells within the row.

The second *xsl:element* within the .xslt file defines the overall body for the document. For example, this element starts with a beginning HTML element and closes with an ending HTML element. The HEAD block assigns a color in hexadecimal notation to the background-color attribute for the table heading (th) element. The BODY block launches a TABLE block and formats the heading for the table. The *xsl:apply-templates* element within the TABLE block specifies the insertion of the first *xsl:element* within the second *xsl:element*. This insertion adds the rows to the table after the table heading. It is critical that the *xsl:apply-templates* element select the *MyRoot* element within the XML document. This is because this element contains all the *Employees* elements within the source XML document to transform. Improperly specifying this select attribute can lead to an empty table.

> **Note** XSLT syntax refers to element and attribute names differently. When referring to an element, you can use its name. For example, use *Employees* when referencing an *Employees* element. When referring to an attribute, prefix the attribute name with the @ sign. For example, refer to a *FirstName* attribute value with *@FirstName*.

```
<?xml version='1.0' encoding='UTF-8'?>
<xsl:stylesheet xmlns:xsl="http://www.w3.org/1999/XSL/
Transform" version="1.0">

    <xsl:template match = 'Employees'>
       <TR>
         <TD><xsl:value-of select = '@FirstName' /></TD>
         <TD><B><I><xsl:value-of select = '@LastName' /></I></B></TD>
       </TR>
    </xsl:template>
    <xsl:template match = '/'>
      <HTML>
        <HEAD>
           <STYLE>th { background-color: #CCCCCC }</STYLE>
        </HEAD>
        <BODY>
         <TABLE border='1' style='width:300;'>
           <TR><TH colspan='2'>Employees</TH></TR>
           <TR><TH >First name</TH><TH>Last name</TH></TR>
           <xsl:apply-templates select = 'MyRoot' />
         </TABLE>
        </BODY>
      </HTML>
    </xsl:template>
</xsl:stylesheet>
```

Formatting Three Columns from the *Shippers* Table

This chapter's final sample demonstrates the preceding approach with another source XML document. Although an XSLT transformation applies to an XML document, you won't normally show the XML document supporting a published

HTML table. Instead, you'll initially specify the *XslPath* property for a *SqlXmlCommand* object when you apply the *ExecuteStream* method. Then, you'll read the stream of HTML to prepare for writing it to a file. This more direct approach doesn't expose the XML document that serves as the source for the HTML table. If you ever find it beneficial to review the XML document, you can always revert to the approach in the preceding sample.

The sample implemented with the *SQLThroughXMLToHTMLForShippers* procedure extracts columns from the *Shippers* table. The *SELECT* statement for the *SqlXmlCommand* object retrieves each column in the *Shippers* table, and the statement includes a *FOR XML* clause to return an XML fragment. The *RootTag* property for the *SqlXmlCommand* object designates *MyRoot* as the unique element that embraces all other elements within the XML document. The *XslPath* property for the *SqlXmlCommand* object points to the MyXSLShippers.xslt file in the root of the XMLSamples folder, which is the folder containing the solution. After instantiating the *SqlXmlCommand* object and specifying its properties, the procedure invokes the *ExecuteStream* method to return an in-memory stream variable with the HTML for the file that the procedure ultimately saves as FormattedShippers.html.

```
Sub SQLThroughXMLToHTMLForShippers()
    'Specify SqlXmlCommand.
    Dim cmd1 As New SqlXmlCommand("Provider=sqloledb;" & _
        "Data Source=(local);" & _
        "Initial Catalog=northwind;Integrated Security=SSPI")
    cmd1.CommandText = _
        "SELECT ShipperID, CompanyName, Phone " & _
        "FROM Shippers FOR XML AUTO"
    cmd1.CommandType = SqlXmlCommandType.Sql
    cmd1.RootTag = "MyRoot"

    'Set the XslPath property to specify
    'the name of the XSLT style sheet.
    cmd1.XslPath = "..\MyXSLShippers.xslt"

    'Return the HTML from cmd1 as an in-memory stream
    'object; then create a stream reader to read the
    'contents of the stream.
    Dim stm1 As Stream
    stm1 = cmd1.ExecuteStream
    Dim srd1 As New StreamReader(stm1)

    'Declare and instantiate a string for the name of
    'the file pointing at the FileStream with the
    'HTML content.
    Dim str1 As String = _
        "c:\SQL Server Development with VBDotNet\" & _
        "Chapter12\FormattedShippers.html"
    Dim fst1 As New FileStream(str1, FileMode.OpenOrCreate)
```

```
        'Declare and instantiate a StreamWriter to populate
        'the file holding the HTML content; then read the
        'StreamReader's contents into a string and write the
        'string to fstl.
        Dim swtl As New StreamWriter(fstl)
        Dim str2 As String = srdl.ReadToEnd
        swtl.Write(str2)

        'Close the file.
        swtl.Close()

    End Sub
```

Figure 12-14 reveals the output from the *SQLThroughXMLToHTMLForShippers* procedure. The Shippers title in the table's header spans three columns in this sample as opposed to the two in the preceding sample. Of course, the table has three columns, and the contents of the first column, listing *ShipperID* values, are centered horizontally. Aside from these differences, the layout of the table follows the design of the preceding sample.

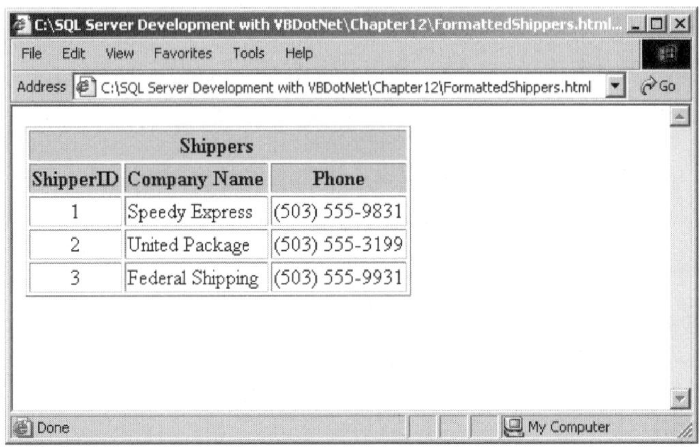

Figure 12-14. The FormattedEmployees.html file contents generated by the *SQLThroughXMLToHTMLForShippers* procedure.

Although I didn't display the XML document because you won't normally show it when preparing an HTML table, a good approximation of the XML document is available for viewing in Figure 12-1. This figure presents the XML output from an earlier sample. That sample creates an XML document from the same *SELECT* statement as the one in this sample. The main distinction between the XML for the two documents is important but subtle. Figure 12-1 reveals that *Shippers* is the root tag for the XML document in the earlier sample. The sample in this section uses *MyRoot* as the document's root tag. The root tag designation is critical because the .xslt file references the designation as it transforms the XML to HTML. If you specify the root tag incorrectly, your HTML will be incorrect as well.

The minor formatting differences between this sample and the preceding one will help to highlight the XSLT syntax issues controlling the layout and formatting of content on an HTML page. You can contrast the MyXSLShippers.xslt listing with the earlier MyXSL.xslt listing used to transform the preceding XML document into an HTML table. As before, the MyXSLShippers.xslt file has two *xsl:template* elements. However, the first element in this file matches the *Shippers* element in the document. This is because the underlying XML document has three separate lines that each start with a *Shippers* element. This element name (*Shippers*) lets you reference the collection of lines in the XML document. Also, notice that the first element contains *xsl:value-of* elements. The preceding MyXSL.xslt file contained only two of these—one for each column. The formatting tags around column values are different in this sample. For example, the *ShipperID* column values have formatting that enforces horizontal centering. In addition, there are no tags for bold or italic styles. Aside from these minor differences, the .xslt files for this sample and the preceding one are the same. The two samples together reinforce one another in demonstrating common XSLT coding techniques for transforming an XML document into an HTML table.

```
<?xml version='1.0' encoding='UTF-8'?>
<xsl:stylesheet xmlns:xsl="http://www.w3.org/1999/XSL/
Transform" version="1.0">
    <xsl:template match = 'Shippers'>
       <TR>
         <TD align = 'middle'><xsl:value-of select = '@ShipperID' /></TD>
         <TD><xsl:value-of select = '@CompanyName' /></TD>
         <TD><xsl:value-of select = '@Phone' /></TD>
       </TR>
    </xsl:template>
    <xsl:template match = '/'>
      <HTML>
        <HEAD>
           <STYLE>th { background-color: #CCCCCC }</STYLE>
        </HEAD>
        <BODY>
         <TABLE border='1' style='width:300;'>
           <TR><TH colspan='3'>Shippers</TH></TR>
           <TR><TH >ShipperID</TH><TH>Company Name</TH><TH>Phone</TH></TR>
           <xsl:apply-templates select = 'MyRoot' />
         </TABLE>
        </BODY>
      </HTML>
    </xsl:template>
</xsl:stylesheet>
```

13

Creating Solutions with XML Web Services

XML Web services offer Visual Basic .NET developers a chance to dramatically extend the reach of their solutions. Although the underpinnings of XML Web services may be unfamiliar to many Visual Basic developers, Visual Studio .NET and the SQL Server 2000 Web Services Toolkit provide implementation techniques that are simple and straightforward. If you have mastered the topics presented in the previous 12 chapters, you can readily learn the content of this chapter. However, the payoff from becoming proficient with XML Web services can be vastly greater than that from learning the content from earlier chapters.

XML Web services, sometimes called Web services, provide a technology for remotely operating an application on another computer. You will typically use Web services with at least two computers, but the technology can tie together many computers in peer-to-peer relationships. At any one time, one computer can support multiple client applications connecting to it. For a pair of computers, one computer will host a Web service application and another computer will host a client application. Because a Web service is a peer-to-peer technology, two computers can each host a Web service even while they are clients of the Web service on the other computer. The computers participating in peer-to-peer relationships exchange information in XML format. The industry momentum building around Web services technology promises wide interoperability across computer platforms and operating systems.

After presenting an overview of core Web services concepts, this chapter presents a series of samples in a hands-on style. The idea is to acquaint you with the basics of building XML Web services. The chapter conveys step-by-step instructions and code samples for creating solutions with Web services. The chapter's content extends and complements the information on Web services that you can find in the Visual Studio .NET documentation and the SQL Server 2000 Web Services Toolkit support materials. Separate sections drill down on creating Web service and client applications using contrasting approaches. For example, you can build both the Web service and client applications with Visual Studio .NET. Alternatively, other sections show how to build a Web service with the Web Services Toolkit and the client application with Visual Studio .NET. The sample presentations describe how to build the solution folders and mention especially important files and procedures for each solution. The chapter's sample files include for your reference the completed solution as I developed them on my system.

Overview of Web services

XML Web services can revolutionize the way applications are delivered to clients in a way that parallels how the Internet changed the delivery of content to computer users over a Web. Web services support a widely adopted set of standards for computers sharing information with one another. Although the consumer of a Web service can be a computer user, it can just as easily be another application. In this way, Web services support distributed computing. Because the Web services standards are so widely adopted and rest on XML format, you can create Web services solutions that have a very far reach in terms of the number of platforms that they can support.

This section builds on the initial introduction to XML Web services in Chapter 8. Instead of highlighting its underlying technologies, this section explores how you can tap these technologies with Visual Basic .NET and SQL Server 2000. In addition, the section examines potential kinds of applications that are especially suitable for Web services solutions.

Elements of Web Services Design

An XML Web service is a technology for invoking procedures remotely on another computer. A Web service server application exposes procedures that are invoked by a Web service client application. As indicated in Chapter 8, XML Web services rest on a mix of open-architecture technologies. This open technology stance and the ability to interchange data between loosely coupled computers in XML format make Web services available across computer manufacturers and software vendors that subscribe to the open standards.

Web services technology is special for a variety of technical and institutional considerations. For example, leading and competing vendors are, in fact, observing the open standards. It seems highly likely that XML Web services will revolutionize how computers from different vendors using different operating systems work together. This enhanced interoperability, in turn, promises to vastly expand the number of software options available for performing typical computer-based tasks, such as customer resource management. Because XML Web services are so easy to implement with Visual Studio .NET and SQL Server 2000, your personal opportunities should advance substantially as you increase your understanding of this emerging technology.

Building a Web service is a multiple-step process that rests on a variety of technologies, such as those discussed in Chapter 8. Happily, the Visual Studio .NET interface shelters developers from many of the details of UDDI, WSDL, and SOAP that implement the plumbing for XML Web services. Visual Studio .NET provides graphical tools for handling some of the details from which it doesn't fully shelter you. A Visual Studio .NET developer can start building a Web services solution as simply as selecting the ASP.NET Web Service template when creating a project. You choose this template from the New Project dialog box in the same way that this book previously described selecting a template for a Windows application or an ASP.NET Web application. Because Visual Studio .NET facilitates building Web services solutions based on ASP.NET, the New Project dialog will attempt to set up a project on a Web server, such as your localhost. For this attempt to succeed, your workstation must have access to a Web server with the .NET Framework—and your account must have authoring permission on the Web server. The Web service application will have a default name, such as Service1.asmx. Although Visual Studio .NET uses ASP.NET to build a new Web service, the extension .asmx especially marks the project as a Web service application.

You can implement a Web service with a class object (although there are other legitimate implementations). Within the class, you can selectively expose some methods. These exposed methods are called *Web methods*. Those methods that you expose are the ones that clients of the Web service can invoke remotely. By thinking of the Web service as an object, you can think of Web methods as the methods of the object. These exposed methods can return a value or a collection of values.

The whole idea behind a Web service is that another application exists that can invoke or consume the Web methods exposed by the Web service. This application can be any client application that can connect to and invoke the Web service, such as a browser, a Windows application, or another Web service. This client application can be loosely coupled to the Web service. In other words, the client can have a connection to the Web service that isn't persistent. In addition, the computers running the client and Web service applications can be running different operating systems (for example, Windows and UNIX).

Client applications must be able to learn about the availability of Web services from vendors before using them. In other words, they need a way to look up available services. This directory function for XML Web services is the role of UDDI (Universal Description, Discovery, and Integration). You can think of it as a yellow page directory of XML Web services. One route for registering and looking up Web services is *http://www.uddi.org*. The UDDI site also provides general support features for the UDDI technology, such as a listing of companies supporting the technologies. As I write this, more than 200 companies have agreed to support the UDDI technology, including Microsoft, IBM, Sun Microsystems, SAP, Compaq, and Dell.

After surveying a list of prospective vendors with XML Web services of the type you seek, you'll likely select one for more due diligence. For example, you'll want to learn about the specific inputs and outputs associated with a Web service. WSDL (Web services Description Language) is an XML-based language for describing the inputs to and outputs from a Web service. The client for a Web service actually interacts with a local proxy for a Web service. WSDL can represent the remote Web service through the local proxy. For typical applications, you don't have to generate the WSDL. This is because Visual Studio .NET generates the WSDL code automatically. However, because WSDL is XML, you can read it.

Typical XML Web Service Applications

In this section, I speculate about what might be some typical Web service applications. I explicitly use the term *speculate* because the technology and its practical application are still in their infancy. Therefore, *you* can use this book to build the next (maybe the first) "killer" Web service. Even if I only get you started on the way to this goal, I will consider this chapter a success. Another outcome for the chapter is to acquaint you with the kinds of inputs and outputs that you can expect to use with Web services.

A Web service can typically do one of three possible tasks.

- **Perform a calculation.** For example, a Web service can amortize a loan or perform advanced statistical or financial computations. As with any Web service, the important point will be to supply a resource not easily or cost-effectively duplicated or one with wide appeal.

- **Look up a result or several results.** You might develop a Web service to generate local taxes in different jurisdictions given the postal code of a buyer. Essentially, this is a lookup operation based on the taxing authorities for a postal code. Many small or medium-size businesses may find it more cost effective to pay a small monthly premium for accessing this tax data automatically than maintain it accurately for their individual operations.
- **Execute an operation,** such as a database insert, delete, or update operation. For example, many small businesses seek a cost-effective solution for adjusting inventory when logging a new order. The new order can lead to one or more inserts in two or more tables. The adjustment to inventory can be a change, specifically a reduction, to the current units on hand for a product.

Web services can exchange data between a client application and Web service application via XML documents. Because the layout of XML formatted data is so flexible (recall that you can have any tags you want), you can adapt XML Web services for working with many different types of business data. For example, suppliers can query manufacturers for the specifics of work orders, including a shipment's quantity and due date. Because XML Web services are accessible from browsers, field employees can enter the time and material charges associated with client visits without returning to the head offices. Concurrently, clients can look up their charges based on visits from field representatives. By securing access to records based on SQL Server or Windows security, a Web service can restrict access to charges for the appropriate client. Other candidates for Web services solutions include remote access and updating of customer resource management systems and order processing from order entry through shipping, order status reports to customers, and billing.

Web Services from Visual Studio .NET

A Web service application built from the ASP.NET Web Service template is a class with a special attribute, namely the *WebService* attribute. You don't have to manually add the attribute that declares the class a Web service, but you will typically want to edit a default attribute setting. The attribute automatically assigns a namespace (namely, *http://tempuri.org*) for the class implementing a Web service. Microsoft strongly recommends that you change the default namespace name because clients require unique namespaces for the Web services that they reference. The *WebService* attribute for a class also enables you to assign a name to the Web service.

Note You will be prompted for your user credentials as you attempt to create a new Web service on a Web server; your credentials must enable authoring on the server. The security for creating or loading a Web service application is more stringent than for a standard ASP.NET application. For example, I found no difficulty creating or loading regular ASP.NET applications using a free Web site hosting account. However, I wasn't able to load an application based on the ASP.NET Web Service template. I suspect that in time some fee-based Internet service providers will start supporting the creation and editing of hosted Web services.

Within a Web service application, you'll need to designate a *WebMethod* attribute for one or more public function procedures within a Web service. Only function procedures with a *WebMethod* attribute are visible to client applications. The method attribute offers six properties. For example, samples in this chapter will demonstrate the use of the *Description* property. This property enables you to assign an extended label to a Web method that may be longer than you prefer for a function procedure's name. See the "Using the WebMethod Attribute" topic in the Visual Studio .NET Help files for a listing of all six properties along with brief summaries and samples illustrating the syntax for controlling property values.

After developing an initial draft of a Web service application, you may want to test or debug your application. One advantage of using the ASP.NET Web Service template is that it offers a built-in interface for testing a Web service application. Figure 13-1 shows the test interface for the initial sample in this chapter. The following note briefly discusses how to open the interface.

Note You can open the interface for testing your application by right-clicking the .asmx file for your Web service in Solution Explorer. Select Build And Browse from the context menu to launch the interface. The Build And Browse command compiles the application, including any changes since the last compile, and opens a new browser window within Visual Studio .NET.

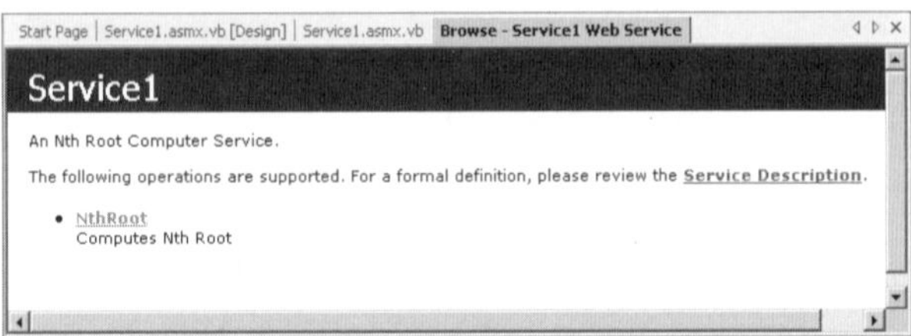

Figure 13-1. The default test interface for a Web service exposes links for launching the Web methods.

I will discuss the design of the sample later. For the moment, let's focus on relating Web service design elements to the testing interface. The filename for the .asmx file appears along the top of the testing Web page. Unless you change the default filename, it will be Service1.asmx. The Web service description that you specify with the *WebService* attribute ("An Nth Root Computer Service.") appears below the filename for the .asmx file. If you like, you can examine the .wsdl file formally describing the Web service application by clicking the Service Description link that appears in the sentence below your personal description for the Web service. The main advantage of the test interface is a bulleted list of links for the Web methods within the Web service. You can invoke a Web method by clicking the link with the function's name for implementing the method. An example is the NthRoot link in Figure 13-1. Immediately below the link for a Web method is the *Description* property that you assign with the *WebMethod* attribute: "Computes Nth Root" in the figure. This space is blank if you don't use the *WebMethod* attribute to assign a string to a Web method's *Description* property. By repeatedly invoking Web methods, you can use traditional techniques for debugging and refining their operation until the methods meet your requirements.

After you've created a Web service application, your next step in creating a Web service solution will be to create a Web service client application. The client application needs a Web reference that points to the Web service application and a proxy variable that instantiates the Web reference within a client application. The client application can be a Windows application or any other type of application that can link to the Web service.

Visual Studio .NET offers tools to simplify the creation of a Web reference. Choose Add Web Reference from the Project menu to open a dialog box for selecting an existing Web service. I'll describe the detailed steps for adding a Web reference later. The important point to recognize is that you can use the menu command to create a Web reference. The Web reference within a client application includes information for discovering the location of a Web service as well as its inputs and outputs. Within the Code Editor for your client application, you can declare and instantiate a proxy object for your Web service. This local proxy object points to the Web service through the Web reference. After instantiating a proxy variable, you can use it to pass inputs and gather return values from a Web service. You can use traditional techniques to test and refine the operation of your client application until it meets your requirements. This capability exists because you can build the client application with standard Visual Basic .NET code.

You typically won't work with the test implementation of your Web service. Instead, you'll deploy the Web service to a virtual directory on an IIS server. I'll cover the detailed steps for deploying a Web service in the discussion of the first sample. The objective of this review of Web services is to acquaint you with the broad outline for creating solutions based on Web services.

Web Services from the Web Services Toolkit

With the SQL Server 2000 Web Services Toolkit, developers can base Web services on stored procedures and user-defined functions, such as those discussed in Chapter 4 and Chapter 5, as well as templates, such as those reviewed in Chapter 6. This technology makes it relatively easy for database administrators and developers who are conversant with T-SQL to build Web services solutions on SQL Server databases. See Chapter 12 for more detail on Web Release 3 and its association with the Web Services Toolkit. The URL for downloading the toolkit along with Web Release 3 is:

http://msdn.microsoft.com/downloads/default.asp?url=/downloads/sample.asp?url=/MSDN-FILES/027/001/872/msdncompositedoc.xml&frame=true

The Web Services Toolkit relies on the setup and configuration of an IIS virtual directory to deliver Web services. You can follow the general guidelines for Web Release 2 when setting up an IIS for Web Release 3, but add some necessary extra steps if you plan to use the directory to deliver Web services from a SQL Server 2000 instance. Of course, one key distinction in the setup of a virtual directory is that you must use Web Release 3, but both release 2 and release 3 share a generally similar Virtual Directory Management utility. See Chapter 6 for a summary of the steps necessary for a standard setup of an IIS virtual directory with Web Release 2. The same general techniques apply to Web Release 3. In addition, this chapter includes a specific set of instructions for creating a virtual directory that hosts a Web service.

Note A note in Chapter 12 offers instructions for upgrading a virtual directory created with Web Release 1 or Web Release 2 for use with Web Release 3.

A Web Release 3 virtual directory offers a new type of object. The type's name is *soap*. You initiate the creation of a *soap* object type by selecting it from the Type drop-down box on the Virtual Names tab of the Virtual Directory Management utility. You can assign the *soap* object any name you want in the Name box, but you must set the Path box to the path for your virtual directory on the Web server. After these selections, clicking Configure will enable you to specify the Web service that you will offer from the virtual directory. However, before configuring a *soap* object, you may need to add database objects to the database to which a virtual directory points or templates directly to the virtual directory or one of its folders.

Clicking Configure on the Virtual Names tab in the Virtual Directory Management utility opens the Soap Virtual Name Configuration dialog box. With this dialog box, you can specify a new Web service and edit an existing Web service associated with a virtual directory. As indicated previously, you can select from among stored procedures, user-defined functions, and templates as resources for the Web service. There are three routes for returning data from the Web service for a virtual directory. First, you can return data as an XML document fragment through an *XMLElement* object. When you use this route, it's up to the client application to process the XML data. Second, if your source returns two or more result sets or you want to explicitly catch returned errors along with result sets, you can specify a *DataSet* objects array as the return route. Each result set occupies a different returned object in the array. It's the client application's job to distinguish between *DataSet* and *SqlMessage* objects. The third route for returning data with the Web Services Toolkit is as a single data set. This route works well when you explicitly decline to accept error messages from SQL Server as *SqlMessage* objects.

Note When working with database objects, namely, stored procedures and user-defined functions, it's imperative that the account you specify on the Security tab of the Virtual Directory Management utility have proper permission to work with the object. For example, if your Web service relies on a stored procedure, the login account for the virtual directory must have EXEC permission for the stored procedure.

There are two styles for row formatting the values returned. By selecting Raw in the Row Formatting group in the Soap Virtual Name Configuration dialog box, you specify that XML formatting be performed on the database server. The second Row Formatting option—Nested—offloads the XML formatting of data from the database server to the Web server hosting the virtual directory. This selection can improve the database processing capability of a SQL Server instance by relieving the database server from performing nondatabase functions, such as formatting a result set with XML tags.

A Web Service to Return a Computed Result

This section demonstrates how to build a Web service to return a computed result with Visual Studio .NET. The main point of presenting the sample is to illustrate the process for creating and deploying a Web service. The particular computation performed by the Web service is of interest only because it allows a review of syntax issues for passing values to and returning a value from a Web service. In addition, the section headings within this section identify the major tasks in creating a solution.

One particularly interesting conclusion that you can derive from this sample is that Web services breathe new life into desktop Windows applications. This is because Windows applications can serve as clients to Web services. Because Web services can run anywhere on the Web and on multiple computing platforms, the Web services paradigm stretches the capabilities of Windows applications accordingly.

Starting to Build a Web Service Application

You can prepare a Web service application to accept Visual Basic code with three steps in Visual Studio .NET. The code does the work for the service, but the plumbing around the code makes your application accessible over the Web, enables clients to discover your Web service, and allows your Web service to return values to clients in XML format. The three steps set up the plumbing into which you can insert the code for your application.

You can launch a Web service from the Visual Studio .NET Start Page. Click New Project. Then, in the New Project dialog box, select the ASP.NET Web Service template. When you do this, Visual Studio .NET automatically prepares to save a new project with the name WebService1. Click OK to complete the first step. Visual Studio will actually set up two folders for your application. One of these folders will reside in the wwwroot folder of the Inetpub directory for your local computer. This folder contains your application's code and related software. You can override both the destination and the name for the folder. For example, Figure 13-2 shows the sample for this section with a new name besides *WebService1*—namely, *TestNthRootService*. Visual Studio also creates a second folder with the same name in its default location for saving Visual Studio .NET projects. This folder contains the .sln file for starting the project for the Web service from within Visual Studio .NET. When you click OK in the New Project dialog box, you conclude the first step.

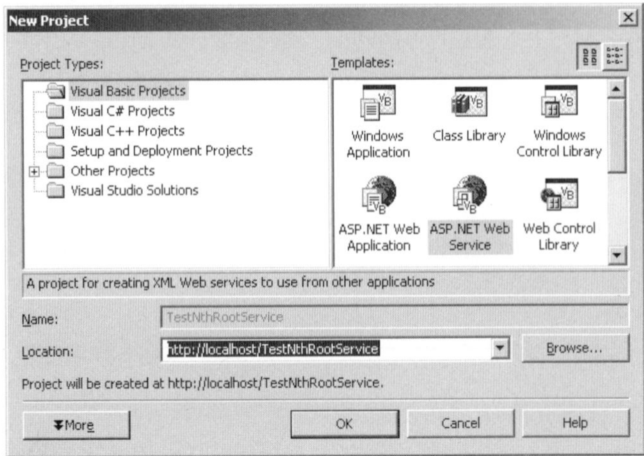

Figure 13-2. The New Project dialog box for starting a Web service named *TestNthRootService*.

Before opening your project, Visual Studio .NET may display the Enter Network Password dialog box, in which you verify your network credentials to confirm your ability to author content on the Web server. Therefore, when you're authoring a Web service, it's important to select a Windows login account with proper permission for authoring a Web site. Windows logins that belong to the VS Developers group can author Web sites on a computer. Assigning the lowest level of permission to perform a task that a login account requires helps to maintain the security on a Web server. Therefore, assigning a login to the VS Developers group is preferable to assigning a login to the Administrators group when a user only needs to author Web sites. Completing the Enter Network Password dialog box concludes the second step for starting a new Web service.

Note Windows 2000 offers a GUI (graphical user interface) for assigning Windows login accounts to Windows groups. From the Windows Start menu, choose Programs, then Administrative Tools, and then Computer Management. In the left pane of the Computer Management window, expand the section for Local Users And Groups and select the Users folder to view individual Windows login accounts. Then click the Help icon on the menu bar. It includes detailed instructions for typical tasks, such as modifying the groups to which an existing login account belongs and adding a new login account.

The third step is to open the Code Editor for your Web service. The project opens to the Service1.asmx.vb[Design] window. In general, your Web services won't have a user design because they are meant for a programming interface as opposed to a user interface. Therefore, you can leave the Design window blank. Right-click anywhere in the Design window, and choose View Code to open the Code Editor.

You need to edit the template-supplied starter design in the Code Editor and add your code so that the service does what you want it to do. Figure 13-3 shows the Code Editor before any editing. The starter design includes some commented code for building a Hello World sample. The Imports statement at the top of the Code Editor allows the code in the window to use items from the System.Web.Services namespace without including the namespace name as a prefix before each item. Notice that the project is a class whose name is *Service1*. After we edit the design and add code, users can invoke the service by referencing from a browser Service1.asmx in the TestNthRootService folder on the localhost Web server. From the Window's title bar in Figure 13-3, you can tell that the name of the project is TestNthRootService. In Solution Explorer, you can assign a new name to the Service1.asmx file that reflects the specific task your service performs. You can achieve this by right-clicking the Service1.asmx item in Solution Explorer and choosing Rename.

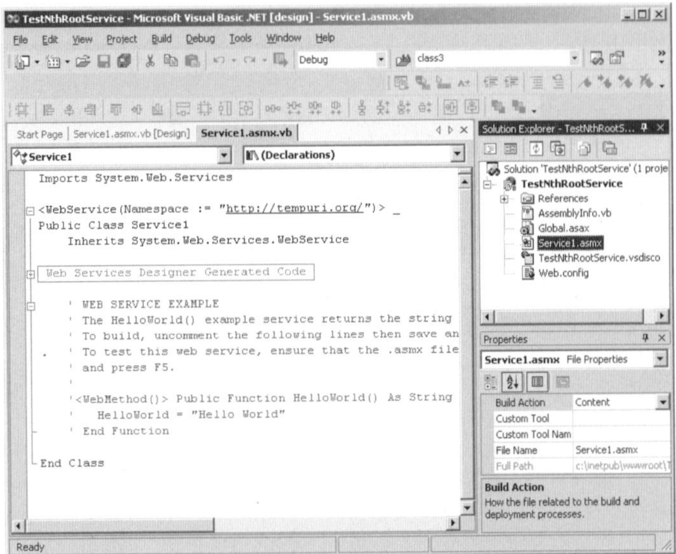

Figure 13-3. The starter design in the Code Editor for a new Web service. Edit this design to configure and code your Web service.

Configuring and Coding Your Web Service Application

The following code listing shows an adaptation of the Visual Studio .NET starter design for a Web services application. The configuration of the starter design includes two attributes—one named *WebService* and another named *WebMethod*. The *WebService* attribute marks the *Service1* class as a Web service. Notice the use of the continuation line marker at the end of the attribute. This ties the attribute to the *Service1* class declaration. The attribute performs two functions through its property settings. First the *Namespace* setting designates a namespace for the service. Recall that you need to make the namespace for each Web service unique. That's why you change the default namespace setting (*http://tempuri.org*) that appears in Figure 13-3. Second the *Description* setting assigns an informal name for the Web service when you are running it in its test interface. This name appears just below *Service1* in Figure 13-1. The *WebMethod* attribute applies to the *NthRoot* function procedure, which implements the *NthRoot* method for the class. This second attribute has a single property setting that assigns an informal description to the method. This description appears as well (just below the method name) in the test interface for the Web service.

The Web service in the following sample computes the *n*th root for a number. For example, the square root of 9 is 3, and the sixth root of 64 is 2. The *NthRoot* function takes two arguments: one for the number, such as 9 or 64, and a second for the root, such as 2 for the square root or 6 for the sixth root. The computation involves taking the log of a number to base 10 and then dividing the log value by the root. The quotient of the division serves as the exponent for 10, which evaluates to the *n*th root for a number. The *NthRoot* procedure passes this value back to the client for the Web service with a *Return* statement.

```
Imports System.Web.Services
'Mark a class with the WebService element to
'declare a Web service; Service1 is default name.
<WebService(Namespace:="http://MyService/XmlWebServices/", _
    Description:="An Nth Root Computer Service.")> _
        Public Class Service1
    Inherits System.Web.Services.WebService

'Web Services Designer Generated Code

    'Mark the function as a Web method.
    <WebMethod(Description:="Computes Nth Root")> _
    Public Function NthRoot(ByVal anumber As Double, _
        ByVal aroot As Double) As Double

        'Compute and return nth root of a number as the
        'antilog of the log of the number (anumber)
        'divided by the root (aroot).
        Dim logvalue As Double = (Math.Log10(anumber))
        Return (10 ^ (logvalue / aroot))

    End Function

End Class
```

Testing a Web Service

When you build a Web service with Visual Studio .NET, you can test it even before you build a client for the Web service. This is advantageous because it allows you to refine the logic of your application and enables you to make sure that your application works as expected.

To test a Web service application from Visual Studio .NET, right-click the page for the Web service in Solution Explorer and choose Build And Browse. This opens a window like the one in Figure 13-1. To test a specific method, click the link for the method, such as *NthRoot*. This opens a new window on the tab labeled Browse - Service1 Web Service for the sample application (as shown at the top of Figure 13-4). Two text boxes allow you to specify the arguments for the *NthRoot* function procedure. Clicking Invoke launches the Web service and collects a return value from the function. The return value appears as a tagged value in an XML document, as shown at the bottom of Figure 13-4.

When you build a client application for a Web service, the client application must pass the arguments programmatically and extract the return value from the XML document that the Web service sends back to the client.

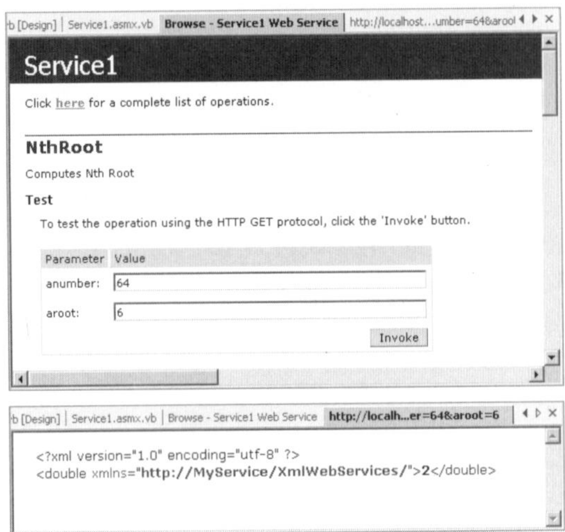

Figure 13-4. The test interface for the *NthRoot* Web method of the *Service1* Web service appears at the top. The XML document with the result for a test appears at the bottom.

Building a Client Application for a Web Service

After you refine your Web service, you will want to develop a client application for it. Although the Web service is a Web application, its clients can be a Windows application or an ASP.NET Web application or even a mobile application, such as one that runs on a personal digital assistant. All the clients in this chapter are part of a Windows application project named XMLWebServiceClients, which is included in this book's sample files. Each form in this application will demonstrate different client application features.

Before you can use a client application with a Web service, the client application must include a Web reference pointing to the Web service. Then the code for your client application can create a proxy variable for the Web reference. The variable exposes the Web methods from the Web service for use in the client application.

You can add a Web reference to a project through the Project menu in Visual Studio .NET. Choose Project, and then choose Add Web Reference to open the dual-paned Add Web Reference dialog box. With this dialog, you can use any of several different techniques for denoting a reference to a Web server. If you are building a client for a Web service on your local Web server, click the

Web References On Local Web Server link at the bottom of the left pane. This populates the right pane with a list of potential links from which you can pick to add a Web reference. The links appear in alphabetical order. For those of you who completed the steps as described to this point, you should discover the following link:

http://localhost/TestNthRootService/TestNthRootService.vsdisco

Visual Studio automatically creates the .vdisco file for your Web service. This file facilitates dynamic discovery of a Web service on a Web server. This style of discovery is appropriate for testing and evaluation purposes on a development computer. However, when you deploy a Web service for production purposes, you will want to use stationary discovery techniques for a Web service based on a .disco file. I'll discuss stationary discovery and .disco files in the next section.

Clicking the preceding link pointing to the .vdisco file changes the display in the Add Web Reference dialog box. (See Figure 13-5, which shows the dialog box after a selection described on the next page.) The right pane shows the URL for the Web reference above links for getting more information about the Web service. Notice that the URL points to the Web service (*http://localhost/TestNthRootService/Service1.asmx*) with the trailing parameter *wsdl* after a question mark (?). Recall that *wsdl* denotes the Web Service Description Language. Clicking the View Contract link in the right pane displays the XML in the .wsdl file for the Web service in the left pane. This file denotes the namespace for the Web service along with the inputs and outputs from the Web methods for the Web service. Clicking the View Documentation link shows the test interface in the left pane. (This is the view of the Add Web Reference dialog box that appears in Figure 13-5.) Clicking Add Reference at the bottom of the dialog box adds a Web reference for the Web service to the client application project. This Web reference appears in Solution Explorer under a Web References heading. A client application can have multiple Web references to different Web services. Within any Web reference are files, such as the .wsdl file for the Web service. You can use the .wsdl file to remind yourself or learn initially to which Web service a Web reference points.

A client application can reasonably offer a user interface, such as a form for users to manipulate. For example, the client for the *TestNthRootService* is *Form1* in the XMLWebServiceClients project (see Figure 13-6). The form includes three text boxes and a button (*Button1*); a label control helps identify the role of each text box, and the Text property setting for *Button1* denotes its purpose. The names for the text boxes from top to bottom on the form are *TextBox1*, *TextBox2*, and *TextBox3*.

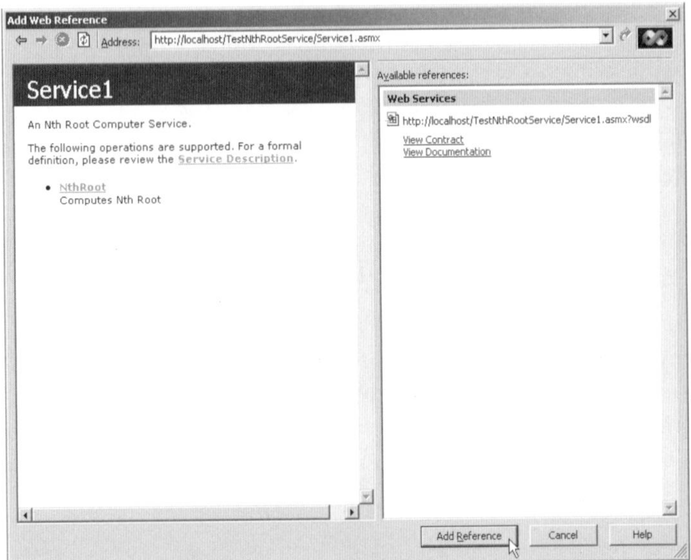

Figure 13-5. The Add Web Reference dialog box after the selection of the View Documentation link for the *Service1* Web service in the TestNthRootService project. Clicking Add Reference adds a Web reference to the project for the *Service1* Web service.

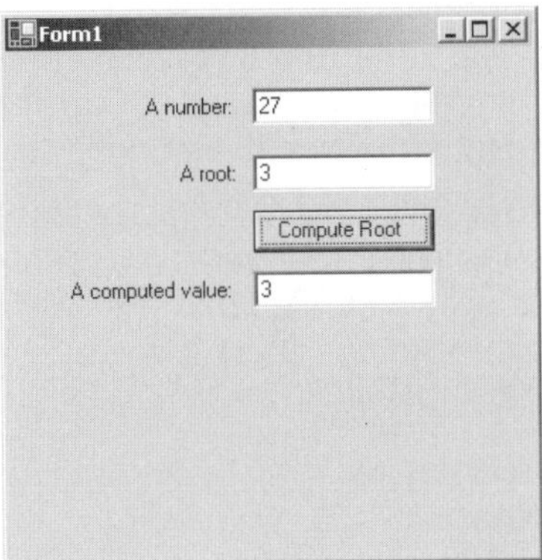

Figure 13-6. The form for the client application of the *Service1* Web service in the TestNthRootService folder shows the cube root for 27 is 3.

After designing the form for a client application that offers user interaction, you can design the code behind the form. The following code listing shows the *Click* event procedure for *Button1* in *Form1*. The *Dim* statement above the procedure creates a variable (*xws1*) for a proxy that points to the *Service1* Web service for computing the *n*th root of a number. Visual Studio lets you specify the Web reference with IntelliSense so that you don't actually have to type the specification for it. The proxy variable lets you refer to the remote Web service. For example, typing **xws1** followed by a period lets you select *NthRoot*. Inserting the open parentheses sign (prompts for the *anumber* and *aroot* arguments for the Web service.

> **Note** Remember that it isn't necessary for a client application to offer user interaction. For example, a Web service for performing currency conversions can accept input from a database and return values for insertion in a database; users need not interact in the process except perhaps to launch a series of conversions. You can even base the launch on a timer, completely eliminating the need for user interaction.

The variable for the Web reference makes it appear as if the procedure were in the current application instead of another one—namely, the Service1.asmx file in the TestNthRootService folder of the wwwroot subdirectory of the Inetpub folder. Because the *NthRoot* function expects arguments with a *double* data type for *anumber* and *aroot*, the procedure converts the values in *TextBox1* and *TextBox2* with the *CDbl* function before submitting them as arguments for the *NthRoot* Web method. The return value from the *NthRoot* Web method is a *double*. Therefore, the procedure converts the value to a string data type before assigning it to *TextBox3*.

```
'Use the Service1 Web service in the TestNthRootService folder.
Dim xws1 As New XMLWebServiceClients.localhost.Service1()

Private Sub Button1_Click(ByVal sender As System.Object, _
    ByVal e As System.EventArgs) Handles Button1.Click

    Dim anumber As Double = CDbl(TextBox1.Text)
    Dim aroot As Double = CDbl(TextBox2.Text)
    Dim myroot As Double = xws1.NthRoot(anumber, aroot)

    TextBox3.Text = myroot.ToString

End Sub
```

Deploying and Discovering a Web Service

There are a couple of ways to deploy a Web service to a Web server. The scenario that I describe assumes that you build and test a Web service on the localhost and deploy on a Web server running FrontPage. You might want to deploy the Web service on another Web server to which the community of users has better access; make sure the Web server to which you deploy a Web service has the .NET Framework installed. The deployment model copies a subset of the files from one Web server to another. In particular, deployment copies a .dll file that includes a compiled version of the service—for example, Service1.asmx.vb—and any related modules that your application might use in the project for the Web service. When you specify a target Web server and virtual directory on the Web server, Visual Studio .NET will automatically copy files to the target Web server. However, you will also have to add a .disco file so that you can create a Web reference for the deployed solution. This section holds your hand through both of these processes.

Before copying your files for a Web service to another server, you should compile your solution and make sure it contains no compile bugs. You can use the Build Solution menu item on the Build menu to accomplish this. With your Web service project open in Visual Studio, choose Copy Project from the Project menu. Change the name of the destination folder as you see fit. For example, if the path initially reads

http://localhost/TestNthRootService

you can change it to

http://myproductionserver/DeployedNthRootService

In the Copy Project dialog box, select FrontPage in the Web Access Method group. In the Copy group, select Only Files Needed To Run This Application. Then click OK. This copies all the files you need to the FrontPage Web site except for one—the .disco file that allows the easy discovery of the Web service.

Recall that the TestNthRootService folder doesn't contain a Service1.disco file, but it contains a Service1.vdisco file. Both files facilitate discovery, but the .vdisco file format is meant only for testing. Other folders will have better security if you use .disco files instead of .vdisco files to mark a folder as containing a production Web service ready for discovery. Happily, you can automatically write to a browser window the .disco file that you need. If you're working with the deployment folder described above, enter the following string in the address box of your browser:

http://localhost/DeployedNthRootService/Service1.asmx?disco

The preceding sample shows the Web service solution deployed to the same local Web server as the original, but it does specify a new folder. This new folder can have permissions for access by more users than the initial folder. In any event, the Web server to which you deploy the solution must have the .NET

Framework installed. Notice that after the URL for the deployed Web service solution there is a question mark (?) followed by the word *disco*. These two items following the URL cause the Web server to return the text for the Service1.disco file in a browser window. (See Figure 13-7.)

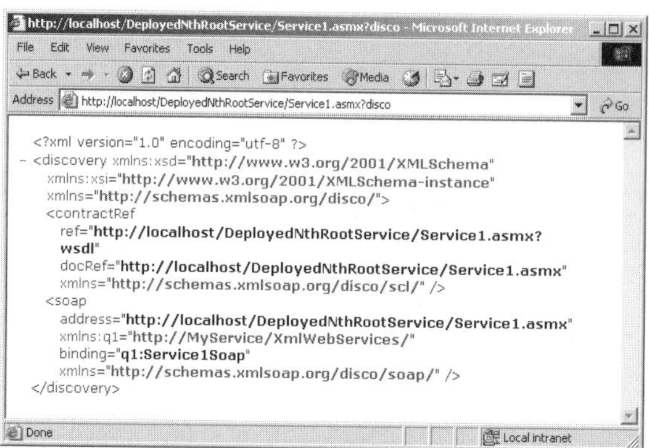

Figure 13-7. This browser window shows an automatically written .disco file for the *Service1* Web service in the DeployedNthRootService virtual directory on the local Web server.

After the .NET Framework has written the .disco file to the browser, copy the contents from the browser's window to your favorite text editor. Remove the leading dash (-) from the *<discovery>* tag. Then save the file in the folder for the deployed Web service, which is c:\inetpub\wwwroot\DeployedNthRootService in the demonstration sample. Use a filename that matches the name of the .asmx file—namely, Service1.disco in our sample.

Now that you have a .disco file, you need to add a Web reference that points to the deployed solution and edit your client solution (or just distribute a new one) so that it uses a proxy for the deployed solution as opposed to the original test solution. With the XMLWebServiceClients project open in Visual Studio .NET, you can create a Web reference for the deployed solution by choosing Add Web Reference from the Project menu. This opens the Add Web Reference dialog box. Then, if your deployed solution is on the local server, click the Web References On Local Web Server link in the left pane. Next scroll down through the Available References list in the right pane until you find the .disco file that you saved for the deployed solution. Figure 13-8 shows the Add Web Reference dialog box with the cursor resting on the saved .disco file. You actually create the reference by selecting the .disco file and then clicking Add Reference at the bottom of the dialog box. By the way, you can also see the discovery file for the test solution toward the bottom of Figure 13-8; notice that this discovery file has the .vdisco extension.

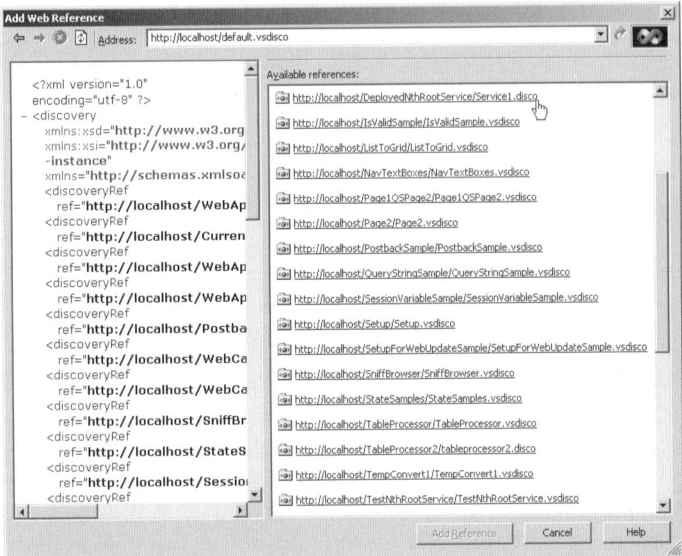

Figure 13-8. The Add Web Reference dialog box just before the selection of the .disco file for the deployed solution.

> **Note** If your solution isn't on the local server, you can type the URL for the deployed Web service's .disco file, such as *http://myproduction-server/DeployedNthRootService/Service1.disco*, in the Address box of the Add Web Reference dialog. Through UDDI, you'll be able to navigate graphically to publicly available Web services.

Finally you can complete the deployed solution by changing the proxy variable, *xws1*, in the client application so that the variable points to the newly added Web reference to the client solution. The sample client application, XMLWebServiceClients, has the code behind *Form1* modified to accomplish this. All you have to do is comment out the *Dim* statement instantiating a Web reference for the test solution (XMLWebServiceClients.localhost.Service1) and uncomment the *Dim* statement for the Web reference pointing to the deployed solution (XMLWebServiceClients.localhost1.Service1). The following lines show how the module-level *Dim* statements should look in the *Form1* module for the deployed solution. This adjustment to the module behind *Form1* in the client application completes the process of deploying the solution so that the client application can access the deployed solution.

```
'Use the Service1 Web service in the TestNthRootService folder.
'Dim xws1 As New XMLWebServiceClients.localhost.Service1()

'New proxy variable pointing at deployed Web service.
Dim xws1 As New XMLWebServiceClients.localhost1.Service1()
```

A Web Service to Return Values from Tables

This section demonstrates how to return values from a table in a database. The sample Web service in this section performs a row count and returns the column values for the first column in any database table on the local SQL Server instance. The client application can specify both the database and table names to determine the return values from Web methods. In addition, the sample client application allows users to select a specific row for which to show a column value. This second level of selection occurs within the client application instead of forcing another call to the Web service. This section doesn't address deployment explicitly because the process is identical to that covered in the preceding section.

Counting and Returning Rows from Any Table in Any Database

The Web service for this section sample works for any table in any database on a database server. You need to specify two input parameters to the Web service. One is the database name. The other is the name of a table within the database. The Web service offers two Web methods. One method returns a count of the number of rows in a table. The other method returns all the values for the first column in the table.

The following listing shows the module for the Web service; I inserted a comment to indicate where the Web Services Designer Generated Code goes. The application exists in the TableProcessor Web services project. I tested the application from Service1.asmx in the TableProcessor folder of the wwwroot subdirectory within the Inetpub directory on my local Web server. As with the preceding sample, a second folder is available in the same place that my system saves Visual Studio projects. This folder also has the name TableProcessor, and it contains the TableProcessor.sln file for Visual Studio to open the project. As you test this application, you will need similar project folders on your system.

The *WebService* attribute for the class specifies *http://MyService/XmlWebServices/* as the namespace for the Web service. If you have another Web service with the same namespace that you are using concurrently, you need to rename the namespace for one of these Web services. The informal description for the Web service is "A Table Processing Service." Recall that this name appears on the test interface for the service. As a consequence, the informal description also appears in the .wsdl file defining the Web service.

After the *Service1* class declaration, the listing declares a pair of module-level variables. The application uses module-level declarations because these variables appear in two or more procedures.

In one sense, the heart of the application is the set of the next two function procedures. Each of these procedures—*RowCount* and *ColumnValues*—implements a Web method named after the function procedure. A slightly longer summary of each method's purpose appears in the *Description* property for the *WebMethod* attribute associated with each function procedure. As with the informal Web service, you can find the function names and their informal descriptions in the .wsdl file for the Web service. The *RowCount* procedure returns a single value just like the preceding sample, except this one is based on a database. The *ColumnValues* procedure returns a collection of values. This represents an opportunity to parse the collection of values if you want to display them individually or select a specific value from the collection. The client application for this Web service demonstrates one approach to this task.

Both function procedures implementing Web methods are just shells for the *ReadRows* sub procedure. The *ReadRows* procedure takes as string arguments the database name and table name that it must process. Then the procedure makes a connection to the database, points a *SqlDataReader* object at the table, and passes through the table's rows to extract values from the first column and count the number of rows. After going through all rows and storing the column values in a local string variable, the procedure inserts (to clarify the meaning of the following data) a short string constant at the beginning of the string variable containing column values. The procedure concludes by closing both the *SqlDataReader* and *Connection* objects.

```
Option Strict On
Imports System.Web.Services

<WebService(Namespace:="http://MyService/XmlWebServices/", _
    Description:="A Table Processing Service.")> _
        Public Class Service1
    Inherits System.Web.Services.WebService

'Web Services Designer Generated Code

'Declare module-level variables.
Dim strValues As String
Dim intCount As Integer

'Mark the function as a Web method.
<WebMethod(Description:="Return row count.")> _
```

(continued)

```
    Public Function RowCount(ByVal adbname As String, _
        ByVal atablename As String) As Integer

        'Pass database and table names to ReadRows procedure.
        ReadRows(adbname, atablename)

        'Return count of rows in table.
        Return intCount

    End Function

    'Mark the function as a Web method.
    <WebMethod(Description:="Return column values.")> _
    Public Function ColumnValues(ByVal adbname As String, _
        ByVal atablename As String) As String

        'Pass database and table names to ReadRows procedure.
        ReadRows(adbname, atablename).

        'Return values from first column in the table.
        Return strValues

    End Function

    Sub ReadRows(ByVal adbname As String, _
        ByVal atablename As String)

        'Open a connection to the database named as
        'an argument.
        Dim strSQL As String = "Data Source=(local);" & _
            "Integrated Security=SSPI;" & _
            "Initial Catalog=" & adbname
        Dim cnn1 As System.Data.SqlClient.SqlConnection = New _
            System.Data.SqlClient.SqlConnection(strSQL)
        cnn1.Open()

        'Declare a command and assign a SQL string to it.
        Dim cmd1 As System.Data.SqlClient.SqlCommand = _
            cnn1.CreateCommand()
        cmd1.CommandText = _
            "SELECT * FROM " & atablename

        'Declare a datareader and copy result set
        'from cmd1 to drd1.
        Dim drd1 As System.Data.SqlClient.SqlDataReader = _
            cmd1.ExecuteReader()

        'Copy and count values in first column.
        Do While drd1.Read()
```

```
            strValues = strValues & CStr(drd1.GetValue(0)) & ", "
            intCount += 1
        Loop
        strValues = "Values in column 1 are: " & strValues

        'Close datareader and connection objects.
        drd1.Close()
        cnn1.Close()

    End Sub

End Class
```

Testing the Web Service in the TableProcessor Folder

After building a Web service application, you can test it to make sure it responds as anticipated. To do this, compile your code and perform preliminary testing with the .NET Framework built-in testing interface. In Solution Explorer, right-click Service1.asmx. Select Build And Browse. This presents a Web page within Visual Studio with links to the Web methods within the Web service.

Click the RowCount link on the *Service1* test screen. This opens another dialog box with a pair of text boxes and a button. Enter **pubs** as the database name in the *adbname* text box. Type **stores** in the *atablename* text box. Then click Invoke. This creates a new page with XML returned by the Web service. (It is, after all, an XML Web service.) If you have *pubs* installed on your database server and you didn't edit the number of stores in the database, it will return the integer value 6. (See Figure 13-9.) You can tell it's an integer by the *int* tags around the number 6. This data type follows from the code for the *RowCount* return value in the preceding section. Its significance is that you must recognize the return value as an integer in any client application that processes values returned by the *RowCount* Web method.

Figure 13-9. The XML returned by the *RowCount* Web method for the Web service in the TableProcessor folder with pubs as the database name and *stores* as the table name.

If you select the test screen for the *RowCount* Web method, you'll notice that it still has pubs and *stores* for the database and table name entries. You can change either or both of these to return the count of rows in another table.

There are no special steps for returning the row count for a table in another database. For example, change the database and table names to Northwind and *Customers*. Then click Invoke. Unless you added or deleted rows in the *Customers* table for the Northwind database, the *RowCount* Web method returns 91 as an integer value.

After verifying the return value for the *RowCount* Web method for the *Customers* table in the Northwind database, you can examine the output for the column values from the *Customers* table. To do this, first close the window returning the *RowCount*; this displays the form for the *RowCount* method. Second go back one screen (for example, using the Web Navigate Back control on the Visual Studio .NET Web toolbar). Then click the ColumnValues link to display the entry form for testing the *ColumnValues* Web method. Type **Northwind** and **Customers** in the blank adbname and atablename text boxes. Then click Invoke. This presents a comma-separated list of *CustomerID* values from the first column in the *Customers* table. (See Figure 13-10.) The string of CustomerID values starts with the string ("Values in column 1 are: ") specified in the *ReadRows* function within the Service1.asmx file for the Web service.

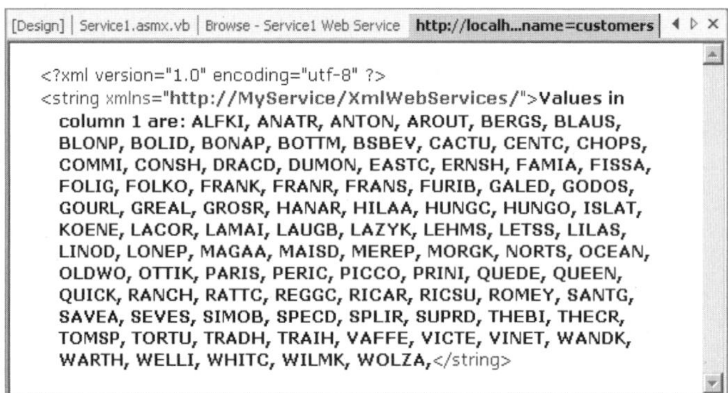

Figure 13-10. The XML returned by the *ColumnValues* Web method for the Web service in the TableProcessor folder with Northwind as the database name and *Customers* as the table name.

Building a Client Application

Any one Web service can work with multiple different client applications. For example, just because the *ColumnValues* method for *Service1* in the TableProcessor folder returns all the values in the first column of a table doesn't mean that a client value has to display all the returned values. The sample client application in this section prompts a user for which row they want from the column and then returns that particular row from the first column. On the other hand, the client application does report the count of rows within a table and returns it as an integer value—exactly as specified by the *RowCount* Web method.

Figure 13-11 shows the form for the client application. In order to run this application by starting the XMLWebServiceClients project, make *Form2* the startup object. Recall from Chapter 9 that you can do this in three steps. First right-click the project name in Solution Explorer. Second select General from Common Properties in the Property Pages dialog box. Third use the Startup object drop-down box to select *Form2*.

The client application displaying its interface through *Form2* has four text boxes with corresponding labels and two buttons. Not all text boxes appear at the same time. When the form initially opens, just the top two of the four text boxes are visible. After valid database and table names are entered, a click of the Row Count button returns the form with three text boxes. These are the initial two text boxes plus a new one showing the count of rows in the table. Clicking the button labeled Get Column Value displays a prompt asking the user which row to return from the table's first column values. The *InputBox* function that produces the prompt returns the default value 1 if the user doesn't specify a row. When *Form2* reappears after the user replies to the prompt, the form shows the first two text boxes with their prior values as well as the fourth text box for displaying a column value. The specific value in the bottom text box is the one matching row specified by the user's reply to the prompt.

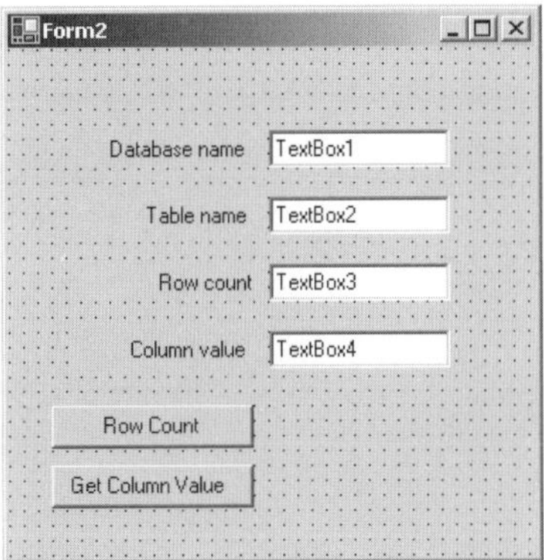

Figure 13-11. The client application form for the *Service1* Web service in the TableProcessor folder.

The processing of the return values from the *ColumnValues* Web method illustrates a typical scenario. A developer engineers an application so that it can accommodate any of several scenarios. For example, a client application makes a selection from the total set of column values to show the column value for just one row instead of the whole set of column values as in Figure 13-10. Figure 13-12 tracks the process from designating database and table names to capturing the reply to the *InputBox* prompt to showing the specific column value that a user wants to view. In the top window, the user designates that they want results from the *Customers* table in the Northwind database before clicking the button labeled Get Column Value. The middle window shows the user indicated that the application should show the column value for the fifth row. By the way, the prompt adjusts automatically to show the maximum number of rows. The application does this by running the *RowCount* Web method when processing a request to show a specific row value from the first column. The bottom window in the figure reveals BERGS as the column value for the fifth row in the first column. You can easily confirm this outcome for yourself by examining the output in Figure 13-10, which shows all the column values for the first column in the *Customers* table from the Northwind database.

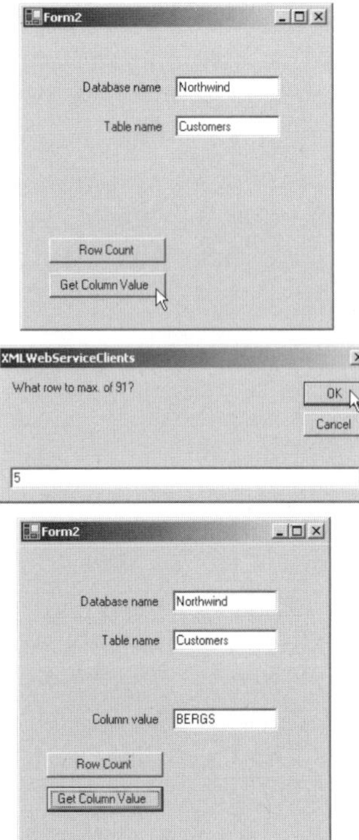

Figure 13-12. The client application for the *Service1* Web service in the TableProcessor folder demonstrating how it handles a request to show a particular column value from the first column of the *Customers* table in the Northwind database.

The following listing shows the code behind *Form2* that manages the behavior of the client application for the Web service in the TableProcessor folder. The listing starts with the instantiation of a module-level variable, *xws1*, for the proxy Web service. Notice how Visual Basic .NET systematically names the second-level reference in the proxy object. The proxy for the first Web service uses *localhost* as its second name. The proxy for the deployed version used *localhost1* as its second name. This proxy variable, which is the third one in the chapter, has *localhost2* as its second name. In all three cases, the first name for a proxy denotes the client application's project—namely, XMLWebServiceClients. Also, the name for the proxy object in each case refers to the .asmx file in the Web service, which has the name *Service1* in all three instances.

The body of the listing includes three event procedures. One is a form *Load* event procedure. This event procedure merely readies the initial look of the form. In particular, it makes the third and fourth text boxes, along with their matching labels, invisible. The application also includes a *Click* event procedure for each button on the form. These event procedures invoke the *RowCount* and *ColumnValues* Web methods as well as processing their return values. As you can see, the *xws1* proxy variable appears in both *Click* event procedures, which is why the listing starts by instantiating the variable at the module level.

The *Button1_Click* event procedure invokes the *RowCount* Web method and displays its result in *TextBox3*. This procedure actually starts by making sure *TextBox4* and its matching label are invisible. These two controls are for displaying a column value and labeling the return value, but a click of the Row Count button (*Button1*) doesn't show any column values. Next the procedure copies the *Text* property values of *TextBox1* and *TextBox2* to memory variables in the client application. These variables store the name of the database and the table for the Web service to examine. After saving the local memory variables, the procedure uses them as arguments while invoking the *RowCount* Web method. The arguments specify for which table in which database to return a row count. The final group of lines in the event procedure makes the text box and label (*TextBox3* and *Label3*) for the row count value visible on the form. The procedure's final line passes the converted value type of the return value from the *RowCount* Web method to the *Text* property of *TextBox3*.

The *Click* event procedure for *Button2* is slightly more sophisticated than the one for *Button1*. There are three reasons for this. First, the *Button2_Click* event procedure invokes two Web methods instead of one. Second, the *Click* event procedure for *Button2* presents a prompt to gather user feedback. Third, the event procedure stores the return value from the *ColumnValues* Web method as an array and then uses the reply to the prompt to pick a value from the array and display it on the form.

Like the event procedure for *Button1*, the *Button2_Click* event procedure starts by making a text box and label invisible. In this case, the text box and label are for the *RowCount* Web method's return value, which a click to *Button2* doesn't show. Just because the procedure doesn't directly show the return value from the *RowCount* Web method doesn't mean the Web method is unused in the procedure. On the contrary, the *RowCount* Web method's return value is used early and often throughout the procedure. In fact, the next three lines save arguments for the Web method, invoke it, and save the return value in a memory variable, *myRowCount*. Next the procedure prompts the user for which row in the first column to show a column value. The procedure uses an *InputBox* function for this with the default value 1.

After obtaining a reply to the *InputBox* function prompt, the procedure concludes its data input phase from the user. All the data it needs is in memory or available via a Web method call. Next the procedure invokes the *ColumnValues* Web method and saves its result as a string. Then the procedure strips off the leading string (`"Values in column 1 are: "`) from the return value and saves the resulting string (*str1*). This leaves *str1* with just the column values from the table named in *TextBox2*.

Perhaps the most interesting aspect of the procedure is the parsing of *str1* to extract individual column values that go into cells in the *myVector* array. The array is dimensioned based on the row count from the table named in *TextBox2*. This value is available via a memory variable (*myRowCount*) from the invocation of the *RowCount* Web method. The procedure then opens a loop that iterates through the column values in *str1*. On each pass through the loop, the code reads the first column value in *str1*, which is a substring up to but not including the first comma. It then saves this value in the first empty cell in the *myVector* array and removes the value, its trailing comma, and the blank space after the comma from the *str1* variable. Therefore, successive passes always have a fresh value as the first column value in *str1*. The procedure concludes by making *TextBox4* with its matching label visible and by selecting a cell from the *myVector* array to show based on the user's response to the *InputBox* function prompt.

```
'Use cabinc_NthRoot Web Service.
Dim xws1 As New XMLWebServiceClients.localhost2.Service1()

Private Sub Form2_Load(ByVal sender As System.Object, _
    ByVal e As System.EventArgs) Handles MyBase.Load

    'Hide RowCount text box and label.
    TextBox3.Visible = False
    Label3.Visible = False
```

```
    'Hide ColumnValue text box and label.
    TextBox4.Visible = False
    Label4.Visible = False

End Sub

Private Sub Button1_Click(ByVal sender As System.Object, _
    ByVal e As System.EventArgs) Handles Button1.Click

    'Hide ColumnValue text box and label.
    Label4.Visible = False
    TextBox4.Visible = False

    'Pass database name and table name from text boxes on
    'the form to the RowCount Web method.
    Dim adbname As String = TextBox1.Text
    Dim atablename As String = TextBox2.Text
    Dim myRowCount As Integer = _
        xws1.RowCount(adbname, atablename)

    'Make the RowCount label and text box visible
    'before populating the text box with a value
    'from the RowCount Web method.
    Label3.Visible = True
    TextBox3.Visible = True
    TextBox3.Text = myRowCount.ToString

End Sub

Private Sub Button2_Click(ByVal sender As System.Object, _
    ByVal e As System.EventArgs) Handles Button2.Click

    'Hide RowCount text box and label.
    Label3.Visible = False
    TextBox3.Visible = False

    'Pass database name and table name from text boxes on
    'the form to the RowCount Web method.
    Dim adbname As String = TextBox1.Text
    Dim atablename As String = TextBox2.Text
    Dim myRowCount As Integer = _
        xws1.RowCount(adbname, atablename)

    'Print out the maximum number of rows as part of a prompt
    'for a selected row from a user.
    Dim strInputMsg = _
        "What row to max. of " & myRowCount.ToString & "?"
    Dim intReturnedRow As Integer = _
        CInt(InputBox(strInputMsg, "", "1"))
```

(continued)

```
        'Pass database name and table name memory values to the
        'ColumnValues Web method and strip off leading string
        'for column values.
        Dim myColumnValues As String = _
            xws1.ColumnValues(adbname, atablename)
        Dim intToColon = InStr(myColumnValues, ":")
        Dim str1 = Mid(myColumnValues, intToColon + 2, _
            Len(myColumnValues))

        'Dimension array and integer variable for loop.
        Dim myVector(myRowCount - 1) As String
        Dim intRow As Integer

        'Pass string of column values to an array.
        For intRow = 0 To myRowCount - 1
            myVector(intRow) = _
                str1.substring(0, InStr(str1, ",") - 1)
            str1 = Mid(str1, InStr(str1, ",") + 2, Len(str1))
        Next

        'Make ColumnValue label and text box visible before
        'passing array value corresponding to user selection in
        'the text box.
        Label4.Visible = True
        TextBox4.Visible = True
        TextBox4.Text = myVector(intReturnedRow - 1)

    End Sub
```

The SQL Server 2000 Web Services Toolkit

The Web Services Toolkit simplifies the creation of Web services based on SQL Server 2000 database objects and templates in IIS virtual directories. Microsoft built on an earlier approach for delivering XML functionality from SQL Server with the Web Services Toolkit—namely, by extending the capability of the IIS virtual directory so that it can host a Web service. The Web service from an IIS virtual directory exposes individual database objects and templates as Web methods.

After the creation of a Web service based on an IIS virtual directory, you still use the same basic approach demonstrated in the preceding two sections for developing a client application for your Web service. This section starts by revealing how to design an IIS virtual directory to offer a Web service. The design of the virtual directory specifies the Web service based on a stored procedure. The review of a core client application and a simple extension of it equip you with the skills to build your own solutions for capturing XML fragments returned from Web methods based on database objects and templates.

Scripting a SQL Server User for a Virtual Directory

Although it isn't essential to designate a SQL Server user when specifying an IIS virtual directory, it can be useful—especially when the virtual directory hosts a Web service. Any Web service emanating from an IIS virtual directory can have a potentially large number of users. By using a special SQL Server user, you can set the permissions for the special SQL Server user and be sure that anyone who connects to the Web service will have permission to perform the tasks enabled through the exposed Web methods. You can also limit the ability to perform tasks through the Web service by limiting the permission for its special SQL Server user.

> **Note** The .NET Framework contains standard security conventions, including techniques for managing the use of encryption that your applications may require for protecting a user's identity, managing data during transmission, and authenticating data from designated clients. See the "Cryptography Overview" topic in the Visual Studio .NET documentation for more detail on this topic. This topic is a major section within the "Security Applications" topic, which you might also want to review.

The following T-SQL script is meant for you to run from Query Analyzer for the SQL Server 2000 instance that you use for the remaining samples throughout this chapter. The script is available among the book's sample files as ScriptsFor13.sql. The sample is built around the notion that this is the local SQL Server 2000 instance. If this isn't the case, you'll need to adjust the sample accordingly. The script drops any prior SQL Server login for the connected SQL Server instance and a prior user for the Northwind database named vbdotnet1. If you incur error messages because the user doesn't exist, simply ignore them because the purpose of the script is to remove a login or user only if it does exist. After making sure vbdotnet1 is free for assignment, the script adds a new user named vbdotnet1 and grants access to the Northwind database. Recall that the Northwind database is one of the SQL Server sample databases. The database's public role grants any user access to most database objects that ship as part of the database. For example, vbdotnet1 has automatic permission to run all stored procedures, such as the *Ten Most Expensive Products* stored procedure, which is one of the built-in user-defined stored procedures for the database.

Notice that this script uses "/*" to mark the beginning of the code comment that stretches over multiple lines, and "*/" to end it.

```
/*Run from member of sysadmin fixed server role.
Ignore errors if user does not already exist.
*/

USE Northwind

EXEC sp_revokedbaccess 'vbdotnet1'
EXEC sp_droplogin @loginame = 'vbdotnet1'
GO

--Add vbdotnet1 user with known permissions.

EXEC sp_addlogin
    @loginame = 'vbdotnet1',
    @passwd = 'passvbdotnet1',
    @defdb = 'Northwind'
EXEC sp_grantdbaccess 'vbdotnet1'
GO
```

Building a Web Service in an IIS Virtual Directory

Now that we have a SQL Server user, we can proceed through the steps for creating an IIS virtual directory. This directory will contain the contract for a Web service. You can create a new IIS virtual directory by choosing Programs from the Windows Start menu, then SQLXML 3.0, and then Configure IIS Support. This opens the IIS Virtual Directory Management utility for SQLXML 3.0. In order to open the utility, you must, of course, have already installed Web Release 3 (SQLXML 3.0). See the "Web Services from the Web Services Toolkit" section for a URL to download Web Release 3 along with the Web Services Toolkit.

With the IIS Virtual Directory Management utility open, expand the folder for the local Web server. Then right-click Default Web Site within the local Web server, choose New, and then choose Virtual Directory. This opens a multi-tabbed dialog box that lets you set the properties of a new virtual directory. You can use the New Virtual Directory Properties dialog box to create the virtual directory by following these instructions:

1. On the General tab, name the directory **Chapter13**, and give the virtual directory the path **c:\inetpub\wwwroot\Chapter13**. You can type the path or use the Browse button to navigate to the folder. Although the utility allows you to create a new folder from within the utility, some may find it easier to create the folder before opening the utility.
2. On the Security tab, select the SQL Server radio button. Then enter **vbdotnet1** in the User Name text box and **passvbdotnet1** in the Password text box. Confirm the password before moving off the tab.

3. On the Data Source tab, accept the default settings of the local SQL Server and default database for the current login.

4. On the Settings tab, leave Allow Template Queries selected and also select Allow POST.

5. On the Virtual Names tab, you set up the virtual directory through which you can deliver Web services. With <New virtual name> highlighted in the Defined Virtual Names list box, enter **SoapFor13** in the Name text box. Then select soap from the Type list. Next, in the Path text box, enter the path for your virtual directory, namely **c:\inetput\wwwroot\Chapter13**. Finally click Save to enable the configuration of your Web service associated with the *SoapFor13* virtual name.

   Once you've clicked Save, the Configure button is enabled.

6. While still in the Virtual Names tab, click Configure (see Figure 13-13) to select SQL Server stored procedures and user-defined functions to expose as Web methods. You can also expose templates through the Web service. Although your database objects and templates must exist before you can expose them, the Web Services Toolkit doesn't expose them until you explicitly configure it to make the Web service offer Web methods based on a stored procedure, user-defined function, or template.

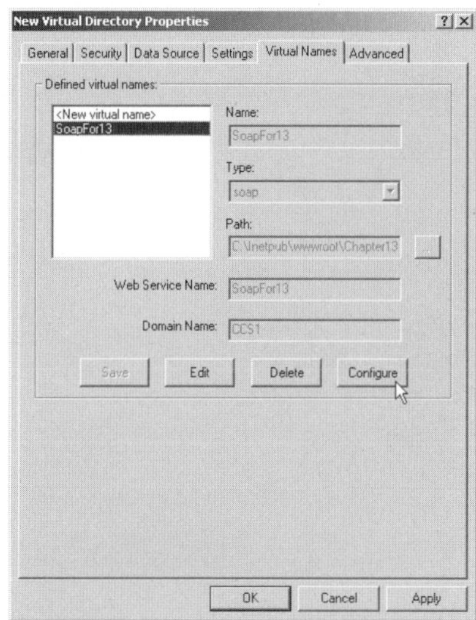

Figure 13-13. The Virtual Name tab for the New Virtual Directory Properties dialog box for the *SoapFor13* Web service in the Chapter13 virtual directory.

7. After you click Configure, the Soap Virtual Name Configuration dialog box opens so that you can specify items to expose as Web methods. If you are going to expose a stored procedure or a user-defined function, designate SP as the Type; otherwise, select Template to designate a template as the source for a Web method. You can designate an item by using the Browse button (…) to browse sources for a Web method in the Web service hosted by the virtual directory. By clicking the Browse button with SP selected as the Type, I was able to pick *Ten Most Expensive Products* as the source for a Web method. I accepted the default selection to return the result set from the stored procedure as XML objects. With this selection, you can retrieve multiple results (or just one) from a stored procedure. Figure 13-14 shows the dialog box just before I click Save to expose the stored procedure as a Web method.

8. Click OK to save the configuration of the Web Service and close the Soap Virtual Name Configuration dialog box.

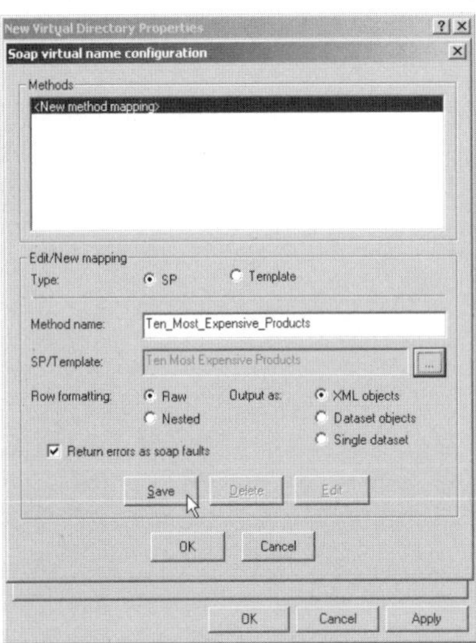

Figure 13-14. The Soap Virtual Name Configuration dialog box displaying the settings for the *Ten_Most_Expensive_Products* Web method just before saving them.

You can improve your debugging process by disabling various caching options.

9. Click the Advanced tab in the New Virtual Directory Properties dialog box. Consider selecting all three options for disabling different types of caching. These selections improve the operation of your Web service, but the caching can be distracting in some debugging and code updating operations.

10. Click OK to save the settings you've chosen and close the New Virtual Directory Properties dialog box.

    Now you're ready to test the Web service. After you finish debugging and refining your Web service, restore the caching features because they speed up the operation of a Web service in normal operation.

> **Note** The book's sample files include the Chapter13 virtual directory folder for reference's sake. In order to create the virtual directory so that you can manage it and use it, you'll need to follow the instructions for its creation in this section. When a subsequent section edits the *SoapFor13* Web service hosted by the Chapter13 virtual directory, you'll need to follow the steps for that as well.

Building a Client Application to Show an XML Fragment

Web services created with the SQL Server 2000 Web Services Toolkit don't have a built-in test interface. In addition, you connect them to a client application slightly differently than Web services, which you build directly with Visual Studio .NET. Nevertheless, the broad outline of the testing process with a client application is similar. In both cases, a .wsdl file formally defines the Web service and specifies any input and outputs associated with individual Web methods. In addition, you must create a Web reference in the client application that points at the Web service.

Create a new form named *Form3* in the XMLWebServiceClients project. Add two label controls. Size the form and controls about as they appear in Figure 13-15 later in this section. (The form is also available in the XMLWebServiceClients project among the book's sample files.) The arrangement and sizing of the form and its controls are intended to accommodate the display of the entire XML fragment returned by the *Ten_Most_Expensive_Products* Web method. Make *Form3* the startup object for the XMLWebServiceClients project so that the form opens when you start the project.

In the module behind *Form3*, add a Web reference to the *SoapFor13* Web service by choosing Add Web Reference from the Project menu. In the address box of the Add Web Reference dialog box, type the following URL with its trailing parameter:

http://localhost/Chapter13/SoapFor13?wsdl

Then press Enter. This populates the left pane of the Add Web Reference dialog box with a representation of the .wsdl file for the *SoapFor13* Web service. The right pane includes a single link with the text View Contract. Click the Add Reference button to create a Web reference for use with a proxy variable. If you have been creating the samples throughout the chapter, the name for this Web reference in the Web References folder of Solution Explorer is *localhost3*. No matter what its name, the reference should include an item named SoapFor13.wsdl. This .wsdl file contains the formal description for the Web service. Any proxy variable based on this Web reference will enable you to run the *Ten_Most_Expensive_Products* Web method and display the result set returned as an XML fragment. The result set from the stored procedure is available as an XML document fragment because the example selected this output format in Figure 13-14.

The next listing shows the code behind the form in Figure 13-15. As you can see, it consists of a single form *Load* event procedure. When the form opens, the procedure connects to the *SoapFor13* Web service and invokes the *Ten_Most_Expensive_Products* Web method. It collects the XML fragment returned by the method in an array of *Response* objects. The *Response* object is the most basic kind of object in Visual Studio .NET; this type of object can accommodate any other kind of object or type. Since the Web service can present either an XML document or a *SqlMessage* object, the application needs *Response* objects to accommodate either outcome. The *SqlMessage* object can return SQL Server error messages and warnings to an application.

Using an array of objects accommodates the possibility of multiple result sets from a single stored procedure or template file. Although this sample has a single result set, the sample's design illustrates the *For* loop syntax for iterating through the members of a Response object array. A *Select…Case* statement sends the *Response* object to the appropriate code for processing. Because this is a very simple application, the code just processes an object containing an XML fragment. The processing consists of a pair of statements that copy the XML fragment in the *Response* object to the *Text* property of the second label on *Form3*. Whenever you choose to output the result set or sets from a Web method as XML objects, you'll have to process the output in this style—that is, with a *Select…Case* statement nested within a *For* loop that iterates through the objects returned from the Web method.

```
Private Sub Form3_Load(ByVal sender As System.Object, _
    ByVal e As System.EventArgs) Handles MyBase.Load

    'Declare Web service xws1 as type named soap in
    'localhost4 Web reference.
    Dim xws1 As New XMLWebServiceClients.localhost3.SoapFor13()

    'Declare object for return from Web service method.
    Dim response As New Object()
    Dim result As System.Xml.XmlElement

    'Declare integer for iterating through multiple
    'result sets that the Web service method can return.
    Dim int1 As Integer

    'Save return from Web service method as an object.
    response = xws1.Ten_Most_Expensive_Products

    'Iterate through result sets.
    For int1 = 0 To UBound(response)

        Select Case response(int1).GetType().ToString()
            Case "System.Xml.XmlElement"
                'Pass int1 result set to result and display
                'in list box and Output window.
                result = response(int1)
                Label2.Text = result.OuterXml
            Case Else
                'Handles end of result sets and other
                'special returns.
        End Select

    Next

End Sub
```

Figure 13-15 shows *Form3* open from the XMLWebServiceClient project. The form contains two labels. The top label has a fixed *Text* property assignment. It always shows "XML fragment:". The contents of the bottom text box can change if the ten most expensive products change because of a price revision, the addition of new products, or the dropping of existing products. The product name and unit price values are delimited by opening and closing tags. Although this format may be convenient for computers to process and is readable by humans, it is verbose. That's because every value has a pair of tags, and there are additional tags to mark the beginning and ending of each row (*<row>* and *</row>*) as well as the beginning and ending of the XML fragment (*<SQLXML>* and *</SQLXML >*).

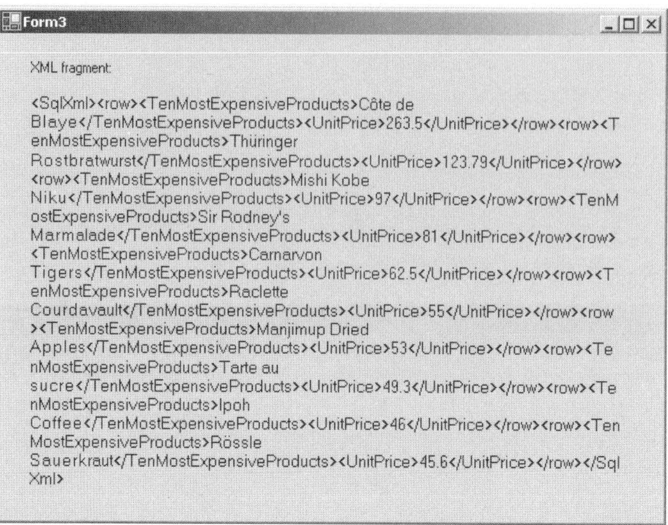

Figure 13-15. *Form3* from the XMLWebServiceClients project showing the output from the *Ten_Most_Expensive_Products* Web method in the *SoapFor13* Web service.

Populating a ListBox Control with an XML Service

Figure 13-15 is interesting, but it's unlikely that you'll want to show many clients of your Web services an XML fragment. It's more likely that they will want to view the tag values in a control than a verbose XML fragment including tags. In the case of the display in Figure 13-15, they might prefer to see a ListBox control with 10 items, showing product name and price in descending order. The sample in this section extends the preceding one to achieve this goal.

You can implement this sample by creating a new form, *Form4*, in the XMLWebServiceClients project. Add a list box control and the code listing in this section. Make *Form4* the startup object for the project. If you have the Web reference defined as in the preceding sample, pressing F5 will cause the form to open and show the ten most expensive products in a list box. (See Figure 13-16.) By adding custom code, such as we will show later in this chapter, you can enable interactivity with data returned by a Web service from within a Windows form control.

Once you understand that your applications can capture the result set from a stored procedure as a *Response* object containing an XML fragment, it's easy to craft a solution like the one in Figure 13-16. All your application has to do is parse the XML fragment to extract the tag values, combine the product name and price in a form suitable for the ListBox control, and then add the combined item to the control.

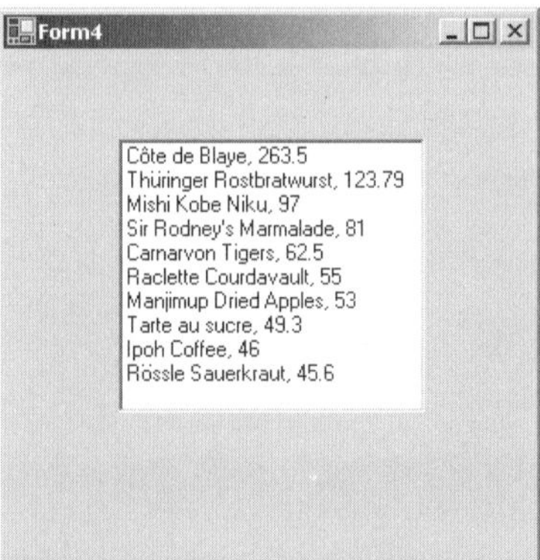

Figure 13-16. A ListBox control on *Form4* showing the processed output from the *Ten_Most_Expensive_Products* Web method in the *SoapFor13* Web service.

The following listing illustrates how you can achieve this. The solution relies on two procedures. The first is an extension of the form *Load* event procedure from the preceding sample. The second procedure is new to this chapter (but you may recall it from Chapter 12). The new code for this procedure as well as the new procedure in this chapter appear in bold type. The primary feature of the extension is the insertion of a *Do…While* loop within the *For* loop that extracts the XML fragment as a response object.

The *Do…While* loop uses two string variables, *str1* and *str2*, to manipulate the XML returned from the response object returned by the *Ten_Most_Expensive_Products* Web method. For example, *str1* stores the current working version of the return value from the Web method. In successive passes through the *Do…While* loop, the procedure extracts the first values for product name and price from the XML fragment. The form *Load* event procedure uses the *MyTagValue* function procedure to extract the product name and price values. The form *Load* event procedure then combines the two values as a new comma-delimited string in *str2*, which the procedure adds as an item to *ListBox1*. Before iterating through the loop again, the code uses the *Right* function to remove from *str1* the XML associated with the added item. When there are no remaining tags in *str1* with price information, the *Do…While* loop releases control to the outer *For* loop, which leads, in turn, to the opening of *Form4* with the populated list box.

As indicated earlier, the *MyTagValue* function procedure initially appeared in Chapter 12. This procedure uses familiar string manipulation techniques to extract tag values from an XML fragment. The calling procedure simply passes the tag name and the XML fragment. The function returns the first tag value in the string with starting and ending tags within the fragment matching the tag name passed to it. The reuse of such a simple procedure from Chapter 12 without any modification illustrates the power of thinking of XML fragments as strings.

```
Private Sub Form3_Load(ByVal sender As System.Object, _
    ByVal e As System.EventArgs) Handles MyBase.Load

'Declare Web service xws1 as type named soap in
'localhost4 Web reference.
Dim xws1 As New XMLWebServiceClients.localhost3.SoapFor13()

'Declare object for return from Web service method.
Dim response As New Object()
Dim result As System.Xml.XmlElement

'Declare integer for iterating through multiple
'result sets that the Web service method can return.
Dim int1 As Integer

'Save return from Web service method as an object.
response = xws1.Ten_Most_Expensive_Products

'Declare variables for processing XML fragment.
Dim str1 As String
Dim str2 As String

'Iterate through result sets.
For int1 = 0 To UBound(response)

    Select Case response(int1).GetType().ToString()
        Case "System.Xml.XmlElement"
            'Pass int1 result set to result and display
            'in list box and Output window.
            result = response(int1)
            str1 = result.OuterXml

            'Iterate through column values in XML string
            'within Web service method output.
            Do While InStr(str1, "</UnitPrice>") > 0
                str2 = MyTagValue("TenMostExpensiveProducts", str1)
                str2 = str2 & ", " & MyTagValue("UnitPrice", str1)
                ListBox1.Items.Add(str2)
                str1 = Microsoft.VisualBasic.Right(str1, _
                    Len(str1) - (InStr(str1, "</UnitPrice>")) - _
                    Len("</UnitPrice></row>") + 1)
            Loop
        Case Else
            'Handles end of result sets and other
            'special returns.
    End Select
```

```
Next

End Sub

Function MyTagValue(ByVal TagName As String, _
    ByVal strXML As String)

    'Declare and compute constants for this tag.
    Dim str1 = "<" & TagName & ">"
    Dim str2 = "</" & TagName & ">"
    Dim int1, int2 As Integer
    int1 = InStr(strXML, str1) + Len(str1)
    int2 = InStr(strXML, str2)

    'Compute tag value and return it.
    'strXML is string with XML to parse.
    'int1 is start position.
    'int2 - int1 calculates number of characters.
    Dim TagValue As String = Mid(strXML, _
        int1, int2 - int1)
    Return TagValue

End Function
```

More on Populating Controls with Web Services

This section drills deeper into building Web services with the SQL Server 2000 Web Services Toolkit and client applications with Visual Studio .NET. In particular, the emphasis is on populating controls on Windows Forms. Client applications created with Windows Forms can interoperate freely with Web services over the Web just as if the client were available locally. In addition to showing how to populate controls, this section also illustrates how to provide interactivity with Web services through Windows Forms. These client features work equally well whether you create your Web service application with the Web Services Toolkit or Visual Studio .NET.

Adding Custom Database Objects as Web Methods

The samples in the preceding section created Web services for an existing stored procedure in the Northwind database. Sometimes our applications benefit from, or even require, the creation of custom database objects. When this is the case for a Web services solution, you need to add the custom database objects to the database. Then, in a separate step, you must expose your new objects through the Web service. Typically, this will require editing a previously existing Web service. The steps described in this section illustrate how to perform these actions.

T-SQL for Creating Sample Database Objects

The next two code samples for client applications will work with result sets returned by two custom database objects for the Northwind database. One of these objects is a stored procedure, and the other is a user-defined function. The stored procedure returns all the *CategoryID* and *CategoryName* column values from the *Categories* table. The user-defined function returns *ProductName* column values from the *Products* table. A *WHERE* clause in the user-defined function causes the function to return just product names that are from a specified category as designated by a *CategoryID* parameter. Therefore, one of the benefits of this database object is that it illustrates the syntax and procedures for using parameters with Web services.

The following T-SQL listing is to be run from Query Analyzer. The listing is available among the book's sample files as ScriptsFor13.sql. If you want, you can adapt the samples for running directly from Visual Studio .NET. (See Chapter 11 for samples demonstrating this approach.) However, it is much easier to run the scripts from Query Analyzer if you're familiar with it. (See the last section in Chapter 1 if you don't already have this background.) Use a login for Query Analyzer that belongs to the sysadmin group.

The scripts for creating the stored procedure and the user-defined function follow parallel paths. First they drop any prior version of the database object. Next they create a new version of the object. Finally they explicitly grant the vbdotnet1 user permission to use the object. Recall that vbdotnet1 is the user for the Chapter13 virtual directory. Without granting the user permission for the object, you won't be able to expose the objects as Web methods for the *SoapFor13* Web service originating from the Chapter13 virtual directory.

```
/*
Run from member of sysadmin fixed server role.
Ignore errors if user does not already exist.
*/

USE Northwind

--Drop udpListOfCategoryNames if it exists.
IF EXISTS (SELECT *
    FROM INFORMATION_SCHEMA.ROUTINES
    WHERE ROUTINE_NAME = 'udpListOfCategoryNames')
    DROP PROCEDURE udpListOfCategoryNames
GO

--Then, create udpListOfCategoryNames, and give
-- vbdotnet1 permission to execute it.
CREATE PROCEDURE udpListOfCategoryNames
AS
SELECT CategoryID, CategoryName
```

```
FROM Categories
GO

GRANT EXEC ON udpListOfCategoryNames TO vbdotnet1
GO

--Drop udfProductsInACategory if it exists.
IF EXISTS(SELECT *
    FROM INFORMATION_SCHEMA.ROUTINES
    WHERE ROUTINE_NAME = 'udfProductsInACategory')
    DROP FUNCTION udfProductsInACategory
GO

--Then, create it, give vbdotnet1
--permission to select from it.
CREATE FUNCTION udfProductsInACategory(@MyCategoryID int)
RETURNS TABLE
AS
RETURN(
    SELECT ProductName
    FROM Products
    WHERE CategoryID = @MyCategoryID
)
GO

GRANT SELECT ON udfProductsInACategory TO vbdotnet1
GO
```

Updating a Web Service with the Web Services Toolkit

After adding custom database objects to a database, you can expose the objects as Web methods through a virtual directory pointing to the database. The virtual directory must have a *soap* virtual name, such as *SoapFor13*, which is the virtual *soap* name for the Chapter13 virtual directory. If you have an existing *soap* name, you can edit it according to the instructions in this section. If you don't already have a *soap* name for a virtual directory, you can use the instructions in the "Building a Web Service in an IIS Virtual Directory" section to create a new *soap* virtual name.

Begin by exposing the two new database objects as Web methods by double-clicking the Chapter13 virtual directory in the IIS Virtual Directory Management utility. On the Virtual Names tab of the Chapter13 Properties dialog box, highlight SoapFor13 and click Configure. This opens the Soap Virtual Name Configuration dialog box. Click the Browse button (…) to select *udpListOfCategoryNames*. Select Single Dataset for the output format. Name the Web method *udpListOfCategoryNamesAsDataset*. Figure 13-17 shows the Soap Virtual Name Configuration dialog box just before saving the settings for the *udpListOfCategoryNamesAsDataset* Web method. Click Save to save the specification for the Web method. You can follow the same general approach to exposing the *udfProductsInACategory* user-defined function as a Web method. Assign *udfProductsInACategoryAsDataset* as its Web method name.

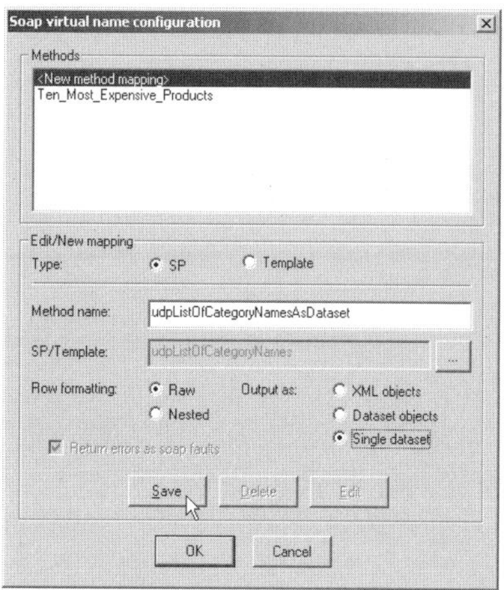

Figure 13-17. The Soap Virtual Name Configuration settings for the *udpListOfCategoryNamesAsDataset* Web method.

Populating a DataGrid and a ListBox with a Web Method

Using the revised Web service gives you a chance to explore more ways of how to tap Web services from within Visual Basic .NET applications. Before you can take advantage of the revisions, you need to refresh the Web reference connecting the XMLWebServiceClients project to the Web service. Curiously, you do this by following the same steps as for adding a new Web reference. Start the refresh process by choosing Add Web Reference from the Project menu within the XMLWebServiceClients project. In the Add Web Reference dialog box that opens, enter **http://localhost/Chapter13/SoapFor13?wsdl** in the Address box. Then press Enter and click Add Reference. This opens the dialog box shown in Figure 13-18. Click Yes to update the Web reference. Without these steps, your client application won't be able to use the Web methods for the *udpListOfCategoryNames* and *udfProductsInACategory* database objects added previously.

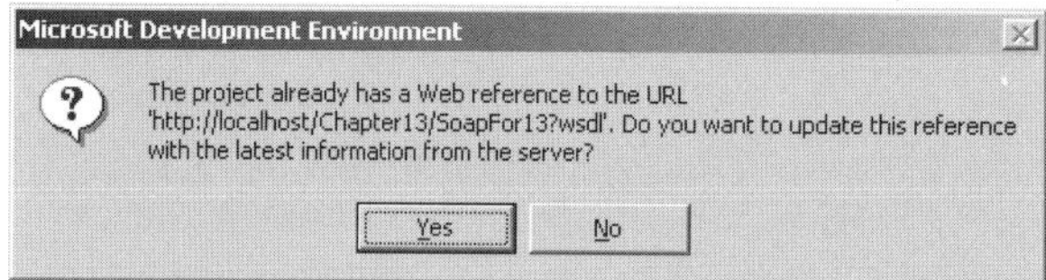

Figure 13-18. Dialog box for updating a Web reference, displayed when you start to add a new Web reference to an updated Web service. Click Yes to update the existing Web reference without adding a new one.

Now that the XMLWebServiceClients project has an updated Web reference, we can put the new Web methods to use. The *udpListOfCategoryNames* stored procedure is similar to the *Ten Most Expensive Products* stored procedure in that neither procedure accepts a parameter. However, the Web methods for the database objects are distinct in ways that affect the syntax for using them. Recall that the *Ten_Most_Expensive_Products* Web method formats its output as XML objects. On the other hand, the *udpListOfCategoryNamesAsDataset* Web method formats its result as a single data set. By specifying its output as a single data set, you know precisely what the format of the return from the Web method will be. (There's no chance of a *SqlMessage* object in the output stream associated with the Web method.) Therefore, the syntax for reading the output can be more straightforward. When you have only one result set from a database object, the Single Dataset format is a great output format for simplifying the processing of your client application.

You can get a hands-on feel for using the *udpListOfCategoryNamesAsDataset* Web method by adding a new form with DataGrid and ListBox controls. *Form5* in Figure 13-19 shows the basic design for the sample. The Design view shows two controls on a Windows form. The left control is an empty DataGrid control; its Properties window shows the control's name as *DataGrid1*. The other control on the form shows its name as *ListBox1*. By making *Form5* the startup object for the XMLWebServiceClients project, you can invoke the form's *Load* event procedure by starting the project. In this event procedure, you can load data from the *SoapFor13* Web service into both controls.

The following listing shows the form *Load* event procedure for *Form5*. It starts by instantiating a proxy variable, *xws1*, for the *SoapFor13* Web service, which is denoted by the Web reference named *localhost3* in the client application. Because I updated the Web reference as described previously, this sample in the XMLWebServiceClients project can invoke the *udpListOfCategoryNamesAsDataset* Web method. This Web method's definition returns a single data set. When returning a result set from a stored procedure as a single data set, you must designate an integer *returnvalue* argument as you invoke the Web method. This *returnvalue* argument makes available the return code for a stored procedure; syntax conventions require the *returnvalue* argument even when the stored procedure has no return code. Chapter 4 refers to return codes from stored procedures as return status values as it illustrates their use.

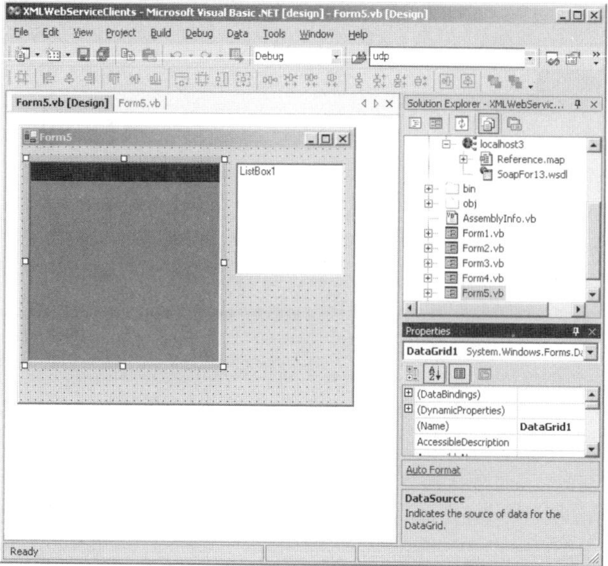

Figure 13-19. *Form5* contains a pair of controls that the code behind the form will populate by invoking the *udpListOfCategoryNamesAs-Dataset* Web method.

> **Note** When a stored procedure has no return code or return status value, the *returnvalue* argument for a Web method assumes the value 0.

After copying the result set from the stored procedure to a data set in the client application, the code assigns the data set to the *DataSource* property of *DataGrid1*. In addition, the procedure passes *–1* as an argument to the *Expand* method for the DataGrid control. This opens the row indicator on *DataGrid1* so that a user can click it to view the data in the control. Without this setting, a user would need to click the Expand control on *DataGrid1* to show the row indicator. (See Figure 13-20 for a view of the row indicator and its parent Expand/ Contract control.)

The last two blocks of code handle iterating through the returned data set from the Web method and populating the items within *ListBox1* based on the column values for *CategoryID* and *CategoryName*. Because *CategoryID* has a SQL Server *int* data type, you gain performance by explicitly specifying it as a string for concatenation with a string constant (", ") and the *CategoryName* column value, which is a string value.

```
Private Sub Form5_Load(ByVal sender As System.Object, _
    ByVal e As System.EventArgs) Handles MyBase.Load

    'Declare Web service xws1 as SoapFor13 in the
    'localhost3 Web reference.
    Dim xws1 As New XMLWebServiceClients.localhost3.SoapFor13()

    'Save return from Web service method as a data set;
    'syntax mandates specification of a returnvalue parameter.
    Dim das1 As System.Data.DataSet
    Dim returnvalue As Integer
    das1 = _
        xws1.udpListOfCategoryNamesAsDataset(returnvalue)

    'Set data grid to display returned data set.
    DataGrid1.DataSource = das1
    DataGrid1.Expand(-1)

    'Declare a row and a string.
    Dim MyRow As DataRow
    Dim str1 As String

    'Iterate through data set rows and insert
    'in the list box column values one row at a time.
    For Each MyRow In das1.Tables(0).Rows
        str1 = MyRow(0) & ", " & MyRow(1)
        ListBox1.Items.Add(str1)
    Next

End Sub
```

Figure 13-20 shows the result of opening the XMLWebServiceClients project with *Form5* as the startup object. The top window shows the form after opening but before the row indicator in the DataGrid control is expanded to reveal the data source behind the data grid. Notice that this row indicator is a child control of an Expand/Contract control within the DataGrid control. Even before the row indicator in the DataGrid control is clicked, the list box shows its values. However, the list box doesn't provide the same degree of data formatting flexibility available with a data grid. The bottom window shows the data grid after a click of the row indicator and after the default width of its second column has been expanded slightly. One of the advantages of the data grid is a user's ability to manipulate the control.

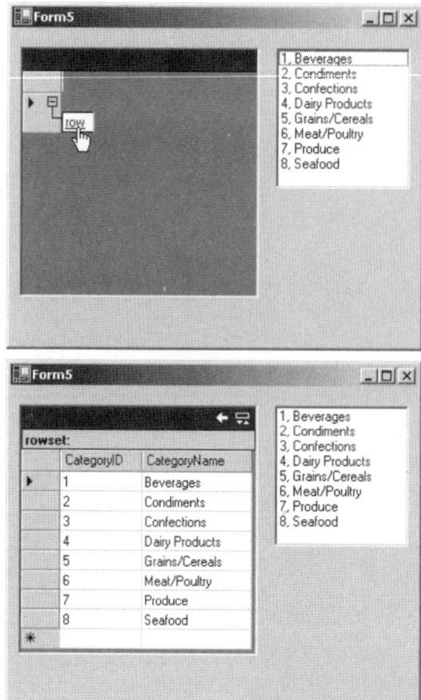

Figure 13-20. The DataGrid control on *Form5* lets the user interact with it to control when the data is displayed and to control the width of the columns.

Dynamically Populating a Control with a Web Method

The last sample in this chapter illustrates how to return values dynamically from a Web service based on a user selection from a list box. The application again draws on the *SoapFor13* Web service. This sample demonstrates how to pass a parameter to a user-defined function in a SQL Server database through a Web service so that the Web method for the user-defined function passes back a result set based on the user's selection from the items in a list box.

The sample uses *Form6*, which you will need to make the startup object for the XMLWebServiceClients project. When a user initially opens the project, it displays an initial list box, a text box, and a second list box like the one in the top window of Figure 13-21. The form automatically selects the first category name in the first ListBox control, displays the *CategoryID* value for the first category name, and displays the products within the category in the second list box. (See the top form window in Figure 13-21.) After the form opens, a user can change the products displayed in the second list box by selecting a new category from the first list box. The bottom form window in Figure 13-21 shows the form after the selection of the Produce category in the first list box. Notice that the selection in the first list box automatically updates the contents of the text box and the second list box. The code behind the form passes an argument to a Web method based on the value showing in the text box; the Web method, in turn, populates the second list box.

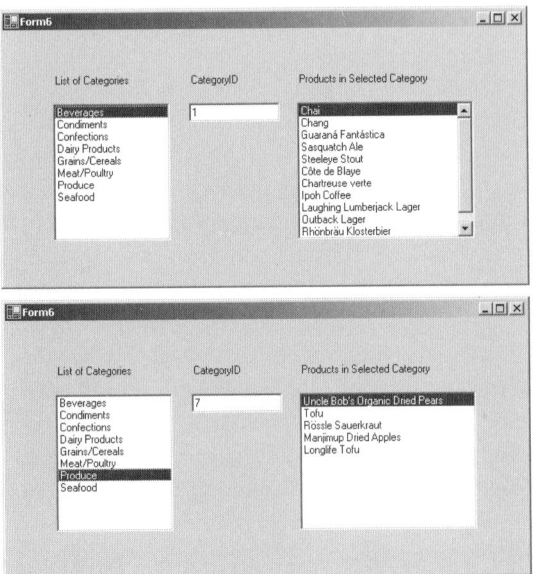

Figure 13-21. *Form6* in the XMLWebServiceClients project automatically adjusts the contents of a text box and list box based on the selection in a list box. Each list box is populated by a separate Web method.

The following listing displays the two short event procedures that control the operation of the sample depicted in Figure 13-21. The *Load* event procedure for *Form6* starts by instantiating a proxy variable for the *SoapFor13* Web service. Next the code uses the proxy variable to invoke the *udpListOfCategoryNamesAsDataset* Web method in the service. As you have seen from the previous sample, this Web method returns a data set containing a data table with *CategoryID* and *CategoryName* column values, in that order. The last block of code explicitly sets the source for *ListBox1* based on the data set returned by the Web method. After setting the *DataSource* for the list box to the table in the local data set, the *Load* event procedure concludes by setting the *DisplayMember* property for the list box to the name for the first column in the local table that serves as the *DataSource* property for the control.

> **Note** When *Form6* initially loads, it automatically selects the first item in *ListBox1*. This, in turn, fires the second event procedure behind the form—*ListBox1_SelectedIndexChanged*. As a consequence, this second procedure sets the *Text* property of *TextBox1* to 1 and the items in *ListBox2* to the names for products belonging to the Beverages category.

The second event procedure populates *TextBox1* based on the index value for the selected item in *ListBox1*. Because this index starts at 0, the procedure adds 1 to the index value so that the range extends from 1 through 8 for each of the *CategoryID* values in the *Categories* table that the *udpListOfCategoryNamesAsDataset* Web method queries. Next the *ListBox1_SelectedIndexChanged* procedure connects to the *SoapFor13* Web service with the *xws1* proxy variable before invoking the *udfProductsInACategoryAsDataset* Web method. The syntax for the statement invoking the Web method illustrates how to pass a parameter to a user-defined function. The parameter is the *Text* property setting for *TextBox1* converted to an *Integer* data type. Because *TextBox1* shows a *CategoryID* value, the Web method returns the *ProductName* column values from the *Products* table in the Northwind database for rows with a matching *CategoryID* value. The procedure comes to an end by using the table in the data set storing the return set from the Web method as the DataSource property for *ListBox2*.

```
Private Sub Form6_Load(ByVal sender As System.Object, _
    ByVal e As System.EventArgs) Handles MyBase.Load
    'Declare Web service xws1 as SoapFor13 in the
    'localhost3 Web reference.
    Dim xws1 As New XMLWebServiceClients.localhost3.SoapFor13()

    'Save return from Web service method as a data set.
    Dim das1 As System.Data.DataSet
    Dim returnvalue As Integer
    das1 = xws1.udpListOfCategoryNamesAsDataset(returnvalue)

    'Populate list box with category names.
    'Automatic selection of first item in ListBox1
    'invokes ListBox1_SelectedIndexChanged event
    'procedure to populate TextBox1 and ListBox2.
    ListBox1.DataSource = das1.Tables(0)
    ListBox1.DisplayMember = _
        CStr(das1.Tables(0).Columns(1).ColumnName)
```

```
End Sub

Private Sub ListBox1_SelectedIndexChanged( _
    ByVal sender As System.Object, _
    ByVal e As System.EventArgs) _
    Handles ListBox1.SelectedIndexChanged

    'Compute CategoryID for selected value.
    TextBox1.Text = ListBox1.SelectedIndex + 1

    'Declare Web service xws1 as SoapFor13 in the
    'localhost3 Web reference.
    Dim xws1 As New XMLWebServiceClients.localhost3.SoapFor13()

    'Save return from Web service method as a data set based on
    'CategoryID value in text box; notice returnvalue parameter
    'is not necessary with a SQL Server function procedure.
    Dim das1 As System.Data.DataSet
    das1 = _
        xws1.udfProductsInACategoryAsDataset(CInt(TextBox1.Text))

    'Populate second list box with product names
    'for products in currently selected category in the
    'first list box.
    ListBox2.DataSource = das1.Tables(0)
    ListBox2.DisplayMember = _
        das1.Tables(0).Columns(0).ColumnName

End Sub
```

Index

A

B

C

D

E

G

H

I

J

O

P

Q

T

V

W

X

Y

About the Author

Rick Dobson, Ph.D., is an author and trainer specializing in Microsoft SQL Server, Microsoft Access, and Web technologies. He is a big fan of programmatic solutions, particularly those that involve Visual Basic .NET, ADO.NET, ASP.NET, XML Web services, and T-SQL—technologies he features prominently in this book. If you look at some of his prior books, you'll discover that he also programs in VBA, ADO, Jet SQL, and SQL-DMO.

This is Rick's fourth book in four years. Both this book and a former one titled *Professional SQL Server Development with Access 2000* (Wrox Press Inc., 2000) focus heavily on the development of SQL Server solutions. While his other two books are on Microsoft Access, they demonstrate his commitment to Microsoft database technology. All of these books include extensive coverage of Web technologies as they relate to database development topics.

Rick and his wife Virginia jointly run their practice, CAB, Inc. (*http://www.cabinc.net*). Rick aims his content production at intermediate and advanced SQL Server, Access, and Web developers. Rick also writes for leading computer resources, such as *SQL Server Magazine*, *MSDN Online Library*, *Microsoft TechNet*, *Visual Basic Programmer's Journal*, and *Microsoft Interactive Developer*. Virginia targets Access power users and beginning developers. She has contributed articles to *http://www.smartcomputing.com*, *http://www.techrepublic.com*, and *Microsoft OfficePro*.

CAB runs two Web sites, *http://www.programmingmsaccess.com* and *http://www.databasedevelopersgroup.com*, as well as its developer seminars. The Web sites feature code samples, live demonstrations, tutorials, FAQs, and links to online resources for SQL Server and Access developers. CAB has offered nationwide seminars about Microsoft database tools annually since 1991. Earlier tours attracted a broad range of database developers and administrators from large and mid-size organizations, such as Ford, EDS at GM, Prudential, the U.S. Navy, State Farm, PACCAR, and Panasonic.

You can get in touch with Rick at rickd@cabinc.net.

Abrasive Wheel

Soldiers used to sharpen their swords by grinding them against especially hard stones, known as grindstones. In the 16th century an unknown inventor attached a grinding surface to a wheel, turned it with a crank, and created the abrasive wheel. Modern abrasive wheels, often made of sandstone or aluminum oxide, are used in fixed bench grinders or in portable hand grinders. They're ideal for sanding and grinding applications such as smoothing welds and castings, removing burrs from metal parts, grinding dies, refinishing rough surfaces on automobiles, and other uses. *Putting your nose to the grindstone* is proverbial for *working hard without a break*, but don't literally put your nose to a rotary grindstone or you'll *cut off your nose to spite your face.*

At Microsoft Press, we use tools to illustrate our books for software developers and IT professionals. Tools very simply and powerfully symbolize human inventiveness. They're a metaphor for people extending their capabilities, precision, and reach. From simple calipers and pliers to digital micrometers and lasers, these stylized illustrations give each book a visual identity, and a personality to the series. With tools and knowledge, there's no limit to creativity and innovation. Our tagline says it all: *the tools you need to put technology to work.*

The manuscript for this book was prepared and galleyed using Microsoft Word. Pages were composed by Microsoft Press using Adobe FrameMaker+SGML for Windows, with text in Garamond and display type in Helvetica Condensed. Composed pages were delivered to the printer as electronic prepress files.

Cover Designer: Methodologie, Inc.
Interior Graphic Designer: James D. Kramer
Principal Compositor: Daniel Latimer
Interior Artist: Joel Panchot
Principal Copy Editor: Shawn Peck
Indexer: Bill Meyers

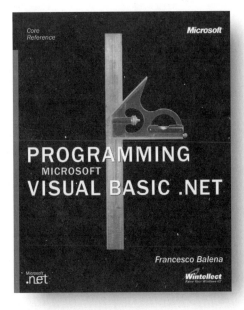

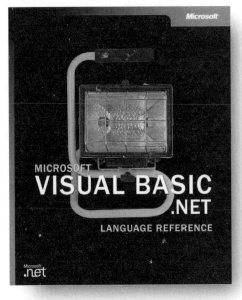

Get a **Free**
e-mail newsletter, updates, special offers, links to related books, and more when you
register on line!

Register your Microsoft Press® title on our Web site and you'll get a FREE subscription to our e-mail newsletter, *Microsoft Press Book Connections.* You'll find out about newly released and upcoming books and learning tools, online events, software downloads, special offers and coupons for Microsoft Press customers, and information about major Microsoft® product releases. You can also read useful additional information about all the titles we publish, such as detailed book descriptions, tables of contents and indexes, sample chapters, links to related books and book series, author biographies, and reviews by other customers.

Registration is easy. Just visit this Web page and fill in your information:

http://www.microsoft.com/mspress/register

Microsoft®

- -

Proof of Purchase

Use this page as proof of purchase if participating in a promotion or rebate offer on this title. Proof of purchase must be used in conjunction with other proof(s) of payment such as your dated sales receipt—see offer details.

Programming Microsoft® SQL Server 2000 with Microsoft Visual Basic® .NET

0-7356-1535-7

____

CUSTOMER NAME

Microsoft Press, PO Box 97017, Redmond, WA 98073-9830

MICROSOFT LICENSE AGREEMENT

Book Companion CD

IMPORTANT—READ CAREFULLY: This Microsoft End-User License Agreement ("EULA") is a legal agreement between you (either an individual or an entity) and Microsoft Corporation for the Microsoft product identified above, which includes computer software and may include associated media, printed materials, and "online" or electronic documentation ("SOFTWARE PRODUCT"). Any component included within the SOFTWARE PRODUCT that is accompanied by a separate End-User License Agreement shall be governed by such agreement and not the terms set forth below. By installing, copying, or otherwise using the SOFTWARE PRODUCT, you agree to be bound by the terms of this EULA. If you do not agree to the terms of this EULA, you are not authorized to install, copy, or otherwise use the SOFTWARE PRODUCT; you may, however, return the SOFTWARE PRODUCT, along with all printed materials and other items that form a part of the Microsoft product that includes the SOFTWARE PRODUCT, to the place you obtained them for a full refund.

SOFTWARE PRODUCT LICENSE

The SOFTWARE PRODUCT is protected by United States copyright laws and international copyright treaties, as well as other intellectual property laws and treaties. The SOFTWARE PRODUCT is licensed, not sold.

1. **GRANT OF LICENSE.** This EULA grants you the following rights:
   a. **Software Product.** You may install and use one copy of the SOFTWARE PRODUCT on a single computer. The primary user of the computer on which the SOFTWARE PRODUCT is installed may make a second copy for his or her exclusive use on a portable computer.
   b. **Storage/Network Use.** You may also store or install a copy of the SOFTWARE PRODUCT on a storage device, such as a network server, used only to install or run the SOFTWARE PRODUCT on your other computers over an internal network; however, you must acquire and dedicate a license for each separate computer on which the SOFTWARE PRODUCT is installed or run from the storage device. A license for the SOFTWARE PRODUCT may not be shared or used concurrently on different computers.
   c. **License Pak.** If you have acquired this EULA in a Microsoft License Pak, you may make the number of additional copies of the computer software portion of the SOFTWARE PRODUCT authorized on the printed copy of this EULA, and you may use each copy in the manner specified above. You are also entitled to make a corresponding number of secondary copies for portable computer use as specified above.
   d. **Sample Code.** Solely with respect to portions, if any, of the SOFTWARE PRODUCT that are identified within the SOFTWARE PRODUCT as sample code (the "SAMPLE CODE"):
      i. **Use and Modification.** Microsoft grants you the right to use and modify the source code version of the SAMPLE CODE, *provided* you comply with subsection (d)(iii) below. You may not distribute the SAMPLE CODE, or any modified version of the SAMPLE CODE, in source code form.
      ii. **Redistributable Files.** Provided you comply with subsection (d)(iii) below, Microsoft grants you a nonexclusive, royalty-free right to reproduce and distribute the object code version of the SAMPLE CODE and of any modified SAMPLE CODE, other than SAMPLE CODE, or any modified version thereof, designated as not redistributable in the Readme file that forms a part of the SOFTWARE PRODUCT (the "Non-Redistributable Sample Code"). All SAMPLE CODE other than the Non-Redistributable Sample Code is collectively referred to as the "REDISTRIBUTABLES."
      iii. **Redistribution Requirements.** If you redistribute the REDISTRIBUTABLES, you agree to: (i) distribute the REDISTRIBUTABLES in object code form only in conjunction with and as a part of your software application product; (ii) not use Microsoft's name, logo, or trademarks to market your software application product; (iii) include a valid copyright notice on your software application product; (iv) indemnify, hold harmless, and defend Microsoft from and against any claims or lawsuits, including attorney's fees, that arise or result from the use or distribution of your software application product; and (v) not permit further distribution of the REDISTRIBUTABLES by your end user. Contact Microsoft for the applicable royalties due and other licensing terms for all other uses and/or distribution of the REDISTRIBUTABLES.

2. **DESCRIPTION OF OTHER RIGHTS AND LIMITATIONS.**
   - **Limitations on Reverse Engineering, Decompilation, and Disassembly.** You may not reverse engineer, decompile, or disassemble the SOFTWARE PRODUCT, except and only to the extent that such activity is expressly permitted by applicable law notwithstanding this limitation.
   - **Separation of Components.** The SOFTWARE PRODUCT is licensed as a single product. Its component parts may not be separated for use on more than one computer.
   - **Rental.** You may not rent, lease, or lend the SOFTWARE PRODUCT.

- **Support Services.** Microsoft may, but is not obligated to, provide you with support services related to the SOFTWARE PRODUCT ("Support Services"). Use of Support Services is governed by the Microsoft policies and programs described in the user manual, in "online" documentation, and/or in other Microsoft-provided materials. Any supplemental software code provided to you as part of the Support Services shall be considered part of the SOFTWARE PRODUCT and subject to the terms and conditions of this EULA. With respect to technical information you provide to Microsoft as part of the Support Services, Microsoft may use such information for its business purposes, including for product support and development. Microsoft will not utilize such technical information in a form that personally identifies you.
- **Software Transfer.** You may permanently transfer all of your rights under this EULA, provided you retain no copies, you transfer all of the SOFTWARE PRODUCT (including all component parts, the media and printed materials, any upgrades, this EULA, and, if applicable, the Certificate of Authenticity), **and** the recipient agrees to the terms of this EULA.
- **Termination.** Without prejudice to any other rights, Microsoft may terminate this EULA if you fail to comply with the terms and conditions of this EULA. In such event, you must destroy all copies of the SOFTWARE PRODUCT and all of its component parts.

3. **COPYRIGHT.** All title and copyrights in and to the SOFTWARE PRODUCT (including but not limited to any images, photographs, animations, video, audio, music, text, SAMPLE CODE, REDISTRIBUTABLES, and "applets" incorporated into the SOFTWARE PRODUCT) and any copies of the SOFTWARE PRODUCT are owned by Microsoft or its suppliers. The SOFTWARE PRODUCT is protected by copyright laws and international treaty provisions. Therefore, you must treat the SOFTWARE PRODUCT like any other copyrighted material **except** that you may install the SOFTWARE PRODUCT on a single computer provided you keep the original solely for backup or archival purposes. You may not copy the printed materials accompanying the SOFTWARE PRODUCT.
4. **U.S. GOVERNMENT RESTRICTED RIGHTS.** The SOFTWARE PRODUCT and documentation are provided with RESTRICTED RIGHTS. Use, duplication, or disclosure by the Government is subject to restrictions as set forth in subparagraph (c)(1)(ii) of the Rights in Technical Data and Computer Software clause at DFARS 252.227-7013 or subparagraphs (c)(1) and (2) of the Commercial Computer Software—Restricted Rights at 48 CFR 52.227-19, as applicable. Manufacturer is Microsoft Corporation/One Microsoft Way/Redmond, WA 98052-6399.
5. **EXPORT RESTRICTIONS.** You agree that you will not export or re-export the SOFTWARE PRODUCT, any part thereof, or any process or service that is the direct product of the SOFTWARE PRODUCT (the foregoing collectively referred to as the "Restricted Components"), to any country, person, entity, or end user subject to U.S. export restrictions. You specifically agree not to export or re-export any of the Restricted Components (i) to any country to which the U.S. has embargoed or restricted the export of goods or services, which currently include, but are not necessarily limited to, Cuba, Iran, Iraq, Libya, North Korea, Sudan, and Syria, or to any national of any such country, wherever located, who intends to transmit or transport the Restricted Components back to such country; (ii) to any end user who you know or have reason to know will utilize the Restricted Components in the design, development, or production of nuclear, chemical, or biological weapons; or (iii) to any end user who has been prohibited from participating in U.S. export transactions by any federal agency of the U.S. government. You warrant and represent that neither the BXA nor any other U.S. federal agency has suspended, revoked, or denied your export privileges.

DISCLAIMER OF WARRANTY

NO WARRANTIES OR CONDITIONS. MICROSOFT EXPRESSLY DISCLAIMS ANY WARRANTY OR CONDITION FOR THE SOFTWARE PRODUCT. THE SOFTWARE PRODUCT AND ANY RELATED DOCUMENTATION ARE PROVIDED "AS IS" WITHOUT WARRANTY OR CONDITION OF ANY KIND, EITHER EXPRESS OR IMPLIED, INCLUDING, WITHOUT LIMITATION, THE IMPLIED WARRANTIES OF MERCHANTABILITY, FITNESS FOR A PARTICULAR PURPOSE, OR NONINFRINGEMENT. THE ENTIRE RISK ARISING OUT OF USE OR PERFORMANCE OF THE SOFTWARE PRODUCT REMAINS WITH YOU.

LIMITATION OF LIABILITY. TO THE MAXIMUM EXTENT PERMITTED BY APPLICABLE LAW, IN NO EVENT SHALL MICROSOFT OR ITS SUPPLIERS BE LIABLE FOR ANY SPECIAL, INCIDENTAL, INDIRECT, OR CONSEQUENTIAL DAMAGES WHATSOEVER (INCLUDING, WITHOUT LIMITATION, DAMAGES FOR LOSS OF BUSINESS PROFITS, BUSINESS INTERRUPTION, LOSS OF BUSINESS INFORMATION, OR ANY OTHER PECUNIARY LOSS) ARISING OUT OF THE USE OF OR INABILITY TO USE THE SOFTWARE PRODUCT OR THE PROVISION OF OR FAILURE TO PROVIDE SUPPORT SERVICES, EVEN IF MICROSOFT HAS BEEN ADVISED OF THE POSSIBILITY OF SUCH DAMAGES. IN ANY CASE, MICROSOFT'S ENTIRE LIABILITY UNDER ANY PROVISION OF THIS EULA SHALL BE LIMITED TO THE GREATER OF THE AMOUNT ACTUALLY PAID BY YOU FOR THE SOFTWARE PRODUCT OR US$5.00; PROVIDED, HOWEVER, IF YOU HAVE ENTERED INTO A MICROSOFT SUPPORT SERVICES AGREEMENT, MICROSOFT'S ENTIRE LIABILITY REGARDING SUPPORT SERVICES SHALL BE GOVERNED BY THE TERMS OF THAT AGREEMENT. BECAUSE SOME STATES AND JURISDICTIONS DO NOT ALLOW THE EXCLUSION OR LIMITATION OF LIABILITY, THE ABOVE LIMITATION MAY NOT APPLY TO YOU.

MISCELLANEOUS

This EULA is governed by the laws of the State of Washington USA, except and only to the extent that applicable law mandates governing law of a different jurisdiction.

Should you have any questions concerning this EULA, or if you desire to contact Microsoft for any reason, please contact the Microsoft subsidiary serving your country, or write: Microsoft Sales Information Center/One Microsoft Way/Redmond, WA 98052-6399.

PN 097-0002296